D0898152

Citizens, Strangers, and In-Betweens

New Perspectives on Law, Culture, and Society

ROBERT W. GORDON AND MARGARET JANE RADIN, SERIES EDITORS

Citizens, Strangers, and In-Betweens: Essays on Immigration and Citizenship, Peter H. Schuck

Why Lawyers Behave As They Do, Paul G. Haskell

Thinking Like a Lawyer, Kenneth J. Vandevelde

Intellect and Craft: The Contributions of Justice Hans Linde to American Constitutionalism, edited by Robert F. Nagel

Property and Persuasion: Normativity and Change in the Jurisprudence of Property, Carol M. Rose

Words That Wound: Critical Race Theory, Assaultive Speech, and the First Amendment, Mari J. Matsuda, Charles R. Lawrence III, Richard Delgado, and Kimberlè Williams Crenshaw

Citizens, Strangers, and In-Betweens

Essays on Immigration and Citizenship

P ETER H. S CHUCK

Westview Press
A Member of the Perseus Books Group

New Perspectives on Law, Culture, and Society

Published in 1998 in the United States of America by Westview Press, 5500 Central Avenue, Boulder, Colorado 80301-2877, and in the United Kingdom by Westview Press, 12 Hid's Copse Road, Cumnor Hill, Oxford OX2 9JJ

Library of Congress Cataloging-in-Publication Data
Schuck, Peter H.
    Citizens, strangers, and in-betweens : essays on immigration and
citizenship / Peter H. Schuck.
        p.   cm. — (New perspectives on law, culture, and society)
    Includes bibliographical references and index.
    ISBN 0-8133-6886-3
    1. United States—Emigration and immigration.   2. Emigration and
immigration law—United States.   3. Emigration and immigration—
Government policy—United States.   4. Citizenship—United States.
I. Title.   II. Series.
JV6465.S37   1998
325.73—dc21

98-11323
CIP

The paper used in this publication meets the requirements of the American National Standard for Permanence of Paper for Printed Library Materials Z39.48-1984.

10   9   8   7   6   5   4   3   2   1

Contents

Preface   xi
Acknowledgments   xvi
Credits   xvii

PART 1
CONTEXTS   1

  1 The Immigration System Today   3

     I.   Demographics, 3
    II.   Public Attitudes, 4
    III. The Evolution of the Immigration Control System, 11
    IV. The Current Legal Admissions System, 13
    V.   The 1996 Legislation: Strengthening Enforcement, 14
    VI. The 1997 Amnesty, 15

PART 2
THE COURTS AND IMMIGRATION   17

  2 The Transformation of Immigration Law   19

     I.   The Classical Conception of Immigration Law, 22
    II.   Pressures for Change, 39
    III. The Communitarian Conception of Immigration Law, 54
    IV. The Future of Immigration Law, 67
    Conclusion, 81

  3 Continuity and Change in the Courts: 1979–1990   82

    Summary of Major Findings, 85
    Conclusion, 86

PART 3
THE POLITICS OF IMMIGRATION   89

4   The Politics of Rapid Legal Change:
Immigration Policy, 1980–1990   91

Introduction, 91
   I.   Periodizing Immigration Reform: The 1980s, 96
   II.   External Events, 100
   III.   Political Entrepreneurship, 102
   IV.   The Changing Balance of Interests, 110
   V.   Ideas, 128
Conclusion, 137

5   Reform Continues: 1990–1998   139

6   The Message of Proposition 187:
Facing Up to Illegal Immigration   149

   I.   Justice Brennan's Legacy, 149
   II.   Why the Court May Turn, 151
   III.   What Voters Were Saying, 154
   IV.   Do Outsiders Have Claims on America? 157
   V.   Elusive Candor, 159

PART 4
CITIZENSHIP AND COMMUNITY   161

7   The Devaluation of American Citizenship   163

   I.   The Equality Principle, 164
   II.   The Due Process Principle, 167
   III.   The Consent Principle, 168
   IV.   An Evaluation of Devaluation, 171

8   The Reevaluation of American Citizenship   176

   I.   Citizenship in the International Domain, 179
   II.   Citizenship in the Domestic Domain, 184
   III.   Citizenship in the Federal System, 193
   IV.   A Brief Note on "Post-National Citizenship," 202
Conclusion, 205

9   Consensual Citizenship   207

10 Plural Citizenships   217

     I.   The Contemporary Debate and Context, 220
    II. Some Policy-Relevant Distinctions, 224
   III. An Assessment of Dual Citizenship, 229
   IV. Possible Reforms, 242

PART 5
CURRENT POLICY DEBATES   249

11 The New Immigration and the Old Civil Rights   251

     I.   Demographic Changes, 253
    II. Legal Changes, 254
   III. Socioeconomic Changes, 255
   IV. Ideological Changes, 257
    V. Political Changes, 261
   VI. Reappraising the Agenda, 262

12 Perpetual Motion: Migrations and Cultures   264

     I.   The Analytic Project, 265
    II. The Question of Culture, 268
   III. The Selectivity and Diversity of Migration, 271
   IV. Discrimination and Immigrant Success, 273
    V. Immigrants in Politics and Markets, 276
   VI. Immigrant Assimilation, 278
  VII. The Future of Immigration Policy, 279

13 Refugee Burden-Sharing: A Modest Proposal   282

     I.   The Current Regime for Protecting Refugees, 287
    II. The Comprehensive Plan of Action, 290
   III. Four Remedial Strategies, 293
   IV. The Proposal: Proportional Burden-Sharing, 301
    V. A Response to (Anticipated) Critics, 318
  Conclusion, 325

14 Alien Rumination: What Immigrants
Have Wrought in America   326

     I.   Demography, 329
    II. Carrying Capacity, 335
   III. Economic Impacts, 337

IV.   Cultural Assimilation, 341
  V.   Politics, 346
Conclusion, 354

Notes   359
Bibliography   460
Index   463

Preface

Exactly one century ago, the United States formally became an imperial nation. But the Treaty of Paris, which concluded the Spanish-American War by transferring the Philippines, Puerto Rico, and other territories to the United States, simply confirmed what had been evident from the nation's inception: It would be a dynamic, expansionist, ethnically polyglot society. Indeed, many of the Constitution's framers viewed the document as a charter for such a "manifest destiny," an imperial enterprise that was swiftly launched with the Louisiana Purchase in 1803 and avidly pursued thereafter as the young nation increasingly projected its political, ideological, military, economic, and cultural power across the continent, hemisphere, and globe. The relentless diffusion of American influence beyond its shores continues today, on the eve of the twenty-first century. (Indeed, as I write, the United States is exploring the terrain of Mars, searching for signs of extraterrestrial life.)

In one of history's great and momentous ironies, however, people have moved in precisely the opposite direction. As America's tendrils spread outward, more than 65 million immigrants thronged to the United States to live. This directional disjunction was hardly accidental. American influence abroad helped to propagate the message that the golden future lay in the United States, a message that inspired a vast throng of immigrants to cast off their destitution and persecution and journey to America but that also proved delusive to the millions who later returned home in failure. Some of America's military and economic ventures abroad created dislocations and relationships that spawned large and recurring migratory streams to the United States from those regions. The four leading sources of immigrants to the United States today—Mexico, the Philippines, Vietnam, and the Dominican Republic—are countries that America once invaded and occupied. This is a particularly striking example of the law of unanticipated consequences, which operates so frequently and remorselessly in the realm of immigration.

This book is about how those 65 million immigrants (plus the more than 5 million who now live in the United States illegally but more or less permanently) have helped to shape American life and law—and vice versa. The notion that these influences are reciprocal—that immigrants both affect and are affected by American society—is perfectly obvious to even the most obtuse observer of the contemporary scene who notices little more than immigration's impact on the food Americans eat, the music they listen to, the languages they speak, and their racial mix. Nevertheless, some of the more complex, particular modes of reciprocal influence remain opaque and elusive to even close students of the subject. I seek in this book to elucidate some of these modes, particularly the legal and policy decisions that shape immigration—again, often in unexpected ways.

The fourteen essays that follow were written for a variety of academic and popular audiences between 1984 and 1997. Half were written in 1996 and 1997; two (Chapters 5 and 10) are published here for the first time; and five others (Chapters 1, 8, 12, 13, and 14) appeared elsewhere only quite recently—all since 1996. Although the essays are wide ranging, they address similar questions. Each of them investigates the nature of the new and extraordinarily difficult challenges that the so-called new (post-1965) immigration has posed to traditional American values and practices. Each essay asks how effectively America's legal and political institutions have dealt with these challenges and how well-suited they are to meet immigration's future demands. Each explores the moral, legal, and political coherence and meaning of the three categories into which immigration law classifies all individuals on U.S. soil: American citizens; illegal or undocumented aliens (literally "strangers," although many are tied to American society in important ways); and the decidedly diverse congeries of aliens who possess a legal right to be in the United States, even if only conditionally and temporarily, many of whom become illegal ("in-betweens").

I have organized the book into five parts. Part 1 provides the context for all that follows. It recounts the historical evolution of the immigration control system; describes the current system, including a summary of the far-reaching changes adopted by Congress in 1996; discusses the principal legal statuses in immigration law (citizens, legal residents, refugees and asylees, illegal aliens, and others); presents statistics on the current demographics of immigration; and analyzes the American public's attitudes toward immigration.

The courts have played an important role in shaping the immigration system, and Part 2 explains how that role has changed, especially since the early 1980s. It traces the transformation of immigration law from what I call its "classical" mode, which the Supreme Court largely constructed in the late nineteenth century to legitimate the government's untrammeled, often arbitrary power over immigration and immigrants, to a contemporary mode in which courts struggle to integrate these classical doctrines and practices into a public law committed to protecting the rights of individuals, including immigrants, against governmental overreaching and procedural unfairness. Drawing upon a variety of methodologies—historical, doctrinal, and empirical—the essays in Part 2 carry the analysis of this struggle forward to 1990.

Part 3 broadens the focus well beyond the courts to encompass the more volatile political forces that drive and shape immigration law and policy in the legislative arenas where public attitudes toward immigration are more directly and forcefully expressed. The essays here detail the politics of immigration legislation in Congress, which in 1990 enacted the current, expansive legal immigration scheme, and in the bellwether, high-immigration state of California, which in 1994 adopted by public referendum a law, Proposition 187, that was designed to crack down on illegal aliens. An understanding of Proposition 187, whose reverberations are still being felt throughout the nation, is essential to an understanding of contemporary immigration law and politics. Chapter 5 updates the developments to April 1998.

Part 4 moves from a consideration of the legal and political processes that regulate immigration to the more fundamental substantive visions of citizenship that compete for public support in the American polity. The four chapters in Part 4 consider issues about which these competing visions differ. Two of them concern the "devaluation" of American citizenship (my term for the narrowing of the differences in the rights of citizens, strangers, and in-betweens that occurred in the 1970s and 1980s), and the current "reevaluation" of citizenship in the wake of public concern about its devaluation. A third chapter explores plural citizenships, the possession by an American citizen of citizenship in one or more other countries as well. The fourth examines birthright citizenship, the constitutional principle that confers automatic citizenship on individuals born in the United States, even if they are here illegally.

Part 5 takes up certain immigration and refugee policy issues that now dominate the political debate. These essays, two of which are extended reflections on highly controversial books by other authors, touch on numerous important and difficult issues. How has recent immigration affected the viability of the public policy agenda—especially the promotion of affirmative action—that the traditional civil rights coalition has been pursuing for the last half-century? Is this immigration causing the coalition to fracture along ethnic and ideological lines? Is the new immigration in general—and bilingual education in particular—threatening the hegemonic position of the English language in American public life? Are multicultural pressures retarding the assimilation of immigrants, or are these pressures facilitating their integration into American life? How is immigration affecting the demand for public services and social welfare entitlements, and how are these demands in turn affecting the public's willingness to support these benefits and shaping the larger debate over the nature of American citizenship? How do discrimination and other forms of adversity affect the economic progress of immigrants? How can international human rights law be reformed to maximize the number of refugees who are protected from persecution?

Let me say a few words about the book's currency and format. Because half of the essays were written since 1996, and most of the others were written only a few years earlier, the analyses and observations that they present continue to be fresh, highly topical, and in my view, valid. The one possible exception to this claim is revealing and instructive—which is why I have included it here. In my very first foray into this field (Chapter 2, published in 1984), I described the traditional ideology and legal order that had shaped classical immigration law until the 1970s, and then adumbrated a still incipient, judicially led evolution toward a quite different, decidedly more "communitarian" conception of the relationship between polity and alien. This evolution was reinforced by important legal and political developments—the communitarian amnesty law of 1986; a series of strikingly pro-alien judicial decisions interpreting that law; the expansionist Immigration Act of 1990 (analyzed in Chapter 4); and the liberalization of the refugee and asylum system in the early 1990s—and it continued, albeit fitfully, into the 1990s.

In 1996, however, Congress acted abruptly but decisively to abort and reverse major elements of this more communitarian legal order. Acting in a political environment that I describe in Chapter 5, Congress rewrote both the immigration statute and the welfare law to reject many of the judicial and legislative innovations at the heart of the transformation that I had prefigured in my 1984 essay, and sought to restore and even extend much of the classical regime, including unprecedented (and perhaps unconstitutional) limitations on judicial review of many immigration enforcement decisions. In addition, the new law requires officials to expedite those decisions; mandates the detention (in some cases, indefinitely) of many aliens pending their removal; expands the grounds for removing aliens; bars reentry of removed aliens, in some cases forever; permits low-level officials to summarily remove aliens with only minimal administrative (and no judicial) review; makes even long-term permanent resident aliens ineligible for a wide range of "safety net" public benefits; greatly restricts aliens' right to seek discretionary relief from removal; subjects aliens' attorneys to serious risks of criminal liability; and many, many other changes.

Taken together, these restrictive changes, which are already under vigorous challenge by immigrant advocates and will be the subject of litigation for many years to come, might be seen as a repudiation of the emergent communitarian order that I thought I had discerned in 1984. Whether or not the courts sustain these restrictions, they bespeak a political impulse that immigration advocates (of which I am one) ignore at their peril.

On the other hand, as I discuss in Chapters 1, 5, and 6, this view is substantially refuted by recent communitarian counter-thrusts on the part of Congress (e.g., the expansionist 1990 law; the 1997 amnesty for a very large group of undocumented aliens; and the restoration of welfare benefits to many legal aliens), of the President (e.g., demands for additional restorations of benefits and for repeal of some of the 1996 law's enforcement provisions), of the courts (e.g., striking down Proposition 187 and some of the 1996 law's restrictions on judicial review), and of state and local governments (e.g., spending their own funds to compensate for the 1996 law's cuts in welfare benefits).

I republish the essays here essentially in their original form—again with one exception. Chapter 3 is a coauthored empirical study of immigration litigation during the 1980s; it consists largely of statistical analysis, the details of which will interest only a small group of specialists who can, if they wish, consult the original for those details. I therefore include only the introduction to that study, a summary of its major findings, the conclusion, and the notes that accompany those passages. In all of the other essays, I excised only those passages whose deletion would prevent repetition or would remove anachronistic data and references. (In such cases, the text does not indicate the excisions.) For the sake of readability, I converted all of the original footnotes (and the textual bibliographical references in chapter 1) to endnotes. In some chapters I excised original notes or added new ones to reflect significant recent developments. In such cases, the notes were renumbered; any cross-references in the notes have been changed to reflect this renumbering. For the same reason, I have augmented some of the original notes. Finally, because some of the 1996 changes have rendered certain statutory citations in the original notes anachronistic, readers seeking citations to the current statutes should not simply rely on my endnote references.

Although all of the essays express my own views on the many legal and policy issues explored in the book, the reader will find my position most crisply summarized in the final essay, "Alien Rumination" (Chapter 14), which takes the form of an extended review of a notorious indictment by journalist Peter Brimelow, in his 1995 book *Alien Nation,* of America's immigration policy in the post-1965 era. Although a review (and a quite negative one, at that) might seem to be an odd format for presenting my affirmative views, I believe that in this case it serves the purpose admirably by enabling me to discuss the available evidence bearing on each of the normative and empirical claims advanced by most contemporary restrictionists. The concluding sentences of that essay capture the credo, which I believe that evidence supports, and the faith animating this book: "Immigration, including the post-1965 wave, has served America well. If properly regulated, there is every reason to expect that it will continue to do so."

Peter H. Schuck

Acknowledgments

For almost two decades, Yale Law School has nourished me and my work. I simply cannot imagine a more congenial and stimulating environment for serious intellectual engagement than this extraordinary institution. In my time there, Yale Law School has been energetically, wisely, and lovingly led by three remarkable deans, Harry Wellington (currently dean of New York Law School, where he has also generously supported my work), Guido Calabresi, and Tony Kronman. Yale's wonderfully quirky faculty and passionate, peerless students have raised many of the fascinating questions surrounding immigration, citizenship, human rights, and ethnic diversity that I have taught, thought, and written about for fifteen years and that I again take up here.

Many other individuals have joined my Yale colleagues in provoking, challenging, correcting, and assisting me as I struggled to formulate the ideas and positions advanced in these essays. I am especially grateful to Ted Wang and Rogers Smith, the coauthors of Chapters 3 and 9, respectively. Other intellectual debts have been acknowledged in the original versions of some of the previously published essays. My editors at Westview Press, Leo Wiegman and Kristin Milavec, shepherded this manuscript with skill and grace.

Finally, I wish to dedicate this book to America's citizens, strangers, and in-betweens—that immense polyglot chorus of erstwhile natives, immigrants, and sojourners who continue to enrich the swelling, inspiring, astonishingly complex ensemble of American life.

P.H.S.
May 1998

Credits

Chapter 1: "The Immigration System Today": excerpted from Schuck, "The Legal Rights of Citizens and Aliens in the United States." Originally Chapter 9 in *Temporary Workers or Future Citizens: Japanese and U.S. Migration Policies,* M. Weiner & T. Hanami, eds. (New York: New York University Press, 1998), pp. 238–290.

Chapter 2: "The Transformation of Immigration Law": from *Columbia Law Review*, vol. 84, January 1984, pp. 1–90.

Chapter 3: "Continuity and Change in the Courts: 1979–1990": excerpted from Peter H. Schuck and Theodore Hsien Wang, "Continuity and Change: Patterns of Immigration Litigation in the Courts, 1979–1990," *Stanford Law Review*, vol. 45, November 1992, pp. 115–183.

Chapter 4: "The Politics of Rapid Legal Change: Immigration Policy 1980–1990": from Schuck, "The Politics of Rapid Legal Change: Immigration Policy in the 1980s" in *Studies in American Political Development*, vol. 6, S. Skowronek & K. Orren, eds. (Cambridge: Cambridge University Press, Spring 1992), pp. 37–92.

Chapter 6: "The Message of Proposition 187: Facing Up to Illegal Immigration": from "The Message of 187," *The American Prospect*, vol. 21, Spring 1995, pp. 87–92.

Chapter 7: "The Devaluation of American Citizenship": from Schuck, "Membership in the Liberal Polity: The Devaluation of American Citizenship," *Georgetown Immigration Law Journal*, vol. 3, Fall 1989, pp. 1–18.

Chapter 8: "The Reevaluation of American Citizenship": from Schuck, "The Re-evaluation of American Citizenship," *Nation-State: Immigration in Western Europe and the United States,* C. Joppke, ed. (Oxford University Press, 1998), pp. 191–230.

Chapter 9: "Consensual Citizenship": from Peter H. Schuck and Rogers M. Smith, "Consensual Citizenship," *Chronicles*, vol. 16, July 1992, pp. 21–25.

Chapter 11: "The New Immigration and the Old Civil Rights": from Schuck, "The New Immigration and the Old Civil Rights," *The American Prospect*, vol. 15, Fall 1993, pp. 102–111.

Chapter 12: "Perpetual Motion: Migrations and Cultures": from Schuck, "Perpetual Motion," *Michigan Law Review*, vol. 95, May 1997, pp. 1738–1760.

Chapter 13: "Refugee Burden-Sharing: A Modest Proposal": from Schuck, "Refugee Burden-Sharing: A Modest Proposal," *Yale Journal of International Law*, vol. 22, Summer 1997, pp. 243–297.

Chapter 14: "Alien Rumination: What Immigrants Have Wrought in America": from Schuck, "Alien Rumination: What Immigrants Have Wrought in America," *Yale Law Journal*, vol. 105, May 1996, pp. 1963–2012.

PART ONE

Contexts

Nothing about America's contemporary immigration policy is more striking than its constant reconsideration and change. It was not always thus. The framework of immigration law remained remarkably stable during more than four otherwise tumultuous decades between 1921 and 1965. Congress did not significantly revise the 1965 system until 1980 when it enacted the Refugee Act, introducing new legal protections and attendant policy dilemmas that persist today. Only in the mid-1980s did the problem of illegal migration receive sustained (but in the event, ineffective) legislative attention.

Since 1986, however, immigration policy has been roiled by fierce political storms and incessant flux. Although few Americans rank it as a high-priority issue, public feelings about immigration run strong and politicians run scared. Congress adopted the most far-reaching changes to date in the 1996 immigration and welfare reform laws. Indeed, it is difficult to exaggerate how radical these reforms are compared to prior law. It is not just that Congress severely restricted the legal rights of both legal and illegal immigrants; these changes also challenge some of the most fundamental precepts of the modern legal order—especially the right of judicial review of agency enforcement decisions and the equal treatment by citizens and aliens—that defines the rights of citizens, strangers, and in-betweens.

And yet . . . The contemporary politics of immigration are too complex and multidimensional, too replete with ambiguities, value conflicts, and contradictions, to allow today's immigrants to be captured in a simple legal category like "discrete and insular minority," a grouping under which they would enjoy heightened constitutional protection. Americans view the relationship among citizens, strangers, and in-betweens in often nuanced ways that combine the symbolic power of myth; the emotional power of deeply held ideals, fears, and antagonisms; the psychological power of family narratives; and the political power of clashing public and private interests.

Chapter 1, which has been updated to reflect conditions existing as of April 1998, discusses the historical, demographic, attitudinal, and legal factors that are propelling and molding these changes; it also furnishes a kind of informational and subject matter map that should help to guide readers as they navigate the remaining chapters.

1

The Immigration System Today

This essay summarizes six aspects of the legal and policy context: the demographic changes that immigration is spawning; the state of public opinion about immigration, which ultimately frames and shapes the legal and policy responses to these changes; the historical evolution of the immigration control system in the United States; the current form of that system; the 1996 immigration reform; and the 1997 amnesty.

I. Demographics

Immigration is producing profound demographic changes in the United States.[1] During the last decade, the number of new immigrants (legal and illegal) exceeded those in any other decade in American history, including the 1905–14 period when 10.1 million immigrants were admitted. From 1987 to 1996, approximately 10 million immigrants were legally admitted, but several million more came or remained in the United States illegally during the decade, and an estimated 5–6 million of them were resident at the end of 1996.[2]

The level of legal admissions remains high. Not counting the almost 2.7 million aliens legalized under the amnesty program (who by 1994 had little inflationary effect on the admissions numbers), 915,000 were admitted in 1996, a large increase over the 720,000 admitted in 1995, and the 804,000 in 1994. As for emigration, an estimated 200,000 Americans leave the United States more or less permanently each year (Warren and Kraly; Dunn). Today, almost 10 percent of the US population—more than 25 million people—are foreign-born. This fraction is well below the 14 percent share in the first decade of this century, well below the share in Canada and Switzerland, and somewhat below that in France and Germany, but it has nearly doubled since 1970.

Because immigrants tend to be younger and have higher fertility rates than the native-born, this proportion is rising steadily; immigrants now ac-

3

count for more than one-third of the population growth in the United States. This may significantly alter the racial and ethnic composition of the population, not only in states like California but in the nation as a whole, although it will have relatively little effect on the nation's median age (Espenshade, 1994). New studies by the US Census Bureau predict that by the year 2020, the white population will shrink to 78.2 percent, people of Hispanic descent (most of whom call themselves white) will increase to 15.7 percent, blacks will increase to 13.9 percent, Asians and Pacific Islanders will increase to 6.9 percent, and Native Americans will increase to 0.9 percent. These changes, moreover, are occurring even faster than the Census Bureau had only recently predicted (*New York Times,* 1994).

II. Public Attitudes

Almost all Americans favor some restrictions on immigration. The principal public debates center on the questions of how much immigration should be permitted, the appropriate criteria and mix for whatever immigration is permitted, and the moral and policy justifications for these criteria. Virtually all Americans want stronger enforcement of existing restrictions, and most also favor reducing legal immigration below current levels, which in 1996 totaled 915,000 aliens admitted as legal permanent residents. In 1996 Congress considered a number of proposals for restrictions on legal immigration, ranging from modest adjustments to major reductions, but these proposals were defeated.

Although those who favor restrictions are commonly seen as monolithic in their views, they are actually a diverse group motivated by different emotions, principles, and interests some of which are misrepresented in public debate. In order to understand restrictionists' views, it is useful to distinguish broadly among four ideological positions, which I call xenophobia, nativism, principled restrictionism, and pragmatic restrictionism. Although these positions can be distinguished analytically, they are often conflated in the political debate over immigration policy. This conflation occurs both because advocates of different positions may advance similar policy proposals and justifications and because conflating them may confer rhetorical and political advantage on particular groups in the intense policy debate.

Although I focus here on restrictionist views, the diversity of expansionist positions should also be noted. Some (like the author) favor moderate increases in legal immigration but tighter controls on illegal aliens. Principled expansionists—libertarians, some economists, and the editorial page of the *Wall Street Journal*—assert that essentially open borders will maximize individuals' rights to engage in voluntary transactions with other individuals and otherwise to do as they like; government, they believe, should not limit these rights by impeding such transactions. Pragmatic expansionists, including many agricultural and other business interests seeking cheap labor or skills in short supply, ethnic groups desiring more members in the United States, and human rights organizations advocating larger refugee quotas, also favor increased immigration.

Xenophobia is an undifferentiated fear of foreigners or strangers as such. Who counts as a foreigner or stranger, of course, depends on the domain of one's primary reference group, which is often much smaller than the nation-state. It may be that the sources of xenophobia are congenital, reflecting some deeply embedded, universal feature of human psychology and identity by which individuals seek to distance themselves from those whom they define as "others" or "strangers." Fortunately, most Americans seem capable of overcoming or "unlearning" this fear as they are exposed to those outside their primary group. In this sense, the scope of xenophobia—the domain of perceived "otherness"—seems to be contracting over time.

One might predict, then, that the development of the so-called global village through advanced communications and transportation technologies and the integration of the world economy would tend to homogenize cultures and reduce the fear of otherness on which xenophobia feeds. No doubt this has occurred to some extent. Public attitudes toward Asians, for example, have grown markedly more favorable and less fearful than they were several decades ago, even as heightened economic competition between the United States and Japan has strained the newer tolerance. On the other hand, the advance of transcendent, cosmopolitan values can engender a sharp backlash in the more parochial enclaves where xenophobia tends to flourish. Sudden migration flows can inflame these attitudes, as has occurred recently in the United States and especially in Europe, including Germany. Some people in these enclaves engage in violence against those whom they view as foreign because of their race, language, appearance, or behavior. This may explain some of the crimes committed in recent years by blacks against Korean-Americans and other immigrant minorities in Los Angeles and Washington, DC. In general, however, the level of xenophobia in the United States has steadily declined and is probably not a significant force today.

Nativism is a more discriminating, specific position than xenophobia. Nativists believe in the moral or racial superiority of the indigenous stock. (In the US context, this refers not to the indigenous stock, which was, of course, Native American, but to the Anglo-Saxons who became demographically, politically, and culturally dominant.) Nativism holds that members of this stock alone exemplify the distinctive values that the nativist associates with the nation-state. The nativist insists that immigrant cultures are inimical to these values and, at least in that sense, inferior. Nativism, then, is a species of racism; it maintains that cultural values inhere in particular racial, ethnic, or national groups and cannot be learned. It demands not only exclusion of the inferior groups but leads ineluctably to doctrines that justify nativist domination of the members of the other groups who are already inside the country.

Nativism, unlike xenophobia, has been a perennial theme in US history; it is as constant as the motifs of welcome, succor, and assimilation mentioned earlier. It has erupted with special force during periods of social upheaval and economic crisis. But even in more stable times, groups of Americans have organized politically for the explicit purposes of ostracizing, excluding, and repatriating immigrants. In his classic study of American nativism during the late nineteenth and early twentieth centuries, John Higham (1970) showed that nativism has appealed to all strata of society at different times. But it has especially attracted those whose economic and social positions are the least secure and who search most desperately for simple explanations, scapegoats, and conspiracies to assuage their painful sense of status vulnerability.

American nativism has assumed many repellent forms. Before (and even after) the Civil War, prominent Americans, including President Abraham Lincoln, proposed sending US blacks back to Africa. Nativist premises have led the federal and state governments to enact harshly discriminatory laws, among them the Chinese Exclusion acts, the national origins quotas, and anti-Japanese policies such as the Gentleman's Agreement and World War II internment. Nativist groups have fomented violence against Catholics, Jews, and other immigrant groups.

As with xenophobia, however, nativism—as distinct from other restrictionist theories—is probably not a significant force in US politics today. Although the question is controversial among immigration scholars and the answer is far from clear (Schuck, 1996: 1966, n. 18), I believe that the support for Proposition 187 in California in 1994 is best understood as an expression of widespread public frustrations with the failures of federal immigration enforcement and the perceived erosion of US sovereignty and control over its borders and demographic destiny, not as a spasm of nativist hatred (Schuck, 1995). The openly nativist candidacy of Patrick Buchanan during the 1992 and 1996 Republican primary campaigns indicates that it does survive and is capable of being mobilized to some extent; the public's decisive rejection of that candidacy, however, suggests that nativism is no longer widespread, even in the conservative wing of the Republican Party. Indeed, some of the most prominent members of that wing, such as the House's Richard Army of Texas, vice presidential candidate Jack Kemp, and commentator William Bennett, are openly pro-immigration, while others such as Speaker Newt Gingrich claim to favor immigration.

In contrast to xenophobia and nativism, *principled restrictionism* is a commonly held position in the United States today. Principled restrictionism is driven neither by a generalized fear of strangers nor by a belief that only certain categories of Americans are capable of civic virtue. Instead, it is the view that current levels of immigration threaten particular policy goals or values advocated by the restrictionist.

Today, the leading principled restrictionists in the United States include some advocates of environmental and demographic controls who maintain that zero (or even negative) population growth is essential to preserve ecological stability and that both the number of immigrants and their high fertility rates threaten that stability. The leading example here is the Federation for American Immigration Reform (FAIR). Some of FAIR's board members are environmental and population control activists, labor union professionals, demographers, and politicians—for example, presidential candidate and former Colorado governor Richard Lamm—who in other areas subscribe to liberal public policy positions.[3] As I write, the Sierra Club is embroiled in a fierce internal debate about whether to call for immigration restrictions.

Many principled restrictionists also express a concern for the effects of contemporary immigration on the interests of low-income Americans. They believe, with some labor economists, that today's levels of immigration—especially illegal (and some legal) migration by low-skill Mexican and Central American workers—displace native workers from jobs, drain scarce welfare benefits intended primarily for American indigent citizens, and consume already overburdened public services (primarily education and health care). Some also point to the adverse effects that large numbers of nonvoting aliens (legal and illegal) have on the political effectiveness of Mexican Americans and other new immigrant groups.

Some principled restrictionists place greater emphasis on values such as national solidarity, linguistic unity, religious tolerance, or cultural coherence. These themes are commonly sounded in congressional speeches, organization newsletters, and private conversations. An example of such a group is U.S. English, founded by the late senator (and linguist S. I. Hayakawa. Many of these principled restrictionists appear to be more conservative in their social policy views than those of the FAIR stripe, but, again, they are well within the mainstream of US politics. Indeed, a number of prominent liberals such as Norman Cousins and Walter Cronkite have been closely associated with U. S. English at one time or another.

Unlike nativism, which most Americans regard as a disreputable position, principled restrictionism contributes significantly to the overt debate about US immigration policy. Because the etiquette of acceptable public discourse forces nativists' views underground, nativists may seek political legitimacy and influence by publicly couching their racist views in the less-objectionable rhetoric of principled restrictionism. Thus it is difficult to determine the extent to which principled restrictionist positions are in fact motivated by nativist and racist views (Schuck, 1996: 1965, n. 14).

Ideally, only the merits of a speaker's position would be relevant in the public debate over immigration, not the speaker's motives. This debate, however, usually proceeds as if motives matter a great deal. Many immigration advocates seek to stigmatize their restrictionist opponents, whether principled or pragmatic, by tarring them with the nativist brush. The reverse is also true: restrictionists deride those favoring more liberal immigration policies as unpatriotic "one-worlders" and "open-borders" advocates. Principled restrictionists are especially vulnerable to this tactic; they cannot easily refute such charges even when they are false.

Pragmatic restrictionism is a common perspective on immigration levels. It resembles principled restrictionism in the policy positions that it supports, but it differs in one important respect. Where principled restrictionists see the threat that immigration poses to their preferred goals or values as inherent in the nature and fact of immigration, pragmatic restrictionists view such conflicts as contingent, not inevitable.

Pragmatists believe, for example, that immigration's actual effects on population, the environment, national unity, cultural consensus, and so forth are empirical questions whose answers depend on a variety of factors. They do not oppose immigration in principle or in general. They may even be prepared to support it if they can be persuaded, for example, that immigrants actually create jobs rather than taking them away from native workers, that they are mastering the English language without undue delay, and that they do not exploit the welfare system or otherwise threaten social cohesion. Although certain labor unions, taxpayer groups, and other interest groups may have closed their minds on these factual questions, the pragmatic restrictionist remains open to persuasion by contrary evidence.

Most Americans, I suspect, are pragmatic restrictionists, although one cannot be certain. That is, they favor lower levels of immigration but are open to argument and evidence about what those levels should be and about what immigration's actual effects are. Thus their views about the wisdom and level of restriction are capable of being changed. In a recent study, political scientists Paul Sniderman and Thomas Piazza examined public attitudes toward race-oriented policy issues and found them notably responsive to counter-argument.[4]

The evidence just cited did not specifically concern attitudes toward immigration policy. But if Americans are open to argument and evidence with respect to the explosive issues surrounding race and welfare, issues on which they presumably have already developed firm attitudes, it must be even truer of immigration about which (as I discuss immediately below) they are already profoundly ambivalent. Attitudes toward aliens, of course, are not the same as attitudes toward either racial minorities or people on public assistance. Nevertheless, two central facts about American society—that white Americans' hostility toward blacks and other racial minorities has declined sharply, and that public benefits for the poor sharply increased between the 1960s and the enactment of the 1996 welfare reform law

(Schuck, 1996: 2010–11)—suggest that negative attitudes toward aliens (as distinguished from attitudes concerning the optimal number who should be admitted to the US) have probably softened as well. I have already noted the markedly more favorable views about Asians since 1965, when they began immigrating to the United States in large numbers.

Surveys of public opinion that specifically inquire about immigration tend to support my claim that most Americans are pragmatic restrictionists (Espenshade and Hempstead). (Interestingly, most *immigrants* hold roughly similar attitudes.) Survey data about many public policy issues often seem puzzling or even incoherent, of course, and those concerning attitudes toward immigration are no exception. These data are sensitive to the respondents' own perceptions about economic and social conditions, the specific wording of the question being asked, and the respondents' willingness to share strong sometimes stigmatized feelings with interviewers who are strangers (Lewontin). In part, however, the data are hard to interpret because of Americans' ambivalent views about immigration.[5]

Some of the evidence of ambivalent or conflicting American attitudes toward immigration may reflect this propensity to draw subtle but important distinctions. According to the survey data, for example, Americans like immigrants more than they like immigration, favor past immigration more than recent immigration, prefer legal immigrants to illegal ones, prefer refugees to other immigrants, support immigrants' access to educational and health benefits but not to welfare or Social Security, and feel that immigrants' distinctive cultures have contributed positively to American life and that diversity continues to strengthen American society today. At the same time, they overwhelmingly resist any conception of multiculturalism that discourages immigrants from learning and using the English language.[6]

One tension most deeply pervades current immigration policy debates: Americans treasure their immigrant roots yet believe that current immigration levels are too high. Anxiety about immigration, it seems, is aroused by the newer immigrant groups, a bias that a 1982 Gallup poll places in a revealing historical light. When asked about its views on the contributions of particular immigrant groups, the public gave the highest scores to precisely the groups that had been widely reviled in the nineteenth and early twentieth centuries; the lowest scoring groups were the newer arrivals (in 1982 Cubans and Haitians). Professor Rita Simon has captured this ambivalence in an arresting metaphor: "We view immigrants with rose-colored glasses turned backwards" (1995). The optimist might infer from this that 75 years hence the public will view today's newcomers—who by then may be seen as old, established groups—with the same solicitude and admiration now generally reserved for Italians, Jews, Slovaks, and other well-assimilated groups. The pessimist, of course, will reject this postdictive prediction, insisting that things really have changed for the worse.

When viewed over time, however, the polling evidence suggests that in attitudes toward immigration as in so many other areas, the more things seem to change, the more they stay the same. The public, it appears, has *always* thought that the immigration levels of their day were too high. Over the course of the past fifty years, Americans asked (in slightly different formulations) whether immigration levels should be increased, reduced, or kept the same have responded in remarkably similar ways. During that period, only 4–13 percent have favored an increase, while 33–66 percent have favored a decrease. In 1993 only 7 percent favored an increase, 61 percent favored a decrease, and 27 percent preferred no change.[7] The trend in attitudes has been toward greater negativity. In 1965, the percentage favoring reduced immigration began rising steadily until the late 1970s, then rose more sharply until the mid-1980s, then declined somewhat for several years, fluctuating until the early 1990s when it again rose sharply. Since about 1980, this attitudinal trend has tracked the trend in the unemployment rate very closely. Hence attitudes can and do change abruptly (Espenshade and Hempstead: 539, 557).

In sum, the survey data indicate that Americans are quite favorably disposed in principle to legal immigration and to cultural diversity but want less of it. They harbor concerns about the impact of immigration and diversity on specific aspects of American life, and also worry about how quickly and completely the newer immigrant groups can be assimilated. As I have noted, these concerns troubled earlier generations of Americans as well.

These data raise another intriguing question: if Americans are indeed ambivalent about immigration and desire even less *legal* immigration, how can we explain the adoption of the Immigration Act of 1990? This was a law, after all, that expanded immigration levels by about 40 percent and will continue those higher levels for the foreseeable future, a law that will thus maintain and perhaps even increase the ethnic and racial diversity of the immigration streams to the United States.[8] This puzzle only deepens when we note that Congress passed the 1990 act during a national and international economic recession, a time when virtually all other immigrant-receiving countries were moving to restrict normal immigration and limit asylum claiming. Why did these enormous anti-immigration pressures fail to convince Congress to follow suit, as so many restrictionists (principled and pragmatic alike) strongly urged it to do? And why did a strenuous restrictionist effort in 1996 fail to cut back these higher legal immigration levels even as it succeeded in restricting legal immigrants' procedural and substantive rights? These questions are addressed in Chapter 5.

One answer is that restrictionist pressures, which often build up in particular regions and localities as a result of the high residential concentration of immigrants in a handful of states and localities, tend to dissipate somewhat when legislation is considered at the national level, where the US Constitution lodges exclusive jurisdiction over immigration policy. In 1995 two-thirds of the legal immigrants intended to settle in only six states: California, New York, Texas, Florida, New Jersey, and Illinois. Almost one in four hoped to live in either of two metropolitan areas, New York or Los Angeles (US Dept. of Justice, 1996: 8). The pronounced regionalization of immigration means that the majority of Americans (and their political leaders) who reside elsewhere only feel its effects on jobs, public service budgets, and cultural unity in an indirect, muted form. Public attitudes about desired immigration levels vary by region (Espenshade and Hempstead: 546, 548).

In addition (and not surprisingly), immigrant enclaves are in precisely those areas where the political groups with a powerful stake in increased immigration, such as growers, church groups, and ethnic organizations, are located. These groups, which enjoy excellent access to the mass media, are often strong enough to counteract the restrictionist pressures that concentrated immigrant populations generate.[9] For whatever reasons, national political leaders, media, prominent commentators, business executives, and other elite groups generally support immigration more than the general public does, and immigration policy tends to reflect their pro-immigration positions.

III. The Evolution of the Immigration Control System

For the first century of American history, the law was not much concerned with immigration. Apart from some state-enforced public health restrictions, US borders were essentially open to both entry and exit (with the notable exception of slavery). Migration patterns were shaped by economic, political, ethnic, and religious developments, not by legal rules.

In 1875, Congress enacted the first federal limitation on immigration (again, apart from laws dealing with the slave trade). Anti-immigrant sentiment increased during subsequent years as immigration from southern and eastern Europe grew rapidly. In 1906, Congress passed a statute requiring English-language proficiency for naturalization, but failed to enact a literacy test for admission. In 1907, as immigration levels swelled, Congress established a national study group (the Dillingham Commission) to review the problem; its massive 1911 report recommended significant restrictions, but none was adopted for another decade. Meanwhile, Congress twice passed literacy requirements for admission, but Presidents Taft and Wilson, like Cleveland before them, vetoed the provisions. In 1917 Congress, reflecting the nationalist passion of the First World War, overrode Wilson's veto and enacted the literacy requirement, while also banning almost all Asian immigration. In 1921, Congress finally adopted the Dillingham approach, enacting a provisional but comprehensive scheme of immigration control. Three years later, this system was institutionalized in the Johnson-

Reed legislation. This National Origins Act provided for an annual limit of 150,000 Europeans, a complete prohibition on Japanese immigration, and a system of quotas that favored migrants from the traditional source countries (primarily the British Isles, Germany, and Scandinavia). Under these quotas, immigration to the United States remained relatively low but rising during the next four decades: 528,000 in the 1930s, 1 million in the 1940s, 2.5 million in the 1950s, and 3.3 million in the 1960s.

Under the powerful influence of the civil rights revolution, the national origins system was finally abandoned in 1965. Under the new law, Asian, African, and Caribbean immigrants became eligible to seek admission, although both the Congress and the Johnson Administration predicted that few non-Europeans, especially Asians, would come. The 1965 law established many elements of what continues to be the structure of the legal immigration system today. These elements include identical per-country quotas and a categorical preference system that emphasized family unification and, to a much lesser degree, occupational skills and refugee status. In 1976 the system was changed to equalize the treatment of Eastern and Western Hemisphere countries, including Mexico, and in 1978 the hemispheric quotas were combined into a single global total of 290,000 visas per year. During the 1970s, legal admissions totaled 4.5 million, the highest since the second decade of the century. It was during this decade, moreover, that concern about illegal migration became a high-visibility political issue in the United States. Most of these migrants were Mexican agricultural workers who had been marooned in the mid-1960s when the long-standing Bracero program was terminated, and in the mid-1970s when the per-country limits were applied for the first time to Mexico.

The period since 1980, as we have seen, has witnessed an enormous increase in immigration levels. Continuing a trend generated by the 1965 law, the source country composition of the migration stream changed dramatically. Between 1985 and 1990, for example, only 8.9 percent of the legal immigrants came from Europe. In contrast, 34 percent were Asian and 54 percent (as well as the vast majority of illegal migrants) were from Mexico, Central America, South America, and the Caribbean. In 1996, when the 1986 amnesty program had ceased dominating these statistics, the shares were 16, 34, and 37 percent, respectively (US Dept. of Justice, 1997). The five leading source countries for legal immigrants in 1996 were Mexico, the Philippines, India, Vietnam, and mainland China. The new immigrants' residential patterns in the United States are highly concentrated, with two-thirds of the legal immigrants settling in only six states: California (especially the Los Angeles area), New York, Texas, Florida, New Jersey, and Illinois (US Department of Justice, 1997).

As immigration levels soared in the 1980s, so did the level of immigration-related political activity at the federal, state, and local levels (Schuck,

1992). In the Refugee Act of 1980, Congress established for the first time a systematic legal structure for controlling refugee admissions and adjudicating refugee and asylum claims. Six years later, in the Immigration Reform and Control Act of 1986 (IRCA), Congress made sweeping changes in immigration enforcement and in admissions. On the enforcement side, it enacted an employer sanctions program that prohibited employers from hiring undocumented workers. The Immigration Marriage Fraud Amendments, passed just before IRCA, also bolstered enforcement by seeking to prevent aliens from using sham marriages to gain admission. Congress also adopted a number of criminal enforcement provisions relating to alien drug trafficking and other criminal conduct.

On the admissions side, IRCA established several amnesty programs (for agricultural workers, other workers, and Cubans and Haitians) authorizing aliens in the United States illegally since 1 January 1982 to apply for temporary legal status, which could eventually lead to permanent legal status and citizenship. Of the 2.76 million who applied, 2.67 million were granted legal status. IRCA also created a temporary "diversity" program designed to favor European (especially Irish) immigrants who would not otherwise qualify for visas. These provisions, which ended up favoring both Irish and Asian immigrants, remain in effect and use a lottery to select these diversity admissions. Finally, IRCA adopted a new anti-discrimination program that was intended to protect legal Hispanic workers against the discrimination that might result from the imposition of sanctions on employers who hired illegals.

IV. THE CURRENT LEGAL ADMISSIONS SYSTEM

Only four years later, Congress passed and President Bush signed the Immigration Act of 1990, then the most far-reaching reform of immigration and naturalization law since 1965, which defines and governs almost all legal admissions under the current immigration and naturalization system. In 1995, the Clinton administration negotiated with Cuba a limited but regularized quota for the admission of up to 20,000 Cubans each year. Legislation enacted in 1996, described below, changes the law relating to asylum claims, aliens convicted of crimes in the US, and the procedures for the deportation and exclusion (now consolidated into "removal" proceedings) of aliens. The resulting system is very complex, but four major elements can, with some necessary simplifications, be briefly summarized.

1. Broadly speaking, three categories of aliens can be admitted: "immigrants," who enjoy the status of permanent resident aliens; "nonimmigrants," who are admitted under restrictions as to the purposes and duration of their visit; and "parolees," who despite their entry are treated legally as if they stood at the border seeking entry.

2. The law establishes an overall cap on non-refugee admissions of 675,000 per year. This cap can be breached, however, if the number of "immediate relatives" (spouses, minor children, and parents of US citizens), who are exempt from this numerical cap, exceeds a certain level. There were 302,000 immediate relative admissions in 1996. The number of overseas refugees is fixed according to the procedures established by the 1980 Act, and asylees are not limited in number. In 1996, more than 128,000 refugees and asylees were adjusted to permanent legal status. For 1997 and 1998, the US planned to admit 78,000 and 83,000 overseas refugees, respectively—a reduction from the level of refugee admissions in recent years—plus an undetermined number of asylees. Also exempt from this numerical cap were Amerasians, "diversity" admissions (from so-called "low-admission" countries), those legalized under IRCA, parolees from the former Soviet Union and Indo-China, and some others.

3. The numerical ceiling of 675,000 is divided into three major categories of immigrants, each governed by its own intricate rules. These categories are: family-sponsored (480,000, further divided into four sub-categories with ceilings); employment-based (140,000, further divided into five sub-categories with ceilings); and diversity (55,000). Although the new system places somewhat greater emphasis than the earlier one did on employment-based admissions (and especially those with higher-level skills), the family-sponsored admissions (including the unlimited "immediate relatives" and accompanying family members) still account for over two-thirds of the total.

4. Within the overall preference ceilings, every country is subject to a further annual ceiling of at least 25,620 with respect to family-sponsored and employment-based admissions. Diversity admissions are subject to a per-country annual ceiling of 3,850. Chargeability to these ceilings depends on the immigrant's country of birth, not country of nationality.

V. The 1996 Legislation: Strengthening Enforcement

The structure and magnitude of legal admissions established in the Immigration Act of 1990 have survived strenuous efforts by restrictionists to alter both. In 1996, however, the government's authority over aliens was vastly strengthened when Congress thoroughly overhauled the basic immigration statute, particularly its enforcement provisions. Two new laws radically limited the procedural and substantive rights that aliens had come to enjoy, greatly extending the tougher enforcement policies that Congress had enacted in a series of measures beginning in 1986. The most comprehensive of the new laws, the Illegal Immigration Reform and Immigrant Responsibility Act of 1996 (IIRIRA), eliminates or restricts the power of the federal courts and of immigration judges to review many types of enforcement decisions; mandates the detention, perhaps indefinitely, of many aliens pending removal (a new category that includes what were traditionally called deportations and exclusions); severely limits the ability of aliens who have committed crimes in the United States to apply for cancellations of removal even in the most compelling circumstances; authorizes the government to remove aliens at the border summarily (i.e., without a hearing before an immigration judge) if they appear to lack proper documents unless they are found to have credible asylum claims; bars aliens who are in the United States illegally from returning later on a legal visa for substantial periods of time; increases the number of offenses that may trigger removal; increases the sanctions for many offenses; imposes new restrictions on those who sponsor new immigrants; adopts numerous other far-reaching changes; and makes many of the new provisions retroactive, thus permitting removal of an alien for conduct that did not subject him to removal when he engaged in it. The constitutionality of some of these provisions, particularly those limiting judicial review for aliens in government custody, is already being challenged in the courts, and it will be many years before the meaning of these fundamental legal changes becomes clear.

VI. THE 1997 AMNESTY

Late in 1997, quite unexpectedly, Congress enacted a new amnesty law that is intended to confer legal status, and ultimately eligibility for citizenship, on more than 400,000 Central Americans who have been residing in the United States for years but have been in legal limbo because of their undocumented status and the pending nature of litigation to determine their right to asylum. The 1997 law will regularize the status of many of them while permitting the others to seek relief from deportation under the more favorable rules that prevailed before the 1996 law limited the availability of such relief. As of this writing, Congress and the Clinton administration were considering whether to extend this relief to other undocumented aliens, including as many as 20,000 Haitians, whose legal status remained uncertain.

PART TWO

The Courts
and Immigration

Today, the courts are leading players in the drama of immigration law and policy. Like so much else in the current immigration regime, this active judicial role marks a profound departure from the traditional pattern. Chapter 2, written in 1984 shortly after I began teaching immigration law, sought to capture and interpret the first stirrings of a then-embryonic shift in the courts' willingness to assimilate even strangers, undocumented migrants, to the mainstream legal order from which even legal immigrants were traditionally isolated to a great extent. This shift was occasioned by a large, sudden flow of migrants from the Caribbean region, many seeking legal protection and residency under a new Refugee Act that had essentially ignored the prospect of the United States becoming a country of massive first asylum. The essay contrasts the "classical" immigration law regime that prevailed through the 1970s with the more communitarian one that the courts seemed to be constructing under the pressures that this new migration had helped to unleash.

As I note in the Introduction to this book, the 1996 amendments described in Chapter 1 call into serious question whether I was wrong, or at least premature, in heralding (and largely praising) this transformation. The accuracy of my judgment remains to be determined, of course, but I predict that the courts will strain to interpret the new law in ways that will preserve many of the procedural protections, especially judicial review, that they fashioned to assimilate strangers and in-betweens to a legal order developed largely for citizens. Chapter 3 attempts to do precisely that. There, Ted Wang and I test empirically the "alien protection jurisprudence" hypothesis that I advanced in Chapter 2. (For those readers who cannot wait to learn the answer, we conclude that immigration litigation during the 1980s generally contradicted but did not conclusively refute this hypothesis. The outcomes in asylum litigation, however, were consistent with the hypothesis.)

2

The Transformation
of Immigration Law

Immigration has long been a maverick, a wild card, in our public law. Probably no other area of American law has been so radically insulated and divergent from those fundamental norms of constitutional right, administrative procedure, and judicial role that animate the rest of our legal system. In a legal firmament transformed by revolutions in due process and equal protection doctrine and by a new conception of judicial role, immigration law remains the realm in which government authority is at the zenith, and individual entitlement is at the nadir.

The distinctiveness of immigration law reflects a number of factors. Since the ideal of nationhood first fired the human imagination, a country's power to decide unilaterally who may enter its domain, under what conditions, and with what legal consequences has been regarded as an essential precondition of its independence and sovereignty.[1] Aliens lack full membership in the moral and political communities that create and sustain our system of justice. They stand outside the gates beseeching the nation to permit them to enter. The relatively few who are fortunate enough to be admitted must remain nonmembers for a time; their moral claims upon us during that hiatus are provisional, contingent, and seldom compelling. Indeed, by calling them "aliens," our law affirms that they remain strangers, objects of our vigilance, our suspicion, and perhaps even our hostility.[2]

The place of immigration law in our larger legal and political system is also a source of uniqueness. Immigration law often implicates the nation's basic foreign policy objectives, a circumstance that has sometimes provoked the Supreme Court, even in nonimmigration contexts, to be less scrupulous in safeguarding constitutional values and more deferential to the other branches of government.[3] The domestic politics of immigration, and hence the laws and policies governing aliens, also reveal unusual patterns. Even lawfully admitted aliens do not vote, of course, and millions of undocumented workers and their families live largely outside the protection of any law.[4] At the psychological and emotional levels, immigration generates complex public attitudes toward outsiders and newcomers. Especially during periods of economic distress, a recurrent nativism has tapped the dark wellsprings of racial and religious bigotry in America, releasing forces that have profoundly shaped the character of immigration and national politics.[5]

A central theme of this essay is the epiphenomenal nature of immigration law. Throughout our history, its changing character has reflected more fundamental social and ideological structures. From the birth of the Republic until the 1880's, American society was consumed by the tasks of populating a vast unsettled continent and exploiting its untapped wealth. These activities were driven by a decidedly open economic and social system and by an ideology that corresponded to a remarkable degree to the tenets of Lockean liberal theory.[6] The liberalism of America's first century conceived of persons as autonomous, self-defining individuals possessing equal moral worth and dignity and equally entitled to society's consideration and respect. This entitlement was in principle universally shared, a natural right deriving not from the particularities of one's time, place, or status, but from one's irreducible humanity. The good society, in this view, was one in which each individual enjoyed maximum liberty to pursue his or her own conception of the good by deciding whether, and on what terms, to enter into contractual relationships with other equally free individuals.[7] Liberal ideology was reflected in a policy of essentially open borders, one that strongly encouraged, indeed actively recruited, mass immigration to the United States.[8]

By the 1880's, the American frontier was closing and the United States turned from agrarian expansion to urban and industrial development. The social milieu in which liberalism had flourished receded, to be replaced by a set of new conditions and attitudes far less congenial to it. Liberal values were challenged by an array of exclusionary impulses—racist and class-based opposition to Chinese laborers, nativist xenophobia, religious bigotry, and political reaction against radical movements drawing upon new immigrant groups.[9] These changes spawned a different ideology, which I shall call "restrictive nationalism," and a corresponding legal order, which I shall call "classical immigration law."

The new ideology and the legal structure that embodied it celebrated norms and countenanced practices that were decidedly, sometimes grotesquely, illiberal. Aliens' natural rights to pursue their self-interest through migration here were now regulated according to considerations of national interest, sovereignty, and power. Consent remained the source of an alien's legal rights and duties, but it was no longer liberalism's consent of freely contracting individuals exercising their natural rights to define their own relationships with others. Restrictive nationalism drew upon the ideological conception of consent-based obligation, but reshaped it to respond to the dictates of an exclusionary sentiment. The new order would be based upon the national government's consent to allow the alien to enter and remain, which consent could be denied or withdrawn on the basis of arbitrary criteria and summary procedures that often transgressed liberal principles.[10]

Classical immigration law proved to be remarkably durable. Indeed, as we shall see, important elements of that system remain in place today, a century after restrictive nationalism began to supplant liberalism as the dominant ideology of immigration policy. Nevertheless, its inconsistency with contemporary public law values has become increasingly evident. The growth of the modern administrative state has magnified its isolation from the dominant developments in American law, throwing its distinctive features into even sharper relief. The currents that have transfigured constitutional jurisprudence, administrative law, civil rights, and judicial ideology since the New Deal, and especially since the 1960's,[11] have largely passed immigration law by, leaving it to navigate its own course.

To be sure, the insularity of immigration law has not gone unnoticed by legal scholars. Many have commented upon its persistence and almost all have vigorously condemned it. Aliens, they have urged, should be brought within the shelter of our dominant legal traditions. Immigration law should be made to embody the more universalistic norms, the more spacious conception of legal and moral community, to which liberalism and contemporary public law aspire.[12]

Today, this chorus of criticism is beginning to find expression in the discourse and doctrines of immigration law. New principles based upon fundamentally different values are beginning to undermine the classical regime and to etch the outlines of a new legal order. I shall call these new principles "communitarian," for their central idea is that the government owes legal duties to all individuals who manage to reach America's shores, even to strangers whom it has never undertaken, and has no wish, to protect. Communitarian immigration values, of course, are linked to those of the past. Although rejecting traditional liberalism's emphasis upon consent as the basis for legal obligations to strangers, for example, communitarianism echoes liberalism's emphasis upon universal rights based upon individuals' essential and equal humanity. What is also striking is their departure from the classical values and their affinity to newly emergent public law norms. These new norms derive the government's legal obligations to individuals from the nature of their social interactions and commitments rather than from the government's consent to be bound as expressed through traditional legal forms and procedures.

Although the infusion of communitarian values may profoundly alter immigration law, their ultimate triumph is by no means assured. Their absorption is still tentative and fragmentary, not yet fully confirmed by the Supreme Court. Moreover, they introduce many contradictions into the immigration system—contradictions among those values, the liberal assumptions that still pervade American law, and the vestiges of restrictive nationalism embedded in the classical immigration structure; contradictions within the communitarian ethos itself; and contradictions between communitarian values and contemporary social realities.

This essay explores the nature and implications of this still-embryonic transformation of immigration law. It does so at a time, perhaps only a fleeting moment, when its dimensions and future direction are widely recognized as urgent questions on the national policy agenda. The essay consists of four sections. In section I, elaborate the essential elements of classical immigration law. In section II, I suggest that a fundamental transformation of the classical system is under way and seek to account for this change by analyzing two interacting fields of force. The first involves a set of changed objective conditions, a new social reality, within which immigration law has developed and is being applied. The second involves a fundamental ideological shift, an altered legal consciousness, concerning the sources and nature of the federal government's legal obligations toward individuals generally. This shift has generated doctrinal currents that has washed over other areas of American law for decades. These currents, however, have left immigration law, isolated in the remote eddies and backwaters of the stream, largely untouched. Together, I argue, these forces are beginning to penetrate classical immigration law, reducing its insularity and moving it closer to the mainstream of public law from which it has been separated by its distinctive conceptions and context. In section III, I explore the character of the communitarian immigration law that I believe is emerging in the cases. The final section discusses some unresolved tensions that this new development is creating, tensions whose resolution poses a fundamental problem for contemporary liberalism and American society.

This essay is as much an exercise in the interpretation of legal change as it is one of causal explanation. Immigration is too intimately linked to the basic processes and structures of American life, its legal doctrines too epiphenomenal, to permit easy causal inferences. Only an integrated work of historical, economic, political, sociological, and legal scholarship could begin to unravel the complex interrelationships and account for the new patterns that we are beginning to observe. This essay has a far more modest ambition. It is to crystalize the still-tentative, often ambiguous changes that have begun to roil the surface of the immigration case reports, and to extract from them some larger meaning for our contemporary public law.

I. THE CLASSICAL CONCEPTION OF IMMIGRATION LAW

Classical immigration law emerged in the late nineteenth and early twentieth centuries as a liberal American polity confronted for the first time the felt need to regulate immigration in significant ways. Not surprisingly, classical immigration law mirrored the highly individualistic values that underlay the prevailing social and legal order.[13] But it added to these values several new and somewhat inconsistent ideological elements. Three features of that order help to reveal the character of the classical view. First, the ethnic, cultural and class composition of the immigrant population changed dramatically between the 1870's and World War I. Unlike the "old" immigrants, who had come to the United States primarily from Northern and Western Europe, most of the "new" immigrants came from Southern and Eastern Europe and—until their entry was sharply restricted in the 1880s—from the Orient.[14] This change triggered the explosive passions of racial and religious prejudice, fears of revolutionary contagion, class conflict, and other deep-seated animosities against the newcomers who appeared to threaten the value system known as "Americanism." Powerful pressures to limit both the level of immigration and the rights of aliens consequently developed.[15] Classical immigration law was launched upon this tide of hostility to strangers.

Second, American society was developing a sense of autonomy and leadership on the international stage. The nation's emergence as an industrializing world power, its acquisition of an overseas empire during the 1890's, and a succession of strong, aggressive presidents from McKinley through Wilson, all contributed to the growth of a "new nationalism" in both the domestic and foreign policy spheres.[16]

Third, the larger legal system, of which classical immigration law was a part, was committed to a very broad definition of individual and governmental sovereignty. Individuals' sovereignty was protected through an array of private property rights. A landowner, for example, enjoyed a plenary right to exclude trespassers, including those who had entered with the owner's permission but had violated the conditions under which the permission was granted. The owner owed no duty to trespassers, except to refrain from willfully injuring them or using unreasonable force in their expulsion.[17] The owner was ruler over his domain; his home, as the saying goes, was his castle. Governments, for their part, were protected by analogous public property rights, as well as by immunity doctrines that severely limited the claims that could be asserted against them.[18] In general, tort law imposed few affirmative legal duties to strangers on governments or private individuals; their only obligations were those that they had voluntarily undertaken.[19]

In such a context, control over which strangers might enter was viewed as a powerful expression of the nation's identity and autonomy—in a word, of its sovereignty. Sovereignty entailed the unlimited power of the nation, like that of the free individual, to decide whether, under what conditions, and with what effects it would consent to enter into a relationship with a stranger. The power implied by that sovereignty was enjoyed by the Nation exclusively and was based wholly upon its explicit undertaking; the government simply owed no other legal obligation to those who sought to enter or remain without its consent. That a stranger was desperate to enter, and had invested a great deal in the effort, was as immaterial as the reasons that prompted the government to refuse her admittance. As the Supreme Court stated in 1892, "It is an accepted maxim of international law, that every sovereign nation has the power, as inherent in sovereignty, and essential to self-preservation, to forbid the entrance of foreigners within its dominions, or to admit them only in such cases and upon such conditions as it may see fit to prescribe."[20] In this sense, the classical idea of sovereignty implied a relationship between government and an alien that resembled the relationship in late nineteenth century private law between a landowner and a trespasser. The essential purpose of immigration law, then, like that of property law, was to preserve and enhance this sovereignty.

The individualistic premises of a liberal legal order, of course, did not lead ineluctably to a restrictive immigration policy and a conception of absolute sovereignty that utterly denied aliens' claims to legal protection. Liberalism, after all, does not merely affirm the primacy of individual consent as the bedrock of political and juridical relationships. It also locates fundamental legal rights in individuals by reason of their universal humanity and without regard to contingencies of their status or condition. Just as the sweeping rights of landowners against trespassers in private law were subject to an exception—quite an elastic one, as it turned out—for "attractive nuisances,"[21] so public international law theorists had long advanced competing principles, also derived from liberal premises, emphasizing the state's obligations to protect strangers who were drawn to enter it.[22] Moreover, a liberal economy, celebrating the laissez-faire values of unimpeded resource flow and exchange, would pursue a policy of free immigration. Indeed, American liberalism maintained essentially that policy from the colonial period until the 1880's. This aspect of liberalism, of course, would suggest a far weaker, more qualified notion of sovereignty, one that would tolerate relatively open borders and at least some protections even for aliens who enjoyed no rights under positive domestic law. In the end, the ideological shift from traditional liberalism to restrictive nationalism reflected the influence of external pressures more than the internal logic of principle.

In what follows, we shall see that these two different ideological threads—the one denying that a society owes aliens any obligation to which it does not consent, the other affirming the existence of certain obligations to aliens owed simply by reason of their humanity—are woven throughout the fabric of immigration law. In the classical period, the first of these, reinforced by a growing sense of nationhood and legitimated by then-current notions of limited public and private obligation, clearly dominated the pattern. As we shall see in sections II and III, however, the second thread, now buttressed by more expansive, communitarian principles of obligation drawn from other moral premises and embedded in other areas of the law, is beginning to challenge the primacy of the first, thereby altering that pattern.

This transformation is proceeding around seven central elements of classical immigration law: (1) the restrictive ideal of national community; (2) the principle of judicial deference; (3) the extraconstitutional status of exclusion; (4) the broad federal power to classify aliens; (5) the civil nature of the deportation sanction; (6) the detention power; and (7) the integration of adjudication and enforcement. Although the emerging changes in these norms and doctrines generally parallel one another, there are important differences. Some, for example, are merely incipient, while others are relatively far advanced. But immigration law's gradual assimilation of the communitarian ideal is shaping all of them to some degree.

The Restrictive Ideal of the National Community

The concept of nationhood expresses political, legal, and social dimensions of community. It entails the mutual acceptance of certain norms, participation in a common public life, commitment to an overarching structure of law, and sharing of the benefits and burdens of national institutions.[23] At this abstract level, the notion of national community is definitional, not operational; it tells us very little about who may or may not become a member, and about what practical difference membership makes in individuals' lives. In American law, at least, the struggle over these questions has revolved around the control and conditions of more specific legal statuses— those of naturalborn citizen, naturalized citizen, citizen born abroad, permanent resident alien, nonimmigrant alien, undocumented alien, and the like.[24] In the positive sense, therefore, our conception of nationhood is revealed by the aggregate of these legal categories and the positive rights and obligations that flow from them. More normatively, however, national community is an ideal toward which we aspire, a way of expressing what it is that we share as a people.

Immigration law necessarily mediates between these two meanings. American society has always prided itself on the inclusive, assimilative conception of nationhood that it embraces and offers to those who would join us. These qualities of openness have been a dominant feature of our self-definition and national myths. Emma Lazarus's verse inscribed on the Statue of Liberty celebrates not only the tens of millions of foreign-born who have flocked to our shores, but also the society that awaited them behind the "golden door."[25]

There is much truth in this account, yet it overlooks much truth as well. Insofar as the availability of the legal status of citizenship is concerned, the ease of acquiring membership in the American community has been striking. As early as the colonial period, citizenship was automatically conferred by birth within the colony; for those born elsewhere, that status could still be readily obtained. Anxious to attract labor and enhance property values, the colonies actively and imaginatively promoted immigration by Europeans. Despite opposition in London, colonial naturalization was converted into a relatively inexpensive, expeditious administrative process based upon consent and available to almost all.[26] When the Republic was created, the right of naturalization was, "generally speaking," immediately extended to all whites who could satisfy a brief residency requirement and make a declaration of loyalty.[27] Citizenship has been conferred automatically by birth in the United States (jus soli)[28] and by birth abroad to American parents (jus sanguinis).[29] The full legal equality of birthright citizens and naturalized citizens was well established early in the nineteenth century,[30] and with the adoption of female suffrage in 1920, political equality between all adult citizens was affirmed, at least as a matter of law.[31] Aliens enjoy the protection of the Constitution once they have "entered" the United States; most of the rights that it recognizes are conferred upon "persons" or "people," rather than only upon citizens or lawful resident aliens.[32]

The inclusiveness of the legal and political communities, thus defined, has often been celebrated; under the conditions of American culture and the ideals of traditional liberalism, this inclusiveness may well have been inevitable. Alexander Bickel, for example, maintained that citizenship was "a simple idea for a simple government," arguing that it could not and should not function as an exclusionary concept in a liberal society.[33]

The story of the steady, progressive enlargement of the national community, however, is more complicated and contradictory than Bickel's account suggests. We have already seen that traditional liberal values fail to account for the emergence and character of the classical immigration order. Moreover, the concept of American citizenship, which Bickel thought unimportant in our constitutional vision,[34] actually seems to have mattered a great deal from the very beginning. Although Bickel contends that the original Constitution made "precious few references to the concept" and "made nothing depend on it explicitly, aside from a few offices,"[35] Justice Rehnquist is probably nearer to the mark in emphasizing that citizenship is a constitutionally significant status "in no less than 11 instances in a political document noted for its brevity."[36] It is, after all, a prerequisite for all high elected officeholders; indeed, the President must be "a natural born Citizen."[37] Citizenship is also required for access to certain categories of federal court jurisdiction,[38] and even for access to the voting rights protected by the post-Civil War amendments.[39] It seems doubtful that at a time when Loyalist disaffection was very much on the minds of American politicians,[40] the Founding Fathers thought citizenship an inconsequential status.

Historically, even the category of citizen has obscured important differences in legal status, the Constitution's unqualified language notwithstanding. That some 125,000 individuals of Japanese descent were American citizens did not prevent them from being driven from their homes into internment camps during World War II solely on the basis of their ancestry.[41] The long struggle over political equality for females, a majority of the population, reflected the Supreme Court's conviction, in Rogers Smith's words, "that participation is extraneous to American citizenship."[42] One century after Congress and the Constitution had overruled the *Dred Scott* decision[43] and decreed the freed slaves to be American citizens,[44] it remained necessary for Congress to enact the Voting Rights Act of 1965[45] to secure the franchise for blacks and other minorities. The legal condition of the American Indian was, if anything, even more degraded and "alienated" than that of blacks.[46]

Perhaps most revealing of the exclusionary possibilities concealed within the broad portmanteau of American citizenship is the legal status of residents of the territories owned by the United States. In *Downes v. Bidwell (The Insular Cases)*,[47] which Bickel unaccountably fails to mention in his article on citizenship, the Supreme Court held that Congress need not confer citizenship on residents of the conquered territories;[48] if it wished, it could create a second-class American citizenship. Indeed, Congress did just that with respect to Puerto Rico, the Virgin Islands, Guam, and the Northern Marianas.[49] And in *Balzac v. People of Porto Rico*,[50] the Court held that United States citizenship for a Puerto Rican conferred no rights under the Constitution except the right to move to the mainland. There, as a state resident, she could "enjoy every right of any other citizen of the United States, civil, social and political."[51]

If classical immigration law permitted Congress to differentiate between American citizens for the purpose of qualifying for full membership in the national community,[52] it is not surprising that the right of aliens to participate equally in American life was severely limited. It is true that aliens were not wholly excluded from constitutional protection. As early as 1886, for example, the Supreme Court strongly affirmed that the Constitution safeguards *all* individuals within the United States, including aliens, from invidious discrimination by the states.[53] Less than twenty years later, the Court ruled that even an excludable alien was entitled to at least a minimal form of administrative due process.[54] But while these holdings demonstrated that the universalistic character of traditional liberalism retained some force during the classical period, they hardly defined an expansive national community. Although the equal protection principle did apply to aliens, for example, the status of alienage applies to a multitude of individuals with very different relationships to American society. That status has always remained a constitutionally permissible ground for classifying individuals for many invidious purposes. Thus, the equal protection principle did not prevent governments at all levels from barring lawfully admitted permanent resident aliens from public employment,[55] employment on public works,[56] ownership of real property,[57] and many, many other kinds of activities through which political and legal communities customarily express their essential character and unity.[58] And while due process was owed to the excludable alien deprived of liberty, the process that was due did not even include a right to a judicial hearing unless the individual claimed that she was in fact a United States citizen.[59]

This restrictive conception of national community was manifested most vividly in the succession of basic federal statutes that regulated immigration during the classical period. Although opposition to aliens has been common throughout American history[60] and certain categories of undesirables, such as prostitutes and public charges, were excluded as early as 1645,[61] blanket federal exclusions began only during the 1880's with laws limiting and then barring the immigration of Chinese laborers. Blanket exclusions continued with the 1917 statute imposing—after many earlier presidential vetoes—a literacy requirement and barring political radicals and some Asians.[62] The 1921 and 1924 laws excluded aliens statutorily ineligible for citizenship, including most Asians. They also imposed quotas based upon the "national origins" of the existing United States population, computed according to a formula decidedly favorable to British immigrants and unfavorable to immigrants from Southern and Eastern Europe.[63] The 1952 Act left this exclusionary structure essentially intact, except to add provisions making all races eligible for naturalization but barring putative subversives.[64] The 1965 amendments, while repealing the national origins system, established for the first time a ceiling on immigration from the Western Hemisphere, designed primarily to limit the influx of Caribbean Basin laborers that had occurred during the earlier Bracero program.[65] In 1978, the hemispheric ceilings were replaced by worldwide and per country limits.[66]

A final feature of the classical conception of national community that is of particular interest here is that it was preeminently a political, not a judicial, artifact. Congress defined the qualifications for, and attributes of, each of the legal statutes that composed it, and the Attorney General administered that definition. Until the 1960's, the federal government created few positive entitlements even for citizens. Moreover, the egalitarian potential of the due process and equal protection safeguards of the fifth and fourteenth amendments,[67] especially as applied to aliens, remained largely undiscovered. Except for a relatively few cases construing open-ended constitutional principles,[68] the courts' role in defining national membership was essentially limited to interpreting and enforcing the requirements for naturalization and other statutory statuses and occasionally construing the relatively determinate citizenship clause.[69]

Because it was Congress that essentially shaped the legal dimensions of the national community, its contours reflected the parochial, temporal political values so characteristic of the legislative process rather than the more cosmopolitan values of universality and pluralism. Citizenship in the liberal American polity, while almost always accessible to residents who desired it, was not available to all. And even citizen status did not always carry with it the full panoply of constitutional protections, either de facto or de jure. For many aliens, full membership was only a distant goal, not a palpable reality. Classical immigration law did not close the golden door, but it narrowed the passageway through it and limited the ways in which one might participate in the society after one had entered.

Judicial Deference

In the canon of classical immigration law, judges should be seen—if absolutely necessary—but not heard. For almost a century, the Court has abjured any significant judicial role in the area of immigration policy. Justice Field penned the classic statement of this position in *The Chinese Exclusion Case:*[70] "[If Congress] considers the presence of foreigners of a different race in this country, who will not assimilate with us, to be dangerous to its peace and security, its determination is conclusive upon the judiciary."[71] Such self-abnegation may strike the contemporary reader, accustomed to lusty assertions of judicial machismo, as a bit faint-hearted, especially when applied to a measure that managed to combine blatant racism, retroactive lawmaking, and a flagrant denial of due process in a noisome statutory stew. Several years later, Justice Gray insisted that courts may not review an immigration inspector's decision concerning the facts underlying an alien's imprisonment and exclusion even in habeas corpus proceedings unless Congress expressly provides otherwise.[72] This statement has a quaint, antique ring when read in an era in which even clear statutory indications of administrative finality have not managed to preclude judicial review.[73] Yet both of these pronouncements apparently remain good law in the Supreme Court.[74] Moreover, the Court has not hesitated to extend this "special judicial deference to congressional policy choices in the immigration context"[75] to administrative officials as well as to Congress.[76]

Judicial rhetoric about deference to the "political branches" and to administrative expertise, of course, is commonplace. Such talk is a venerable aspect of the courts' protective coloration and should not necessarily be taken too seriously. The rhetoric of judicial deference in immigration cases prior to the 1980's, however, was striking in that courts almost invariably meant what they said. With a few exceptions,[77] the Supreme Court reflexively confirmed the deference principle with a decision on the merits in favor of the government rather than using that principle, as it did in many other administrative law contexts, merely as a disarming prelude to judicial self-assertion.[78]

It is worthwhile pausing to consider why this deference persisted for so long. One might suspect that judicial reluctance to challenge the power of the other branches reflected the weak political support for aliens. Yet even the Warren Court, whose case reports are filled with decisions checking governmental authorities on behalf of politically vulnerable groups,[79] was abjectly deferential in the context of immigration law and thus firmly within the classical tradition.[80] A lack of political influence, therefore, fails to explain why courts that eagerly picked up the cudgels to protect convicted criminals did not do so for aliens.

Other possible explanations for judicial deference seem equally dubious. The Immigration and Naturalization Service (INS), whose administrative competence and fairness have often been harshly criticized,[81] would seem an odd repository for judicial trust. Nor has the congressional record in the immigration area been one to inspire much judicial confidence;[82] legislative threats to constitutional values have been common.[83] Another rationale for extraordinary judicial deference in classical immigration cases—the presence of foreign policy, national security, or other questions of an essentially nonadjudicatory nature—has explicitly been disavowed by the Court.[84] And even if one remains skeptical of this disclaimer—even if one believes that immigration cases often present questions of legislative fact and foreign policy with which courts are and should be profoundly uncomfortable—that rationale can hardly explain the striking pattern of judicial deference in cases decided as late as the 1970's in which daunting questions of that kind were either inconsequential or wholly absent.[85] Indeed, judicial deference cannot even be explained on the grounds that only the claims of aliens are involved: the plaintiffs in some of these decisions asserted claims—unsuccessfully, as it turned out—based primarily upon the rights of United States *citizens,* not of aliens.[86]

A wholly satisfactory answer to this puzzle still eludes us. I suspect, however, that the pronounced judicial passivity in classical immigration law has been subtly linked to the powerful conception of national sovereignty that lies at the heart of that tradition, and arises from the impact of that conception on the judge. In a constitutional system marked by an extraordinary degree of political, institutional, and social fragmentation, manifestations of solidarity and nationhood can exercise a potent hold over the judicial, as well as the lay, imagination. The flag, the President, the American moon landings—these are compelling symbols of our national spirit and collective will, all the more awesome for their rarity in our atomized lives.[87] The idea of sovereignty, so elusive in our domestic constitutional structure, may come closest to being reified and recognizable when a unified national government deploys its laws against one who is plausibly seen as an outsider—as, quite literally, alien.

Other considerations reinforce the power of the sovereignty concept as an explanation for judicial deference. For over a century, the states have been consistently excluded from any significant role in the administration of immigration policy.[88] Moreover, immigration policy has enjoyed a considerable consensus as among the President, Congress, and the bureaucracy; one searches the immigration cases in vain for a titanic interbranch struggle like those that have occurred in other areas of public law.[89] One measure of this consensus is that Congress has chosen to confer exceedingly broad discretion over the most far-reaching immigration decisions,[90] has delegated this discretion not merely to the executive branch but to a cabinet official who traditionally is a close political confidant of the President, and has done so not only for matters obviously requiring the weighing of many administrative considerations but also for those impinging upon fundamental civil liberties.[91]

In the face of broad, express congressional delegations of authority to the executive branch in the area of external relations, in which the President also enjoys substantial constitutional power in his own right, in view of the strong consensus between the political branches, and in light of the minimal moral claims upon us of those deemed to be outside the national community, judicial power is most problematic and the President's authority, in Justice Jackson's words, "is at its maximum." There, "[he may] be said (for what it may be worth) to personify the federal sovereignty."[92]

The Extraconstitutional Status of Exclusion

In the classical tradition, the exclusion process—the process for determining which aliens may enter the United States for the first time, or which aliens, having entered previously, may reenter after a significant absence or may remain after having been "paroled" into the country—is essentially freed from any significant constitutional constraints. Concerning excludable aliens, classical immigration law holds that "the decisions of . . . administrative officers, acting within powers expressly conferred by Congress, are due process of law."[93] Here, at least, the Constitution, not just politics, seems to stop at the water's edge.[94]

Congress and the Attorney General, by statute and regulation, long ago provided certain procedural rights to excludable aliens equivalent to those enjoyed by aliens who have "entered" the United States and who therefore can claim the Constitution's protection.[95] Still, the extraconstitutional status of exclusion proceedings remains far more than a formal or academic matter. Some important differences between exclusion and deportation procedures persist.[96] Moreover, what Congress and the Attorney General have given, they may also take away—unless, of course, that procedure is constitutionally required. Such a withdrawal of procedural rights is not merely a theoretical possibility. As unprecedented numbers of excludable aliens seek entry,[97] immigration officials desperately seek to manage their caseloads by economizing on procedures. The Simpson-Mazzoli immigration reform legislation recently derailed in Congress, for example, would authorize summary exclusion—without administrative hearing or court review—of aliens seeking to enter without adequate documentation.[98]

Finally, exclusion's extraconstitutional status has encouraged and legitimated some of the most deplorable governmental conduct toward both aliens and American citizens ever recorded in the annals of the Supreme Court. In *United States ex rel. Knauff v. Shaughnessy,*[99] to cite a notorious example, the Court allowed the wife of an American citizen who had served in the United States Army and been honorably discharged to be permanently excluded from the United States without any hearing. Her exclusion was based upon an administrative finding that admission would be "prejudicial to the interests of the United States"; this finding in turn was based upon confidential information disclosed neither to the wife, her husband, nor the Court. In an even more infamous case, *Shaughnessy v. United States ex rel. Mezei,*[100] the Court countenanced the exclusion and two-year incarceration[101] of a lawful United States resident of twenty-five years' standing on the basis of these same ex parte procedures.[102]

While these decisions are easy to denounce and their reasoning is not difficult to demolish,[103] they cannot simply be dismissed as McCarthy-era aberrations, anachronistic monuments to cold war hysteria.[104] The Supreme Court continues to cite them with apparent approval.[105] Indeed, their teaching remains enshrined in the current immigration statute. If, for example, a consular officer just out of Foreign Service training "has reason to believe" that an alien seeks to enter "incidentally to engage in activities which would be prejudicial to the public interest,"[106] she may deny the alien entry; her decision is final, subject only to administrative review.[107] Moreover, if an alien "may appear" to an immigration officer to be excludable on that or several other political grounds and the Attorney General agrees that the alien should be excluded on the basis of confidential information that he thinks should not be disclosed, that essentially ends the matter.[108]

The Power to Classify Aliens

The extraconstitutional status of exclusion procedures has been extended and strengthened by yoking it to another distinctive feature of the classical conception—the virtually unlimited power of the federal government to classify aliens on the basis of *substantive* considerations.[109] The equal protection principle enshrined in the fifth and fourteenth amendments prohibits the irrational or invidious exercise of legislative and executive power. Its requirement that legal classifications be related to a proper governmental objective[110] has, in other areas of public law, annihilated a formidable number of statutes, regulations and other official actions of every kind and description. Yet classical immigration law has essentially neutralized this principle.

In the immigration context Congress "regularly makes rules that would be unacceptable if applied to citizens."[111] It would be difficult indeed to make sense of the history of American immigration law were that observation not manifestly true. There is little question, for example, that the squalid prejudice that led Congress summarily to exclude Chinese laborers,[112] to preserve the ethnic distribution of an earlier era through national origin quotas,[113] and to preclude Asian-Americans for decades from becoming naturalized United States citizens,[114] only withstood equal protection scrutiny because they involved aliens and were instituted by the federal government.[115] Yet the Supreme Court did not hesitate to bless these and other such practices.[116]

In fact, the equal protection principle has been applied less rigorously to federal alienage classifications than to the states';[117] the Court has not required the former to demonstrate even a "rational basis," much less the "compelling" governmental interest required of the latter.[118] Although there are substantial arguments based upon constitutional text, structure, and intent in favor of a more general differentiation of equal protection standards as between federal and state classifications,[119] the Court has taken that dual standard approach for only a few classifications. The most notable of these is alienage.

As with judicial deference in the immigration area generally, it is not at all obvious why federal alienage classifications have been singled out for kid-glove treatment. One theory might hold that aliens are more "discrete and insular" in state politics and therefore more deserving of special judicial solicitude than they are in federal politics. This argument is plausible but not convincing. It is true that federal responsibilities for foreign affairs, national economic growth, and immigration generate certain policies that almost all aliens, despite their heterogeneity, might be expected to favor. Moreover, certain specialized organs of the federal government, including the INS and the relevant House and Senate judiciary subcommittees, are especially concerned about such matters and—at least theoretically—provide a forum in which aliens' interests can be advanced.[120] On the other hand, aliens and their ethnic compatriots who are citizens are concentrated in a handful of states, a fact of great political significance.[121] In at least some of those states, such as California, Texas, and New York, these ethnic groups, sometimes even including the disenfranchised aliens themselves, exert considerable influence upon local, state, congressional, and even presidential politics.[122] Although the situation might well be different in other states in which aliens' interests are less well-represented, it is far from clear that the political influence of aliens will generally be greater at the national level where their voting and organizational powers are more diffuse.

A second argument in favor of the essentially unlimited federal power to classify aliens might be grounded in the constitutional text itself. The difficulty, however, is that the only explicit reference in the Constitution to this question, apart from references to United States citizenship[123] and the slave trade,[124] is the provision authorizing Congress "[t]o establish an uniform Rule of Naturalization."[125] This hardly qualifies as a sweeping grant of power over immigration, much less as a ringing endorsement of invidious federal alienage classifications having nothing whatever to do with the naturalization process. Although the precise source of the exclusive congressional power to regulate immigration is far from clear,[126] it is nonetheless well-established.[127] But because this power is implicit rather than textual, it tells us little about the appropriate relationship between the equal protection principle and the federal government's power to classify.

To account for the privileged status that federal alienage classifications enjoy in classical immigration law, we must look, I suspect, neither to the alien's condition nor to the Constitution's text. Rather, the explanation can be found in the classical tradition's self-consciously political definition of national community and in its norm of extraordinary judicial deference to that choice. By the very nature of this definition, citizens and aliens are almost *never* "similarly situated," while the federal government's interests in emphasizing that difference—for example, giving preference to citizens in order to encourage aliens to naturalize and thus join the national community[128]—is almost *always* deemed compelling.[129]

The "Civil" Nature of Deportation

A fundamental tenet of classical immigration law holds that deportation is a civil, administrative proceeding, not a criminal prosecution. Deportation, Justice Holmes wrote without elaboration, is not "a punishment; it is simply a refusal by the Government to harbor persons whom it does not want."[130] This distinction possesses little logical power: at least concerning aliens who have established a foothold in American society, it is a legal fiction with nothing, other than considerations of cost and perhaps administrative convenience, to recommend it.[131] Nevertheless, it has proved to possess the staying power that Holmes knew to be far more important in law than logic.[132]

The legal consequences of classifying deportation as civil and not punitive are considerable. Certain constitutional rights, such as those protected by the sixth amendment,[133] are expressly limited to criminal proceedings. Others, such as the prohibition against ex post facto laws,[134] have been held to apply only to criminal or quasi-criminal "punishments."[135] In the immigration context, at least, the applicability of the exclusionary rule, the allocation of the burden of proof, and even the right to judicial review itself, may depend upon how the action is classified.[136]

With so many legal rights turning upon the assignment of the proceeding to one category or the other, we should expect that the hoary characterization of deportation as civil rather than punitive would be firmly rooted in the importance of its real world consequences to aliens. Deportation, however, has little in common with civil sanctions. Not only is it often imposed for conduct that also constitutes a crime, a feature that civil sanctions only occasionally exhibit, but it often results in incarceration.[137] Deportation, in fact, serves as an important adjunct and supplement to criminal law enforcement, and it reflects judgments, essentially indistinguishable from those that the criminal law routinely makes, concerning the moral worth of individual conduct.[138] For those deportees who cannot acquire American citizenship[139] and will therefore remain stateless, deportation may be catastrophic.[140] Even deportees who will not be rendered stateless may nevertheless be unable to return to their country of nationality due to perilous economic or political conditions prevailing there,[141] while deportation to a third country may mean having to live as a stranger in a strange land. Even those who can return to their country of nationality may be expelled from the only society to which they feel some attachment and be obliged to go instead to a place with which they have only the most tenuous link.[142] In addition to causing profound estrangement,[143] deportation, unlike conventional criminal punishment, imposes upon the alien a more or less permanent disability. Once deported, an alien may be prevented from ever returning legally; indeed, merely reapplying for admission constitutes a felony unless she first obtains the Attorney General's express consent.[144]

In view of what is inevitably and personally at stake, then, it is undeniable that deportation punishes the alien and punishes her severely.[145] To maintain, as classical immigration law consistently has done, that deportation resembles a sanction like being ejected from a national park rather than that of being banished or sentenced to jail, suggests that something deeply symbolic, not dryly logical, has been at work in the shaping of the doctrine. In condoning the deportation of the alien without the safeguards that government must ordinarily afford before it can impose grave punishment,[146] the law affirms the contingent nature of her claims on the community.[147] The government's obligations to the alien are viewed as resting upon her formal status rather than upon her actual relationship to the society. Since under the classical order the alien's entry was conceived of as a privilege whose continued enjoyment was conditional upon her compliance with the formal terms that the government prescribed, deportation was simply the revocation of her license, a reversion to the status quo ante. No special procedural safeguards for this reversion were thought to be necessary.[148]

The Power to Detain

In classical immigration law, the detention of aliens[149]—often involving incarceration—has been an important tool of program administration and law enforcement: it ensures that aliens will appear for their hearings, commit no offenses, be inclined to cooperate with the immigration authorities, and, if in the country illegally, not compete for jobs with lawful aliens and citizens. The statute therefore expressly authorizes the Attorney General to detain aliens in a variety of circumstances.[150] But the detention authority is more than a programmatic resource, ancillary to the power to exclude and deport. Detention is also an awesome power in its own right.

Shaughnessy v. United States ex rel. Mezei[151] most vividly illustrates this point.[152] Mezei, a long-time resident of the United States who had journeyed abroad to visit his mother, was excluded on undisclosed security grounds when he returned. After some sixteen months in custody, the government announced that it had abandoned its futile efforts to find a country to which he could be deported. Thereafter, Mezei remained on Ellis Island in what Justice Black in dissent described as an "island prison" in which Mezei must "stay indefinitely, maybe for life."[153] The Supreme Court summarily rejected Mezei's challenge to his exclusion. Having never seen the government's evidence,[154] there was of course little for the Court to say. Mezei, it noted, was actually the beneficiary of "legislative grace"; as an excludable alien, the authorities could have kept him aboard the vessel that brought him here rather than extending "temporary harborage" at Ellis Island.[155] Mezei's complaint was with the countries that would not accept him, not with the American government: "[A]n alien in [Mezei's] position," the Court concluded, "is no more ours than theirs."[156]

Mezei was unusual only in the potentially indefinite duration of the detention. Prior to 1954, INS policy was to detain almost all aliens at the port of entry pending a determination of admissibility.[157] Although the Supreme Court expressly upheld this policy, at least regarding Communists, who were denied any bail,[158] some lower courts resisted it.[159] In 1954, the Justice Department decided to change its detention policy, closed Ellis Island, and began to parole aliens into the country pending determination of their admissibility. Detention was reserved for situations in which the alien was likely to abscond or considerations of national security or public safety required continued confinement.[160] In the Court's words, detention thereafter became "the exception, not the rule"; although parole was a matter of administrative grace that in no way altered the alien's status as an outsider seeking entry, the new policy reflected "the humane qualities of an enlightened civilization."[161]

If that was true, humanity and enlightenment were more transient than the Court supposed. In 1981, when South Florida was besieged by aliens from the Caribbean Basin, the pre-1954 policy of routine detention with limited exceptions was reestablished.[162] The effect of this influx upon detention was dramatic and immediate; during 1982, more than one million person-days were spent in INS detention, almost double the figure for 1980.[163] The mass, routine incarceration of aliens, sometimes for long periods of time and often under overcrowded and unpleasant conditions, had once again become a fundament of our immigration policy.[164] It reaffirmed two classical conceptions. First, it implied that aliens remain wholly outside the national community unless and until the formal requirements of membership are satisfied. Second, it implied a strong view of national sovereignty, one holding that the nation cannot be obliged against its will to enter into a continuing relationship with an intruder.[165] Under the classical model, such an individual has thrust herself upon the nation and may therefore be treated as the utter stranger that she is; she may be unceremoniously separated from our midst. In the *Mezei* Court's revealing phrase, she is "no more ours than theirs."[166]

Non-Independent Adjudication

Under our system of public administration, it is common for agencies to integrate investigative, prosecutorial, and adjudicatory functions within one bureaucracy. Regulatory commissions and boards are typically organized in that fashion, and due process is not thereby offended.[167] But of all the federal agencies that dispense "mass justice" to individuals,[168] the INS has been unusual, if not unique, in operating a system in which those who receive evidence and formally adjudicate individuals' rights are subject to the direct administrative supervision of officials empowered to interrogate, arrest, detain, and impose severe sanctions upon individuals.[169] Traditionally, the immigration judges[170] who must decide which aliens shall be excluded and deported were an integral part of the INS and, like the INS law enforcement agents, were subject to the direct and indirect influence of its political leadership.[171]

In the immigration setting, adjudications by nonindependent decisionmakers raise especially troublesome questions. In *Wong Yang Sung v. Mc-Grath*,[172] the Court seemed to agree. The case came before the Court in 1950 under the then-applicable 1917 immigration statute, which required deportation hearings to be conducted by immigration inspectors whose duties were not limited to these adjudications; in addition, they investigated similar cases and might have performed some prosecutorial functions in the very cases that came before them for adjudication. The Court denounced this system, finding it "particularly" objectionable in deportation proceedings, which involve "a voteless class of litigants" unfamiliar with American law and custom, and often, the English language.[173] Noting that the Administrative Procedure Act (APA)[174] did not permit this practice,[175] the Court seemed to hold that a deportation hearing before an independent decisionmaker was constitutionally required.[176] But this concern for independence soon vanished—or at least was easily mollified. For when Congress responded to the Court's decision shortly thereafter by establishing a system of immigration judges who performed only adjudicatory duties but worked under the administrative aegis of the more enforcement-oriented INS district directors, the Court found no constitutional defect.[177] What had occurred to change the Court's view? Therein lies a confusing tale.

As early as 1948, Congress had considered legislation[178] to exempt the INS from the APA provisions that required trial-type procedures, including a substantially independent hearing officer, for certain kinds of adjudications.[179] Advocates of such exemption had argued, inter alia, that creating a corps of independent decisionmakers would be too costly and that immigration was too closely linked to political functions and foreign affairs to be subject to the APA's more scrupulous procedures.[180] After the Court in *Wong Yang Sung* suggested that the APA's separation-of-functions provisions were constitutionally required for deportation adjudications, Congress in 1950 adopted a rider to the Justice Department's supplemental appropriation that exempted exclusion and deportation proceedings from those APA requirements.[181] In 1952, Congress enacted a new and comprehensive immigration statute that included a separation-of-functions provision only slightly broader than that in the 1917 law, which had provided only that a hearing officer could not decide the same case that he had investigated,[182] but narrower than that in the APA. The 1952 provision, which remains in effect today, prohibits a hearing officer from conducting a proceeding in a case in which she has performed either investigative or prosecuting functions.[183] This procedure is to be "the sole and exclusive" deportation procedure.[184]

A sharply divided Court upheld these new provisions three years later in *Marcello v. Bonds*,[185] but its reasoning defies comprehension even today. An alien, Carlos Marcello, had challenged the 1952 Act's deportation procedures on the grounds that, inter alia, they left the hearing officer subject to the supervision and control of INS investigators and prosecutors, thereby violating the APA's separation-of-functions requirement and Marcello's due process rights.[186] The Court characterized the statutory issue as whether Congress in the 1952 immigration act had reversed its decision in the 1950 appropriations rider to exempt deportation cases from APA procedural requirements and had in effect reinstated *Wong Yang Sung* by making the APA's hearing provisions directly applicable to deportation proceedings. Concluding that Congress had not done so, it rejected Marcello's claim.[187]

The Court, however, failed even to acknowledge the real question: how could the 1950 appropriations rider possibly have overruled *Wong Yang Sung?* That decision, although ambiguous about precisely how much separation of functions due process required, was clear that the *Constitution itself* demanded a more impartial tribunal than Congress or the INS had yet afforded.[188] That being so, the Court's comparison of the APA provisions and 1952 Act's deportation procedures was quite beside the point. For purposes of constitutional analysis, the relevant comparison was between the 1952 Act's procedures and the earlier ones invalidated in *Wong Yang Sung*, for the issue was whether the new procedures met the Court's constitutional objections to the old ones.

The most generous interpretation of the Court's performance in *Marcello* would be that the Court, reasoning sub silentio, had made that comparison and had discerned sufficient differences between the two statutes to render *Wong Yang Sung* irrelevant. To have done so explicitly, of course, would have required the Court to say just how much independence the Constitution demanded of adjudicators in deportation cases. But the Court was not then prepared to confront that question, nor has it been since. Indeed, when the Court turned to Marcello's due process claim, which invoked *Wong Yang Sung*, the Court could manage only a one-sentence evasion of the issue:

> The contention is without substance when considered against the long-standing practice in deportation proceedings, judicially approved in numerous decisions in the federal courts, and against the special considerations applicable to deportation which the Congress may take into account in exercising its particularly broad discretion in immigration matters.[189]

Classical immigration law, the Court seemed to be saying, sanctioned a system of adjudication in which the hierarchy of legitimate legal succession is completely reversed. Here, where sovereignty confronts strangers, the Constitution can be subordinated to a congressional statute, indeed, to mere administrative practice. The Red Queen could not have said it better.

II. Pressures for Change

Each of these sturdy redoubts of classical immigration law—a restrictive notion of national community; extraordinary judicial deference; the extra-constitutional status of exclusion; the unlimited federal power to classify; the civil nature of deportation proceedings; broad detention power; and nonindependent adjudication—is under siege today. Capitulation seems only a matter of time for some of these doctrines, while for others the outcome remains highly uncertain. The forces of change, however, are insistently hammering at the gate, threatening the autonomy and insularity that have long sheltered classical immigration law from developments elsewhere in the legal culture.

The assaults upon the classical legal order in immigration come from two different kinds of pressure. The first includes what might be called *structural* changes. These are shifts in the basic economic, demographic, social, and political institutions and relationships that inescapably shape immigration policy. The second consists of changes in *ideology* or legal consciousness. These are altered beliefs about the meaning of justice, the rightness or wrongness of certain actions, and the proper role of law and of particular legal institutions in society.

It is important to recognize that the legal and policy implications of these changes are to some degree indeterminate. Each structural change, for example, poses problems for immigration law that might generate a variety of possible responses. Thus, it is not at all inevitable, though I think it likely, that the recent massive influx of undocumented aliens would lead to expanded, rather than reduced, legal protections for them. By the same token, new values concerning the sources and nature of obligations to strangers in public and private law contain internally contradictory elements that may tend to drive immigration law and policy in quite different directions. We saw earlier that this contradiction can be traced to a tension within the interwoven strands of liberalism and restrictive nationalism upon which classical immigration law has drawn.[190]

In addition to those ambiguities, both structure and ideology bear a complex relationship to the system of immigration law and administration that is already in place. As the experience with the Caribbean immigration of the 1980's suggests, structure and ideology are autonomous to some degree, influenced by their own ebbs and flows and by conditions over which immigration law can exercise little effective control. Yet as that same experience shows, structure and ideology are also shaped by the existing system. Finally, the precise relationship between these two factors, legal ideology and social structure, is uncertain, as is the causal contribution that each makes to observed changes in immigration policy.[191]

Structural Changes

Structural conditions, by their nature, do not appear as discrete, clearly bounded phenomena. Instead, they are multifaceted, interrelated, and causally complex. For analytical purposes, however, one can distinguish a number of structural changes that are beginning to impinge upon immigration law in important ways. I shall discuss five: the constraining of American foreign policy; changes in economic conditions; mass refugee and asylum claims; the influx of undocumented aliens; and shifts in political forces. Taken together, these structural changes call into serious question the continued plausibility and relevance of the assumptions concerning consent-derived obligation, strong sovereignty, and restrictive national community that linked and legitimated the elements of classical immigration law.

The Constraining of American Foreign Policy.   Classical immigration law developed during a period in which the United States emerged from relative isolation into a position of international power and, for a time, unchallenged supremacy. Only toward the end of this period, in the 1960's, did the nation begin to face any serious threats of military and diplomatic vulnerability. The last decade, however, has witnessed a significant erosion of the power of the United States to work its will in the world. During the post-Vietnam period, a succession of economic, political, and military crises has occurred in areas of the world of great strategic importance to the United States. Examples include the Arab oil embargo; wars in the Middle East; the Iranian revolution; confrontations with the Soviet Union over Afghanistan, Poland, Africa, and Southeast Asia; continuing instability and repression by Caribbean basin and other Third World regimes; economic and political weakness among some of our allies; the emergence of Japan, Korea, and other Asian countries as effective competitors in world markets; the near-collapse of the Mexican economy; and protracted world recession. These crises have left the United States more dependent than ever upon the goodwill of other nations for the attainment of its policy objectives. We probably enjoy less freedom of action today on the world stage than we have since we came to maturity as a world power at the end of the last century, when the ideology of restrictive nationalism and the structure of classical immigration law took root.[192]

This adjustment in the international balance of power inevitably affects our immigration policy. For example, the United States' thirst for Mexican oil and gas and its desire to sustain stable, politically moderate regimes in the volatile Caribbean basin have almost certainly discouraged the INS from controlling the southern border as tightly as it might. Similarly, strong United States opposition to Soviet-sponsored regimes such as those in Afghanistan, Cuba, and Kampuchea, coupled with its firm support for authoritarian regimes in Central America and the Philippines, has made the administration of the Refugee Act of 1980 seem incoherent and arbitrary.[193] The growing reluctance of the United Kingdom, Australia, and other previously "open" countries to admit Third World immigrants[194] has intensified pressures on the United States to relax its own restrictions.

Dependency, of course, is an exceedingly volatile, complex, and poorly understood psychological phenomenon at the level of individuals.[195] It is surely no less so at the level of nations. With respect to immigration law, a number of quite different, perhaps inconsistent, responses by the political branches and by the courts are possible. Congress might react defensively, hoping to restore our diminished sense of autonomy and well-being by restricting both immigration levels and alien rights, much as the United Kingdom has recently done.[196] Courts might see the matter differently. They might regard the interdependence between nations as a justification for a more permissive stance, softening the sharp boundary between subject and object, government and alien, us and them, that has characterized classical immigration law. What seems clear, however, is that feelings of greater dependency can modify our concepts of national sovereignty and community in subtle ways, altering immigration law in the process.

Economic Changes.   Classical immigration law emerged from a society in which rapid economic growth, with the exception of the Depression era, was more or less constant and taken for granted.[197] Immigration has consistently been viewed as a valuable device for influencing the labor market.[198] Prior to the 1920's, that generally meant relatively unlimited immigration—except for Orientals—to supply cheap manpower for an industrializing economy. In more recent years, it has meant limiting non-family legal immigration to workers capable of meeting specialized needs,[199] adopting special programs to supply agricultural laborers for farms in the Southwest,[200] and tolerating large numbers of undocumented workers who fill the lowest rungs of the occupational ladder.[201]

During the last decade, however, economic conditions have deteriorated. Low rates of growth, high unemployment and underemployment, and chronic inflation[202] have created a climate of economic uncertainty in which immigration policy is being pulled in several different directions. In part, this reflects the fact that immigration now creates a more intricate pattern of effects upon the domestic economy than ever before. The issue of undocumented aliens is an example. Labor economists are sharply divided concerning whether and to what extent undocumented workers displace domestic labor.[203] There seems little doubt, however, that at least in particular economic sectors, such as low-margin service establishments and certain agricultural industries, undocumented workers willing to work at or below the minimum wage rate preserve and create many jobs that would not survive in a more restricted, higher-wage labor market.[204]

For the vast majority of Americans who do not have to compete with undocumented aliens for jobs, housing, or services, this productive activity almost certainly constitutes a significant net benefit by creating anti-inflationary pressures and generating greater, wealth throughout the society.[205] By helping American products to meet low-wage competition from abroad, such labor is an important national resource. At a time of fiscal stringency, American taxpayers are also probably advantaged on balance by the presence of undocumented aliens, who appear to pay a good deal more in direct state and local sales taxes, Social Security and withholding tax, and indirect taxes than they receive in governmental benefits.[206]

Other interactions between a changing economy and immigration are also important. For example, immigration is already altering both the short-term and long-term demographic profiles of the United States in ways that may have enormous implications for the future shape of the economy.[207] Aliens admitted to the United States under labor certifications also increase the society's wealth and efficiency by meeting labor market shortages and providing the means for flexible adjustments to new economic conditions. In certain occupational areas, such as the staffing of municipal hospital systems, they have filled crucial gaps, permitting some breathing space for longer-term development of specialized domestic manpower.[208]

These examples, of course, do not begin to tell the whole economic story. For the many domestic workers who do not enjoy any easy insulation from the competitive effects of a large pool of undocumented aliens, the presence of relatively docile, desperate aliens willing and even anxious to accept very low wages and often illegal working conditions may be nothing less than a calamity. The easy availability of such workers has probably retarded technological innovation in some industries, encouraged employers to violate labor standards, and accelerated the decline of labor unions. Certain public services in particular localities have been severely burdened by undocumented aliens. Other economic effects are even more ambiguous. Demographic changes, and their economic consequences, are notoriously difficult to predict.[209] Even the system of labor certification for alien workers has had mixed consequences. It is said to have been abused by employers and putative employees alike, to suffer from administrative and other inefficiencies, and to have produced low-quality services in some important instances.[210]

If the precise relationship between immigration and economic changes is opaque, however, the importance of that relationship is transparently clear. Classical immigration law, as we have seen, responded in part to the rhythms of the labor market.[211] In this respect, the 1980's are likely to be no different. The new economic order that the United States now confronts, especially the intensified competitive pressures that are spurring it at a time of lagging productivity growth, constitutes a structural change of which the political branches and the courts will surely take account in deciding the kind of society that immigration law is to fashion and defend.

Refugee and Asylum Claims.   Unlike the world in which classical immigration law first evolved, today's world is teeming with refugees—individuals displaced from their homes and countries by convulsive events such as civil war, persecution, natural disaster, and unimaginable destitution.[212] There have always been refugees, of course, but the brutality of modern warfare, the ferocity of political struggle, and the disruptiveness of social and economic changes have dramatically altered the scale of displacement and devastation. In 1982, there were some ten million refugees, and the number may well be increasing.[213] Hundreds of thousands are in overseas refugee camps awaiting resettlement in the United States; during fiscal 1984, the United States is expected to accept no more than 72,000.[214] What is unprecedented, however, is not the number of refugees abroad who seek resettlement here—the upheaval of World War II displaced at least eight million persons[215]—but the number of refugees who manage to reach American shores to seek asylum, and the kinds of societies from which they have come.

Prior to 1972, relatively few asylum claims—under 500 on average each year—were filed in the United States; these were often prominent defectors from Soviet-bloc countries. These claims were handled informally and according to ad hoc procedures; neither the immigration statute nor INS regulations addressed the question of asylum.[216] INS regulations did not establish procedures and standards for resolving asylum claims until January 1975,[217] and only the enactment of the Refugee Act of 1980[218] created a legislative basis for an asylum status and a systematic basis for determining it.

During the middle and late 1970's, the number and national origins of asylum claimants began to change. In 1977, the INS received 3,702 asylum applications and two years later, the number was 5,801, a significant increase, to be sure, but still manageable. Indeed, the Refugee Act that President Carter signed on March 17, 1980 had little to say about asylum; to the drafters of the Act, it was essentially an afterthought.[219] Within weeks of the signing, however, Fidel Castro expelled large numbers of Cubans, the Mariel boatlift brought them to the United States, and the asylum question occupied center stage. Between March 1980 and July 1981, over 53,000 asylum claims were filed, as Mariel Cubans and undocumented Haitians streamed into southern Florida.[220] Since then, they have been joined by asylum claimants from other Caribbean Basin trouble spots, the Middle East, and elsewhere.

These numbers may somewhat exaggerate both the seriousness and the uncontrollable nature of the backlog, especially if one assumes that the status of the Mariel Cubans eventually will be regularized through legislation, and recognizes that United States policy actually encouraged the filing of many of these claims.[221] Nevertheless, there is no question that the flood of asylum claimants presents extremely difficult problems for immigration law and policy. Most come not from the Soviet bloc but from nations with which the United States has, or until recently had, close political ties. These nations, such as Haiti and El Salvador, would bitterly resent our granting asylum to their citizens. Many asylum claimants come from nearby Caribbean nations and allege patterns of persecution that are presumably common in those countries. Migrating from largely rural, preindustrial societies that are culturally quite distinct from ours, many face serious obstacles to assimilation here. Most probably cannot qualify for asylum status under the existing law.[222] These features have created considerable concern by the INS that favorable action on these claims would open the floodgates even wider.

Regardless of their prospects for success, the incentives for aliens to claim asylum are powerful, often overwhelming. Merely by filing the claim, an alien apprehended by the INS automatically wins a delay in deportation until all avenues of administrative and judicial review have been exhausted. For one who wishes to remain as long as possible, this delay can be extremely valuable in itself. Beyond that, the claimant, if not detained, may be able to obtain work, melt into the surrounding population, and avoid detection. She may be able to establish ties that ultimately prevent the INS from ever deporting her. In any event, she asserts constitutionally protected life and liberty interests so great that extensive procedural rights are probably triggered by her claim. The stakes in delay being so high and the filing of a claim being essentially costless to the alien, she has little to lose and much to gain by doing so. Indeed, even if the INS denies her claim and is in a position to expel her, it may nevertheless decide to defer deportation indefinitely, as it has done in the past with respect to Poles, Ethiopians, and many other groups.[223]

In sum, the ease of asserting asylum claims has made illegal immigration far more difficult to deter. It now imposes serious strains on the INS's administrative system and enforcement strategies quite apart from the substantial resources required simply to adjudicate the claims themselves. Finally, mass asylum claims have encouraged the INS to adopt an explicit policy of mass incarceration of undocumented aliens, reversing a long-standing, judicially ratified preference for parole,[224] and raising urgent legal and policy issues.[225]

The large, steadily increasing number of asylum claims, then, presents classical immigration law with unprecedented dilemmas of a legal, moral, and administrative nature. This development exerts massive pressure upon the notions of sovereignty, consent-based obligation, and restrictive national community that have supported the structure of classical immigration law. It does so, moreover, in the context of uniquely poignant, compelling human claims to justice.[226]

Undocumented Aliens. Perhaps the central fact about immigration with which social policymakers must deal today is the presence of an immense population of aliens in the United States in apparent violation of the immigration laws.[227]

The complex effects of undocumented aliens upon the domestic economy were discussed earlier. But the massive influx of undocumented aliens challenges classical immigration law on grounds far more fundamental than those of economics. When a routine external event such as the decline in value of the Mexican peso can generate a torrent of illegal border crossings that the INS is largely powerless to prevent,[228] confidence in the efficacy of our law, in our capacity to control events, is threatened. Indeed, as the INS has shifted its personnel to the Mexican border and the South, illegal entries across the far longer and essentially unpatrolled Canadian border, hitherto only a very minor problem, have increased significantly.[229] Significantly, this deluge is occurring at a time when INS border apprehensions are actually at record levels.[230] In view of these developments, it has become something of a political cliché, indispensable for congressional testimony and press conferences alike, to affirm that our ability to regulate entry and exit is perhaps the basic attribute of national sovereignty, and that the easy, continual and largely unimpeded entry of undocumented aliens demonstrates that "we have lost control of our borders."[231]

The central social fact about undocumented aliens is this: once they enter illegally, and especially if they decide to remain more or less permanently,[232] they quickly begin to establish significant relationships with the individuals and institutions in the locales to which they gravitate. Some bring or are joined by their spouses, others marry here. If they bring children, those children usually attend local schools and acquire American customs; if their children are born here, the children are automatically United States citizens.[233] Virtually all find employment, pay taxes, and have access to certain public benefits.[234] Many establish ties with churches and other voluntary associations.[235] And a substantial proportion will continue to reside in the United States for the rest of their lives, the immigration law notwithstanding.

Suppose that an anthropologist or sociologist, intimately familiar with American culture but innocent of any knowledge concerning aliens' legal status, were to observe life in the Haitian section of Miami or the barrios of El Paso. She would undoubtedly notice that some residents tend to live furtively and seem especially vulnerable to exploitation. But she would surely also conclude that these same individuals are neither strangers nor outcasts but are vital elements in their neighborhoods, sinking deep roots into the local society and participating in many aspects of community life.

The challenge that this development poses to the continued coherence and integrity of classical immigration law can scarcely be exaggerated. Just as the hard facts of hopelessly porous borders demand a new understanding of sovereignty, the reality of undocumented aliens' humanity and their steady integration into communal life here undermines some of the traditional conceptions that that law reflected. New "social contracts" between these aliens and American society are being negotiated each day, and these cannot easily be nullified with invocations of sovereignty, as classically understood. These understandings often represent commitments valued not only by the aliens who seek to acquire legal status but also by the substantial number of Americans who apparently benefit from their contribution to our society.[236] It is also true, however, that most undocumented aliens have come here uninvited,[237] that they remain here in knowing violation of our laws, and that any moral claims they may have must be compared to those of the numerous would-be immigrants who wait patiently, often at great personal cost, for legal admission. Conventional ideas about morality and community simply cannot adequately capture the complex, ambiguous character of the relationship between undocumented aliens and American society.

Political Shifts. The character and magnitude of the structural changes that I have been discussing are certain to engender far-reaching alterations in demography, public attitudes and power relationships. These alterations have themselves become part of the context and background against which the adequacy of classical immigration law must be appraised. Three seem particularly significant: the rise of Hispanic and Asian Americans as formidable political forces; the skewed geographical distribution of aliens; and the unusually broad public consensus on the need for legal change.

In a democracy, demography is political destiny. In the American context, that destiny is one in which the traditionally dominant ethnic groups of European ancestry will gradually yield political ground to those of Hispanic and Asian descent.[238] Projections, of course, are highly fallible and sensitive to assumptions about difficult-to-predict variables, especially fertility and migration rates. Nevertheless, their orders of magnitude suggest that extremely important political changes impend, changes that are certain to affect future struggles over the direction of immigration law.[239] Indeed, these changes are already evident, for example, in the growing number of Hispanic elected officials,[240] and in the considerable influence exerted by Hispanic groups over the shape and likely fate of current legislative proposals for immigration reform.[241]

Political influence, however, is a function not simply of aggregate votes but also of the geographical location of those voting, not simply a matter of the benefits and costs of a policy change but also of the distribution of those benefits and costs.[242] And the voters most directly concerned with immigration policy, as well as the benefits and costs of that policy, are concentrated in a small number of politically important states, especially California, Texas, Florida, New York, New Jersey, and Illinois. Indeed, one estimate is that of the 5.5 million eligible Hispanic voters, ninety-three percent reside in nine states that account for three-fourths of the electoral votes needed to elect a Presidential candidate.[243] The great majority of undocumented aliens apparently go to those states as well,[244] and despite efforts to distribute them more evenly, most refugees have also migrated there.[245]

This geographic concentration, of course, is hardly surprising. Immigrants, like most other people, tend to go where there are jobs and people of similar background who can help them to find work, establish social ties, and begin the difficult transition into the American culture. For present purposes, however, the more far-reaching implications are that immigration policy will acquire an increasing political urgency, and that aspects of immigration law that impose significant costs upon those regions are not likely to be tolerated for long.

Perhaps the most important political change is related to the above factors but is not fully explained by them. There now exists a shared conviction that the traditional immigration system, especially in light of the structural changes described earlier, has become fundamentally incoherent; its assumptions and values seem to diverge from the evolving moral basis of the larger legal system of which it has become an increasingly insular, incongruous, and discordant part. Public opinion polls indicate a growing anxiety over the inability of the government to control the influx of undocumented workers.[246, 247] Another piece of evidence that a perceived incongruity exists between traditional assumptions and the changing social order lies in the recent judicial efforts to dismantle the structure of classical immigration law. This development, which is the subject of section III of this essay, not only reflects but is helping to transform the politics of immigration.

Ideological Changes

We saw in section I that classical immigration law arose within a legal order in which nationalistic, exclusionary values were superimposed upon the earlier individualistic and universalistic ideology of traditional liberalism. The resulting ideology of restrictive nationalism emphasized three related aspects of the government-alien relationship. The government's legal obligation to aliens rested almost entirely upon the terms and conditions upon which its consent to their entry had been granted and to which they had at least implicitly agreed. This consent principle legitimated, and in turn was legitimated by, a strong conception of sovereignty, in which the alien's relationship with American society was defined in legal, formal terms prescribed by the government. Finally, membership in the national community, while nominally universal for those within the United States, was in fact and in law graduated and restrictive for aliens. In recent years, however, profound changes have been wrought in the individualistic underpinnings of these basic conceptions, especially the idea of consent-based legal obligation. In the process, the moral and legal foundations of classical immigration law have eroded.

Individualism and the Right-Privilege Distinction. Duncan Kennedy's analysis of the individualistic legal order affords some insight into the evolving legal meanings of consent, sovereignty, and national community in classical immigration law.[248] Although his work concerns private-law contract rules, it isolates certain fundamental values that have also shaped the ideology of immigration law. To Kennedy, conflicts in the law over three recurring issues reveal the nature of individualistic values. The first concerns the extent to which one party should be obliged against its will to defer to another's interest. Individualism assumes that people are independent and self-sufficient. It seeks to limit reciprocal obligations of sharing and sacrifice, the scope of legal duties, and the force of equitable claims.[249] The second concerns the extent to which the parties' bargaining power should determine legal outcomes. An individualistic system recognizes only limited constraints upon the balance of forces in the state of nature, and accepts the outcomes that even highly unequal bargaining power generates.[250] The third issue concerns the extent to which a court is justified in overriding a party's expressed intention in the interest of some broader notion of justice. Individualism denies any such justification.[251]

The fundamental elements of classical immigration law analyzed in section I substantially reflected an individualistic ideology emphasizing the ideas of consent, sovereignty, and restrictive national community. Not being bound by any transcendent conception of community, for example, the government was free to define the American commonwealth as it saw fit, acknowledging only those claims or interests to which it was prepared, out of considerations of national interest, to consent. As *Downes v. Bidwell (The Insular Cases)*[252] and the qualified legal rights of women and racial minorities during this period suggest,[253] this design was often restrictive in practice even when it was expansive in principle. A concept of national sovereignty that applied the individualistic values of autonomy, self-determination, and consent in the immigration context, where nationalistic goals challenged traditional liberal ideals and altered their meanings,[254] would also find congenial the other substantive elements of the classical tradition—the extraconstitutional status of exclusion, plenary federal power to classify aliens, "civil" deportation, broad detention power, and nonindependent adjudication. Rhetorically, it would seek some principle to harmonize these doctrines and render them coherent.

Restrictive nationalism, the ideology underlying classical immigration law, found such a principle in the "right-privilege" distinction. This idea was sententiously formulated by Justice Holmes, who rejected a policeman's first amendment challenge to his discharge by observing that "[t]he petitioner may have a constitutional right to talk politics, but has no constitutional right to be a policeman. . . . The servant cannot complain, as he takes the employment on the terms which are offered him."[255] Like many other areas of public law, immigration doctrine found the power of this principle to be irresistible. If government employment was not a "right" but only a "privilege," defeasible at the instance of the employer without constitutional impediment, how much more contingent was the alien's ability to enter the United States and enjoy equal benefits there, especially under a regime of sharply restricted immigration?[256] By conceiving of entry as a privilege conditioned upon the alien's consent to the decidedly limited rights and inferior status that classical immigration law offered her, restrictive nationalism sought to reconcile the illiberal elements of classical immigration law with the individualistic values that it drew from traditional liberalism. Indeed, when the "demise" of the right-privilege distinction in the law generally was announced during the 1960's[257]—quite prematurely, as it turned out[258]—immigration law took little notice. In that isolated realm, and especially with respect to doctrines relating to exclusion, the distinction remained a seductive principle through which the dominant ideas of consent, sovereignty, and national community could be vindicated.

Restrictive nationalism's use of individualistic values to validate whatever outcomes existing power differentials happened to produce—its refusal to disturb the conditions imposed by the government upon aliens—left little independent role for the courts. Rather than legitimating judicial infusion of equitable, extraconsensual, or communitarian values into immigration law, individualism—or at least that philosophical thread of individualism that emphasized consent as the source of legal obligation—seemed to demand the kind of abject judicial deference to the sovereign's immigration authorities that, as section I suggested, became a hallmark of the classical tradition.

Toward a Communitarian Legal Order. During the last decade, however, the ideological stability and coherence of classical immigration law have been threatened simultaneously from two different directions. First, our legal system has dramatically expanded the circumstances under which the law imposes legally enforceable duties upon both government and private individuals or groups. Second, there has been a related movement, especially but not exclusively in public law, from a preoccupation with the rights of individuals to an increasing emphasis upon the vindication of group rights.[259]

In the classical view, as we have seen, government owed essentially no duty to aliens that it had not already imposed upon itself through positive law. This idea of autonomy married a central theme in liberal ideology—the primacy of consent as the source of legal obligation—to a growing nationalistic concern with America's sovereignty in its burgeoning international relations. But liberalism has always contained another, somewhat contradictory theme—the universality of certain natural rights.[260] Such rights are anchored not in the accidental contingency of one's birthplace or previous nationality, but in the common humanity, rationality, and dignity of all individuals.

The legal order, animated by the emergence of new, "communitarian" public law norms,[261] has gradually begun to generalize from this natural rights dimension of liberalism. These norms are expanding and transfiguring the sources of, and justifications for, legal obligation to individuals whom public and private law traditionally conceived of as "strangers." These norms, however, are grounded in a fundamentally nonliberal intuition—the perception that individuals, societies and nations are bound to each other by pervasive interdependencies. These interdependencies are thought to imply certain moral and legal consequences that neither liberalism nor restrictive nationalism would accept. They imply that socially accepted values should augment consent as a basis for imputing legal duties; that the conception of national sovereignty should be weakened in order to define the relationship between the United States and aliens in terms of morally significant, informal social interactions; and that membership in our national community should depend not upon formalistic criteria but upon the functional social linkages actually forged between aliens and the American people. Thus, communitarian norms grow out of the universal human rights aspect of traditional liberalism. They diverge, however, both from liberalism's individualistic ethos and from the restrictive nationalistic values that underlie classical immigration law.[262]

The Scope of Obligation in Private Law. Well before immigration law began to feel the influence of communitarian values, these values had already limited the sway and reshaped the contours of the consent principle in private law. The most notable effect occurred in contract law, where the bargain principle, which imposed legal obligation only for consensual, intentional exchanges, was augmented by more encompassing theories of obligation that have nothing to do with consent, such as detrimental reliance and unjust enrichment. This movement from contract to tort[263] premises liability not only upon the expressed will of the parties but also upon widely shared norms concerning what is fair. It recognizes that individuals are neither independent nor self-sufficient, and that spillover effects pervade not only the marketplace but the moral domains of our collective life. Our concern for the welfare of others clearly transcends the realm of contract, extending to nonmarket values such as procedural fairness and humane treatment as well. Courts increasingly eschew the individualistic liberal values of autonomy and self-determination in favor of communitarian values emphasizing paternalistic protection and social justice. For example, they now commonly refuse to enforce contracts of adhesion,[264] and often relieve promisors of the consequences of mistakes.[265] Ian MacNeil has sought to capture the essence of these developments, writing of a change from "discrete contract" to "relational contract" conceptions, in which social structures, relationships, and values play a crucial role in defining the scope and content of legal obligation.[266] More generally, an increasing preoccupation with substantive, rather than formal, criteria of justice is leading courts to emphasize flexible, tort-like standards such as "reasonableness" and "fairness," standards more capable of assimilating communitarian norms.[267]

In tort law proper, an analogous evolution has occurred. During most of the classical period, tort liability was relatively confined, reflecting a highly focused, restrictive definition of the individual injury-producing event and employing narrow criteria of relevance. Increasingly, however, tort obligation grows out of the larger social context in which such interactions occur. The entire matrix of social relationships—the expectations and nonmarket values that they generate, such as distributive justice, economic efficiency, social equality, and human dignity—have become relevant to the scope and content of legal duties. Landlords, by reason of their presumably superior knowledge, access, and power, must compensate losses due to crimes perpetrated on their property.[268] Property owners, for much the same reasons, are obliged to protect trespassers against certain injuries sustained on their premises.[269] Similarly, psychiatrists have a duty to prevent assaults by their patients,[270] physicians must obtain informed consent,[271] and novel fiduciary obligations have been extended to new groups such as insurers.[272]

The Scope of Obligation in Public Law. Thus, the domain within which private autonomy, action, and property may be exploited without regard to the interests of strangers has been progressively abridged by judicially imposed duties. It does not require a great leap of imagination to suppose that the same moral ideas and legal consciousness that generated such a pronounced restriction of individual sovereignty in private law have begun to influence the evolving conception of governmental sovereignty in the public law of immigration as well. Such an influence has been reinforced by parallel developments in public law itself, where a counterpart to the movement from contract to tort has fundamentally altered administrative and constitutional law conceptions of obligation during recent decades.

Richard Stewart has chronicled an evolution in administrative law away from what he calls the "traditional" model. In the traditional model, private property rights are taken as a given. The state may intrude upon those rights only to the extent that the legislature has expressly commanded it, and administrative decision procedures and judicial review must be tailored to facilitate the enforcement of that limitation.[273] The palpable inadequacy of this model, Stewart argues, lies in its failure to come to grips with the inescapably problematic nature of administrative discretion in the contemporary welfare state.[274] This failure has recently given rise to what Stewart calls an "interest representation" model of administrative law. In this model, the state, before deciding whether and how to act, is obliged to establish and enforce administrative and judicial procedures that are designed to generate a plausible approximation of the "public interest"—that is, procedures that facilitate participation by all interests that may be affected by those decisions.[275]

This "interest representation" model has assumed many doctrinal forms, such as judicial and statutory rules expanding opportunities for standing, intervention, and fee-shifting, and more searching judicial review that holds administrative officials to higher standards of rationality and procedural justice.[276] For purposes of the present discussion, perhaps the most far-reaching consequence of this reconceptualization of administrative law is the emergence of group litigation as a crucial strategy of legal change. This development has enlarged not only the number and types of claimants but the kinds of claims that may be pursued against government in the courts.[277] The vast expansion of group rights and remedies against governmental entities and officials has generated new forms of injunctive relief,[278] and secured new conceptions of property rights.[279]

Even more than its counterpart in private law, this evolution of administrative law doctrine toward the vindication of group rights has increasingly emphasized relational, social expectancy, group, and other communitarian values, in addition to individual rights based upon traditional notions of private property.[280] Group litigation has not only made it economically possible to challenge governmental policies more effectively and to press new kinds of values on courts; it has also raised the stakes in judicial decisions, making it more difficult for courts to regard cases as isolated disputes on the private-law model. Such cases have helped to reshape judges' conceptions of their role, of the sources of governmental misconduct, of the functions of litigation, and of the remedial obligations of government.[281] As we shall see in section III, these transformations wrought by the rise of group litigation and group rights have been especially significant in a number of the important class action immigration cases of the early 1980's.[282]

The reformation of administrative law that Stewart describes has been paralleled by a radical change in constitutional law, particularly in the Supreme Court's understanding of what constitutional due process and equal protection requires. These developments generally have received enormous scholarly attention[283] and need not be repeated here. Two aspects, however, are particularly relevant to immigration law. First, constitutional law has accorded greater prominence to precisely those values—procedural fairness and equal treatment—that the consent, sovereignty, and restrictive national community conceptions of classical immigration law tended to depreciate. Second, it extended protection to many groups, including criminal defendants, convicted prisoners, and students, that are not obviously more deserving or needful of special judicial protection than the aliens to whom classical immigration law denied significant protection.

The Implications for Immigration Law. Each of these ideological changes, then—in private law, administrative law, and constitutional law—has contributed to the erosion of the moral and legal foundations of classical immigration law. Each has responded to deeper changes in social structures and patterns of legitimation. Each reflects the waning of the individualistic emphasis upon consent as the principal basis of legal obligation, the rise of communitarian values, and the rapid growth of the administrative state. Just as the imposition of private obligation has come to be justified by fluid, relational, tort-like norms, so the closed, formalistic, property-oriented values of administrative and constitutional law have yielded to those emphasizing open processes and the protection and advancement of diffuse nonmarket values.[284] These changes do not simply constitute significant evolutions in legal doctrine. They exemplify a fundamentally changed understanding of moral, political, and social reality, an understanding from which immigration law can no longer be isolated.

III. The Communitarian Conception of Immigration Law

In section I, I distilled the fundamental, distinctive ideological basis and doctrinal elements of classical immigration law that were developed by the Supreme Court as early as the 1880's and confirmed by it well into the 1970's. In section II, I suggested some structural and ideological changes that are beginning to cause different principles, already well-established in other areas of law, to penetrate immigration law. It remains to examine the lines along which the basic elements of immigration law are being transformed today, a task undertaken in this section, and to consider in section IV some of the implications of these transformations for the future character and consequences of immigration law.

Broadening the National Community: Plyler v. Doe

The Supreme Court's decision in *Plyler v. Doe*,[285] compelling a state to provide the children of undocumented aliens with a free public education, may ultimately come to have the same epochal significance for that group that *Brown v. Board of Education*[286] has had for black Americans.[287] In one sense, of course, *Plyler* may be read narrowly as nothing more than an equal protection case in which the state failed to adduce a "substantial purpose" for treating the children of undocumented aliens differently than it treated their documented alien or citizen peers.[288] In this view, the question of how the national community ought to be defined was not even at issue: *Plyler*, after all, invalidated a state law, not a federal one, and only the latter can prescribe the contours of that community. But in another, broader sense, the decision may mark a fundamental break with classical immigration law's concept of national community and of the scope of congressional power to decide who is entitled to the benefits of membership.

Plyler effects this change on three different levels. First, it inducts into the national community a new group of uncertain size and composition. These uncertainties do not simply reflect our ignorance about which aliens are here illegally and how numerous they are, for even the defining characteristic of the new group remains opaque. Previous expansions of the national community, most notably the fourteenth amendment's extension of citizenship to the freed slaves[289] and the nineteenth amendment's extension of suffrage to women,[290] admitted well-defined, undifferentiated categories of individuals;

within those categories, membership was universal. But neither *Plyler*'s holding about public benefits nor its more general spirit necessarily embraces undocumented aliens as an undifferentiated group. To be sure, the Court reaffirmed a principle that had been clearly established for a century[291]—that all aliens "within" the United States, whatever their legal status, are entitled to some constitutional protection. But it was the "innocent" children, not their "guilty" parents, to whom Texas denied equal protection; although it is children, not parents, who attend public school, the unconstitutionality of the state law involved more than the withholding of educational benefits from aliens in general. Had Texas adopted an analogous system of free public *adult* education or job training, for example, the Court apparently would not have upheld an equal protection claim by the *parents*.[292] The enduring importance of education benefits for *children*, moreover, accounted both for the level of scrutiny selected and the extent of the right created.[293]

These narrowing distinctions—between undocumented alien parents and their children, and between education and other services—raise a number of significant problems with the Court's reasoning, and suggest that those distinctions may be difficult to sustain in future cases. For example, the Court failed to explain why denying educational benefits to an innocent child differs from the denial of other governmental benefits to her undocumented parent, upon whose income and well-being the child's welfare ultimately depends. If Texas may not harm innocent children by depriving them of access to public education, why may it harm these same innocents—who may actually be United States *citizens*—even more grievously by denying their parents access to welfare benefits or public or private employment, which provides their essential economic support?[294] Does *Plyler* mean that a state may not exclude from public housing a family in which an adult has committed a crime? Can the Court's "innocent children" rationale be harmonized with its willingness to allow the routine deportation of children who are not only innocent of their parents' wrongdoing but are United States citizens?[295] Are not these deprivations as directly a result of parental status or wrongdoing as the deprivation that the Court refused to countenance in *Plyler?* Because the Court addressed none of these questions, the potential scope of *Plyler* remains an open question.

Second, *Plyler* not only enlarged the national community to uncertain dimensions and on the basis of uncertain principles, but did so in the face of a congressional policy to exclude undocumented aliens from the country *altogether.* Some have doubted that such a policy can even be said to exist, given the historical ambivalence of Southern States toward the entry of low-cost agricultural labor.[296] In *Plyler,* the Court went so far as to deny that the Texas statute "corresponds to any identifiable congressional policy," or "operate[s] harmoniously within the federal program."[297]

This proposition is demonstrably false, at least under current conditions. Unauthorized entry, after all, is a federal crime.[298] In recent years, considerable law enforcement effort has been devoted to preventing it.[299] Congress has excluded undocumented aliens from numerous federal benefit programs.[300] Indeed, the Court only six years earlier in *De Canas v. Bica*[301] had deemed Congress's policy against illegal aliens to be strong enough to sustain a state statute barring their employment; it was enough for the Court that the statute was consistent with federal law.[302] The *Plyler* majority's effort to distinguish *De Canas* is utterly unpersuasive.[303] Its other arguments—that because some undocumented aliens might ultimately escape deportation and because denial of benefits did not stem the influx of illegal aliens, Texas's approach was thereby rendered irrational[304]—stand on no firmer ground. If substantial effectiveness were the criterion, most regulatory statutes would probably be doomed.[305] Certainly, there are few areas in which the public policy options are as problematic as in the control of illegal immigration. What is disturbing about *Plyler* is not that it makes the policymaker's task more difficult—any judicial invalidation of a statute does that. *Plyler*'s peculiar vice is that it uses the inherent difficulty of a problem as a justification for making it even more intractable.[306]

Third, *Plyler* could perhaps be understood and even defended as a case of federal preemption that merely reaffirms the exclusive, plenary power of Congress to regulate immigration. This view, however, is undercut by the Court's previous decision in *De Canas*. That case announced a broad tolerance for state legislation that discourages immigration in areas traditionally of local concern, such as labor markets and public education, in ways that are generally consistent with federal policy. Unless this aspect of *De Canas* has been overruled sub silentio, *Plyler* must be seen as the germination of a new and quite different principle. This principle seems to be that a state may not seek to discourage illegal entry by means of disincentives that may harm the children of those who, because the disincentives are ineffective, decide to enter anyway. This principle, of course, would have dictated a different result in *De Canas*, since it would have invalidated the statute in that case.[307] Even more important, the principle would seem to require that result even if *Congress*, rather than a state, enacted the statute.[308]

If that is the meaning of *Plyler*, it constitutes a conceptual watershed in immigration law, the most powerful rejection to date of classical immigration law's notion of plenary national sovereignty over our borders. If those to whom we have refused entry are entitled by their mere presence—together with the presence of their children—to claim not only constitutional procedural protections,[309] but also the significant substantive entitlements that legislatures grant to lawful residents,[310] then immigration law's ideal of national community has also been transformed. In the classical view, the political branches of government defined the boundaries of that community and the consequences of exclusion. That definition, responsive to the political values, local interests, and policy concerns that animate Congress, has tended to exclude those whose entry was believed to threaten these interests. The most important meaning of *Plyler* may be that the courts are beginning to assert a coordinate, if not supervisory, role in defining the dimensions and meaning of national community in the immigration context. Courts are expositors of a constitutional tradition that increasingly emphasizes not the parochial and the situational, but the universal, transcendent values of equality and fairness imminent in the due process and equal protection principles. In that capacity, they have also asserted a larger role in the creation and distribution of opportunities and status in the administrative state. In *Plyler,* the Supreme Court moved boldly on both fronts. In doing so, the Court seems to have begun to redefine the community to include all those whose destinies have somehow, even in violation of our law, become linked with ours.

Judicial Self-Assertion

On this reading of *Plyler,* the days of extraordinary judicial deference to Congress in the immigration field may be over. Still, by setting *De Canas* to one side, it is possible to view *Plyler* not as a case about the contours of community or the equal protection principle but simply as a straightforward federal preemption case dressed up in equal protection garb, the kind of state regulation of immigration that courts have long rejected. But even if one rejects the view that such a reading of *Plyler* may be too narrow, the judicial boldness apparent in the increasing number of recent decisions confronting *federal* exercises of power over immigration cannot be dismissed so lightly.

To be sure, the emergent judicial assertiveness in the face of federal regulation of immigration essentially remains a lower court phenomenon, *Plyler* aside, as does most of the transformation of immigration law to date.[311] Moreover, some of these cases have arisen in a deportation context, in which due process rights of aliens are well established. Significantly, however, many innovative rulings involve exclusion proceedings,[312] where the powers of Congress and the Attorney General are at their greatest.

One district court decision, *Hotel & Restaurant Employees Union, Local 25 v. Smith,*[313] suggests the extraordinary flavor of these cases. The unconventional procedural posture in which the court decided the case is itself a sign of deeper changes. *Employees Union* did not arise in an exclusion or deportation proceeding, nor did it involve a detained plaintiff. Indeed, the plaintiff was not an alien at all but a union local, and it challenged not a particular adjudication but a general administrative practice known as "extended voluntary departure" (EVD).[314] Under this practice, the Attorney General may accede to a State Department request that no action be taken to deport nationals of a particular country due to dangerous, unsettled conditions there, such as civil war, invasion or repression.[315] EVD is generally used in situations in which returning the alien to her country of origin might be hazardous but in which asylum probably cannot legally be granted.[316] EVD, then, provides temporary refuge for an indefinite period to all nationals of that country who are here at a particular time. Since 1960, it has been granted to nationals of fifteen countries; today, it is enjoyed by Poles, Afghans, Ethiopians, and Ugandans, among others.[317]

In *Employees Union,* the plaintiff challenged the Attorney General's decision denying EVD status to Salvadorans while granting it to other groups.[318] It alleged violations of section 4 of the Administrative Procedure Act,[319] and of the constitutional guarantees of equal protection and due process.[320] The Attorney General moved to dismiss the complaint, contending that a decision to grant or deny EVD was a highly delicate, discretionary judgment based upon a variety of difficult and confidential foreign policy considerations. To be compelled to articulate those considerations publicly, he maintained, would hamper the President's conduct of foreign policy and jeopardize the interests of Americans and other innocent people outside the United States. EVD decisions, he insisted, are made in close consultation with Congress; for the courts to second-guess such decisions would constitute an unwarranted intrusion into the delicate realm of high-stakes foreign policy in which it was essential that the United States speak with one voice.[321]

In the context of EVD decisions, these foreign policy and national sovereignty arguments have great force and plausibility, certainly far more than the similar arguments advanced by the government and readily embraced by the Supreme Court in some deportation cases decided during the 1970's.[322] The purpose of EVD, after all, is to create a flexible alternative to conventional legal categories—deportation, exclusion, asylum, voluntary departure. It is designed to be an additional administrative tool capable of responding to rapidly changing, politically charged events. EVD, far from depriving an alien of her opportunities to pursue the traditional avenues of relief from exclusion or deportation, actually creates a new remedy for situations in which the others may be unavailable or inadequate. To surround this device with constitutional constraints not applicable to excludable aliens generally could reduce and perhaps even eliminate its usefulness to the government and to aliens. If granting it to one group meant that the Attorney General was legally obliged to grant it to another, he might grant it more sparingly in the first instance. In that event, excludable aliens faced with dangerous conditions at home might well be made worse off. As is sometimes the case, more law might in the end mean less justice.[323]

The district judge, however, would have none of this. He found no difficulty in discerning a judicially manageable standard for evaluating grants or denials of EVD, despite the sensitive nature of the political and foreign policy issues presented, and despite considerable doubt that such a standard exists or can even be formulated. Indeed, the standard that the judge relied upon—"'widespread fighting, destruction and breakdown of public services and order'"[324]—has been disclaimed by the government as a workable basis for EVD decisions;[325] moreover, it appears to require data not easily obtainable[326] and calls for a comparative assessment of international conditions that would be most difficult for a court to make.[327]

Undaunted by such obstacles, however, the judge went on to suggest that "prudential considerations" did not preclude judicial review. He speculated that "since there has been criticism of American treatment of Salvadoran refugees," reversing the EVD denial might enhance American credibility abroad.[328] This non sequitur is singularly unpersuasive. There is probably no United States foreign policy that does not ignite some criticism; certainly, those domestic and foreign interests that support our current EVD policy would protest its reversal. The judge also failed to explain why he refused to credit the contention that the United States must "speak with one voice" on this matter.[329] Instead, brushing aside all other objections, the court concluded that plaintiffs had stated a legal claim and could proceed to trial.[330]

Perhaps *Employees Union* is an isolated, unrepresentative case—a single district judge doing no more than interpreting plaintiffs' claims generously, as he must, on a motion to dismiss. Yet until the early 1980's, it was almost inconceivable that a court would haul the government into court primarily at the behest of excludable or deportable aliens and require it to defend a policy such as that concerning EVD, a policy that is plainly and appropriately discretionary in nature, intimately intertwined with the most delicate and volatile aspects of our foreign policy, and reflective of political negotiation between Congress and the president.[331] In embryonic form, *Employees Union* bears the distinctive marks of much contemporary public law judging—deep skepticism if not indignation about the propriety of political compromises reached by the other branches, boundless faith in the courts' ability to analyze, comprehend, and predict the real-world consequences of complex policy alternatives, and serene confidence about the capacity of constitutional litigation and procedural reforms to harmonize the relevant public values.[332] What is surprising is not that this judicial style has become commonplace in other areas of the law; the truly remarkable development is that it is beginning to appear for the first time in immigration cases.

The Constitutionalizing of Exclusion

It is only since 1980 that the courts have started to bring the exclusion process into the mainstream of constitutional law. Litigation challenging the mass detention of excludable aliens in the wake of the recent Cuban,

Haitian and Salvadoran influxes has generated most of this change. As we shall see below, courts have begun to create extensive procedural and even substantive rights to avoid or terminate detention.[333] Glimmerings of this new approach, however, are also discernible in some nondetention cases.

The Supreme Court's own contribution to this development has been quite modest. In *Landon v. Plasencia*,[334] the Court reaffirmed earlier holdings that a lawful permanent resident who returns to the United States after a very brief trip outside the country is entitled to a due process hearing when the government seeks to exclude her on the theory that she has made a new "entry."[335] Similarly, the Court also reaffirmed the classical doctrine on the legal status of aliens seeking initial entry, the far more common and important situation.[336]

The lower courts, however, have begun to stir. Of the nondetention cases, two are of particular interest. In *In re Phelisna*,[337] the court held that the burden of proof on the question of whether the alien, when apprehended, had already made an initial "entry"—and therefore is entitled to the due process that deportation proceedings afford—rests upon the government, not the alien.[338] Because earlier immigration decisions made "entry" turn in part upon the alien's subjective state of mind,[339] a matter obviously difficult for the government to prove, such a shift in the burden of proof could enable aliens to obtain deportation hearings—and thus eligibility for immigration benefits, including discretionary relief from deportation under a variety of statutory provisions—in many cases now governed by exclusion procedures.

Traditionally, as we have seen, the substantive grounds for exclusion have been even more immune from constitutional review than the procedural ones.[340] Even here, however, that immunity has begun to erode, at least in some lower courts. In *Lesbian/Gay Freedom Day Committee, Inc. v. INS*,[341] the court, reasoning in the shadow cast by an earlier Supreme Court case[342] that had rejected a constitutional challenge to the long-standing policy of excluding homosexuals, proceeded to invalidate that policy on statutory construction grounds. It went on to hold that even if the statute were interpreted to bar alien homosexuals, it would violate the first amendment rights of homosexuals in the United States to communicate and associate with such aliens,[343] a theory criticized, although not clearly rejected; a decade earlier by the Supreme Court.[344]

These decisions may be harbingers of a view of exclusion that differs radically from that represented by the relevant Supreme Court precedents.[345, 346] The classical notion drastically limited the circumstances under which the government would be subjected to a procedural or substantive duty that it did not wish to acknowledge. Its explicit willingness to enter into a relationship with the alien, and its express consent to particular limitations upon its power to expel, were the sole measures of that duty. Today, however, obligation is increasingly imputed to the government on the basis of more abstract principles gleaned from the congeries of domestic law norms, including constitutional due process and equal protection, the Refugee Act of 1980,[347] and judicially elaborated communitarian values. Under these norms, even strangers can, by a kind of proxy relationship to citizens, claim some legal protections.

The Supreme Court in 1972 discerned and warned against the implications of this new view: "[C]ourts in each case would be required to weigh the strength of the audience's interest against that of the Government in [excluding] the particular alien applicant, according to some as yet undetermined standard."[348] While this caution may be amply warranted, it is also somewhat disingenuous. For that, of course, is precisely the kind of interest-balancing process that judges, with the encouragement of the Court and most legal scholars, routinely perform today in areas of the law as disparate as abortion regulation[349] and first amendment cases.[350] Once the excludable alien's rights are defined not by her compliance with government-prescribed forms and conditions but in terms of her relationship with and benefit to American citizens,[351] the genie is out of the bottle. Under that approach, the sovereign's consent no longer constitutes the limiting principle from which the government's duty can be derived, and the courts' role can no longer be confined to enforcing the government's willingness or refusal to acknowledge the existence of rights in the alien.

Limiting the Federal Power to Classify Aliens

The classical view of Congress's power to classify aliens—one of essentially unlimited scope—would seem to be securely entrenched. The Supreme Court's most recent decisions affirming this view, *Mathews v. Diaz*[352] and *Fiallo v. Bell*,[353] are less than a decade old. And the one threat to this principle—a novel constitutional theory announced by a bare majority of the Court in *Hampton v. Mow Sun Wong*[354] to condemn a century-old bar to federal employment of aliens—has not prospered.[355]

Still, the seeds of judicial intervention have been planted, and under the new conditions described in section II, they may yet take root. *Diaz* seemed to concede that even federal alienage classifications were reviewable, albeit under a "narrow standard of review,"[356] and *Fiallo* affirmed that it must be based upon a "facially legitimate and bona fide reason."[357] Great and imposing structures of judicial power have been built upon far less prepossessing foundations than these.[358] It seems likely that, just as the Court earlier imposed constitutional limits on Congress's broad power to regulate the acquisition and loss of American citizenship,[359] the Court will not continue indefinitely to tolerate, as it did in *Diaz*, unprincipled discrimination against aliens who sociologically, economically, morally—indeed, in all respects except legally—have become vital members of the community. I have suggested that *Plyler v. Doe*,[360] although involving a state classification, may evince an increasing judicial hostility to federal alienage classifications as well, at least where the power to define "political community" is not plausibly at issue.[361] Less ambiguously, the decision in *Hotel & Restaurant Employees Union, Local 25 v. Smith*,[362] and the detention cases discussed below suggest a growing judicial solicitude for those whom Congress may unquestionably exclude but who may now draw upon other sources of legal obligation once they make it inside our gates.

Deportation and Due Process

The principle that deportation is a civil, administrative proceeding, with its corollary that certain procedural safeguards need not be provided, is a fixture of classical immigration law. It shows no signs of being jettisoned. This result was unexceptionable when individualistic premises emphasizing consent and formalism animated the legal system, when deportation plausibly could be viewed as the revocation of a conditional "privilege" or license, and when such remedies did not trigger due process requirements.[363] In today's altered ideological and doctrinal setting, however, deportation appears in a rather different light. In a system that increasingly recognizes communitarian values, courts can be expected to take notice of the fact that deportation wrenches and uproots the alien from her most profound human attachments, attachments valued by the larger community from which she is torn as well as by the alien herself. They are unlikely to ignore the fact that even where she has failed to fulfill the conditions under which she gained entry, her presence here has spawned new social relationships, generating expectations and obligations that may transcend in importance those that she violated.

The lower courts have begun to respond to this new normative environment. In 1983, for example, the Ninth Circuit, overruling the Board of Immigration Appeals, applied the exclusionary rule to bar introduction of illegally obtained evidence into deportation proceedings.[364] The same court has also applied the fourth amendment to limit the INS's "area control" method of questioning deportable aliens.[365] Another court has suggested that due process requires free, appointed counsel for indigents at deportation hearings "[whenever] an unrepresented indigent alien would require counsel to present his position adequately to an immigration judge."[366] Courts have also found various due process violations in the mass, summary processing of deportable aliens with potential asylum claims.[367]

Despite some congressional resistance,[368] this judicial assimilation into the deportation process of rights drawn from criminal procedure has been spasmodic and fragmentary[369] but seems likely to continue. Doctrinally, this evolution may take any of several forms: expanded notions of what "fundamental fairness" requires; classification of deportation as a "quasi-criminal" proceeding;[370] or application to deportation decisions of equal protection standards[371] or general administrative law principles governing the decision-making process.[372] Normatively, this evolution reflects the courts' growing conviction, manifested in the reformation of administrative law that Stewart describes and in the increasing influence of communitarian values generally, that our society has as important a stake as aliens do in a fair, accurate and dignified public law process for deciding who shall remain among us.

Empirically, however, it remains unclear whether judicializing deportation procedures further would actually yield such a process. The question is complex for several reasons. The sheer number of deportable aliens apprehended each year suggests that more formal procedures might require an enormous reallocation of resources from other activities to adjudication.[373] If even a modest fraction of these aliens had to be processed through judicially mandated formal procedures, the INS would almost certainly be obliged to rely upon informal deportation practices to an even greater extent than it does now. Yet these practices could be rendered ineffective if illegal aliens could, by invoking more formal deportation procedures, impose substantial costs and delay upon the enforcement process.[374] In addition, a further formalization of deportation might affect decisions on aliens' applications for discretionary relief from deportation in unpredictable, perhaps undesirable ways.

Finally, it is far from clear that more formal procedures would actually enhance the accuracy or fairness of deportation decisions. The central reality of immigration administration is the overwhelming caseload of the immigration judges; in fiscal 1983, they were expected to decide an average of 5.35 deportation and exclusion cases *per day,* yet this assembly-line justice would not even keep the backlog from growing.[375] It is not difficult to imagine either the quality of the procedural forms that can be provided to aliens under such conditions or the effect upon the process of requiring new ones. In short, until we know much more about the actual relationships between procedural forms, substantive outcomes and process values in the peculiar setting of the deportation sanction, the law's treatment of that sanction as a merely "civil" one may be a necessary compromise with the uncertainties surrounding the dynamics of immigration administration.

Detention and Due Process

No single development has animated and shaped the current transformation of immigration law more powerfully than the massive influx and subsequent detention of aliens from Cuba, Haiti, El Salvador, and other

Caribbean Basin countries since 1980. The prolonged incarceration of thousands of aliens, most of them innocent victims of severe economic deprivation, indiscriminate armed conflict, or intense political persecution, has seared the judicial conscience as few events since the civil rights struggles of the 1950's and 1960's have done.[376]

Several aspects of this mass detention have especially troubled the courts. First, the conditions of confinement are often harsh and oppressive. These include chronic overcrowding, lack of recreation, violent disturbances, legal uncertainties, and the volatile mixture of different age groups and of as many as forty different nationalities in a given facility.[377] These individuals are not being held for criminal prosecution yet are detained without bond, a situation that clearly raises the most serious questions of denial of due process.[378] In addition, many of those so confined have at least colorable claims to various kinds of legal protections under domestic and international law notwithstanding their undocumented status. These include claims to asylum under the Refugee Act of 1980,[379] withholding of deportation if return would threaten the alien's life or freedom due to persecution,[380] extended voluntary departure,[381] so-called "deferred action,"[382] and relief through private legislation.[383] It also appears that certain actions by both the Carter and Reagan administrations actually encouraged aliens to assert these claims.[384] Finally, the INS has approached its undeniably difficult administrative task with an exceedingly heavy and arbitrary hand. The list of INS's adjudicated, post-1980 violations of the constitutional and statutory rights of aliens and of its own regulations is long, varied, and profoundly dispiriting.[385]

Under these circumstances, the courts are understandably less willing to credit the conventional administrative law presumption that the agency, if left to its own devices and to only sporadic congressional oversight, will comply with the law. As the lower court precedents granting injunctive relief against the INS accumulate, judges are naturally less hesitant to intervene. In the past, courts exercising their habeas corpus jurisdiction occasionally intervened to limit detention of individual deportable or excludable aliens.[386, 387] Recently, however, judges have demonstrated a willingness to grant broad, class relief to large numbers of aliens, enjoining INS's efforts to use detention as a way of deterring what the courts themselves acknowledge to be a tidal wave of undocumented entrants. Thus, within the last two years alone, the courts have invalidated some of INS's key detention initiatives. These include a general policy decision to detain all undocumented aliens who do not establish a prima facie case for admission;[388] its program of mass deportation of detained, undocumented Haitians coupled with mass processing and denial of their asylum claims;[389] its mass detention, deportation, and coerced voluntary departure of Salvadorans, coupled with failure to notify them of their right to apply for asylum;[390] and its prolonged detention of excludable Cubans pending deportation.[391]

In detention cases, the courts have transmuted classical immigration law's conception of the nature of the government-alien relationship into a rather different one in which rights against the government accrue to aliens without the government's consent and without the formal conditions for immigration having been observed. This conception lies at the core of the district court decision in *Fernandez-Roque v. Smith*.[392] In *Fernandez-Roque*, the individuals being detained were not simply aliens subject to future exclusion proceedings. Some apparently had already received statutory exclusion hearings and were subject to final orders of exclusion; the others had been administratively determined to have had criminal records in Cuba. Many of the plaintiffs had been detained since their initial arrival here.[393] Plainly, if any aliens could be considered total strangers to American society the plaintiffs in *Fernandez-Roque* could. Despite this fact, the court extended to these excludable aliens an array of constitutionally derived procedural rights that were actually far more extensive than those enjoyed by deportable aliens—indeed more extensive than those enjoyed by American citizens who challenged revocation of parole after a criminal conviction. It also created "a presumption of releasability" with the government bearing the burden of proof on the ultimate issue.[394] As a practical matter, this ostensibly procedural decision amounts to granting a *substantive* right to remain in this country indefinitely to many aliens who are clearly excludable under our laws.

This new conception of the government-alien relationship is also revealed in the emerging law of asylum. Far from viewing the alien as classical immigration law did, as an utter stranger with no legal claims upon the government other than those the government has agreed to recognize, the emerging law of asylum now enables any alien to acquire rights against the government to which the latter has not expressly consented, rights about which the Refugee Act of 1980 is silent.[395] These new rights—for example, timely notice of the right to apply for asylum[396]—reflect what David Martin has called "the procedural exuberance of the lower courts."[397] But some of them—for example, the rights to stay deportation proceedings pending final resolution of an asylum claim[398] and to be free from unnecessary or prolonged detention in the interim[399]—may have far-reaching substantive effects. These rights may as a practical matter amount to the right to work and live in the United States indefinitely. To enjoy them, all the alien need do is reach our shores. If she can also qualify as a refugee, she may then claim further statuses to which the government *has* expressly consented—asylum and the probability of adjusting to permanent legal residence.[400] Even if she cannot qualify as a refugee, she may be able to obtain withholding of deportation under section 1253(h).[401]

In limiting the permissible detention of aliens who have not yet "entered" the country,[402] then, the courts have found new nonconsensual sources of legal rights in an excludable alien's constitutionally protected interest in liberty, a potential asylum applicant's statutory interest in protection from persecution, and more general communitarian values. To define such rights and obligations, a court does not simply content itself with assessing the government's compliance with legal forms or its expressed intention, but appraises the alien's social context—her relationships, fears, expectations, and alternatives. *Mutatis mutandis,* a similar kind of inquiry directed at similar kinds of questions underlies modern theories of liability in private law and other areas of public law. Substantive justice, not the forms of consent and sovereignty, has become the principal touchstone of legal analysis.

The Separation of Adjudication and Law Enforcement

We saw earlier that the structural integration of adjudication and law enforcement has been a distinctive element of classical immigration law.[403] The government, by integrating these functions, has sought to enhance policy control and administrative efficiency. Like civil deportation and extraconstitutional exclusion, this decision structure is simply seen as part of the price that the alien must pay—literally, the price of admission—in order to enjoy the privilege that the government offers. If the alien is dissatisfied, she is free to try to do better by going elsewhere.[404] But when the individualistic, consent-based legal order gives way to one that seeks to vindicate universal human rights, communitarian values, and imputed social duties, the legitimacy of the original structure is seriously undermined. A society—or at least a federal judiciary—committed to these norms expects the government to exercise its awesome power over aliens fairly, in a way that preserves their dignity, protects their interest, and minimizes the risk of arbitrariness and error. This is true even if meeting this expectation makes life more difficult or costly for the government.

It is not surprising, then, that like the other features of classical immigration law, the integration of adjudication and enforcement is now under attack. Objections to this practice are neither theoretical nor purely historical. For example, in *Haitian Refugee Center v. Smith,*[405] a 1982 decision, the Court of Appeals affirmed the trial court's finding that the immigration judges had cooperated with the INS prosecutors in administering a program of mass, summary injustice.[406] Other abuses in earlier times have often been alleged.[407]

Limited reforms have already been instituted. In 1983, an administrative reorganization formally moved the immigration judges outside of the administrative control of the INS and placed them, along with the Board of

Immigration Appeals (BIA), into a new Executive Office for Immigration Review.[408] This new unit is not independent of the Justice Department, for it remains under the supervision of the Deputy Attorney General. The administrative adjudication of immigration cases, therefore, continues to be conducted under the direct supervision of the Attorney General, the Nation's chief prosecutorial official. Moreover, training and career lines increase the possibility of bias; most immigration judges come from many years of service in the ranks of the INS. Thoroughgoing changes, such as an independent administrative law judge system, have successfully been resisted.[409] In this respect, even more than in others that we have discussed, the transformation of immigration law remains embryonic, tentative, and incomplete.

IV. THE FUTURE OF IMMIGRATION LAW

Although still partial and fragmentary, the signs of incipient change are abundant and unmistakable. The courts' almost complete deference to Congress and the immigration authorities, long a keystone of the classical structure, is beginning to give way to a new understanding and rhetoric of judicial role, as unusual in immigration cases as it is now commonplace in other domains of public law.[410] Perhaps emboldened by the declining legitimacy of the existing system and the compelling human dilemmas presented in recent cases, lower courts are testing and sometimes transcending the confines of the classical canons. The Supreme Court, it must be emphasized, has not yet spoken on the post-1980 cases. Nevertheless, the Court has seemed to provide the lower courts with ample leeway within which to innovate.[411] The administrative apparatus of the immigration system, virtually overwhelmed by the numbers and novelty of the problems it confronts, is in such serious disarray that the courts appear increasingly unwilling to countenance INS's business as usual.[412] Congress, which only manages to reassess immigration policy in a fundamental way every thirty years or so, has just abandoned a half-decade's effort—perhaps the last for years to come—to enact the most far-reaching changes in immigration law since the McCarran-Walters Act of 1952.[413] In an important sense, the lower courts are on their own. If *Plyler v. Doe* is any guide, the Supreme Court is not inclined to rein them in.

To say that the individualistic structure of the classical immigration system is gradually being supplanted by one increasingly based upon communitarian norms is not to say that the particular forms that change is taking are inevitable. The relatively open immigration policy and easy access to citizenship that largely prevailed prior to the 1880's[414] represented one model of the government-alien relationship; the restrictive nationalism embodied in the 1917 and 1924 statutes[415] represented quite another. The Bracero and

H-2 programs, which allowed foreign workers to enter the country on a limited basis,[416] and the employer sanction, legalization, and summary exclusion schemes represent still others.[417] The United Kingdom, although sharing a common legal tradition, has recently taken a very different, still more restrictive path.[418] These choices and others were and remain open to us so long as we affirm the somewhat inconsistent ideals of consent-based obligation, universal human rights, and strong national sovereignty.

Why, then, has immigration law begun to move in the particular directions that section III described? Although a fully satisfactory causal explanation lies well outside the scope of this essay, I have tried to suggest the beginnings of an answer. I have noted that the foundations of classical immigration law were laid at a time when the assumptions of traditional liberalism, qualified and reshaped by the very different assumptions of restrictive nationalism, dominated legal thought about the meaning of national sovereignty and about the sources and scope of the government's obligation to individuals in general and to aliens in particular. Important economic and social changes, however, have rendered both ideologies increasingly incoherent and irrelevant as applied to immigration problems. Consequently, they gradually have been supplanted by theories of obligation derived not from the forms of consent by a sovereign government, but from a new communitarian ethos that grounds obligation in social relationships and notions of substantive justice.

Courts adjudicating under these changed structural and ideological conditions and drawing upon principles and moral intuitions that have long dominated private, administrative, and constitutional law, are now beginning to fuse these ideas into a new and radically different system of immigration law. In doing so, judges are both responding to and accelerating the penetration of communitarian values into *all* areas of contemporary law and life, as collectively imposed duties and bureaucratic institutions replace the individualistic values and decentralized structures of the market.[419] Immigration law, with its political and institutional insularities and eccentricities, has simply assimilated these pervasive changes in the legal culture more slowly and equivocally than have other areas of law.

If these structural and ideological conditions help to explain the course that immigration law has followed and to identify the coordinates of its present location, they suggest little about its ultimate destination. Legal history, like all history, reveals few continuities or uninterrupted patterns.[420] In the social sciences, projections into the future on the basis of predictive models and extrapolations from current trends are notoriously unreliable.[421] And law, it need hardly be added, is far from being a science.

In fact, the transformation of immigration law has significantly increased its indeterminacy by aggravating certain tensions and contradictions long embedded within the classical structure, and by creating new ones peculiar to a communitarian legal system. Three facets of this transformation reveal its problematic nature most starkly, and also seem likely to affect the future development of immigration law in particularly important ways. These relate to the legitimacy of immigration law, the role of the courts in developing the law, and the conception of community that the law embodies.

Legitimacy

Law's ability to influence human conduct derives ultimately from its moral legitimacy. This legitimacy in turn is significantly affected by the incentive structure—the array of costs and benefits—that the law in fact creates.[422] Immigration law deals with private activity that is quintessentially deliberate and calculating, activity therefore in which incentives are highly and directly salient to motivation.[423] Classical immigration law, as we have seen, took an uncompromising but detached view of the relationship between government and aliens. If admitted, an alien was bound by the terms of her privilege or license, as prescribed by the visa or parole conditions. When the INS sought to enforce those conditions against her in deportation or exclusion proceedings, the INS almost always prevailed. If equities in favor of the alien had developed subsequent to her admission, of course, she might seek relief by way of a private bill or, after 1952, by administrative suspension of deportation. But the legislative route was unpromising,[424] administrative relief was highly discretionary, and the courts characteristically deferred to that discretionary judgment.[425]

Today, the incentive structure of immigration law has shifted—to the marked advantage of these aliens who are undocumented or out of status but also wish to remain. Evasion, delay, surreptitious reentry, and administrative overload in the immigration system are the most precious resources of such aliens, and a more communitarian law is increasingly making those resources abundantly available to them. As the gap widens between the standards of living and working in the United States and in the countries that are the major sources of undocumented aliens, the rewards for entering and remaining are correspondingly greater. In a classic demonstration of how procedure and substance are intimately related, the courts have expanded aliens' procedural rights in the various ways discussed in section III, thereby increasing the probability that aliens will in fact obtain the ultimate substantive benefits—avoidance of deportation and receipt of the right to work here. They can utilize the numerous avenues of discretionary administrative relief that exist, invoke administrative and judicial review of each administrative decision, and move to stay and reopen proceedings at each stage of each administrative and judicial process—while steadily accumulating new relationships and equities that will enable them to delay deportation, obtain work authorization, and perhaps permanently legalize their status.[426] Concerning those who are ultimately expelled from this country, the vast majority choose to leave "voluntarily" and can subsequently—often only hours later—return unnoticed, only to begin the process once again.[427] "Beating the system" has become a game, it seems, that almost any resourceful alien equipped with easily obtained fraudulent documents[428] or a competent lawyer can successfully play.

The judicial innovations that have begun to transform immigration law cannot properly be evaluated without considering these intractable realities. It is not simply that these reforms have increased the cost of administering the immigration system; greater cost, after all, almost inevitably attends new procedural rights and cannot alone be a decisive factor. The more important concern is the loss of credibility and deterrence that a legal apparatus suffers when it cannot effectively execute its own rules and intentions, and when its impotence is both widespread and apparent to those who are expected to comply. In the case of immigration law, this includes aliens, employers, smugglers, and others who know of or participate in violations of that law.

Strengthened incentives to "beat the system" would be of relatively little concern if that system possessed the capacity to defend itself against this threat. Increasingly, however, it does not. Immigration law is being altered in ways that make it far more time-consuming, costly, and difficult for the INS to apprehend, interrogate, search, arrest, detain, deport, assign status to, and allocate benefits among aliens. At the same time, the administrative resources of the INS, never adequate to its responsibilities, are actually being reduced in real—and in some respects, even in nominal—terms.[429] One crude but revealing index of one important dimension of the INS's enforcement program is that the number of Border Patrol officers is little more than twice the number of guards patrolling the United States Capitol.[430] There are few powerful political constituencies seeking stronger border enforcement.

In such a situation, an effective enforcement program simply is not feasible. When fewer staff must perform far more complex and demanding tasks, when more formal, individualized, humane, and accurate decisions must be made with respect to more numerous and strategically sophisticated aliens, the gap between the demands of the law and the realities of administration may pass beyond the inevitable and tolerable, attaining truly critical dimensions.

Edwin Harwood has suggested another measure of the magnitude of this moral and administrative predicament. In 1961, over twelve percent of all illegal aliens who were ordered by the INS to leave were formally deported rather than allowed "voluntary departure"; by 1982, fewer than two percent were deported.[431] As the number of undocumented aliens entering the United States has grown, INS border enforcement has come to depend almost entirely upon its ability to persuade the vast majority of the deportable aliens whom it apprehends that they should admit to illegal status and depart voluntarily. If a substantial fraction of them were to begin to stand mute, claim to be citizens, or invoke their right to a due process deportation hearing, the INS enforcement machinery would grind to a virtual halt, at least without substantial infusions of additional budget and manpower resources.[432] As Harwood puts it, "[e]nforcement works to the extent it does only because aliens are either insufficiently informed of the law's vulnerability in this regard, or because they are basically honest and unable to persist in a deception."[433] In short, the viability of immigration enforcement today depends largely upon the continuation of two conditions that may well prove transitory—aliens' ignorant waiver of their legal rights and their candor in the face of powerful incentives to dissemble.

The total collapse of a credible enforcement posture could result from legal developments that enhance the strategic position of undocumented aliens, developments the administrative implications of which are only now beginning to be perceived. First, whatever their compensating benefits, new procedural protections, such as the application of the exclusionary rule to immigration enforcement proceedings and a right, in effect, to have free appointed counsel,[434] must inevitably strengthen the bargaining position of the numerous illegal aliens who wish to resist or delay deportation. Second, the dramatic increase in asylum applications growing out of the chaotic conditions in Central America in part reflects legal and strategic advice rendered to aliens by lawyers and organizations that, quite appropriately, seek to delay or defeat deportation of their clients. Many international developments outside of anyone's control could unleash new waves of undocumented entries and asylum petitions. Third, expanded procedural rights, such as those extended to excludable aliens in *Fernandez-Roque v. Smith*[435] also enhance their bargaining power by making the expulsion process more costly, protracted, and uncertain. There is some evidence suggesting that such a situation can exacerbate these problems by attracting additional aliens who see strategic opportunities in the system's marasmus.[436] Finally, several of the pending Simpson-Mazzoli legislative proposals, particularly the amnesty for illegal aliens, would not only create additional opportunities to delay and prevent legitimate expulsions of aliens already here; in addition, they probably would attract new illegal entrants who hope, through use of fraudulent documents, to qualify for amnesty and legal permanent residence status.[437]

At some point, administrative incapacity prefigures a critical loss of legitimacy. In the case of immigration, it is entirely possible that this point has already been reached. In this sense, the lamentation that "we have lost control of our borders" is more than an expression of profound frustration, more than a rhetorical *cri de coeur*. The tidal wave of undocumented aliens who cannot be effectively deterred from crossing into the United States has swept away the credibility of INS enforcement. At the same time, only three years after enactment of the Refugee Act, a backlog of more than 166,000 pending asylum applications[438] is encouraging, if not requiring, policies of mass detention. These policies have led to judicially mandated mass releases into the community and pressures for crude categorical relief.[439] These simultaneous, parallel explosions in the number of putative refugees and in the number of illegal aliens have, as Alexander Aleinikoff puts it, imposed humanitarian and process demands regarding respect to the former that, if applied to the latter, will effectively immobilize enforcement.[440]

These contradictions do not simply confirm that the law's promises have outstripped its capacity to deliver. Far more important; they are sapping immigration law of its moral force in the eyes of aliens, employers, officials and the general public. Law without legitimacy is little more than naked force, the power, as it has been said, that comes out of the barrel of a gun. And because immigration law reflects some of our most deeply held values concerning community, self-definition, national autonomy, and social justice, any diminution of its legitimacy entails a profound, perhaps irretrievable, loss.

Unlike some problems that government faces, the problem of restoring legitimacy to immigration law is partly one of money. Additional resources and staff could accelerate exclusion, deportation, and asylum decisions, reducing the need for prolonged detention of aliens and reducing the period during which they can acquire the ties that a more communitarian immigration law is most reluctant to sever. More funds could also improve the INS's border control and investigation activities, although serious difficulties would remain under even the most optimistic foreseeable budgetary conditions.[441] Coupled with other reforms, such as effective employer sanctions and an amnesty program,[442] it might at least contain the influx of undocumented aliens. Until Congress appropriates funds and authorizes personnel levels that are adequate to the scale of the challenge, however, immigration law will continue to teeter on the brink of moral and programmatic bankruptcy.

But even dramatically increased funds could not wholly solve immigration law's legitimacy problem, at least in the short run. The more spacious conception of community revealed in cases such as *Plyler v. Doe*[443] is also working to undermine the legitimacy of immigration policies directed at the apprehension and exclusion of undocumented aliens. Two very recent examples suggest the dimensions of this conflict. The first involves the insistence by the police chief of Santa Ana, California, probably repeated less candidly in many other communities near the Mexican border, that federal immigration officials who seek to apprehend illegals are not welcome in that city. According to another Santa Ana official, "we never invited the undocumented alien population to settle in our city but now that they have, we are going to work with them. You can't afford to have 25 percent of the population hostile towards the Police Department."[444]

The second example involves the willingness of a steadily increasing number of churches and individuals, now estimated at up to 30,000, to defy the immigration authorities by openly offering sanctuary to undocumented aliens, especially those from Central America and Caribbean countries who are unlikely to be granted asylum status in the near future.[445] By providing this sanctuary, these individuals almost certainly violate criminal provisions that impose possible sanctions of fine and imprisonment.[446] Such attitudes betray a growing sense of moral commitment and obligation to strangers. But while these attitudes and the acts of personal witness that they inspire may be morally admirable, they bode ill for the effective enforcement of immigration law.

Indeed, communitarian values are themselves antithetical to vigorous immigration enforcement, especially when reinforced by traditional liberalism's human rights dimension, which Americans continue to cherish. By regarding all who arrive here not as strangers but as members, along with Americans, of a universal moral community in which abstract principles of exclusion yield to the more palpable claims of actual and potential human linkage, communitarian values deprive administrative deportation efforts of the moral legitimacy that the classical order managed to sustain for so long. If that is so, the collapse of immigration enforcement may actually generate a profound public reaction against aliens and the communitarian values that increasingly protect them, reviving the nativist impulses that have always been an important, albeit often deplorable, element of our national character.

Judicial Role

The transformation of immigration law also casts into bold relief a set of contradictions surrounding the parallel, intimately related transformation of the function of courts in the American legal system. Few areas of public law are so susceptible to administrative abuse and lawlessness as immigration law. The INS is among the most insular and chronically understaffed of federal agencies; it is vulnerable to manipulation and neglect by Congress and to political reprisals by powerful employer interests opposed to vigorous law enforcement. Aliens, the nominal clients of the system, are politically and economically weak, unfamiliar with legal forms, procedures, and the language, and often reluctant or unable to assert their rights. Unlike welfare recipients, school children, and mental hospital patients, for example, aliens often exist in a kind of *social* vacuum, outside any structures of institutional, programmatic, administrative, or professional support.

INS decisions, moreover, have low visibility; they occur in isolated adjudicatory contexts in which their larger policy consequences, if any, are fragmented and thus difficult to discern or monitor. Decision errors are likely to
be common, and the distribution of costs and benefits of such errors makes
their detection unlikely. Thus positive errors—in which the agency erroneously admits or grants a benefit to one who is not entitled to it—do not affect the agency's budget and will not be challenged unless Congress does
so.[447] Negative errors—in which the INS erroneously excludes, deports or
denies a benefit to an alien who is entitled to it—only affect the agency's budget if it is challenged, and then only to the extent of the resources necessary to
contest the appeal. Negative errors, of course, are highly salient to aliens,
perhaps even life threatening, but they often are not in a position to challenge
such errors in administrative or judicial review proceedings or in Congress.

Federal judges must be presumed to be aware of these realities, and it
would not be surprising if many of them concluded that such a decisional
context cries out for judicial intervention. Courts of general jurisdiction
might be expected to hold the INS to the same constitutional and administrative standards to which other federal agencies are held—indeed, to
higher standards in view of the life and liberty interests so often at stake in
immigration cases, especially those involving detention, asylum, and
EVD.[448] In conjunction with the changes discussed in section II, these factors surely help to explain and perhaps even to justify the emergent judicial
assertiveness that is both a hallmark and a necessary condition of immigration law's incipient transformation.

Perhaps paradoxically, however, an active, intrusive judicial role in immigration cases raises serious dilemmas, the resolution of which will shape the
future of immigration law. Some of the manifest difficulties of devising a
new constitutional order in an area of law that has long defied one are revealed in *Plyler v. Doe*,[449] in which the Court felt obliged to turn conventional legal categories and precedents inside out in order to reach a morally
appealing result. Others are revealed in *Fernandez-Roque*, in which the
court created an entire procedural system out of whole cloth, one that
places some excludable aliens in an even better legal and strategic position
than deportable aliens, many of whom have already become more or less
integrated into our society. Still other difficulties are apparent in *Hotel &
Restaurant Employees Union, Local 25 v. Smith*,[450] in which the court proceeded as if the justiciability of EVD for particular nationality groups were
no different than the justiciability of an individual detention or adjudication case, as if the intricacies of contemporary foreign policy in Central
America were simply an irrelevant smokescreen thrown up by the government in order to confuse the court.

In addition to the courts' problematic efforts to fashion a new order in
an area that historically has been resistant to judicial involvement, obsta-

cles to effective intervention inhere in immigration law's own administrative structure. The broad substantive discretion that the statute confers upon the Attorney General in almost all areas of immigration policy suggests the distinct possibility that judicially mandated procedural changes would not significantly affect outcomes. Instead, they may simply make the agency's journey to the same substantive result more costly and cumbersome. By adversely affecting the agency's bargaining position vis-à-vis illegal aliens, such changes may succeed in incapacitating the informal enforcement process as well. Yet if courts attempt to avoid these difficulties by ordering reform of a more structural, systemic nature, they will encounter not only the same kinds of pitfalls that have plagued judicial efforts to constitutionalize other areas of governmental activity[451]—lack of manageable standards, inadequate policymaking tools, limited inducements, implementation problems, questions of institutional legitimacy, and the like—but also some others that are more or less peculiar to the immigration field.[452]

If this analysis is correct, the conflicts over judicial role engendered by the transformation of immigration law can probably be best resolved in the broad middle ground between the abject judicial deference of the classical tradition and the sweeping structural relief sometimes granted in other policy areas, precursors of which are beginning to appear in immigration cases as well.[453] Courts should actively scrutinize INS adjudications, demanding decisionmaking procedures of high accuracy, fairness and dignity. Although courts can certainly do this in the context of reviewing those individual adjudications that are appealed, the peculiarities of the immigration decision process—especially the weakness of politics and litigation as controls over administrative abuse, and the high costs to aliens, and citizens, of negative errors—argue strongly that courts should insist that administrators install more systematic quality-assurance techniques at the INS and BIA levels over decisions,[454] rather than demanding ever more formalized, extensive hearing procedures whose effects, apart from increased cost and delays, are uncertain and quite possibly perverse.[455]

Courts should also be more discriminating in their approach to reviewing immigration decisions. In particular, they should distinguish between congressional and executive branch decisions that do not involve delicate foreign policy judgments, such as many deportation decisions,[456] and those that do, such as policies on EVD. They should feel much freer to apply conventional constitutional and administrative law principles to the former than to the latter. Where life and liberty interests collide with powerful foreign policy, law enforcement, or other governmental interests, courts should seek relatively flexible solutions, such as "clear statement" requirements or remands to the agency with instructions to develop new approaches, rather than finding refuge in rigid constitutional rulings.[457] Similarly, courts in appropriate cases should require the INS to issue standards that narrow and guide its vast discretion, thereby putting aliens and low-level officials on notice concerning what the law requires and enabling administrative superiors, Congress and the courts to hold the INS to those standards.[458]

In urging the courts to take these steps, however, we should not imagine that any set of immigration adjudications are likely to constitute an adequate solution to the contradictions and problems that this transformation is engendering. The crucial determinants of INS policy—resources, political support, international developments, the inherent vulnerability of illegal aliens—lie well outside judicial control. Because judges can affect these matters only marginally, if at all, they cannot really ease the profoundly difficult moral and policy choices that make immigration policy so unmanageable today. Those choices involve tradeoffs that only Congress can effectively address. Unfortunately, as the recent derailment of the Simpson-Mazzoli legislation vividly suggests, Congress remains politically stalemated on precisely these questions.

Regardless of whether or not Congress is prepared to act, however, a communitarian immigration law will demand a great deal of courts. They must maintain their traditional concern for the protection of individual rights and procedural fairness values. Indeed, if the INS cannot be made to respect these values, judicial vigilance is bound to become more intense. At the same time, however, courts must recognize the dangers to political control and effective administration of immigration policy posed by judicial pursuit of communitarian ideals that, however appealing in the abstract, are still only weakly rooted in our collective attitudes toward contemporary immigration.

Community

Community, as Carl Friedrich observed, is "the central concept of politics."[459] It follows, then, that immigration law is a fulcrum of our political system. By seeking to define, mold and protect the American community, it undertakes to answer the first questions that any society must put to itself: What are we? What do we wish to become? How shall we reach that goal? And most fundamentally, which individuals constitute the "we" who shall decide these questions?[460] A liberal polity asks these questions with a special intensity and self-consciousness. To most Americans, they cannot be neatly resolved by invoking divine guidance, settled traditions, or some imminent, organic principle. Instead, these questions can only be addressed through the never-ending processes of rational argument, irrational commitments and political choice.

Liberalism has never satisfactorily answered these questions and probably never will. It regards any fixed or exclusive definition of community with profound suspicion. Indeed, in a truly liberal polity, it would be difficult to justify a restrictive immigration law or perhaps any immigration law at all. National barriers to movement would be anomalous. Criteria of inclusion and exclusion based upon accidents of birth, criteria that label some individuals as insiders and others as outsiders, would be odious. Wealth, security, and freedom would not be allocated on such grounds, especially in a world in which the initial distribution of those goods is so unequal.[461] Instead, individuals would remain free to come and go, to form attachments, and to make choices according to their own aspirations, consistent with the equal right of others to do likewise. No self-defining, self-limiting group could deny to nonmembers the individual freedom of action that liberalism distinctively celebrates. In essence, this was the conception of community—one embracing all who wished to come and remain here—that prevailed until the 1880's. Indeed, just as the period of open borders was coming to a close, the Supreme Court breathed additional constitutional life into that communal ideal by extending the succor of the equal protection principle, and thus the protection of the constitutional community, to all "persons" in the United States, whether citizen or alien.[462]

In the second American century, immigration law, shaped by a burgeoning sense of American nationhood and international stature, narrowed this ideal in the interests of defining a *national* community. As the flood of "new immigrants" prior to World War I attests, this definition was not always or inevitably a static one. Nevertheless, it eventually placed severe limits upon the potential character and membership of that community, constricting it from an essentially universalistic one to a legal artifact self-consciously constricted by Congress. The felt necessity to restrict the community compelled liberalism for the first time to try to develop criteria of exclusion. But the idea of a restrictive community based not upon universal human rights but upon contingent national interests proved to be a very hard one for liberalism to integrate. Its meaning shifted depending upon who was defining it, for what purposes and in what context.

If immigration law were to promote some ideal of community, then, it must first identify what the grounds of community formation should be. Those grounds, however, are as varied as the patterns and motives of human association. Earlier idealizations of community—the intimacy of the Greek *polis*[463] or the spiritual unity of a universal religion,[464] for example—were obviously irrelevant to conditions in America. Liberal theory provided no guidance either. For all its universality, liberalism essentially viewed society as a contrivance animated solely by individuals' self-interest, by their need for protection against strangers and against each other. It denied the natural sociability and shared values that the ancients had taken to be the fundamental basis of political life.

Indeed, it is no exaggeration to say that traditional liberalism articulated no real theory of community at all. Its vision of the good society was one of privatistic acquisitiveness, not social solidarity and common purpose.[465] Unable to stake out any middle ground between the utopian community of all mankind and the ahistorical community of individuals freely contracting in the state of nature, liberalism could not furnish immigration law with a coherent definition of the relevant community. In that ideological vacuum, the decidedly illiberal, nationalistic features of classical immigration law— the national origins quota and the fortress mentality that underlay summary, extraconstitutional exclusion procedures, for example—were able to flourish.

As America's third century begins, the struggle over the dominant conception of community—and thus over the contemporary meaning, relevance, and relative significance of liberal, nationalistic, and collectivist values—continues. But this struggle is now being waged in a new legal and political context. Today, large numbers of migrants can easily, inexpensively, and surreptitiously enter United States territory, where they can readily form social and economic attachments that the government cannot easily sever. Here, they find a society in which private property increasingly consists of advantages—including public benefits and legal alien status— that only the government can confer, a society in which the stakes in defining community, in inclusion or exclusion, are therefore higher than ever. They also find a legal order that is in great flux, one whose premises are shifting from individualistic values, which emphasize consent as the source of duty, to communitarian values, which ground duty in expanding social relationships, interdependencies and expectations. From the point of view of the undocumented alien, who under present conditions often cannot be apprehended much less expelled until she has had an opportunity to form these attachments, these developments add up to good news indeed.

These brute facts present liberalism with a poignant predicament. Committed to the rule of law but confronted by individuals who, sociologically speaking, have found community in America only after flouting that law, liberalism cannot legitimate their presence. Committed to the moral primacy of consent, liberalism cannot embrace those who enter by stealth. Committed to universal human rights, liberalism cannot secure those rights in the real world without rooting itself in political institutions that are actually capable of instantiating its values. Today and for the foreseeable future, those political institutions are the institutions of the *nation*.

As section I revealed, moreover, even a liberal nation has powerful propensities toward illiberal, exclusionary practices. The very idea of nationhood implies a coherence of shared tradition, experiences and values—a national community. This community is inevitably parochial and inward-turning; just as it affirms a core of common commitments, it also sets the nation apart from, if not above, the rest of humanity.[466] Moreover, the nation has ordained an activist government that seeks to assure at least a minimal level of economic security and well-being for individuals. It cannot possibly provide this assurance to mankind in general; instead, it must restrict its primary concerns to those to whom it has undertaken a special political responsibility. Even this more limited task is impossible if masses of destitute people, many ill-equipped to live and work in a postindustrial society, may acquire legally enforceable claims against it merely by reaching its shores. Finally, the nation inevitably seeks to mobilize its people's passions and energies against real or imagined threats, as in wartime or domestic crisis. To accomplish this, it must make powerful emotional appeals to national unity and sacrifice. Whether the goal is the realization of universal liberal values—"making the world safe for democracy," for example—or more parochial ones—such as "manifest destiny" or "the great society"—the individual wills that liberalism glorifies must be merged into an almost mystical embodiment of national character and patriotic purpose.

For liberal values to triumph, then, liberalism is obliged to accommodate a competing, illiberal conception of community that threatens those values even as it promises to actualize them—albeit for only a limited portion of humanity. By investing the distinction between insiders and outsiders with moral and political significance, nationalism—the ideal of national community—rejects liberalism's own communal visions. The universal brotherhood of man enjoying natural rights and the society of strangers linked by little more than contract are both too impractical and alienating, and represent too impoverished a view of what our society and political natures require, to fully realize our humanity. Both ignore our basic need for what Michael Walzer has called "communities of character, historically stable, ongoing associations of men and women with some special commitment to one another and some special sense of their common life."[467] For the liberal welfare state to enlist the active public support necessary if it is to do its affirmative, individuality-enhancing work, some such community is essential. Our psychological natures also seem to link mutual commitments to some degree of human propinquity. Thus, as Walzer observes, the very notion of a meaningful community, liberal or otherwise, probably implies some exclusion for at least some purposes. The relevant questions are how much exclusion the sense of community requires, and upon what basis it should proceed.

Liberalism rules out certain answers to these questions—exclusion based upon race, for example. In practice and probably in principle, however, it also leaves open many possibilities. It remains to be seen whether the communitarian values that are increasingly shaping our legal order can supply immigration law with appropriate criteria of inclusion and exclusion. Certainly, these new values reflect important sociological facts about how social linkage and expectations evolve, facts that no just legal order, no ideal of legal community, can ignore.

Yet a communitarian conception of immigration law provides some grounds for concern. Once society's duty to aliens is no longer moored to the classical norms of mutual consent and compliance with publicly sanctioned legal procedures but is derived from vague, even circular, notions of social expectations and relationships, the legal order is cast adrift upon a sea whose ungovernable tides may carry it to realms unknown, unimagined, and fraught with dangers.[468] The problem is not simply one of a limited American capacity to assimilate newcomers. Our history testifies eloquently to the greatness and durability of that capacity. It is not inexhaustible, of course, and as noted earlier, the conditions of a postindustrial society may make the effort to assimilate masses of migrants from premodern societies especially problematic today. Still, when one recalls that more than fourteen percent of the United States population in 1910 was foreign-born compared to four and a half percent in 1970 and that eight other industrialized countries now have a higher percentage of foreign-born than the United States does.[469] The prospect of even several million new immigrants joining a nation of 226.5 million people,[470] especially one that is rapidly aging and has an historically low fertility rate, seems considerably less daunting.[471]

The sheer *number* of immigrants, then, is unlikely in itself to create unmanageable difficulties, even assuming a range of admissions far more generous than current policy permits. Two other considerations, however, are more troubling. First, there is a risk that a communitarian immigration law will encourage further social and cultural fragmentation, intergroup hostility, distributional inequities, and intensified political conflict, and that these conditions will at some point degrade the quality of American democracy. The discord between English-speaking and French-speaking Canadians, not to say the civil strife that afflicts so many other polyglot societies, looms as a haunting reminder of this danger.

Second, the tension between liberalism's universal aspirations and our need as a society to achieve the degree of solidarity that effective activist government requires must be resolved at *some* level of exclusion. Although it remains unclear what this level should be, it is imperative that America make this choice self-consciously rather than having it preempted by the self-interested actions of others. When courts wielding some conception of communitarian values decide to empower strangers unilaterally to create and enforce substantial claims against American society, that process of self-definition is seriously impeded. If the American community's power to define its common purposes and obligations is no greater than the power of strangers to cross our borders undetected and to acquire interests here, our capacity to pursue liberal values—to decide as individuals and as a society what we wish to be—may be critically impaired.

Conclusion

Social conditions and a changed legal consciousness have begun to undermine the foundations of classical immigration law. In its growing decrepitude, we can glimpse both the remnants of the individualistic legal order that once gave it life and legitimacy, and the outlines of the communitarian one that promises to transform it. The courts are busily razing the old structure and designing the new one, largely along the lines laid down by the contemporary administrative and constitutional orders. Immigration is gradually rejoining the mainstream of our public law.

3

Continuity and Change
in the Courts: 1979–1990

Immigration to the United States increased dramatically during the 1980s.[1] This flow of immigrants has already transformed the face of many American cities and will dramatically alter the composition of our society. High levels of immigration profoundly affect many different facets of life in the nation, such as ethnic and language mix, fertility rates, religious affiliations, popular culture, the labor force, and political coalitions.

Increased immigration in the 1980s also created enormous pressure for legal change. Congress responded by enacting three major pieces of legislation—the Refugee Act of 1980,[2] the Immigration Reform and Control Act of 1986,[3] and the Immigration Act of 1990[4]—which renovated virtually the entire legal structure for handling immigration.[5]

The increase in immigration, combined with statutory changes, presented new administrative and judicial challenges. Asylum claims, relatively inconspicuous in the 1970s, became a major focus of agency and court adjudication.[6] The immigration court, the adjudicator of first resort in exclusion and deportation cases, acquired new independence and importance in 1983 when it was removed from the Immigration and Naturalization Service (INS) and put under the auspices of the Executive Office for Immigration Review (EOIR).[7] Immigration matters began to emerge as a major component of the administrative law caseload in the federal courts.[8] In addition, affirmative challenges to INS policies, uncommon before 1980, had by the end of the decade become a prominent, policy-shaping category of immigration litigation.[9]

The scholars who have analyzed the increase in immigration during the 1980s have taken at least two cognizable approaches. Political scientists, economists, and demographers have examined the broad social significance of immigration in a social science context.[10] Immigration law scholars, however, have taken a narrower approach, looking at how recent immigration has affected particular legal doctrines such as the rights of undocumented workers,[11] the standards governing asylum claims,[12] and the operation of the ideological exclusion provisions.[13] However, between these broad social and narrow doctrinal studies lies a phenomenon that has received almost no systematic attention: the changing patterns of immigration litigation and adjudication in the courts during the 1980s.

Addressing this phenomenon, I have argued that a number of developments during the 1980s, including illegal migration, the United States' new role in the world, and fundamental changes in American constitutional and administrative law, gradually shifted immigration law away from its exclusionary history and toward a more pro-alien focus.[14] Judges became less deferential to the government's asserted interests in national sovereignty and border control, and became more protective of aliens whom the government was seeking to exclude or deport.[15] Recently, the same author reviewed immigration legislation during the 1980s and concluded that it, too, had acquired a decidedly pro-immigrant character as the decade progressed.[16] While this "alien protection jurisprudence" hypothesis seemed consistent with leading court decisions and other legal developments, it had yet to be tested with systematic evidence.

This essay tests the "alien protection jurisprudence" hypothesis by systematically analyzing a large sample of immigration cases adjudicated throughout the decade. To the extent this hypothesis is correct,[17] then, all other things remaining constant, at least two patterns should emerge. First, changes in the nature of immigration litigation should have made it easier for aliens to challenge the government's immigration control policies. Aliens could raise these challenges either defensively, by seeking to defeat deportation and exclusion proceedings brought against them, or offensively, by initiating challenges to government policies and practices. Second, case outcomes should have changed, with aliens prevailing at a higher rate.

We recognize, however, that the disputes adjudicated by the courts are not a random sample of all immigration disputes; certain factors beyond our control may affect our analysis. For example, the character of the claims that reach the courts reflects a winnowing process shaped by administration policies, INS and EOIR decisionmaking, immigrants' access to counsel, settlement of cases, and other factors that change over time.[18] In addition, because we have collected data solely from cases that reached final judgment and were reported either in a bound volume or on an electronic database, our analysis may be skewed by a litigation selection effect, which can distort the findings of any research that seeks to draw inferences about legal trends from a subset of cases. A litigation selection effect may arise, in part, as a result of the costs of litigation and the disputants' estimated likelihood of success; these factors strongly affect the decisions of parties whether or not to litigate. Thus, the disputes selected for litigation constitute neither a random, nor a necessarily representative, sample of the complete set of all disputes. However, for reasons explained in more detail in the accompanying note, we believe that litigation selection effects are minimized in immigration litigation and do not affect the major findings of this study. First, any selection effects would largely be limited to our analysis of litigation outcomes, and would not affect many of the other topics we discuss, such as caseload, criminal cases, and remands. Second, to the extent that a selection effect influences our analysis of outcomes, it may actually make our findings more striking.[19]

Bearing in mind the possibility of selection effects, we analyze a large number of immigration cases, and provide statistical evidence about the kinds of claims that were brought to court during the 1980s and how those claims were decided, in order to test the "alien protection jurisprudence" hypothesis. Section I describes our other objectives in undertaking this study, as well as the procedures employed in generating our data, and the inherent limitations of those data.*

Section II describes the changing patterns of immigration litigation during the 1980s by analyzing the characteristics of the immigration caseload of the federal courts. We present aggregate data for 1979, 1985, 1989, and 1990[20] on the following aspects of the caseload: (a) case volume and forums; (b) divisions within the circuit courts; (c) nationality of alien claimants; (d) types of proceedings; and (e) types of relief sought. Here and throughout the article, we compare Ninth Circuit litigation patterns to those of the other circuits to determine whether and to what extent the Ninth Circuit is uniquely pro-alien.[21]

Sections III, IV, and V discuss three distinct categories of immigration cases in the courts. Section III focuses on "affirmative challenges," a relatively new and increasingly important category of cases. Unlike typical INS-initiated deportation or exclusion proceedings, affirmative challenges are cases initiated by aliens, labor unions, or others seeking to directly challenge governmental policies or practices. We analyze several aspects of this category: (a) the volume of cases in various circuits; (b) the goals of those initiating the challenges; (c) the distinction between "impact" litigation and other kinds of affirmative challenges; (d) the issues in contention; (e) the grounds on which the challenges are based; and (f) the ultimate success rates of the claims.

Section IV focuses on criminal immigration cases. This discussion is brief because our data on criminal prosecutions are limited to caseload volume, the nature of the criminal charges, and the outcomes of the cases.

Section V examines statutory review cases, which involve direct judicial review of administrative decisions—primarily exclusions, deportations, visa denials, and employer sanctions. We analyze how these cases were decided by

---

*Sections I–VI are not included in this synopsis, but can be found in the original source.

examining: (a) the types of relief sought by aliens; (b) aliens' success rates; (c) how reviewing courts disposed of the cases on appeal (e.g., affirmance, reversal, remand, etc.); (d) how the Supreme Court's decision in *Chevron, U.S.A., Inc. v. Natural Resources Defense Council, Inc.*[22] affected the dispositions of reviewing courts in non-criminal immigration cases; and (e) the results in cases remanded by district and circuit courts to INS, BIA, or immigration judges.[23]

Finally, section VI summarizes our most significant findings and briefly suggests their implications for the management of immigration litigation.

* * *

VI. Summary of Major Findings

Our principal findings can be summarized as follows:

1. The 1980s witnessed a significant growth in immigration litigation in the district courts and especially in the circuit courts. The Ninth Circuit consistently heard approximately half of the circuit court immigration litigation throughout the decade. The Ninth Circuit's share of the district court caseload was much smaller.
2. Contrary to the investment hypothesis, which predicts that aliens from further away will fare better in immigration cases, aliens from regions neighboring the United States tended to have higher overall success rates in the courts than those from more distant regions.
3. The number of appeals from deportation orders rose dramatically during the decade. Exclusion cases, in contrast, grew more slowly. They composed a very small share of the circuit court caseload, especially in the Ninth Circuit, where deportation cases are concentrated, and an even smaller share in the district courts.
4. Affirmative challenges, common even in 1979, composed a declining share of the overall caseload, despite an increase in absolute numbers. However, the impact litigation component of the affirmative challenge category—challenges to statutes, regulations, and practices of general applicability—grew substantially as a percentage of the caseload. Aliens enjoyed an impressive success rate in such cases, particularly in the courts of the Ninth Circuit, where they won the majority of their impact lawsuits.
5. Asylum litigation grew only slowly before 1985 but increased rapidly thereafter. Salvadorans enjoyed a high success rate, while asylum claimants from the Middle East, a region traditionally favored by U.S. refugee law, fared much worse.
6. In general, the data contradict, but do not conclusively refute, the alien protection jurisprudence hypothesis, which posits the emergence of a pro-immigrant legal climate. The overall success rate for

aliens in court declined from 36 percent in 1979 to 27 percent in the 1989–1990 period.

7. Our data tend to support the alien protection jurisprudence hypothesis, however, with respect to several subsets of cases. Asylum claimants fared better by the end of the decade, winning 37 percent of their cases in the 1989–1990 period. In 1989–1990, the Ninth Circuit produced more pro-alien asylum decisions compared with other circuits, and compared with its own decisions in 1979. Aliens also fared better in impact litigation as the decade progressed, especially in the Ninth Circuit.

8. Throughout the decade, reviewing courts proved increasingly likely to affirm INS and BIA decisions in statutory review cases. The affirmance rate reached 70 percent by 1989–1990. But despite this increase, our re-examination of data from the earlier Schuck-Elliott study indicates that: (a) the affirmance rate actually declined after the Supreme Court's *Chevron* decision; and (b) the Ninth Circuit's relatively pro-alien decisions may have been responsible for most of that reduction.

9. Although our interview data concerning what occurred after remand are sketchy, we were struck by the lack of vigor with which the INS and the BIA pursue the cases that the courts remand to them. Their passivity may be due to the belief that most of the cases will be resolved collaterally.

CONCLUSION

This study represented an effort to learn more about contemporary immigration litigation in the courts. It sought to: (a) establish a profile of the immigration caseload; (b) discern some of the effects of certain immigration policy reforms on that caseload; (c) emphasize the growing importance of affirmative challenge litigation, especially impact cases, in the immigration area; and (d) determine what occurs when federal courts remand immigration cases to the INS and the administrative immigration court. The study was meant to be descriptive, not normative.

Still, we could not have completed such an analysis without gaining some impressions, however sketchy, about the organization, conduct, and possible reforms of immigration litigation. Our findings indicate that aliens often prevail over the INS in asylum litigation and impact litigation. These results suggest that the government currently contests many meritorious claims by aliens, which in the interests of all parties would best be resolved at an early, pre-litigation stage.

In particular, aliens were successful in overturning administrative denials of asylum requests. They won 36 percent of their asylum claims in statutory review cases during the 1989–1990 period; the Salvadoran success rate was an even higher 55 percent. Moreover, aliens' success rates in asylum cases at the end of the decade seemed to be on an upward trend.[24] The fact that all these valid claims had been considered at least once at the administrative level by the EOIR, and in many cases by district directors as well, is indicative of a major failing in the Justice Department's processes for screening, adjudicating, and deciding to litigate these claims, and thus presents important opportunities for reform.[25] Furthermore, aliens and advocacy groups were also highly successful in impact lawsuits, most of which challenged the INS's failure to implement new immigration policies in the manner prescribed by Congress. The nature and quantity of these lawsuits, coupled with Congress's failure to overturn their results, provide a clear signal that some important aspects of the INS's administrative performance are deeply and systematically flawed.

We are hardly the first observers to call attention to the INS's recent administrative failures; severe and widespread criticism was directed at the agency throughout the 1980s.[26] Moreover, our study was not designed to provide an evidentiary basis for diagnosing the INS's problems, or for proposing specific solutions. Nevertheless, our impact litigation data furnish much unmistakable evidence that the INS's enforcement orientation has often hindered its ability to provide effective services and fair adjudication.[27] The many successful challenges to the INS's asylum and legalization programs suggest that the problem of integrating enforcement, service, and adjudication functions to produce consistent, judicially approved standards may be an endemic one.[28] Nevertheless, the Justice Department has recently sought to address its administrative difficulties by establishing a new system for reviewing asylum claims at the INS level.[29] It remains to be seen whether the problem has been solved or whether additional changes will be necessary.

The patterns of impact litigation against the INS also suggest a need for the agency to solicit outside advice from advocacy groups before developing and implementing new programs. Such collaboration is by no means uncommon, and the INS has recently undertaken several such efforts. For example, upon the advice of the Lawyers' Committee for Human Rights, the INS has developed a project designed to reduce detention of aliens seeking asylum.[30] In addition, the INS's General Counsel has worked with aliens' advocates to develop a handbook, given to all INS asylum officers, explaining the legal standards that are supposed to govern asylum adjudications.[31] These and other collaborative relationships could inform the INS about future implementation problems, could avoid costly litigation that often hinders the INS's policy role, and could take advantage of the expertise and political support of outside groups. This dialogue should continue during the implementation phase of programs, when new and unforeseen problems are certain to arise.

PART THREE

The Politics of Immigration

Immigration politics varies considerably depending on whether the subject is the number and types of aliens who may lawfully enter the United States (legal immigration policy), the enforcement of laws barring aliens who have no right to enter or remain (illegal immigration policy), or the substantive rights to which legal and illegal aliens are entitled once they are in the United States (immigrant policy). The chapters in Part 3 call attention to the different political patterns that characterize these three policy domains.

The Immigration Act of 1990 significantly increased immigration quotas, confirmed and even extended the ethnic diversity of the post-1965 immigration, regularized the status of many aliens, and eliminated certain ideological grounds for exclusion and deportation. Although restrictionists mounted an energetic effort in 1996 to reverse these changes and limit legal immigration, they failed. Congress declined to amend the 1990 Act, turning instead to a major redesign of the enforcement machinery for removing illegal aliens. Thus the 1990 Act remains the charter of America's legal immigration policy, and in Chapter 4 I detail its political and legal history. My account of the 1990 Act highlights the diverse political roles that ideas about immigration, as distinct from the clash of organized interests, played in the public debate leading to its enactment. Chapter 5 analyzes the post-1990 developments in light of this emphasis on the evolution of politically relevant ideas about immigration.

In Chapter 6, I analyze Proposition 187, whose adoption by referendum in California in November 1994 was surely one of the most convulsive, consequential political events in the long history of U.S. immigration policy. Proposition 187 mandated discrimination against illegal aliens in a broad range of state-administered income support and social service programs. It spawned similar proposals in other states. More important, it prefigured the 1996 federal laws in which Congress sought to accelerate the removal of illegal and deportable aliens and to require government programs at all levels to deny benefits to illegals and deportables. But in a radical reversal of long-standing immigrant policy, Congress also denied such benefits to most legal immigrants as well. (The 1997 budget legislation restored some of these benefits, but this restoration affects only a subset of this legal immigrant category: those admitted to the United States before August 22, 1996, and otherwise eligible for Supplemental Security Income (SSI). In 1998, the Clinton administration proposed legislation to restore some of the Food Stamp benefits that had been cut and to modify some of the harsh enforcement measures that were enacted in 1996.

4

The Politics of Rapid Legal Change: Immigration Policy, 1980–1990

INTRODUCTION

Conventional wisdom maintains that the enduring structures of American politics make rapid policy change unlikely. This proposition is confirmed by much political science. Our institutions are designed to bridle and domesticate reform impulses, dissipating the constant pressures for new political and social arrangements. The separation of powers establishes numerous veto points, making initiatives of any kind difficult. The political culture's firm commitment to broad participation and due process places a much higher value on consultation than on decisiveness or direction. Special interests tolerate only incremental changes. The major parties clothe themselves in the familiar as they move toward the political center and its embrace of the status quo. New ideas are of only marginal importance; their transformative power is routinely blunted by one of America's oldest ideas, pragmatism. Stability, not innovation, is the master theme of our politics.

There are exceptions, of course, but they tend to prove the rule. Progressive Era reforms occurred only after a long period of resistance by the instrumentalities of the 19th-century "state of courts and parties." Implementing the New Deal required an unprecedented economic collapse, a national crisis, and a presidential campaign against the Supreme Court. The Great Society legislation of the 1960s was only made possible by the assassination of a president, important demographic changes, and the conjunction of the civil rights, environmental, and consumer movements. The resurgence of congressional policy initiatives in the 1970s was a direct outgrowth of Watergate, our greatest political scandal, as well as the most unpopular war in American history.[1] Even the fabled "Reagan Revolution," one might argue, exemplifies the norm of policy stability, at least when a longer time frame is used.[2]

These characteristic policy continuities make all the more interesting and curious the innovations in immigration politics and policy that were adopted during the 1980s. By 1990, a fundamental redesign of U.S. immigration policy had occurred, one that may endure. The new immigration law regime pointed in quite different directions than its predecessors. It also contrasted sharply with the increasingly restrictionist, even xenophobic, immigration policies that many other Western industrialized nations were instituting at precisely the same time.

The decade's reforms will expand legal immigration to the United States for years to come. While conscripting employers into the campaign against illegal immigration, the new laws also established a process that will eventually confer legal status on millions of undocumented workers and their families. They diversified the ethnic composition of the immigration stream. Jettisoning Cold War-hardened principles of exclusion, they also liberalized asylum policies and established a possibility of safe-haven for hundreds of thousands of dislocated individuals ineligible for asylum. They made the statuses of citizens and aliens more equal. They strengthened enforcement against criminal aliens.

Genuine policy innovations such as these are unusual in American politics, and immigration policy is no exception. Immigration has always engendered fierce passions, inflamed rhetoric, and bitter divisions. From World War I until the 1980s, debates about immigration almost invariably led to restrictive policies.[3] The 1965 law, which eliminated the national origins quotas, was also restrictive in some respects.[4] Subsequent reform proposals were mired in political stalemate. What happened in the 1980s, then, to produce immigration policies that are remarkably liberal and expansive by historical standards? And why did no sophisticated immigration analysts in 1980 predict such policy changes (except, perhaps, for employer sanctions)?

These questions challenge the leading paradigms of causal explanation advanced by political scientists. Their theories—interest group liberalism, "muddling through" incrementalism, rational choice, and "the new institutionalism"—can explain (that is, post-dict) rather well the small policy shifts and the programmatic give-and-take that are so familiar in American politics.[5] These theories explain continuities most easily; they expect political conflicts to yield fairly stable equilibria while allowing for some change around the edges. They are less successful at explaining major policy innovations that occur suddenly in areas of high political visibility and contention.

Most of these causal theories (incrementalism is a notable exception) view political interests and preferences as largely exogenous. Groups organize around these interests and bargain to a solution. The theories seldom acknowledge the political importance of difficult-to-quantify variables such as happenstance, creativity, sharp changes in values, persuasion through rational argument, statesmanship, self-sacrifice, and passions (as distinguished from interests). When these factors are mentioned, their roles are ordinarily of the "black box" or deus ex machina variety. Perhaps because such factors are more elusive, evanescent, and unmeasureable than votes, rules, formal institutions, and other "harder" phenomena, the leading theories tend to treat them as residual and marginal, or to use them to account for large unexplained variances.[6]

Immigration policy changes during the 1980s fit rather uneasily into these theoretical paradigms.[7] If these policy shifts had proceeded gradually over a long period of time or had culminated in profound social upheaval or major regime change, the fit might have been less awkward. In fact, the movement to a much more expansive immigration policy, stymied for so long, occurred with remarkable speed.

Why did this happen, and why did it happen when it did? My answer is to a considerable degree consistent with standard pluralistic and rational choice explanations. In my account, mass migrations, international crises, and other events in the late 1970s and early 1980s set the stage for the subsequent debate, raising the political stakes and salience of immigration policy and deepening the broad public concern about illegal aliens. As the decade wore on, the perceptions, strategies, and influence of the major interest groups—growers, labor, business, ethnic groups, and human rights advocates—changed, shifting the political equilibrium toward more expansive policies. Political entrepreneurs reshaped the issue agenda. They logrolled among a broad array of special interests, manipulated public symbols and ideals, and mobilized elite and grassroots support into a strong coalition. Institutions structured their activity, bringing Congress, party leaders, interest groups, the immigration bureaucracy, the courts, the media, and other political actors into a complex series of negotiations. In my account of immigration politics between 1980 and 1990, then, external events, political entrepreneurs, and group interests all played essential parts in the decade's immigration reforms. If Occam's Razor can cut this cleanly, why seek a more refined, complex explanation?

These factors, while necessary to explain recent immigration politics, are simply not sufficient, for at least three reasons. First, these factors fail to explain why long-stalemated immigration reforms were finally enacted. This decade, after all, was dominated by militantly conservative politics and by presidential administrations with little commitment to more expansive immigration. No national crisis or social convulsion generated pressures for sharp policy changes.[8] Instead, "normal politics" prevailed.[9] Congress, traditionally the dominant player in immigration politics,[10] was fairly stable in both its partisan and its ideological composition.[11] The White House, of course, remained in Republican hands beginning in January 1981.

Until well into the decade (late 1986, to be exact), the prospects for *any* meaningful immigration reform, restrictive *or* expansionist, seemed decidedly bleak. Experts viewed immigration policy as the Vietnam of domestic politics, an arena of bitter, protracted warfare from which no one emerged unharmed. No enterprising politician, it seemed, would invest much time or capital in immigration reform.[12] The interests most directly affected—growers, business, organized labor, ethnic groups, and human rights groups—had been at loggerheads for many years. The cast of characters in congress had changed little; in the Senate, it was virtually the same. The legislative process in general had become even more congested and immobilized. A less propitious time for ambitious immigration policy reform could scarcely be imagined.

Second, even if events, entrepreneurs, and interests could adequately explain why Congress addressed immigration issues when it did, these factors cannot explain why Congress *expanded* immigration benefits—and not just for legal aliens but for illegal aliens as well. One would have predicted precisely the opposite policy outcome. If historical patterns continued, the main forces driving immigration politics during the 1980s—especially the tide of illegal migration and the recessions that struck the economy at the decade's beginning and end—should have generated powerful pressures to *restrict* immigration. Indeed Senator Alan Simpson of Wyoming, the politician who would exercise the most influence over the shape of the new legislation during the 1980s, began the decade by proclaiming his strong restrictionist leanings.[13]

Interest group pressures also should have yielded either continued stalemate or a more restrictive policy. In the late 1970s, moreover, an aggressive alliance of environmental, population control and some labor interests joined the fray. The newly formed Federation of American Immigration Reform (FAIR) claimed that immigration was adversely affecting the quality of life. FAIR sought to mobilize Americans concerned about protecting the environment against overcrowding, preserving English as the common language, and promoting public safety. By 1980, the smart money would have bet that this new coalition would bolster the existing anti-immigration forces to produce a more restrictionist policy equilibrium.

Finally, events, entrepreneurs, and interests fail to explain a striking aspect of the decade's immigration politics: xenophobia and racism retreated to the margins, leaving relatively few traces on the new laws. The Haitian and Marielito migrations in the early 1980s as we shall see, did produce considerable anti-immigration sentiment. Little of it, however, evidenced the kind of widely shared animus against foreigners or racial minorities that had marked earlier immigration politics. Such attitudes became even less prominent as time went on, and were notably absent from the congressional campaigns and pre-presidential debates of the late 1980s and early

1990s, at least until Patrick Buchanan entered the race for the Republican presidential nomination in early 1992.[14] At a time when events, entrepreneurs, and interests were causing some of the leading Western democracies to close their doors to immigrants, often harshly, with openly xenophobic rhetoric proclaimed by significant parliamentary parties,[15] American politics was producing just the opposite behavior.

If the standard pluralistic model fails to predict the historically unique expansionist policies that the decade produced, we must seek a more complex explanation. In order to fill out the story, I emphasize another causal factor: the power of *ideas*—our values and other generalizations that frame our understanding of the world. Here and in section V, I maintain that these ideas were crucial to the triumph of immigration reform and expansion.

The political role of ideas has not gone unnoticed by positive political theorists. Their theories, however, tend to view ideas as epiphenomenal rather than causal, instrumental rather than normative. These theories note that innovative politicians use agendas, voting, and issues strategically; and that these resources may include new ideas.[16] But ideas in this view are little more than additional tools in politicians' kit bags. From the theorists' perspective, ideas may even be *less*—if they obscure the "real" interests that lie beneath them.

I do not propose to challenge these theories or their arguments about how ideas are deployed in politics. Indeed, I have already said that my account provides much empirical evidence to support the theories. Instead I stress an importantly different political function of ideas which the literature has tended to neglect.[17] Ideas can precede interests as well as advance them. They not only help political actors to fulfill their existing political agendas; they also affect how those actors construct their agendas in the first place. Ideas can alter how people perceive the world, decide what to value, and organize to attain it. In this way, they redefine ends and means and may even supply new ones. Immigration politics in the 1980s exemplifies this independent causal role of ideas. Certain distinctive notions about immigration and its effects propelled the reform impulse in directions that were more expansionist than interests, entrepreneurship, and events alone would have dictated. Among the most important ideas shaping the political debate were the following. Global competition strategy and immigration policy ought to be tightly linked. Ethnic diversity in the United States population should be confirmed and extended. Family unification should continue to be a paramount value. Illegal migration poses a serious threat to social stability and equity. This threat must be reduced before legal migration is expanded. Human rights should constitute a major, permanent component of United States immigration policy. The job skills required by the economy and those supplied by domestic workers, were seriously mismatched, which immigration policy could and should cure. Civil liberties, civil rights, and due process norms should govern the law's treatment of aliens, even illegal ones. The social benefits of expanded immigration could be achieved at little or no cost.

Few of these ideas, of course, were really new. None of them, however, had previously been effectively mobilized to support an expansive immigration policy. Even the most familiar ideas became more salient to the immigration debate as conditions changed. Some ideas—the constitutional principles of due process and equal protection are perhaps the best examples—were well established in other areas of public law but had not generally been applied previously to immigration. Policy intellectuals and advocates forcefully advanced these ideas, and the media brokered them, helping to galvanize a consensus around an expansive immigration policy and to influence the specific forms that the new policies took.

There are pitfalls in emphasizing ideas' causal role in politics. Peter Hall notes one of them: "Any attempt to specify the conditions under which ideas acquire political influence inevitably teeters on the brink of reductionism, while the failure to make such an attempt leaves a large lacuna at the center of our understanding of public policy." Political science, Hall claims, has neglected the influence of ideas in favor of structuralist (and, one might add, rational choice) accounts of public policy and political change. This traditional approach exaggerates the constraints on and the incremental character of policy development while undervaluing the creative, even transformative, agency of ideas. Hall urges that political analysis not content itself with invoking ideas but instead seek to identify the conditions that lend political force to one idea rather than another, and at one time rather than another.[18]

This is a tall order. Compared with votes, institutions, interests, events, and the other palpable phenomena that political analysts can observe and even measure, ideas are elusive and their effects on outcomes are harder to gauge. Ideas may simultaneously alter what political actors perceive and pursue. At the same time, those actors may deploy ideas rhetorically and instrumentally. Thus, ideas' independent causal force in politics must be revealed through inference and the testimony of those most intimately involved. We are wise to be skeptical of such evidence but we would be foolish to ignore it simply because it is less tangible and quantifiable.

I. Periodizing Immigration Reform: The 1980s

In this section, I briefly summarize the chronology of immigration reform in the 1980s. This summary provides a context for the detailed narrative and analysis that follow. It also explains why I have selected this particular decade as the unit of analysis.

The period begins with an epochal event in U.S. immigration history: the Mariel boatlift from Cuba early in 1980. That year also roughly corresponds to a number of other crucial immigration-related developments: in Central America, Iran, the Soviet Union, Poland, and elsewhere. Finally, 1980 was an election year and ushered into the White House a new, conservative, and generally pro-immigration administration. The period ends with the enactment of the Immigration Act of 1990, which marks the culmination of the pro-immigration forces that the events surrounding 1980 put in train.

The significance of this decade for immigration politics can best be grasped by comparing the prospects for reform as they appeared in 1980 with the reality of reform in 1990. In 1980 the Carter administration was in its final death throes, struggling with the political legacy of two straight years of double-digit inflation, high unemployment (soon to go higher), and a debilitating hostage crisis in Iran. These crises made politicians and their constituents edgy, cautious, and inward looking. When boatloads of Haitians and Cubans sought refuge in South Florida early in the year, the authorities greeted them with initial hospitality followed by undisguised hysteria and hostility. Between 1975 and 1979 alone, the United States, in the aftermath of the Vietnam War, admitted over 300,000 Indochinese refugees and asylees, more than it had accepted from any other country or region during any comparable period in American history.[19] Also, between 1971 and 1980, over 200,000 refugees and asylees including the Marielitos arrived from Cuba. Refugees from the Soviet Union and other regions raised the total refugee cohort from 106,000 in 1976 to an historic high of 350,000 in 1980.[20]

Overseas refugee admissions were within the government's control, but illegal migration across the Southern border manifestly was not. The growing volume of these illegal crossings during the 1970s caused environmental and population control organizations to form FAIR in 1979 to lobby for restrictive immigration legislation. Some civil rights groups concerned about minority job losses shared FAIR's concerns, while usually spurning its rhetoric.[21] In that same year, Senate Judiciary Committee Chairman Edward Kennedy, concerned that growing illegal migration could trigger a political backlash against immigration, persuaded Congress to establish a Select Commission on Immigration and Refugee Policy (SCIRP) to propose new, hopefully prudent solutions. Father Theodore Hesburgh, then president of the University of Notre Dame, chaired the commission for most of its life.[22]

When the Reagan administration assumed office in 1981 and the Republicans also gained control of the Senate, these stirrings seemed especially auspicious for reform. Except for the 1965 abolition of the national origins quota system, Congress had paid little attention to immigration policy since the early 1950s. With illegal migration now certified as a national issue, a new president determined (in the words of his attorney general, William French Smith) to "regain control of our borders,"[23] widespread concerns expressed about growing welfare rolls, "compassion fatigue"[24] in the air, and ethnic conflict becoming a staple of TV evening news programs, reformers on Main Street and Pennsylvania Avenue geared up to do battle.

Restrictionism, if not outright xenophobia, was in the air. In 1981, Senator Simpson, who along with Senator Edward M. Kennedy of Massachusetts would shape the immigration legislation of the 1980s more powerfully than perhaps anyone else in Congress, appended an avowedly restrictionist separate statement to the SCIRP report.[25] In response to that report, the Reagan White House proposed its own restrictions on illegal migration, emphasizing that an "immigration emergency" existed.[26] In August 1982, Senator Walter (Dee) Huddleston of Kentucky, FAIR's chief advocate in the Senate for tighter limits on legal immigration, mobilized considerable support for a decidedly restrictive bill. It would have capped all legal immigration (including refugees and "immediate relatives," neither of which categories was capped at that time) at 425,000, a level far below the almost 600,000 immigrants and refugees admitted that year.[27] With the economy sliding into a deep recession, representatives of organized labor redoubled their traditional efforts to preserve American jobs for American workers.

Appearances, however, are often deceiving in politics, where illusion counts for so much. Less than a decade later, Congress had substantially liberalized immigration policy. In 1986 it enacted the Immigration Reform and Control Act (IRCA). This measure was widely but somewhat misleadingly billed as restrictive. In one very important respect it was: IRCA for the first time penalized employers who hired illegal aliens. But many of its other provisions—the amnesty and agricultural labor sections, as well as its updating of the registry for long-term illegal aliens—were remarkably generous to illegal and temporary workers. In addition, it reserved 10,000 visas for "diversity" admissions,[28] a harbinger of a new strategy for expanding legal admissions that would become firmly embedded in the Immigration Act of 1990 (hereinafter referred to as the 1990 act). As events unfolded, these liberal policies proved to be more momentous, and perhaps also more politically durable, than the much-publicized employer sanctions.[29] Within a few years, these changes would create new immigration and citizenship opportunities for millions of low-skilled and illegal workers.

Only four years later, Congress approved the 1990 act, which was also generous to both legal and illegal aliens, especially the former.[30] The new law, which FAIR strongly opposed, will increase annual legal immigration totals by about one-third.[31] It bestowed work authorization and possible citizenship upon an estimated 250,000 close family members of amnestied aliens. It also conferred protected status upon almost two hundred thousand undocumented Salvadorans[32] and, by codifying the previously discretionary practice of "extended voluntary departure," created the possibility of protected status for members of other nationality groups illegally in the United States. Among other liberalizing provisions, the new statute also embodied a firm commitment to ethnic diversity in admissions, expedited naturalization, and for the first time *narrowed* the INS's power to exclude aliens on ideological and a variety of other grounds.

Any remaining doubts about the political and legal forces propelling the new expansionist ethos were dispelled only a few weeks after passage. Litigation pressures forced the Bush administration to provide new asylum hearings under liberalized standards and procedures for an estimated 150,000 Salvadorans and Guatemalans whose claims (some dating back to 1980) had been denied or were still pending.[33] The attorney general, who late in 1989 had permitted thousands of Chinese students to remain in the United States despite their visa restrictions, also granted temporary protected status under the new law to over 50,000 Kuwaitis, Liberians, and Lebanese aliens in the United States.[34]

The 1990 act's expansionist character is even more remarkable when one considers the inhospitable political climate in which it was enacted. First, the 1965 reform had dramatically and unexpectedly shifted the source-country pattern toward high-volume Asian and Hispanic flows. Equally unexpected, the asylum provisions of the 1980 Refugee Act had further stimulated illegal migration by Hispanics. There was considerable sentiment, not all of it restrictionist, that an imbalance had developed, which needed redressing. Second, successful implementation of IRCA's employer sanctions program was widely viewed as a political precondition for seeking to expand legal immigration, yet mounting evidence in 1990 indicated that three years into the program, the "back door" of illegal migration remained wide open.[35] Third, the restrictionists could also argue that IRCA's amnesty programs were all *too* successful, in contrast to the sanctions. They had already produced in 1989 the highest legal admissions total (almost 1.1 million) in seventy-five years, an increase of 70 percent over the previous year. (The 1990 figure, not published until 1991, would soar to over 1.5 million, a record by far.[36]) Perhaps most important, economic recession, which historically had spawned strong restrictionist sentiments and policies, was already under way. Despite these formidable obstacles, however, the 1990 act passed, and by lopsided margins.[37]

These rapid and dramatic changes in immigration politics and policy are particularly significant because immigration is a bedrock, traditionally divisive political issue. Immigration does not simply operate on the surface of politics, nor is it driven by transitory, faddish concerns. Instead, it engages the enduring economic, political, and cultural interests of powerful social groups in visible, palpable, often emotional ways. Politicians and citizens know that immigration, as much as any other area of public policy, defines who and what Americans wish to be. Understanding how we forged a new consensus on immigration may therefore reveal some of the forces that are reshaping contemporary American politics.

II. EXTERNAL EVENTS

In the years just before and after 1980, a number of international developments magnified the migratory pressures on the United States. These included political and economic upheaval in Southeast Asia and the Caribbean Basin; the Soviet decision to permit higher Jewish emigration; the Iranian Revolution; and a new surge of illegal migration. Although American foreign and economic policy certainly influenced these events, they were largely beyond our control.

The United States withdrawal from Vietnam and other parts of Southeast Asia left the region in a state of social chaos. Millions of people fled their homes, journeying by boat and on foot to the more secure, if still perilous, haven of refugee camps in Thailand, Malaysia, Indonesia, Hong Kong, and other areas on the perimeter of the conflict. A refugee crisis might only be avoided if the United States could somehow induce these countries of first asylum,[38] which often sought to repel the refugees through "pushbacks" and other brutal means, to maintain and enlarge their camps. To accomplish this, the United States had to assure those countries that it would eventually resettle the refugees here if repatriation and other measures failed. To make good on these promises, the United States agreed to admit hundreds of thousands of Vietnamese, Laotians, Thai, and Cambodians during the 1970s and 1980s.

Before 1980, no regular legal mechanism existed for admitting them. The pre-1980 law permitted only 17,400 refugee admissions annually, a number completely inadequate to the situation. The law limited such relief to those who had fled either the Middle East or Communist-dominated countries. To avoid these limitations, refugee groups either had to seek special authority for these admissions or—more commonly in a refugee emergency—persuade the attorney general to invoke his general statutory authority to "parole" them into the United States for public interest reasons. Between 1975 and 1979, at least ten separate paroles—each limited in duration and numbers and overwhelmed by the next refugee crisis—had been used to admit over 300,000 Indochinese refugees.[39] Hundreds of thousands more would come from this region during the 1980s.

Detente during the late 1970s in connection with the effort to ratify the SALT II accord also led to increased exit visas for Jewish emigrees from the Soviet Union; more than 50,000 left in 1979 alone, and many made their way to the United States. And, at that time, Iranians composed the largest group of temporary visitors ("nonimmigrants") to the United States. The Shah's fall in 1979 left a quarter million Iranian students stranded here.[40] The Soviet invasion of Afghanistan had similar effects, though on a much smaller scale.

Migratory pressures from Latin America had also intensified. The Sandinistas' overthrow of the Somoza dictatorship in mid-1979 left a large contingent of Nicaraguans, whose deportation had been stayed, in the United States with no assurance that they could return home safely. Agricultural workers from the Dominican Republic and Haiti had come during the late 1970s, and hundreds of thousands remained illegally, many settling in New York and South Florida.

Throughout the 1970s, congressional committees had expressed growing frustration with how the executive branch handled these spasmodic, essentially uncontrolled refugee flows, and with how far U.S. refugee policy deviated from the principles of human rights law embodied in treaties and in emerging international custom and practices. By the end of the decade, the committees' leaders could mobilize support for a new refugee admissions system. They envisioned a process that would be more predictable, manageable, and consultative, that would enhance Congress's policy influence, and that would limit the administration's parole power. The Refugee Act, signed by President Carter in March 1980, was the result of this vision.

Most migration to the United States in the 1970s was gradual and largely invisible outside of the newcomers' enclaves. But when 125,000 Cubans arrived by boat in South Florida, they immediately became front-page news not only there but throughout the country. The Marielitos' dramatic flight and their determination to remain here occurred less than a month after the Refugee Act was signed. It severely embarrassed the Carter administration. The flotilla of Cubans, several thousand of whom bore the stigma of Castro's prisons and mental hospitals, seemed like a hostile "invasion" to many Americans. Coinciding with new flows of undocumented aliens to Sunbelt cities, the arrival of the Marielitos aggravated the strain on public facilities, services, institutions, and values. Coming so soon after other refugee crises, this new incursion triggered public anger at the government's fecklessness, and weariness at the seemingly infinite line of human victims knocking at, or clambering over, the gates.

The Marielitos and the Haitians, who had become coming during the 1970s, also made the United States a major first-asylum country, an unprecedented event in its history. Initially encouraged by officials, Cubans and Haitians in large numbers began to apply for asylum under the new Refugee Act. Those who did so could not be deported pending decision on their claims. Signaling a new way to gain a foothold in the United States, the torrent of asylum claims drew additional migration. Other groups did the same, and within a few years the asylum backlog reached almost

200,000. The phenomenon of first-asylum claiming dramatized a new, politically explosive fact: the United States was increasingly vulnerable to uncontrollable external forces. Many Americans feared in this vulnerability a diminution—or at least a redefinition—of the nation's sovereignty. The United States, it seemed, no longer controlled its own destiny; its fate was now inexorably linked to the rest of the world. Taking various forms, this theme would become a central political preoccupation of the 1980s.

The Marielito incident also drew the federal courts, armed with hoary constitutional principles, into the immigration debate. Their forceful participation had far-reaching effects on public and governmental attitudes toward immigration and thus on immigration politics and law. This is discussed in section V.

III. POLITICAL ENTREPRENEURSHIP

As has often been noted, the same Chinese ideogram denotes both crisis and opportunity. In the 1980s, shrewd politicians in Congress seized upon these external events and the feelings that the events aroused, magnifying an already acute fear of change into a deep sense of crisis. By defining the crisis in ways that invited certain policy solutions that lay near at hand, they succeeded in creating political opportunity. The politician's art depends upon this interaction between crisis definition and remedy formulation. The immigration reforms of the last decade reveal this art in a particularly transparent form.

The sense of crisis was captured and created in a phrase: "We have lost control of our borders." This slogan—proclaimed constantly on editorial pages, in the halls of Congress, and from the Justice Department—fueled deep anxieties about the erosion of economic security, national autonomy, and the "social contract" that legitimates the modern welfare state. A deep recession was destroying millions of American jobs. Coming after several years of high inflation, new job competition from low-skilled, low-wage, unorganized foreign workers who came during this period threatened Americans whose economic status was most fragile. The slogan revealed doubts that Americans could still dictate the terms on which they dealt with foreigners. Customary ways of life seemed in jeopardy in urban areas like Miami and Los Angeles where the newcomers concentrated, quickly altering social patterns and political arrangements. An immigration policy designed to preserve the familiar now seemed unable to do so. As welfare burdens on taxpayers grew, immigrants became easy scapegoats.

The fact that these fears were frequently exaggerated or misplaced was less important politically than the fact that they were intense and could not be readily refuted or allayed. These fears created both risks and opportunities for politicians in both parties, at both ends of Pennsylvania Avenue, and in the severely affected states. In Congress, which has long dominated immigration politics,[41] employer sanctions bills had been proposed at the behest of organized labor in the 1960s. A bill passed the House twice during the early 1970s with presidential backing, only to die in committee on the Senate side where opposition by growers, other employers, and Hispanic groups—an unlikely coalition except in the exotic politics of immigration—proved decisive. Even after Peter Rodino, Chairman of the House Judiciary Committee, grafted a legalization proposal onto employer sanctions in 1975, they failed.

The Carter administration, politically vulnerable due to the wide currency given to an earlier exaggerated estimate of twelve million illegals,[42] again broached the idea in 1977. Rodino, however, was now gun shy and the proposal again went nowhere.[43] The White House and congressional leaders, unable to reach consensus but under pressure to act, sought a way out. Hoping to deflect growing restrictionist pressures and passions, they agreed to create a blue-ribbon panel, the Hesburgh Commission,[44] to study the problem, shape a consensus, and recommend policy changes to solve the illegal alien problem.

This was not the first time that political leaders had established a study commission to help resolve an impasse over immigration legislation. The Dillingham Commission, which urged literacy tests in its 1910 report, set an infamous precedent with its racist rhetoric and restrictionist policy recommendations. The Hesburgh group, however, was very different in composition, staffing, and processes. Its members and staff were highly sympathetic to immigration and ethnic diversity; half of its members were descendants of the very groups that the Dillingham Commission, composed entirely of men with English and Scottish roots, had stigmatized. And the new commission was preoccupied with a new problem: illegal migration.[45]

The Hesburgh Commission would play a central role in the immigration politics of the 1980s. Some of its congressional members became the leading protagonists in the decade's struggles over immigration. The commission staff deliberately emphasized ideas that could appeal across partisan, ethnic, and economic group lines; as SCIRP Director Lawrence Fuchs later put it, "the central strategy was to take xenophobia, race, and even economic conflict out of the debate."[46] The policy agenda that the commission laid out in its 1981 report—linkage between control of illegal migration and expansion of legal admissions; a three-track system of admissions (family related, independents selected for economic reasons, and refugees); adherence to civil rights and civil liberties values—set the terms of the subsequent debate. Indeed, IRCA and the Immigration Act of 1990 can be viewed as having largely fulfilled the agenda that the commission advanced a decade earlier.[47]

Senators Kennedy and Simpson, two strikingly different politicians, played especially significant roles. Their successful collaboration on immigration policy throughout the 1980s certainly qualifies them as one of the oddest "odd couples" in modern politics.[48] Of the two, Kennedy's position favoring a liberalized immigration and refugee policy was the more predictable. As a freshman senator, he had managed the 1965 reform bill. During the 1970s he had chaired the Judiciary subcommittee on refugees, and he had steered the Refugee Act of 1980 through Congress. He also considered himself, and was viewed by others, as continuing his brother Robert's leadership of the ethnic-civil rights coalition in the Senate. Kennedy's liberalizing agenda, although sometimes constrained by his close ties to organized labor and the Hispanic caucus's abhorrence of sanctions, was hardly surprising.

Simpson was another story entirely. Nothing in his personal or political background prepared him for his decisive role in the immigration debates of the 1980s, much less for his sponsorship and management of legislation that would substantially expand and diversify legal immigration. Even his appointment to the Hesburgh Commission had been fortuitous, occurring only after Strom Thurmond declined to serve. A conservative Republican whose father had been a senator, Simpson was still in his first term in the early 1980s. His state, Wyoming, contained few immigrants, legal or illegal. From a narrow electoral perspective, it made as much sense for Simpson to invest his energy in immigration policy for more than a decade as for George Bush to spend his time on our relations with Iceland.

Even from a broader vantage point, immigration reform was a quagmire. It was conventionally viewed by politicians as a "no win" issue, a lost cause, the domestic equivalent of Vietnam.[49] This was especially true during the pre-IRCA period, when the focus of legislation was on illegal aliens who aroused negative feelings even among otherwise pro-immigration Americans. Immigration, moreover, was an issue that primarily excited people in Florida, Texas, California, New York, and a few cities in which residents felt inundated by undocumented workers, wanted more of their ethnic compatriots admitted, or both. In the rest of the country, there were even fewer political points to be scored by immigration reformers. Simpson's devotion to this cause over the course of a decade, then, is simply inexplicable in terms of the traditional careerist goals that animate most legislators.

Simpson became fascinated by immigration and plunged into the commission's work with gusto as soon as he was appointed to it early in 1979.[50] Prior to then, his views on immigration had been relatively unformed. As a young man, he had been disturbed by the treatment of Japanese internees in the Hart Mountain center in Wyoming and by the exploitation of farmworkers under the old Bracero program. But illegal migration also troubled him deeply. He feared its economic effects on do-mestic workers, its creation of growing enclaves of people outside of the law's protection, and the cultural separatism that it might engender among unassimilated aliens unable to speak English. Perhaps most worrisome was the disrespect for the law that it engendered.

A witty, spontaneous, outspoken, and sometimes belligerent, cranky man, Simpson had to learn the delicate punctilio of immigration discourse, one in which those who espouse limits and articulate concerns about assim-ilation open themselves to being depicted as racists.[51] But learn he did. In 1981, when the Republicans took control of the Senate and just before the Hesburgh Commission's final report was to be issued, he convinced the new Judiciary Chairman Strom Thurmond to recreate an immigration subcom-mittee[52] with Simpson as chairman. From this perch, he would orchestrate the legislative politics on immigration during the decade.

While the leadership on immigration issues in the Senate remained stable during the 1980s, the roster of influentials in the House changed after IRCA's enactment in 1986. Before that, Rodino and Romano Mazzoli were the key players. Rodino, Judiciary Committee chairman since 1973, was an urban liberal who had helped secure the 1965 immigration reforms. De-spite the more restrictionist views of his chief counsel and immigration ex-pert, Garner Kline, Rodino was an ardently pro-immigration. Mazzoli, who became chairman of the immigration subcommittee in 1981, was a moderate Democrat from Louisville, Kentucky. Like Simpson, he began with amorphous views on immigration issues.[53] Also like Simpson, he was under few constituent pressures on immigration and was not thought to harbor higher political ambitions. Simpson and Mazzoli, then, were uniquely situated to rise above narrow electoral interests in seeking reform should they be motivated to do so.[54]

Simpson and Mazzoli developed a close working relationship and de-cided to pursue an unusual joint legislative strategy.[55] Early in 1981, the Hesburgh Commission had issued its report proposing (among other re-forms) employer sanctions linked to a secure employee verification system, a legalization program, and some relief for the growers whose labor supply would be reduced by sanctions and legalization.[56] This package, the com-mission hoped, would break the political logjam that had long blocked re-form, although the three special interest members had not budged from their initial positions.[57] Although Simpson generally endorsed the commis-sion's approach, he advanced a more restrictionist position on several spe-cific policy issues.[58]

Simpson and Mazzoli decided to use the commission's proposals, ignor-ing the White House "immigration emergency" package, as a starting point for their own bill. Then, to the surprise of old immigration hands, William French Smith, Reagan's attorney general and friend, endorsed the soundness of their general approach. Simpson sensed, however, that the White House staff did not share Smith's enthusiasm. In Simpson's meetings with the president in the Oval Office, Reagan would applaud Simpson's efforts and Reagan's aides would nod in assent. In practice, however, the White House failed to give Simpson any meaningful political support on immigration legislation. This lack of significant presidential involvement in the legislative struggles over immigration would continue throughout the decade.[59]

The two legislators introduced identical bills in May 1982, and held joint hearings. Simpson skillfully steered his bill, containing a generous legalization program, through a conservative, Republican-controlled Senate; it carried by a lopsided vote, 80–19. Here, as in immigration reform legislation throughout the 1980s, Kennedy's political contribution was crucial to the bill's success, especially in the Senate, where most Democrats looked to him to signal what was and was not acceptable to liberals in this policy area. Had Kennedy resolved to kill an immigration bill, he could readily have done so in a number of ways. Thus his cooperation with Simpson, particularly prior to IRCA's passage when the Republicans still controlled the Senate, coupled with his willingness to press his Democratic colleagues on the House committee to take action on these bills, was decisive.

As Congress neared adjournment, however, the House bill got stalled in the crush of other closing business. Although there was a postelection session, the House bill seemed doomed. The Rules Committee yielded to Hispanic groups that opposed both employer sanctions and rigorous identification requirements, and allowed virtually unlimited floor amendments. Speaker Tip O'Neill said that he had scheduled the bill for floor action only as a courtesy to the White House. The bill died with the 98th Congress, the House having considered only two of some three hundred pending amendments. The House nevertheless gave Mazzoli a standing ovation, an extraordinary gesture recognizing the heroic effort necessary to bring immigration reform even that far.

In 1983, Simpson and Mazzoli decided to try again, this time with separate bills containing the provisions supported in their chambers the year before. The prospects for reform seemed dimmer than ever. Bruce Morrison, a liberal Democrat from New Haven, Connecticut who had just been elected to the House and would be a leading force in immigration legislation at the end of the decade, recalls how the rancorous atmosphere then caused him to avoid appointment to the Immigration subcommittee despite the lure of a possible chairmanship in the near future. The policy issues—illegal workers, border control, and amnesty—made it particularly difficult for urban liberal Democrats to take positions without arousing ethnic tensions and resentments. "The politics of illegal migration," he says, "were all negative; restrictionists had the upper hand. It was a political minefield."[60]

The main problem was not in the Senate, which again (with Kennedy's blessing) approved Simpson's bill quickly, adding a transition period for the growers. As always in immigration legislation, the politics in the House was more complex. No fewer than five different committees—Judiciary, Agriculture, Education and Labor, Energy and Commerce, and Rules—held hearings and proposed amendments. As the election approached, the Hispanic caucus and the growers whipsawed the proponents. Each of these groups (albeit for altogether different reasons) opposed sanctions, the growers opposed legalization, and both groups would wield influence during the impending primaries. O'Neill feared the bill as a Trojan horse designed by Republicans to divide his party during a presidential election campaign and to attract Hispanic support with the promise of a Reagan veto. Insisting that reform had "no constituency," he delayed bringing it to the floor until well into 1984, when he was moved by media criticism and by certain assurances from Simpson. No veto was forthcoming, Simpson said, but should the president change his mind and decide to veto the bill, Simpson would inform O'Neill far enough in advance so that the Democrats would not be out on a limb.

A deeply fractured House approved the bill 216–211, only after additional concessions to the growers and bitter division over sanctions and legalization. Time ran out, however, when the conference became embroiled in disputes over federal payments to the states to cover legalization-related costs and, to a lesser degree, over remedies for sanctions-related discrimination against Hispanics. Congress adjourned, requiring the proponents to start all over again in Reagan's second term.

The tortured progress of immigration reform in Congress from 1981 through 1984 revealed several clues to the evolving pattern of immigration politics. First, politicians would not seriously consider expanding legal immigration until they felt that the problem of illegal immigration had been addressed. In the commission's words, the back door must be closed before the front door could be opened.[61]

Second, a reformist majority would be exceedingly difficult to assemble. It might perhaps be cobbled together by designing a package of interconnected and somewhat incompatible measures: sanctions, legalization, a generous farmworker program, antidiscrimination remedies, and federal subsidies to state and local governments. But this package—by pitting Hispanics against blacks, urban areas against rural, Washington against state capitols and city halls, unions and environmentalists against ethnics, and interest group leaders against their own rank and file—would be riddled with policy inconsistencies and would further divide a Democratic party already severely weakened by another presidential defeat. The Hispanic Caucus and the growers were essential to any viable reform package and must be appeased to pass a bill, yet their interests conflicted on many points. The legalization proposal had become increasingly generous as time went on with respect to both eligibility and federal subsidies, yet liberal amnesty provisions would threaten state and local government support and might prompt a presidential veto.

Third, and more encouraging, the immigration debate was being conducted at a higher level than ever before. Few traces of racism or nativism could be found. Indeed, the nation's opinion leaders—politicians, editorial writers, interest groups, and academics—seemed determined to transcend traditionally parochial concerns about immigration. They seemed genuinely committed to finding a path to reform.

Still, the prospects for reform in the new Congress that convened in 1985 were hardly rosy. The proponents, especially in the House, were reluctant to bloody themselves once again in what seemed like a hopeless struggle. Indeed, some of the obstacles had grown more formidable, especially the political influence of the growers of perishable crops who were determined to maintain their supply of cheap labor. This was apparent when Simpson, who was now assistant majority leader, was obliged to accept a large temporary worker program in order to get his bill through the Senate. Characteristically in immigration legislation, this addition only served to complicate matters in the House, where further increases in the illegal population had fueled restrictionist sentiment and where the Hispanic caucus opposed the farmworker program as well as sanctions. Amnesty was the major attraction for Hispanics and many liberals, yet polling evidence indicated that public support for it, which was never significant to begin with, was now eroding.

The only way to forge a majority coalition would be somehow to persuade the growers to accept a farmworker program that met liberal demands for worker protection. Charles Schumer, a very junior member from Brooklyn, devised such a proposal with Rodino's blessing, and began to negotiate with the growers and the California delegation. It would grant illegal farmworkers temporary legal status on quite generous terms, allowing them to go on to become legal residents and ultimately citizens and with no obligation to remain in agriculture, while assuring growers a future supply of imported "replenishment" workers should the need arise. The Schumer amendment passed the Judiciary Committee in late June on a close vote, 19–15, and then won a nearly pyrrhic victory in the Rules Committee, which voted to send the bill to the floor under a rule that barred consideration of an amendment that would have deleted Schumer's compromise and substituted a plan, approved in the Senate version, to admit as many as 350,000 guestworkers (nicknamed "Wilson workers" for Senator Pete Wilson), but without any amnesty for them. In late September, the House voted 202–180 to reject the liberals' rule and, with Congress scheduled to adjourn on October 10, time was running out. Rodino had been burned before by the alliance of growers and Hispanics. Noting that the ball was now in the administration's court, he indicated no plan to seek a new rule.

While the press exerted strong pressure on both sides to compromise, Attorney General Edwin Meese entered the fray. He prompted House Republicans to seek to bring the bill to the floor without any rule at all, but the Democrats defeated this effort on October 1 by a vote of 235–177. Simpson, however, was determined to revive the stalled bill and although he did not like Schumer's proposal, or indeed any legalization not preceded by credible, enhanced enforcement, he favored compromise. The bill's supporters from both chambers convened a preconference meeting and worked out a deal even before House passage. After diluting the Schumer provision somewhat, the embryonic conference announced that, if the House would approve a bill, the House and Senate could reach agreement. Encouraged by these developments, the House voted 278–129 to bring the bill to the floor, along with fourteen amendments. After an amendment that would have eliminated legalization and thus killed the bill was narrowly defeated, 199–192, the House approved the bill, 230–166. Simpson told the press, "I guess we just jump-started a corpse."[62]

Because Congress's adjournment had been postponed, there was time for the conference, which Simpson effectively controlled. He hammered out an agreement on the key issue that troubled the White House: the cost of funding benefits for legalized aliens. A crucial trade occurred when the House conferees agreed to drop their demand to attach a sunset provision to employer sanctions, in exchange for Senate agreement to require a later General Accounting Office (GAO) study and report on sanctions' discriminatory effects. The Schumer provisions largely survived as a generous amnesty for illegal farmworkers. With editorial opinion in the media strongly favorable to the compromise, the conference bill passed the House. After an attempt to prevent its consideration in the Senate was defeated, 75–21, the Senate also passed the bill. It was opposed by many conservatives, including Phil Gramm, and by some liberals, including Ted Kennedy, who echoed the Hispanic caucus's argument (which was actually rejected by its leaders in the House vote) that the antidiscrimination safeguards were inadequate. When the president signed the legislation on November 6, he insisted that those provisions required resident aliens to prove discriminatory intent, not just disparate impact, an interpretation hotly disputed by Barney Frank, who sponsored the provisions.[63] IRCA, "the corpse that would not die,"[64] became law.

For present purposes, there are two important things to be noted about IRCA. First, its passage was anything but inevitable. The key votes were remarkably close in the House, and any of a number of possible circumstances could have brought about its demise. Given the kind of compromise package that it represented, there was little real enthusiasm for the final bill. There was plenty in it for anyone to dislike, and its enactment said as much about the members' exhaustion as it did about the bill's political support. If it had not passed then, it is not at all clear that Senator Simpson and other key sponsors would have tried again in the next Congress, especially since the next legislative struggle would take them into a presidential election season.

Second, it was on balance a law that would expand immigration. This is most apparent, of course, in its legalization provisions. These granted the opportunity for amnesty to workers in general, agricultural workers, and Cuban and Haitian immigrants. IRCA also updated an earlier, general amnesty provision to protect other aliens who had been in the United States since 1972. These provisions, moreover, were fairly liberal—especially for farmworkers—with respect to eligibility criteria,[65] time periods, and access to benefits, permanent legal status, and citizenship. But the law's pro-immigrant character is also evident in its antidiscrimination provisions, which were designed to protect legal Hispanic workers; in its raising of the quotas for colonies; in its expanded program (H-2) for agricultural workers; and in the special provisions making five thousand extra visas available to immigrants from countries (the Irish were the intended beneficiaries) "adversely affected" by the 1965 repeal of the national origins system—the precursor to the diversity provisions that would be such a striking feature of the 1990 act.

The pattern of interest group views about IRCA likewise confirms its pro-immigration tenor. Perhaps most telling was the lament by the head of FAIR, the leading restrictionist lobby: "We wanted a Cadillac, we were promised a Chevy, and we got a wreck."[66] Groups seeking more legal immigration and generous treatment of undocumented workers tended to support IRCA. Even the employer sanctions, the principal provisions restricting immigration, were solicitous of employers' interests, were weakened by the absence of a secure identification card, and thus lacked rigor. For example, the provisions contained generous grandfathering rules and created broad defenses for employers.

IV. THE CHANGING BALANCE OF INTERESTS

Immigration politics had obviously changed by 1986; IRCA was compelling evidence of this.[67] And it would change even more in the same direction by 1990, as we shall see. But why? The *dramatis personae* were much the same (although control of the Senate would return to the Democrats in 1987), and no immigration crises comparable to those at the beginning of the decade occurred in the late 1980s. The combination of political entrepreneurs and external events can explain just so much. A successful merchandiser, after all, must have something to sell that people want to buy.

A fuller answer, I think, can largely be found in two broad secular changes that occurred or culminated during the decade: a shift in interest groups' relative strength, and the prominence of ideas capable of galvanizing a new cultural consensus favoring expanded immigration. These two developments, of course, are inextricably linked: interests both promote and reflect values, and interests and values are both redefined through the political process.[68] My discussion treats them separately nonetheless. This section considers the evolving pattern of interest group influence, while section V considers the ideas that have infused new immigration values into the political debate.

During the decade, the terms of trade among the crucial organized interests with high stakes in immigration policy—Western growers, labor unions, business, ethnic groups, and human rights advocates—changed. As a result, the political equilibrium, the compromises that were struck, moved in a sharply pro-immigration direction. This change strained an already fractured Democratic party coalition in Congress. As the power of the ethnic and human rights groups waxed and the power of organized labor waned, restrictionist influence in the party declined. FAIR had a staunch advocate on the Senate floor in Dee Huddleston, but, after Huddleston's election defeat in 1984, FAIR's influence, which had peaked at the beginning of the decade, steadily declined.

In addition, immigration advocates hoped to neutralize the main institutional centers of restrictionist sentiment. These were the state and local governments that would be saddled with most of the costs of the public benefits and services claimed by the new immigrants or by the workers they displaced. These governments did not oppose increased immigration in principle; their growing Hispanic and Asian populations, buttressed by the willingness of most black leaders to support these groups' family unification claims for expansion,[69] would have made restrictionism politically suicidal. Instead, their chief concern was simply to defray the immigration-related costs, which might be accomplished with federal subsidies. (The amount of the subsidies, of course, remained subject to much haggling.)

In the remainder of this section, I describe how the growers, unions, business, ethnic, and human rights interests influenced immigration legislation during the 1980s. Even before doing so, however, I wish to call attention to—and reject—one way of interpreting the decade's events. It is tempting to understand what happened simply as a demonstration of the political strength of organized business interests and the corresponding weakness of organized labor. In this view, business,[70] which generally favored expanded immigration, won while labor, which generally sought to restrict both permanent and temporary skills-related admissions, lost. There is certainly some truth to this explanation, as we shall see. Business did gain politically at the expense of labor during the decade in many policy areas, not just immigration, and this change affected political outcomes. But this account elides two inescapable facts. Business interests have *always* been powerful and had almost always favored increased immigration, yet restrictionist policies have been the rule for the last seventy-five years. By the same token, restrictionism's triumph was most complete during the 1920s, when labor's political influence was at its nadir.

Factors other than the power of business and labor, then, must have affected the political equation in the 1980s. One such factor was the changed status of nativist and racist arguments for restriction, arguments that had become largely illegitimate morally and irrelevant politically as purported justifications for limiting immigration. Another, discussed in section V, was the new role of ideas in immigration policy debates.

Since the interest groups concerned with immigration policy interacted constantly in the legislative process, I risk some artificiality by discussing them separately. This is especially true of labor and business; I therefore treat those two together after discussing the growers.

Growers

The agricultural interests, especially the growers of perishable commodities, exercised enormous influence over IRCA. Mounting a political strategy that stretched back to their opposition to the Chinese exclusion laws a century earlier and to Mexican border controls more recently,[71] the growers hoped to defeat employer sanctions and institute a large guestworker program that would guarantee their labor supply. Although they did not get their way entirely, they did achieve enough of their agenda that little remained at stake for them in the post-IRCA legislative debates over legal immigration policy. The growers' interests were well represented in the California, Florida, and Texas delegations in Congress, and after 1981 in the White House as well. This representation placed their goals within reach, but the growing public indignation over undocumented workers during the pre-IRCA years forced them to compromise. As other enforcement efforts proved ineffective, some sanctions program came to seem inevitable.

Growers were also met with alarming reports on Europe's experience with guestworker programs. These programs invited Third World workers to come without their families when the labor supply was tight, with no hope of permanent residence or political rights. When labor needs slackened, however, the guestworkers refused to leave even when their "hosts" offered them large subsidies. Living as single men in enclaves of poverty, crime, and hopelessness, the guestworkers aroused strong nativist backlash among voters, which simply increased their isolation. This experience, coupled with vehement opposition by Hispanic groups and their allies, generated congressional resistance to such a program.

The growers were therefore obliged to adopt the more limited goals of weakening the sanctions and assuring that they would not shut off the supply of cheap labor. Coupled with an enlarged H-2 program negotiated between grower interests and Congressman Howard Berman, the Schumer plan satisfied these goals by giving the growers an amnestied work force and a guarantee of "replenishment agricultural workers" (RAWs) if their supply of labor became tight. In exchange, he extracted a concession—generous legalization terms for agricultural workers—that was vitally important to the Hispanics and liberals while costing the growers little so long as amnestied workers and, if need be, RAWs could be relied upon.

Labor and Business

Organized labor's hold over immigration legislation gradually weakened during the 1980s as the number of union members continued to decline and labor's reputation for political effectiveness lost its luster. Still, labor succeeded in protecting its vital interests in immigration policy throughout the decade, including the 1990 act. For a century, the unions, like most of their rank and file, had favored restrictions on immigration. During the 1970s, ethnic tensions, status anxieties, and fears of competition over jobs, housing, and public services led most unions to oppose increased admissions, amnesties for illegal aliens, and importation of temporary farmworkers, while favoring employer sanctions and stepped-up border enforcement.

In the pre-IRCA period, the main immigration policy issues concerned how illegal aliens and agricultural guestworkers were treated. Organized labor's position on these issues was clear and long-established, and it usually got its way. In 1964, the AFL-CIO had succeeded in engineering the termination of the Bracero program, which had permitted seasonal farmworkers from Mexico to enter to work on American crops without much protection, undermining domestic wage levels. During the 1970s, labor had been the principal force propelling the employer sanctions proposals that surfaced in Congress and passed the House only to fail in the Senate. As the 1980s began, the Hesburgh Commission member representing the AFL-CIO expressed the unions' continued, uncompromising hostility to any guestworker program, however protective it might be of American workers.[72]

In IRCA, however, organized labor enjoyed only modest success. It did obtain its long-sought goal of employer sanctions, but the sanctions were widely viewed as weak, readily undermined by a combination of document fraud by workers, broad defenses by employers, and an anticipated lack of official zeal in prosecuting such cases. The unions supported legalization inasmuch as it would improve the enforcement of the labor laws. Here too, however, widespread fraud in the farmworker program made the amnesty more open-ended than some of the unions may have either anticipated or desired.[73] After IRCA, labor's influence in Congress generally continued to wane,[74] as revealed in its declining membership base and its defeats in its high-priority battles on common-situs picketing, plant-closing legislation, and fast-track authority for the U.S.–Mexico free-trade agreement.

The post-IRCA politics of immigration, however, were quite different. With the rancorous debate over illegal migration behind it (as least for the time being), Congress could now turn to the question of legal immigration. Having closed the "back door," it would be easier to pry open the front door. Pre-IRCA, illegals were the target and so restrictionists had the upper hand. Thus expansionists had to use up all of their political capital seeking to soften the effect of sanctions through an amnesty, which was unpopular with the general public. After IRCA, expansionists had more valuable things to trade, and a logrolling strategy of granting more visas to favored groups became attractive.

In this setting, even a weakened labor movement was better situated to protect and promote its positions. Moreover, Senator Kennedy, a staunch ally and political hero of the AFL-CIO, had assured its president, Lane Kirkland, and other labor leaders that he would protect the unions' vital interests in any immigration legislation. Labor defined those interests as protecting domestic jobs and wage levels, and it sought to advance them primarily by limiting temporary labor visas. Significantly, labor did not seek to limit family-oriented admissions; to the contrary, it sought to expand them despite the fact that those entering under family visas are more likely to compete for the jobs that the unions covet than those entering under employment visas, who are (especially after the 1990 act) more highly skilled workers. Indeed, workers admitted as family members need not even obtain labor certifications. "The unions fight over fewer than 200,000 worker slots," Bruce Morrison noted, "but they support the more than 500,000 slots for family members, refugees, and ethnic diversity."[75] Refugee admissions, which Kirkland personally favored,[76] were also endorsed by organized labor.

During the 1980s, industrial, commercial, and professional organizations exercised growing influence over immigration policy. As in some other areas of public policy, business dissatisfaction with the inefficiencies of the status quo spurred it to become a leading advocate of reform.[77] The Reagan and Bush administrations were decidedly attentive to business interests, which converged with more general public anxieties about U.S. competitiveness and the increasing globalization of labor markets.

These interests, of course, were not monolithic. Employers of low-skilled workers in the garment industry, hotel and restaurant services, and other sectors dependent upon illegal labor lobbied to preserve their access to cheap labor by defeating or at least weakening employer sanctions. In IRCA, as we have seen, they succeeded in accomplishing the latter. Many other employers had a more complex agenda. IRCA might affect the status of their highly skilled employees who came to the United States on temporary visas, but violated their terms and were now just as illegal as the clandestine border-crossers. Nonetheless many firms, including the large multinational corporations, were less concerned about IRCA's employer sanctions and legalization provisions than about the anachronistic system of employment-related visas. This slow, rigid system often prevented them from hiring and moving their employees about efficiently. The American Immigration Lawyers Association, a group whose members increasingly represented large multinational employers rather than just individual aliens challenging deportation, similarly supported reform of legal immigration standards and procedures.

Reform of legal immigration, however, would pit business directly against two formidable forces: organized labor, which sought to restrict temporary labor visas in order to reduce job competition from low-wage immigrants; and the coalition of ethnic, denominational, and human rights groups, which sought more visas for family unification and humanitarian reasons. Business interests hoped that with IRCA and illegal immigration issues out of the way, Congress would turn next to urgently needed reforms of legal immigration, but neither Mazzoli nor Rodino nor the administration was anxious to move on these issues. Before opening the front door, they insisted on assessing IRCA's effects in order to see whether it had indeed closed the back door.

In 1988 the Senate, again under Democratic control, overwhelmingly passed a Kennedy-Simpson bill after only seven hours of debate. This bill established the baseline for all future negotiations on immigration reform. It began its long legislative journey with three major agenda items, reflecting a compromise between Simpson's and Kennedy's views. First, it sought to limit chain migration by restricting the existing law's fifth preference (for citizens' adult siblings and these siblings' spouses and children) to include only never-married siblings of citizens,[78] and by limiting the second preference (for resident aliens' spouses and unmarried children) to only those children under age twenty-six.

The bill also added a new category of "independent" workers, who possessed skills needed in the United States, but had no employer to file for labor certification on their behalf. This category, which was to be administered by lottery for all those above a threshold level on a point system, combined two themes: an emphasis on skills-based admissions and on source-country diversity. The new "independent" admissions policy was designed to favor English speakers; Irish and Western Europeans would have benefited, as well as Indians, Filipinos, Nigerians, and English-speaking natives of the Caribbean. Reflecting a political strategy devised by Senator Kennedy's staff, an Irish spokesman, Daire O'Criodain, noted "We never would have gotten Simpson's support with an Irish-only bill."[79] Another provision, admitting those willing to invest two million dollars here (reduced on the Senate floor to one million dollars) and employ at least ten Americans, was similar in its emphasis on immigrants' economic contributions.[80]

Finally, the bill imposed the first-ever overall numerical ceiling on legal immigration, although one exceeding then-current levels. Kennedy had accepted the cap as a necessary price for obtaining Simpson's support for higher overall numbers. Kennedy knew that a cap was particularly important to Simpson, who viewed it as a symbol of the nation's sovereign power and its willingness to control immigration in the face of relentless demographic and political pressures for expansion. In proposing this cap, however, Simpson pitted immediate relatives of citizens, whose visa numbers were unlimited under current law, against other family-based admissions, whose value he viewed as exaggerated.[81]

This bill was not enacted. Mazzoli and Rodino were simply not sufficiently interested in pressing reform on a reluctant Congress, and there was substantial opposition to a point system and a cap. Instead, Congress responded in a less contentious way to the growing ethnic group pressures for more admissions. Embracing the diversity slogan the groups used to legitimate their special claims, it passed a law enlarging the special IRCA-created preference for "adversely affected" countries (primarily Ireland) and adding a new one for "underrepresented" ones, which would turn out to favor the Indian subcontinent.[82] The same Congress also enacted a statute facilitating the deportation of certain criminal aliens, another reform raising few political difficulties.[83]

None of this, however, seriously addressed business's concerns; indeed, several personnel changes in the new Congress that convened in 1989 dimmed the prospects for business-oriented reforms. Jack Brooks, a Texan with little immigration policy expertise, had replaced the retired Rodino as chairman of the House Judiciary Committee. Bruce Morrison, who like Kennedy in the Senate enjoyed strong organized labor backing, had taken over the chairmanship of the Immigration subcommittee from Mazzoli, who other committee Democrats felt lacked party loyalty. (He had spoken on the floor against seating the Democrat in the disputed 1984 Indiana election, and was thought to curry favor with the Republicans.)[84]

Unlike Mazzoli, however, Morrison was a highly partisan activist and a quick study. Some of his congressional colleagues, however, found him mercurial and difficult to deal with, especially as he began to maneuver toward a tough race for governor of Connecticut in 1990. His talents were amply displayed in the jockeying that led up to the 1990 act. Morrison had only joined the subcommittee in 1987, just after IRCA, when he saw certain, new, interesting avenues opening up for immigration reform. He had known nothing about the field but he was brash and he learned quickly. Although junior in terms of service in the House, on the full committee, and even on the subcommittee he now chaired, he itched to take the lead. It was a sign of the times in Congress that he was able to do so. Before the post-Watergate reforms in committee structure and other political changes that reduced members' reliance on the party hierarchy in the House, a member so junior and (until then) so unspecialized would almost certainly have been barred from exercising policy leadership in such a controversial area.

By 1989, Morrison had begun to focus on three main areas for reform. First, he viewed the limits on visas for the spouses and minor children of resident aliens as inhumane and foolish, simply encouraging illegal migration. Second, he echoed the complaints, confirmed by a congressional consultant's report, that temporary employment visas were being abused and converted into what was in effect permanent employment. Third, he saw the political appeal of diversity admissions; indeed, he viewed them as politically essential to immigration expansion.[85] Even before he took over the subcommittee, he and his liberal colleagues had been impressed by pro-diversity testimony at a set of meetings that Mazzoli had chaired in the prior Congress. Morrison was convinced that ethnic groups must feel that their members had access to the United States or else they would simply circumvent the system. One of his first acts as chairman was to visit Miami and South Texas, where he observed the devastating effects on local public services in areas of high immigrant concentration. Sensitive to both the merit of greater federal support to defray local immigration-related costs and to the political value of using cash payments to mute local government opposition to wider reforms, he advocated "immigration emergency" subsidies.[86]

While Morrison was fashioning his strategy Kennedy and Simpson, whose own bill had been close enough to Kennedy's to enable them to combine forces, again moved their bill swiftly in the Senate. It was almost identical to their joint bill of the year before, with one important alteration: this time, it increased the number and proportion of employment-based visas. Senate passage, however, was not so easy as it had been in 1988. In order to get the bill through the Judiciary Committee, Simpson was forced to drop his proposed changes to the preference system, through which he hoped to limit chain migration by restricting visas for unmarried siblings. The provision valuing English-speaking skills in the "independent" visa point system, which Kennedy had also strongly favored (partly as a boost to Irish applicants), was deleted in the committee. Perhaps most important, Simpson was decisively defeated (62–36) when the Senate approved a Hatch-DeConcini amendment placing a floor under the immediate relatives category. This would make the cap "pierceable"; in effect the cap would be nonexistent. Before approving the bill (S. 358) in July, 1989, the Senate also raised the number of scheduled visas from the bill's proposed 590,000 to 630,000, as well as approving a stay of deportation for close family members of aliens legalized under IRCA. In addition, the final Senate version placed some restrictions on federal benefits for illegal aliens.

Kennedy, who was determined to win passage of the Senate bill (or something like it) in the House, made a politic gesture of deference to the other chamber by paying a visit to committee chairman Jack Brooks and subcommittee chairman Morrison. Kennedy confided that he had no more time to waste on unsuccessful immigration bills and that reform would be achieved either now or never. Brooks agreed to move legislation through his committee as soon as Morrison's subcommittee completed its work. As it turned out, however, this took a long time.

The Senate bill had avoided a politically explosive issue: the temporary (nonimmigrant) visas, which the unions wanted to restrict and business wanted to expand. In addition, the Senate, as in 1988, dealt only indirectly with the issue of diversity visas. Ethnic, union, and business dissatisfaction, however, demanded that these issues be addressed head-on in the House, as became clear in the unusually extensive set of hearings that Morrison held in his subcommittee and jointly with the Education and Labor Committee in late 1989 and early 1990. Business wanted more numerous and flexible employment-related visas, elimination of employment preference backlogs that had increased sharply since IRCA, and the use of immigration policy to serve labor market needs as it did in other countries competing with the United States. The AFL-CIO attacked the numerically unlimited aspect of temporary employment visas, which it viewed as a wage-reducing end run around the preference system. The union also challenged the notion that immigration could be used to reduce particular labor shortages, pointing out that efforts to do so in the areas of nursing and agriculture had not eliminated the shortages. The problem could only be solved, it claimed, through better wages and working conditions.

Morrison's approach had little in common with the Senate bill. Opposed to a cap, Morrison wanted instead to expand immigration. He believed that the climate for liberal reform would not persist; a recession was widely predicted and Kennedy seemed unlikely to try again if this effort failed. He therefore fixed on a new strategy. Rather than responding to what people feared about immigration, which Morrison saw as the politics of the pre-IRCA era, he would seek to institutionalize what each particular constituency liked about it. He hoped to logroll his way to a majority with an omnibus bill built around a coalition of intense, pro-immigration special interests. This was a familiar political device, but it had not previously been used in immigration bills because restrictionists were too strong. It was also dangerous, especially in an election year, because it threatened to increase the number and intensity of opponents.

Central to this strategy was Morrison's effort to attract and meld labor and business support. He launched this effort with a bold but politically risky tactic, announcing that he favored reforming *both* permanent and temporary employment visas. In consultation with labor, he floated several new proposals. These included a cap on temporary employment visas and a tax on employers importing workers under permanent visas, the proceeds to be used for retraining domestic workers. Under no illusions that he could get such a tax through the Ways and Means Committee, Morrison hoped to use the idea as a way to open a debate about employer-financed worker retraining. (He later proposed a nontax alternative, mandatory employer training of workers on the job or in local schools, but it went nowhere.)

When Morrison introduced his bill (H.R. 4300), it contained provisions that would produce substantially higher admissions, which organized labor opposed but which everyone also knew would have to be reduced if the bill were to be politically viable. But Morrison's bill also contained two other new elements that labor ardently supported: a cap on temporary employment visas, and a labor recruitment test as a precondition for temporary skilled worker visas. When business protested, he neutralized their opposition by increasing the number of permanent employment visas and relaxing the labor recruitment requirement. Simpson, who had done little to secure business support for his immigration proposals in the past, did not really address them in the pending Senate bill either.[87] Thus Morrison's concessions were important in attracting business support for his approach when the crucial conference stage was reached.

Ethnic Groups

Ethnic groups composed the other crucial component of Morrison's coalition. To a considerable degree, immigration politics is, and has always been, ethnic politics. In the struggle for preferred access to limited immigration benefits, some groups have fared much better than others.[88] Hence the cooperation among different ethnic groups is by no means predestined; they often make uneasy coalition partners. Quite apart from these competitive anxieties among ethnic groups, deep differences in ideology, perceptions, interest, organizational skills, and other political resources may divide them. Even within particular groups, class and generational divisions may impede cooperation on specific political issues. Recent experience suggests that "rainbow coalitions" are much easier to envision than to create and maintain.[89]

In the immigration reform context, the ethnic groups did not lack for political advantages. They could invoke themes like family unity, ethnic or source-country diversity, redress for past injustices, and foreign policy goals that resonated deeply with the public and Congress. Their geographical concentration in a few politically important states gave them especially great political influence in the House. And their numbers, constantly growing as the newly naturalized joined the voting rolls, swelled the chorus of voices demanding more immigration.[90]

For purposes of understanding the politics of immigration reform in the post-IRCA period, it is useful to divide ethnics into two groups: the Irish and the others. The Irish, of course, were not alone in seeking favored access to the United States for their fellow ethnics. But because family reunification would not bring over many Irish, they *were* unique among ethnic groups in their downplaying of the importance of family-related visas. Instead, they emphasized education, English competency, knowledge of U.S. history, and other requirements that putative Irish immigrants could readily fulfill.

The Irish also held some unusually strong political cards in the House. Since many of them had come after IRCA's 1982 amnesty deadline, they could claim special hardship in the prospect of deportation. They also formed an important constituency in Connecticut, where Morrison had launched an uphill campaign for governor against an incumbent named O'Neill, a member of his own party. Morrison thus needed to play the "Irish card" for all it was worth. The Irish viewed the "independent" admissions approach, adopted by the Senate in 1988 and again in 1989 with them in mind, as too limited and uncertain to help them much. The Irish recognized that they would often be "outskilled" by other English-speaking workers from India, Pakistan, Jamaica, and Hong Kong. They naturally preferred a sure thing: a "diversity" program defined to favor the Irish. This was also a viable option in the Senate. Although Simpson opposed it, his deep commitments to an overall cap on admissions and to the provisions strengthening enforcement and making it easier to deport criminal aliens made him willing to make major concessions in order to obtain them. And higher Irish immigration was among Kennedy's key policy goals.[91]

The term "diversity" seems a bit curious when one considers the historical context and beneficiaries of the new provisions. Morrison's bill would extend, alter, and institutionalize both the limited, temporary diversity program adopted in IRCA (called NP-5, for countries "disadvantaged" by the 1965 law) and another program enacted on a similar basis in 1988 (called OP-1 or "Berman," for "underrepresented" countries). More than 75 percent of the visas under the NP-5 program went to four countries whose emigrants were already very well represented in the United States: Ireland (41 percent), Canada (18 percent); Great Britain and Northern Ireland (9 percent), and Poland (9 percent).[92] The OP-1 program, in contrast, did benefit Third World countries; Bangladeshis, for example, received 22 percent of the Berman visas in 1990.[93]

In the debates leading up to the 1990 act, proponents of such diversity programs commonly sought to rationalize them by invoking civil rights rhetoric, arguing that the 1965 law had "discriminated against" or "disadvantaged" Europeans and other "old seed" groups. One could only make this argument, however, by ignoring the history of pre-1965 immigration. In enacting the 1965 reforms, Congress had intended to favor these same Northern and Western European groups, which had been previously advantaged by the national origins quotas jettisoned in the 1965 act. As it turned out, however, the new system was exploited most effectively by immigrants from Asia, the Pacific region, Latin America, and (to a far less extent) Africa,[94] who had been obliged by the national origins quotas to languish on endless queues but who now quickly turned the tables using the family-based admissions categories to bring in their relatives.

This wholly unexpected turnabout sparked the political interest in diversity programs during the 1980s. Congress had responded to these pressures in IRCA and in 1988. It was especially responsive in the 1990 act. It knew full well, of course, that the new provisions would disproportionately favor Europeans, especially the Irish.[95] Congress appreciated that these groups are already well represented in both the legal and illegal[96] U.S. population, and that they are well represented precisely because of their advantaged pre-1965 immigration patterns.[97] Indeed, much of the "disadvantage" cited by the beneficiaries of the new provisions actually reflects the fact that they, like the Italians, had been in the United States for so many generations that they could no longer gain much help from the 1965 law's preferences for immediate family members and siblings.

Other ethnic groups also demanded special relief. Sometimes they marched under the banner of diversity, whereas at other times they invoked human rights and family unification themes. Working with the Organization of Chinese Americans and other ethnic coalitions, Morrison had been instrumental in promoting group-specific legislation in 1989 protecting Chinese students after Tiananmen Square.[98] Along with Senator Frank Lautenberg, he had won an amendment giving Soviet Jews who wished to emigrate here special advantages under the Refugee Act. Steven Solarz, an influential member of the House Foreign Affairs Committee, was actively promoting the cause of Hong Kong residents, who were regarded in Congress as model immigrants due to the skill levels, wealth, English language ability, and ties to U.S. multinational corporations that many of them possessed. He argued that U.S. foreign policy interests dictated encouraging them to remain in Hong Kong as long as they were still safe there. He also stressed, however, that the United States should give those who chose to leave strong incentives to choose the United States over Canada and Australia, which were also wooing them. We should therefore assure Hong Kong residents *now* that, after China took over the colony in 1997, they could still use their visas to the United States.

Hispanic organizations, in coalition with the AFL-CIO and other ethnic and denominational groups, lobbied vigorously to protect and increase family preferences. They found an eager advocate in Morrison, who proposed a thorough revamping of the preference system. Among other changes, he followed earlier reformers in seeking explicitly to separate the immigration flow into distinct streams,[99] one for family members and one for independent workers, and allot visas to each stream. At the same time, he recognized family unity as the dominant norm in immigration politics. He proposed a higher allotment for the existing second and fifth preferences, which Simpson hoped to limit. He also favored backlog reductions and "family fairness" admissions (for immediate relatives of IRCA-legalized aliens). There was little support for an overall cap in the House, and Morrison did not propose one. In addition to the increase in numerically limited visas, he would maintain the unlimited admission of citizens' immediate relatives.

As Lawrence Fuchs has noted,[100] the willingness of the older immigrant groups, notably the Jews and Italians, to support higher Asian and Hispanic immigration levels was a remarkable feature of the politics that produced the 1990 act. These groups, Fuchs points out, endorsed expansionist principles even though they could anticipate that Asians and Hispanics, rather than their own fellow ethnics, would be the main beneficiaries of those principles. At least in the short run, there was little prospect for Soviet Jews coming here after the invasion of Afghanistan in 1979, and by 1990 most of those who got out were being diverted to Israel, not the United States. Italians, as noted earlier, could no longer gain many admissions through the family-related preferences precisely because they had been here so long. Yet these groups helped to prevent a reduction of the fifth preference, which was now as important to the Asian and Hispanic groups as it had been to the Italians at an earlier stage.[101] In part, this may have reflected more long-range considerations; should there be a new influx of Jews and Italians, that preference would be available to bring their siblings here. More fundamentally, however, the behavior of these groups was one more sign of the emergent expansionism, a new politics that reflected the interplay between a growing consensus on pro-immigration ideas and a broader coalition mobilized by ethnic logrolling.

Human Rights Groups

The human rights groups—the American Civil Liberties Union (ACLU), Amnesty International, religious groups, and others—were concerned about several other policies: protected status for those Salvadorans (and hopefully other groups) who did not technically qualify as refugees but would face danger if they returned home; repeal of the so-called ideological exclusion provisions enacted during the Cold War era; a softening of the Procrustean marriage fraud provisions enacted in 1986; and the fate of Tibetans displaced by Chinese oppression (a cause championed by Barney

Frank and matinee idol Richard Gere). The last three concerns were easily accommodated. Some of the ideological exclusions had been temporarily repealed earlier as to nonimmigrants,[102] and it was hard to imagine why permanent residents should be treated less generously. Only the INS and Senator Simpson seemed committed to the existing marriage fraud provisions; here, as elsewhere, the INS's agenda enjoyed little credibility with Congress. The Tibetan's plight appealed to the entire political spectrum, diehard anti-Communists as well as militant liberals.

In contrast, the issue of protected status for Salvadorans implicated fierce partisan struggles over American policy toward Central America, not just immigration. Congress was bitterly divided over it. While the House had passed some version of the Moakley-DeConcini bill, which would protect Salvadorans, on four occasions, Simpson adamantly opposed it and had always killed it in the Senate. This time, however, Moakley was chairman of the House Rules Committee. Since his committee regulated the process of floor amendment, which could make or break an immigration bill by fracturing the fragile coalition supporting it, Moakley had to be reckoned with and mollified. Simpson and the White House tried to ignore this fact, but Morrison, who favored the human rights agenda anyway, did not. He knew that Moakley suspected that the Salvadoran's cause would not receive fair consideration in the Senate, which had failed in 1986 to bring his bill to a vote as part of IRCA. Morrison also knew that Moakley feared that a generic safe-haven bill would do little good for the Salvadorans since a Reagan or Bush White House would never designate them for specific protection.

Morrison therefore proposed to Moakley packaging a generic safe-haven provision along with a specific designation of protected status for the Salvadorans and Chinese. Morrison knew that the Senate would do nothing on this package until the House passed a legal immigration reform bill; at that point he would include these pieces in his omnibus bill, along with other narrow reforms such as administrative naturalization and citizenship for Filipino war veterans. Meanwhile, he would have Moakley's vital support.[103]

Morrison's larger coalition-building strategy took a long time to put together, and Kennedy, who provided important help by keeping Brooks on board and by getting the Senate to adopt specific pieces of Morrison's package, was becoming nervous and impatient as the end of the Congress approached. Morrison's omnibus bill was not approved by the full committee until August 1, and it elicited the Justice Department's "fundamental opposition" and a presidential veto threat due primarily to the high immigration levels that the bill would authorize. The committee report was not issued until after Labor Day. When it reached the floor for debate, however, its supporting coalition was broad and powerful. The only serious complaint lodged against it there was business's concern about the restrictions on temporary workers, which Morrison promised to address in conference. Congressman John Bryant, a Texas Democrat on the immigration subcommittee, proposed an amendment to delete all provisions of the bill except those relating to family reunification. His position, however, was decisively rejected, 257–165, and the House passed the committee's omnibus bill on October 3. Still, there was great cause for concern. First, the margin of victory was a slender thirty-one votes, a sign that Morrison's bill could be vulnerable to amendment during the forthcoming conference. Second, the House bill bore little resemblance to the Senate version. Finally, time was running out. The leadership planned to adjourn within a few weeks, and the power of opponents increases geometrically at the end of a Congress. Kennedy, on the Senate side, was particularly worried about the time factor since it could encourage any Senator, including Simpson, to demand concessions on controversial issues and thereby derail the legislation again. For example, Jesse Helms might insist on retaining the provision in existing law, which he had authored and which was anathema to many liberals, excluding aliens who tested HIV positive. (The provision was later repealed in the conference bill, Helms notwithstanding).

The White House had signaled its support for the Senate bill and its opposition to Morrison's. Beyond this, however, it had played no significant role in using its muscle to line up votes or otherwise shape the legislative process.[104] The INS, a long-troubled agency under relatively new and shaky leadership, deferred to the attorney general's initiative, which was seldom forthcoming. In this negative posture, the administration would neither negotiate nor even discuss compromises between the two bills. It indicated some flexibility only after the *Wall Street Journal* praised Morrison's bill for its higher ceilings for skilled workers. The *Journal* ran two editorials twitting Republicans for blocking the legislation, the first headlined "Democrats for Vitality," and the second called "Stonewall Simpson:" "Mr. Simpson is so afraid of Mexicans," the editors wrote, "that he's now backing away from the immigration bill that he personally led through the Senate." They also criticized the administration's silence, eliciting a letter to the editor from Michael Boskin, the chief White House economist, indicating his support. Two days later, the chastened Simpson also responded.[105] Roger Porter, the president's domestic policy adviser, concluded that the administration was on the wrong side on the issue and should support enactment of a bill.[106]

The negotiations leading up to the Senate-House conference were delicate. Simpson was adamantly opposed to many of the provisions in the highly expansionist House bill, so much so that he might have preferred to see the legislation die—indeed, he threatened to filibuster it to death—rather than accept those provisions. He wanted to reduce the proportion of family visas; eliminate the family backlog reductions; retain the increases in permanent employment visas but reduce or eliminate visas for unskilled workers;[107] eliminate or raise any cap imposed on temporary worker visas for entry-level professionals; make it easier for employers to obtain Department of Labor certification of domestic worker unavailability; adopt an earlier cutoff date for the family fairness relief; drop Moakley-DeConcini; and—most important to him because of their symbolic value—adopt an overall cap and strict border enforcement and deportation provisions to close the "back door" to illegal immigration.

Kennedy, however, was also resolute. Fearing that the next Congress, which would extend through the presidential election, would be unable to agree on immigration reform, he was not prepared to give up the present opportunity in the vain hope of passing a more liberal bill later on. Kennedy promised that if Simpson did not try to block the conference, Kennedy would not sign a conference report embodying legislation that Simpson found unacceptable. Simpson accepted Kennedy's proposal and then confronted the House conferees with his demands. He began the negotiations by asking the other key conferees whether they too had "bottom lines" for the bill. Morrison insisted on provisions favorable to the Irish.[108] Moakley demanded asylum for the Salvadorans. Berman required generous treatment of Asian and Hispanic family groups. Schumer insisted on the new diversity programs. The negotiations were very delicate and rancorous. At times both Kennedy and Simpson lost their tempers as House members shifted their positions, making bargaining more difficult. Kennedy, Simpson, and Brooks—three of the most powerful men in Congress—often had to cool their heels waiting for Morrison, who was frequently absent or late due to his hectic campaigning in Connecticut. Their patience with this junior member, who many considered abrasive and arrogant, was sorely tested, and they were only mollified by the constant entreaties of more popular members like Berman and Schumer.[109]

Faced with the challenge from Simpson (who was supported by Kennedy),[110] the House surrendered on many fronts. On the issue of a cap, however, it held fast. The ceiling, set at 700,000 visas for the first three years and dropping to 675,000 thereafter (not counting refugees and asylees), remained pierceable whenever the number of admissions of citizens' immediate relatives exceeded 226,000 a year. Even without piercing the ceiling, the bill authorized an increase of 40 percent over current levels, which was well above the increase in the Senate bill. Indeed, even at that high level, the cap did not include refugee/asylee admissions.

The House conferees were obliged to make important concessions in exchange for this substantial increase in legal admissions. The family fairness cutoff date was moved back to 1988. Restrictions on temporary workers were retained but diluted. Employer attestation was permitted on an experimental basis. Finally, Simpson obtained both beefed-up border enforcement measures and stronger (some would say Draconian) provisions restricting the rights of aliens who commit crimes, limiting their appeals, and accelerating their deportation. In focusing on drug-related offenses, of course, Simpson was riding a wave of drug-war rhetoric deployed by the administration and Democrats alike. To achieve these gains, however, Simpson was obliged to accept a number of provisions that he opposed but Kennedy and the House conferees favored: a transitional and permanent diversity program (the former reserved 40 percent of its visas for the Irish); another year's extension of the period in which IRCA legalization applicants could apply for permanent status; and other provisions providing special relief for the Tibetans, Hong Kong residents, and (again) the Irish.

The last obstacle to a conference agreement was the Moakley-DeConcini provision establishing a safe haven for Salvadorans. Simpson opposed any country-specific relief, making the long-familiar argument that Salvadorans were only economic migrants, not refugees. Moakley, who controlled crucial votes on the Rules Committee that would be critical if a conference report returned to the House, insisted that he would kill the bill unless it provided specific relief for the Salvadorans. Simpson proposed a more generic relief provision that the president would apply to specific situations, but Moakley was adamant. When Simpson quipped that "this turkey gets more feathers every day," the conferees looked at Moakley. Brooks, who was presiding over the conference, "reminded" the assemblage that Moakley was chairman of Rules. Asking whether there was some way to accommodate Moakley, Brooks—who had never been viewed as an expansionist and who therefore had far greater credibility with Simpson than Rodino would have had—called a recess.

At that point, Simpson decided to relent in the interests of getting a bill passed, and the White House quickly fell into line.[111] When the conference reconvened, there was movement. Moakley proposed a thirty-six-month temporary protected status (TPS) period for the Salvadorans; he compromised on eighteen. Simpson extracted promises from Moakley that deportation notices would be sent out to Salvadorans at the end of the eighteen-month period, that neither Moakley nor DeConcini would seek to legislate legal status for them at that point, and that it would take an extraordinary majority (three-fifths of the Senate) to pass such legislation.[112] In return, Simpson accepted a generic safe-haven provision that Moakley, with specific protection for Salvadorans now in hand, very much wanted.

It was, as Simpson said, an "anguishing compromise,"[113] but the Senate immediately ratified it, 89–8. As usual with immigration legislation, House approval posed more of a problem. At the eleventh hour, the Hispanic Caucus, led by Ed Roybal, challenged a Simpson-sponsored provision in the compromise report that would establish a pilot program in three states to test a more secure driver's license as an identification document for purposes of verifying work authorization under the employer sanctions title.

With considerable hyperbole, they argued that this proposal would lead to a national identification card, which in turn would lead to massive violation of civil liberties—an argument that the ACLU had long advocated.

Although the unions and others in the expansionist coalition also opposed ID cards, they did not feel strongly enough about it to view it as a possible deal breaker.[114] The Hispanic groups, however, pressed the coalition hard to go along with their adamant refusal to accept ID cards. Perhaps most important to the political fate of the bill, they convinced the Black Congressional Caucus, which few politicians wished to offend, to support their position.

This eagerness of the black leadership to use an immigration issue to cement ties with the Hispanics is an especially striking feature of the politics of the 1990 act. Black leaders had sought in earlier immigration debates to mobilize their supporters around opposition to expansion. Now, however, they were willing to mute or forego this traditional restrictionism in the hopes of mollifying a group with whom they were increasingly competing over redistricting, patronage, access to housing, control of public schools, representation on the Supreme Court, and other issues.[115] The conciliatory stance of the black groups was a dramatic confirmation of the burgeoning power of Hispanics in national politics.

Armed with black support, the Hispanic Caucus prevailed on a key vote governing the rule for floor debate on the conference report. It now found itself in the catbird's seat: it could kill the bill if its demand was not met. At this point the bill was much closer to being a corpse than IRCA had ever been.[116]

If the Hispanic Caucus was bluffing, it was not at all clear that the bluff would succeed. Simpson, after all, had already had to make many concessions, perhaps too many from his point of view. Unable to get his overall cap of admissions and displeased with many of the provisions that had been logrolled into the bill, he might be tempted to let it die, especially since the caucus, which was often at odds with him politically, would probably end up bearing public responsibility for its death.[117]

Barney Frank, who saw this mortal danger to a bill that he desperately wanted to pass, moved to break the impasse. In a late night meeting, Frank argued to Simpson that the bill could be saved if Simpson would drop his drivers' license proposal, in return for which Frank would try to convince Senate liberals to consider the proposal in the next Congress. Simpson now found himself in an oddly familiar position. During the final act of the IRCA drama, he had had the votes to defeat the liberals' move to broaden the amnesty by extending the residency cutoff date. Now he again held the fate of immigration reform in his hands.[118] And once again, as in 1986, Simpson decided to yield in order to secure a bill. Agreeing to Frank's plan, he allowed the pilot program to be deleted. With this resolved, the House proceeded to approve the conference report, 264–118.[119]

V. IDEAS

The Immigration Act of 1990 was a pastiche of many influential groups' policy agendas, but it was also considerably more than that. The immigration debate of the 1980s revolved around ideas as well as interests. Indeed, as I explained in the Introduction, one cannot adequately account for IRCA and the 1990 act without understanding how ideas about immigration altered the legislative politics of the 1980s.

It is not easy, even in theory, to distinguish ideas from interests. We can hardly conceive of our interests without drawing upon ideas, and we often use our ideas to advance our interests.[120] But in another sense and in certain contexts, we can readily distinguish them. Voters, for example, are aware both of their own interests and of the idea of public interests that transcend their own interests, and they know—and routinely act on—that difference.[121]

How do ideas influence legislative outcomes in general, and how did they do so in the specific case of immigration policy? Ideas perform at least five functions in politics: coalition building, belief changing, symbol mobilizing, regime reinforcing, and dissonance reducing.[122] These functions, of course, are only separable at an analytical level; in practice, particular ideas may perform several of them simultaneously. This was certainly true of ideas about immigration in the 1980s. The exogenous force of ideas, moreover, is greater for some of these functions (belief changing is the clearest example) than for others. In the remainder of section V, I show how immigration ideas were used to perform each of these political functions and then show how the ideas shaped immigration policy at three different levels of normativity: constitutionalism, policy purposes, and specific policy design.

Coalition Building

Ideas are the glue of a pluralistic politics. Appealing to general ideas is necessary if groups with disparate conceptions of self-interest and public interest are to form coalitions. And since policies must almost invariably be justified in public interest terms in order to win broad support, ideas can supply the necessary language in which that discourse of justification is conducted.[123] In this respect, an idea's ambiguity may contribute to its power to facilitate coalition building.

The idea of "diversity," which played such a crucial role in the enactment of the 1990 act, is an example. Although this notion might have been defined exclusively, as it was under the national origins quota system, its usefulness in fashioning and maintaining an expansionist coalition depended upon it being defined so capaciously that a large number of countries could qualify and their supporters in Congress could be placated. Much the same may be said of the idea of international human rights. In a world in which the number of refugees vastly exceeds the willingness of receiving nations to accept them, admission of one group on the basis of human rights principles can be viewed by others as little more than special interest group favoritism.[124] The idea of universal humanitarian principles, while violated in many cases, helped to contain this favoritism and thus maintain the coalition.

Perhaps the most influential coalition-building idea during the 1980s was the emphasis by the Hesburgh Commission, echoed by many of its members such as Senators Kennedy and Simpson throughout the decade, on the need to control illegal migration as a precondition for expanding legal immigration. This idea of linkage enabled liberals and conservatives to join forces in otherwise unlike coalitions to support legislation that at once "closed the back door" and "opened the front door." The wedding of employer sanctions and legalization in IRCA and of tougher enforcement provisions and expanded immigration quotas in the 1990 act must be understood in terms of the moral force and political logic of this idea.

Belief Changing

Ideas can affect how policy intellectuals and other experts who influence decisionmakers think about an issue. Ideas call attention to new empirical relationships and alter the weight accorded to different values. For example, ideas about the benefits and costs of a policy and how they are distributed among individuals and groups fuel all politics, immigration included.

Certain ideas that gained sway during the immigration debates of the late 1980s encouraged many decisionmakers to believe in the existence of a mismatch between job skills needed in the evolving economy and those that new immigrants are bringing with them; some also came to believe in a looming labor shortage. Labor economists testified that the existing system of legal admissions was highly inefficient, aggravating these conditions, and that a restructured system expanding admissions of the "right" kind of immigrants could create immense social benefits while imposing few social costs. Although many business interests had long embraced these ideas, the general hostility to immigration evident at the beginning of the decade had pushed them to the margins of the debate. But the decade's free market, libertarian *zeitgeist*, nurtured by prominent academics, influential mass media, and conservative think tanks, succeeded in grounding and sharpening these notions. Influential conservatives like Alan Simpson and liberals like Bruce Morrison came to accept them and to incorporate them into their policy proposals.

Symbol Mobilizing

In the immigration debate, the fund of pro-immigration ideas was not confined to the efficiency-oriented calculations of neoclassical or labor economists. Ideas can also evoke the symbolic dimension of politics, linking workaday policies with our deepest emotional and normative commitments.

The civil rights movement supplied immigration advocates with a powerful imagery of struggle and rhetoric of egalitarian ideals. During the 1980s, Americans' tolerance for ethnic differences continued to grow.[125] The celebrations of the Statue of Liberty's centennial and the Constitution's bicentennial also imparted strong emotional, even romantic, resonances to the connections between ethnic diversity and national pride and strength, to the image of the United States as a haven for the persecuted, and to the idea that aliens should not be excluded because of their political speech.

Not all of the symbolism evoked by ideas, of course, carried pro-immigration connotations. The notions that the United States was unable to control its borders and that immigrants took jobs away from American workers aroused deep fears about both waning sovereignty and economic decline. These ideas competed vigorously for public allegiance with the more optimistic ones.

Regime Reinforcing

Ideas, even those that call for policy changes, can reaffirm and thus support elements of the status quo. Ideas, Hall points out, are more warmly received to the extent that they converge with existing government institutions, policies, and implementation capacities, and are consistent with social norms concerning the appropriate role of the state in society.[126]

Immigration policy debates during the 1980s provided many instances of this kind of reinforcement. Employer sanctions, for example, were adopted out of a widespread recognition that the INS's limited enforcement capabilities must be augmented with the enforcement resources of the private sector. The notion that alienage raises fundamental equal protection issues, which led to IRCA's antidiscrimination provisions, drew upon an explicit analogy to civil rights and fair employment principles that had long been established for the rest of the population. Similarly, the idea of restricting ideological exclusions reaffirmed the First Amendment protections applicable to the rest of society. These examples also suggest that ideas, by appealing to social continuities and legal traditions, often have the considerable political advantage of masking the extent to which change is in fact being effected.

Dissonance Reducing

Ideas can give eloquent voice to a previously inarticulate sense among members of the public that social values and ways of thinking are changing and that policies therefore need to be brought into harmony with these new practices. By engendering a kind of cognitive dissonance, ideas can underscore tensions into our political life, stimulating the search for new modes of behavior or governance.[127]

There were many examples of this dynamic in the immigration debate. The perceived economic inefficiency of the existing immigration regime prompted a demand for the admission of more higher-skilled workers. The new limits on ideological exclusion reflected the idea the Cold War attitudes had become anachronistic. The adoption of liberal safe-haven policies was an acknowledgment that the traditional "refugee" definition was inadequate to deal with contemporary migration flows. Due process safeguards long withheld from aliens were included at many points. The 1990 act's generous "family fairness" protections for illegal aliens related to amnesty applicants bespoke a recognition that deporting those individuals under the existing rules would often be cruel and self-defeating.

If ideas have different political functions and their autonomy from interests varies, they also shape policy at different levels of normativity. In the immigration debate of the 1980s, we can distinguish three such levels. The most foundational is that of the *rule of law*. The courts during the 1980s infused immigration decision making with certain transcendent principles of equal protection and due process that had long been conventional in virtually all areas of public policy except immigration. These principles obliged the government—"the potent, the omnipresent teacher" in Brandeis's phrase[128]—to treat immigrants more like citizens than ever before, in both substantive and procedural terms. At a second, more pragmatic level, the new ideas shaped *policy purposes*. The most important example was the conviction, shared by most policy elites[129] during the decade, that the United States was engaged in a high-stakes global competition spurred by the drive for economic efficiency, and that expanded immigration could help us win it at little or no cost to other social values. At the third, most operational level, ideas shaped *policy design*. Here, ideas about immigration helped to forge a consensus on techniques for implementing new and old policies.

Rule of Law

As noted in the Introduction, the Marielito incident drew the federal courts into the vortex of immigration policy as never before.[130] In order to discourage illegal migration and asylum claims, the Reagan administration in the early 1980s adopted harsh, often arbitrary policies of exclusion and incarceration. These policies starkly raised the issue of whether and how the rule of law would apply to undocumented aliens. The courts, moreover, had to resolve this issue at a time when other trends in public and private law called into question the legal rules that had traditionally governed aliens.

The principle of rigorous court review of immigration policy was not widely accepted in 1981. Before then judges had upheld almost all federal immigration policies, viewing them as expressions of U.S. sovereignty to which ordinary constitutional principles simply did not apply. They accorded the Congress and its agent, the INS, "plenary power" to regulate immigration and protect national borders pretty much as they saw fit. Policies that in other contexts would have been flatly unconstitutional easily passed judicial muster.

In the early 1980s, however, something had begun to change.[131] The courts, far more insulated from the pressures of organized interest than the other branches, were especially responsive to the influence of public interest ideas—here, the ideas of equal treatment, due process, and social integration. While the courts continued to cite the same old precedents and acknowledge the government's plenary power over immigration, the immigrants began to win some important cases. Drawing upon constitutional and administrative law norms long established in other policy areas, the courts invalidated key INS policies and practices,[132] barred the states from denying public education to undocumented alien children,[133] limited the federal government's power to bar controversial figures from entering on purely ideological grounds,[134] and enlarged the procedural rights of aliens resisting expulsion.[135]

In order to protect asylum claimants, for example, the courts eased the standard of proof, upheld claims by those who had been politically neutral, and pressured the INS into granting a work authorization (the brass ring in the immigration merry-go-round) to any alien presenting a "non-frivolous" asylum claim. The INS's policy of confining thousands of undocumented aliens under conditions resembling criminal punishment obliged the courts to devise legal norms to control agency abuses. In still other areas, the courts reduced the gap between the (nonpolitical) rights of citizens and of aliens almost to the vanishing point.[136] A particularly dramatic example of this occurred in 1989 when a federal judge held that a statutory ground of deportation was unconstitutional, the first such holding ever.[137]

Coming when and in the form that they did, these principled thrusts helped to transform the political issue in Congress and in the country. In particular, the civil rights movement's broad legitimacy altered the nature of politically acceptable discourse and empowered groups organized to combat bigotry. As noted in the Introduction, the racism and nativism that poisoned earlier American attitudes toward immigrants had declined dramatically among elites and the general public by the 1980s. The courts' insistence on protecting the procedural and constitutional rights of aliens during this period affected how politicians and citizens thought about them. By exploiting the deference to judicial ideals that marks American political culture, the courts helped to guide the normative debate in universalistic, human-rights–oriented, pro-immigration directions.

Policy Purpose

Global competitiveness and labor market efficiency were important political touchstones during the 1980s. The rhetorical power of these slogans was stoked by the spectacle of rapid economic growth along the Pacific Rim and in West Germany at a time of recession in the United States. Policy elites raised alarms about looming shortages of high-skilled workers in the United States, the reluctance of many low-skilled Americans to do the menial work that a modern society required, the decline of our educational system, and the need to compete internationally.

These concerns had important political effects. Congress was bound to respond when the Hudson Institute and Booz, Allen & Hamilton issued well-publicized reports predicting labor shortages in key sectors of the economy if the employment visa system was not reformed; when Tom Campbell, an articulate House Republican from the Silicon Valley, regaled his Judiciary Committee colleagues about the stunningly high proportion of new U.S. engineers who were foreign-born; when business representatives decried the lack of domestic workers willing to work at the minimum wage; when Morrison warned the House that employers seeking critically needed skills unavailable domestically could move offshore; when demographer-publicist Ben Wattenberg testified about the economic and social dangers posed by the "baby bust." Despite the implausibility of using immigration policy to fine-tune domestic labor markets, the idea gained powerful support, leaving its imprint on many provisions of the 1990 act, including the new employment visa provisions and the "McDonald's exception" permitting foreign students to work off-campus to fill jobs that Americans seemed to disdain.

This idea was reinforced by the writings of free market economists and libertarian commentators. Their theories were supported and disseminated by an effective network of academic institutions, think tanks, and prominent media, which included the Heritage Foundation, the Cato Institute, and the *Wall Street Journal*. These writers self-consciously sought to transform the "policy paradigms"[138] employed by the public and policy-makers in immigration and other policy areas, and they succeeded. Their writings appeared just in time to influence the congressional hearings that assembled the political and evidentiary bases for the 1990 act. They argued that recent immigration policy had been deeply misguided, and that our preoccupation with undocumented aliens and generous family-oriented admissions had diverted us from more important issues: How many aliens should we admit? Which kind should we seek? What should be their role in the economy? How should we go about encouraging them to come?

Although these commentators' specific answers to these questions often differed, they usually agreed on a set of decidedly pro-immigration ideas: that immigrants tend to be especially productive and entrepreneurial; that immigration promotes economic growth and makes almost everyone better off; that it neither reduces the wage and employment levels of domestic workers nor consumes significant welfare benefits; and that immigration policy should be more carefully tailored to our economic needs than it had been in the recent past. Indeed some economists—Julian Simon was perhaps the most notable—came perilously close to saying that open immigration, like free trade, would provide us with a free lunch![139] These ideas flooded TV and radio talk shows, congressional hearings, and the editorial pages of major newspapers.

Even those participants in the policy debates who reject this remorselessly Panglossian view of immigration[140] agree that these ideas played an important role in shaping the 1990 act. By emphasizing immigration's efficiency, its ability to enlarge society's aggregate wealth, these ideas appeared to soften the bitter *distributional* conflicts that lie just beneath the more placid, cooperative surface of American life. It was somehow reassuring to think that the important zero-sum game was an international competition between the United States and other nations for investment and jobs, rather than a domestic conflict among low-income groups in America's cities—an assurance belied by the smoldering political struggles between native-born blacks and recently arrived Hispanics.

The new emphasis on global competition and resource mobility had another ideational resonance, which also inclined the public toward a more liberal immigration policy. It made the old idea of national sovereignty seem anachronistic, perhaps moribund. If, as the economists claimed, borders are and ought to be porous—if people cross them for much the same reason that Toyotas, computer programs, and Eurodollars do—then the idea of sovereignty could no longer carry the normatively satisfying meaning that it once had to those who invoked it to limit immigration. Politicians might conjure the idea and citizens might find solace in it, but it would increasingly be hollow and merely rhetorical. If a nation's policy independence increasingly connotes isolation and irrelevance, if our fate in matters as diverse as trade, security, scientific progress, and refugee movements is inexorably linked with the policies of other nations, then a pragmatic people would feel impelled to use immigration policy affirmatively to shape its destiny, rather than having outsiders and events thrust that destiny upon it.

These notions helped to galvanize the debate and the majority coalition. But although the new ideas made remarkable headway by the time Congress completed its work, they did not displace all the old ones. In particular, they failed to dislodge family unification as the core immigration policy value; it continued to trump all others as it had for over a quarter-century.

An affirmative case could be (and was) made, of course, that economic and family goals were in harmony because family links would actually advance labor market efficiency by providing valuable social, emotional and economic supports to immigrants, helping them to produce and succeed.[141] Thus was an old idea pressed into new service. Any competition between family-based and employment-based visas, moreover, was muted by Morrison's successful logrolling strategy, which sought to increase the numbers in *all* admission categories, making the pie large enough so that it would no longer seem worth fighting over the relative size of the various slices. Morrison's strategy was evident in the title of his version of the immigration bill: the Family Unity and Employment Opportunities Act of 1990.

Still, a strategy of conflict-suppressing expansion clearly has its political limits, and the 1990 act may reach those limits, especially if illegal migration continues to grow. The trade-off between family unity and skills, for example, probably cannot be ignored forever. Recent evidence suggests that U.S. income is lower—six billion dollars a year lower, according to a recent estimate—than it would be if immigrants' skill levels had not declined as a result of the family unity preferences.[142] This may not seem like much in a five-and-one-half-trillion-dollar economy, but it suggests that some price is being paid for the family unity trump.

The 1990 act continued to accord primacy to family unity goals but did give labor market concerns somewhat more weight. In 1990, 20 percent of the legal immigrants admitted under numerical quotas (54,000 out of 270,000) were admitted under skills-related visas, and although the 1990 act increased the number of such admissions to 140,000, their share of the new total (675,000 for the first three years plus citizens' "immediate relatives" in excess of 226,000) remained at 20 percent.[143] However, the 55,000 diversity visas, which also carry a skills requirement, does increase that share to as much as 28 percent. (To the extent that immediate family admissions grow and pierce the cap, of course, these proportions [although not the numbers] of skills-based visas will decline.) In addition to increasing the numbers, Congress also placed a much stronger emphasis in the employment-related visa categories on higher-level skills. More flexible labor certification procedures were also added. Still, the family category's share still accounts for two-thirds or more of the visas (again, depending upon the number of immediate relatives who come).

Policy Design

As the ideas of the rule of law, free labor markets, more selective admissions, diversity, and human rights joined family unity in shaping the decade's immigration debates, they helped to generate and rationalize a number of specific policies, adopted in the 1990 act, which were designed to implement these more general goals in a major way. Five of these policies, already discussed, are particularly important: (1) higher overall immigration levels; (2) more skills-oriented admissions criteria; (3) the primacy of family-based admissions; (4) enhanced enforcement against documented aliens; and (5) the elimination of certain grounds for exclusion that raised serious constitutional questions.[144] Both the 1988 and 1990 laws adopted another prominent, politically attractive policy: a crackdown on aliens convicted of drug-related and other serious offenses. But this policy did not really grow out of these five ideas.

One additional policy—the use of presumptively universalistic criteria for source-country and humanitarian admissions—merits separate discussion because of its highly contested status. No firm consensus in favor of universalism in admissions has ever been established, as demonstrated both by the pre-1965 national originals quotas for immigrant admissions, and by our country-specific refugee policies during the entire postwar period.[145] Yet the universalistic ideal did prompt Congress to repeal the national origins quotas in 1965 and adopt the 1980 Refugee Act, which regularized refugee and asylum criteria and procedures in the interest of equal treatment while preserving discretion to favor some countries and regions over others.

During the 1980s, even this ambivalent universalism was thrown into a headlong retreat. In the refugee area, where pre-1980 policies had expressly targeted certain geographic areas and political ideologies for special protection, favoritism was extended through administrative practices and statutory changes. Soviet Jews and Pentecostals, Salvadorans, Tibetans, and a few other groups with powerful patrons in Congress received special preference. Some favoritism is to be expected, of course, in any political system in which well-organized, cohesive interests enjoy special access and influence. Indeed, it is inescapable in a world in which the United States must decide each year which 130,000 or so of the roughly fifteen million refugees it will admit. A properly constrained favoritism may even be a legitimate instrument of a sound and moral foreign policy. Yet the facts that 74 percent of those approved for admission in 1990 came from two areas (the Soviet Union and Indochina),[146] that most of these remained in their own countries rather than having crossed international borders (an exceptional situation for relief under the Refugee Act), and that the vast majority of the world's refugees live in areas that are disfavored, remain troubling.

The source-country bias represented by the new transitional and permanent diversity programs and other country-specific benefits under the 1990 act[147] also demonstrates the continuing power of well-positioned special interests to shape policy on legal immigration. These programs may fairly be viewed as affirmative action programs for the favored groups, programs in which admission, social welfare benefits, and the power to bring family members here are the valuable prizes. Perhaps some members of Congress view source-country favoritism as a form of indirect compensation for those who claim to suffer "reverse discrimination" in domestic programs. Diversity programs, in this view, function as political safety valves, diffusing some resentment by earlier immigrant groups against the Asians and Hispanics who account for most recent immigration.[148] On the other hand, such programs might also engender bitter resentment among the new groups. They might see diversity programs as a continuation and magnification of the effects of earlier, long discredited racist and nativist policies, and they might therefore agitate for new provisions that, in the guise of redressing an injustice to them, would perpetuate an injustice on others. If the history of immigration policy teaches us anything, it is that *any* system of limited admissions discriminates against *some* nationality groups. The playing field cannot be made perfectly level.

CONCLUSION

An important political question remains: What is the relationship between the beleaguered universalistic ideal and the durability of the political coalition that produced the 1990 act? If the 1990 act was a marriage of convenience among a broad array of special interest advocates in which the diversity provisions were politically essential, as Bruce Morrison thinks, its enactment may not in fact demonstrate any long-term public commitment to increased immigration. Instead, the 1990 act may simply reflect a unique resolution of conflicting forces, a temporary truce owing more to the political dynamics of a particular logroll at a particular point in time than to any broad political consensus in favor of an expansionist future.

Few things in American politics, of course, are settled forever. Most settlements are precarious, established by coalitions whose political fortunes wax and wane with the contingencies of events, leadership, interests, and ideas. Immigration policy is no exception. Because it arouses powerful emotions, is sensitively linked to economic conditions, responds to the flux of ethnic group politics, and continually infuses into the polity newly naturalized voters seeking more immigrants like themselves, immigration engenders constant pressures for change. The events of the 1980s, culminating in the 1990 act, demonstrates just how rapidly these pressures can affect immigration politics and policy.[149]

But the power of the immigration reform impulse during the 1980s only deepens the mystery of why these pressures produced a highly expansionist result by 1990. The restrictionist road, along which U.S. immigration law had traveled for over six decades, well into the 1980s, again beckoned, yet this time it was not taken. Interests advocating ideals of restriction or homogeneity exerted countervailing pressures,[150] and the political environment was in some ways quite favorable to their cause. IRCA had not really closed the back door. Many Americans believed that the 1965 and 1980 reforms had opened the front door too wide and that the immigrants passing through it added relatively little economic value to society. A recession had begun and the Persian Gulf war impended. In the end, however, those who wanted fewer and similar immigrants lost while those who sought more and different ones won. The values of expansion and diversity prevailed over those of restriction and homogeneity.[151] Although some existing policies were reaffirmed (especially family unification), policy innovation was the order of the day.

Few political commentators in 1980 would have predicted such an outcome within a decade. Indeed, it is no easy thing to explain even after the fact. The phenomenon of rapid and radical policy change adopted by institutions and actors that ordinarily prefer continuity remains a fascinating intellectual puzzle.[152] Important clues to that puzzle, I have argued, can be found in new and renovated ideas about immigration and its role in American life.

That political entrepreneurs and special interests exploited these ideas for their own policy ends is hardly remarkable, but this did not render the ideas epiphenomenal; they were not simply markers in a game in which the "real" stakes were elsewhere. Rather, these ideas helped to form an agenda, define the terms of debate, and structure the conflict. They possessed independent political significance—and for us, explanatory power.

Whether all of these ideas prove to be sound, and whether the policies they produced will endure, are of course questions for future historians.[153] What today's scholar can say with some confidence is that the course of U.S. immigration politics in the 1980s reveals a society that takes new ideas ever more seriously.

5

Reform Continues:
1990–1998

To hear some immigration advocates tell it, Americans in the 1990s have slammed the golden door shut in a fit of xenophobic hysteria, bolting it against newcomers and expelling many long-resident, law-abiding aliens. *New York Times* columnist Tony Lewis recounts almost weekly a new horror story of INS bungling or cruelty. The hapless agency, which is required to implement even foolish or unjust congressional mandates, gives Lewis plenty of ammunition. For example, the INS seeks to deport immigrants who have committed minor, long-forgotten crimes in their youth but have since led blameless lives. It forces long-resident illegal aliens who are about to receive legal visas to leave the country so that they will not be barred from reentering later. It summarily excludes aliens whose documents may be perfectly valid if an inspector doubts their authenticity. Prominent academics publish a book entitled *Immigrants Out! The New Nativism and the Anti-Immigrant Impulse in the United States*. Amnesty International lumps an attack on American policies together with its critique of dictatorships. Ethnic advocacy groups like the Mexican American Legal Defense and Education Fund depict U.S. immigration policy as nativist and brutal.

Fortunately, this is a false picture; indeed the opposite is more nearly true. America's immigration policy is more generous, color-blind, and politically durable (barring an economic crisis) than ever before. Restrictionists constantly assail this policy but succeed in hitting only the easy targets: undocumented aliens, visa violators, and criminals. And even most of these still manage to elude INS enforcement and remain in the country.

Americans have complex, nuanced ideas about immigration. They value their country's ethnic diversity, honor their immigrant tradition, and admire the immigrants they know personally. However, they also want to admit fewer legal immigrants, steadfastly oppose illegal ones, and do not want any of them on the public dole. Politicians who favor more immigration must somehow allay these anxieties, so they promise to keep out illegal aliens, prevent legal ones from abusing the system, and hold the line on numbers. Since these are difficult promises to keep, those who favor current immigration levels are always fighting an uphill battle, and any victories they achieve are vulnerable to populist attacks.

Given this public ambivalence, U.S. immigration policies often seem inconsistent. But though they may seem schizoid, they are not anti-immigrant. In 1996, for example, Congress made it easier to deport illegal aliens quickly and without court review, and ended public benefits for many legal immigrants. But in that same year, it also admitted the largest, most ethnically diverse group of new immigrants since 1914; it rejected restrictionists' efforts to cut back on admissions (while raising sponsors' income requirements); and it also greased the skids for legalizing over 400,000 undocumented aliens from Central America—and thousands more from Haiti, if President Clinton has his way.

Recent immigration history reflects this pattern. In 1965 the United States admitted fewer than 300,000 immigrants (roughly the number admitted fifteen years earlier); the vast majority were whites from Europe and Canada. That same year, Congress replaced the racist national origins quotas, which dated from the 1920s, with a system emphasizing family and employment ties. The new law literally transformed the complexion of U.S. immigration. By 1980, most legal immigrants came from Asia, Africa, Latin America, and the Caribbean; illegal entrants came primarily from Mexico; while most, entering legally and then violating the terms of their visas, came from Ireland and eastern Europe. In 1980 almost 500,000 Cuban, Haitian, and other illegal aliens, aided by the new Refugee Act, gained a foothold in the United States through a new asylum process that helped them resist deportation and often work legally while their claims languished in legal limbo. By 1986 the Border Patrol was arresting over 1.7 million each year; 5 to 6 million remained in the United States, with more than 200,000 new undocumented immigrants swelling this underground population each year. The chronically understaffed, incompetent INS careened from crisis to crisis.

In this political tinderbox, Congress played an intricate, confusing kind of good cop, bad cop game. While it attacked immigrant marriage fraud and barred firms from hiring the undocumented, it also legalized 2.7 million long-resident illegal aliens. In 1988 it moved against the growing number of criminal aliens, allowing the INS to quickly deport "aggravated felons," a new and elastic category. Yet in 1990 Congress adopted an expansive new system increasing legal admissions to 50 percent above the pre-amnesty level. This law, the Immigration Act of 1990, also mandated new "diversity" visas for groups excluded by the 1965 law (though most of these same groups had benefited from the old national origins quotas), eased controls on alien workers, and limited the INS's power to deport for ideological reasons. New INS rules treated asylum claims more liberally.

The 1990 law remains the centerpiece of U.S. legal immigration policy. It emerged from a potent pro-immigration coalition of business and grower interests, ethnic and human rights groups, political entrepreneurs, pro-immigration mass media, and other social elites. This legislative victory was especially impressive because the new law's advocates faced some unusual political obstacles in addition to the usual ones. The economy was in recession. Illegal immigration had returned to 1986 levels. Scarce public services were increasingly strained by the swelling ranks of newly amnestied aliens, mostly politically unpopular Mexicans. Media reports about the criminal aliens filling American prisons and stalking American streets caused public alarm. Europe, roiled by ugly nativism and fearful of mass influxes from eastern Europe and North Africa, was steadily tightening its already exclusionary policies, giving confidence—and a model—to American restrictionists. Still, the pro-immigration consensus forged in 1990 prevailed and has proved remarkably durable.

The first challenge to the new law came from Pat Buchanan's populist presidential campaign in 1992, which charged that the law betrayed U.S. sovereignty and threatened its political identity and ethnic cohesion. His efforts to exploit public fears about immigration to attack the North American Free Trade Agreement (NAFTA), however, attracted little support. In 1994, immigration became a central issue in high-immigration states like California. There, Governor Pete Wilson promoted Proposition 187, which aimed to bar illegal aliens from public schools and other state-funded social services, as a central motif of his reelection bid and presidential aspirations. Although Proposition 187's passage received enormous media attention, its political significance is hard to assess. The measure was aimed at illegal aliens, not legal ones, but proponents' subtly coded language (referring to illegals "flooding" the state) and provocative images (of opponents waving Mexican flags) surely obscured the distinction. Proposition 187, which has been a dead letter since a court has enjoined it, was supported not only by most white, black, and Asian voters but also by many Latinos who resented competition for jobs, housing, and public services by newcomers. Politicians in other states, emboldened by 187's electoral success, jumped on the bandwagon, although none of those movements achieved 187's success.

But while politicians run few risks in attacking undocumented and criminal aliens, they have found it harder to cut back on legal immigrants who enrich the economy or to deny them the public benefits that their taxes support. The politicians know that many of these immigrants will soon become voters and that some of their friends and relatives already are. For these reasons, the "Contract with America," which helped Republicans gain control of Congress in 1994, finessed the immigration issue. The GOP has been struggling without success to define a defensible party line on this issue.

When the new Congress convened in 1995, restrictionists in the California and Texas delegations swung into action. Lamar Smith, a Texas Republican who favored restriction, became chairman of the House immigration subcommittee and held hearings on proposals to cut back on admissions, end birthright citizenship for the U.S.-born children of illegal aliens, and strengthen INS enforcement against undocumented, out-of-status, and criminal aliens.

Although these initiatives attracted some Democratic support, they inflamed tensions within the GOP. Restrictionists cited the popularity of Proposition 187, the effect of high immigrant fertility rates on environmental and demographic conditions, welfare abuses by aliens, multicultural excesses, and the criminal alien problem, in support of their proposals. But Jack Kemp, William Bennett, William Kristol, and other party strategists argued that restrictionism was a political dead end that violated the party's deep commitment to free markets, economic growth, entrepreneurial energy, and social optimism. House Speaker Newt Gingrich spoke glowingly of immigrants' contributions to American society, Senate Majority Leader Richard Armey insisted that America could never have enough good immigrants, and Texas Governor George Bush praised them as economic assets. These Republican leaders contended that forward-looking realpolitik also argued against restrictionism. Just as the party's militant anticommunism had once attracted the support of Cubans and immigrants from the former Iron Curtain countries, a pro-immigrant image could secure future political gains with entrepreneurial Asians, refugees from Latin American conflicts, and other ethnics drawn to Republican ideals, rather than pushing these voters into the Democrats' waiting arms.

These arguments fell on deaf ears. Goaded by the Federation for American Immigration Reform (or FAIR, a lobbying group led by activists in the labor, English-language, population control, and environmental movements), many restrictionists saw new political opportunities in Clinton's unpopular fiscal bailout of Mexico, the apparently relentless surge of illegal migration across the country's southern border, criminal aliens in the cities, and the use of public benefits by many aliens at a time when even the president was calling for radical welfare reform. Buchanan's nativist appeals early in the 1996 presidential campaign widened these Republican divisions. In April, national outrage over the Oklahoma City bombing prompted an immediate, bipartisan, and ham-handed response from Congress: the Anti-Terrorism and Effective Death Penalty Act of 1996 (AEDPA). Lifting various items from the reform bills then percolating through the immigration subcommittees, Congress enacted many tough enforcement provisions, including secret deportation tribunals for suspected terrorists. (Ironically, the bombers turned out to be Americans from the heartland.) The AEDPA mandated swift detention and removal of criminal and illegal aliens and of those who could be even tenuously linked to terrorist groups. It also limited or ended traditional hardship waivers and appeal rights for certain alien categories and made many of these changes retroactive. These harsh rules, however, were anticriminal, not anti-immigrant. None was aimed at legal aliens who had not committed crimes in the United States.

Those who insist that America has turned its back on immigrants point to the 1996 welfare and immigration reforms. Even these laws, however, do not make the critics' case; they merely show that the appropriate balance between securing the advantages of expansive immigration without suffering the disadvantages is a difficult one to strike and that the United States has sometimes gotten it wrong. The welfare reform statute, which made many legal aliens ineligible for important public benefits, also cut the benefits of millions of *citizens*. Although immigrants in general did not receive means-tested benefits more than did demographically comparable Americans, some subgroups (e.g., elderly aliens on Supplemental Security Income, or SSI) received them at much higher rates. Many voters objected to benefits for aliens not out of anti-immigrant animus but because immigrants arrived under the explicit provision that they have jobs or citizen sponsors who promised to support them if and when necessary. It is neither nativist nor anti-immigrant to believe that poor citizens have a stronger claim to shrinking resources than immigrants who have been admitted on the condition that they not become "public charges." From this perspective, it was a fair and prudent compromise to use the large savings from alien ineligibility (especially since Clinton vowed to reverse them) to help preserve benefits for destitute U.S. citizens, although this priority would never satisfy immigrant advocates who rejected all citizen-alien distinctions (other than voting). In 1997, Congress restored many of the SSI and related benefits to those who were eligible under the earlier law and to the newly disabled. Moreover, President Clinton proposed in his January 1998 State of the Union message to restore the provision of food stamps to families with children. Meanwhile, New York, California, New Jersey, and other high-immigration states have filled some of the remaining gap with their own funds, thereby refuting the claims of many who predicted that immigrants were so politically friendless that the states, in a headlong "race to the bottom," would cut their benefits even more in the hope that they would leave.

The Illegal Immigration Reform and Immigrant Responsibility Act (IIRIRA), which Congress enacted quickly and with little debate, is another story. This statute is the most radical reform of immigration law in decades—or perhaps ever. It thoroughly revamps the enforcement process and extends the AEDPA in ways that even many INS officials find arbitrary, unfair, and unadministrable. For example, it requires the INS to exclude aliens at the border summarily and without judicial review if they seem to lack proper documentation. The IIRIRA makes asylum claiming more difficult and bars the INS from granting discretionary relief from deportation to many aliens even for compelling humanitarian reasons as the previous law permitted. It mandates the detention of many removable aliens—perhaps forever if they come from a country like Vietnam that refuses to take them back. It equates the rights of aliens who entered illegally and live in the United States with those of aliens with no ties in the United States. It limits the rights of illegal aliens to reenter legally. It further expands the category of "aggravated felon" aliens, who can be deported summarily even if they have been long-term residents of the country. It bars judicial review of INS decisions to deport them. (The definition of "aggravated felony" is now so broad that it includes almost all drug, weapons, and other nonpetty offences; it even covers subway fare beating.)

Much in this new law is harsh and unjust, will have perverse effects, and needs to be changed. To be sure, Congress was properly concerned about the endless procedural delays that illegal aliens (or their lawyers) have employed to prolong their stays while they work and search for a way to remain permanently through marriage, employment, amnesty, the visa lottery that Congress foolishly created, or by going underground if necessary. But fair, accurate adjudication, backstopped by access to the federal courts for those at risk of deportation, is essential not only to aliens but also to the many Americans with strong family, employment, religious, and social ties to them. These high stakes, along with a long tradition of INS lawlessness and incompetence that improved management has not yet eliminated, make judicially protected due process all the more necessary. (The agency's performance is so dismal that the U.S. Commission on Immigration Reform, chaired by the late Barbara Jordan, has proposed abolishing it altogether, allocating its tasks elsewhere.)

Procedural protection for aliens is not merely a sound policy prescription; the Constitution demands it. In a free society, officials who deprive individuals of personal liberty—as when they arrest, detain, and deport immigrants—must meet rigorous legal standards. For centuries, courts have ensured this legality through the "Great Writ" of habeas corpus, which requires officials with custody over an individual to appear promptly before a judge and show that the restraint on liberty is legally justified. The Suspension Clause of the Constitution preserves habeas corpus except in cases of rebellion or invasion. Congress has protected this right statutorily since 1789, and aliens have always used habeas corpus to challenge the legality of detention and deportation decisions. Most of the lower federal courts have so far interpreted the IIRIRA narrowly to maintain judicial review for aliens in INS custody; otherwise, the law would be unconstitutional. (No relevant IIRIRA or AEDPA case has yet reached the Supreme Court.) Law professor Lenni Benson sees an irony in this: The IIRIRA may induce the courts to intrude into immigration enforcement even more than before, as they defend their institutional and constitutional prerogatives and jurisdiction by confronting the more frequent abuses that the INS's new immunity from review surely encourages.

Some other IIRIRA provisions are also extreme and counterproductive. Eliminating the possibility of discretionary relief in hardship cases prevents the INS from making the humane, prudent adjustments that are often needed to respond to the diverse circumstances of aliens and the citizens to whom they relate. Such relief can also enable the agency to use its scarce enforcement resources most effectively and to avoid the severe public censure and embarrassment that the INS inevitably reaps when its absurdly and cruelly inflexible decisions are brought to light. The law's summary removal procedure for undocumented asylum claimants gives even the lowliest, most poorly informed inspector enormous discretion, and practically final say, over such life-and-death issues as whether the individual will face the risk of persecution if returned to his country of origin. Since the INS had recently instituted promising reforms in the asylum area, this radical statutory change may have been unnecessary as well as unwise.

But even the IIRIRA's recklessness and unfairness should not obscure a fundamental fact about immigration politics: Challenges to the high levels of *legal* immigration set in the 1990 law, such as the Jordan Commission's proposal to reduce legal admissions by more than one-third, have all failed. Tough on undocumented and criminal aliens, and arbitrary toward asylum seekers and deportation hardship cases, the IIRIRA has had only one serious effect on law-abiding immigrants: to raise their sponsors' income requirements. Indeed, Congress may soon increase the quota for high-skilled foreign workers.

Perhaps the best evidence of the strength of today's pro-immigration consensus lies in Congress's treatment of *illegal* aliens. Targeting them is the moral, political, and policy equivalent of motherhood and apple pie. Illegal aliens are, well, *illegal*. Whether surreptitious border crossers or visa violators (the INS estimates roughly equal numbers of each), they broke our law and have no right to be in the United States. Yet even here, the powerful pro-immigrant lobby has convinced Congress to let them remain. In addition to legalizing 2.7 million illegal immigrants in the late 1980s, Congress enacted a new amnesty in November 1997 for some 400,000 more, these from Central America. At the same time, it grandfathered in still other illegal aliens under a now-lapsed provision allowing them to gain permanent residence simply by paying a $1,000 fee and filing their green cards in the United States, relieving them even of the inconvenience of going home to apply for U.S. admission. But American ambivalence (if not hypocrisy) about illegal immigration is even more pronounced than this. The same politicians who have now bestowed amnesty on more than three million illegal aliens have also enlarged the Border Patrol until it is now the federal government's largest domestic uniformed service. The same legislators who denounce the INS for incompetence have doubled its budget in the last four years, making it one of the fastest-growing agencies in government; yet the agency (according to a recent General Accounting Office [GAO] report) still has no formal management plan to evaluate its multi-billion-dollar enforcement program.

Even convicted criminal aliens enjoy a perverse kind of protection. Unlike illegal aliens, they have no political sponsors at all, yet they manage to remain in the United States in large numbers—*even when they are already under lock and key and thus should be easy to deport*. Although aliens in general are apparently less crime-prone than citizens, the criminal alien population has nevertheless soared. In 1980, fewer than 1,000 federal inmates were foreign-born, 3.6 percent of the total. By 1996, the numbers had grown to almost 31,000 (29 percent of the total). The foreign-born population in state prisons has also risen from 8,000 in 1980 (2.6 percent) to 77,000 (7.6 percent) in 1996. Foreign-born individuals account for an estimated 21 percent of California's prisoners and 13 percent of New York's. Nationwide, 300,000 or more deportable criminal aliens are in custody or under other legal supervision—almost ten times as many as in 1980—at an estimated cost of $6 billion a year. Despite a high-priority INS effort to deport these criminals, the agency managed to remove only 50,000 of them in 1997, fewer than 15 percent of those in custody or under supervision. The real scandal is that this figure actually represents a major improvement for the agency over previous years. The INS's slow progress in deporting criminal aliens caused Congress in the IIRIRA to adopt extreme remedies such as mandating the detention and removal of all criminal aliens and barring them from seeking discretionary hardship relief, judicial review, or subsequent readmission. Even if these new rules survive challenges in the courts, however, the INS cannot effectively implement them unless it can obtain more detention space and deportation officers and can induce closer cooperation from the local law enforcement agencies on whom it must depend to process criminal aliens.

Recent immigration trends have presented restrictionists with much political ammunition for their struggle to reduce admissions, especially of nonwhites. For example, illegal immigration continues at very high levels and even legal immigrants are more numerous and racially, linguistically, and religiously heterogeneous than ever before—and more so in the United States than anywhere else in the world (though Canada admits more immigrants per capita). Of the ten top source countries, only Jamaica sends predominantly English-speaking immigrants, so urban school systems must educate students who speak dozens of languages for which teachers cannot readily be found. Bilingual education has become a major curricular and fiscal battleground, as evidence mounts that many costly programs actually retard English fluency. About half the states have established English as their official language; some, like California, have also tried to limit illegal aliens' access to public schools. The politicization of ethnicity and attacks on the traditional assimilative ideal have aggravated long-standing anxieties about what Arthur Schlesinger (an emblematic liberal and surely no nativist) calls the "disuniting of America." The affirmative action debate has been sharpened by the anomaly that newcomers who never suffered discrimination in the United States compete for preferences with already beleaguered descendants of African Americans who were slaves. Immigration probably accounts for a significant share of the widening wage gap between high- and low-skill workers, especially blacks. Even citizenship has come under a cloud. Federal indictments allege the falsification of over 13,000 naturalization exams, and the GAO reports that taxpayers bear significant public costs because U.S.-born children of illegal aliens are automatic birthright citizens entitled to all government benefits.

Despite these political opportunities, the restrictionists have failed to dislodge the high immigration status quo. The feisty Republican debate over immigration seems particularly favorable to its continuation. Conservative flirtations with restrictionist and even nativist rhetoric have proved to be internally divisive, perhaps even suicidal. Laws like California's Proposition 187 have made little headway in other states. In Los Angeles, New York, and other immigrant cities, successful Republican politicians are appealing to first- and second-generation Asians and Hispanics. On balance, they gain more votes by supporting legal immigration. Many of the party's corporate allies, especially high-tech companies that depend on skilled foreign-born workers, are pressing Congress to admit more of them, and the Republican chairman of the Senate immigration subcommittee, Spencer Abraham, has introduced legislation to accomplish this, which is also supported by Lamar Smith, his more restrictionist counterpart in the House. Many Republicans see that the social conservatism, upward mobility, and entrepreneurial spirit of many immigrant groups may attract them to the GOP.

As the majority party in Congress, the Republican Party is the arena in which American ambivalences over immigration policy are being debated and politically resolved. The results have been good, bad, and sometimes ugly. But even liberal groups exhibit this ambivalence, as evidenced by the fight within the Sierra Club and labor unions over whether or not to support restriction. For advocates of moderate legal immigration (and I am one), the best way to sustain the pro-immigration consensus is not to idealize all immigrants as ethnic Horatio Algers but to attend to legitimate concerns about criminal and undocumented aliens, visa violators, naturalization fraud, welfare abuse, bilingual education, affirmative action, and unfair competition for low-income domestic workers. We should decry the new laws' excesses while celebrating Americans' openness to self-supporting, law-abiding newcomers who don't demand special breaks. And we should stop crying wolf about nativism.

6

The Message of Proposition 187:
Facing Up to Illegal Immigration

The latest earthquake out of California is political, not seismic. The reverberations of Proposition 187, the anti–illegal immigrant initiative on the state's November 1994 ballot, have already registered high on the Richter scales in state capitals and in Washington, where politicians see that Pete Wilson's firm identification with Proposition 187 was largely responsible for his sweeping reelection victory. The law's aftershocks are even unsettling Europe, where leaders in almost every country face their own immigration crises, desperately seek solutions, and often look to U.S. experience for guidance.

Is Proposition 187 a firebell in the night (as was said of the *Dred Scott* decision), warning of imminent civil conflict? Or is it instead just a flash in the pan, one more California exotic that flourishes in that state's unique climate but fails to take firm root elsewhere? Proposition 187, I believe, lies somewhere in between. It is less a spasm of nativist hatred than an expression of public frustration with a government and civil society that seem out of touch and out of control, and with external convulsions that America's borders can no longer contain. Although the alarms that motivated Proposition 187 are exaggerated and widely misunderstood, the law is nevertheless a warning—a primal scream, as one political commentator called it—to all of those who are friends of immigration and have slumbered in the wistful hope that illegal residents and the political problems that they create would, quite literally, go away.

I. JUSTICE BRENNAN'S LEGACY

Proposition 187 is a melange of different policies that seeks to stem the flow of illegal aliens into California, encourage the state's roughly 1.4 million illegal residents to go home, and expel those who do not leave voluntarily. The most controversial provisions would bar anyone who is not a citizen, legal permanent resident (green-card holder), or legal temporary visitor from receiving public social services, health care, and education. The provisions differ slightly for each service, but they generally impose three duties on all service providers: to verify the immigration status of all who seek services, to promptly notify state officials and the INS about whoever is "determined or reasonably suspected to be" violating the immigration laws, and to notify the alien (or in the case of children, their parent or guardian) of their apparently illegal status. Proposition 187 is no ordinary law; it provides that the legislature cannot amend it "except to further its purposes" and then only by a recorded supermajority vote in each house of the legislature or by another voter initiative.

As a practical matter, the parts of Proposition 187 that would deny public services may never be implemented. Immediately after voters approved it, immigrant advocate groups and some local officials filed a blizzard of legal challenges to the constitutionality of the heart of the measure's services denial and reporting provisions. (Since Proposition 187 provides that its sections are severable, some might survive even if others are struck down.) A federal judge immediately enjoined it pending trial, and most commentators believe that the courts will ultimately strike down some if not most of the measure.

But the legal challenge against Proposition 187 is not nearly as solid as many say. Indeed, a closer look at the relevant constitutional precedents suggests that the courts could uphold the law if they have a mind to do so.

The courts have long prohibited the states from discriminating against legal immigrants, largely on the grounds that the states' authority in this area is subordinate to the federal government's. But until recently, the courts had never addressed illegal immigration. It simply had not been a major issue.

That started changing about thirty years ago. INS arrests—a crude, unsatisfactory indicator of illegal entries—swelled from 1.6 million in the 1960s to 8.3 million in the 1970s, and then continued to rise in the early 1980s. When states and localities sought to protect their education and health care budgets by imposing restrictions on the newcomers' access to benefits, the courts could no longer duck the issue. In 1982, the Supreme Court decided *Plyler v. Doe,* a class-action suit brought on behalf of undocumented Mexican children living in Texas. Upholding the ruling of a lower court, a five-to-four majority struck down a statute that withheld from local school districts any state funds for the education of any child who had not been legally admitted into the United States.

The constitutional challenge to Proposition 187 rests mainly on this precedent. Writing for the *Plyler* majority, Justice William Brennan argued that the Texas law would inevitably harm children. These children would eventually obtain legal status in this country, yet would be "permanently locked into the lowest socioeconomic class." Brennan acknowledged that the state had some leeway in such matters: Under equal-protection principles, illegal alien status does not constitute a "suspect class" like race or religion, and education is not a "fundamental right." Hence, it did not require heightened judicial scrutiny. Nevertheless, Brennan said, a law that denied children "the ability to live within the structure of our civic institutions . . . can hardly be considered rational unless it furthers some substantial goal of the State."

Brennan conceded that keeping illegal aliens out of the state might be a legitimate state goal. But the trial court had found that the Texas law had neither the purpose nor the effect of doing that, and Brennan agreed. The Texas law might save some money, according to Brennan, but Texas had failed to establish that illegal aliens imposed a significant fiscal burden on state coffers or that their exclusion would improve the quality of education. Besides, Brennan said, federal immigration policy was not concerned with conserving state educational resources, much less with denying an education "to a child enjoying an inchoate federal permission to remain." (This referred to the possibility that an illegal alien might obtain discretionary relief from deportation.) All the Texas law would serve to do, Brennan said, was promote "the creation and perpetuation of a subclass of illiterates," who would be socially dysfunctional and a burden to society. That, he said, clearly was not something the states were allowed to do.

The parallels to Proposition 187 are obvious. Both would in effect bar undocumented children from the public schools; if anything, California's new ban on enrolling such children is even more categorical and rigid than the Texas statute invalidated by *Plyler,* which simply denied state funding to those who were enrolled. Any court that accepted Brennan's premises in *Plyler* would have a hard time sustaining Proposition 187.

II. Why the Court May Turn

Brennan's opinion, with its plea on behalf of "innocent children" and its recognition that many of these children will grow up in the United States anyway, has an undeniably powerful resonance. Yet Brennan's argument had its soft spots, including an unwarranted emphasis on the uniqueness of education benefits in justifying special constitutional protection for children. It is one thing to say that children should not be penalized for their parents' illegality. But Brennan never explained how the denial of schooling to a child differs from the denial of other governmental benefits to an undocumented parent, upon whose income and well-being the child's welfare ultimately depends. The Court has always permitted the government to deny undocumented parents access to the private employment and public benefits that provide their children's essential economic support, arguably harming the children (who may actually be U.S. citizens) even more grievously.

If a state may do that, why can't it deny those same children access to the schools? Does *Plyler* mean that a state may not exclude from public housing a family in which an adult has committed a serious crime? Is the Court's rationale consistent with the INS's clear power to deport the undocumented parents of children—children who not only had no role in their parents' wrongdoing but may be U.S. citizens themselves? In each of these cases, the child suffers because of the parent's illegal status, at least as much as under the Texas law.

A second weakness in Brennan's reasoning—his denial that the Texas law corresponded to any identifiable congressional policy or operated harmoniously within the federal program—has grown even more glaring in the post-*Plyler* years. Even in 1982, the federal policy against illegal aliens was clear enough: Illegal entry was a federal crime. Congress was spending more and more money to prevent it and had expressly barred illegal aliens from numerous federal benefit programs, and the Court had upheld California's own employer sanctions law on the ground that it was consistent with federal policy. Since then, Congress has implemented a much more comprehensive strategy of immigration enforcement. Post-*Plyler* measures include employer sanctions, severe penalties against smuggling and immigration marriage fraud, expedited deportation procedures for criminal aliens, streamlined asylum procedures, assistance to states in detecting welfare claims by illegal aliens, tighter visa screening, new enforcement technologies, and a huge funding increase for border control at a time when other agency budgets were frozen. As discussed in chapters 1 and 5, the 1996 immigration reform statute added still more enforcement authority. These changes have not been terribly effective. Eight years after Congress imposed employer sanctions, for example, illegal entries are back to the pre-1986 level (although they would almost certainly have been even higher had employer sanctions not been instituted). Other reforms have also yielded disappointing results.

Yet substantial effectiveness cannot be the touchstone of constitutionality; if it were, many public policies would probably be doomed. And what would be the benchmark of effectiveness to which the Court would compare the law being challenged? In effect, Brennan used the inherent difficulty of immigration control as a justification for making it even more intractable. He assumed that exclusion from the schools was a wholly ineffective way to influence migrants' behavior, yet it is surely true that at least some parents are less likely to immigrate if they know their children will be denied schooling. Illegal aliens always have alternatives: They can return home or refrain from coming in the first place. These options may seem harsh but they follow directly from the premise of national territorial sovereignty, a premise that the Court has always affirmed.

Subsequent developments may also invalidate the other cornerstone of Brennan's decision—the fact that Texas was unable to prove financial harm from illegal immigration. In California, 1.4 million illegal residents constitute 43 percent of the national total and account for nearly 5 percent of the state's own population. An Urban Institute study has provided the first objective assessment of how this concentration affects communities—an assessment that was not available when *Plyler* was decided. The study covered only three cost categories: education and emergency medical services to which illegal aliens are legally entitled and the costs of incarcerating those convicted of crimes. (One in five inmates in California state prisons is a deportable alien.) Those costs are substantial—about $1.75 billion a year in California alone. The study, moreover, did not include either the benefits that illegals fraudulently obtain or the other costs that they impose. Partly offsetting this $1.75 billion, the study estimated, is $732 million in revenues generated from sales, property, and income taxes on illegal aliens in California. (The fact that many illegal alien workers pay federal payroll taxes but do not claim Social Security benefits does little for California, although it certainly affects the overall calculus of the benefits and costs that they represent for the nation as a whole.) These arguments will become even stronger if the devaluation of the peso sends a new stream of Mexicans north.

Of course, the legal challenge to Proposition 187 does not rest entirely on the strength of Brennan's opinion; indeed, a decision to strike down the law could well rely on two other arguments.

First, while the federal government has moved to curb illegal immigrants, it has never cut off certain of their benefits, notably including public education in federally assisted schools and emergency Medicaid services. The courts could take this inaction to mean that Congress remains satisfied with *Plyler* and does not wish to undermine the decision's rationale.

Second, a court wishing to invalidate Proposition 187 could cite the many practical problems that implementation would present in order to show that the law is so irrational as to be unconstitutional. How, for example, will California school officials know whom to exclude? Federal law protects the privacy of any "personally identifiable information" in students' educational records and severely sanctions violations. (Immigration expert Wayne Cornelius predicts that if Proposition 187 is found to violate the privacy law, California could lose up to $15 billion in federal funds.) The Fourth Amendment bars officials from stopping and questioning people without having "a particularized, reasonable suspicion based on specific articulable facts." Neither skin color nor surname alone satisfies that test. So unless aliens volunteer their illegal status, due process principles almost surely require a hearing before the state may withdraw benefits previously granted. Much litigation would ensue.

Meanwhile, many U.S. citizens and legal aliens would get caught up in the dragnet, provoking an even worse political backlash than what is now generated by clumsy INS enforcement sweeps of shops and factories where many legal employees also work. The dragnet problem would also plague the many families in which some members have legal status and thus qualify for benefits whereas others are undocumented and do not. INS efforts to deport the undocumented members would trigger even more legal wrangling because existing immigration law provides several discretionary remedies that are designed to avoid precisely this kind of family-splitting and personal hardship.[1] Many service providers have also said that they will ignore the new law even if the Court upholds it. Hence, it is unlikely to be vigorously implemented.

The challenge to Proposition 187, then, could go either way. A court eager to invalidate the legislation could emphasize its resemblance to the law Brennan struck down in *Plyler*. Even a court uneasy with *Plyler's* rationale could stress Proposition 187's bluntness as a policy instrument for a problem largely outside California's constitutional authority. Only two of the *Plyler* dissenters, William Rehnquist and Sandra Day O'Connor, remain on the court; even if Antonin Scalia and Clarence Thomas joined them they might be unable to pick up a fifth vote.

But a court determined to uphold Proposition 187 by overruling *Plyler* or by distinguishing it away would at least have plausible grounds for doing so. Although justices are usually reluctant to overturn precedents, a standard argument against doing so—that the precedent has engendered legitimate expectations and stakes in the status quo—seems particularly weak because illegal aliens can have no legitimate expectations of remaining here, much less of receiving public benefits. The court could focus on the analytical soft spots in Brennan's "innocent children" logic, on the fact that today's federal policies against illegal aliens are far more comprehensive than they were when *Plyler* was decided, and on California's high costs of educating illegal alien children, costs that the federal government does little to help defray.

Moreover, this court could simply limit the new decision to its facts, invalidating Proposition 187's ban on basic schooling—thus preserving *Plyler*—while upholding its ban on social services, nonemergency health care, and higher education, as well as the reporting provisions. A court sympathetic to California's policy might also allow the state to repair some of the law's defects through narrowing regulations.

III. What Voters Were Saying

If Proposition 187 does survive the legal challenge, many other states—and perhaps the federal government—are likely to consider similarly restrictive measures. Virginia, for instance, recently required its schools to verify the legal status of all students over eighteen years of age enrolled in English as a Second Language programs, and of all students over twenty who entered the United States after the age of twelve, or risk losing some state funding.

It is tempting to dismiss this legislative impulse as mere nativism or racism, as so many on the left have done. But the anger behind Proposition 187 focused on illegals, not legal immigrants. Governor Pete Wilson took great pains to underscore that distinction on the campaign trail. In his advertisements and public statements, he praised legal immigrants' contributions to society while accusing the undocumented of taking jobs away from Californians and consuming scarce public services. (The precise magnitude of the adverse effects and the offsetting benefits generated by illegal aliens remain hotly contested issues that he failed to discuss.) A survey conducted by Ron Unz, Wilson's opponent in the primaries, found that most supporters of Proposition 187 were primarily motivated by perceived welfare dependency by undocumented immigrants—not by immigrants per se. A majority of Asians and blacks, plus nearly a third of Latinos—hardly a nativist coalition—voted for the measure. (In Texas, an even larger percentage of Latino voters indicated they would have supported such a measure had it been on the ballot in their state.)

Proposition 187, like the "official English" laws approved in California and elsewhere since the mid-1980s, was a symbolic message to policy elites. Both measures are grand gestures with few practical consequences other than to convince politicians that many voters now view American society as increasingly alien (literally) and uncontrollable. These voters responded angrily to the vivid television images of Mexican officials denouncing the measure and to the marchers in Los Angeles waving Mexican flags and protesting its limits on welfare benefits. On election day, the voters said that illegal immigrants, industrious as they may be, are part of the problem and that Proposition 187, crude as it is, is part of the solution. It is no solution, of course, but that only underscores the need for a sounder political response in order to forestall future initiatives of this kind.

This response should begin with the candid recognition by leaders that illegal immigration, even at current levels, is not an unmitigated evil and that immigration enforcement competes for resources with other social goals. Although it is hard for Americans to admit that they tolerate some lawbreakers as a matter of policy, the fact is that they do—and they always will. This is especially true when the illegal transactions are between consenting adults and arguably make everyone better off on balance. The United States is a large country with relatively low population densities even in the cities, and with a vast economy that needs more unskilled labor than domestic workers are willing to supply at current wage levels. The country can continue to assimilate a significant number of illegal aliens so long as the costs are not too high or too localized.

Granted, illegal aliens do impose a cost on society. But the cost may be lower than many critics say. Restrictionists stress the recession in California, but then what about the booms in places like Texas or South Florida? Labor economists are divided on many fundamental methodological and empirical questions: Is the low-wage labor market in which most illegal aliens work segmented or unitary? Are citizens and other legal workers displaced by illegal workers, or would they not accept the jobs and wages that illegal workers take? How many jobs do illegal aliens—who are producers and consumers—create? What are the long-term effects on the economy of retaining low-skill jobs rather than moving to more technologically advanced ones? Can labor market effects be assessed by examining a metropolitan area, or must we also examine illegal aliens' effects on legal workers who are discouraged from migrating to areas where illegal aliens are concentrated? Do illegal immigrants work at lower wages for the same work? (Most evidence suggests otherwise.) Their work and consumption enables all Americans to enjoy lower prices, better services, and a more efficient economy, at least in the short run. (Of course, the benefit-to-cost ratio favors those who live far from the enclaves in which illegal aliens are concentrated—those who need not compete with illegal aliens for public services and entry-level jobs.)

It is true that the absolute number of new immigrants, legal and illegal, has never been higher. But it is also true that the proportion of America's foreign-born population is lower than it was at the beginning of the twentieth century (9 percent versus 14 percent), and about half what it is in Canada today (about 16 percent). New immigrants' share of the U.S. population is far below the share in the high-immigration years prior to World War I. The vast majority of aliens who enter illegally are more or less seasonal migrants; only 300,000 a year become long-term residents, a number somewhat higher than the 200,000 American citizens and legal resident aliens who are estimated to leave the country each year to live elsewhere permanently. Many of the illegal aliens who remain will manage to obtain legal status by successfully obtaining asylum or persuading the INS to adjust their status.

Even if the government decided it wanted to eliminate illegal immigration completely, it could not do so. For almost a decade, the INS enforcement budget has grown at a more rapid rate than that of almost any agency in government. Yet illegal immigration has not fallen off (though it surely would have increased were it not for the increased INS funding). Americans could have expanded the border patrol line along the country's entire southern border shoulder to shoulder, but Congress has concluded, probably wisely, that these funds would be better spent on other things. Effective enforcement requires a secure national identity card, yet this would be costly, bitterly controversial, and perhaps technically unworkable.

To tighten the borders effectively, better consular and asylum screening would also be critical; half the illegal aliens enter on visas issued by U.S.

foreign service officers abroad and many others successfully exploit the procedurally complex asylum system. Low-level visa decisions, however, are notoriously difficult to make and hard to control, and the INS's brand-new asylum procedures remain untested—both in the field and in the courts. At Congress's insistence, deporting the estimated 300,000 criminal aliens now in federal and state prisons or under criminal justice supervision has become a top INS priority, but this too will require increased resources and sustained management attention, from an agency historically renowned for its incompetence.

Proposition 187 will probably reduce some migration, especially by women and their small children, who constitute a growing fraction of the illegal flow. But the enormous legal and practical obstacles to implementing laws like Proposition 187 will always limit their effectiveness. A vast, prosperous nation with strong due process and equal protection values and a 2,000-mile border with the Third World cannot eliminate illegal migration; it can only hope to manage it. America's leaders must tread this thin line.

IV. Do Outsiders Have Claims on America?

Even so, Proposition 187 insists that government need not provide public services for those illegal immigrants. Although the constitution protects illegals as "persons," Congress can exclude them from public education if it wishes—even though the states cannot unless Congress permits them to do so.

Such a move would be perverse. If U.S. enforcement policy "allows" illegal aliens to enter and remain long-term (but illegal) residents, then Brennan was surely right: There is little point, and even less justice, in consigning them to lives of ignorance, dependency, and discrimination by denying them education—a denial that would injure not only them but the American communities in which they will live and work. For much the same reason, they should also receive emergency medical care.

Beyond that, however, the moral claims of illegal aliens are much harder to justify. Most Americans doubt that illegal aliens have legitimate claims to public benefits such as Aid for Dependent Children (AFDC), food stamps, housing subsidies, and higher education. Whatever net financial burden illegal alien residents impose upon state and local governments should also be distributed more fairly. Although Washington has exclusive power to control the border and deport illegal aliens, the costs of federal enforcement failures fall on the states. The federal constitution now requires the states to provide illegal immigrants with public education, the most costly service, yet Congress pays only a minuscule fraction of the bill. Federal law mandates that legal and in some cases illegal aliens receive a host of other public benefits and services. But although states bear about two-thirds of the costs for such services, two-thirds of the taxes legal and illegal aliens pay go straight to Washington. This fiscal mismatch is even greater in the case of illegal aliens, who pay federal payroll taxes but claim relatively fewer benefits than legal aliens and citizens.

Calculating this imbalance will not be easy. Marginal benefits and costs are hard to measure and set off against one another. Remedying the imbalance may be even harder, given the experience with the old "impacted aid" program for communities with military installations and the more recent program to defray the state costs of the amnesty program for illegal aliens. Congress's new interest in unfunded mandates reflects less a desire to rectify intergovernmental inequities than a desperate search for budget savings; if the savings do not materialize, congressional enthusiasm in this area will quickly evaporate, leaving the states no better off. Still, even crude justice is better than none.

Congress is now considering proposals to reduce benefits for legal immigrants as well. In 1993 Congress limited Supplemental Security Income (SSI) benefits for low-income elderly legal aliens in response to a dramatic increase in claims. This affected almost 700,000 immigrants, 10 percent of the SSI caseload. Now, with the victory of Proposition 187, members of both parties have proposed even broader restrictions on benefits for legal immigrants. House Speaker Newt Gingrich calls himself "very pro legal immigration" and has criticized such proposals, as have GOP stalwarts Alan Simpson, Jack Kemp, and William Bennett.[2]

Proposals to deny legal aliens federal benefits raise a fundamental issue that Americans have avoided since the McCarthy era—the nature of membership in a liberal polity. Are legal permanent residents like taxpaying citizens who lack only the franchise? Or are they on probation, obliged to demonstrate good behavior and financial independence unless and until they naturalize? In its 1976 *Mathews v. Diaz* decision, the Supreme Court seemed to endorse the "probation" model, broadly upholding Congress's power to discriminate between citizens and all (or only some) aliens in distributing public benefits. In general, however, Congress has tended to treat all legal resident aliens like full members in most important respects, including benefits.

To be sure, circumstances have changed since *Diaz*. Immigration (legal and illegal) and public benefits (especially education, health care, and SSI) have grown enormously. Welfare receipt by some legal immigrant groups, including refugees from Indochina and immigrants from the Dominican Republic, is very high and often long term. To produce a hoped-for $22 billion in savings over five years, Congress would not even have to pass a new law; the federal government could enforce an existing but rarely used law that requires the U.S. relatives of family-based immigrants to make good on pledges of financial support for the immigrants.[3]

But as with Proposition 187, the savings from excluding legal aliens may prove illusory. Many Indo-Chinese refugees, for example, combine low education and few skills with strong political claims to at least temporary assistance. Even if cutting off federal benefits would save Washington some money, the states will have to fill much of the gap; the Supreme Court has ruled that it cannot discriminate against legal residents without congressional approval. State general assistance programs constitute the final safety nets for indigents who are ineligible for federal benefits, and cuts in federal benefits will drop some legal permanent immigrants into those nets. These federal cuts could also have the unintended effect of encouraging legal permanent residents to naturalize quickly to protect their access to benefits. Although increased naturalization is highly desirable, it will dissipate the savings that Congress seeks.[4]

V. Elusive Candor

Proposition 187, in its most important provisions, constitutes perverse public policy that has come at a politically propitious moment. Responsible leadership should recognize the practical and moral arguments against these provisions and should concentrate on setting immigration limits that Americans are prepared to enforce.

But from where will such candor come? Certainly not from the likes of California Governor Wilson. During the debate over the Immigration Reform and Control Act of 1986 (IRCA), which enacted employer sanctions and legalized over 2 million undocumented workers, then-Senator Wilson held the fragile legislative compromise hostage until he won approval for programs increasing the number of "temporary" farmworkers available to California's growers. By ensuring that the agricultural amnesty and guest worker programs were so open-ended that the INS could not prevent widespread fraud, Wilson enabled hundreds of thousands of undocumented workers to enter and work in the state. Although most of them are now legalized, they were subsequently joined by their spouses and children who are and will presumably remain illegal for some time and who are major consumers of the public services that Wilson sought to limit under Proposition 187.

Only ten days after Proposition 187 was approved, Wilson reverted to his 1986 ways by proposing to the Heritage Foundation that still more "temporary" workers be imported to harvest California's crops. Wilson surely knows that Proposition 187 could have dire practical consequences for his state, and he may secretly hope that an activist court will rescue him by striking it down. Reliance on such a judicial deus ex machina exposes the ideological expediency of many court-bashing conservatives of Wilson's stripe.

In truth, some immigration advocates haven't been much more forthright. After working tirelessly and effectively to stymie INS enforcement, they now express wonder and dismay when the public demands swift, heavy-handed responses to this complex problem. They insist that aliens who enter surreptitiously should be called "undocumented" rather than "illegal" because their legal status remains uncertain for months or years during which the aliens can usually obtain work permits—an uncertainty that is largely the product of the advocates' own skillful manipulations of an increasingly vulnerable administrative system.

As long as policy elites continue to evade realities and responsibilities, restrictive measures such as Proposition 187 will flourish. But misguided though such measures are, they do have at least one salutary effect: forcing Americans to consider anew what it means for the United States to be a nation of immigrants at a time when the core values of legality, national sovereignty, and self-reliance are under extraordinary pressures from within and without.

PART FOUR

Citizenship
and Community

In a sense, virtually all of immigration law and policy can be viewed as an effort to implement one or another vision of citizenship. Each of them instantiates a distinctive conception of the liberal political community by defining the nature of membership, the criteria for attaining and losing it, and the rights and obligations of citizens toward each other and toward the various categories of nonmembers ("strangers" and "in-betweens").

Two transformations of the dominant vision of American citizenship have occurred since the early 1960s, when the law reflected the traditional view of citizenship, closely aligned with the classical conception of immigration law elaborated in Chapter 2. This traditional conception allowed the federal and state governments to treat citizens and aliens differently in important respects. Beginning in the late 1960s, Congress and the Supreme Court moved to embrace a more egalitarian vision in which those differences (at least if imposed by state governments) became constitutionally suspect. An important consequence of narrowing these differences was to "devalue" the status of citizenship in the eyes of many Americans by making it easier to acquire and harder to lose and by reducing the distinctive advantages associated with that status. This is the subject of Chapter 7, which was written in 1989. More recently, however, Congress has responded to public anxieties about this and other developments by seeking to "revalue" citizenship through a variety of measures designed to reinvigorate its meaning and content. These measures include permitting and in some cases mandating discrimination against aliens. Chapter 8 analyzes this cycle of devaluation and reevaluation.

Chapter 9 considers a traditional element of U.S. citizenship law—birthright citizenship—in one of its most controversial applications. This chapter, which is an abbreviated version of my coauthored 1985 book, *Citizenship Without Consent: Illegal Aliens in the American Polity,* explores the deep tension between the distinctive (though not unique) *jus soli* rule, which confers automatic citizenship on those born on American soil without regard to their legal status, and the principle that a liberal democratic polity must be constituted through the consent of its members. In a society that celebrates the rule of law and seeks to discourage illegal immigration through increasingly severe measures, the practice of giving birthright citizenship to the U.S.-born children of illegal aliens raises this tension to an acute level. These are individuals, after all, whose very presence violates American law and whose parents may legally be deported. On the other hand, the desire to avoid creating a hereditary class of illegal outcasts, many of whom will grow up in the United States and perhaps spend their entire lives there, demands recognition as well. Hence the dilemma.

To many who are concerned about the devaluation of citizenship, the practice of dual citizenship—according to which an American citizen may hold citizenship in another polity—epitomizes the problem by diluting the dual citizen's commitment to American society and creating divided loyalties. For a number of legal, political, and demographic reasons, dual (and even triple) citizenship has become more common and became even more so in March 1998 when a new Mexican law went into effect permitting Mexican citizens to naturalize in the United States without thereby relinquishing their Mexican nationality and facilitating their reacquisition of Mexican nationality if previously lost. Chapter 10 develops the arguments for and against a liberal policy permitting plural citizenships, concluding with a proposal for a change in the renunciation oath required of naturalizing citizens that more accurately reflects the limited risks of conflicting loyalties created by plural citizenships today.

7

The Devaluation of
American Citizenship

Citizenship, Alexander Bickel wrote, "is at best a simple idea for a simple government."[1] His point was that full membership in the American political community has been widely and easily available at least since the 14th Amendment was adopted, and that the nature of this inclusive citizenship—in particular, the legal rights and obligations attached to that status—has long ceased to be an important or divisive public issue. There is merit in Bickel's observation; indeed, it is probably truer today than in 1973 when he made it. For United States citizenship—relative to most other countries and to earlier periods in American history—is notably easy to obtain, difficult to lose, and confers few legal or economic advantages over the status of permanent resident alien.

This pattern is entirely consistent with the philosophical premises of the American polity. The same liberal ethos that has dominated political institutions in this country has also profoundly shaped the legal, political, and social significance of citizenship. Liberalism's influence reflects the generative force in American life of three fundamental principles. The "equality principle" established a strong presumption that government must treat alike all individuals who are similarly situated. The "due process" principle requires the government to deal fairly with all individuals over whom it exercises coercive power. The "consent principle" emphasizes that political membership must be grounded in a continuing consensual relationship between the state and its citizens.

In this essay, I contend that the distinctive meaning of American citizenship, as revealed by the distinctive rights and obligations it entails, has been transformed in recent decades by a public philosophy that is steadily expanding the equality and due process principles in the pursuit of liberal values. These changes have reduced almost to the vanishing point the marginal value of citizenship as compared to resident alien status. These changes have not only minimized the alien's incentive to naturalize; they have also altered the social significance of citizenship.[2] From the points of view of the society and of aliens, these developments have been quite consistent with the consent principle.

Sections I, II, and III explore how the equality, due process, and consent principles have evolved in ways that devalue citizenship. Section IV seeks to appraise this development. The discussion assumes throughout that the United States possesses not only a legal right but also a moral justification to limit the right to enter its territory and to participate fully in its political life.[3] Although this premise can be contested on a number of grounds,[4] such arguments are outside the scope of this essay.

I. The Equality Principle

From the Republic's earliest days, American citizenship was relatively easy to acquire, at least for white men.[5] It was first defined constitutionally in the 14th Amendment, ratified in 1868. That Amendment was primarily intended to overrule the Supreme Court's infamous *Dred Scott* decision[6] and enfranchise the newly freed blacks. In its first sentence (the "Citizenship Clause"), the Amendment conferred citizenship upon "all persons born in the United States and subject to the jurisdiction thereof,"[7] virtually universalizing citizenship for persons born on American soil.[8, 9] The statutory prerequisites for naturalization are also readily satisfied and have been liberally construed by the courts,[10] and the political process reinforces the easy access to citizenship that the law protects.[11]

For present purposes, however, it is the 14th Amendment's Equal Protection Clause[12] that is chiefly of interest. That clause (and the body of civil rights legislation that implements it) is the fountainhead of the equality principle. In its most general formulation that principle holds that government may not arbitrarily or irrationally classify people and that in adopting legislative or administrative distinctions among people, it must treat alike all persons who are similarly situated.

Beneath the grandeur and simplicity of the equality principle, however, lie three deep tensions that have important implications for the meaning of American citizenship. First, the equality principle is empty in an important sense; while affirming that like situations must be treated alike, it fails to supply any criteria of relevant differences, criteria that might tell us *in what respects* government may legitimately take differences among people into account.[13] Since no two situations are identical, the equality principle raises a recurring question: which differences between situations or between people justify differential treatment? This question converts the principle into a battleground for competing norms that purport to provide an answer to it.

This problem is especially acute when government seeks to treat citizens and aliens differently, for citizens are by definition full members of the polity while aliens, also by definition, are not.[14] At the same time, a society that respects and celebrates individual freedom accords certain basic rights to all persons simply by virtue of their humanity, without regard to their contingent statuses.[15] Without a coherent theory of relevant differences, however, the equality principle cannot bridge the vast gulf between these two positions.

The second tension is between majoritarianism and minority rights. The equality principle constrains the constitutional power of majorities by limiting the kinds of distinctions that they may make in the rules they adopt. No political system based on the consent of the governed can endure if majorities consistently fail to get their way. Yet just as clearly, no system committed to the liberal value of individual freedom can consistently subordinate minorities' vital interests to the majority's untrammeled will. American constitutionalism manages this conflict in a number of ways—through a constitutional structure that fragments and limits majority power, a bill of rights enforced by an independent judiciary, political and religious traditions of tolerance and accommodation, and a diverse private sector that provides market and nonprofit alternatives to governmentally imposed uniformity. But the basic tension remains, and it is especially great in the area of aliens' rights. There, the citizens who control the political process are permitted to make decisions that profoundly affect the interests of noncitizens. Yet the latter not only constitute a minority and thus are politically subordinate to begin with;[16] they are denied the vote altogether.

The third tension is between the values of equality and liberty. Although the American polity cherishes both values, they conflict in fundamental ways. Where liberty (at least in the negative form stressed by classical liberalism)[17] is the principal value, inequalities of wealth, status, and opportunity are certain to flourish. But when government seeks to attack these inequalities by mandating substantive equality, some persons' liberties must inevitably be limited. This is most obviously true when the goal is economic equality, which can only be created and then maintained (if at all) through constant governmental intervention. But the tension also persists when other forms of equality are pursued. Citizenship issues sharply implicate this tension because aliens (especially undocumented ones) tend to be disadvantaged with regard to wealth, education, mastery of English, or other socially valued resources whose cumulative effects upon well-being are great.[18]

American law has approached these three tensions in a characteristically pragmatic and theoretically messy way. It seeks to provide the equality principle with a theory of relevant differences by requiring governments to justify any legally imposed disadvantages; how demanding these justifications must be in order to pass judicial muster depends upon the nature of the disadvantaged group. Alienage classifications, in particular, must be more than merely rational; generally, they must be justified by a "compelling governmental interest," one that could not be secured by a more carefully tailored classification.[19] In the area of citizenship policy, this equal protection approach to the liberty-equality tension has two important implications. First, birthright and naturalized citizens must be treated alike.[20] Second, citizens and legal resident aliens must be treated alike in most respects (e.g., access to public services),[21] although discrimination continues to be permitted in certain limited areas (e.g., access to certain public jobs).[22]

The equality principle, then, extends to legal resident aliens almost all of the significant rights and obligations that attach to American citizenship.[23] Five remaining disadvantages, however, are worth noting. Although none of these is trivial, only two of them are likely to interfere seriously with the quality of life or opportunity of many aliens.[24]

Three exceptions to the equality principle are political in nature; they involve the right to vote, the right to serve on juries, and the rights to run for certain high elective offices and to be appointed to some high (and not-so-high) administrative positions. Each of these restrictions seems to be premised on one or more of the following assumptions: that aliens' political socialization is too fragmentary and embryonic to be trusted in matters of public choice; that confining political participation of this kind to citizens carries an important symbolic message about the value and significance of full membership; and that exclusion of aliens from such participation encourages them to naturalize as soon as possible. It is not obvious that these propositions are correct, nor does it follow that even if they were correct they would justify the kinds of restrictions being imposed. Modern tradition and political inertia, more than sound policy, account for their durability.[25]

Although aliens enjoyed the franchise in many states during the 19th century,[26] only U.S. citizens may exercise it today. This restriction certainly limits the political influence of aliens as a collectivity and as members of smaller national or ethnic groups with distinctive political identities and interests, but it is unlikely to be of great concern to an individual alien.[27] Service on federal and many state juries is also withheld from aliens,[28] but the practical consequences of this exclusion seem slight; indeed, many citizens regard such service as a burdensome chore of which they would just as soon be relieved. (It is, after all, commonly called "jury *duty*.")

Limitations on aliens' access to government employment present a somewhat more complex pattern. I see no merit in denying voters or elected officials the opportunity to place aliens in the kind of high elective or appointive offices from which the law sometimes bars them regardless of their ability. As a practical matter, however, few of them are likely to seek such positions. But the same cannot be said of aliens' exclusion from all federal civil service positions[29] and from many state government jobs that are thought to involve a "political function."[30] At a time of growing public employment, these restrictions impose a far more onerous burden on aliens, and presumably affect a significant number of individuals.

A fourth important disadvantage for many aliens concerns their lesser ability to reunite with their family members who wish to come to the United States for permanent residence. Citizens are entitled to a preferred immigration status for their "immediate relatives"[31] without regard to numerical quotas, and for their siblings and their adult children under the numerical quota system. In contrast, the spouses and unmarried children of resident aliens qualify for only a numerically limited preference,[32] and their siblings receive no preference at all.

The other important inequality concerns the right to remain here. Citizens, whether through birthright or naturalization, are not subject to deportation,[33] but resident aliens are. The deprivations that deportation of a long-term resident can wreak upon aliens and their families and friends are potentially enormous. Although the Supreme Court has repeatedly stated that deportation is not punishment and therefore does not implicate the constitutional guarantees that surround the imposition of criminal sanctions,[34] there can be no question that, as Justice Douglas put it, deportation "may deprive a man and his family of all that makes life worthwhile."[35]

My point, then, is certainly not that deportation is inconsequential. It is that an individual alien's actual risk of deportation is far lower than might be suggested by the numerous grounds for deportation[36] and the INS's broad discretion in interpreting and applying them. The reason why this risk is now so low can be found in the recent evolution of the "due process" principle.

II. The Due Process Principle

The due process principle, established by the 5th and 14th Amendments to the Constitution, requires government to observe high standards of procedural fairness in adjudicating rights. This principle sharply constrains governmental efforts to deport resident aliens who might otherwise be eligible for citizenship or to regulate the acquisition and loss of the citizenship status itself. In that sense, it diminishes the urgency of naturalization and thus shapes the incentives for, and the social significance of, American citizenship.

Although the immigration statute contains numerous grounds for deportation, a resident alien who does not engage in patently criminal behavior actually faces almost no risk of being expelled. Aliens facing possible deportation can invoke extensive procedural safeguards established by statute, regulation, and judicial practice.[37] In fact, the government obviously finds it difficult to deport legal resident aliens (as distinguished from those who entered illegally or violated their visa restrictions). Statistically speaking, deportation of legal resident aliens is quite rare; the risk that a long-term resident alien who has not been convicted of a serious crime will be deported appears to be vanishingly small.[38] As a practical and legal matter, the right of such an alien to remain in the United States is almost as secure as a citizen's.

The due process principle affects the value of American citizenship even more directly than through limitations on deportation of aliens. I have already emphasized that as a matter of law, citizenship can be acquired relatively easily. Equally important, United States citizenship, once acquired, is also almost impossible to lose without the citizen's consent. Supreme Court decisions since the 1960s have severely restricted the government's power to denaturalize a citizen for reasons of disloyalty, divided allegiance, or otherwise. Today, the government cannot prevail against a birthright citizen unless it can prove that the citizen specifically intended to renounce his or her citizenship.[39]

The due process principle has made this standard difficult to satisfy—as it should be. Relatively few denaturalization proceedings are brought and the number of successful ones appears to be declining.[40] Denaturalization proceedings against citizens who procured citizenship by misrepresenting their backgrounds or through other illegality are largely directed against Nazi and Soviet persecutors, and the standards that the government must satisfy to prevail have become more demanding.[41] Dual citizenship, although still disfavored by the government, is legally protected (except when a foreign national seeks naturalization in the United States)[42] and is in fact increasingly common.[43]

III. The Consent Principle

The consent principle occupies an important place in the liberal tradition. It holds that political membership should not be ascribed to an individual on the basis of the contingent circumstances of his or her birth. Instead, it must reflect the individual's free choice to join the polity, as well as the polity's concurrence in that choice.[44]

Two striking facts suggest that many aliens do not consent to citizenship: a large number of aliens who are eligible to naturalize fail to do so, and most of those who do naturalize do not apply until well after they become eligible. According to one analysis of the 1980 census, more than twenty-five percent of the foreign born who had resided here for more than ten years had failed to naturalize. For "Latinos" (the term used in the study), fifty-six percent had failed to naturalize; even for those who had resided here for more than twenty years, the figure was forty-four percent.[45] Naturalization rates also vary considerably among different ethnic groups. Mexicans and other Central Americans, for example, naturalize at much lower rates than Asians do.[46]

The precise causes of so many aliens' lack of interest in naturalizing remain uncertain. Doubtless, some of it reflects many aliens' continuing hope to return to their native land to live. This hope is a realistic one for many individuals, such as Mexicans, whose countries are nearby and whose domestic politics are relatively stable. For others, such as Cambodians and Vietnamese who have migrated great distances and whose homelands are firmly controlled by brutal regimes, that hope—the so-called myth of return—is unlikely to be fulfilled. The reluctance to acquire American citizenship may also reflect property restrictions and other disadvantages to which those who naturalize here and thus renounce their foreign nationalities might be subjected were they to return to their native lands. Finally, INS backlogs and administrative priorities have impeded some naturalization.

To these well-understood motives for resisting American citizenship, another less-discussed one may be added: the courts, by interpreting the equality and due process principles more expansively, have substantially reduced the value of citizenship to legal resident aliens. Today, the marginal benefits to most aliens of moving from legal resident status to full membership are slight. Indeed they have never been smaller.

We have seen that the right to vote is probably unimportant to most aliens and that for the law-abiding ones (that is, almost all of them), the risk of deportation is practically nil. Moreover, aliens are eligible for all but a relatively small number of elective or appointive jobs, and virtually all public services and benefits are now equally available to legal resident aliens as a matter of law.[47] Military conscription, which was abolished during the early 1970s, applied to citizens and resident aliens alike. On the other side of the equation, American citizenship carries some risks. For example, a new citizen must renounce allegiance to her country of origin in order to naturalize here. Shedding her former nationality may impose a psychic loss as well as jeopardize her property and other interest there.

Of course, many aliens prefer to be on the safe side and more than 280,000 of them, probably motivated by a desire to obtain higher immigration preferences for family members or stirred by the emotional and symbolic attractions of identifying as full Americans, did naturalize in 1986.[48] And there is some evidence that newly arrived immigrants are naturalizing at a somewhat higher rate in recent years.[49] Still, the naturalization rate remains low, especially for Hispanics, and particularly compared to that prevailing in Canada, another immigrant society similar in important respects to the United States.[50] Part of the reason may be the weak incentives for legal aliens to naturalize.

Presumably, the same is true of illegal aliens. What seems to matter most to them is legal status, not citizenship. Indeed, the recently concluded amnesty program suggests that many illegal aliens, especially non-Mexicans, are not even prepared to seek legal status, much less citizenship. Obviously, any illegal alien prefers legal status so long as it can be obtained at low cost. But most amnesty programs, including the American version, involve some risks to aliens.[51] The INS's calculated ambiguity on its split-family status policy, for example, discouraged many amnesty-eligible aliens, even though the INS apparently lived up to its promise.[52]

It is possible, of course, that once the newly legalized aliens become eligible for citizenship, they will seek it more energetically than those aliens who have always resided here legally. Illegal aliens, after all, occupy a precarious status, one to which the equality and due process principles have only a limited (albeit increasing) applicability.[53] Because they must daily confront the risks of exploitation, arbitrary treatment, and deportation, the security that citizenship provides may seem more important to those who have suffered most from not having it. On the other hand, more than seventy percent of the aliens who will be legalized through the amnesty program are Mexicans, a group in which even those with legal resident status tend to naturalize at low rates. Once legalized, these individuals may conclude—as their previously legal counterparts have so often concluded—that American citizenship is a status that they do not particularly need or want.

If the only consent that mattered were the individual alien's, the consent principle would raise few problems. Each alien would simply decide upon the level of social and political integration into American life that he or she desired. A decision to forego naturalization, if truly voluntary and informed, would be a matter of indifference to the polity: that decision would properly be viewed as satisfying the consent principle as fully as a citizen's knowing decision to expatriate him or herself. But the consensual citizenship to which liberalism is committed is a two-way street. As Rogers Smith and I have explained elsewhere,[54] the consent principle does not look only to the individual's choice: instead, it requires *mutual* consent to citizenship and what valuation of citizenship that consent implies.

The American polity has consented to citizenship for aliens in several different ways. For naturalizing aliens and foreign-born children of citizens, that consent is statutory.[55] For native-born children of citizens and legal resident aliens, the Citizenship Clause expresses a categorical, constitutional consent (albeit one subject, as we have seen, to several established exceptions). That consent also extends to those legal resident alien who choose not to naturalize. The Immigration and Nationality Act permits them to remain in that status indefinitely; it does not require naturalization, or impose any penalty for that failure.

But American society's valuation of citizenship is perhaps most strikingly revealed in its willingness to confer automatic birthright citizenship upon the native-born children of illegal aliens and nonimmigrants (temporary visitors).[56] Until recently, this practice, which may be unique to the United States, had no practical or symbolic importance and thus attracted little attention. Illegal migration across the southern border, which had been common ever since the 19th century, was viewed as a manageable flow, one that benefited American society and was tolerated if not encouraged.[57] By the mid-1980s, however, the flow had reached crisis proportions and Congress finally decided to adopt more meaningful restrictions.[58] By then, an estimated 75,000 or more children were being born in the United States each year to parents who came here in flagrant violation of American law, parents who often crossed the border simply to procure American citizenship for their new children.[59]

In itself, this practice does not tell us much about aliens' valuation of that status. The Mexican woman who is carried across the Rio Grande to obtain citizenship for her child, after all, demonstrates only that she believes that it is worth crossing the river for. But the law's response to her action—its willingness to grant automatic citizenship to the child in exchange for so little effort and affinity—says more; it says that American society is prepared to dispense citizenship at a very low price to individuals who are perfect strangers. This suggests that citizenship has been devalued in another sense. Not only do aliens need or want less; many of those who do want it for their children need expend remarkably little in order to get it.[60]

IV. AN EVALUATION OF DEVALUATION

But the devaluation of citizenship only serves to raise a further question: so what? Should we be concerned that American citizenship has manifestly little appeal for many aliens, or should we instead view this development with indifference or even satisfaction?

There are at least four dangers lurking in a devalued citizenship. The first is political: a concern for the quality of both the governmental process and the policy outcomes that it generates. Sound governance demands that those who are affected by the business of government participate in those decisions. The consent that invigorates liberal democracy must be as broad as the society that is coerced and governed in its name. But if millions of adult individuals subject to the exercise of governmental power are non-citizens who are largely disabled from voting, politicians have little incentive to learn about and respond to their claims. Under those conditions, the gap between power and accountability widens and the potential for exploiting non-citizens grows. When vitally affected interests remain voteless and (to that extent) voiceless, policy decisions are seriously deformed.[61]

A second danger of a devalued citizenship is cultural in nature. An effective society—one that can accomplish its common goals, facilitate the private ends of its members, and nourish its system of values—requires that newcomers achieve at least a modest degree of assimilation into its culture. At a minimum, this must involve attaining competence in the common language in which that culture expresses and changes itself, but it also demands some comprehension of the nation's institutions and traditions. If newcomers do not value citizenship, if they fail to acquire the mastery of language and social knowledge that citizenship requires, they jeopardize their own well-being and (if they are sufficiently numerous) that of their adopted society. They create practical obstacles to the success of their own projects, while encouraging others to view them as strangers rather than as collaborators, as outsiders rather than as integrated members of the community.

The third danger created by the devaluation of citizenship is spiritual in nature. Democracy is more than a mechanism for governmental decisions, more that a technology for getting the public's work done well. It is also a normative order, an ethos that legitimizes certain process values and nourishes particular ways of thinking about the means and ends of politics. Its success depends upon the discipline of self-restraint; a willingness to sacrifice advantages and share burdens; a concern for the public interest; the capacity to inspire and accept leadership; a reverence for law, and pride in one's political community.

A polity that devalues citizenship may discourage the development and diffusion of these civic virtues. Although citizenship cannot guarantee any of these virtues, it seems to be a necessary or at least instrumental condition for most of them. If non-citizens can claim the same benefits that citizens enjoy without having to bear the obligations of full membership, they may acquire an "entitlement mentality" that can erode those virtues. Most non-citizens are manifestly law-abiding and socially productive; they are presumably no less altruistic than other people. But by withholding their participation in and commitment to our civic life, they decline to be public-spirited in the fullest sense. To that extent, they may impoverish the democratic spirit of their communities.

A final danger concerns the emotional consequences of devalued citizenship. Fred Schauer has noted that citizenship serves as an especially important bond among individuals in a polyglot society like ours in which there are relatively few other affective linkages or commonalities.[62] The ethnic, wealth, gender, religious, and lingual differences that divide us, Schauer points out, are inherently difficult for individuals to control or change. Citizenship, in contrast, is a status that can enable us to transcend these more enduring differences and achieve some common ground. If citizenship is to perform this special office, it must be accessible to all. But if it comes too readily accessible, it may lose much of its capacity to bind us together in a meaningful, emotionally satisfying community.

Schauer's observation is really a point about how national communities are constituted and kept cohesive. Michael Walzer has hinted at an underlying emotional dynamic of such communities in his assertion that "neighborhoods can be open only if countries are at least potentially closed."[63] This suggestion, if true, has an important implication for citizenship. If we need the warmth and immediacy of parochial attachments to feel truly human, if there are spatial limits to our capacity for communal spirit,[64] then citizenship may be a way to crystallize those attachments and define their outer boundaries. A liberal society committed to the equality and due process principles seeks to rationalize and bureaucratize relationships among individuals and with the state by appealing to universal, abstract standards. At the same time, its members commonly feel a heightened need for some refuge from that universalizing impulse, some enclave in which they can define themselves and their allegiances more locally and emotionally.

National citizenship is certainly not the only haven from universality, and it has never been the most satisfying one; for most people, that succor is more fully provided by family, friendships, neighborhoods, ethnicity, religion, and other less cosmopolitan attachments. But if, as Bickel showed, citizenship has not been particularly important in American law, it has surely affected how Americans feel about and define themselves and others. As citizenship's value and significance decline, therefore, we should expect that people's more parochial loyalties may loom correspondingly larger and may be asserted with greater intensity. Such a shift may yield neighborly pride, ethnic solidarity, and other emotional satisfactions. But it may also encourage a retreat from civic commitment toward some darker feelings that are never wholly absent from American life: xenophobia, petty localism, intolerance, and privatistic self-absorption.

The existence of these dangers reinforces a point that is often obscured by the liberal, minimalist conception of citizenship celebrated by Bickel and dominant in American law: society's interest in the value of citizenship transcends the valuation that the individuals in the society place upon it. Even if aliens' decisions to forgo naturalization were truly voluntary and fully informed—indeed, even if those choices did not expose them to political exploitation or injustice at the hands of citizens—society might be justified in concluding that in the aggregate those choices debase, perhaps even imperil, the quality of its political life. Put another way, the level of political, and hence, social assimilation that aliens find perfectly congenial may seem inadequate from society's point of view.

But there is another side to this ledger. As we have seen, the devaluation of citizenship has been accomplished in part through the medium of the equality and due process principles, which have significantly reduced the differences between the rights of citizens and resident aliens. If this devaluation represents a loss to the distinctiveness of the citizenship status and involves some dangers, it also represents an immense gain for the liberal values of inclusiveness and equal treatment. These values, no less than the civic virtues described earlier, enhance the quality of political life. By maximizing individual opportunity and preventing the formation of a legally disabled underclass, the equality and due process principles have fostered the social mobility and optimism that seem essential to the success of American democracy. If the distinctiveness of citizenship is a casualty of this policy of individual empowerment and social amelioration, then (one might say) so much the worse for citizenship.

It must also be conceded that the dangers of which I have written are for the most part still theoretical rather than imminent. Only the cultural danger—the risk posed by the failure of many Hispanics to master English and thus to gain the access to the society that only competency in the common language affords—arguably threatens the stability and well-being of American society. The others remain speculative and their potential magnitude is difficult to assess. Moreover, while a devalued citizenship may plausibly be linked to these dangers, the actual strength of these relationships is not at all clear. The incentive structure that the equality and due process principles have altered is surely relevant to aliens' decisions about whether or not to naturalize (or migrate in the hope of conferring birthright citizenship on their children). But it would be foolish to think that decisions of that kind turn entirely upon these sorts of incentives or even that those decisions are wholly rational ones. The question, then, of whether and to what extent the devaluation of citizenship constitutes a serious problem has no simple answer. But although there are substantial arguments on both sides, these arguments are not in equipoise. In fact, there are reasons to believe that the devaluation of citizenship is not, on balance, a cause for great concern. As we have just seen, most of the dangers seem remote. And even if these dangers were more proximate than they appear to be, it is not obvious either that altering our citizenship policy would forestall them or that we would know which particular alterations would be effective.

In addition, the devaluation of citizenship is probably irreversible, and necessity here should be seen as a virtue. The constitutional jurisprudence through which the equality and due process principles have helped to devalue citizenship cannot properly be viewed as either a doctrinal sport or a temporary ideological compromise. Rather, that jurisprudence reflects some fundamental dynamics in domestic law and international relations—the growing integration of the United States into the world economy, the emergence of group rights, the invigoration of judicial review—that are reshaping immigration law.[65] These structural changes appear to have widespread support and are likely to be permanent.[66]

Finally, and perhaps most fundamentally, the conception of membership that drives political institutions has steadily grown more fluid, functional, and context-dependent and seems likely to become even more so in the future. Before the rise of the modern nation-state, political membership was usually based upon kinship and ethnic ties. Today, at least in a liberal polity like the United States, membership is a far more complex, variegated, multipurpose idea. For certain purposes, such as voting, citizenship is the crucial status, but for others, such as the attribution of most constitutional rights, mere territorial presence suffices.[67] For still other purposes, such as participation in an economic common market, membership is constituted by supranational groupings such as the recently established United States–Canada free trade zone or the still-evolving European Community.

We live in an increasingly integrated world. Transnational economic relationships are ubiquitous, international travel has become inexpensive, migratory pressures are already enormous and are steadily increasing, environmental problems are global, scientific and cultural exchange are highly valued, and political cooperation among nations is more essential than ever before. Even within our borders, citizenship represents an increasingly hollow ideal. It neither confers a distinctively advantageous status nor demands much of the individuals who possess it.

It would be premature, nonetheless, to conclude that national citizenship today is anachronistic. I have suggested that it provides a focus of political allegiance and emotional energy on a scale capable of satisfying deep human longings for solidarity, symbolic identification, and community. Such a focus may be especially important in a liberal ethos whose centrifugal, cosmopolitan aspirations for global principles and universal human rights must somehow be balanced against the more parochial imperatives of organizing societies dominated by the more limited commitments to family, locality, region, and nation.

If the political and emotional aspects of citizenship remain significant, we nevertheless seem resolved as a society that little else of consequence should be allowed to turn upon it. But within that general understanding and social consensus, the precise role that citizenship should play and the special rights and obligations that ought to attach to it are emphatically open, contingent questions. As to these questions, only one proposition seems certain: today's conception of citizenship may not be adequate to meet tomorrow's needs.

8

The Reevaluation of American Citizenship

Citizenship is very much on America's collective mind. Congress is busily redefining it. Intellectuals are writing books about it. Citizens are debating whether it has lost its meaning. Aliens are lining up to apply for it in unprecedented numbers. What, one may ask, is going on here?

Citizenship talk proceeds through several different tropes. Sometimes we advance it as a powerful aspirational ideal. In this normative usage, it serves as a proxy, or placeholder, for our deepest commitments to a common life. Citizens, in this view, mutually pledge their trust and concern for each other and their full participation in shared civic and civil cultures. Sometimes—perhaps even at the same time—we also deploy citizenship as a positive concept. In this positive usage, it describes a legal-political status that some individuals enjoy, some can only aspire to, and still others have little hope of ever attaining. Here, citizenship describes a relationship between individuals and the polity in which citizens owe allegiance to their polity—they must not betray it and may have to serve it—while the polity owes its citizens the fullest measure of protection that its law affords, including (except for minors and some convicted felons) the right to vote.

These two uses of citizenship—the normative and the positive—are linked rhetorically, and perhaps even psychologically. Like the serpents on a caduceus, they are tightly intertwined. We often use the ideal of citizenship as a standard against which to evaluate the actual conduct of others, hurling the ideal as an accusation, bitterly condemning what we do not like about contemporary life and ascribing it to the defects of our fellow citizens. Whether the offense is the despoilment of public spaces in our cities, the failure to vote in our elections, the violence in our schools and neighborhoods, or the erosion of our families, we indict not only the individual perpetrators but the polity that, by debasing citizenship, has fostered or at least countenanced these wrongs. At times—and today, seems such a time—our despair may be so great that we wonder whether we remain one people dedicated to common purposes. The most disillusioned of us may conclude that citizenship should be a privilege that requires us to be better in order to claim it, a prize that can be earned only through greater rectitude.

It is precisely at these censorious moments, however, that citizenship's positive meaning can check the harsh, exclusionary impulses that its normative meaning reflexively arouses in us. When we are tempted to say (or feel) that our fellow citizens should, "shape up or ship out," or should "love our country or leave it," we may recall that our law does not view citizenship as a reward for civic virtue. The target of criticism may respond with what he imagines is a rhetorical trump: "It's a free country." But far from silencing the critic, this reply simply invites a rebuttal in which he invokes his underlying conception of freedom—and of citizenship. So the conversation goes.

In the United States today, this conversation is particularly heated. Not since the McCarthy era in the early 1950s, when many Americans aggressively questioned the loyalty of their fellow citizens, relatively few immigrants were admitted, and relatively few of those sought to become citizens, has citizenship talk been so energetic and morally charged. In Congress, at the bar of public opinion, and even in the courts, citizenship in both its normative and positive dimensions is being closely re-examined. Indeed, Congress adopted welfare reform and immigration control laws in 1996 that were intended, among other goals, to increase sharply the value of American citizenship while reducing the value of permanent legal resident status. As of April 1998, moreover, some members of Congress were calling for legislation that would restrict the availability of naturalized citizenship, birthright *(jus soli)* citizenship, and plural citizenships.

In this essay, I explore the reasons why Americans are arguing more passionately about citizenship today, and why some of the rules that have long structured citizenship status are under vigorous assault. I shall argue that the intensity of this debate reflects the tensions that arise within and among three analytically distinct relational domains, each of which is characterized by a distinctive problematic, a wrenching conflict between competing and deeply held values.

The first domain is international law and politics. Here the nation defines the scope of its sovereignty by classifying all individuals as either insiders or outsiders. By insiders, I mean those whom the polity brings into its constitutional community by granting them legal rights against it. The American constitutional community includes citizens, legal resident aliens, and in some cases, illegal aliens. Outsiders are everybody else in the world. The United States defines its sovereignty in this international domain largely, but not exclusively, in terms of its power over territory; its constitutional community embraces virtually all individuals within its national borders and territories, as well as some who are outside them but to whom the United States has acknowledged some special political and legal relationship. The distinctive problematic in this domain is a tension between the values of national sovereignty and autonomy and the reality that many outsiders possess the power to transform themselves into insiders without the nation's consent and beyond its effective control.

The second domain is national politics. Here, public law classifies the body of insiders into different categories, defining what the polity owes to each of them and what they in turn owe to the polity. Its distinctive problematic is a tension between the values of equal treatment and communal self-definition, and the reality of limited resources. This tension is particularly delicate because it encourages the marginalization not only of outsiders but of some insiders as well. The meaning of citizenship in the national political domain is highly controversial in the United States today because it is intimately connected to bitterly divisive questions about the welfare state—its essential legitimacy, its moral character, its purposes, its programmatic scope, and its availability to citizens and to various categories of aliens.

The third domain is federalism—the structural division of the American polity into multiple, overlapping sovereignties.[1] Each individual possesses a civic status in the national polity and in a state polity. She may also live in a private enclave in which her status is regulated, often extensively, by contract. Different rights and duties attach to these diverse statuses. Federalism's distinctive problematic is a tension between the values of equality and uniformity, which the nation can promote through its power to unify the same policy throughout its territory, and the value of diversity among, and responsiveness to, the policies advanced by different states and contractual regimes. In this domain, as in that of national politics, Americans are bitterly debating the meaning of citizenship in the most divisive of contexts: a fundamental reconsideration of the welfare state. In August 1996, the United States adopted a welfare reform law—forged through a remarkable bipartisan consensus—that constitutes perhaps the most far-reaching change in American social policy since the foundations of its welfare state were established during the New Deal. I discuss these reforms in a later section on citizenship in the federal system.

The essay is divided into three sections, corresponding to these three domains of citizenship. In each, I discuss how changing conditions, ideas, and values have provoked a re-evaluation of American citizenship by deepening its characteristic tensions. Before concluding the essay, I offer some brief and tentative observations on the notion, which has recently come into academic vogue, of what is commonly called "post-national citizenship."

I. Citizenship in
the International Domain

In dividing up the world's population into insiders and outsiders, the United States is remarkably inclusive, at least relative to other polities. This inclusiveness takes a number of different forms. First, the United States has adopted a very liberal legal immigration policy, admitting approximately 800,000 aliens each year (the precise number fluctuates considerably) for permanent residence.[2] This annual influx probably exceeds the legal admissions totals of the rest of the world combined. Moreover, the United States has increased its legal admissions during the 1990s, a period during which other countries have been restricting them. When Congress overhauled U.S. immigration laws in 1996, it resisted intense political pressures to reduce the number of legal admissions. Hence, the post-1990 growth in the legal immigration system remains in place. Second, the United States in the 1980s and early 1990s extended legal permanent resident status to nearly 2.7 million illegal aliens through a massive amnesty, a program to legalize illegals' dependents, and more conventional immigration remedies. Third, a combination of expansive *jus sanguinis* and *jus soli* rules extends citizenship very broadly—to essentially all individuals who are born on U.S. soil, regardless of their parents' legal status, all children born abroad to two American parents, and many children born abroad to one American parent. Fourth, U.S. naturalization requirements are relatively easy—indeed, some say, too easy—to satisfy. From 1990 to 1995 the United States naturalized between 240,000 and 488,000 aliens a year; in 1996 alone, more than one million individuals were naturalized, the largest cohort in history. Propelled by welfare law changes that restrict many benefits to citizens, further increases in petitions—up to an estimated 1.8 million in 1997—are expected.[3] Fifth, dual (and even triple) citizenship is increasingly common, and the State Department no longer opposes it in principle.

Finally, more than one million aliens enter the United States illegally each year; some 250,000 to 300,000 of these individuals remain in illegal status more or less permanently, producing an illegal population now estimated at over 5 million. Simply by virtue of their presence in the United States, illegal immigrants can claim extensive procedural rights, and in some cases, substantive entitlements as well, under the Constitution, statutes, and administrative rules, although the 1996 amendments to the immigration statute severely limited some of these rights, especially for those who entered the United States illegally. Even excludable aliens stopped at the border, who possess only the most elementary constitutional rights, such as access to the courts and freedom from physical abuse, can claim many statutory rights under U.S. laws.

In the international arena, the principal force reshaping Americans' conceptions of citizenship is the growing anxiety aroused by their perception that their national sovereignty is under serious challenge. Three recent developments are particularly salient: the globalization of the U.S. economy; the increase in immigration, particularly illegal immigration; and a more general diminution of American autonomy in the world.

Globalization

The integration of the world economy—its "globalization," in the already hackneyed phrase—has proceeded at an ever-quickening pace. This integration, moreover, is comprehensive, encompassing all factors of production, distribution, and communication including goods, services, capital, technology, intellectual property rules, and (most pertinent for present purposes) labor. The U.S. economy, while primarily focused on its enormous domestic market,[4] has in recent years become a nimble exporter and importer of capital and, to a lesser extent, of jobs. A number of factors strongly suggest that this trend will continue. Powerful economic and political interests are driving this trend, while enfeebled labor unions lack the bargaining-power to arrest, much less reverse, it. American producers, no longer able to count on policies protecting them from foreign competition, are rationalizing their operations by sending low-skill jobs abroad while importing high-skill technicians, managers, and professionals where needed.

Nowhere is the force of this globalization dynamic more apparent than in the formation of regional free trade blocs and their gradual extension—through the inclusion of new members, mergers with other such blocs, and coverage of additional goods and services. This dynamic first occurred in Europe with the progressive expansion of the Treaty of Rome, leading to the establishment of the European Union, which has grown to include much of the former European Free Trade Area as well as other new members and trade sectors. For the United States, of course, the crucial development has been the creation of the North American Free Trade Agreement (NAFTA), which is likely to be enlarged eventually to include Chile and perhaps other hemispheric nations, as well as being extended to include other areas of economic activity. Long before NAFTA, of course, the United States and Mexican governments had concluded a number of formal and informal arrangements involving economic activities in the border areas and the control of migration to the United States from South and Central America. NAFTA has altered and extended these arrangements, with consequences that will not be well understood for years to come.

For present purposes, the important point is that these developments signal a growing recognition by the U.S. government that America's fate is increasingly linked to that of her neighbors, her other trading partners, and the rest of the world. These linked fates are not merely economic but are also demographic, social, and political. The United States is increasingly vulnerable to the immense migratory pressures being generated by conditions beyond her borders and her control. These "push" factors are magnified and reinforced by powerful, indeed tidal, "pull" factors: a vast and burgeoning American economy that often prefers foreign workers to domestic ones, a dynamic American culture that promises immigrants great personal freedom and mobility, and grooved pathways of kinship-based chain migration that constantly creates and replenishes immigrant and ethnic communities in the United States.

Migration

Since 1965, immigration to the United States has been transformed in virtually every vital aspect.[5] The legal immigration streams have swelled in both absolute terms and as a percentage of the overall population. Even more important than the size of those streams, the "look and feel" of American society has changed dramatically with the changing mix of the newcomers' national origins, races, and languages. All of this has occurred in a relatively short period of time, generating cultural, economic, and social anxieties among many Americans.

But it is *illegal* migration that is primarily driving the political dimension of this debate. The volume of illegal migration has grown fairly steadily during the last three decades except for the period immediately following the enactment of the employer sanctions provisions of the Immigration Reform and Control Act of 1986, when the number declined. This decline, however, proved to be brief; by 1990, the number of illegal immigrants in the United States had already returned approximately to its pre-1986 level; the permanent illegal population now exceeds 5 million. Even the growth in the resources devoted to border control during the last five years—extraordinary especially when compared to the retrenchment in other federal programs—shows no clear sign of stemming this influx (as opposed to rechanneling it). The continuing ineffectiveness of border control is a source of enormous frustration to Americans and their politicians, especially in the relatively small number of communities with high concentrations of illegals. At the same time, Americans have become more dependent on illegal workers and more aware of this dependence, which for many employers, consumers, and communities can approach an addiction. These competing feelings can produce hypocrisy of comical dimensions. California Governor Pete Wilson, for example, sought to build a political movement by denouncing illegal aliens, many of whom had been admitted earlier as temporary workers under a program that he had sponsored as a Senator, only to be caught employing them in his household and then failing to pay their social security benefits!

Because many Americans feel beleaguered and victimized by illegal immigration, it is profoundly affecting their political identity. These feelings are intensifying as the large number of former illegal aliens who received amnesty in the late 1980s begin to become U.S. citizens, many motivated by a desire to secure their access to welfare state benefits in the United States. Moreover, the families of these amnestied illegals are now exerting strong pressures on the *legal* immigration system, competing with the often more compelling claims of legal immigrants' relatives who wish to join their families in the United States. Congress is also considering whether to eliminate automatic birthright (*jus soli*) citizenship for the U.S.-born children of illegal alien parents. None of these proposals, however, is likely to be enacted. Congress is also taking up the less controversial question of whether the naturalization law should be changed in light of concerns that many immigrants are naturalizing fraudulently, for the wrong motives, or too easily.

As the number of illegal aliens grows, their position in the American polity becomes increasingly anomalous. Americans admire the tenacity, hard work, and resourcefulness of illegal aliens (at least the majority who do not commit crimes in the United States) but at the same time, deeply resent their furtive success in penetrating U.S. territory, working in U.S. jobs, earning (and exporting) dollars, and securing legal status—even the ultimate prize, citizenship—for themselves and their families. As the data on the individuals who voted in favor of California's Proposition 187 illustrated, many legal resident aliens and recently naturalized citizens are also strongly opposed to illegal migration.[6] The fact that the United States has long countenanced illegal migrants, derived tax revenues and other economic benefits from them, and built important sectors of her economy around their continued flow arouses cognitive dissonance, but it does not really alter the fact of resentment.

The number of illegals residing in the United States now is probably higher than the number whose plight prompted the 1986 legalization. Responding to this reality, Congress in late 1997 enacted a new amnesty for approximately 150,000 Nicaraguans and Cubans. It also eased the legalization rules for another 250,000 Guatemalans and Salvadorans, and the Clinton Administration moved to extend relief to more than 15,000 Haitian asylum seekers as well. Americans believe that illegal aliens impose large costs on American society, but even if they did not believe this, they would still demand the interdiction and expulsion of illegals. After all, illegals are like trespassers; they have no right to enter or remain. Control of illegal migration, then, is not merely a pragmatic policy goal; it assumes the character of a legal duty and a moral crusade, as evidenced by the far-reaching immigration control legislation enacted in 1996. Americans' conceptions of citizenship reflect these imperatives.

Diminished Autonomy

The massive breaching of American borders by illegal aliens is vivid evidence of the nation's vulnerability; "invasion" and "flood" are the metaphors that are conventionally used to describe the influx. Americans, however, are experiencing a more general sense of unease that their national destiny is moving beyond their control. This anxiety springs from many sources. I have already mentioned growing U.S. reliance on the global economy; American prosperity now depends almost as much on public and private decisions in Tokyo, Bonn, and Hong Kong as it does on those in Washington or Wall Street. But the loss of control is not confined to the economic realm. The protracted trauma of the Vietnam War convinced many Americans that the United States can no longer work its will in the world militarily. The geopolitical fragmentation encouraged by the end of the Cold War has left the United States as the sole remaining superpower, yet the American Goliath is now at the mercy of myriad ethnic rivalries and subnational conflicts that defy international intervention and order. Even threats to public health, traditionally the province of national governments, increasingly cross national borders, as the recent examples of AIDS, dengue fever, tuberculosis, and other communicable diseases suggest. Public concern with international terrorism, galvanized by several notorious bombing incidents, adds to Americans' anxieties about this loss of control.

The world has always been a dangerous place. Most Americans probably believe that it is more dangerous today than ever before, although precisely the opposite is true—at least for them but also for many others. They evidently feel growing insecurity about their jobs, marriages, safety, and personal future. People in such a state of uncertainty naturally search for safe havens from these storms. Their citizenship serves as a dependable anchorage; it gives them a secure mooring in an increasingly intrusive, turbulent, uncontrollable "worldwind." A valuable legal status, it can never be taken away. It defines who is a member of the extended political family, which, like its natural counterpart, offers some consolation in a harsh world. We imagine that we can count on the company of citizens to join us in a search for common good. Our concern for our fellow citizens is usually greater than that for the rest of humankind. Fellow citizens share our lifeboat and are in it for the long haul.

Citizenship thus imparts to the polity a special shape and expectancy—in the United States, a common claim to enjoy the "American way of life." The more perplexing and menacing we find the world and the more buffeting its gales of change, the more tenaciously we cling to our citizenship's value and insist on maintaining it. David Jacobson, drawing on the conceptions of Mircea Eliade and Benedict Anderson, suggests that this tenacity is driven by an even more profound disorientation—a crisis of what Jacobson calls the desacralization of territory. "The nation," he writes,

> is the primordial center, the ultimate point of reference, for its members. . . . In being boundary oriented, the (nation)-state depends on those boundaries being effectively maintained. The entry of undocumented or illegal immigrants, or the settlement of guest workers, is not simply a violation of the law of the recipient country. It is a violation of sacred space and of a primordial category.[7]

II. Citizenship in the Domestic Domain

If citizenship provides succor to Americans in their confrontation with the outside world, it also promises them political and social standing and national identity in the domestic one. Here, citizenship crowns a hierarchy of statuses, with each one bearing a distinctive set of legal rights and obligations.[8] David Martin has suggested that this domain may be represented metaphorically by concentric circles; a community of citizens at the central core is surrounded by a series of more peripheral status categories, with ever more attenuated ties to the polity, weaker claims on it, and more limited rights against it.[9] Citizenship's normative meaning can be inferred from (among other things) the magnitude and nature of the gap between the citizens and those in the outer circles with respect to their rights and duties.

American citizenship, as Alexander Bickel famously observed, "is at best a simple idea for a simple government."[10] By this, Bickel meant that the ratification of the Fourteenth Amendment to the Constitution made membership in the American polity widely and easily available, that the legal rights and duties associated with citizenship have long ceased to be an important or divisive public issue, and that this consensus has been both firm and highly desirable. In an article published in 1989, I found merit in Bickel's point and suggested that it was probably truer then than it had been in 1973 when he first asserted it.[11]

Today, however, Bickel's (and my) confident assurances seem embarrassingly premature. In a radically altered political environment, the question of citizenship is now both salient and divisive. To understand the larger significance of what has transpired, it is necessary to describe the basic structure of U.S. citizenship law, and the differences between the rights and duties of citizens and those of legal permanent residents (LPRs). I shall then discuss the reevaluation of citizenship that is now occurring in the United States in the shadow of more fundamental debates—notably, debates concerning the role of immigration in America's future and the legitimacy and shape of the welfare state.

The Structure of U.S. Citizenship Law

United States citizenship can be acquired in three ways. The most common way—citizenship by birth in the United States—reflects the Anglo-American tradition of *jus soli*,[12] a right protected by the Fourteenth Amendment's Citizenship Clause.[13] Judicial interpretation of the Citizenship Clause has long been understood as extending this status to native-born children of aliens who are in the country, even if present illegally or on a temporary visa. This interpretation has never been seriously questioned in the courts, although it has recently come under scrutiny, and some criticism, from politicians, commentators, and scholars.[14]

A second route to citizenship is through naturalization. In 1996, more than one million individuals were naturalized, more than twice the 1995 total, which itself had set a record. To naturalize, an LPR must have resided in the United States with that status for five years, be of good moral character, demonstrate an ability to speak, read, and write English; and demonstrate a basic knowledge of U.S. government and history. More than eighty-five percent of all naturalizations take place under these general provisions, although some people are permitted to use less restrictive procedures. Spouses of American citizens can naturalize after only three years; children who immigrate with their parents can be naturalized more or less automatically (simply by obtaining a certificate) when their parents naturalize; and adopted children of U.S. citizens can also naturalize in that fashion. Certain aliens who served with the American military during past wars may naturalize easily. Some individual or group naturalizations are effectuated directly by statute. It is significant that a large number of citizenship-eligible aliens choose not to naturalize.[15]

The third route to citizenship is through descent from one or more American parents. This principle, known as *jus sanguinis,* is codified in the immigration statute. For example, a child of two citizen parents born outside of the United States is a citizen if one of the parents resided in the United States prior to the child's birth. If one of the parents is an alien but the citizen parent was physically present in the Untied States or an outlying possession for a period or periods totaling five years, two of which were after the age of fourteen, the child is a citizen. Over time, Congress has liberalized these eligibility requirements, and the Supreme Court is now considering a constitutional challenge to a gender-based distinction in the statute.

Plural citizenships are quite common in the United States due to the combination of the American *jus soli* rule with the various *jus sanguinis* rules of other countries. Thus, aliens who naturalize in the United States must renounce their prior allegiance. This renunciation may or may not effectively terminate the individual's foreign citizenship under the foreign state's law, but U.S. naturalization law—unlike Germany's—does not require that the renunciation actually have that legal effect. As a result of this policy, as well as its policy of allowing U.S. citizens to naturalize elsewhere, the U.S. government tolerates and protects plural citizenships.[16] Since most of the countries of origin from which the largest groups of immigrants to the United States come—Mexico, the Philippines, the Dominican Republic, Canada, and India—recognize children born to their nationals abroad as citizens, plural citizenship among Americans is rapidly increasing.[17]

United States citizenship, once acquired, is virtually impossible to lose without the citizen's express consent. Supreme Court decisions since the 1960s have severely restricted the government's power to denationalize a citizen for reasons of disloyalty, divided allegiance, or otherwise. Today, the government cannot prevail against a birthright or *jus sanguinis* citizen unless it can prove that the citizen specifically intended to renounce his or her citizenship. This standard is difficult to satisfy—as it should be. Relatively few denationalization proceedings are brought and the number of successful ones is probably declining. Denaturalization proceedings against citizens who procured citizenship by misrepresenting their backgrounds or through other illegal means are largely directed against Nazi and Soviet persecutors, and under the 1988 Supreme Court decision, *Kungys v. United States,*[18] the standards that the government must satisfy to prevail are quite demanding.

Advantages of Citizenship Status

Until the statutory changes adopted by Congress in 1996, the differences between the legal rights enjoyed by citizens and those enjoyed by LPRs were more political than legal or economic, and those differences had narrowed considerably over time. In the same 1989 article referred to earlier, I argued that the narrowing of these differences constituted a "devaluation" of citizenship, one that raised important questions about the evolving political identity of the United States. Today, partly in response to widespread dissatisfaction with this previous devaluation, a re-evaluation of citizenship is in progress, one in which the differentiation of the rights of citizens and LPRs is a central theme.

The power of Congress to treat citizens and LPRs differently is subject to certain constitutional constraints. United States courts have established that the constitutionality of government-imposed discriminations between citizens and aliens turns in part on whether the discrimination being challenged is imposed by the federal government or by a state. In several Supreme Court decisions during the 1970s, the Court held that Congress could exclude resident aliens from public benefits under Medicare (and presumably under other federal programs as well), but that states could not do so without the federal government's blessing. Since then, the constitutional rationale for decisions restricting the states' power to discriminate may have changed. The Court originally seemed to view state law discrimination on the basis of alienage as a "suspect classification" like race. Under the Equal Protection Clause, the State would be required to show that its interest in discriminating against aliens was "compelling" and narrowly tailored to achieve its purpose, a very difficult burden to satisfy. In subsequent cases, however, the Court relied on a different constitutional theory based on the Supremacy Clause, not the Equal Protection Clause. This latter theory, known as "federal pre-emption," is discussed below and in the next section, "Citizenship in the Federal System," as are the recent developments in federalism reflected in the 1996 welfare reform law.

Despite these constitutional constraints on discrimination against aliens, some noteworthy differences in legal rights between LPRs and citizens had emerged long before the enactment of the 1996 changes, which significantly increased those differences. Three are political in nature: the right to vote, the right to serve on federal and many state juries, and the right to run for certain high elective offices and to be appointed to some high (and not-so-high) appointive offices. Each of these restrictions seems to be premised on one or more of the following assumptions: that aliens' political socialization is too fragmentary and embryonic to be trusted in matters of public choice; that confining political participation of this kind to citizens carries an important symbolic message about the value and significance of full membership; and that exclusion of aliens from such participation encourages them to naturalize as soon as possible.

Although aliens enjoyed the franchise in various American states during the nineteenth century, only U.S. citizens may exercise it today—a rule that applies in virtually all other countries as well, at least in national elections. A number of local communities have allowed aliens (some even include illegals) to vote in some or all of their local elections, and proposals to extend the franchise to aliens have been advanced in several large cities, including Washington and Los Angeles. In addition, some academic commentators support such a change, drawing on the historical precedent for alien voting and on liberal, republican, and natural rights theories.[19]

Most individual LPRs (as distinct from immigrants' rights advocates) probably do not view the inability to vote as a major disadvantage, although they may well resent the second-class status that this disability implies.[20] Immigrants' collective political identities have emphasized their ethnicities much more than their alienage per se; most empowerment campaigns have been mounted by ethnic organizations and promote naturalization, not legal changes to allow aliens to vote. Indeed, in 1996 Congress made it a federal crime for aliens to vote in federal elections, and made voting in violation of any federal, state, or local law grounds for removal. But now that Congress is changing the law to disadvantage legal aliens as a class, the political salience of alienage per se, and hence, the value that aliens place on the vote, are likely to increase in the future.

Citizenship requirements for jury service are less of an issue in the United States. In the framing of the Bill of Rights, which protected the right to trial by jury in both criminal and civil cases, jury service was seen as an important political, as well as legal, institution protecting the people from the oppression of governmental and private elites. Prior to the notorious O. J. Simpson trial, Americans esteemed the institution of the jury. Although most serve on it conscientiously, many also view it as less a privilege than a burden. Proposals to permit aliens to vote in local elections emerge periodically, but the notion of extending jury service to aliens has not surfaced in the recent public debate about improving the jury system.

The U.S. policy of barring aliens from federal employment, which is similar to the practice of most nations,[21] is likely to be a greater concern to aliens than the bar to jury service for most aliens. Few if any LPRs are likely to seek high elective or appointive offices prior to naturalization. Many LPRs, however, might want to pursue employment in the federal, state, and local civil service systems. In two Supreme Court decisions in the mid-1970s, the Court applied the constitutional principles relating to discrimination against aliens in the civil service setting. It held that the Constitution permitted Congress and the president to limit federal civil service jobs to citizens (which has been done since the 1880s) but that the states could not impose citizenship requirements for their own civil service systems. The Court emphasized the exclusive federal interest in regulating immigration, a principle that is discussed more fully below. It recognized, however, the state's power to exclude LPRs from particular job categories that represented the state's "political function," such as schoolteachers and police officers. This distinction, between jobs involving a political function and those that do not, has proved exceedingly difficult to apply but continues to enjoy the Court's support.

Two other disadvantages to LPRs are worth mentioning. First, LPRs have a lesser right to sponsor their family members for immigration. As noted earlier, immediate relatives of citizens receive a preferred immigration status without regard to numerical quotas, and citizens' siblings and adult children have a preferred status under the numerical quota system. In contrast, the spouses and unmarried children of resident aliens qualify for a numerically limited preference, and their siblings receive no preference at all.

Many policy-makers, including members of the U.S. Commission on Immigration Reform, are concerned about the chain migration effects that will be generated by the almost 2.7 million illegal aliens who were legalized under the 1986 amnesty program, are now LPRs and will soon be citizens. This will enable their immediate family members—and in turn *their* family members—to immigrate legally to the United States in large numbers. Congress, under considerable political pressure to reduce legal immigration, could decide to limit LPRs' family immigration rights further, or even to limit the family immigration rights of U.S. citizens who achieved that status only by virtue of the amnesty program enacted in 1986. If enacted, such a policy would raise novel and important constitutional questions concerning whether Congress may discriminate among U.S. citizens based on their prior immigration status.

In addition to different sponsorship rights, citizens and LPRs differ with respect to the right to remain in the United States. LPRs are subject to deportation (after the 1996 immigration control legislation, the term is "removal"); citizens (whether by birth, naturalization, or statute) are not. Deportation of a long-term resident can wreak enormous suffering upon aliens and their families and friends. Although the Supreme Court has repeatedly held that removal is not punishment and therefore does not implicate Due Process and other constitutional guarantees that surround the imposition of criminal sanctions, the fact is that, as Justice Douglas once put it, removal "may deprive a man and his family of all that makes life worthwhile."[22]

Still, it is important to place this risk in realistic context. The actual risk of removal for non-criminal LPRs living in the United States has been vanishingly small.[23] Even after the 1996 immigration control legislation, formal removal of legal aliens, especially non-criminal LPRs, remains a costly process for the INS to effectuate. Statutes, regulations, and judicial rulings require the INS to observe high standards of procedural fairness in adjudicating whether LPRs may remain in the United States. Severe administrative difficulties further limit the INS's ability to implement even the relatively few formal removal orders and the far more numerous informal departure agreements that it does manage to obtain. Except at the border, where the INS can often effectuate the "voluntary departure" of aliens, the agency has been notoriously ineffective at actually removing aliens who want to remain in the United States—even the "aggravated felons" against whom the Congress has provided special summary enforcement and removal powers.[24] As a legal and practical matter, then, a long-term, non-criminal LPR's chances of remaining in the United States if he wishes have been almost as great as those of a citizen. The 1996 law, intended to facilitate the removal of aliens who are inadmissible, commit crimes in the United States, lack credible asylum claims, or are otherwise out of status, is unlikely to increase this risk significantly.

Today the most controversial issue concerning the rights of LPRs concerns their access to public benefits to which citizens are entitled. Prior to the 1996 welfare reforms, LPRs and some other legal aliens who would likely gain LPR status sometime in the future (such as family members of amnestied aliens, refugees and asylum seekers, parolees, and Cuban-Haitian entrants) were eligible for many cash assistance, medical care, food, education, housing, and other social programs, albeit subject to some restrictions.[25] In addition, LPRs were often eligible for benefit programs, such as low tuition in state university systems. The 1996 welfare reforms significantly limit the eligibility of LPRs for all or virtually all federal cash assistance programs.[26]

These legal differences in the United States between the social program benefits that are available to citizens and to LPRs have no parallel in the increasingly beleaguered welfare states of the European Union. In the United States, however, these differences are somewhat palliated by several facts. Some states and cities (New York is a notable example) have been lax and even obstructionist in their enforcement of these limitations. Many LPRs and illegal aliens have managed to circumvent them through fraudulent applications. Most importantly, the vast majority of LPRs can easily escape the limitations on benefits by naturalizing within five years (three if they marry a citizen). Much of the remarkable surge in the naturalization petitions since the 1994 election apparently reflects precisely this kind of calculation on the part of LPRs, who anticipated the kinds of restriction on their entitlements that Congress adopted in 1996.

The Reevaluation of Citizenship

In recent years, public discourse about citizenship has returned to first principles: its nature, sources, and significance. So fundamental are these principles that the new discourse amounts to a reevaluation of American citizenship in both its normative and its positive dimensions. This reevaluation has been prompted by deep concerns about the unity and coherence of the civic culture in the United States, concerns that flow from five developments in the post-1965 era. They are the accumulation of multicultural pressures; the loss of a unifying ideology; technological change; the expansion and consolidation of the welfare state; and the devaluation of citizenship.

Multicultural Pressures

With the enactment of the 1965 immigration law, the composition of the immigration stream to the United States changed radically. Of the top source countries, only the Philippines and India sent large numbers of English-speaking immigrants. Bilingual education thus became a major issue in public education, and teaching in dozens of languages became necessary in many urban school systems. With the growing politicization of ethnicity and widespread attacks on the traditional assimilative ideal, anxieties about linguistic and cultural fragmentation increased. These anxieties have led to public referendums in California and other states establishing English as the official language. Proposals to limit affirmative action and bilingual education have been adopted or are under consideration.

Meanwhile, as genuine racial integration proved elusive, the civil rights movement took a turn towards separatism. Blacks, already severely disadvantaged, were increasingly obliged to cede political and economic influence to more recently arrived Hispanic and Asian voters. Many of the newer groups qualified for affirmative action programs, which exacerbated tensions among the groups and magnified fears that immigration and affirmative action were fragmenting American society. Certain economic sectors came to depend almost entirely upon immigrant workers, legal and illegal. Relatively parochial immigrant enclaves grew larger. These multicultural pressures caused many Americans to feel more and more like strangers in their own country.

Loss of Unifying Ideology

The end of the Cold War deprived the United States of an ideology, anti-communism, that had served for many decades as a unifying, coherent force in American political culture and as an obsessive preoccupation and goal in U.S. foreign policy. No alternative ideology has yet emerged to replace it. Only constitutionalism, our civic religion, seems potentially capable of performing the function of binding together a nation of diverse peoples.

Technological Change

Rapid changes in transportation and communication technologies have transformed a world of sovereign nations into a global web of multinational enterprises and interdependent societies. Migration has become less expensive. Immigrants no longer need to make an irrevocable commitment to their new society; they can more easily retain emotional and other ties to their countries and cultures of origin. On the other hand, there is growing concern that television tends to assimilate second-generation immigrant youths into an underclass culture rather than into the mainstream American culture.

Welfare State Expansion

In the United States, the welfare state—especially the creation of entitlements to income support, food stamps, medical care, and subsidized housing—expanded rapidly during a brief period of time, at least when compared to the more gradual, long-term evolution of European social support systems.[27] With this growth, the behavior, values, and economic progress of immigrants became matters of great fiscal significance and public policy concern. In contrast to the historical pattern, immigration no longer ebbed and flowed with the business cycle—presumably because of the growth of the social safety net. Immigration increasingly pitted citizens and aliens against one another as they competed for scarce public resources. The perennial debate over how the polity should conceive of community, affinity, and mutual obligation took on a new significance as the stakes in the outcome grew larger. Demands that Americans' obsession with legal rights be balanced by an equal concern for their social and civic responsibilities were increasingly heard in the land.[28]

In August 1996, this long-simmering debate culminated in the radical restructuring of the Aid to Families with Dependent Children (AFDC) program (known and often stigmatized in the United States as "welfare") and some other federally funded cash and social services programs. In the next section, I analyze in some detail the implications of this change for U.S. citizenship in a federal system.

Devaluation of Citizenship

The egalitarian thrust of the welfare state, its nourishing of entitlement as an ideal, and the repeal of the military draft led to a progressive erosion of citizenship as a distinctive status bearing special privileges and demanding special commitments and obligations. The rights of LPRs converged with those of citizens until there was little to separate them but the franchise, citizens' greater immigration sponsorship privileges, and their eligibility for the federal civil service. Americans began to feel that U.S. citizenship had lost much of its value and that it should somehow count for more.[29]

These concerns, which have parallels in other countries,[30] have prompted calls for a revitalization of citizenship. One type of proposal, which led to the enactment in 1993 of the National Community Service Corps, looks to the creation of a spirit of public service among young people. Another approach, a centerpiece of both the 1988 and 1996 welfare reform legislation, seeks to combat the entitlement mentality by insisting that able-bodied citizens work or get training, and eventually leave welfare altogether.

A third approach, exemplified by the 1996 restrictions on immigrants' access to public benefits, is largely motivated by the desire to save scarce public resources and to favor citizens in the allocation of those resources. Its incidental effect, however, will be to increase the value of citizenship by widening the gap between the rights of citizens and aliens, thereby creating stronger incentives for the latter to naturalize. Whether this incentive is the kind of motivation for naturalization that proponents of a more robust citizenship have in mind is a question that is seldom asked.

Two other types of reform aim directly at citizenship itself. The current INS commissioner is firmly committed to enhancing the attractiveness of the naturalization process, thereby encouraging more LPRs to acquire citizenship. This effort, however, has been caught up in a congressional investigation of fraud in and partisan manipulation of the naturalization process before the 1996 elections, a review that has already produced administrative reform and may prompt changes in the naturalization law.

A more radical proposal, not at all inconsistent with encouraging naturalization would deny citizenship to some who would otherwise obtain it automatically. This approach would alter the traditional understanding of the *jus soli* rule, embodied in the Citizenship Clause of the Fourteenth Amendment, under which one becomes a citizen merely by being born in the United States, even if the one's parents are in the country illegally or only as temporary residents. Such proposals, which have also been advanced in Canada,[31] would eliminate this type of birthright citizenship either by constitutional amendment or by statute. Advocates of such a change emphasize the importance of mutual consent—the polity's as well as the alien's—in legitimizing American citizenship. They also point to the irrationality of permitting a Mexican woman with no claims on the United States to be able to confer American citizenship on her new child simply by crossing the border and giving birth, perhaps at public expense, in an American hospital. Defenders of birthright citizenship stress the importance of avoiding the creation and perpetuation of an underclass of long-term residents who do not qualify as citizens, a condition similar to that of many guest workers and their descendants stranded in countries that reject the *jus soli* principle.

Congress is unlikely to eliminate birthright citizenship per se although, as noted earlier, political support for this idea has grown recently. Many other nations also apply a birthright citizenship rule. Some others, notably Germany, have been moving towards it, although remaining well short of the American position. Nevertheless, some modification of the traditional birthright citizenship rule might attract wider support in the United States. For example, the law might deny automatic citizenship for those who are born in the United States in illegal status but still enable those native-born illegals who continue to reside here for many years to naturalize at some point. Alternatively, it might reduce somewhat the perverse incentive effects of the current birthright citizenship rule by denying to illegal parents any immigration benefits derived through their birthright citizen children.

III. Citizenship in the Federal System

Among the most striking features of contemporary geopolitics is the fragmentation of national political authority, and its devolution—through the collapse of centralized regimes, civil wars, negotiated agreements, and other decentralizing processes—to smaller, subnational, often ethnically defined groups. This devolution, of course, is still very much in flux. Indeed, as the economic, military, and political disadvantages of radical decentralization become more manifest, some recentralization is bound to occur.

Nevertheless, the rapidity and militancy with which devolution has proceeded are remarkable. This has been most apparent in the former Soviet Union, which fractured in the aftermath of the Cold War. But even before the dissolution of the Soviet Empire, the weaker states of Africa and Asia had been disintegrating into chaos. Devolution is also occurring, albeit more slowly and less dramatically, in older nation-states like Italy, Belgium, and Mexico, and in paradigmatically strong ones like the United Kingdom and France. It is even occurring in nation-states like Canada, which already has highly decentralized federal systems in place.

The United States falls into this last category. Devolution to the states is perhaps the most prominent area of policy innovation pursued by the Republican congressional majority since the 1994 elections. The programs that compose the modern welfare state are being reassessed and, in some cases, fundamentally reshaped to give the states control of central aspects of the policy process: policy design, financing, eligibility, administration, evaluation, and enforcement. The recasting of the AFDC program is the most dramatic example of a fundamental curtailment of federal power and augmentation of states' authority. Although Congress has not yet overhauled the Medicaid, food stamp, and supplemental security income (SSI) programs as thoroughly as AFDC, the precise division of authority between the federal and state governments remains the subject of bitter struggle and intense negotiations. Devolution of control over social programs, along with deregulation and privatization initiatives in a number of other policy areas, reflects a significant repudiation of the New Deal and Great Society; even the Democratic Party has acceded to it. The nationalizing trajectory of American political development has not merely been interrupted; it has been reversed.

These changes are not merely ephemeral. Instead, they reflect deep and abiding forces in U.S. society[32]—and elsewhere in the world. The structures supporting national power will be almost impossible to restore once they are dismantled, for restoration would require three conditions to converge: a convulsive national crisis equivalent to the Great Depression; a renewal of public confidence in the efficacy of centralized power and of national governmental solutions; and a surrender by the states of their hard-won powers. None of these conditions, much less all three, seems likely.

In emphasizing the changing conceptions and roles of national and state citizenship, one must also take note of another institutional development— the private residential enclave—that is becoming an increasingly significant locus of civic membership and governance in the United States.[33] Whether these enclaves take the form of urban apartment condominiums, suburban homeowners' associations, or other co-operative community arrangements, these territorial organizations create new kinds of governance regimes that exercise far-reaching powers over millions of Americans. Although such enclaves are more creatures of private law than public law, and the relationship of people and activities within them are structured more by contracts than by political constitutions, they nevertheless regulate important aspects of their members' lives in ways that closely resemble the powers of government. They too devolve authority—here, from the states, which ordinarily regulate property rights and community development, to private organizations.

These reconfigurations of governance amount to a reconstruction of American citizenship. By redefining the relationships between the citizen and the nation, the citizen and the states, and the citizen and his or her community, these devolutions are fundamentally transforming the rights and duties of membership in the various layers of American polities. In doing so, they are also transforming the meanings that attach to those memberships and those polities.

An important, if relatively unremarked, aspect of this devolution-driven redefinition of citizenship is its possible effect on the status of aliens. The role of the states in defining the rights of aliens in the United States has a somewhat complex history. Until 1875, when the first federal statute restricting immigration was enacted, the states exercised broad authority over aliens' entry and legal rights. Although a Supreme Court decision in 1849 (the *Passenger Cases*) indicated that states could not regulate immigration per se but still possessed a residual constitutional responsibility for protecting the health, safety, and morals of those within their jurisdiction, including aliens. States often exercised their jurisdiction over aliens during this early period in ways that had the effect of limiting immigration, especially by aliens who were poor, ill, or otherwise considered undesirable.[34]

Even after the federal government entered and occupied the field of general immigration control and the Supreme Court invalidated some state laws regulating aliens, states continued to enforce local laws that limited aliens' rights with respect to employment, property ownership, use of public resources, eligibility for public benefits, and other matters. With some exceptions, these statutes were generally upheld by the courts until the 1970s, when the Supreme Court began to apply strict scrutiny to almost all state laws limiting aliens' rights. Relying on the federal government's exclusive, or plenary power, over immigration, the Court went so far as to invalidate even those state law discriminations that tended to reinforce federal policies against illegal aliens by disadvantaging them. In perhaps no other area of legislation has the federal government's primacy been more firmly established and the power of the states more clearly circumscribed.[35]

The plenary power doctrine is a double-edged sword. It has been criticized by many legal scholars (and I count myself among them) who find no textual warrant for it in the Constitution and who contend that the structural and policy justifications that have been used to support it, such as the need for a single voice in foreign affairs, are either weak or over-broad.[36] These scholars believe that the federal government's power over aliens, while broad, must be subject to some constitutional limitations. At the same time, these scholars have generally applauded the courts' reliance on the plenary power doctrine's federal pre-emption logic when used to constrain states' power to regulate and discriminate against aliens. Deepening this tension is the fact that differences between citizens and aliens make the main alternative doctrinal constraint on state alienage discrimination—heightened scrutiny under the Equal Protection Clause—difficult to apply.

The question, then, is how fair treatment of aliens can be assured in a federal system in which the national government possesses plenary, or at least primary, responsibility for regulating aliens while the states, which sometimes have fiscal and political incentives to discriminate against them, possess some degree of policy autonomy, especially in a devolutionary era.

Today, however, this old question has taken on a new coloration. The United States has entered a period of extraordinary constitutional ferment in which the federal government's constitutional authority—even over subjects as to which it has long played the exclusive or dominant policy-making role—is being increasingly challenged. The most dramatic example of this ferment occurred in the Supreme Court's *United States v. Lopez*[37] decision, rendered in 1995. In *Lopez*, a sharply divided Court invalidated a federal statute that prohibited the possession of firearms near schools. It did so on the ground that the federal power to regulate under the Commerce Clause of the Constitution did not extend to such a local activity. Although the decision's scope and significance remain unclear, it cast doubt on almost sixty years of jurisprudence that construed the Commerce Clause to permit virtually any regulation that Congress wished to enact. *Lopez* has already provoked new challenges to long-established laws in policy areas involving highly localized impacts—for example, environmental regulation, drug enforcement, and abortion—which had previously been considered well within the ambit of federal power.

Federal regulation of immigration, of course, would survive a constitutional challenge under *Lopez*. As noted above, more than a century of Supreme Court decisions have emphasized the national sovereignty and foreign policy implications of immigration law, the exclusive federal prerogatives in this area, and the dangers of state encroachment. This traditional approach remains essentially sound, and it is difficult to imagine that the Court, ironically radical as some of its constitutional law conservatism is, would jettison it.

It is not the Constitution, however, that has restricted state responsibility in the immigration field. In a series of decisions invalidating state laws on federal pre-emption grounds, the Court has clearly indicated that Congress remains free as a matter of *policy* to authorize, or perhaps even require, the states to act in this area. The real impediment to a greater state role is Congress, which has long chosen to occupy the field of immigration policy through federal legislation. In recent years, Congress has prescribed only a very limited role for the states in immigration policy—to provide federally mandated social services for refugees. The recent federal court decision invalidating most of California's Proposition 187 on pre-emption grounds is only the most recent example of the limits placed on state policy discretion when it conflicts with federal policy, the state targets illegal aliens.[38]

This situation, however, could change. Nothing in the nature of immigration policy requires that it be an exclusively national responsibility. Although immigration control is a national function in all countries, subnational units in some federal systems—Canada and Germany, for example—do exercise important policy-making functions with respect to immigration. With devolution occurring in so many other areas of public policy traditionally controlled at the center, can immigration regulation remain impervious to the trend? And if the states were to assume a more significant, independent role in immigration policy, a role that Congress might encourage and that the courts might therefore sustain, how would this development alter the nature of citizenship in the American polities?

These questions are by no means academic. Some of the same economic, social, political, and ideological forces that are propelling devolution in other policy areas also affect immigration politics. Immigrants are not distributed randomly across the nation. Quite the contrary; immigration is a largely *regional* phenomenon, with the vast majority of immigrants tending to live in a handful of states and metropolitan areas. However great the economic and other benefits of immigration to the nation as a whole may be, its costs—especially those resulting from immigrants' use of schools, hospitals, prisons, and other public services—are highly concentrated in these few high-impact states and metropolitan areas, while the rest of the country need not incur immigration's costs in order to enjoy many of its benefits. For proposals like Proposition 187 have been prompted by frustration with the costs of services demanded by large immigrant concentrations. For these high-impact states, immigration is as salient as any policy area with which they deal.

That these state-level impacts also have enormous *political* significance is obvious when one considers, as politicians surely do, that the seven states with the largest immigrant populations account for two-thirds of the electoral votes needed to win the presidency.[39] This fact places immigration reform high on the *national* political agenda—and it is from the national level, principally from Congress, that devolution of power over immigration policy must ultimately issue. Signs of movement in this direction appeared in the 1995 federal law limiting unfunded national mandates on states and localities, and in the 1996 welfare reform legislation discussed earlier. One of the practices prompting the unfunded mandates law was the federal government's recent policy of admitting a growing number of refugees while at the same time reducing its funding for resettlement support, thus forcing states, localities, and non-governmental organizations to pick up the tab for the increasing deficit.[40] The 1996 welfare reform law restricts federal policy initiative even further, transmuting AFDC into block grants and leaving the states largely free to determine how to distribute those funds among U.S. citizens while barring the states from spending them on certain alien categories. State laws that impose restrictions on state-financed programs consistent with the new federal restrictions will almost certainly survive constitutional challenge in the courts.

In a recent article, Professor Peter Spiro develops a more sweeping rationale for the devolution of immigration policy to the states.[41] He argues that the interests in national uniformity and control over foreign relations, which constitute the traditional justifications for federal pre-emption in immigration policy, are no longer decisive in a "post-national world order." In that order, according to Spiro, states are the major fiscal and political stakeholders in immigration policy. They also play larger, more independent roles in their dealings with foreign nations. He attributes the more robust state role in foreign relations to the globalization of information, communications, and travel, and to the economic and cultural ties that states have increasingly forged with foreign governments and communities. "This international engagement on the states' part," Spiro writes, "has inevitably undermined the [traditional pre-emption] doctrine's more fundamental underpinning, viz., that other countries will not distinguish the states and their actions from the nation's."[42]

Spiro's argument is less important for his prescriptions, which I find quite problematic, than for his empirical claim that the federal government's monopoly of authority and influence in foreign relations and immigration is steadily (and, in his view, irrevocably) eroding, as the states and private nongovernmental organizations operate more independently of Washington.[43] Assuming that he is correct about this, however, it does not follow that Congress will devolve authority over immigration policy to the states—even if it continues to do so in other policy domains. Congress may instead conclude that immigration is simply *different*, perhaps because, it believes, contrary to Spiro that immigration's foreign policy implications and the need to speak with one voice are considerations of overriding importance.

Alternatively, Congress might adopt a middle path. Congress might decide that *as a matter of national policy*, it is prepared to tolerate greater diversity among states in their treatment of aliens. By adopting an affirmative national policy that allows states to discriminate against aliens in certain areas such as welfare benefits or student loans, Congress could continue to uphold the principle of federal pre-emption while encouraging policy diversity among the states. Such a national policy might well pass constitutional muster as an exercise of Congress's plenary federal power. If so, the courts might then uphold— as consistent with and in furtherance of this federal plenary power—discriminatory state laws that would otherwise raise serious constitutional questions. They might distinguish *Graham v. Richardson*[44] and its progeny on the ground that the discriminations invalidated in those decisions were not authorized by this kind of clearly expressed congressional policy.

In the welfare reform legislation enacted in August 1996, Congress took precisely this middle path on the question of aliens' eligibility for welfare and other public benefit programs. The legislation is very complex. It creates a new legal category ("qualified aliens"); differentiates among particular programs, governmental levels, and alien categories; carves out many exceptions; contains "grandfather" clauses; and provides special transitional rules. Consequently, its specific meanings will remain uncertain for years to come. But, what is of greater interest for present purposes is this: *Congress sought to "revalue" U.S. citizenship by adopting a firm national policy favoring discrimination against LPRs (not just illegal aliens) in the distribution of public benefits and by conscripting the states in the implementation of that new policy.*

In the 1996 law, Congress defined four different policy modalities along a spectrum running from prescription to complete deference. Interestingly, these modalities do not simply track the distinction between federal and state programs (although that distinction is obviously at work in the chosen level of prescription). Moreover, Congress is somewhat prescriptive even where it is deferential.

The first modality, which deals with federal benefits (defined broadly) and is highly prescriptive, precludes any contrary state policies. It bars aliens other than LPRs, refugees and asylum-seekers, and a few other categories of immigrants from access to all federal benefits. The law also bars all *current* LPRs and other aliens with legal status, except for three favored groups,[45] from the fully federal SSI and food stamp programs.[46] Finally, it bars *new* LPRs and other legal aliens (other than those three groups) during their first five years in the United States from all federal means-tested programs such as AFDC and its successor. The law also contains a large number of exceptions including emergency Medicaid, disaster relief, child nutrition, some training, and education.

In its second modality, Congress is more deferential to the states' policies toward aliens—even relating to some federal programs. It *allows*, but does not require, states to bar aliens from three federal programs including: the block grants for temporary assistance for needy families, social services block grants, and non-emergency Medicaid. In contrast, Congress *requires* states to provide these benefits—which in the case of Medicaid benefits are very costly—to the three favored alien groups.

In its third modality, Congress adopts a prescriptive mode regarding most *state and local* benefit programs. States are prohibited from allowing any aliens other than LPRs, temporary visitors, and some other categories to receive state and local public benefits, except for certain emergency programs. States are allowed however, to make *illegal* aliens eligible for those state and local benefit programs, but only if they do so by new, specific legislation. Oddly, this empowers states to place illegal aliens in a better position than certain categories of legal aliens to whom, under the new law, the state may not provide state and local benefits. A fourth modality—deference to state programs—*allows* states to bar legal aliens, other than the three favored groups, from state programs altogether.

This crazy-quilt pattern is not accidental; it is emblematic of the complexity of U.S. policies, federal structure, and public administration. From the perspective of the polity's valuation of citizenship, however, two aspects of the new law's treatment of aliens are particularly striking. First, the federal government has now made a clear, comprehensive policy choice, albeit on that is confusing in its details, in favor of a national policy to discriminate against aliens in its federal programs, and to either require or permit the states to do so in their programs. This policy fundamentally reverses the recent law in this area. With a few exceptions, such as the wholly federal program at issue in *Mathews v. Diaz*,[47] the federal government had largely abandoned the practice of discriminating against aliens and, because Supreme Court decisions held the states to the same rules as a matter of constitutional law, the states could not discriminate either.

New York City, Florida, and other plaintiffs immediately challenged the new federal policy on equal protection grounds. A federal district court in New York, however, has upheld the statute as being rationally related to the federal government's interests in controlling program costs, encouraging aliens to naturalize and to be self-sufficient, and removing an incentive for immigration.[48]

The second noteworthy feature of this new federal mandate to discriminate is that it is part of a statute that vastly enlarges the states' discretion over most other aspects of welfare policy. This means that the new policy on alien benefits is unusual not only substantively, in that it requires discrimination that in other contexts would be unconstitutional, but also structurally, in that it presumes, contrary to the now-dominant thinking about federalism, that Washington knows best and should enforce its "one-size-fits-all" policy preferences on the states.

In general, however, the rights and obligations of individuals—U.S. citizens and aliens alike—will now depend more on state law and less on federal law than at any time since the New Deal. To the extent that Congress devolves immigration policy to the states, *state* citizenship could become more salient than in the past, and the constitutional limits on states' power to discriminate—constraints derived from state constitutions as well as from the U.S. Constitution—will become more significant. State citizenship is a status that has received little scholarly attention of late; it ceased to have much practical significance once states barred aliens from voting in their elections, American Indians received U.S. citizenship, and the Supreme Court interpreted the Constitution's Privileges and Immunities Clause to limit the states' power to discriminate against citizens of other states.

This might change if Congress expressly permitted the states to favor their own state citizens over aliens in areas other than those public benefits covered by the 1996 welfare reform law, however, this might change. The plenary power doctrine might then preclude aliens from challenging Congress's decision to do so under the U.S. Constitution; in that event, aliens' only recourse might be to challenge the state law discrimination under the applicable state constitution. State constitutions typically contain equal protection clauses, and those clauses proscribe many kinds of discrimination—in some cases more completely than the federal Constitution does. But the extent to which state constitutions would limit alienage discrimination would be unclear, particularly where the constitutional issues arise in a novel context in which states exercise new powers and operate outside the shadow cast by traditional federal pre-emption principles—or indeed operate consistently with federal policies favoring discrimination against aliens.

If devolution thus transforms the structure of American federalism, the nature of citizenship in the American polities must also be transformed. The legal, political, and social relationships between an individual alien and the larger juridical communities that affect her relative status and well-being—the national government, state governments, and local self-governing enclaves—will in effect be redefined.

Like so much else in this new devolutionary regime, it is difficult to predict how aliens will fare under it. Some aliens will be better off than they are now, while others will be worse off. Some states and local communities already embrace legal aliens at least as warmly as the federal government does. In such states, this favorable reception is driven by enduring forces; it will probably continue even after the 1996 changes in the welfare and immigration laws are fully implemented. There, aliens are regarded as valuable economic and cultural assets, and politicians anticipate that immigrants may soon become citizens and voters and these politicians may seek support from already established ethnic communities concerned about the newcomers' welfare. State governments in Texas and New Jersey, for example, seem to view legal immigrants as beneficial to their states.[49] Even Pete Wilson, the California governor who promoted Proposition 187, has defended the welfare benefit rights of legal aliens, extending their entitlements under federally funded programs as long as possible. State and city politicians in New York and Massachusetts have welcomed even illegal aliens.[50]

Other states and communities, however, may view at least certain types of immigrants as unwanted invaders, as fiscal and political burdens that the state can hope to shift to other states. The possibility of a so-called race to the bottom, in which states seek to discourage some categories of immigration by adopting more discriminatory policies than sister states, is a powerful argument in favor of pre-empting state immigration policies in a federal system or at least for imposing limits on permissible state discrimination.[51] It is a possibility, moreover, which the 1996 welfare reform magnifies. The experience of other federal nations in dealing with this risk of immigration policy fragmentation should be of special interest to the United States in this devolutionary era.

IV. A Brief Note on "Post-National Citizenship"

In recent years a number of scholars have pointed to a new development in thinking about citizenship—what Yasemin Soysal and others have called the idea of "post-national citizenship." Its "main thrust," according to Soysal, "is that individual rights, historically defined on the basis of nationality, are increasingly codified into a different scheme that emphasizes universal personhood."[52] In this conception, transnational diasporic communities of individuals bearing multiple, collective identities make, and, ideally, enforce claims against states. In contrast to a traditional "national" model of citizenship, individuals—simply by virtue of their personhood—can legitimately assert claims on the basis of their universal human rights (as devolved by evolving principles of international law) whether or not they are citizens, or even residents, of those states.

In somewhat similar terms, David Jacobson notes the emergence of a "deterritorialized identity" that is transforming the nature of, and relationships among, the community, polity, and state, and he cites some judicial decisions that seem to be propelling this transformation. A new dispensation, Jacobson believes, is inevitable:

> The multiplicity of ethnic groups and the absence of contiguity of such groups make any notion of territorially based self-determination patently impossible. However, in so far as such groups can make claims on states on the basis of international human rights law and, hence, become recognized actors in the international arena, territoriality becomes less critical to self determination.[53]

Jacobson quickly adds that this bright promise of post-national citizenship is being realized only in western Europe and North America, acknowledging that eastern Europe is experiencing the very opposite: "the territorialization of communal identity."[54]

These visions of post-national citizenship are undeniably attractive. A just state will respect and vindicate minority groups' claims to cultural diversity and autonomy. Detaching the legitimacy of these claims from their conventional territorial moorings in "normal politics"[55] and traditional citizenship law, as post-national citizenship seeks to do, may sometimes promote their recognition. Indeed, Soysal's own work on the progress of Muslim communities in western Europe suggests this outcome.[56] Some court decisions, which have required polities to extend procedural and even substantive rights to strangers who come within their jurisdiction and claim judicial protection, also seem to point in this direction.[57]

Those decisions, however, remain exceptional and some have been overturned in the United States by the 1996 immigration and welfare reform laws. But a more important set of questions about the character and implications of post-national citizenship are raised by recent events elsewhere in the world. Bosnia, Somalia, Rwanda, Burundi, Cambodia, and all too many other areas of conflict should remind us that the ostensible goals of post-national citizenship—human rights, cultural autonomy, and full participation in a rich civil society—are tragically elusive, and that its achievements are extremely fragile.

The problem is not merely that partisans of exclusion and discrimination will oppose post-national citizenship at every turn and often succeed in establishing illiberal policies in traditional nation-states. The more fundamental problem is that post-national citizenship ultimately depends on its ability to transcend, or at least enlarge, the domains of normal politics and law. After all, if those domains would accept the post-national agenda, there would be no need to advocate it as an alternative to traditional national citizenship and hence no problem. Such a transcendence of normal politics, however, would leave post-national human rights naked and vulnerable with no firm political and institutional grounding. Without such a grounding, national courts enforcing international law principles are unlikely to provide durable, reliable protection.[58] The often feckless international human rights tribunals are even less plausible guarantors of those principles.

Soysal and Jacobson might acknowledge this point yet respond that some protection for post-national citizenship, however episodic, is better than none. But this response does little to shore up post-national citizenship, for its grounding only in adjudication would risk more than an incomplete fulfillment. The problem is not simply that courts are institutionally ill-equipped to defend their rulings in the political arena, or even, as Mr. Dooley famously put it, that the Supreme Court follows the election returns.[59] The greater risk is that the normative foundation of a post-national citizenship may be so thin and shallow that it can easily be swept away by the tides of tribalism or nationalism. As formulated by Soysal in her work on civil society, post-national citizenship, unless it includes rights already established under national laws, possesses only a limited institutional status, largely confined to some courts. Of course, if it were more fully institutionalized than this, the new ideal would be superfluous. Beyond this, Soysal argues, post-national citizenship is built on a "discourse of rights," one that explicitly renounces the Habermasian effort to fuse reason and will in pursuit of a non-coercive consensus. Instead, this discourse chooses "to focus on agendas of contestation and provide space for strategic action, rather than consensus building."[60]

I am not at all certain what this means, but it strikes me as ominous. I worry when normative commitments on which the lives and welfare of vulnerable minorities depend is premised on something as insubstantial, transitory, and manipulable as a "discourse," even a discourse of rights. Discourses of rights are double-edged swords, and my metaphor is grimly apt. The slain in the former Yugoslavia call out an unmistakable warning from their mass graves. Their murderers, after all, were and are participants in a discourse of rights. They too are transnational communities that plausibly invoke universal human rights to legitimize their claims to group autonomy, cultural integrity, and political self-determination. They too believe that these rights are threatened by other communities, even as those other communities, with tragic irony, claim similar rights and perceive similar threats. In this furious competition for communal power, the discourse of rights—universal in form but fatally tribalistic in practice—has legitimized genocidal holocausts. This discourse has been far more destructive of human life, property, and values than all of the well-known limitations of normal politics in democratic polities.

In reasonably democratic states—and post-national citizenship is only possible and meaningful in such states—even an imperfect constitution recognizing minority rights, and even a majoritarian politics in which groups must compete for acceptance of their communal aspirations, are likely to provide more certain guarantees of liberal human rights than a discursive ideal. This is especially true to the extent that the post-national, trans-national ideal is institutionally grounded only in politically isolated courts and lends itself, because of its substantive indeterminacy, to repressive applications. A discourse whose success requires overcoming the messy exigencies of normal politics where expansive conceptions of human rights must contend for legal recognition seems destined to be either irrelevant or anti-democratic.

There is, however, a valuable role that the notion of post-national citizenship can and should fulfill. It should serve as a compelling vision of tolerance, diversity, and integration that people of good will can aspire to, that normal politics in democratic states can sometimes realize, and against which their failures can be fairly judged and condemned. This is the role that it has begun to play in the United States. To claim more for it, or to promote it as an alternative to, or as a cure for, the weaknesses of democratic politics, would ultimately discredit the humane agenda that its proponents advocate. If it can succeed in mobilizing normal politics to win that recognition in positive law, however, it will be truly transformative even as it thereby ceases, in an important sense, to be "post national."

Conclusion

Citizenship is a status whose meaning in any particular society depends entirely on the political commitments and understandings to which its members subscribe. In the United States, many of these commitments and understandings have always been tenuous, contestable, and contested; and some still are.[61] Of no political arrangement is this more true than the American welfare state. It was first established only sixty years ago and it only reached its current form in the 1970s and 1980s, with the rapid expansion of the food stamp, Medicaid, and social security programs.[62] In this mature form,[63] then, the welfare state is less than three decades old. During most of this period, moreover, its legitimacy has been under constant attack by much of the political and intellectual establishment; the present political struggle will determine precisely how firm its hold on the public's allegiance actually is.[64]

This feverish debate over the welfare state, which has continued and in some ways deepened since its inception in the New Deal era, has inevitably shaped Americans' conception of the meaning and incidents of citizenship. In this sense, the American debate might be seen as yet another example of what has tendentiously been called "American exceptionalism"—the notion that, for a variety of complex historical reasons, some of the patterns that have shaped the character of European democracies do not apply, or apply quite differently, to the United States. In this case, however, I believe that such a perception would be mistaken. More likely, the American debate prefigures a re-evaluation of citizenship in Europe.

Such a re-evaluation appears to be inescapable in light of a number of extremely important developments: the enlarged scope and ambition of the European Union; the migration and asylum pressures unleashed by the fall of the Iron Curtain; the social tensions created by large, unassimilated alien populations with limited access to citizenship; the recognition among many European leaders that recent budget deficits are both unsustainable and inconsistent with further monetary and political integration; and the sclerotic performance in recent years of the high-cost European economies in the intensely competitive global markets. Although this debate may resemble the

American one in some respects, it will be distinctively European in many others. As the social, economic, and political conditions of Europe and the United States increasingly converge, we shall have unprecedented opportunities to learn from one another—from our triumphs as well as our mistakes.

9

Consensual Citizenship

The customary division of national laws of citizenship into the "principles" of *jus soli* (place of birth) or *jus sanguinis* (line of descent) denotes the objective criteria most often used to determine one's citizenship. But the conceptions of political membership that have vied for supremacy in Anglo-American law implicate a different, more fundamental dichotomy—one between the rival principles of ascription and consent. These principles reflect quite distinct understandings of the origins, nature, and obligations of political communities, and each promotes certain values that Anglo-American legislators and judges have embraced at different times and often simultaneously. At least since the 18th century, Anglo-American law has embodied compromise doctrines that combine certain features drawn from each conception in the hope of producing pragmatic satisfaction, if not theoretical coherence. As we shall see, however, the two principles are not so easily blended.

In its purest form, the principle of *ascription* holds that one's political membership is entirely and irrevocably determined by some objective circumstance—in this case, birth within a particular sovereign's allegiance or jurisdiction. According to this conception, human preferences do not affect political membership, only the natural, immutable circumstances of one's birth are considered relevant. The principle of *consent* advances radically different premises. It holds that political membership can result only from free individual choices. In the consensualist view, the circumstances of one's origins may of course influence one's preferences for political affiliation, but they are not determinative.

English law assumed from antiquity that all persons born within the dominions of the crown, whether of English or alien parents, were English subjects. Yet neither members of the royal family nor the children of English subjects could lose any rights due to birth outside the king's domain. No theory of membership that could account for these diverse precedents was formally elaborated until 1608, when Sir Edward Coke in the landmark *Calvin's Case* elaborated "the first comprehensive theory of English subjectship." His theory based that status firmly on the ascriptive principle. Through it Coke established once and for all the common membership of Scots and Englishmen in one united community of allegiance, regardless of any contrary indications in any past or future man-made law. To reach this result, Coke appealed to natural law, thereby giving birthright political membership the strongest possible sanction.

Natural law dictated, he held, that one's political identity is automatically assigned by the circumstances of one's birth. Coke understood political identity as being at root a question of one's allegiance as a subject to some sovereign. At birth, every person acquired such an allegiance. The subject owed complete obedience and service; the sovereign owed physical protection and just governance. Being imposed by the eternal law of nature, which was prior to all man-made law, both obligations were perpetual and immutable. Expatriation and denationalization—termination of the allegiance between a natural-born subject and his sovereign by either the individual or the government—were considered contrary to natural law and therefore impossible for either party.

The ascriptive view of Coke, although deployed for particular political purposes, has more universal attractions. It captures a widely shared moral intuition: many persons feel indebted to those who have nurtured them, including the broader political community into which they were born, despite the fact that they did not initially choose to receive that aid. Because our community shapes our identity, our sense of who we are, it may indeed seem natural to feel that one belongs in one's country and owes it allegiance in a way that can never be entirely extinguished. Many also feel that the nation should take responsibility for all those who, through no fault of their own, depend upon it in their most vulnerable years. Indifference to the needs of infants is obviously cruel, and the ascriptive view promises protection to all those thus situated. On a more mundane level, ascription appears to provide clear, simple rules that avoid many complicated questions of nationality and allegiance.

But for all this, the ascriptive view entails several serious problems. First, it significantly constrains individual freedom, however one defines that concept. Birth binds one irrevocably to a particular community of allegiance. According to most modern notions of political freedom, it seems morally wrong to ascribe to an infant inescapable obligations that may, for example, eventually require him to violate his conscience or even jeopardize his life by participating in a war he thinks unjust. Second, ascription significantly constrains governmental control over membership and can compel the state to provide protection to those, most notably illegal aliens, whose entrance into the country it has actively endeavored to prevent. Finally, the formulations of the ascriptive principle provided by Coke create multiple allegiances. Coke explicitly permits weaker, more consensual, but still valid allegiances to coexist with the fundamental obligation to the sovereign who provided protection in one's infancy. When conflicts arise, the ascriptive view cannot resolve them. In *Calvin's Case,* for example, a sovereign wished to assert the primacy of natural subjectship, but in other circumstances he would have favored a different priority, emphasizing instead his claims to the overriding allegiance of children born of his subjects abroad, of naturalized subjects, or of resident aliens. Today, this problem persists in the ambiguous and inconsistent relationships created by dual citizenship.

The assaults on the medieval world of Coke that produced political and ideological revolutions in England and America challenged not only governmental absolutism but also patriarchal supremacy. That dual focus was necessary because paternal and political rule were both defended as ordained by nature, and apologists for autocracy often relied on the more apparently natural authority of fathers to buttress monarchical claims, especially the claim to the perpetual birthright allegiance of native-born subjects. Consequently, when Enlightenment proponents of limited, consensual government sought to challenge absolutist views, they had to reconsider the "natural" authority of fathers over children, its implications for state power, and thus how the circumstances of birth defined one's political membership.

This reconsideration appeared most clearly in the works of John Locke. For example, in each of his *Two Treatises of Government,* Locke took as his main opponents those defenders of the old order who argued that "Everyone is born a Subject to his Father, or his Prince, and is therefore under the perpetual tye of Subjection and Allegiance." The historian James Kettner views Locke as the theorist who best exemplified the transition from ascriptive subjectship to consensual citizenship. Despite some recent reservations about the influence of Locke's *Second Treatise* in America, the choice is appropriate.

Locke's familiar doctrine of government by consent, with its attendant right of revolution, was based on his radically view of the relationship of children to their parents and to the polity, a view that stemmed in turn from a thoroughgoing rejection of the medieval portrait of society as a natural, organic hierarchy. To Locke, the most fundamental fact about children was that they were creatures of God, intended to occupy that equal and independent status that is the natural condition of mature, rational beings. This fact, for Locke, defined limited nature of parental and political authority. Locke agreed that the family was a natural social unit and that parents properly possessed some dominion over their offspring during minority. He maintained, however, that this authority rightfully belonged to both parents, not simply to the patriarchal father. And he insisted, even more vehemently, that parents possessed only limited, tutelary authority over their children, and possessed this authority only while the latter remained incapable of rational self-governance.

The state also possessed a limited jurisdiction over children, for its duties stemmed not only from the consensual will of its citizens. It also had to conform to the obligations posed by the natural human rights that Locke held to be inviolable and inalienable endowment of all persons. As an authorized executor of the law of nature, the state thus had to protect the child's right to life, property, and education should the parents arbitrarily violate their duties to the child. A child, however, could not be a government's subject because subjectship must be based on the tacit or explicit consent of an individual who had reached the age of rational discretion. Locke insisted: *"A Child is born a subject of no Country and Government. He is under his Father's Tuition and Authority, till come to Age of Discretion; and then he is a Free-man, at liberty what Government he will put himself under; what body politick he will unite himself to."*

Locke reveals most of the attractions and limits of the consent principle. Its attractions are considerable: indeed, leading contemporary writers on citizenship and international law insist even more strongly than Lockean Enlightenment and public law writers did that only consent is an appropriate basis political membership. Consensualism encourages genuine personal commitment and development, permitting affirmation of one's values through voluntary affiliation with others. At the same time, as the political philosopher Michael Walzer has argued, permitting a democratic community the power to shape its own destiny by granting or refusing its consents new members is essential if the community is to be able to protect its interests, maintain harmony, and achieve a unifying sense of shared values. When it is combined with liberalism's stress on universally held natural rights, moreover, consent principle recognizes the aspirations and dignity of all humanity, for it urges a world in which all will be linked politically only by bonds of mutual agreement. Because these values of personal autonomy and communal self-definition are so widely shared in American society today, a morally credible doctrine of civic membership must give central importance to membership based on actual, mutual consent.

But like ascription, consent also poses serious problems Although some of these problems can be resolved or minimized without great difficulty, others are more troubling. First, of course, there is a problem of proof. Especially after fact, it will often be hard to determine who has and has consented to membership in a particular regime, expressly or tacitly. Second, there is a problem of unjust exclusion. As most liberals have accepted, consent to membership must be mutual, expressed by the existing community as well as by the individual. Otherwise, existing members will be coerced and their free choices nullified. But this requirement might imply that a society could deny outsiders opportunities for membership in ways that are harshly restrictive or discriminatory. It might also mean that a society could freely denationalize citizens against their will, reducing their security and status, perhaps even leaving them stateless. In both these instances, adherence to consent may well violate liberalism's other deep commitment to insuring that the basic human rights of all be secured as fully as possible. As noted above, the tension between government by consent and full protection for inalienable rights, visible in liberal theory almost from its inception, is dramatically evident if a democratic government denies all obligation to those who are compelled to turn to it but who are not admitted to be its citizens.

The difficulty points in turn to a third, related problem. The notion of consent is far from being a self-defining concept. It necessarily requires assumptions about several highly controversial questions, such as the scope of free will, the nature of informed choice, and the availability of alternatives. By relying upon notions such as tacit agreement, it may even smuggle in elements of ascription. In the context of consensual citizenship, moreover, the requirement of mutuality may seem to render individual consent hollow in practice because those to whom a state refuses consent may have no practical option to go elsewhere. Persons faced with a choice of only limited, exceedingly harsh alternatives may be more aptly described as compelled than free to choose. More generally, no clear, unproblematic boundary exists between the realms of consent and coercion.

Fourth, there is a problem of unlimited expatriation. The consensual principle in its purest form is literally anarchical, jeopardizing all memberships and allegiances. Although some liberals insist that rational individuals can recognize the imprudence of promoting social instability, political societies probably could not survive if their citizens felt free to renounce their memberships unilaterally whenever it seemed convenient to do so. A fifth and related problem of pure consensualism is its narrow, desiccated rationalism. By limiting moral obligations only to those incurred by rational choice, it denies the validity of widespread beliefs that individuals owe something to their family, community, state, and other social groups, and that these groups owe something to their members. The reality of these affective attachments calls into question the adequacy of basing obligation on rational consent alone.

Both the ascriptive and consent principles are thus attractive and problematic in their pure forms. It is tempting, then, to think that the best features of each can be integrated into a coherent law of citizenship without sacrificing some values that we cherish. Doubtless, that hope explains why American law has combined the two and has varied the mix of ascriptive and consensual elements—especially of birthright citizenship and the right of expatriation—over time. But American law has never adequately reconciled these elements; no combination of consent or ascription that is either theoretically satisfying or practically efficacious, especially in light of current conditions, has yet been achieved. For example, two recent and somewhat related developments have begun to place far greater strain on the ideological compromises between ascription and consent in America's citizenship law. The massive increase in illegal migration to the United States and the equally dramatic rise of the welfare state have transformed perhaps the greatest advantage of birthright citizenship from a modern liberal viewpoint—its automatic inclusiveness—into something of a disadvantage. By underscoring the growing practical importance of consent as the chief constitutive political principle of a liberal society, these developments invite us to reconsider birthright citizenship on legal and policy as well as philosophical grounds. They lead us to reject the traditional rule and to propose a more consensualist law of citizenship in which ascribed status at birth plays a correspondingly reduced role.

When the framers of the Fourteenth Amendment's Citizenship Clause adopted (in a significantly compromised form) the common-law rule of birthright citizenship, immigration to the United States was entirely unregulated. In 1998, the number of illegal aliens residing in the United States is estimated at between 5 and 6 million, with the number increasing by approximately 200,000 annually. More than 400,000 of these people will eventually receive legal status under the 1997 amnesty law, but the vast majority of the illegal aliens are not eligible for this relief.

If mutual consent is the irreducible condition of membership in the American polity, questions arise about a practice that extends birthright citizenship to the native-born children of such illegal aliens. The parents of such children are, by definition, individuals whose presence within the jurisdiction of the United States is prohibited by law and to whom the society has explicitly and self-consciously decided to deny membership. And if the society has refused to consent to their membership, it can hardly be said to have consented to that of their children who happen to be born while their parents are here in violation of American law.

The present guarantee under American law of automatic birthright citizenship to the children of illegal aliens can operate, at the margin, as one more incentive to illegal migration and violation by nonimmigrant (temporary visitor) aliens already here of their time-limited visa restrictions. When this attraction is combined with the powerful lure of the expanded entitlements conferred upon citizen children and their families by the modern welfare state, the total incentive effect of birthright citizenship may well become significant. In addition to anecdotal evidence that many aliens do cross the border illegally to assure United States citizenship for their soon-to-be-born children, a recent study illuminates two features of this phenomenon. First, the number of births in the United States to illegal alien parents is not trivial; a conservative estimate places the number as in excess of seventy-five thousand each year. Second, these births—and the public costs that they entail—are disproportionately concentrated in a relatively few urban areas.

Congress has the power to respond to this infringement of consensualism if it so desires. Although the Citizenship Clause of the Fourteenth Amendment has been assumed to guarantee birthright citizenship to such children *ex proprio vigore,* the question of the citizenship status of the native-born children of illegal aliens never arose during its adoption for the simple reason that no illegal aliens existed at that time, or indeed for some time thereafter.

The debates also establish that the framers of the Citizenship Clause had no intention of establishing a universal rule of birthright citizenship. To be sure, they intended to do more than simply extend citizenship to native-born blacks by overruling the reasoning and result in *Dred Scott.* But they also intended, through the clause's jurisdiction requirement, to limit the scope of birthright citizenship. The essential limiting principle, discernible from the debates (especially those concerned with the citizenship status of Native Americans) was consensualist in nature. Citizenship, as qualified by this principle, was not satisfied by mere birth on the soil or by naked governmental power or legal jurisdiction over the individual. Citizenship required in addition the existence of conditions indicating mutual consent to political membership.

Our interpretation certainly does not imply that children of illegal aliens are not entitled to any constitutional protection. Indeed, those children (and perhaps their parents as well) may have legitimate moral or humanitarian claims upon American society. We may be said to have incurred moral obligations to illegal aliens by encouraging them to migrate here, by enriching ourselves through their labor, by absorbing them into our communities, by inviting legitimate expectations of humane treatment, and by other behavior. But even if moral obligations to illegal aliens exist and are compelling, they by no means imply birthright entitlement to American citizenship. Again, that does not mean that policy toward illegal aliens is morally unconstrained. For children who have already been born here of illegal alien parents, for example, a retroactive change in the law depriving them of their citizenship status would violate important expectation and reliance interests and create great confusion and uncertainty.

But these concessions to prudence, fairness, and humanitarianism should not be taken to deny to the American community the essence of a consensual political identity—the power and obligation to seek to define its own boundaries and enforce them. If Congress should conclude that the

prospective denial of birthright citizenship to the children of illegal aliens
would be a valuable adjunct of such national self-definition, the Constitution should not be interpreted in a way that impedes that effort. Citizenship
status is not necessary to afford illegal aliens and their children at least minimal protection and public benefits. They do and should possess certain
rights by reason of their presence within the United States. Protection
against any risk of statelessness can assured by statute. Thus, the Constitution need not and should not be woodenly interpreted either to guarantee
their children citizenship or to cast them into outer darkness.

In the end, the question of birthright citizenship for the children of illegal and nonimmigrant aliens should be resolved in the light of broader
ideals of constitutional meaning, morality, and political community.
These ideas militate against *constitutionally* ascribed birthright citizenship in circumstances. Beyond the issue of the Citizenship Clause's intent,
it is morally questionable to reward lawbreaking conferring the valued
status of citizenship, and it is even questionable to plant that guarantee in
the Constitution. This true even though the lawbreakers are often individuals whose ambition, resourcefulness, and family values most American
would admire. Those characteristics might lead Congress to confer citizenship broadly and easily, but as a matter informed choice, not constitutional inadvertence.

Three basic steps are required to achieve a law of citizenship at birth that
is theoretically consistent, practical addressing current policy problems,
and consonant with the nation's fundamental claim that its government
rests on the consent of the governed. The first step requires a reinterpretation of the Citizenship Clause of the Fourteenth Amendment. Its guarantee
of citizenship to those born "subject to the jurisdiction" of the United
States should be read to embody the principle of consensual membership,
and therefore refer only to children of those legally admitted to permanent
residence in the American community—that is, citizens legal resident aliens.

On our consensualist reading, those born "subject to the jurisdiction" of
the United States would be citizens at provisionally, in the sense that they
would have the opportunity upon attaining majority to renounce that citizenship if they so desired. At no time, however, would they be vulnerable
any denial of consent to their membership on the part of the state. Native-
born children of legal resident aliens would be provisional citizens at birth
and during their minority would enjoy the same right to expatriation. Citizenship at birth would not be guaranteed to the native-born child those
persons—illegal aliens and "nonimmigrant" aliens—who have never received the nation's consent to their consent residence. Even the citizenship
law of the United Kingdom, for whose antecedents our common-law citizenship was originally derived, and which continues to adhere to the

birthright citizenship principle, does not extend it to the native-born children of either illegal aliens or temporary resident aliens. The same is true of other Western Europe countries. Since the proposed doctrine would require a reinterpretation of the Citizenship Clause, the change should be made prospectively, assuring citizenship to those born in the United States while the current understanding has be effect.

Congress, which bears the ultimate responsibility for fashioning the structure of our immigration policy, would also decide the role of the birthright citizenship for the children of illegal and nonimmigrant aliens. That decision is obviously only a small piece of immigration policy. Congress must carefully weigh the moral claims of these children to membership relative to the claims of other groups, assessing the likely effects on illegal immigration of eliminating their present guarantee of citizenship, and considering how such a change should relate to the more comprehensive, systematic measures for reducing illegal immigration. We are genuinely uncertain about how such an evaluation would or should come out. It is an issue on which reasonable people can differ.

The second step necessary to realize a consistent, consensual law of citizenship at birth is to render the right of expatriation more meaningful. We propose that a formal procedure be established and publicized under which any citizen, at the age of majority, may expatriate himself (preserving citizens' rights to do so subsequently as well). Despite recurring calls for legislation fully prescribing formal expatriation procedures, there is no legislated procedure for expatriating oneself within the United States under normal circumstances. As a result, few know that an expatriation right exists, and it is procedurally difficult to exercise. In that sense, citizenship is more ascribed than consensual.

We would not only permit native-born citizens to seek another nationality, but would also guarantee them permanent residence in the United States if they wished it. Our proposal would thus retain the asymmetry, created by Supreme Court rulings, between affirming the individual's right to self-expatriation, while denying the nation's power to denationalize those who are already members. Although a thoroughgoing commitment to pure consensual membership might seem to imply a national power to denationalize citizens at will, the existence of such a power might threaten the vigorous exercise of basic constitutional freedoms, such as First Amendment political rights, or might create a condition of involuntary statelessness and thus of acute human vulnerability.

In *Citizenship Without Consent*, Rogers Smith and I consider a number of objections to our proposal to reinterpret the constitutional guarantee of birthright citizenship. The most troubling objective is that our position does little to address the problem of the influx and status of illegal aliens. Indeed, by eliminating constitutionally mandated birthright citizenship for their native-born children, the proposal could (depending upon the magnitude of its countervailing disincentives to illegal migration) actually increase the number of individuals in illegal status. In this view, the current birthright citizenship rule has at least one virtue that our proposal lacks. It recognizes that in fact (due largely to ineffective immigration enforcement) many native-born children of illegal aliens, along with their parents, will manage to remain here indefinitely. Denying birthright citizenship to those children would add one more obstacle and disadvantage, one more source of stigma and discrimination, to those they must endure as they continue living in American society, as many will be able to do. This dilemma is compounded by the fact that these children's life prospects would be clouded by the action of others over whom they have no control—in this case, the illegal entry of their parents. Better (defenders of the current rule might argue) to eliminate their cruel disability at the moment of birth than to maintain it thereafter.

Although appealing, this argument from life prospects is ultimately unpersuasive. Our proposal to make one's national status turn, at least provisionally, on the national status of one's parents seem more morally acceptable and less determinative of one's life prospects than many other contingent factors—such as inherited wealth, upbringing, or genetic endowment—that are far more likely to shape those prospects in fundamental ways. Indeed, our proposal seems less arbitrary in terms of life prospects than the fundamental concept of birthright citizenship itself, which bases national status wholly upon the accident of geographical location at birth. And even if the innocence of the child and allied concern for his life prospects are accepted as morally or legally relevant, it does not follow that *citizenship,* as distinguished from mere nondiscrimination, should be the prize for that innocence. Nondiscrimination does not necessarily imply the same rights and benefits that citizenship or legal residence status confers. These children and their parents, by being denied birthright citizenship, would not be treated as the *Dred Scott* decision treated blacks; they would not be denied the law's protection. They would instead be required to choose among continuing to live in illegal status, with more limited equal protection and due rights; seeking to obtain legal status; or returning to their home countries.

Our proposed interpretation would, moreover, produce at least one benefit. The government of a more truly consensual polity could more truthfully proclaim to citizens, resident aliens, and illegal aliens alike that American citizenship stands on a firm foundation of freely willed membership. It could more credibly claim the contemporaneous allegiance and, if necessary, the personal sacrifice of its citizens than it was able to do during the Vietnam War and other corrosive national conflicts. It could more persuasively invoke what it now can only baldly assert—a legitimacy grounded in a fresh, vital, and always revocable consent.

10

Plural Citizenships

To reflect deeply on citizenship is to enter a bewildering gyre of reasoning. It is commonly held that citizenship entails a kind of membership, but there the consensus ceases and the contention begins. Membership in what? Why, in the polity of course. And what is a polity? It is a community of citizens. Oh. And does the polity include those who are not citizens? Well, it includes them in some senses but not in others. If it is the citizens who decide on the nature and conditions of non-citizens' inclusion, by what right did they acquire that power and under what limitations do they exercise it? Hmmm.

One cannot really answer these questions without first formulating some theory that can either justify or criticize existing practice. Failing that, a metaphor can sometimes serve as a placeholder or surrogate for theory; it is a kind of theory manqué whose power to persuade lies in its compressed, immediate, deeply felt associations and imagery. For this reason, citizenship-talk usually unleashes a high-stakes rhetorical battle of metaphors. One portrays citizens as members of a family of origin, individuals who are linked to one another irrevocably by blood or by some equally binding historical integument. Another conceives of citizenship as a normative fellowship of belief, a dense community of shared value, what Robert Cover called a *nomos*. A third depicts citizens as members of a club who join and disaffiliate for their own purposes as and when they wish—so long as they meet eligibility standards and their dues are fully paid up. A fourth image of the civic relationship is that of a marriage—formalized through solemn vows, designed to be permanent, and dissolved only with the consent of the state and upon certain proofs.[1]

Each of these metaphors captures certain features of constitutive relationships like that between citizen and state. The idealized family imagery evokes our desires for security, permanence, and unquestioning devotion, a web of mutual commitments beyond choice or calculation; yet it also presupposes a common experience and affinity of descent that are infrequent in a society as radically heterogeneous and open as that of the United

States. The *nomos* metaphor, like that of marriage, draws much of its rhetorical power from our yearnings for commitments that are so intense and unique that they occupy our spiritual domain. The consensuality of marriage, however, preserves room for considerable self-definition and autonomy, whereas the totalizing tendency of religion and the ascriptive tie of family tend to constrict such a space. The club is the most instrumental of these communal forms. Like marriage, club membership is contractual in nature and may generate affective ties but arises out of more calculating, reversible choices. Like markets, clubs require only a partial, episodic commitment from a member; they lay claim to a relatively narrow range of a member's identity.

When the debate turns to dual citizenship or nationality[2] and the question of divided loyalty arises, these metaphors continue to both clash and converge. For those who invoke the family or *nomos* as the dominant image, dual citizenship[3] is an impossibility, a condition utterly at war with the logical, spiritual, emotional, and psychological presuppositions of such communities. For those who liken the polity to a marital relationship, dual citizenship amounts to polygamy, a diffusion of allegiance and affection that threatens the integrity of both relationships. In contrast, those who prefer the club metaphor are quite comfortable with multiple memberships, each for limited purposes defined by the member. Alternatively, one might abandon these relational metaphors altogether and view acquired citizenship as a "new political birth,"[4] or, focusing on citizenship's traditionally territorial-spatial dimension, regard it as a more or less permanent home.

This debate, of course, will not end there. One remains free to question the appropriateness of each of these metaphors as applied to a political community. One can also challenge the metaphors' normative integrity by pointing to certain inconsistent social practices that seem to compromise their coherence—for example, America's separation of the religious and political domains; the multiplicity of family groupings to which American's belong; the blending of families and the generation of new ones through marriage and remarriage; and the cessation of relationships through divorce.[5] Such challenges invite the suspicion that although each of these images captures some significant aspect of citizenship, none provides an adequate account of it.

In this chapter, I hope to move beyond these metaphors by focusing instead on how we might think about dual citizenship without being distracted by such familiar, freighted, and powerful images. This discussion will underscore the profoundly value-laden character of the increasingly incendiary dual citizenship debate, which threatens to polarize Americans in positions that will be difficult to compromise.

Section I of this chapter begins by explaining why dual citizenship is becoming both more common and more controversial. This requires some discussion of the legal and social contexts in which dual citizenship has been liberalized[6] and citizenship itself is being reassessed. Others have ably and recently covered this ground, so my summary can be brief.[7] Section II develops some distinctions that can add texture to our understanding of dual citizenship and help us to identify some leverage points for possible policy change. Section III—the heart of the chapter—analyzes the arguments for and against permitting dual citizenship; it explores both the normative claims and the often-suppressed empirical issues that underlie the normative debate.

Based on this analysis, section IV considers how dual citizenship law might be reformed. I generally applaud the recent trend in U.S. law to accept dual citizenship and believe that this emerging regime should be refined rather than either rejected or extended. I focus on two problems with existing dual citizenship law that deserve reformers' attention. First, the statutory requirement that a naturalizing citizen "renounce and abjure absolutely and entirely all allegiance and fidelity to any" other state, language that dates back to 1795, is broader than necessary to secure the loyalty that the U.S. needs and has a right to expect of its citizens. This broad, indiscriminate formulation obscures what the oath should clarify: the kinds of ties to other states that are inconsistent with American citizenship and must therefore be renounced. It may suggest to new citizens that they are being asked to renounce more than a liberal polity should demand. Second, the renunciation requirement applies only to naturalizing citizens, not to those dual citizens who acquired their U.S. citizenship by birth or descent. This difference creates an inequality among citizens that is difficult to justify and that appears to contradict fundamental constitutional principles. This inequality warrants public scrutiny and debate. By refining and clarifying the renunciation requirement and by calling on Congress to make the rights and obligations of citizens—old and new alike—as equal as possible, I hope to remedy both problems.

I readily acknowledge that if my approach to the first problem were adopted—if the oath were modified to require new citizens to renounce only the core political allegiance that they bear to another state—the U.S. dual citizenship policy and practice might change little. Americans (whether single or dual citizens) might continue to view their political rights and duties much as they do now, naturalization officials and the courts might interpret the standards as before, and aliens' incentives and propensity to seek naturalization might remain largely unaffected. Even if my proposal would change little in practice, however, this is hardly ground for objection. Since I do not regard the current permissive dual citizenship policy as being fundamentally "broke," I see no strong reason to "fix" it except for refining the renunciation language in the oath. On the other hand, my approach to the second problem—reducing the inequality among citizens with respect to their right to acquire dual citizenship—would affect the right of existing U.S. citizens to acquire additional nationalities in the future and to act accordingly.

Some commentators on citizenship issues, including me, have expressed doubts about the dominant conceptions of citizenship, the distribution of rights and responsibilities among those who reside in the polity, and the justifications advanced to support this distribution.[8] Although these criticisms raise interesting and important issues concerning citizenship, none of them doubts the fact that strong normative arguments can be made for retaining some distinctive citizenship status, although disagreement exists about which arguments are most persuasive. In what follows, I shall assume the essential validity of the status of citizenship,[9] even as I question certain conventional ways of thinking about and regulating it.

I. The Contemporary Debate and Context

It is only a matter of time before Congress takes up the dual citizenship issue. A number of structural changes are stoking Americans' anxieties about the course of the nation's political development and about the coherence of its national identity. These changes include the globalization of the economy; easier travel; instantaneous and inexpensive communications; increased immigration, especially by the undocumented; diminished American autonomy in the world; the expansion of multinational corporations and the emergence of influential transnational nongovernmental organizations; growing multicultural pressures prompting concerns about immigrant assimilation and English language acquisition; the loss of a unifying ideology; dizzying technological changes; the expansion and consolidation of the welfare state; and what many perceive to be a devaluation of American citizenship.

In analyzing these developments, I have suggested that together they are already precipitating a re-evaluation of the meaning of citizenship and of the legal and political practices that give shape and texture to that meaning.[10] This re-evaluation of citizenship is broader, more robust, and more radical[11] than perhaps any consideration of the subject since the 19th Amendment was adopted in 1920. It is even more remarkable because much of the law governing citizenship is both old and relatively stable. With several extremely important exceptions—the 1798–1801 period when the Alien and Sedition Acts were in effect, the elimination of racial and gender barriers to eligibility in 1870, 1920, and 1952, and the more durable ideological exclusion and English language requirement added in 1906[12]—the legal requirements for naturalization have changed little since the First Congress. The principle of birthright citizenship (*jus soli*) was established even earlier; indeed, its English roots have been traced back to 1290.[13]

Despite (or perhaps because of) their antiquity, both naturalization and birthright citizenship principles are now under active reconsideration. In the wake of the political and legal imbroglio arising out of the naturalization of thousands of ineligible aliens shortly before the 1996 elections,[14] as well as prosecutions of private naturalization testing organizations for large-scale fraud,[15] Congress is investigating the administration of the naturalization program and reviewing the naturalization standards themselves. Legislation to limit birthright citizenship for the native-born children of illegal aliens is also under active consideration.[16]

Because dual citizenship is a product, among other things, of naturalization and birthright citizenship rules, controversy over those rules necessarily implicates dual citizenship as well. But dual citizenship raises a host of other controversial questions that extend well beyond the issues raised by naturalization and birthright citizenship. The context in which dual citizenship operates, moreover, is being transformed. It is not surprising, then, that prominent academics and policy-oriented foundations are now taking a lively interest in the subject and are publishing important critiques of existing practices.[17] The INS itself has commissioned an outside consultant to study the possibility of "re-engineering" the naturalization process.

No reliable data exist on the number of Americans holding dual citizenship, but there can be little doubt that the total is growing rapidly. With current legal and illegal immigration approaching record levels, naturalization petitions quintupling in the last five years to almost 2 million a year, and legal changes in some of the largest source countries that encourage (and are often designed to encourage) naturalization in the U.S., dual citizenship is bound to proliferate. This fact alone would justify Congress's reconsidering U.S. dual citizenship policy.

But this reassessment reflects more than simply the growth of dual citizenship. Modern transportation and communication technology makes residence and effective participation in two polities easier than ever, converting many merely "technical" dual nationals into functional ones.[18] Many Americans believe that immigrants today are naturalizing for "selfish" reasons—for example, to obtain social benefits for which only citizens are eligible—and that the rules should be changed to require, or at least encourage, purer motives for naturalization. A decade ago, many commentators expressed consternation over Rupert Murdoch's naturalization, which appeared to have been prompted primarily by Murdoch's desire to qualify under Federal Communications Commission rules limiting ownership of multiple media properties to U.S. citizens.[19] More recently, controversy over the judicial decision to free convicted rapist Alex Kelly on bail led critics to allege that he and his parents had acquired Irish citizenship for the sole purpose of facilitating his flight from the U.S. should he decide to become a fugitive rather than face prison.

The government does not maintain a registry documenting the incidence of dual citizenship (much less indicating how and why it is acquired) so it is far from clear that the "opportunistic" use of the practice has increased.[20] But there is a more fundamental reason why we cannot answer this question. Even if it were possible to discern and disentangle the complex mix of feelings that surround a decision to naturalize, no social or political consensus exists on the normative question of which motives are and are not legitimate; indeed, this issue has scarcely been discussed.

Whatever aliens' motives for naturalizing may be, the road to dual citizenship seems easier to travel today than it was in the past. Both of the social behaviors that create new opportunities for dual citizenship—marriage between individuals with different nationalities and international migration by individuals—have become more common, and the legal rules that govern dual citizenship are also changing in ways that permit migrants to exploit these opportunities. The interaction between these behaviors and rules, then, has increased the dual citizen population.[21] Many of the principal countries of origin have amended their nationality laws to enable their nationals in the U.S. to acquire American citizenship more easily.[22] Mexico, the Philippines, the Dominican Republic, Canada, and India, for example, now confer their nationality on the children born to their nationals in the U.S.; these infants simultaneously acquire birthright citizenship in America.[23] The Council of Europe is also moving in this direction; its draft convention would permit those who become dual nationals in member states by birth to retain both nationalities.[24] To the extent that states like Germany, which traditionally accepted few permanent immigrants and refugees begin to accept more of them—a course that the U.S. increasingly urges upon them—they will be under greater pressure to liberalize their policies toward dual citizenship in order to facilitate the assimilation of these newcomers.[25]

More important for present purposes, major source countries are also making it easier for their nationals to retain that nationality when they naturalize in the U.S.—and easier to reacquire it thereafter if it is subsequently lost, as through mandatory renunciation in the course of naturalizing in the U.S. Some of these countries have repealed provisions that required those wishing to renaturalize in their country of origin to renounce their other nationalities, while others decline to give effect to their own nationals' renunciations if those renunciations are required by the second state as a condition for naturalizing (as in the U.S.).[26] Moreover, many countries of origin that might be prepared to effectuate their nationals' renunciation of citizenship may nevertheless fail as a practical matter to learn of the renunciations and thus will continue to treat them as their nationals.

An important instance of this liberalizing trend—at least in terms of the number of individuals who may be affected—is a new Mexican law that took effect in March 1998. It reverses longstanding constitutional limitations on Mexican dual nationality and enable Mexicans who naturalize in the U.S.—estimated to exceed 100,000 in 1996—to retain (or reacquire) their Mexican nationality, which confers many economic rights in Mexico but not the franchise. (Mexico would continue to require, as the U.S. does, that those who naturalize there must renounce their other citizenships). A second change limits its *jus sanguinis* transmission of citizenship/nationality to the first generation; children born in the U.S. to Mexican citizens will be Mexican nationals but their children will not (unless, of course, they naturalized there).[27] Although estimates of the number of Mexicans eligible to do so range from 2.3 to 5 million,[28] the new balance of incentives created by this law, coupled with legal and policy developments in the U.S. that are prompting record levels of aliens to petition for naturalization, strongly implies that the number of Mexicans seeking to naturalize will be much larger than would be predicted from the group's traditionally low rate of naturalization in the U.S.[29] In India, another major source country, a major political party supports similar liberalization of its dual citizenship law.[30]

These changes clearly demonstrate the most significant change of all: other states increasingly *want* their own nationals to acquire U.S. citizenship—a striking departure from the historical pattern.[31] Approximately 60 percent of Swiss nationals now live abroad as dual citizens, a fact evidently desired by the Swiss state.[32] Sending states in Central America attach enormous importance to the remittances by their nationals of funds earned in the U.S., which are likely to increase if those migrants can acquire dual citizenship.[33] The "transnational communities" created through their nationals' dual citizenship in the U.S.—communities often reinforced by multinational enterprises and international nongovernmental organizations—increase the flow to these states not only of remittances but of technology, skills, and tourism.[34] These states also welcome the growing prospect that their nationals, once naturalized and able to vote in the U.S., may succeed in influencing American politics in ways that will serve the interests of the states of origin.[35]

The growth of the U.S. dual citizen population, however, reflects changes in domestic law as well as developments in foreign law. The U.S. has acquiesced in these external changes by not attempting to counter them, but it has also magnified their effects simply by its growing toleration of dual citizenship. For example, the INS has steadily increased the resources and visibility that it devotes to the promotion of naturalization. Yet the U.S. has also refrained from taking any meaningful steps to ensure that its new citizens' renunciation oaths are legally effective in their countries of origin (which, as just noted, usually make little or no effort to do so).

Since the 1960s, moreover, the U.S. courts have limited the government's authority either to denationalize its citizens or to denaturalize those who have acquired citizenship through misrepresentation.[36] Congress might have responded to these limits by framing narrower standards capable of surviving judicial scrutiny but it has not done so. Indeed, it has enlarged dual citizenship over time by narrowing the severe gender bias in prior law that made it easier for females to lose their U.S. nationality by marrying foreigners and made it harder for females to transmit *jus sanguinis* citizenship to their children born abroad.[37] By substantially raising the level of legal immigration, the U.S. has multiplied the number of aliens who will eventually naturalize and who will, despite the renunciation requirement, retain or reacquire their prior nationalities. The U.S. State Department, bowing to such realities, has gradually shifted its official policy from one of opposition to dual citizenship to one of grudging acceptance.[38]

These liberalizations in law and policy advance important humanitarian goals. They reflect both efforts by countries of origin to facilitate their nationals' naturalization in the U.S. (and elsewhere) by not automatically denationalizing them when they do so, and efforts by the U.S. to reduce the tension between the unwanted growth of dual citizenship and a commendable desire to avoid the potentially harsh effects of denationalization and denaturalization on individuals who often possess strong ties to the United States.

Noteworthy as these liberalizations have been, they do not necessarily mark an inexorable trend. Because they also entail some risks to the polity's interests (discussed in section III), they can generate a political reaction and reversal. Canada has recently had some second thoughts about its liberalized law,[39] and the U.S. is likely to reconsider its own changes in light of new developments, especially the new Mexican nationality law, which heighten the doubts and anxieties about dual citizenship that many Americans harbor.

II. Some Policy-Relevant Distinctions

Before turning to the putative advantages and disadvantages of dual citizenship, it is worth briefly considering five distinctions that may help to clarify the debate over the effects, merits, and possible reform of dual citizenship policy. These distinctions concern (1) who is affected by dual citizenship; (2) the role of consent in citizenship law; (3) how Congress may regulate political and non-political rights; (4) the different treatments of original and newly acquired citizenship; and (5) the effectiveness of renunciation of prior citizenships.

1. Entities Affected.   Different entities may be affected by dual citizenship policy and will therefore seek to shape the rules governing it. (An appraisal of these effects is deferred until section III).

Dual citizenship most obviously affects the *individuals* who may acquire, or be denied, that status. Many procedural and substantive rights turn on whether one is a citizen of the polity in which one lives or does business. Moreover, polities define the specific content of those rights differently, although international law seeks to reduce those differences. For example, one's ability or willingness to migrate and to work or receive public benefits in the destination state will vary with the state (or states) in which one can claim and exercise those rights.

Dual citizenship affects the interests of *states* quite apart from its impact on individuals. Because dual citizenship rules affect the incentive and opportunity to migrate to and remain in the destination state, they help to shape the political identities of states and their inhabitants, as well as the contours of public programs and budgets. Historically, at least, dual citizenship policies have also had far-reaching impacts on the military, diplomatic, political, and commercial relationships among states, which has occasioned bilateral and multilateral conventions seeking to regulate dual citizenship.[40] For these reasons, dual citizenship also affects the interests of the states' existing citizens. They will have strong feelings, of course, about who belongs to their community and under what terms. Like stockholders facing a possible dilution of their shares, they do not wish to see their own membership devalued by extending membership to others "too cheaply." As taxpayers, they want to ensure that their fiscal burdens are not increased unduly.

Finally, the *international community* possesses a discrete interest in dual citizenship rules insofar as it hopes to minimize the risk that individuals will be rendered stateless, a goal that it has long sought to achieve through international agreements. States' general, *ex ante* interest in a system that minimizes statelessness, of course, is not inconsistent with the *ex post* reality that particular states, when confronted with a potentially stateless individual's claim for citizenship in their polity, may decide to oppose that individual's claim. Although this interest might seem superfluous—dual citizenship, after all, presupposes an existing nationality in some other state—it is not. In a world of mass migration, poor record keeping, uncertain citizenship rules, and state incentives to deny nationality to some individuals who may claim it or to withdraw it from some who already possess it, the international community may view dual nationality as a kind of safety net for those who might otherwise fall between the cracks of the state system.[41]

2. Consent. Broadly speaking, one may acquire or lose citizenship consensually or nonconsensually. Naturalization, of course, is the paradigmatically consensual mode of acquisition, at least as for adults. (Parents' naturalization can confer nationality on children without the latter's consent.)

The more nonconsensual modes of acquisition include citizenship conferred at birth and descent through the operation of *jus soli* and *jus sanguinis*. Marriage is a hybrid mode of acquiring citizenship; one might view it as either consensual or nonconsensual, depending on whether one focuses on the individual's awareness of the nationality consequences when marrying or on the automaticity of citizenship upon marriage (where that is the rule). Citizenship may be lost consensually through expatriation where one has renounced citizenship or performed some other act that has that legal effect. (Under U.S. law, one must also *intend* that it have that effect). It may be lost nonconsensually through a state's denationalization or denaturalization of a citizen without that alien's knowledge or assent, where the state's rule permits this.

The perceived consensuality of one's acquisition or loss of dual citizenship may affect the way in which it is evaluated by others and hence the consequences that they may wish to attach to that acquisition or loss. This is not to say that consent is the only criterion of legitimacy, only that it is, in some form, the most widely accepted and important.[42]

In one view of the matter (and other things being equal), a citizenship that one actively seeks through naturalization—especially if accompanied by an express renunciation of another allegiance—is likely to be viewed as more genuine, deliberate, and morally deserving of recognition than one that is acquired adventitiously and without some measure of personal commitment or at least continuing connection to the polity. The perceived fairness and legitimacy of a citizenship acquired passively and automatically through one's parents may vary depending on whether the nationality-conferring event is defined as birth in a state to which the parents are significantly linked (what might be termed "qualified" *jus soli*), birth in a state where the parents simply happen to find themselves at nativity (absolute *jus soli*), or birth to these parents *wherever* they may be located (*jus sanguinis*). By the same token, a loss of citizenship caused by a voluntary, knowing act of expatriation will probably be perceived as fairer and more legitimate than an involuntary, state-imposed denationalization. This is not to deny that one's political or national identity may be powerfully shaped by a citizenship that is acquired nonconsensually; it is merely to call attention to the normative appeal of consent as a standard legitimating many important social practices.[43]

If the consensuality of an acquisition or loss of citizenship is viewed as an important indicator of its legitimacy, then the methods that a state uses to regulate acquisition and loss are likely to be designed to test its knowing, voluntary character. Requiring the individual to take a naturalization oath is one such technique; mandating that the individual elect one nationality, as through renunciation of other allegiances or designation of one nationality as "primary,"[44] is another. Some states are more lenient in permitting their nationals to retain a second citizenship if it was acquired involuntarily (as through *jus soli*) rather than through naturalization. This same purpose of measuring and ensuring consent explains the requirement that a parent (or under now-repealed law, the individual in question) establish some period of residence in the U.S. in order to acquire *jus sanguinis* citizenship, a requirement that the Supreme Court has held to be constitutional (*Rogers v. Bellei*).[45] It also explains the constitutional (and now statutory) requirement that expatriation occur only through an unambiguous act and formal procedures giving some assurance that the relinquishment of citizenship will be both knowledgeable and voluntary.[46]

3. Regulating Political and Non-Political Rights. Political membership in the polity is the hallmark of citizenship, and political rights are usually limited to citizens.[47] The most important of these, of course, is the right to vote, but other political rights such as eligibility to hold high public office and to contribute money to political campaigns may also be restricted to citizens. Congress defines political and non-political rights and decides how they are to be distributed among citizens, non-citizen nationals, and aliens; in this way it establishes the functional significance of these statuses.

This power is subject to constitutional constraints. The two most important ones are the mandate that naturalization rules be "uniform" and the equal protection principle, which the Supreme Court has interpreted to preclude distinctions between naturalized and other citizens, at least in the expatriation context.[48] On the other hand, these principles might not prevent Congress from providing that U.S. citizens who subsequently naturalize in other countries may not exercise political rights there, so long as Congress did not discriminate unfairly between groups of U.S. citizens. Indeed, Congress might possess the constitutional power to prohibit U.S. citizens from naturalizing elsewhere at all, even though *Afroyim* might preclude it from enforcing this prohibition through the harsh and thus constitutionally limited sanction of expatriation.

4. Original Versus New Nationality. The coexistence of these congressional powers and constitutional constraints render even more doubtful the continuing differences between those who already possess U.S. citizenship and those who wish to acquire it through naturalization, with respect to their opportunities to enjoy dual nationality. After all, the latter are required as a condition of naturalization to renounce their earlier allegiances and thus be limited to a single citizenship, whereas the former are free to acquire new ones as they wish. How can this be justified in light of the *Schneider* principle of legal equality between all citizens? The truth is that little or no attention has been devoted to the question.

In both the debate about and the practice of dual citizenship, the assumption seems to be that one's original nationality is more binding and deeply felt and thus less problematic than one's subsequently acquired nationality. Americans seem to worry much more about the divided loyalties of those who are nationals of other states and wish to naturalize in the U.S. than they do about the loyalty of American citizens who choose to naturalize in other countries while retaining their American citizenship (as other states increasingly permit them to do). This interesting premise seems to drive the renunciation requirement which is at the heart of American dual citizenship law. Why else would the law require naturalizing citizens to renounce other national allegiances while permitting U.S. citizens to acquire other nationalities without constraint?

Yet the basis for this premise is far from clear. Recall that one can only naturalize in the U.S. by actively and solemnly renouncing one's original nationality—an act that provides some affirmative evidence of loyalty and commitment to the U.S. In contrast, American citizens who naturalize elsewhere may have never been obliged to acknowledge or even confront seriously their sentiments about the U.S.; rather, Americans simply infer allegiance from their continued residence and minimal law abidingness—surely weaker indicia of loyalty and commitment. As Sanford Levinson puts it, "American law tolerates political bigamy so long as the second political marriage follows, rather than precedes, the acquiring of United States citizenship."[49]

The explanations for this practice may be more chauvinistic than rational.[50] Perhaps Americans imagine that fellow citizens who naturalize elsewhere (or who take up residence in their country of origin) without renouncing their U.S. citizenship must be taking this step not out of dissatisfaction with American society but in order to serve some instrumental purpose (say, retirement or business) or to affirm a religious or ethnic tie (as with Ireland or Israel), and that doing so is not inconsistent with retaining their political loyalty to the U.S. Only if they use their new citizenship to shirk obligations to American society, such as avoiding taxes or military service, do their fellow Americans begin to question their suitability for continued citizenship.[51]

A more psychological explanation would be that the first allegiance (like first love?), because it grows out of an earlier acculturation in another society, is the dominant, deeper, and more durable one unless it is renounced (and perhaps even then); a newer allegiance thus seems more opportunistic and shallow, thus less legitimate. The opposite assumption, of course, also seems plausible. That is, an allegiance explicitly acknowledged during maturity and after some study of American institutions is likely to be more genuine than one for which no acknowledgement has been required and that may have never been put to a serious test.

Even if the premise is true on average (how would we know?), it is surely both underinclusive and overinclusive. After all, many of those who naturalize do so after having resided in the U.S. for quite a long period of time during which they may have become fully assimilated, whereas birthright or *jus sanginis* citizens may have spent little or no time in the U.S. (The requirements of physical presence and residence in the United States, which sometimes condition the transmission of *jus sanguinis* citizenship, now apply to the parents, not to the child who thereby gains citizenship.)

The Supreme Court has also played its part in creating and legitimating this asymmetry by refusing in *Afroyim* to recognize the effectiveness of congressionally defined expatriating acts unless they are voluntarily performed with the specific intention of relinquishing U.S. citizenship, a ruling that Congress accepted and codified in 1986. Although the Court primarily invoked textual and rights-based justifications for the position, it may well have been influenced by the assumptions that a first citizenship is less vulnerable to dilution than a subsequently acquired one and that Congress can always ensure the integrity of the latter by prescribing standards for naturalization if it wishes.

5. Formal Versus Effective Renunciation.   U.S. law requires those who wish to naturalize to renounce their other political allegiances as a formal matter. Unlike Germany, however, the United States does not require that these prospective aliens make such renunciation legally effective by successfully expatriating themselves under the other state's law, much less that they provide proof of such expatriation to the naturalization court. As Gerald Neuman has shown, even the German practice provides for exceptions (such as when expatriation is not possible or is unreasonable), and in any event this requirement is far from foolproof.[52] Evasion (by the naturalizing citizen, the country of origin, or both) and non-enforcement are likely to be common in any such system. The arguments for and against requiring a truly effective renunciation are of course the arguments for and against dual citizenship, a subject to which I now turn.

III. An Assessment of Dual Citizenship

Dual citizenship, like other complex social-legal phenomena, is difficult to evaluate. It is not simply that the normative criteria to be applied to it are deeply contested—although they are. It is also that the empirical consequences of the current regime of dual citizenship, and of the various reforms that might be adopted, are highly uncertain. We know what the rules of dual citizenship are (they are admirably clear, except for the standards for denaturalization),[53] but we lack any reliable information concerning how those rules actually affect the sensibilities and behavior of would-be and existing citizens and how those effects might change if the rules were altered in one way or another.

To render the evaluative enterprise manageable, one is tempted to elaborate models designed to capture the disparate values that might be brought to bear on it. In an earlier effort to appraise naturalization policy, for example, Gerald Neuman did just that, sketching four "simple normative models" or perspectives that he called unilateral liberal, bilateral liberal, republican, and communitarian.[54] Although Neuman's article contained some very useful insights, his models did little analytical work for him. What was interesting in his analysis did not derive from the models, in part because they were characterized at so high a level of generality that many naturalization practices could be justified under several or all of the models.[55]

I doubt that an effort to develop more rigorously specified normative models of dual citizenship would be worth the trouble. Instead, I shall employ the less systematic but perhaps more effective approach of canvassing the advantages and the disadvantages for the American polity of dual citizenship (in various possible forms), drawing on a variety of normative perspectives including those that are suggested by Neuman's models. In each case, I shall try to highlight the most important but unanswered empirical questions on which the integrity of such evaluations may ultimately depend. The answers to such empirical questions will obviously determine—from a given normative perspective—the magnitude of benefits and costs that the evaluator will assign to some aspect of dual citizenship. Obviously, the variety of possible normative perspectives merely compounds these uncertainties by raising a further, more fundamental question of whether one should characterize dual citizenship as a benefit or as a cost in the first place.

In light of the indeterminacy of any overall assessment under these (quite common) conditions, it should not be surprising that I do not reach any crisp, rigorously derived evaluative conclusions. Nevertheless, at the end of the day I am inclined to think that the growth of dual citizenship is on balance a good thing. Moreover, I am able in section IV to recommend a nontrivial (or so it seems to me) policy change that seems broadly consistent with *all* of the leading normative perspectives.

Benefits of Dual Citizenship.   As noted in section II, dual citizenship's benefits flow to a number of different entities. For individuals who hold dual citizenship, the status is advantageous because it provides them with additional options—an alternative country in which to live, work, and invest, an additional locus and source of rights, obligations, and communal ties.[56] Despite the growing and enthusiastic literature on transnational communities,[57] it is a fair question whether the quality of dual citizens' relationships to their polities and civil societies is diluted by the possible diffusion of attention, affection, and commitment that dual citizenship may entail. People who commute between two communities, for example, often report that they feel a bit alienated from both and fully attached to neither.

On the other hand, many people who are members of two nuclear families (perhaps through divorce and remarriage) seem to feel intense ties to both. Even if the quality (somehow defined) of each relationship were diminished, it might well be that the total satisfaction derived from the two families taken together is greater than before.

It is hard to know how to answer such questions, just as it is hard to know which of these (or other) analogies to dual citizenship is most appropriate in thinking about it. What is clear, however, is that the individual's choice is always a necessary, albeit not sufficient, condition of dual citizenship. Because it is usually acquired voluntarily and can be renounced when it is not (or no longer) desired, no individual is compelled to be a dual citizen against his will for very long (although the law may prevent some who wish to be dual citizens from becoming or remaining one). The individual who perceives dual citizenship to be a benefit will become (or remain) one if he can (i.e., if the law permits it); otherwise not. From a liberal perspective—and perhaps under some versions of republicanism and communitarianism as well—this is justification enough for dual citizenship.

U.S.-based business firms also benefit from dual citizenship. Employees, by acquiring dual citizenship, become more valuable to a firm because they can travel and work abroad more easily, are more likely to be bilingual, and can more readily build transnational market networks that will advantage the firm. By the same token, other states and their citizens benefit from the liberal availability of dual citizenship in the U.S. I have already noted that the steady flow of remittances from the U.S. is essential to the social and economic viability of many other societies, but the dynamic is a more general one. Just as genuinely free trade among nations tends to benefit all participants, so too does the international flow of human, financial, and technological capital that dual citizenship facilitates. For the same reason—and also because (as noted earlier) dual citizenship reduces the risk of statelessness, which all countries have a strong interest in minimizing—the international community of states benefits.

Finally, dual citizenship confers significant benefits on American society as a whole. In addition to the economic advantages (including tax revenues) generated by a population with many dual nationals, there are exceedingly important social and political advantages. Citizenship probably facilitates (as well as reflects) the assimilation of newcomers by imparting a sense of welcome and belonging, reinforcing their attachment to American values and improving their English language skills.[58] Citizenship also helps to legitimate the exercise over them (and others) of governmental power; it reduces the risk that they will be subject to discriminatory treatment. To the extent that a liberal dual nationality policy encourages long-term immigrants to naturalize—a causal relationship, as assumed by most commentators[59]—it advances the essential democratic value of full political and social participation by all individuals who are subject to the polity's coercive authority.

Even a liberal state, which more than republican and communitarian polities, values individuals' rights to decide for themselves whether and how to participate, may nevertheless have a strong interest in actively encouraging resident aliens to naturalize. The reason, I have noted elsewhere, is that "[a]t some point . . . the ratio of aliens to citizens might become so high that aliens' lack of direct or indirect political participation and representation would present a serious problem for democratic governance. . . . "[60] Sanford Levinson put the point this way: "[O]ne must ask if a country consisting primarily of resident aliens can sustain itself as a community with ideals worth professing."[61] Such a scenario, I suggest, is by no means far-fetched; if current trends continue, almost one-third of Germany's population by 2030 will consist of foreign nationals, and in large cities the figure could reach 45 percent.[62]

Peter Spiro sees an additional attraction of dual citizenship. Citing as an example the 1996 elections in the Dominican Republic in which many U.S. dual citizens voted, he imagines that if those who acquire U.S. citizenship thereby absorb American constitutional values, they "may put those values to work not only in the U.S. but also in the country of origin. . . . Dual nationality . . . could become a part of the U.S. strategy to enlarge global democracy." The desirability of having U.S. citizens who retain their political links to other countries is thus an argument for eliminating the renunciation requirement in U.S. law.[63]

Costs of Dual Citizenship. Were these benefits the only consequences of dual citizenship, it would hardly be the contentious public issue that it is— and will increasingly become. A liberal dual citizenship policy entails costs, however, and they must be taken into consideration in evaluating its merits.

Some of these costs are rather mundane and unlikely to have much weight in any overall evaluation of the merits of dual citizenship policy. For example, dual citizenship can magnify legal uncertainties and hence the transaction costs associated with resolving them. Under conventional conflict of laws principles, an individual's citizenship can be a factor in determining the jurisdiction whose law applies to that person's conduct, transactions, or status. This determination becomes correspondingly more difficult where the person possesses two nationalities.

A more significant cost of dual citizenship, which arises from the 1996 welfare reform statute, is fiscal in nature. Under this statute, which departs radically from prior law, most aliens—including those who have lived in the U.S. for many years—are no longer eligible for some valuable public benefits and services to which citizens may be entitled. Providing these benefits and services to resident aliens imposed a substantial fiscal burden on the federal government, which was a major reason why aliens were targeted as part of the deficit reduction effort in the first place.[64] (The assumption of these fiscal burdens by the state and local governments, which have moved with surprising speed to narrow the gap created by the federal statute,[65] has merely shifted the costs rather than eliminating them.) To the extent that a liberal dual citizenship policy confers public benefit entitlements on individuals who, if they remained aliens, would not otherwise receive them, those budgetary costs would again be borne by government.[66] And to the extent that those marginal costs are occasioned by individuals who did not contribute commensurate taxes to the U.S., this fiscal effect will be even more objectionable to many existing citizens.[67]

Less quantifiable is the effect of dual citizenship on the state's obligation to provide diplomatic protection to its citizens. Peter Spiro recently analyzed this consideration, noting that the traditionally unfettered right of a state to treat its own citizens pretty much as it likes sometimes clashes with the second state's right and obligation to protect its citizens (single or dual) when they are abroad, including when they are in their other country of nationality where the second state's protection responsibility was traditionally not applicable.[68] He maintains, however, that the establishment of a regime of general international human rights, in which a state may protest another states' mistreatment of individuals regardless of whether or not they are nationals of the protesting state, effectively reduces the protesting state's diplomatic protection burden. Spiro acknowledges that dual citizenship may intensify such interstate conflicts but asserts that this "will be more a matter of politics than of law, and in any event the factor is unlikely to push anyone over the brink." He also argues that one state is unlikely to hold another state responsible for the actions of its (their) citizen because "states so clearly have lost the capacity to control the international activities of their citizens."[69]

Spiro's assertions concerning tendencies and probabilities may well be correct as a general matter. It seems plausible that when compared with other factors that influence state actions in the international sphere, the motivational significance of dual citizenship may have declined. At the margin, however, it also seems plausible that a state will intervene more readily and energetically on behalf of its own nationals than on behalf of strangers to whom it owes no special duty of protection, and that where the state's arguments for intervening are closely balanced, the existence of such a duty might furnish a real or pretextual reason that might affect, or even tip, the balance.[70] Ultimately, the magnitude of the protection burden posed by dual citizenship is one of those empirical questions to which we simply have no reliable answers, especially since it is likely to depend on many factors and thus vary from situation to situation.

In the debate over liberalizing dual citizenship, the most divisive and worrisome concerns are of a fundamentally political nature. The fact that these concerns are perhaps the most speculative and least quantifiable of the consequences of dual citizenship does not mean that they are insubstantial and thus easily dismissed. Indeed, it is precisely the elusiveness of these political concerns that makes them such powerful rhetorical weapons in the hands of partisans.

Consider first the electoral implications of dual citizenship. Assume that a dual citizen is eligible to vote in the elections of both countries.[71] Should this be troubling to Americans? To the extent that the interests of the U.S. and those of the other country do not conflict, it is hard to see any good reason for objecting to a situation in which the individual asserts one set of interests in the American election and another, not inconsistent set of interests in the other election. Here, Spiro's speculation seems plausible.

Sometimes, however, those interests will conflict in the sense that the other state's election may shape that state's policies—on trade or foreign policy, for example—in ways that either benefit or adversely affect the U.S. It is true—indeed, *increasingly* true given the growing diversity of the U.S. population in terms of national origin—that American citizens/voters often have policy preferences that accord some weight to the interests of other countries. This has always been the case—and always a source of concern to other members of the polity who think themselves exempt from such conflicts. Such preferences in fact exist whether or not the citizens/voters are also citizens of those other countries, and whether or not those other-country interests might, under some views of America's national interests, be adverse to those interests.

Somewhat more controversially, I believe that we should conceive of the national interest of the U.S. as including those preferences. After all, if the national interest is in some fundamental democratic sense an (indeterminate) aggregation of the interests perceived by citizens/voters,[72] then this aggregation cannot exclude preferences that accord some weight to other-country interests. As Spiro puts it: "A dual Mexican-American who advocates policies that benefit Mexico is little different from a Catholic who advocates policies endorsed by the church or a member of Amnesty International who writes his congressman at the organization's behest. There are no questions here of disloyalty, only of interests and identities and of different modes of social contribution."[73] This seems correct, at least within very broad limits—that is, so long as Mexico, like the church and Amnesty International, is not an enemy of the U.S. capable of doing her great harm.[74]

Spiro also posits the harder case in which the Mexican government endorses candidates in American elections and seeks to influence the votes of its dual nationals in the U.S. (Given Mexico's well-publicized protests against Governor Pete Wilson's position on Proposition 187 in California's 1994 elections, this scenario is not at all fanciful.) Spiro dismisses this concern, arguing that states of origin have little leverage over their nationals in the U.S. and even less inclination to use it, and that retention of Mexican nationality would add little to the dual national's existing propensity, shared with other hyphenated Americans, to give weight to ethnic affiliations. Again, this seems persuasive, at least given the current U.S.-Mexico alliance, the long-standing attitudinal differences among groups of people in the U.S. with Mexican ancestry,[75] and the propensity of voters, including hyphenated Americans, to focus on local issues.

Voting, of course, is not the only way in which dual aliens participate in U.S. elections by dual citizens. Like single citizens and legal resident aliens, they may contribute to political campaigns and make independent expenditures seeking to influence the public debate. Although recent congressional hearings concerning apparently illegal campaign contributions by foreign companies and individuals fronting for them may eventually lead to additional restrictions on these practices (proposals to limit or ban legal aliens' campaign contributions are pending in Congress), extending such restrictions to dual citizens would be unwise and almost certainly unconstitutional. Their full participation benefits American politics for the same reasons that the participation of other citizens (and legal aliens) does.[76]

The reverse situation, in which U.S. citizens participate in elections in countries where they hold dual citizenship—conduct that once triggered denationalization under U.S. law but due to the Supreme Court's ruling in *Afroyim* no longer does—also seems unproblematic from the American point of view, at least so long as this participation does not embroil the U.S. in unwanted disputes with the other country or involve situations in which the voter subordinates the interests of the U.S. to those of the other country, as distinguished from merely taking the latter into account in determining the former. Indeed, Spiro's point, noted earlier, bears repetition here: this participation could help to disseminate abroad the liberal democratic values that the American polity seeks to inculcate in its citizens.

This analysis suggests that the electoral conflicts engendered by dual citizenship are in principle quite consistent with the aggregation of preferences that we call the national interest. It is true, of course, that the government will ordinarily find it impossible as a practical matter to discern, much less prove in a denaturalization or expatriation proceeding, that the voter has in fact preferred another country's interests to those of the U.S. (properly defined). Accordingly, we must assess the risk of disloyalty in this sense on the basis of probabilities and magnitudes—the probability that a U.S. voter will subordinate American interests, and the number of Americans who are likely to go to the trouble of voting in foreign elections. Both seem exceedingly low.

All of this, of course, still begs the most basic question raised by dual citizenship: who should be permitted to become U.S. citizens and thus to vote and have their preferences counted in that aggregation process? In order to address this question, we must look beyond possible electoral conflicts to more transcendent concerns having to do with political unity, identity, community, and loyalty.

If citizenship is anything, it is membership in a political community with a more or less distinct political identity—a set of public values about governance and law that are widely shared by those within it. As already noted, the United States does not require birthright and *jus sanguinis* citizens to affirm a commitment to those values and that identity, yet it permits U.S. citizens to acquire other citizenships without limit and without affirming their solidarity with and loyalty to American society. How, then, might dual citizenship threaten this American political identity?[77]

One answer is that although all citizens who are also members of other polities may threaten this identity, the government is in a position to minimize that danger by exerting a leverage (the oath requirement) over the individual who wishes to naturalize that it lacks over its existing citizens. This answer, however, ignores several possibilities. Congress could require existing U.S. citizens too to take a loyalty oath,[78] as they now do when they apply for passports and certain jobs. It might also limit their freedom to naturalize abroad or, if they are allowed to naturalize, might limit their freedom to take certain actions, such as voting in other countries' elections. As discussed earlier, such legislation should not raise constitutional difficulties so long as Congress neither discriminates among citizens in this regard nor seeks to enforce its restrictions by expatriating them.

One can also argue that dual citizenship threatens America's political unity and identity regardless of whether one thinks that it is inconsistent to require only naturalizing citizens to swear an oath. In this view, dual citizenship dilutes America's political identity by adding members who are committed to other polities with other values. Put another way, in terms elaborated by Albert Hirschman, dual citizenship weakens loyalty by making exit easier.[79] To be sure, a citizen in a federal system may owe simultaneous allegiance to two polities, but if both share essentially the same values, as in the American case, the danger of disunity would be less than in cases where the citizen is a member of two polities with quite different political cultures.

At least two responses to this claim are possible. One is to deny that this identity is unique; the claim is that the polities from which most immigrants come today are committed to the same principles of governance to which the U.S. subscribes. This claim, however, is not convincing, at least in practice. Of the ten leading source countries in 1996, only Mexico, the Philippines, India, the Dominican Republic, and Jamaica even arguably qualified.[80] Another response, conceding that American values are indeed unique, might nevertheless despair of our ability to reduce them to a verbal formulation that can serve as a more discriminating naturalization criterion than the existing standards, tests, and oaths. In this view, there is little choice but to continue administering them in essentially their current form. This assumes, however, that Americans know what they are asking the individual to affirm and renounce. I challenge this assumption below.

Two variations on these disunity and dilution themes should be noted. The first was made by a Canadian parliamentary committee, which expressed a fear that dual citizens might "import and perpetuate their strident ethnic or nationalistic self-interests here in their new country"; they might "bring foreign quarrels to Canada."[81] Insofar as this is not simply another way of voicing the electoral concerns discussed earlier, it seems to envision a more general threat to political civility and accommodation posed by certain types of conflicts that dual citizens are thought more likely to inflame.

The second variation is that many dual citizens naturalize for the "wrong" (i.e., selfish or opportunistic) reasons.[82] This characterization is already being made of the flood of naturalization petitions following the 1996 welfare reform law that will likely be used to disparage naturalizations by Mexicans once the new Mexican law becomes effective. There is evidence that many aliens are indeed naturalizing to preserve or obtain welfare benefits,[83] and this perception has had powerful political ramifications. In addition, Aleinikoff cites a study of a 1994 change in the Dominican Republic's citizenship law similar to that being adopted in Mexico, which shows that the desire to facilitate Dominicans' naturalization in the U.S. without reducing their ties to the home country was an important argument for the change.[84]

Nevertheless, it is not clear what we should make of this "wrong reasons" argument. It implies that we know and can define what the "right" reasons for naturalizing are, that right and wrong reasons either do not coexist or can be disentangled, that we can render transparent through evidence the motivational mix that particular individuals possess, and that existing citizens do not value their *own* citizenship, at least in part, for instrumental reasons. None of these propositions, however, has been demonstrated or appears likely. It is true—as public opinion surveys and the political support for the 1996 welfare reform law suggest—that most Americans are repelled by the notion that some aliens are naturalizing in order to gain access to the welfare system. But as Aleinikoff points out, other instrumental reasons, such as a desire to integrate and actively participate in American society and politics, are not only viewed as praiseworthy but reflect values that "we look for in native-born citizens."[85] Lines that are both morally satisfying and administrable are exceedingly difficult to draw here.

This leads to a final complaint about the relation between dual citizenship and political community and identity—concerns about immigrants' ability to assimilate socially.[86] Dual citizenship, the argument goes, retards assimilation by encouraging newcomers to cling to old ties and refrain from unequivocally casting their lot with the U.S.[87] Dan Stein, a leading opponent of dual citizenship, states that immigrants "ought to get on board or get out."[88] Naturalization and assimilation are surely correlated, if only because one must have already achieved some level of English proficiency and knowledge about American society in order to qualify in the first place. But naturalization does not merely reflect assimilation; it probably also accelerates it, as discussed earlier. For this reason, one can argue that the government has an interest in promoting naturalization more energetically than it does, rather than essentially relying on individual aliens' initiative.[89]

For present purposes, however, the relevant question is not how naturalization affects assimilation but how *dual* citizenship, as distinguished from single citizenship, affects it at the *margin*. It may be, as Spiro asserts, that "retention of former nationality will not in itself retard the process by which the new citizen deepens his identification with the community of his naturalized homeland," but he cites no evidence to support his assertion and I know of none one way or the other.[90] There are reasons, however, to question his claim. If it is true that dual citizenship helps to build and reinforce "transnational communities," that any individual possesses only limited affective and attentional resources, and that allocating those resources between two communities necessarily reduces the level of commitment to either one, then it seems to follow that this lower level of commitment to the American community will slow the rate of assimilation into it. To recur to the family metaphor, it is doubtful (although possible) that parents with two sets of children from different marriages manage to devote the same amount of time to each child as they would if they had only one set of children to raise.

Even if this is true, of course, countervailing considerations may nonetheless support a more liberal dual citizenship policy. Spiro immediately adds, for example, that "denying the possibility of naturalization (or of raising its price too high, by requiring renunciation) *will* retard that process and weaken the bonds of community, at least as delimited in territorial terms (italics original)."[91] Again, he cites no support for this important and plausible empirical claim about how the price of naturalization (including renunciation) affects the speed and quality of assimilation. But the opposite claim—that immigrants whom the law requires to make a firm, undiluted commitment to American society may assimilate sooner and better than those who can naturalize without having to affirm that commitment—is also plausible. In the end, we are left with no evidence but an important research issue. In my view, the question of the marginal effects of dual citizenship on assimilation is indeed pivotal, but regretfully it is also unanswerable at present except on the basis of supposition.

Beyond the concern about assimilation, the debate on dual citizenship revolves around the issue of dual nationals' loyalty to the U.S. The anxiety, of course, is that their allegiance to America is wanting—at best divided and at worst subordinate to their earlier allegiance. This is partly a concern about national security. In this view, people whose loyalties are either divided or lie elsewhere may be tempted to subvert the nation's safety and well-being in service to another state, even to the point of treason.

Traitors[92] do indeed dot American history, but it is doubtful that dual citizens—or even aliens, who have not sworn allegiance to the U.S.—are disproportionately represented among them. Spiro believes that the national security risk posed by dual citizenship is minimal. As with diplomatic protection, he emphasizes historic shifts that have reduced the differential danger posed by dual citizens as compared with others. Specifically, he argues that the spread of democracy in the world has lowered the prospect of war, especially the kind in which dual nationals might pose a security threat. "Lightning wars conducted by volunteer armies," he suggests, "present few opportunities for shadowy fifth columns." Moreover, the undemocratic regimes with which the U.S. might now go to war are "less likely to instill the real loyalties of dual nationals even where they command their formal ones."[93]

As with diplomatic protection, one can acknowledge the general tendencies that Spiro identifies while still doubting that they will apply in every case and reduce the risks to zero. Our world is one in which hostilities may take the form not only of formal military campaigns[94] but also of clandestine acts of terrorism or theft of valuable technologies undertaken on behalf of undemocratic regimes that nevertheless can claim the fervent political and religious loyalty of their people.[95] Although legal or illegal aliens can also engage in such conduct, citizens probably have somewhat greater opportunities at the margin to do so. In such a world, Spiro's assurances may be too optimistic. The fact that few dual nationals pose any greater danger of disloyalty than those with only one nationality does not preclude the risk that the dual citizenship of those few may place them in a better position to wreak immense damage. This risk is a cost (to be discounted, of course, by its presumably low probability) that must be assessed against a policy of more liberal dual citizenship. Again, any effort to quantify it raises empirical questions for which there are no obvious answers.

But to view public concerns about the loyalty of dual citizens as being limited to the fear of treason is to risk trivializing those concerns. Even if divided loyalty does not culminate in active betrayal, it may create practical and moral conflicts—as when both countries demand military service of their citizens. Beyond such concerns, such divided loyalties surely offend common-sense conceptions of the desired citizen-state relationship. I have already alluded to the variety of competing metaphors that may plausibly frame those popular views. As I also noted, these metaphors should not impoverish a reflective deliberation about dual citizenship; metaphors, after all, should serve us rather than rule us. At the same time, however, such a deliberation should take seriously the public values that are embedded in the metaphors that American society invokes.

My guess—and it is of course only a guess—is that most thoughtful Americans, if asked to characterize the relationship between citizen and state that naturalization and the oath ought to affirm and reify, would view marriage and the marriage vow as the most closely analogous. Americans simply do not think of their polity as a mere club—a transitory affiliation affording easy entry and exit for purely instrumental reasons with few strings attached[96]—and they don not think of naturalizing citizens as entering an ideologically or spiritually defined *nomos* or a blood relationship.

If we think that naturalizing citizens are entering into a kind of marital relationship with the polity, it might seem natural and morally compelling to insist that they make a firm choice of one polity or another. The law, after all, sometimes obliges us to make a firm choice between competing claims on our allegiance and identity. We must choose one U.S. state of residence,[97] one political party,[98] one name,[99] and one marriage at a time. Why not require us to choose one national citizenship? In marriage, we expect a certain exclusivity or (where not exclusive) at least a clear priority of commitment. One who marries, of course, does not thereby renounce all non-marital affections, obligations, and trusts; the vow surely contemplates the maintenance of other deep attachments and other duties of emotional or financial support. But virtually all marrying couples, not to mention the larger society, certainly expect that some of the most essential marital commitments, such as procreation and sexual intercourse, will indeed be exclusive whereas others, such as friendship and Wednesday evenings, may be more widely diffused. Yet even here, we expect the spouse to enjoy unequivocal pride of place in the event of conflict.

Is the analogy of citizenship to marriage accurate? It is of course far from perfect. In particular, the intense intimacy that marriage entails is not always replicated in the relation of citizen to policy—and vice-versa, as many unsuccessful marriages attest. Moreover, American political culture apparently does not regard dual citizenship as bigamous, for it now permits U.S. citizens to acquire other nationalities without constraint, which suggests that such conduct is not regarded as tantamount to bigamy. It is also true that the "transformed consciousness" of which Levinson speaks in connection with marriage (drawing on Hegel and David Hartman) is not quite the same as the "new political birth" to which naturalization is sometimes likened. Likewise, it is hard to imagine the civic counterpart of procreation, unless it be citizens' inculcation of American values in their children.

Despite these differences, however, I nevertheless believe that marriage probably comes closer than any other common relationship to capturing the quality of enduring loyalty and priority of affection and concern that most Americans expect from those who apply to become their fellow citizens. And if this is true, certain implications might follow. First, the exclusive loyalty demanded of a citizen, like that demanded of a spouse, would be a circumscribed loyalty, one limited to the domain of political loyalty appropriate to the relationship between citizen and state in a liberal democratic polity. Even within that domain, loyalty is perfectly consistent with the most severe public criticism of the polity and its officials, and outside that domain loyalty is simply not a question, as the citizen's only essential duty is to observe the law (which may of course impose other duties on citizens), not to love the country.

Second, just as marital duties apply to all married persons equally and categorically, the political loyalty required of naturalized citizens should be the same—no more, no less—as that required of all other citizens, regardless of how they acquired their citizenship. This principle, affirmed in *Schneider v. Rusk*, lies at the heart of any polity committed to equal protection of the laws. Such a polity—especially one whose civil society and public philosophy countenance large inequalities in private goods—cannot flourish unless its members regard and treat each other as political and legal equals. In this sense, second-class citizenship is a pernicious oxymoron. Deviations from the equality-among-citizens principle should be tolerated only for the most compelling reasons.

As already noted, naturalization imposes some requirements on would-be citizens that birthright and *jus sanguinis* citizens need not satisfy. Neuman calls these "asymmetries." Some are procedural and to that extent are inescapable in the case of naturalization, but others such as good moral character and the renunciation of prior allegiances are deeply substantive. If the principle of equality among citizens means anything, it must mean that these substantive asymmetries demand justification. Neuman shows that some of the requirements themselves can be criticized from certain normative perspectives, but he does not view the asymmetries as problematic because the former do not yet possess their U.S. citizenship, and "a power to revoke is more dangerous than a power to withhold in the first place."[100]

Rather than justifying the asymmetries, however, Neuman's assertion begs the most significant questions about them.[101] First, the power to revoke is not always more dangerous than the power to withhold; for example, one who already has something may be in a better position to defend it (e.g., through political mobilization) than one who still lacks it.[102] Second, the persuasiveness of the revoke/withhold distinction depends on the nature of the asymmetry at issue. For example, the good moral character asymmetry probably strikes most people as less objectionable than, say, the ideological asymmetry, which excludes otherwise desirable citizens simply because they subscribe to unpopular views that existing citizens are perfectly entitled to advocate.[103]

Third, different asymmetries may have different rationales and no single justification is likely to work for all of them. The asymmetric requirements concerning knowledge of the English language and American government, for example, might be defended on the basis of a strong presumption—not true in every case, of course—that by adulthood birthright citizens have lived and been schooled in the U.S. long enough to acquire this knowledge, and that *jus sanguinis* citizens acquire it through their families. The good moral character asymmetry might be justified by a presumption that living in American society nurtures such character (this would be quite a stretch) or by the intuition that anyone applying for membership in a community should be expected to satisfy so minimal a requirement.[104]

Finally, none of these rationales can serve to justify either the ideological or renunciation asymmetries. Many existing citizens hold ideological views that might preclude their naturalization, and many others have acquired plural nationalities along with the risk of divided loyalties, which the naturalizing citizen must renounce. A defense of these asymmetries, then, must be based on something like the leverage argument that I noted earlier, which of course is less a justification than a raw assertion of power.

This analysis narrows, but does not resolve, the question of which forms of disloyalty other than treason should be counted as costs of dual citizenship. If (as I believe and Spiro does not) even a polity committed to a liberal dual citizenship policy can properly demand that new citizens affirm their exclusive political loyalty to the U.S., we must still decide what we mean by "exclusive political loyalty to the U.S." and which kinds of continuing commitments to other polities are deemed consistent with that loyalty. The answers, I believe, should be consistent with the content of the oath itself.

IV. Possible Reforms

Particular anxieties about dual citizenship imply particular questions that must be addressed and particular remedies that might then be proposed. Some concerns go to the standards and processes by which one may acquire and lose citizenship; others go to the rights and duties that attach to the status. Some concerns go to the criteria for naturalization whereas others go to the criteria for dual citizenship. Overlap obviously abounds; as we have seen, the debate over dual citizenship today is largely a debate about what the appropriate standards for naturalization should be. Reforms directed at particular concerns, then, risk being overly broad and should be carefully targeted at the specific problem that is perceived.

One set of possible solutions is based on the premise that dual citizenship is now acquired too easily and/or for the wrong reasons. I have already expressed doubts about this premise but if that is the diagnosis, then certain remedial options would follow. For example, Congress could fashion eligibility standards for dual citizenship that are more stringent than they are now or than they are for single citizenship naturalizations. Instead (or in addition), it could reduce the benefits flowing from dual citizenship. In either case, it could distinguish these standards and rights from those that apply to people who naturalize for single citizenship. Again, however, any effort to create distinct classes of citizens—particularly with respect to their legal rights[105]—would raise constitutional difficulties.

I shall not discuss these possibilities further here, as I believe that the reformers have not met the burden of proof, which I think they must bear, that a significant problem in fact exists as to either the standards or the motivations for acquiring dual citizenship. I shall instead focus my attention on the naturalization oath itself and on how it might be modified to address the threats to political identity and loyalty that I discussed in section III. I do so for several reasons. First, many Americans already take these threats seriously.[106] Second, these anxieties are likely to intensify in the future as the national origins of the immigration stream continues to diversify. Third, there is much merit, quite apart from whether these anxieties are justified, in attempting to be clearer about what it is America imagines it is asking new citizens to affirm in their oaths. The delightfully archaic formulation of the oath, as well as its ambiguities, together make for considerable uncertainty as to its meaning and practical effects.[107] If consent (as I believe) is the master concept underlying America's political arrangements, that consent should be knowing, discriminating, and authentic.[108] I argue below that the current oath, particularly the renunciation provision, fails these tests.

Before turning to my proposal,[109] let me make certain premises explicit. First, it should go without saying that I take the naturalization oath requirement, and hence the content of the oath itself, seriously, as do most oath takers.[110] Drawing on analogies to nuptial and religious vows, Levinson has reviewed the arguments for and against loyalty oaths, including the inconsistency of their professions with certain social realities and their possible ineffectiveness, hypocrisy, and even cynical uses. He correctly notes, however, that oaths—at least when solemnly performed in an appropriately focused and dignified setting—have the capacity not only to bind one in a psychological sense but also to generate "a transformed (and socialized) consciousness."[111] Having observed naturalization ceremonies and discussed them with presiding judges and new citizens, I find that this claim rings true.[112]

Second, I believe that an effort by some immigration proponents to eliminate the renunciation requirement in the oath would constitute a colossal, even tragic political blunder. Such an effort, which Spiro urges, would arouse intense, widespread political opposition and animus, which would be directed against immigrants in general and naturalizing immigrants, especially Mexican-Americans and other Spanish-speaking groups, in particular. The renunciation requirement would swiftly be transformed into a sacred shibboleth, a symbol of the integrity and security of the American polity with a prominence out of all proportion to its genuine significance.

On the other hand, a suitably modified renunciation requirement should be embraced, even by those who now doubt its efficacy, as a useful instrument of immigrant assimilation, regardless of how that controversial idea is defined. The reason is that after all is said and done—after one acknowledges both the unpersuasiveness of some rationales for renunciation and the inconsistency between even the most persuasive rationales and some actual practices—few would seriously contest the notion that the U.S. may legitimately insist that those who naturalize in the United States owe it a core political loyalty. They will surely disagree about which sorts of commitments constitute that core, which of these are exclusive and which merely primary, and which commitments lie outside the core and thus may be made to other polities without violating a properly refined renunciation oath. My own view, which follows, is that the core is properly quite small, limited to those obligations that are essential to the flourishing of a polity as liberal as America's is. But that there is *some* core that the U.S. may demand in exchange for the rights and blessings of citizenship seems indubitable.

A third premise is that the current oath, which requires one to renounce "absolutely and entirely all allegiance and fidelity to" another polity, utterly fails to define any such core. As already noted, its terms are simply too archaic, broad, and unqualified to communicate which duties Americans would truly place within this core were they to deliberate about the question. Because of this vague generality, the current renunciation oath cannot elicit the knowing, discriminating, and authentic consent of the oath takers, which is necessary both to confer their full membership in the polity and to legitimate its exercise of power over them. People taking a solemn oath of renunciation should know precisely what they are accepting and forswearing. Accordingly, the requirement should be reformulated to provide a clearer, more refined definition of those loyalties that must—and those that need not—be renounced.

Finally, certain aspects of loyalty that the U.S. can legitimately demand of its new dual citizens are already encompassed in other parts of the naturalization oath. Hence they need not be among those aspects of loyalty to which a redefined renunciation requirement should apply. Specifically, these aspects of loyalty include the duty "to support and defend the Constitution and the laws of the United States . . . "; the duty "to bear true faith and allegiance to the same"[113]; and the duty to bear arms or to perform equivalent public service. These duties obviously (though they do not say it in so many words) encompass an obligation to obey U.S. law.

Which aspects of loyalty, then, do dual citizens owe exclusively or primarily[114] to the U.S. such that there is something that they must renounce?

I am inclined to place only two duties of loyalty in that core. First, the naturalizing citizen should be obliged to prefer the interests of the U.S. over those of any other polity. This duty to accept the primacy or superiority[115] of America's claim on a dual citizen will seldom come into question except in cases of war and other serious conflicts between the U.S. and the dual citizen's other country of nationality. In such situations, dual citizens may be obliged to make decisions (perhaps in voting or about military service) knowing that the interests of the two countries inescapably clash and that they must therefore choose between them, as distinguished from simply taking the interests of the other state into account in forming their views about where the national interests of the U.S. lie. Ordinarily, moreover, the oath taker's true state of mind and affection cannot be challenged as a practical matter. Since the government may not (and even if it could, should not) seek to control or punish oath takers' thoughts or feelings, their bad faith (if it exists) cannot be effectively sanctioned unless it relates to objective facts that they have misstated and that might be the subject of denaturalization proceedings. Still, these realities do not render the duty meaningless. The fact that it will generally be unenforceable does not distinguish it from many other significant duties that we owe to others but whose observance must ultimately rest on our conscientious moral commitments.

Even this relatively constrained duty of primary loyalty, however, can be challenged as going too far. Stephen Legomsky, for example, argues that naturalizing citizens should be required at most to accord *equal*, not greater, weight to U.S. interests in the event of a conflict, and he wonders how I think the U.S. should respond if other countries required primary loyalty from their dual nationals who are U.S. citizens and if such individuals took such an oath in the other country.[116] My answer, which presupposes that citizenship should be more demanding and hence exclusive than mere membership in a voluntary club, is that a nation has a legitimate claim to its citizens' primary loyalty (as I have narrowly defined it), and that one who cannot muster that minimal degree of loyalty should not be granted citizenship. Whether the government should be able to expatriate an American citizen who voluntarily, knowingly, and solemnly pledges primary loyalty to another state in derogation of primary loyalty to the U.S. (again, as narrowly defined) is a separate question turning on several considerations, but in principle, and under current law as legitimated by the Supreme Court and confirmed by Congress in 1986, the answer is yes.

The second core duty is that the new citizen must not hold a high public office in another polity.[117] Although this proscription is likely to be overbroad in the sense that many official decisions that such an individual makes would not actually impinge on U.S. interests, a relatively clear prophylactic rule nevertheless seems warranted. Some of the official's decisions may create conflicts with that official's first duty to prefer the interests of the U.S., the stakes to the U.S. in these decisions may be disproportionately great, and drawing distinctions in general or on a case-by-case basis would be very difficult. Even so, some line-drawing would be necessary. For example, the offices that are "high" enough to trigger this duty should probably depend on the breadth of their policymaking responsibilities, a familiar form of legal classification. Ordinary military service in another nation not at war with the U.S. would not necessarily implicate this duty but perhaps a military leadership position should.

Plausible objections to this duty can be anticipated as well. One is that the government could not constitutionally (or now, even statutorily) expatriate or denaturalize a U.S. citizen for holding office in another nation unless that person specifically intended thereby to renounce American citizenship. The Supreme Court, however, has never so held; *Afroyim* involved only voting in a foreign election, which as I have just noted poses a smaller risk of conflicting loyalties. But even if the Constitution does bar the government from depriving a foreign officeholder of U.S. citizenship, it would probably not bar Congress from imposing other sanctions on that person. The question may be more one of appropriate remedy than of the power to implement a policy against foreign office-holding.

Stephen Legomsky makes another objection. Noting my belief that American citizens may properly take the interests of other groups and even countries into account in deciding where U.S. national interest lies, he wonders why I should be troubled by a U.S. citizen holding high office in another nation any more than if that person were holding high office in a corporation or other interest group and favoring that group's interests at the expense of the U.S. national interest.[118] My answer is that the risk of conflict in the government-government situation is likely to be far greater, the stakes for the U.S. in how such conflicts are resolved far higher, and the number of individuals who would be burdened by this duty far fewer than in the government-private entity situation that Legomsky posits.[119] Like my first response, this one will not satisfy those who find no justification for citizenship as a distinctive status carrying certain rights and responsibilities denied to non-citizens. As I noted in the Introduction, however, I am not such a person.

By solemnly affirming their primary loyalty to the United States and renouncing any inconsistent political allegiances in their naturalization oaths, new dual citizens would minimize any risks to the American polity that their divided loyalties might seem to pose. They should not be required to renounce any ties to their other country that do not pose these risks—for example, the intention to vote in foreign elections, serve in non-policymaking offices abroad, or seek to advance another country's interests. The naturalization oath can be easily and succinctly revised to express these principles. The revised oath can take the form of either a renunciation or an affirmation. What is essential is that it define the core aspects of loyalty that the new citizen must accept.

This change, however, would not remedy the anomaly in current citizenship law, noted earlier, that naturalized citizens are obliged to accept these duties and renounce inconsistent allegiances whereas citizens who are Americans through birthright or *jus sanguinis* are not and may indeed acquire new allegiances (short of treason) without taking, much less violating, any oath.

Congress could address this anomaly (if anomaly it is)[120] by seeking to eliminate the differential treatment. It could do so by making these duties applicable to *all* citizens in two ways. First, it could oblige existing citizens to take the same loyalty oath. Precisely because many (like the author) would find such a requirement obnoxious, it would focus their minds on the troubling implications of demanding more of their new countrymen than they do of themselves.[121] Congress could also (or instead) limit existing citizens' freedom to acquire new citizenships or to act upon them in particular ways (for example, voting) that naturalizing citizens are obliged to renounce or forego. If new citizens can be forced to affirm their loyalty publicly, then why not existing ones? If existing citizens are unwilling to do this, then they may conclude that they should not force new ones to do so either. This conclusion would demonstrate once again the value-clarifying, unfairness-constraining function that the principle of legal equality among all citizens can play in democratic discourse and politics.

PART FIVE

Current Policy Debates

Immigration constantly transforms America. It does so in many different ways—by altering the country's demographic profile, by infusing it with moved religious values and secular practices, by refreshing its energy and optimism, by engendering new conflicts, and by unsettling old assumptions. Historically, these transformations have convulsed American society, throwing up new social challenges going well beyond (and beneath) the now-familiar preoccupation of contemporary politicians and commentators with the problem of illegal aliens and the imperative of border control. These challenges are social and cultural in the very deepest sense, but they also can arise in more prosaic forms, prompting specific public policy proposals and ongoing debates. The four essays in this final part explore some of these proposals and debates.

Chapter 11 considers a problem that is bound to intensify in the future, if only for demographic reasons: the clash between the traditional civil rights agenda of black America and the growing aspirations of immigrant groups who demand political recognition and social advance, often at the expense of blacks and with little sympathy for their long struggle and special status in American politics and law. The attitudes of immigrants toward policies designed to facilitate the social progress of blacks and certain other minorities inevitably reflect the distinctive ways in which the newcomers conducted their own struggles to join the American mainstream. Chapter 12 illuminates these attitudes by reviewing a provocative study comparing the cultural patterns and assimilative strategies that six different ethnic groups—the Chinese, Japanese, Jews, Germans, Italians, and Indians— have employed over long periods of time in their migrations to the United States and elsewhere across the globe.

Immigration is almost always fueled by self-interest—that of both the immigrant, who leaves everything that is familiar in order to make a fresh start, and the receiving country, which carefully considers its national interest in choosing which categories of newcomers it will admit. Many decisions by countries to protect refugees, however, are somewhat different. Although national interest defined in terms of domestic politics, ethnic affinities, international alliances, and other factors of realpolitik contribute to the determination of which particular refugees a country will protect, purely humanitarian values also play a role, sometimes a decisive one. Chapter 13, which advances a novel proposal to establish nearly universal, tradable refugee quotas, seeks to exploit both of these motivations—national self-interest and human rights principles—in the hope of increasing the number of refugees to whom at least minimal protection will be extended.

The concluding essay, Chapter 14, uses a book review as a vehicle for analyzing a number of important but contested empirical issues concerning the demographic, environmental, political, economic, and cultural consequences of immigration as well as the normative values that one may bring to these disputes. In this essay, I also explore how immigration shapes multiculturalism, English language usage, affirmative action, and other bitter policy conflicts, suggesting my approach to resolving them.

11

The New Immigration and the Old Civil Rights

The political rhetoric of civil rights—its ideology, iconography, and martyrology—has always kept the stirring black struggle for equality on center stage. At the same time, this rhetoric has treated the immigrant's drama as peripheral, rather like Shakespeare's (not Stoppard's) treatment of Rosencrantz and Guildenstern. There are signs, however, that the audience's attention has begun to wander, diverted by the performances of immigrant groups on other stags. These developments make the relationship between civil rights and immigration ripe for reexamination.

The traditional civil rights coalition—black, Jewish, and labor groups supported by liberal media, intellectuals, urban politicians, and (intermittently) Latino organizations—succeeded in forging a common programmatic agenda. Dominated by the policy preoccupations of black leaders, this agenda gave priority to governmental action designed to enlarge and protect the member groups' claims to legal, social, and political equality in American life. Although the precise meaning of equality and the specific policies for gaining it have long been contested within the coalition and even within its constituent groups, it has centered on three principles: nondiscrimination, equal opportunity, and (more controversially) affirmative action. In its most robust form, affirmative action is defined as race-based, government-enforced group preferences in the distribution of socially valuable, centrally allocated resources.

The civil rights coalition can lay claim to a glorious, heroic past. Beginning with the postwar integration of the armed forces, it won many landmark victories. It renovated public law and reshaped public opinion, advancing equal opportunity in education, housing, voting rights, public accommodations, and numerous public programs and private activities. In the 1960s and increasingly during the 1970s and 1980s, the coalition expanded to include other groups—including the disabled, the elderly, women, aliens, gay men and lesbians, children, Latinos, Asians, native Americans—by grounding civil rights claims in a more universal ethos of human rights. These new groups invigorated the coalition and, like their predecessors, helped to alter public values and reform private institutions. This broader coalition won new civil rights victories even during the Reagan-Bush years: the Americans with Disabilities Act of 1990, the Immigration Act of 1990, the Civil Rights Amendments of 1991, and the extension of many state and local civil rights laws to protect women and gay men and lesbians. As if to seal the alliance, the National Association for the Advancement of Colored People early in 1993 organized its first Hispanic chapter in New York City.

Despite these impressive gains, the coalition's salad days may be over. The internal disarray and drift of the NAACP, the movement's flagship, and Bill Clinton's downplaying of black civil rights issues during the presidential campaign are signs of danger. Furthermore, the coalition has been unable to prevent clashes (politically and in the streets) among black, Latino, and Asian groups. The power of organized labor, urban voters, and left-wing Democrats has been declining. And many states have sought to reverse protections for gay men and lesbians, who (to the annoyance of many blacks) claim continuity with the black struggle for civil rights.

Other issues, including the deficit, health care, economic reform, and global competition, now dominate the policy agenda, shouldering civil rights aside and marginalizing the coalition in favor of other claimants whom politicians find more compelling. More ominous in the long run, however, may be the growing gap between how the coalition and the general public think about civil rights. To traditional activists, discrimination—both intentional and structural—is a, if not *the*, central cause of minority group crime, substance abuse, dependency, school-leaving, teen pregnancy, and abandonment. The general public, on the other hand, places far greater blame on debased family values, failed public programs, and individual immorality.

To these stresses on the civil rights coalition, burgeoning immigration has added new ones. The catalyst was the 1965 immigration reform, which repealed the detestable decades-old national origins quotas and enabled many new immigrants from Asia, Latin America, and Africa to come to the United States. This law was in fact a momentous civil rights victory, extending the notion of equal treatment beyond U.S. borders to national and ethnic groups traditionally disfavored by our immigration laws. That it also contributed to the coalition's future decline is an arresting political irony. No one expected this reform to unleash demographic, legal, socio economic, ideological, and political forces that, several decades later, would threaten the civil rights coalition that worked so hard to enact it.

I. DEMOGRAPHIC CHANGES

The new immigration's effects on the future size and shape of the U.S. population are enormous. The 1980s brought more legal immigrants to the United States (though not as a percentage of the population) than any other decade since 1910, and immigration has continued to rise during the 1990s. Including illegal entrants would make total immigration for the 1980s the highest for any decade in American history. (Out-migration during the period might reduce this total by about 1.5 million.) When the Census Bureau combines legal and "permanent" illegal immigration trends, moreover, it estimates that, in the future, immigration will increase by as much as 1.4 million annually.

How will this affect civil rights politics? In a democracy like ours, ethnic demography is political destiny. By that remorseless standard, blacks are steadily losing power relative to other groups, including some of their traditional coalition partners. First, the ethnic groups that comprised most of the 1980s immigration flow have grown rapidly, dwarfing the black cohort's rate of increase. During that decade, the Asian population increased by 107 percent, the Hispanic (as defined by the Census) by 53 percent, and the black by only 13.2 percent. The immigrant groups, of course, start from a much smaller population base than blacks, but their fertility rates remain higher than those of both Americans in general and black Americans in particular (though the immigrant fertility rates, like those of other groups in the U.S., are likely to decline over time).

Political influence, moreover, reflects not just raw numbers but the way in which those numbers are aggregated in elections: effective voting power. In an electoral system dominated by single-member districting, effective voting power is a function (among other things) of geographic concentration and voter turnout. New immigrants, both legal and illegal, are heavily clustered in a relatively small number of metropolitan areas, and half of the top ten metropolitan areas of residence were in California; the largest concentration was in Los Angeles–Long Beach. On the other hand, because housing discrimination in urban areas tends to be far greater against blacks than against Latinos and Asians with similar income levels, blacks tend to be more residentially concentrated. This has a compensating effect of enhancing black voting power, as measured by bloc control of particular legislative seats. The struggle over representation on the Los Angeles City Council, in which Latinos, Asians, and blacks competed to control the redistricting plan, undoubtedly prefigures bitter conflicts to come.

II. Legal Changes

Legislative policy and judicial decisions have altered the law in ways that will probably favor precisely those aliens most likely to compete with American blacks for jobs, voting power, public benefits, patronage, and housing.

IRCA and the 1990 act substantially increased the numbers of both legal and formerly illegal immigrants admitted now and in the future. As already noted, the amnesty program and larger visa allotments added millions to the legal population. The 1990 law's provisions on "family fairness," temporary protected status, and "diversity" (which strongly favor white Europeans, especially the Irish) also favor visa applications by many others who are in the U.S. illegally. Other provisions make it easier for aliens, once admitted, to naturalize (and thus vote) than it was in the past. Indeed, their growing numbers have led some cities such as Takoma Park, Maryland, to permit legal resident aliens to vote in local elections even without naturalization. Moreover, anti-discrimination provisions in the 1986 law, strengthened in 1990, protect the employment opportunities of aliens who compete with black Americans for scarce jobs. Although the 1990 law favors the admission of higher skilled workers more than the earlier one did, the continued influx of illegal workers is certain to heighten job competition further for low-skilled black Americans.

During the 1980s the courts also rendered many pro-alien decisions concerning the asylum, due process, and equal protection rights of deportable aliens. These decisions made it easier for undocumented workers to enter, remain, work, raise families, and resist deportation. The huge backlog of asylum claims, together with severe budget constraints on detention facilities and more liberal asylum adjudication and work authorization rules, create powerful pressures on the INS to release undocumented workers into the community and the job market, pending their hearings. A settlement in one case protected from deportation almost 200,000 undocumented Central Americans until their hearings.[1]

The courts during the 1980s and 1990s also altered affirmative action law in ways that are exacerbating ethnic tensions between blacks and their recently arrived competitors. In *City of Richmond v. J. A. Croson*, for example, the Supreme Court limited the power of local governments to use affirmative action to promote minority contracting in public projects. Not coincidentally, *Croson* originated in Richmond, Virginia, where, as in a growing number of cities, blacks controlled the city government and hence could give patronage to their own firms.

At the same time, the Court *supported* race-based affirmative action in the context of electoral districting under the Voting Rights Act. Egged on by the Reagan and Bush Justice Departments and Republican political strategists, as well as by traditional civil rights activists, the Court interpreted the act to maximize minority representation by creating what are in effect safe legislative and judicial seats for residentially concentrated racial and ethnic groups. This approach confers clear personal benefits on minority legislators but, as Lani Guinier, Carol Swain, and others have shown, it has dubious consequences for their minority constituents. In New York, Miami, Los Angeles, and other cities, blacks, Latinos, Asians, and even Jews (in Brooklyn) are locked in a zero-sum struggle over the safe seats. The Court's more recent decisions, beginning with *Reno v. Shaw,* have greatly complicated this struggle, introducing new legal considerations that several pending redistricting cases from multi-ethnic cities will need to clarify.

For several reasons, an ethnic approach to districting disadvantages many black Americans who support liberal candidates. First, especially given their typically low turnout, more blacks must be "packed" into a district in order to guarantee their control of the seat, leaving smaller and less influential minorities in adjoining districts. This in turn tends to make those districts more conservative than they would otherwise be. Such gerrymandering also makes race and ethnicity even more pivotal markers in political conflicts that—being racially defined and polarized—are perceived as zero-sum. This perception may soon be heightened when the Supreme Court decides a pending redistricting case from Dade County, Florida, pitting Hispanics and blacks against one another.

III. Socioeconomic Changes

Although socioeconomic competition between black Americans and other ethnic groups goes back to colonial times, the immigration of the 1980s and 1990s has added new twists. Four aspects of the conflict are especially important: job competition, competition for public benefits, differentiation *within* the black community, and differentiation *among* ethnic groups.[2]

Job Competition

To what extent does immigration affect the job opportunities and wage levels of American workers in general and black Americans in particular? In analyzing this crucial question, one must distinguish between the facts and people's perceptions of the facts.[3]

The labor market effects of immigration are complex and the evidence is rather inconclusive. Almost all labor economists seem to agree that immigration increases the nation's aggregate wealth and has to some degree displaced jobs and reduced wages, especially for low-skilled blacks. But economists keenly dispute the magnitude, duration, and distribution of these effects. Some relevant factors have been suggested: how segmented a particular labor market is, how immigration affects the level of migration of American workers to the cities, how complementary Americans' and immigrants' labor skills and consumption patterns are, and how intensive immigration enforcement is. An analysis by Thomas Muller of employment and wage effects on blacks in cities with the highest immigrant concentrations concludes that the effects overall are positive. Politically more compelling, however, is anecdotal evidence that black American workers are being displaced by Cuban immigrants in Miami, Koreans in New York and Los Angeles, Mexicans in Texas, and Indochinese in Denver.

Competition over Public Benefits

Competition over divisible public benefits is essentially a zero-sum game; to the extent that aliens receive them, there are fewer left for other citizens, including low-income blacks.[3] This is true as a political matter even where, as with Aid to Families with Dependent Children and food stamps, all eligible individuals are entitled to the benefit. Indeed, public benefits may be a *negative*-sum game; if the voters believe that too many unentitled aliens are receiving them, they may insist that benefit levels be reduced. The studies indicating that immigrants in fact generate more tax revenues than they consume in benefits are beside the point politically; the levels of government that collect the taxes (mostly federal and state) are different from those that fund the benefits (mostly state and local).

It is hard to know to what extent aliens use public benefits. With unreliable data, analysts often cannot distinguish between legal and illegal aliens, different nationality groups, different labor-market skill profiles, and different communities. Drawing on earlier data, labor economist George Borjas finds that immigrants in general are only slightly more likely than citizens to claim welfare benefits, but that among certain groups such as legal Cubans and Mexicans, the utilization rates are quite high; among female-headed Dominican households, the rate exceeds 30 percent. Other studies indicate that illegal aliens and their children (who are often U.S. citizens) frequently use public hospitals and public schools in many cities. Competition for cheap housing, public and private, between blacks and immigrant groups is also intense, as are the competing demands by different groups for their share of police protection. These public costs and group conflicts have aroused immigration-related backlashes against public benefits in many communities, even ones with traditionally liberal policies on public benefits.

Differentiation Within the Black Community

Rapid growth of the black middle class is one of the most striking features of American social change since World War II. Among young intact families, blacks have almost gained parity with whites in income (although not in wealth), a remarkable achievement given their vastly inferior position only a short time ago. And, though still vulnerable to racial discrimination (most notably in housing), many blacks have acquired new class interests that separate them from those they left behind. These upwardly mobile families and individuals, like their white class counterparts but unlike many lower-income blacks, have important economic stakes in increased immigration, which increases social wealth without threatening their own jobs. Indeed, immigration probably *increases* their job opportunities on balance, especially since they disproportionately are public employees who provide a variety of education, health, welfare, and other social services to immigrants. Some black immigrant groups share the black middle-class perspective. Studies indicate that West Indians and, to a lesser extent, Haitians tend to be more optimistic than comparable American-born blacks and have made relatively rapid economic progress in the United States.

One result of this social differentiation among blacks is that their positions on immigration issues have become far more diverse, making it even more difficult for them to speak with a unified political voice. This fragmentation is exemplified by opinion polls in which black Americans are deeply divided over whether immigration should continue at current or increased levels or whether the levels should be decreased. This growing class differentiation further weakens the cohesion among blacks.

Differentiation Among Ethnic Groups

An exceedingly delicate but important phenomenon in inter-group relations, and hence in the solidarity of the civil rights coalition, is the variable rate of economic progress made by different ethnic groups in the United States. Simply (and perhaps indelicately) stated, a number of relative newcomer groups from Asia and the Caribbean basin have "leapfrogged" American blacks as a group in standard indices of economic success such as income (especially family income) and entrepreneurship (blacks own only two-thirds as many businesses per capita as Hispanics). If present trends continue, moreover, other groups will eventually pass them. While the causes and the magnitude of this differential progress are still in dispute, the fact of inter-group difference is incontrovertible. As I shall suggest, this fact will profoundly affect the politics of civil rights.

IV. IDEOLOGICAL CHANGES

The mythology and imagery of immigration have always been powerful ideological forces in American life. During the 1980s these forces produced some striking shifts in public policies and attitudes in favor of expanded immigration. I have already discussed some of these shifts.

The stories about immigration that we Americans, hyphenated and otherwise, tell ourselves invariably rest on a historical claim. This claim depicts gradual progress through dogged self-help and relentless hard work in the face of harsh prejudice against the group. These stories are inscribed in our family memories, our civic culture, and our national iconography. The fact that some of these immigration stories (or myths, if you prefer) are false is less relevant politically than the fact that they tend to undermine the *group* claims and status of blacks. Political elites, ordinary citizens, scholars, and journalists, in polite company as well as on radio call-in shows, are increasingly making comparisons between American blacks and immigrant ethnics. Such comparisons often focus on sensitive topics: economic status, attitudes toward work and welfare dependency, family values and stability, crime and violence, school completion, entrepreneurial spirit, and labor force attachment. Those who make the comparisons share a strong normative consensus, or a conventional ideology of group behavior: all social groups must exhibit the same public and private rectitude that other paragon groups are thought to have displayed in the past. The group being judged must *perform* under the watchful eye and to the satisfaction of these paragon groups.

The crucial, incendiary political fact about these comparisons is that they often disfavor American blacks as a *group*. When black groups seek race-based preferences, they invite such comparisons—a cruel paradox. After all, when a group claims a preferential entitlement for itself *as a group,* it spotlights its underlying claims about uniqueness, desert, opportunity, and performance. Other groups that feel themselves disadvantaged by the preferential policies to which such claims lead are bound to reflect on their *own* feelings of uniqueness, desert, opportunity, and performance. In a meritocratic society that glorifies upward mobility and economic success, group claims imply group comparisons, which in turn underscore group differences. Black calls for group preferences have given such comparisons, long a staple of private conversation, greater salience and visibility in the public domain, where a subtle rhetorical etiquette governs the discourse.

How does a pluralistic society think and speak about groups and their differences? Broadly speaking, we might distinguish between two perspectives: professional social science and folk social thought. Professional practitioners and consumers of social science methodically gather, analyze, and study large bodies of socioeconomic data bearing on group and subgroup performances, rendering their judgments accordingly. Lay people with strong opinions about group differences, however, appraise group performances largely on the basis of their own experiences, intuitions, and impressions, mediated by the commentary of other folk social thinkers. By virtue of their number (comprising virtually the entire population) and the intensity of their opinions, their views also loom large in the public debate, especially when cleansed of the tincture of explicit racism that is now unacceptable in national public discourse.

Both perspectives yield group comparisons that undermine the idea that blacks deserve preferential treatment. To isolate how discrimination affects groups, the social scientist must control for socioeconomic factors that correlate with performance differences without necessarily causing them. An important example is the age distribution of different racial and ethnic groups. Jews are much older than blacks on average, while blacks as a group are older than Latinos. One would predict higher income (if the age differences apply to the groups' working age cohorts) and lower crime rates for the older groups, independent of differentials in performance. Another example is geographical location; inter-group variations in income differ by labor market. But beyond clear-cut variables like age and location, identifying spurious correlations is harder. Jews and other immigrant groups were urbanized much earlier than blacks, which would affect their relative performance, but in complex, poorly understood ways. For example, urban experience can breed skills needed for economic success but may also weaken family stability. To complicate matters, even family stability may retard economic progress where, as with earlier Italian immigrants, family solidarity conflicts with individual ambition.

Even if we control for educational level, the variable most highly correlated with success, bitter disputes remain about how to measure, interpret, and compare group differences in performance. Unlike age and gender, education is not immutable but reflects human choice; it is a costly investment in human capital that invites value judgments. Indeed, Americans appraise this choice so highly that they view groups who have made it as having performed well both socially and morally.

Educational level, however, is also socially determined to some degree, reflecting discrimination's effects on the student's family stability, self-image, and aspirations. Thus the fact that some recent immigrant groups, notably Asians, have higher educational levels than American blacks only raises another set of questions. One such question—the extent to which a better-educated group possessed this advantage *before* its members immigrated to the U.S.—may be answerable, but others are much harder to grapple with. If immigrants did not bring their educational advantage with them to the United States, did they face obstacles to educational attainment similar to those that discrimination created for native-born blacks? How much does discrimination actually affect educational choices? Why does discrimination appear to spur achievement for some groups while inhibiting it for others? Why are the performance differences *within* groups often even greater than those among groups?

Where social science is inconclusive on these questions, folk thought often speaks with smug clarity—in informal conversations, on call-in shows, and in individual musings. Impressionistic, anecdotal, and subjective, folk thought is authenticated by vivid personal experience and emotional engagement. For precisely these reasons, however, it also carries higher risks of error, ideological bias, casual group stereotyping, and even racism.

Folk thought has always emphasized cultural-attitudinal explanations for group differences rather than demographic or historical ones. This emphasis tends to make the comparisons more morally charged and invidious since folk thinking often assumes that values are simply matters of *choice*. It is significant, then, that social scientists, who appreciate how deeply embedded values can be, are increasingly converging on cultural-attitudinal explanations for residual differences in group performance. This turn toward cultural explanation is observable not only among liberal sociologists like Christopher Jencks and William Julius Wilson and more radical theologians like Cornel West, who might be expected to find a focus on group values congenial. Economists, who usually prefer "harder" variables, also engage in cultural explanation.

Regardless of how and by whom group comparisons are made, they are certain to become more common. Pressed into political service by the newer, more mobile immigrant groups who wish to fortify their own competitive positions against blacks, these comparisons will probably also be more pointed. As their political influence grows, Asians and other groups whose immigrant ancestors also faced virulent racial discrimination here and who bear no group responsibility for black slavery or subordination may be somewhat less sympathetic to traditional affirmative action claims when these claims conflict with their own. Some of the bitterness growing out of inter-group clashes in Los Angeles, New York, and other cities where blacks and immigrants (and assimilated and first-generation immigrants) live cheek-by-jowl competing for scarce jobs and other resources surely reflects feelings of moral superiority and animus inspired by these group comparisons. Even when these feelings do not boil over into the violence and vituperation that are now staples of media reports, they persist just beneath the surface.

The mythic, evocative immigration stories that Americans and immigrants tell themselves have inspired great achievements by countless black *individuals,* just as they have motivated members of other groups. But this powerful ideology is increasingly being turned against blacks as a *group*. By using their political capital to obtain race-based preferences that other groups either dispute or wish to gain for themselves, blacks inflame resentments within the civil rights coalition and opposition without, aggravating their already heavy political disability.

V. POLITICAL CHANGES

As I have noted, much of the political friction within the coalition reflects tensions among groups with different interests and ideologies. On many important policy issues, from affirmative action to defense spending, Hispanics and Asians are more conservative than blacks. They perceive less discrimination against themselves than blacks do. And they often fail to support black candidates for office. But there has also been tension *within* groups as a result of the growing value differentiation between the organizations' leadership and the rank and file. Black leaders are caught between traditional black opposition to immigration (which goes back at least to the infamous Chinese Exclusion legislation more than a century ago) and the need to collaborate with other coalition groups that are more pro-immigration. Similarly, Latino activists differ from their rank and file on issues like bilingual education and immigration control. These fissures further weaken the coalition.

The evolution of recent immigration enforcement legislation reveals how this split plays out politically. In the 1984 immigration reform bill, all twenty black members of Congress voted *against* both employer sanctions for the hiring of illegal aliens and an English language precondition for legalization. When the issues arose again two years later in IRCA, the Black Caucus split its votes only after the Hispanic Caucus decided to split. In the pivotal negotiations leading up to the 1990 Act, moreover, the Black Caucus supported the Hispanic Caucus in its opposition to an enforcement-enhancing identity card. Had the black members not done so, the 1990 Act almost surely would have died—a result that polls suggest would have delighted many, perhaps most, rank-and-file black voters.

Two other kinds of differentiation within the civil rights coalition also threaten its political cohesion and agenda. Ethnic groups have moved out of central cities and into the suburbs at varying rates due in part to group-specific differences in economic mobility and in vulnerability to housing discrimination. Perhaps more important are differences within groups: individuals of the same ethnicity have developed different understandings of their own ethnic identities, as new experiences in the United States transform certain loyalties and identifications. Political analysis shows, for example, that changes in party loyalties of Latino and Asian voters reflect changes in the significance to them of their minority group membership, anticommunist émigré feelings, and economic status. More generally, as language, ethnicity, historical experiences, and other attributes that underlie conventional groupings of individuals become less determinative and predictive of their behavior, the word "group" begins to lose some of its meaning as a political descriptor. While this has progressed further and faster for some groups than for others, it is proceeding in all of them.

As groups assimilate at different rates, shedding their traditional identities and acquiring new ones, the coalition's salience and solidarity will erode—a process revealed in the recent mayoral election in Los Angeles and the Texas senatorial contest, where the Republican candidates attracted many previously Democratic Hispanic voters but few black ones. As sociologists have long predicted, commonalities of class and culture are gradually supplanting racial and ethnic solidarity.

VI. Reappraising the Agenda

Lest I seem unduly pessimistic about the coalition's political prospects, I must make several qualifications. There are strong countervailing forces. The steep rise in both white and minority group educational levels and in integrationist sentiment has spurred a growing public sympathy for the coalition's equal opportunity and non-discrimination goals, although not for its stronger versions of race-based affirmative action. The "social standing" of blacks in the eyes of the white majority has also improved dramatically since the mid-1960s. Demographic and legal changes during the 1980s produced new district lines that helped to increase the number of black members of Congress, including one senator. (This increase, however, may be difficult to sustain in the next reapportionment.) And as noted earlier, the coalition in recent years succeeded not only in resisting legislative and judicial efforts to reverse earlier civil rights gains, but in actually extending federal civil rights protections to women, aliens, and the disabled. Civil rights groups, then, have demonstrated impressive resilience, innovation, and capacity for growth in the face of new challenges and inauspicious political conditions.

This brings me to a second qualification: the coalition's incentive to change policy direction. I have argued that the new immigration has complicated the coalition's search for programmatic consensus within and among its member groups and with erstwhile allies outside the coalition, and that race-based preferences may be a special casualty of this more complex politics. In their place, however, many stalwart friends of civil rights will seek to redefine the traditional agenda to emphasize conceptions of social need and justifications for state intervention based on measures of economic distress and desert rather than on ascriptions of race or ethnicity that are inaccurate—and, for many Americans, morally objectionable.

There are intriguing signs that some members of the black community, as well as some of their traditional allies, have already begun the painful process of reappraising the assumptions and programmatic directions of civil rights under the conditions of the 1990s. Skepticism about some applications of race-based preferences has recently been expressed by a younger cadre of black intellectuals like Stephen Carter, Randall Kennedy, and other contributors to *Reconstruction* and other new journals of black commentary, as well as by writers on race issues like Shelby Steele, Hugh Price, William Raspberry, and Glenn Loury. Though some in this group are often described as neo-conservatives, they actually share much common ground with more liberal or social-democratic analysts such as William Julius Wilson, Theda Skocpol, Christopher Jencks, Cornel West, and Paul Starr. While these scholars possess impeccable civil rights credentials, they urge that need or even more universalistic criteria be substituted for race in distributing resources.

Immigration is swiftly magnifying both racial diversity and intra-group differentiation. Political progress for civil rights in this setting demands need-based policies capable of reaching across racial and ethnic divides while also appealing to working- and middle-class voters—the opposite of racial preferences. There are many promising possibilities, including increased funding for Head Start, stronger enforcement of child-support obligations, an expanded earned income tax credit in lieu of minimum wage increases, and health care coverage for many who are now uninsured. While such policies use nonracial eligibility criteria, they would still disproportionately favor racial minorities and poorer whites. Voting Right Act enforcement that avoided gerrymandering blacks into a few districts controlled by black incumbents could encourage legislators to promote new multi-racial coalitions on an even broader scale by forcing them to compete for black support. Moreover, as innovative Republicans like Jack Kemp have realized, these coalitions need not be limited to the Democratic Party.

Once launched, this reappraisal cannot easily be confined. It will naturally extent to the broader set of policy issues on which civil rights traditionalists have long dictated the liberal orthodoxy: urban education, immigration controls, public housing, criminal justice reform, privatization of public programs, youth minimum wage laws and many others.

The new immigration is transforming the conception, complexion, and contours of civil rights politics. New leaders, affirming continuity with venerable civil rights approaches, will nevertheless invoke new symbols, form new alliances, and take new positions. Many traditionalists will resist, but the political and social forces that immigration has triggered are well beyond their control, rendering old strategies unworkable and increasingly unthinkable.

12

Perpetual Motion:
Migrations and Cultures

Human beings are constantly on the move. Americans are probably the most peripatetic people in the industrialized world, with nearly twenty percent of us each year changing the location of our homes within the United States.[1] Our mobility, however, is insignificant when compared with the migrations of peoples who cross the ocean leaving their societies far behind and casting their lots with new, altogether alien ones.

Intercontinental migrations of this kind, of course, have proceeded ever since the first communities dispersed by foot across the globe in search of food, water, land, and security. In migrating, these groups have transported more than their families and possessions; they have also carried with them their language, art, religion, values, skills, practices, perspectives, and social institutions—their unique cultures.

The distinctiveness of these migrant cultures, and the myriad ways in which they have altered the societies in which they have been transplanted, are the subjects of Thomas Sowell's stimulating book, Migrations and Cultures: A World View, Sowell, an academic economist who has long been a senior fellow at the Hoover Institution at Stanford, has devoted a long and distinguished career to exploring these phenomena empirically, usually relying heavily on the field research of others. In his earlier works,[2] Sowell amassed social science and historical data, much of it cross-national, to challenge certain assumptions that are widespread among policymaking and intellectual elites as well as much of the general public. Exhibiting an admirable combination of academic technique, analytical seriousness, iconoclastic audacity, and ideological pugnacity, he rejected the credo of universalistic liberals and egalitarians that humans are really all the same beneath the surface. Quite the contrary, he insisted, individuals differ from one another in the most fundamental respects—in how they perceive, think, value, express themselves, and behave. These differences, moreover, are most dramatically manifested in their economic performance, which reflects different commitments to a variety of economic virtues. These virtues include the propensity to work incredibly hard at jobs often disdained by the native population,[3] be unusually productive,[4] take entrepreneurial risks,[5] build strong families and communal institutions, invest in education and other human capital, practice extreme thrift and self-denial, constantly innovate, and so on.

Opposing the view of most social reformers, Sowell maintained that these different commitments do not primarily reflect differences in the objective conditions that prevail in the larger societies where the individuals live, such as the level of economic development and discriminatory attitudes. Instead, he argued, these differences in economic and social behavior have almost everything to do with the individuals' underlying values and practices, which in turn are shaped by the distinctive cultural patterns of their ethnic and religious groups. Finally, and most emphatically, Sowell rejected the notion, cherished by some advocates of multiculturalism, that because all cultures are different, each of them equally deserves society's respect and protection, if not nurturance. Instead, he insisted, some cultures are more economically successful and hence more worthy of emulation than others—at least if wealth is a value.[6]

I. THE ANALYTIC PROJECT

Migrations and Cultures recapitulates these themes of individual striving, cultural determinism, group differences, and economic standards of achievement—but it plays them out on a global scale. Sowell has selected six ethnic groups for special attention: Germans, Japanese, Italians, Chinese, Jews, and the Indians of south Asia. In their destination countries, large fractions of each of these groups, albeit to different extents,[7] acted as a "middleman minority," by which Sowell means that its members predominate in occupations that facilitate the movement of goods and services from the producer or supplier to the consumer, without necessarily physically transforming such goods and services. Middleman functions include retailing, wholesaling, moneylending, brokerage, and the like. Throughout the world, Sowell notes, the economic functions performed by middlemen are widely misunderstood and underappreciated. The middlemen who perform these functions, moreover, tend to cultivate different skills and attitudes than the rest of the population and arouse particularly virulent hostility and discrimination. As a result, these groups have been obliged to develop unusually adroit survival skills (pp. 27–35). *Migrations and Cultures* is both a catalogue of those skills and an account of how the six groups have deployed them as minorities in societies across the globe.

Drawing on an impressive array of secondary sources ranging widely over time and space, Sowell traces each group's dispersion around the world and describes the patterns of family, communal and religious life, occupations, economic activity, political participation, and institution building that the groups' members have exhibited in the diverse nations and regions in which they have settled.[8]

All six groups have been economically successful in their destination countries.[9] Indeed, they have usually become more successful than the native populations with whom they had to compete there, despite daunting initial disadvantages and continuing barriers.[10] Their successes, however, were invariably hard won and took considerable time to consolidate. What makes their progress even more extraordinary is the fact that in almost every case, certain personal attributes that the groups brought to the destination country, or the social conditions that they encountered there, posed enormous obstacles to their progress, or even survival. The list of disadvantages is long: abject poverty and lack of skills,[11] ignorance of the native language, racial difference, disease, ethnic insularity, harsh discrimination, and sometimes violence at the hands of the native population, limited opportunities to marry and form families, and political exclusion. Often, moreover, they were also greeted by unpromising material and economic conditions, sometimes even less propitious than the ones from which they had so desperately fled. In some cases, as with the Black Sea Germans, the Jews in Germany and eastern Europe, and the Indians in some African regions, the newcomers' economic vitality generated bitter hostility from the native populations, forcing them to remigrate. Although obliged to start over with many of the same disadvantages that they encountered in their earlier migrations, these groups nevertheless managed to replicate and even enlarge their success.

Sowell hopes to explain why these remarkable records of accomplishment against long odds are so consistent within and, to some extent, across these groups.[12] As a methodological matter, the global context of his study provides a provocative setting in which to draw explanatory inferences. First, the six groups differed enormously from one another with respect to race, language, religion, and other demographic variables, even including the gender ratio of their migrating populations.[13]

Second, some of the countries of origin generated remarkably diverse *intragroup* migrations. The Indian migrants, for example, included Gujaratis who went primarily to Africa, Guyana, and Fiji where they have dominated commerce; Tamils who settled in Malaya and Ceylon where most worked as laborers; Chettyars who went to other parts of Asia where they often dominated the moneylending business; and Jains who took their diamond industry skills overseas (pp. 311–12, 367–68).

Third, the groups' countries of origin were very different in terms of their geophysical features—climate, soil, terrain, water supply. The migrants had adapted to these features in their countries of origin by adopting patterns of occupation, agricultural practice, community life, diet, and dress that were peculiarly suited to those countries. But the diversity among migrants in their original conditions and cultures went well beyond the differences among the countries from which they came. Even *within* countries of origin—especially the immense land masses of China and India but also within the smaller ones of Italy, Germany, and Japan—localities exhibited their own distinctive geophysical conditions and cultural patterns. Migrants from those localities brought those further variations with them to their new homes. As migrant streams often flowed disproportionately from particular localities within each country of origin,[14] the migrants transplanted these intragroup differences to the destination country.

Fourth, the destinations of the six groups differed. All of the groups sent sizable cohorts to the United States and Australia, and the groups overlapped to an extent in some other countries, but the six migration streams established their own distinctive axes.[15] Finally, the groups' migrations also occurred at different times,[16] were prompted by different historical circumstances, and were received differently by the native populations and by their governments.[17]

This striking heterogeneity in the geographical and demographic patterns of migration makes for an exceedingly complicated and potentially messy story. The great challenge for the analyst, then, is to extract from this welter of diversity some general truths about the determinants of the economic success and social integration of outsider groups. Sowell's methodological strategy is to exploit the fact, strongly established by his data, that some remarkable commonalities can be discerned within these evident differences. If these six groups, so heterogeneous vis-à-vis one another and internally, nevertheless managed to achieve so much economic progress despite such formidable obstacles in so many and varied venues, their common success might provide important information bearing on why ethnic groups perform as they do and why some do better than others. At the very least, their common successes under such disparate conditions would tend to cast doubt on some familiar explanations of group differentials, particularly explanations that emphasize conditions such as poverty, ignorance, hostility, and discrimination, which all of these groups faced but still managed to overcome in inhospitable country after inhospitable country.[18] If the analyst can also extract from this bewildering heterogeneity certain common cultural and behavioral patterns, and if he can then link those patterns to the groups' economic successes, alternative explanations of those successes—and perhaps of other groups' failures[19]—may emerge.

Such linkages, if firmly established, might even support prescriptions for programmatic change. Sowell stresses, for example, a strong theme in much of his earlier work: the folly and mischief of judging the discriminatory character of a society or economy, as some affirmative action advocates do, according to how different groups are distributed in particular occupations. Skills, he maintains, are not randomly distributed in any one society, and they hardly become more equally distributed when they are transported across borders or oceans (p. 375).

> [O]ne of the clearest facts to emerge from these worldwide histories of various racial and ethnic groups is that gross statistical disparities in the "representation" of groups in different occupations, industries, income levels, and educational institutions have been the rule—not the exception—all across the planet. Moreover, many of these disparities have persisted for generations or even centuries.[20]

Disparities in achievement, he insists, can reflect differences in values and lifestyle,[21] which in turn can be—indeed, must have been—at some point in the past for all groups—self-consciously (or group consciously)—cultivated or rejected. Thus, Sowell's analysis may yield practical and policy payoffs as well as intellectual ones.

On the other hand, attempts to identify, explain, and influence group differences are famously controversial, even incendiary. Such efforts frequently generate allegations—some well-founded, some not—of racism, sexism, or other invidious attitudes that emphasize and exploit such differences. The bitter dispute over studies purporting to establish the magnitude and sources of group-specific differences in I.Q. is a cautionary tale,[22] as is the ugly history of eugenics, a movement fueled largely by efforts to isolate and stigmatize certain groups as inferior and to locate the root of their inferiority in biological endowment.[23] Where highly and almost universally valued goals such as academic achievement and economic success are concerned, observations about group disparities are likely to be seen as normatively loaded assertions about which groups or cultures are superior or inferior rather than simply as descriptive statements about varied group preferences of the some-like-chocolate, others-like-vanilla genre. Such analyses must therefore be undertaken with the utmost care and seriousness; at the same time, punches should not be pulled. *Migrations and Cultures* easily passes this test.

II. THE QUESTION OF CULTURE

Sowell maintains that the economic successes of migrant ethnic groups are rooted in culture, and not in biology, environment, or even history (pp. 375–77). He believes that certain ensembles of values and practices constitute distinct cultures and that certain of these cultures are more successful economically than others. Members of groups in which those cultures already flourish may have easier access to these values and practices, just as fluency in a particular language comes more readily to those who have been reared in households where it is habitually spoken. But it is these values and practices that conduce to economic success, not membership in any ascriptively defined group.

The idea of culture, then, is utterly foundational in Sowell's analysis. It is unfortunate, therefore, that this notion is also suspiciously flexible, maddeningly ambiguous, and ultimately elusive. He evidently conceives of the cultures that promote economic success at a level of generality so abstract that they can include quite different ways of life that quite different groups have crystallized in quite different economic forms. Precisely such abstraction, of course, is essential to his analytical project. After all, he is seeking both to explain how certain ways of life are transformed as they are carried to and transplanted in new environments, and also to identify the values and practices that animate those transformations. He writes:

> It is easy enough to understand how immigrants from an agricultural background in the cold lands of Scandinavia would settle in agricultural communities in the cold lands of Minnesota or Wisconsin, or how Chettyar moneylenders from India would become money-lenders in Burma or Malaya. What is more challenging is to understand how unskilled workers from southern China would become retailers throughout Southeast Asia and in the Caribbean and North America. . . . [p. 8]

Cultures, he says, "cover a broad spectrum of human concerns, from things as superficial as modes of dress to things as deeply felt as what one is prepared to die for" (p. 379). Between these extremes are the values and practices—the "human capital"—of special interest to Sowell, the economist: meticulous work habits, perseverance, social cohesion, law abidingness, risk taking, family unity, future orientation, and the like.[24]

How do we know these precious cultural attributes when we see them and how do we know that they exist in certain groups more than others? These are important questions, given the subjectivity of values and the ambiguous signification of practices. Sowell does not really discuss these conceptual and methodological issues. Instead, he employs three main indicia of cultural values and practices: groups' cultural reputations as reported by his mostly academic sources, descriptions of certain objective institutions and practices that group members have established, and inferences about cultural values that he draws from the fact of their economic success in the face of obstacles. These indicia, of course, are merely proxies (and crude ones at that) for the underlying phenomena that are truly of interest to us, and such indicia beg a number of fundamental questions about evidence and causality. Still, if these data and interpretations are not as rigorous as one might wish, they are nonetheless highly plausible. We would be foolish to dismiss them until we have something better.

What is the source of these cultural values and practices? What, according to Sowell, made the southern Italians notably hard working and yet lacking in entrepreneurial initiative,[25] while their countrymen from the north were disproportionately successful as entrepreneurs in the United States (pp. 164, 167)? Sowell ascribes the southerners' industriousness to the exigencies of their hard-scrabble life on unyielding soil in Italy; elsewhere he opines that having brought few occupational skills with them they nevertheless managed to exploit their "inner strength and inner values" (p. 174). But where did these inner values come from, and why did the northerners, on this theory, evidently possess them in even greater degree?

Sowell does not advance a comprehensive theory of the formation and change of cultures; he simply asserts that they exist and that they somehow persist over time and space. Yet how cultures arise and then manage to endure are questions that both go to the heart of his theory and lack self-evident answers. Indeed, the very existence of a culture should puzzle an economist like Sowell. In economic or evolutionary theory, of course, it is not difficult to explain why some cultures endure while others decline. Some values and practices are more economically efficient, politically sustaining, militarily functional, and morally and spiritually fulfilling than others. As such, they possess strong properties of survivability when cultures clash and compete—as they inevitably do in trade, migration, religious struggle, and war.

But again, what causes a culture to establish itself in the first place? In the language of economic theory, after all, a culture is a pure public good[26] and a costly one at that. Until it takes hold and becomes habitual, it requires of its practitioners much sacrifice—time, self-discipline, imagination, and experimentation—without any assurance that it will survive. However, those who wish to produce a public good like culture cannot appropriate its benefits for themselves but must share them with free riders who will not bear any of its costs. Since everyone would prefer to be a free rider, no one will make the investment necessary to produce and sustain the culture.

All of this assumes rationality, of course, and one might say that cultures are the very antithesis of rational products, arising instead out of more opaque spiritual and psychological needs and the little-understood processes that propel communal identity formation. Sowell, however, does not make this move. Insofar as one can discern his implicit theory of culture, it seems largely materialist, rationalist, and functionalist—fully in the spirit of economic theory. Thus he emphasizes the value-shaping role of soil, climate, topography, and water supply, and the rational, functional adaptations of people to these geophysical factors as they develop their occupational patterns and social mores.

Here, Sowell sometimes seeks to have it both ways. Thus, he attributes both the meticulousness of the Japanese and the brute physicality of the southern Italians to the poor agricultural conditions in their homelands (pp. 111, 146). Nor can such geophysical factors adequately explain the pronounced cultural differences that sometimes persist between groups that live for long periods of time in close proximity and material similarity to one another, such as Native Americans and their immediate neighbors. And while he mentions some striking instances in which cultures decline (he cites Rome) or suddenly flourish (the Scottish Enlightenment of the late eighteenth century), he fails to explain why these and other abrupt reversals of cultural fate and effectiveness, despite apparent geophysical, normative, and habitual continuities, do not count as evidence against his theory that culture—which is supposed to reflect these continuities—drives performance (pp. 380–81). In the end, then, he does not really dispel the deep and fascinating mystery about the ultimate sources and economic consequences of culture.

III. THE SELECTIVITY AND DIVERSITY OF MIGRATION

Migration, we know, is a highly selective process. Migrants are not simply a random sample of the population in the country of origin. Even before leaving their homeland, they are special, differing in a number of important respects from the demographically similar people whom they leave behind. They also differ from the migrants from other countries and from the natives of the countries to which they go. After all, the mere fact that migrants are prepared to uproot themselves, abandon all that is familiar (and sometimes familial), and trust that they can establish themselves in a strange land and prosper there suggests that they are more audacious, enterprising, self-confident, and risk taking than those who stay at home. Migrants are seldom the most abjectly poor in the country of origin; "[t]hose a notch or so higher on the economic scale could more readily gather together the passage money and might be a notch or so higher because they had more initiative or more skills or experience."[27] Nor do migrants always go from poorer countries to wealthier ones; the more general pattern, exemplified by the German and Flemish migrants to eastern Europe, is that migrants go to places, rich or poor, where they can be more productive.[28]

If immigrants are already special before they migrate, their experiences in the destination country make them even more so. Those who migrate and later return to their countries of origin—a significant fraction of all non-refugee migrants[29]—find themselves to be even more different from the countrymen whom they left behind than they were when they originally departed. In a sense, they become aliens in their own countries, different not only in their new skills and lifestyle but in ideas and values (pp. 22–25). These differences can become so great that the returning migrants feel a need to cluster with other returnees in enclaves that are quite distinct from the surrounding society and that engender its resentment (pp. 22 nn. 110 and

111, 145). Often, one supposes, those back home welcome the remittances that migrants send back more than the returning migrants themselves.[30]

The economic progress of those migrants who settle permanently in the destination country does not necessarily ensure their rapid integration into the larger society. One of Sowell's most interesting findings is that some of the same social conditions that facilitate the group's economic success may also retard its assimilation. Perhaps the most important factor promoting assimilation is the rate at which the immigrant group marries members of the destination society.[31] This intermarriage rate is in turn powerfully affected by the sex ratio of the migrants, which can vary considerably even within a particular group going to the same country. For Germans in the state of South Australia in the last half of the nineteenth century, he reports, there were almost as many female immigrants as male ones; as a consequence, they continued to marry within the group and established isolated German-speaking enclaves. In contrast, the sex ratio among German immigrants in the state of Victoria was four males for each female, which resulted in frequent intermarriage with non-Germans and relatively few ethnic enclaves.[32] The sex ratio among the Japanese in Brazil was about 3:2 (p. 131), and almost all Japanese in Brazil came in family groups (p. 131). In Brazil, the resulting high rate of in-group marriages minimized the degree of the group's interaction and competition with the host society (p. 131). The remarkably insular Italian marriage patterns in the United States represent another example.[33] In the short run, migrants' intermarriage with natives engendered increased interaction, competition, and hostility toward migrants in the host society; in the long run, however, it surely promoted assimilation and the attenuation of ethnic identities.

Like a person rummaging through a fine antique store, the reader of Sowell's account of migrations can hardly avoid coming across some interesting but unexpected miscellany. Many claims are surprising only because they reflect a comparative perspective often lacking in even the most thoughtful commentators on immigration. Examples include his claims that: the World War II internment of Japanese civilians was "an even bigger disaster . . . in Canada than in the U.S." (p. 123); that German prejudice against Jews and other groups historically "tended to be less rather than more prevalent, as compared to other Europeans—or to Asians or Africans, for that matter" (p. 103); that the prejudice against the Chinese has been greater and more violent in Asia than elsewhere (p. 227); and that the Japanese communities in the United States during World War II felt much greater loyalty to the United States than those in Brazil felt to Brazil, despite being subjected to harsher treatment here (p. 107). Some of his data are shocking and must indelibly alter our images of earlier migrations. He notes, for example, that seventeen percent of the immigrants on ships bound for the United States during the mid-nineteenth century died either on the way or on arrival (p. 39), a mortality rate that begins to approach even the ghastly toll of the "middle passage" voyages of the slave trade.[34]

IV. DISCRIMINATION AND IMMIGRANT SUCCESS

At a time when all immigrant-receiving countries—other than the United States—are accepting fewer legal immigrants, it is worthwhile to consider how government policies toward immigration have evolved. Some countries once welcomed and even subsidized immigrants, recognizing their potential for spurring economic development. The Czars, for example, invested heavily in creating settlements for the Volga Germans whom they hoped would serve as agrarian models for their own, more backward subjects (p. 59). Brazil, like many American states in the nineteenth century, also subsidized immigrants whom they hoped would settle and develop their vast frontiers (p. 156). But it is dismaying to observe how even national economic self-interest often yielded to xenophobia, as governments initiated, or capitulated to, the most repressive policies excluding, harassing, exploiting, expelling, and killing even their most productive immigrants.[35]

Some immigrant groups were resilient enough to survive even the harshest forms of discrimination. Sowell reports, for example, that although the internment of the Japanese in the United States reduced the internees' income in the immediate post-war years, they achieved economic parity with Americans by 1959; in Canada, where the internments were even more damaging economically, their rebound was "spectacular" (pp. 118, 124). The growing social acceptance of the Japanese after their internments in countries as disparate as Peru, Australia, and the United States was also stunning (p. 139). In 1959, only sixteen years after the repeal of the virulently racist Chinese Exclusion Act, Chinese family income in the United States approximated the national average (p. 226).

What are we to make of these remarkable triumphs of so many immigrant groups in so many unwelcoming societies? Could it be that anti-immigrant animus, which so cruelly and perversely disadvantaged these groups in the short run, actually strengthened their economic and often social positions in the long run? In some paradoxical way, might hostility and discrimination promote the survival and prosperity of the very group (if not always of each member) that they hope to exclude?

This is an intriguing question. Given the fact that most if not all destination countries today display xenophobic attitudes and policies,[36] it is also an extremely timely and relevant one. To ask it, of course, is emphatically *not* to countenance discrimination, which inflicts undeserved suffering on innocent, admirable people.[37] Instead, such a question invites us to consider the subtle dynamics of immigrants' progress, to reconsider some long-held assumptions, and to wonder anew at the strength of the human spirit and the persistence of coherent cultures under conditions of extreme adversity. It is to this question that I devote the remainder of this review.

Before considering how discrimination might paradoxically work to the eventual advantage of a victimized immigrant group (although not to all individual members), one should recognize three important complications that Sowell does not, and perhaps cannot, adequately explain. First, not all immigrants' stories have happy endings; indeed, many do not, at least if we look only at the first generation—the immigrant himself. I previously noted that Sowell's data reveal the immense return migration flows experienced by some groups.[38] He suggests that many of these returnees succeeded as immigrants and came home as wealthy men. We must assume, however, that many, perhaps even most, of the returnees did not fulfill the dreams that had impelled them to migrate and many of these came home to resume the limited opportunities that they had hoped to escape.

Second, Sowell's data, while impressive in their range and depth, are necessarily limited to the six ethnic and national groups that he describes. Although their diasporas were quite large (especially the Chinese and Indians), they do not begin to include all of the great migrations in recent history. The representativeness of his data, then, remains uncertain. They exclude, for example, the out-flows from the Arabian peninsula, many Asian migrants, groups from the Mahgreb and sub-Saharan Africa, those from eastern Europe (other than the primary migration of Jews and the secondary migration of Germans), and the immense flows north from the Caribbean and South and Central America. Some of the groups that Sowell canvasses have been more successful than others; so too have some of the groups that he does not include.[39]

Third and most important, the diverse immigration experiences *within* Sowell's six groups cast considerable doubt on the adequacy of his cultural explanation for group successes abroad. As noted earlier, he attributes these differences in economic performance largely to the *premigration* variations in local cultures, habits, skills, economic opportunities, and physical resources that divided each group in its country (or in the case of Jews, countries) of origin. To be sure, he does mention some of the *postmigration* conditions—economic geography, local attitudes toward migrants, the availability of market niches, demographic pressures for intermarriage, and so on—that greeted each diaspora's subgroups as they settled in different destination communities and countries. He maintains that these conditions, together with the traditions and values the group's members carried with them, shaped their experiences in their new homelands. But if these conditions contributed to their success in the destination countries as well, then it was not the group's *premigration* culture (as Sowell would have it) that explains their success but rather some unspecified, perhaps indeterminate, combination of pre- and postmigration factors.

It seems almost self-evident that any persuasive theory purporting to explain differential success among immigrant groups would have to take account of such a combination of pre- and postmigration factors. After all, how else are we to explain the fact that immigrant groups that have succeeded in the United States and Canada have fared relatively poorly in some of their other destination countries? A leading migration scholar, Myron Weiner, makes the point cogently:

> Second-generation Arabs and Turks appear to be doing better in the United States than they are in France and Germany. Culture in these cases is presumably the same, yet the outcomes differ. The ease with which citizenship is acquired, the acceptance of cultural and religious diversity by the host population, and educational opportunities may be factors in explaining the differences.[40]

In short, an immigrant group's performance may be powerfully shaped by its values, habits, and skills, but those factors are inevitably mediated by more external, less controllable factors such as legal and political institutions and the attitudes and behavior of inhabitants in the destination country.

Sowell would surely not deny the importance of these external factors. After all, if a group's culture is powerfully influenced by the geophysical and institutional conditions in its country of origin, as he insists, then it can hardly be doubted that the same kinds of factors would influence the group's success in the destination country. Nevertheless, Sowell makes a problematic choice in his selective theoretical account: he emphasizes group culture as the crucial intervening variable between those conditions in the country of origin and the group's performance in the destination country, but then fails to incorporate the destination country's institutional and attitudinal variables into his causal theory. He wants to insist on the explanatory power of a single factor—albeit one, as we saw, that is diffusely defined—that social scientists (not to speak of more careless commentators) too often neglect. By doing so, however, he forgoes the opportunity to incorporate other factors into his theory—factors that would produce a less striking and original[41] but more comprehensive and ultimately persuasive account of immigrants' diverse experiences.

Invidious discrimination, as Sowell painstakingly demonstrates, is an important part of those experiences in almost all cases. Even when the host government welcomed immigrants, as in the case of Czarist Russia and the Volga Germans, the populace tended to receive them with hostility and recrimination.[42] The great puzzle is to understand why this discrimination did not in the end defeat the efforts of the newcomers to prosper and assimilate. An answer might be of great value to contemporary immigrant groups and ethnic minorities that must devise strategies for dealing with the continuing animus that their presence arouses in almost all societies.

V. Immigrants in Politics and Markets

Sowell offers a solution, and it is one that will seem counter-intuitive, perhaps even subversive, to many readers. I also suspect that it will particularly offend those who actively advocate the group interests of immigrants and minorities in the public domain. Sowell believes that immigrants' interests are best advanced not through political action but through successful participation in the market. Paradoxically, discrimination can promote economically functional behavior by immigrants. Because they are excluded by the majority from ethnic preferences in certain politicized sectors of the economy, they may redouble their efforts to acquire education and economic skills that will make such preferences unnecessary. They may also gravitate to other less politicized sectors where they face reduced competition and can accumulate enduring advantages.[43] Deprived of opportunities in the extractive or manufacturing industries or as corporate employees, they may gain expertise in the middleman functions so vital to modern economies and in the professions where potentially lucrative self-employment and independence beckon.[44] Thrown back by discrimination on their own resources, they may rely upon family members and community ties which can entail economic efficiencies.

Sowell explains the dramatic decline in virulent anti-Japanese discrimination thus: "behavior and performance are more effective ways of changing other people's minds than moral crusades or emotional denunciations" (p. 139). But the social consequences of a group's success are more convoluted and remorselessly perverse than this Pollyannaish lesson suggests. Indeed, as Sowell shows elsewhere in this book and as others have also shown, a group's economic success has often heightened, rather than reduced, such hostility.[45] Indeed, he himself reports that the Chinese have aroused more hostility than other immigrant and minority groups that are much more prosperous than the Chinese (p. 228), that Jewish achievements have magnified anti-Semitism everywhere, indeed particularly "in those societies most desperately in need of the special skills of Jews" (p. 307), and that the economic success of the Tamils in Ceylon has engendered bitter hostility and discrimination by the native Sinhalese (p. 354). Surely then the larger truth, which Sowell's evidence supports but his tendentiousness obscures, is that both responses to immigrant success, admiration and animus, can coexist; indeed, they can and do coexist at the same time, in the same society, even in the same individual.[46]

As a well-known neo-conservative economist, Sowell's preference for market-based solutions to social problems hardly comes as a shock. Even so, the historical evidence that he adduces on the relationship between immigrant groups' economic progress in the destination countries and their lack of involvement in the politics of those countries is provocative. He reports that in destination country after destination country, economic assimilation of the group *precedes* its acquisition of political influence, not the other way around. The most prosperous immigrant groups, he states, have not advanced themselves through ethnic group politics; their political activity has occurred *after* they gained economic power.[47]

An aversion to politics in the destination countries would not be surprising. After all, these groups originated in societies governed by nonparticipatory or repressive regimes; hence they bore with them no tradition of organized pluralistic politics even when they migrated to relatively participatory societies. Moreover, none of these groups, with the exception of the Chinese in Malaysia, constituted a large enough fraction of their new society for ethnic group solidarity to seem like a viable strategy for political success.[48] Indeed, group-based political action would carry grave risks of bitter retaliation by the dominant ethnic groups.[49] Finally, it was often the public sector that most actively excluded immigrant groups, as South Africa did with respect to Indians (pp. 330–31).

Where members of immigrant groups have played prominent or leadership roles in politics—for example, Germans and Italians in the United States, Jews in Australia, and Japanese in Peru—they have almost always done so, Sowell claims, as otherwise-established, economically independent individuals rather than as ethnic group activists or representatives.[50] Many immigrants, of course, participated in political organizations in which ethnic solidarity was viewed as an important electoral asset, as in the "machine" organizations that dominated the governments of some American cities. Typically, however, these ethnic groups joined such organizations as elements of larger, multiethnic and transethnic coalitions in which the dominant incentives for action were individual material benefits, not group-oriented programmatic goals and public goods. Moreover, as Sowell and others have argued, those groups, such as the Irish in the United States, that managed to gain political patronage and public sector jobs through such organizations paid a high price for their political success, though one not noticed at the time. They were slower to achieve market power, economic independence, and social assimilation than those groups that eschewed politics for private sector rewards by focusing their energies on the cultivation of entrepreneurial, market-oriented skills.[51]

Again, this trade-off is not surprising. All individuals, whether native born or immigrants, must make an ensemble of strategic decisions about how they will invest their scarce resources. Compared with the native born, immigrants have ordinarily been more constrained in their choices because they traditionally entered their new society with more limited resources.[52] Their most important choice, like that of all individuals, is whether to invest in present and near-term rewards or instead to sacrifice those rewards in the hope of longer-term returns. This choice in turn leads to other, more specific ones—between investing in themselves or in their families; between immediate employment or education; between consumption and saving; between cultural insularity or assimilation; between learning the new language rapidly or more slowly; between pursuing individual goals or group goals; between public sector and private sector occupations. In reality, of course, such choices are not always quite as stark as I have presented them; for example, immigrants may work full time *and* go to school, and they may retain their cultures of origin while *also* seeking to learn new folkways. Inevitably, however, their tradeoffs are difficult and poignant. They must choose, and their choices, on average, will have far-reaching consequences for them and their families. The aggregate of such choices will significantly affect the future of their group and of their new society.

VI. Immigrant Assimilation

Sowell's evidence strongly suggests that the most economically successful immigrant groups have chosen to devote their energies and resources primarily to the pursuit of relatively future-oriented, family-oriented, market-oriented, assimilationist, apolitical, and individualistic strategies of economic and social advancement.

Of these strategies, assimilation seems the most elusive; its definition is ambiguous and its preconditions are both temporally and behaviorally uncertain.[53] The terms of trade between the immigrant's retention of his traditional culture (even as he transforms it under the influence of the destination society) and his induction into, and acceptance by, the new are under constant negotiation.[54] Even the effects of assimilation on group survival are not clear cut; as Sowell reminds us, the degree of Jewish assimilation had little effect on their ultimate fate during the Holocaust; they were more fully integrated into German and Polish society than elsewhere in Europe, yet they suffered annihilating losses there as well as in countries like the Soviet Union where they were less assimilated (pp. 267–70).

Even for the stunningly successful groups that Sowell presents, for example, the *pace* of assimilation has varied among and within different immigrant groups over time and place according to demographic factors (for example, sex ratio) that affect intermarriage rates, geophysical and cultural insularity, popular hostility, and other conditions. Moreover, some behaviors that can retard assimilation in the short run may foster it in the longer term. Sowell notes, for example, that the Japanese in Brazil, like other upwardly mobile but slow-to-assimilate groups, advanced largely through self-employment.[55] George Borjas, a labor economist who specializes in immigration, argues that the traditional immigrants' strategy of exploiting ethnic market niches such as specialized restaurants and retailing, a strategy that is usually viewed as promoting economic skills, entrepreneurship, and assimilation, has its darker side. Such a strategy, he suggests, may consign immigrants to their ethnically defined enclaves, making it more difficult for them to break out and compete in larger, more cosmopolitan markets in which scale economies and new products, services, and skills are rewarded (p. 137). On the other hand, sociologists of immigration like Alejandro Portes emphasize that communal insularity, while delaying full assimilation, may nevertheless create a vital breathing space for the immigrants' children, the crucial second generation. This allows these children to learn the language and essential norms of mainstream society while at the same time rejecting, under the intense cultural tutelage of their immigrant parents, the more destructive, adversarial native subcultures that surround and threaten to seduce them.[56]

Sowell's theory and data cannot resolve these somewhat competing claims about assimilation any more than they can rigorously differentiate the interrelated roles of immigrant values and skills, geophysical and demographic factors, and destination country institutions and receptiveness in shaping the fates of immigrant groups. But in underscoring both the primacy of individual economic achievement in the social progress of groups and the relative insignificance of ethnic politics to that progress, he turns on its head much of the conventional wisdom among ethnic group leaders in the United States and elsewhere. In this respect, Sowell heightens the relevance of the work of social scientists—work that he does not cite—who are skeptical about the tenor and effectiveness of modern ethnic politics, especially in the United States. In contrast to those who view ethnic and panethnic appeals as providing a solid grounding for the advancement of immigrants' interests,[57] these skeptics argue that contemporary minority group politics tends to emphasize the rhetoric of protest, symbolism, and separatism at the cost of strong political organization, accountable leadership, broad coalition building, sound policies, and real economic gains.[58] In their view—and in Sowell's—such a politics constitutes a model for acceptance that upwardly mobile immigrants should not emulate. At best, in this view, it distracts them from their vital need to acquire individual economic skills, construct durable communities, and adopt social identities and linkages firmly anchored in the American mainstream. At worst, it encourages them to adopt ideological styles and agendas that can help to generate the kind of harsh, backlash politics that in 1996 produced the most xenophobic spate of legislation in more than four decades.[59]

VII. The Future of Immigration Policy

Sowell says little about the present and future of immigration policy, yet his subject—the migration of cultures—is so central to the immigration debate that he cannot help but offer some general advice. Migrating cultures compete with those that they encounter in their diasporas, and the competition proceeds at many levels—economic, military, religious, linguistic, technological, ideological, aesthetic, normative, physiological, and even bacteriological. Often, the immigrants demand or evoke responses from the dominant culture of the receiving country. In some cases—he mentions affirmative action and multicultural policies in the United States, Canada, and Australia—the demands for change may come less from the immigrants than from the natives, and they may increase the costs of absorbing immigrants, including the level of natives' hostility (p. 387).

After noting that immigration has both positive and negative consequences for the receiving country depending on the cultures that the immigrants carry with them, Sowell makes two acute, interesting observations. First, "domestic ideological agendas may make it impossible to be selective in admitting immigrants from different nations, leaving as alternatives only loss of control of the borders or restrictive policies toward immigrants in general" (p. 388). This seems a fair characterization of the way in which Congress has perceived the politics of immigration in the United States and explains much of the harshness of the 1996 legislation.[60] Second, after noting that formal schooling and desirable human capital are not the same, he states that "the transportation of bodies and the dissemination of human capital have become increasingly separable operations, so that the historic role of immigration in advancing nations need not apply to its future role. . . . Neither technological nor managerial human capital requires mass immigration for its diffusion" (pp. 389–90). Whether other forms of human capital such as "can-do" optimism and energy, a strong work ethic, future orientation, religious piety, traditional family values, and faith in education and in America do in fact require—and justify—continued immigration he does not say. It remains, however, a crucial question for American public debate.

The future of American immigration policy, and indeed the future course of American society more generally, may well depend on which prescription for immigrant progress—Sowell's individualistic, apolitical, market-oriented strategy of human and social capital accumulation, or the politics of ethnic protest advocated by many minority group leaders—gains the allegiance of the large number of recently arrived and future immigrants. If past is prologue, the vast majority of them will continue to follow Sowell's preferred path to full membership in American society. In that process, they will—often with some sense of loss—gradually attenuate, transform, and shed their ethnic group identities.

But past is not always prologue. Indeed, it is not even past; instead, it survives to help shape the future. The experiences of recent immigrants to the United States are almost certainly more diverse than at any other time in American history, if only because our immigration stream is now more diverse than ever before in national origins, linguistic, racial, cultural, and relative educational and skill-level terms. This kaleidoscopic range of experiences and perspectives, which have served us well in the past, provides much reason for optimism about immigration; it also gives some ground for fresh concern.[61] Only time will tell whether the optimism or the concerns are borne out. In the meanwhile, the perennially stirring, compelling drama of individual and cultural migration continues.

13

Refugee Burden-Sharing: A Modest Proposal

The world is awash in refugees.[1] According to the most recent estimates, more than fifteen million individuals are already outside their countries and in need of international protection and assistance.[2] This population, already immense, is growing steadily and remorselessly with the proliferation of refugee-producing and migration-facilitating conditions: political repression, armed conflict, civil strife, environmental disaster, famine, social and economic disintegration, wretched governmental policies, and improvements in communications and transportation opportunities.[3] Refugee emergencies have become so endemic that the rhetoric of crisis today is as likely to numb as it is to energize.[4]

The current legal and political arrangements for managing refugee flows were established to manage European cross-border refugee flows during the post-World War II era. The cause of these flows became much more varied as time went on, their locus shifted during the 1960s, 1970s, and 1980s to other regions, notably Africa, south and southeast Asia, the Middle East, and the Caribbean, and internally displaced individuals became more numerous than the border-crossing refugees.[5] By the 1980s, Europe had come to think of the refugee burden as more of a problem for the Third World and the United States than for itself. Protected from large-scale refugee movements by an impregnable Iron Curtain in the east, Europe seemed relatively immune to the threat.

It is no longer possible to entertain this comforting illusion. With the dissolution of the Soviet Union, Germany's reunification, the militarization of bitter ethnic conflicts in the Balkans, and the failure of many former European colonies to establish viable political and economic systems, refugees are once again pouring into the very heart of Europe. Moreover, new migration routes, facilitated by cheap transportation and intricate social networks, are bringing migrants to Europe (and thence to the United States) from Asia, Africa, and the Pacific archipelago.[6] Although few of these migrants are likely to meet the legal qualifications for Convention refugee status,[7] many of them nevertheless seek some form of temporary or permanent protection and must be processed in one or another European state until their status can be determined—with the attendant fiscal, social, and political burdens on the receiving state that such processing ordinarily entails.[8] Europe thus joins the Third World, North America (the United States and Canada),[9] and the other traditional receiving regions in facing the prospect of additional flows of migrants claiming protection through the international refugee system, broadly defined.

Virtually all discussions of refugee law and policy focus on the acute vulnerability of refugees. These commentators seek ways to alleviate refugees' sufferings, either by fulfilling or extending the protections to which they are entitled or by eliminating the political conditions that impel them to flee from their homelands. The reason for this focus on the refugees themselves is as obvious as it is sound and humane: Refugees present egregious cases of injustice and compelling claims for some form of international protection. Their claims are compelling not so much because they often live in conditions of poverty, unemployment, rude shelter, and mistreatment. After all, these are the conditions of daily life for most other human beings unfortunate enough to have been born into the wrong social class in the wrong place at the wrong time. These conditions are also those in which most refugees lived before their flight made them objects of international law's concern. Instead, what marks refugees off for particular solicitude is their radical, enforced dislocation and isolation and their uncertain legal status as aliens. They are of special humanitarian concern because they were compelled to abandon the only protections and solaces that can render the harsh vicissitudes of life endurable: the assistance (however minimal) of their own governments and the social supports of their customary communities.

The perspective of this essay, however, is quite different. Rather than focus on the suffering that refugees endure or the root causes of their flight, I take these remorseless facts as tragically given. I emphasize instead the burdens that the sudden, massive refugee flows that are now endemic impose on states. I do so not because these burdens are more than the international order, taken as a whole, can or should bear (they are not) but because I am convinced of the following three propositions. First, the emerging state responses to these burdens are seriously jeopardizing the viability of any meaningful regime of international human rights protection. Second, any realistic solution to this problem must somehow forestall these responses by easing these burdens in exchange for a set of obligations that states are more willing to accept and implement. Third, this can only be accomplished by distributing obligations more widely and fairly among states over time.

Doubtless, my effort to salvage a meaningful human rights regime from the carcass of state sovereignty will seem rather odd to many well-informed commentators on refugee law and policy in the academy and in the field. They often maintain that state sovereignty constitutes perhaps the chief threat and impediment to the fulfillment of human rights goals. To them, state sovereignty is the problem, not the solution.

This view is certainly plausible. After all, nation-states are today the principal designers and executors of human rights violations. They also encourage, abet, condone, or at least fail to prevent many human rights violations committed by ostensibly private groups. Finally, the principle of state sovereignty often delegitimates and stymies proposed interventions by states and supranational groups into the offending state's territory—interventions that might prevent or rectify violations occurring entirely within national borders. In each of these ways, the nation-state has indeed impeded and confounded human rights goals, just as its critics suggest.[10]

This line of argument is true as far as it goes, but it does not go nearly far enough. For it is also true that for the foreseeable future, genuine human rights protections—particularly the protection of refugees—can only be enforced and implemented by sovereign states or by other entities such as supranational agencies and nongovernmental organizations (NGOs) working with their assistance or sufferance. This is a brutal reality of which any practicable, meaningful reform proposal must take full account. To ignore or deny it is to engage in a dangerous fatuity.

But the link between sovereignty and protection is more than a regrettable necessity. While malefactors have committed great crimes in the name of state sovereignty, the nation-state has also been an essential, powerful force for justice. The mature nation-state is a unique formation conceived through communal imagination, cemented by history, fueled by political ideology, and equilibrated by institutions. Its combination of scale, power, predictability, and normativity enable it to generate levels of self-sacrifice and coordinated action in the common interest of which other groupings, whether larger or smaller, seem incapable.

But however one appraises the overall relationship between nation-states and human rights, the analysis and proposal that follow are constructed on a premise that few knowledgeable observers of the current refugee regime can seriously dispute. My premise is that the current refugee regime is "broke"—in the limited but important sense that it fails to afford adequate protection to the enormous and growing number of people fleeing from what seem to be, and often are, intolerable conditions—and that it needs fixing. This is not to deny the many important and often heroic responses that the international community has mounted to address human rights emergencies. Indeed, I describe one such response, the Comprehensive Plan of Action and Orderly Departure Program in Southeast Asia (CPA), in some detail. It is simply to say that much more needs to be done as these emergencies continue to proliferate.

This essay proceeds in several sections. In section I, I discuss some of the reasons why the current refugee protection regime is inadequate. In section II, I summarize the CPA experience, the most important example of a negotiated refugee burden-sharing arrangement, which suggests both the value of international burden-sharing quotas and the need to create a more reliable, effective structure for prescribing and administering them.

In section III, I consider four broad strategies for improving refugee protection. In the order of their abstract desirability, they are: (1) eliminating the root causes of refugee flows; (2) prompt repatriation of refugees; (3) temporary protection of refugees; and (4) permanent resettlement of refugees in third countries.[11] I conclude (with virtually all other commentators) that each of these is problematic and that the practical realities of refugee crises and international refugee politics often require resort to the strategies of temporary protection and permanent resettlement because the more desirable ones are simply not available.

In section IV, I describe my proposal, which is intended to ameliorate some,[12] but certainly not all, of the most important inadequacies in the current system. Details aside, the proposal consists of two main elements. First, a group of states would agree to observe a strong norm of proportional burden-sharing for refugees, would seek to induce other states to join the group, and would arrange for an existing or newly established international agency to assign to each participating state a refugee protection quota. A state's quota would commit it to assure temporary protection or permanent resettlement for a certain number of refugees over a certain time period. Second, the participating states would then be permitted to trade their quotas by paying others to fulfill their obligations. As noted immediately below, states would participate in the quota-cum-market system voluntarily, albeit under the influence of their more powerful neighbors. Accordingly, the system should require only limited regulation by the agency. As discussed in section IV, its chief responsibilities would be to administer the system, including the quotas and the flow of information about refugees, and to ascertain whether the requisite protection is actually being delivered.

I propose that this scheme be entirely consensual on the part of the participating states and that it be established on a regional or even a subregional basis, rather than on a global one. These states would define the refugees who might look to them for protection according to agreed-upon criteria. For example, the criteria might prefer refugees from countries of origin located in the region, refugees in first-asylum states located there, or refugees from countries with historical ties to participating states.

A regionally structured system would possess several important advantages over a more global one. It could exploit a tradition of regional responsibility for localized refugee flows and solutions, the greater commonality of interests and values that regions tend to share, and the more intense patterns of interaction that they exhibit. It would minimize the psychological, fiscal, and other costs of having to relocate refugees over long distances and of locating them farther from their homes. Its limited size and consensual character would also make it administratively more manageable. As with other groups seeking gains from trade, however, participating states would have an incentive to expand the membership over time if the scheme proved successful.[13]

I also discuss in section IV why this unusual burden-sharing scheme might actually be politically acceptable and practically workable. Such a happy outcome, however, is far from clear. Under the existing regime, after all, states that are not states of origin or of first asylum are entirely free to join in, or refrain from, refugee protection efforts, as their interests dictate. Why then would they choose to surrender that freedom of action and accept a burden-sharing obligation that is likely to be costly, risk domestic political tensions, and probably ratchet upwards over time?

Some states will probably reject such an obligation out of hand; they will point out that they neither generate refugee flows nor are likely to receive them. They may also point to the fact that the kind of massive refugee flows that have occurred in Rwanda and the former Yugoslavia are the exception, not the rule. The larger, wealthier, and more stable states can often absorb smaller, more gradual refugee movements without resorting to extraordinary measures.

Even these states, however, might be attracted to burden-sharing for the same reason that many individuals are attracted to catastrophic health insurance: States may rationally prefer to incur a small and predictable protection burden now in order to avoid bearing large, sudden, unpredictable, unwanted, and unstoppable refugee inflows in the future. They might prefer a system that created strong incentives for more states to support temporary protection of refugees, largely in the Third World, over the current one, which generates strong pressures for an even more dreaded (from their perspective) form of relief: permanent resettlement.

As the world grows smaller and more interconnected, and as an increasing number of refugees can more easily reach more places and claim protection there, such "refugee crisis insurance" might well be a "good buy"—perhaps even for relatively insular states. By introducing a market in quota obligations, the scheme would permit even greater flexibility. For many states, then, this burden-sharing scheme would be fairer and more rational than the status quo—especially if, as I propose, it were established on a regional basis. So, at least, I shall argue.

Section IV concludes by discussing how such a scheme would be enforced. Briefly, I suggest that while the scheme would be administered and to some extent enforced by an international agency, it is the states with the greatest interest in a better refugee protection system—those in North America and Western Europe—that would have the strongest incentives to deploy the various carrots and sticks of international diplomacy at their disposal (trade benefits, other forms of assistance, security guarantees, etc.) in order to secure both initial agreement and subsequent compliance.

The United States has compelling reasons to seize the initiative on this issue. As the only remaining superpower and the leading funder of the existing international refugee system, it has the greatest stake in assuring a just and stable world order. The Bosnian tragedy revealed a vacuum of leadership in European refugee crises that only the United States can fill. Finally, the United States continues to be vulnerable to its own sudden refugee flows from the Caribbean, which it has experienced from time to time since 1980.

So far as I know, this proposal is a novel one—although it resembles in some respects an approach adumbrated by Professor James C. Hathaway several years ago,[14] and its quotas feature seeks to build on the embryonic burden-sharing norm that the CPA experience, detailed in section II, exemplified. Because the proposal will certainly be controversial in the refugee-policy community, section V defends it against a variety of anticipated objections, particularly to its market element, which is bound to arouse the most opposition. At the outset, however, I wish to emphasize a point that should inform one's reaction to the entire analysis. Although the proposal entails many problems, virtually all of those problems already exist, sometimes to an even greater degree, in the current system. For this reason, I urge the reader to keep the "compared to what" question firmly in mind as she ponders these problems.

I. THE CURRENT REGIME FOR PROTECTING REFUGEES

The existing system of refugee protection is almost universally criticized by those individuals and organizations most committed to human rights goals,[15] and by governments that are affected by its functioning. The bill of particulars in the various indictments converge in many respects. All commentators recognize that the system was designed in the post–World War II era to deal with a predominantly European displaced population facing prospects quite different from those confronting today's refugees. Modern globalization of the world economy, the revolutions in transportation and communications, and the dissolution of colonial empires into a plethora of weak and often oppressive states—changes so consequential for the magnitude and character of contemporary refugee flows—all lay in the future.[16]

The system that developed is one in which each state of first asylum must determine the status of the claimant—in particular, whether she qualifies as a refugee under the 1951 Convention Relating to the Status of Refugees.[17] If so, she may be entitled as a matter of international, and perhaps domestic, law to the panoply of rights that the Convention accords refugees.[18]

From the perspective of refugees seeking protection, this system suffers from a number of serious flaws. Since all of these flaws have already received much attention and extensive critical analysis from refugee advocates, international organizations, and scholars of international human rights law, I shall discuss them only briefly. The core legal concepts embedded in the refugee definition—persecution on account of race, religion, national origin, political opinion, or membership in a particular social group—are expansive and ambiguous enough to have engendered enormous uncertainties when they are applied to particular cases. On the other hand, these concepts are quite narrow relative to the diverse circumstances and motives that may prompt individuals to leave their countries in haste and in vulnerable condition.[19]

The refugee protection system, however, has less to do with the legal niceties of the Refugee Convention than with the political prerogatives of sovereign states. Each state judges for itself whether a particular migrant or group of migrants who reaches its territory or seeks resettlement there will receive that, or any, relief. Each state, moreover, possesses powerful disincentives to provide relief, especially on its own territory. Such relief is costly to provide; at a minimum, it includes food, clothing, shelter, and information. If the state does not allow the migrants to come and go as they please, it must keep them in custody or under close surveillance. If they remain in custody in close quarters and enforced idleness, the risks of violence, crime, and other social pathologies are correspondingly great. Although refugees are often kept in the most squalid conditions, those conditions may nevertheless be superior to those in which most citizens of the receiving state live.

In any event, the admission and maintenance of even small numbers of refugees over long periods of time are almost certain to occasion bitter political opposition within the receiving state, especially if the refugees are permitted to compete for scarce jobs. The presence of refugee populations can create serious foreign policy embarrassments. In sufficient numbers and under certain conditions, the mere presence of refugees can constitute a genuine national security threat to the receiving state. They may prompt domestic rioting, ethnic violence, and the destabilization, perhaps even overthrow, of the regime.[20] In this sense, refugee protection is not simply a human rights issue; it can also be a matter of geopolitical significance affecting the security of the international order.

Nor are these risks equally distributed across the globe. To the contrary, this distribution is decidedly lumpy. Until the demise of the former Soviet Union and the outbreak of hostilities in the former Yugoslavia, Europe had generated and received relatively few refugees for decades. Even today, most refugee flows occur in Africa and southern Asia, and the brunt of refugee burdens by far is borne by neighboring states in those regions.

A state inclined to comply with only the letter of the Refugee Convention is not obliged to afford much protection to the migrant. The duty of *non-refoulement*—the obligation not to return a refugee to conditions of persecution—is clear enough, but most of the other rights-defining provisions of the Convention contain qualifying phrases and other limitations designed to protect the interests and prerogatives of the receiving state.[21]

It appears, however, that most states are not so inclined. For them, free-riding appears to be the rational strategy in the area of refugee protection. This means accepting as few refugees as possible in the hope that others will assume the burdens of resettling or otherwise dealing with them. The pursuit of a free-rider strategy is constrained only by whatever pressures can be exerted by domestic refugee advocates, international human rights organizations, and other states that can deploy a variety of carrots or sticks.

The primary institutional advocates for refugees within the system, and the most insistent voices calling for state compliance with its norms, are the United Nations High Commissioner for Refugees (UNHCR) and the many secular and religious nongovernmental organizations (NGOs) working in the refugee field. Yet both UNHCR and the NGOs are chronically under-funded relative to their growing protection responsibilities, and they are vulnerable to political attack by the receiving states on whom they must rely for their operating authority, budget, cooperation, and legitimacy. In reality, these forces compromise them at every turn. Under the exceedingly difficult circumstances in which UNHCR and the NGOs must usually work, the wonder is that they perform as effectively as they do.

For these and other reasons, refugee protection has proven to be woefully inadequate—a conclusion to which countless human victims bear grim and silent witness. This inadequacy is especially apparent during refugee emergencies such as those in southeastern Asia during the 1970s and 1980s, and Africa and the former Yugoslavia in the 1990s. Here, however, I wish to emphasize one systemic, institutional failure that I believe contributes substantially to all of the others: the failure of refugee burden-sharing among states. If meaningful reform of the refugee protection system is to occur, it must start here.

The problem is simpler to state than to solve. Although the entire international community ought to shoulder the burdens of dealing with massive refugee flows, only a relatively small number of nations and regions actually do so. Some of those least capable of bearing these burdens have in fact carried a disproportionately large share of them. This is most strikingly true of some African states that often serve as countries of first asylum for many of the most wretched refugees. Conversely, some of the states that are most capable of incurring refugee burdens have stood on the sidelines watching.

No strong norm of refugee burden-sharing currently exists in international law or practice. This is not to say that the appeal of such a norm has gone unremarked. In recent years, a number of commentators have called for the creation or recognition by the international community of a norm of equitable burden-sharing.[22] Some have inferred a principle of international solidarity from more abstract principles of justice or have discerned such a principle from existing international instruments[23] from which the norm of equitable burden-sharing of refugees might be derived as a logical and normatively desirable corollary.[24] Such inferences, however, are more in the nature of moral exhortation and prudential argument than expositions of authoritative legal principles.[25] In practice, there have been very few instances of large-scale burden-sharing arrangements designed to expand rather than restrict refugee protection.[26] The most important example is the CPA.[27]

II. THE COMPREHENSIVE PLAN OF ACTION

The CPA resettlement program provides a useful study of the conditions under which burden-sharing can succeed. They developed and were refined over an extended period of time, and involved intensive bilateral and multilateral negotiations conducted in a crisis atmosphere in which national self-interest was the main driving force and jerry-built, practical solutions were the principal desiderata.[28]

After the sweep of communist victories in southeast Asia in 1975, well over two million people fled Vietnam, Cambodia, and Laos for "first asylum" in neighboring countries.[29] Before 1979, these people received relatively little international assistance, and refugee camps were poorly organized.[30] A coordinated international response began in July 1979, when the United Nations convened an international conference in Geneva to seek solutions to the burgeoning refugee crisis. Conference participants were attentive to the differing abilities of countries to assist the refugees. In its report on the conference, UNHCR noted that "[s]ince the countries of first asylum were developing countries confronted with serious economic and social constraints, it was essential that countries outside the area assumed the principal responsibility for resettlement."[31]

The sixty-five governments attending the Geneva conference agreed to three principal commitments:[32] (1) countries in the region would provide at least temporary asylum;[33] (2) the international community would offer resettlement places for those who had already fled;[34] and (3) the countries of origin would discourage hazardous departures and would cooperate with the United Nations and other countries to promote direct outflows through an Orderly Departure Program (ODP).

The 1979 accord reflected the national self-interest of the conference participants.[35] Resettlement countries wanted to preserve the precarious temporary refuge policies of first-asylum countries, which were not signatories to the 1951 Refugee Convention or to its 1967 Protocol. The United States in particular was committed to protecting its wartime allies,[36] and to providing "a noncommunist alternative to the peoples of Indochina."[37] In addition to providing humanitarian assistance, the U.S. interest was served by a system that accorded presumptive refugee status to all those fleeing the southeast Asian communist regimes.[38] The resettlement program also supported the conventional immigration policy goals of resettlement countries.[39]

First-asylum countries in southeast Asia, burdened by the expense and political difficulties of providing refuge, hoped to stem the tide of refugees and spread the costs of assistance. As one observer noted, these countries were persuaded to provide first asylum by the "assurance that the international community will effectively take care of the refugees, and the smooth operation of a resettlement programme aiming at an equitable sharing of the burden imposed on the southeast Asian countries."[40] The cooperation of the first-asylum countries was also bolstered by Vietnam's agreement to reduce the outflows by resuming its dubious policy of prohibiting illegal departures[41] and by creating an in-country Orderly Departure Program (ODP). Finally, the costs to first-asylum countries were reduced by agreements to place some first-asylum camps under UNHCR auspices and to have UNHCR cover the direct costs of their operation.[42]

The Geneva conference produced immediate results. In 1979, thirty-eight countries accepted Indochinese refugees for resettlement.[43] Vietnam clamped down on smuggling operations, causing an immediate decline in refugee outflows.[44] Resettlement rates increased, causing the population of boat people in the region to decline from 205,000 in mid-1979 to 40,000 three years later.[45] From 1979 until 1989, over 1.7 million Indochinese refugees were resettled under the framework laid out at the 1979 conference,[46] and over 150,000 left through the ODP.[47]

In addition to the confluence of national self-interests, the Indochinese resettlement program demonstrates three points about burden-sharing. First, full-scale international cooperation was implemented under the leadership of the United States and UNHCR. UNHCR coordinated international discussions, established refugee camps and holding centers, channeled funds to care for the refugees, and monitored the implementation of the resettlement programs. The United States, the largest resettlement country, shouldered a significant share of the costs.[48] The sheer number of cooperating countries reflected, at least in part, U.S. leadership.[49] Had the United States and UNHCR not borne the brunt of the resettlement and organizational burdens, the international consensus might have unraveled.

Second, the program's success depended upon the full cooperation of all countries involved; any shirking of one country's responsibilities could upset the precarious international balance. Several incidents illustrate this point. In May 1989, Malaysia instituted a policy of turning back boatloads of Vietnamese refugees and migrants,[50] likely causing some neighboring countries to experience a drastic increase in boat arrivals. In Indonesia, for instance, 3,787 Vietnamese arrived in May alone—the highest figure since the beginning of the outflow.[51] Another such example occurred in 1986, when Vietnam suspended interviews of ODP applicants for U.S. departures.[52] As a result, illegal departures from Vietnam surged, along with the number of arrivals in first-asylum countries. The neighboring countries responded by refusing asylum to the new arrivals. Thailand, for example, began sending back boats and denied those migrants who were admitted an opportunity to seek resettlement. Similar reactions occurred in Indonesia and Hong Kong.[53] In sum, one country's defection triggered exclusionary reactions in others;[54] interlocking interests contributed not only to the implementation of burden-sharing programs, but also to their effective maintenance.

Third, effective burden-sharing requires efforts to reduce the burdens on all countries and spread them over time. As the Indochinese resettlement program progressed, countries began worrying that it caused a "pull effect" by encouraging people to flee their countries in search of resettlement in the West.[55] As the number of boat arrivals increased and the average stay in the refugee camps lengthened in the late 1980s, first-asylum countries began taking unilateral and sometimes inhumane measures to deter further arrivals and to reduce camp populations.

In response to these concerns, the resettlement program was refined in 1989 at a second Geneva conference on Indochinese refugees. The conference participants adopted a new program, the Comprehensive Plan of Action (CPA), to address the Vietnamese and Lao refugee problems.[56] The CPA, which was scheduled to expire on June 30, 1996, preserved the basic framework of the earlier resettlement program, with one modification. Under the CPA, refugee status was no longer conferred automatically on all those who arrived in first-asylum countries; instead, arrivals were subject to refugee screening by local immigration officials. Those screened in were eligible to seek resettlement in a third country, while those screened out remained in holding centers and faced eventual repatriation.[57] To balance concerns over national sovereignty and human rights, conference participants agreed to establish a "region-wide refugee status-determination process . . . in accordance with national legislation and internationally accepted practice," including UNHCR training and oversight.[58] To secure the support of first-asylum countries, resettlement countries committed to expedited resettlement of all refugees who arrived prior to the cut-off date set by the CPA.[59] The CPA also called for additional countries to join the resettlement effort.[60]

At the time of the sixth follow-up meeting of the Steering Committee of the International Conference on Indochinese Refugees in March 1995, there remained 36,339 screened-out Vietnamese and 2,048 with refugee status in first-asylum countries.[61] Although the Steering Committee called for the completion of all repatriation and resettlement by the end of 1995, the process was delayed both because a number of screened-out Vietnamese refused to be repatriated at all costs, and because the United States proposed to offer screened-out boat people a second chance to apply for refugee status according to U.S., not CPA, refugee criteria.[62] Word of the U.S. proposal caused "violent anti-repatriation protests" in the camps and impeded the repatriation and resettlement under the CPA.[63] In early 1996, the Vietnamese government and the United States agreed to procedures whereby "[p]otential returnees would register for a U.S. interview before departing the camps. Upon return to Vietnam, they would go back to their areas of origin to await their interview. Those accepted would be processed for U.S. resettlement."[64] UNHCR announced that the CPA would formally end on June 30, 1996.

III. FOUR REMEDIAL STRATEGIES

Broadly speaking, the problem of massive refugee flows can be addressed in only four ways.[65] I shall call these the root cause, repatriation, temporary protection, and permanent resettlement strategies. Each has its own distinctive advantages and disadvantages. In section IV of this essay, I describe, and in section V defend, a novel version of the temporary protection and permanent resettlement strategies, which I call proportional burden-sharing.

It is essential to emphasize at the outset (and I shall repeat this point later on) that although I focus on temporary protection and resettlement through proportional burden-sharing, they are the *least attractive* of the four strategies in principle, and sometimes even in practice. In short, they are—particularly resettlement—strategies of last resort, but all too often they are the *only* resorts. The grim reality is that the root cause and repatriation strategies are often either unavailable or implemented in ways that fail to protect refugees as well as even an imperfect system of proportional burden-sharing might.

One may argue that this need for large-scale temporary protection and resettlement was historically contingent, a function of the political and military patterns associated with the Cold War. According to this view, the end of the Cold War meant the cessation of long, remorseless wars of national liberation fueled by Soviet-sponsored regimes implacably hostile to returning refugees. With the spread of democratic governance (so the argument runs), the refugee flows of today and tomorrow are more environmentally than politically or ideologically driven; hence refugees can readily return once the environmental crisis is over.[66]

This cheerier scenario may come to pass, but there is as yet little evidence to support this optimism and, in fact, some that tends to contradict it. The most recent empirical study suggests that although the sources of refugee flows are indeed changing, the violence and the distribution of weaponry per conflict are increasing, making refugee repatriation more difficult.[67] As for the future, there are ominous signs of possible refugee flows from Hong Kong now that it is under the control of the People's Republic of China.

Nevertheless, my argument in favor of a burden-sharing system does not rest on any strong claim about the particular level of protection that future crises may require. To support my argument, it is enough that significant protection is likely to become a compelling need sometime within the political time horizon of the major receiving states; that the uncertainties about the timing, magnitude, duration, and resolution of the precipitating refugee crises are seriously problematic for these states (not to mention for the refugees); and that these states view as unsatisfactory the ad hoc improvisations that have been used to handle this problem in the past.

My argument for a formal system of proportional burden-sharing, then, is a decidedly qualified one. It proposes that in situations in which the root causes of a refugee crisis can be prevented or eliminated, or in which repatriation can be safely accomplished, those strategies are preferable to proportional burden-sharing and should be pursued.[68] Only in situations in which these conditions cannot be satisfied does a system of proportional burden-sharing, implemented through either temporary protection or, in the last resort, permanent resettlement, become salient.

The Root Cause Strategy

Eliminating or preventing the political, economic, environmental, and cultural conditions that prompt refugees to flee their homes and countries in the first place is the most attractive approach by far. Obviously, this strategy, if effective, precludes the necessity for flight and hence forestalls the suffering that attends it.

The difficulty with a root cause strategy, of course, is that it is extremely difficult to execute.[69] One must be able to identify accurately the conditions ultimately prompting flight and then be able to rectify those conditions. Both identification and rectification are daunting obstacles.

The easiest case for identifying root causes should be the environmental disaster. Yet even here, causal patterns are often complex and elusive, as when environmental conditions interact with underlying economic and social practices to produce a catastrophe that would not have occurred otherwise.[70] As for persecution-induced flight, even a readily identified malefactor or regime, such as Castro's Cuba or Hussein's Iraq, may not be the root cause. As in the environmental case, the brutal regime's hegemony could be epiphenomenal, with the true causes embedded in underlying political or cultural traditions—habituation to authoritarianism, for example—that would probably survive the regime.[71]

An even more serious obstacle to a successful root cause strategy, however, is the problem of rectification. Even those root causes that can be accurately identified are often impossible to change—at least in the short run and with the limited policy instruments available even to states willing (within limits) to act to prevent human rights abuses. The fecklessness of the United Nations in dealing with refugee-producing atrocities committed by local satrapies in the former Yugoslavia is a particularly telling and grim example. In part, this impotence reflects the constraints on intervention posed by the strong norm of national sovereignty in international law and politics.[72] Despite several recent instances in which this norm has been overridden in the name of human rights,[73] that norm continues to be a formidable limitation on our ability to mount and deploy a root cause strategy in other states. Even if the norm against intervention did not exist, the underlying social realities are notoriously hard to reform—even in one's own country, not to mention in other societies whose workings we understand far less. In such circumstances, the law of unintended consequences operates with a particularly remorseless logic.

Not surprisingly, the most common and uncontroversial means through which states seek to prevent the flow of refugees and other migrants from source countries are the consensual policies of trade, investment, development assistance, and other forms of foreign aid. Along with border controls, such policies—culminating in NAFTA—have been the cornerstone of U.S. efforts to reduce the flow of undocumented workers and their families from Mexico.[74] But while these policies may be mutually beneficial and highly desirable on their own terms, their potential for strengthening the source country's economy, polity, and society in ways that will reduce refugee and immigrant flows—at least in the short run—is relatively limited.[75]

Indeed, economic development in the source country may actually have the opposite effect. By increasing the education and mobility levels of potential migrants, improving their information about conditions and opportunities in destination countries, and raising their expectations, economic development can encourage those with the greatest energy, courage, and determination to try their luck elsewhere. Development also tends to create a middle class that demands political liberalization from undemocratic regimes, which may respond with the kinds of repressive measures that often generate refugee flows.[76] Again, the capacity of economic and political development to ameliorate human rights abuses and stem refugee and immigrant flows cannot seriously be questioned. However, the course and pace of such development and its effects on migration patterns are poorly understood and notoriously unpredictable. Root cause strategies that are premised on the easy cultivation and rapid success of development are likely to be disappointing.

The Repatriation Strategy

If, as is usually the case, the root causes of refugee flows cannot be prevented or eliminated, it follows that refugees will flee. In that event, the paramount goal of a human-rights strategy must be to restore the normalcy of refugees' lives by returning them to their homes and families as soon as possible. This approach is more practicable than the root cause strategy and is likely to be far less expensive, as it does not require (indeed, it hopes to prevent) refugees from establishing new roots in the country of refuge.

In fact, many refugees are eventually repatriated,[77] some within a relatively short period of time after their initial flight. For the others, however, "eventually" can be a very long time indeed.[78] In principle, repatriation should not occur until conditions in the source country have stabilized enough for the refugees to return safely. If the regime that persecuted them remains in power, such a return may be dangerous. Their homes and businesses may have been seized, occupied, or formally expropriated by the regime or private marauders, leaving them little to which they can return. They also may have reason to fear death or other reprisals at home should they return. For these reasons, voluntary repatriation may not be possible for years, even for those refugees who ardently wish to return to their homelands, while forcible repatriation may be resisted even to the point of violence or suicide.[79]

The "end-game" of the CPA, which was scheduled to expire on June 30, 1996, presented a variation on the same theme. With more than one million Indochinese refugees resettled since 1975, mostly in the United States, approximately 33,000 boat people, whose claims to refugee status had been repeatedly rejected, remained in southeast Asian camps. Under the CPA, these people were to be repatriated—by force, if necessary. In the United States, Senator Jesse Helms, Congressman Christopher Smith, and other elected officials opposed repatriation, insisting that these refugees would face persecution if returned to Vietnam and that they should instead be permitted to resettle in the United States. This, in turn, emboldened the remaining boat people to resist repatriation to the point of violent rioting, destroying camp buildings, taking hostages, and in many cases escaping. The United States, unwilling to face the prospect of effectuating a forcible repatriation that might require it to spill the blood of innocents who had already suffered for years in the camps, reached an eleventh-hour agreement with Vietnam for a repatriation that for many of the returnees may only be brief. Under the agreement, they will be returned to Vietnam where they will be permitted to file yet another claim for refugee status and apply once again for resettlement in the United States. It was expected that thousands of these claims would succeed.[80] In this way, the United States has adopted a new sub-strategy—what might be called "temporary repatriation."

The Temporary Protection Strategy

If conditions in the source country make immediate repatriation (whether temporary or permanent) impossible, one must adopt an interim approach until the refugees can be safely returned. This, of course, is the purpose of granting political asylum; it is a temporary protected status that may, but need not, lead to a right of permanent residence. Indeed, if the conditions in the source country change so that the threat of persecution no longer exists, asylum may be properly rescinded.[81]

But although traditional refugee law is preoccupied with questions of asylum eligibility, determination, and rights, the number of individuals granted asylum is but a tiny fraction of those who actually receive protection and an even smaller fraction of those who genuinely *need* protection. Most countries of first asylum have concluded that the fiscal and political costs of adjudicating mass asylum claims, granting employment and residence rights while those claims are pending, and permanently integrating asylees into their societies are simply unacceptable.[82] As a result, asylum law has become less and less relevant to the protection problem in mass influx situations.[83] Better solutions are desperately needed.

Instead of granting asylum, the more common response of states faced with large refugee influxes—even those with highly developed asylum determination systems and absorptive capacity—has been to provide some form of temporary protection in the protecting state.[84] Properly and humanely deployed,[85] it can be a flexible, practicable regime of protection in mass influx situations so long as states observe certain safeguards—especially decent living standards, access to a fair asylum determination process, and genuine *non-refoulement*.

If these conditions are met, there should be no objection to a protecting state "renting space" outside of its territory to provide temporary safe haven.[86] Indeed, temporary protection has the great virtue that it can usually be effectuated in or near the first-asylum state, which tends to be near the refugee's country of origin. It therefore minimizes the psychological and economic costs of moving the refugee again, safely maintaining her in her present location and close to her past and hopefully future home. Moreover, because grants of asylum or permanent resettlement are relatively rare, and safe repatriation may be impossible, the refugee's options are likely to be temporary protection or nothing.

Temporary protection is also a desirable strategy from the perspective of industrialized states' narrow self-interest. It is a way to keep refugees safely (in both senses) in the Third World from which most of them come, thereby alleviating the pressures to grant them permanent resettlement in the First World. Any refugee protection scheme that does not promise to accomplish these goals is unlikely to attract the necessary political support by industrialized states. It is for this reason that a meaningful system of refugee protection must rest on the foundation of a viable temporary refuge option.

Even so, temporary protection can impose serious costs on industrialized states. If temporary protection is to succeed in deterring migration to their territories, these states must ensure that the migrants are protected under conditions of detention, isolation, and privation with little hope of gaining legal status, while also providing levels of safety and hygiene demanded by their domestic standards of decency, if not by the vague common-denominator norms of international refugee law. This is an exceedingly difficult balance to strike, and even such minimal levels of amenity can be very costly for the government to maintain, especially over a long period of time.[87]

Time, then, is of the essence. The protecting state may find that "temporary" safe haven is something of an illusion, if not an oxymoron—that what was justified as short-term relief has a way of becoming, in effect, permanent resettlement.[88] This development is of the utmost importance for the future of refugee protection. If potential protecting states come to believe that refuge granted on a nominally "temporary" basis is likely to become permanent, they will be more reluctant to offer it.

This is increasingly the case in the United States, where temporary protection either on or near American soil has recently been ratcheted upward into more or less permanent residence. The most important example of this concerns the Salvadorans who entered the United States illegally during the 1980s and who, after having successfully avoided deportation, were granted temporary protected status (TPS)[89] under the special provisions of the Immigration Act of 1990. The Act authorized such relief on the understanding that the Salvadorans would return to El Salvador once conditions there stabilized.[90] During the early 1990s, the administration and Congress extended the departure dates several times and when the program finally expired in December 1994, the Immigration and Naturalization Service (INS) granted nine more months for the Salvadorans to file for asylum or seek legal status. This concession reflected the fact that the INS had massively violated Salvadorans' legal rights in processing and rejecting their asylum claims during the 1980s. Approximately 150,000 of them reapplied.

Most experts predict that few of the almost 200,000 original TPS Salvadorans will ever have to leave.[91] The remaining TPS Salvadorans can now have their claims reheard, although changed circumstances have made most of these claims harder to sustain than they would have been during the 1980s. This process will drag on for years due to a current and growing backlog of over 400,000 asylum cases.[92] The INS does not know what happened to the original 187,000 TPS Salvadorans, or how many remain (the estimate is 100,000), much less their names or locations. Most probably melted into the population, managed to secure legal status, or returned to El Salvador on their own. As many skeptics had predicted, TPS turned out in the Salvadoran case to be "a slow way of saying yes."[93] It remains to be seen whether the six other countries' nationals who now enjoy TPS will similarly be able to bootstrap their presence in the United States into permanent residence. In any event, the Salvadoran experience makes it doubtful that the U.S. government will grant temporary protection as readily in the future.

Even when the United States moved its temporary protection program offshore by placing Cuban migrants on Guantanamo and in Panama, most of them ended up receiving permanent residence, despite the frequent insistence by the President and Attorney General that these Cubans would never be permitted to enter the United States.[94] These Cubans managed to convert temporary protection into permanent status not because the United States deemed them refugees—quite the contrary—but because the U.S. government, for a combination of political and fiscal reasons, was not prepared to return them to Cuba or to continue their temporary protection status in the Guantanamo and Panama camps.[95]

Several other forms of temporary protection have been attempted. In some cases, military action or U.N. fiat has established putatively safe enclaves in the countries of origin, as in northern Iraq and the former Yugoslavia. The conditions necessary to create and maintain such enclaves, however, are quite limited. In other cases, the destination state has negotiated bilateral or multilateral "readmission agreements" with third countries (usually countries of transit) to admit (or readmit) certain categories of migrants and to provide them with certain services and protections until they can be repatriated or their status otherwise regularized. Germany has concluded these agreements with Poland, the Czech Republic, and Romania.[96] The principal purpose of such agreements, of course, is not humanitarian but more effective border control by enlisting the cooperation of neighboring states through which the migrants pass.[97] From the perspective of the destination state, however, this assistance by the transit states may be costly to procure. Such arrangements, moreover, also risk human rights violations by the transit states, whose citizens are likely to be hostile to the migrants' presence. This hostility can be expected to increase as time goes on.

Temporary refuge is the keystone of the refugee protection structure. If past is prologue, states will always confine their grants of asylum and permanent resettlement to a relatively small number of refugees; for most refugees, the best that they can hope for is temporary protection. Unless the system can credibly assure states that the temporary protection they grant will indeed be temporary, its availability to refugees is likely to be under-mined, with tragic effects. Thus an important test of the value of any re-form is whether it can maintain that credibility. I hope to demonstrate in section IV that proportional burden-sharing, through marketable quotas, would create the incentives to satisfy that test.

Permanent Resettlement

As I noted earlier, resettlement must be the protective strategy of last re-sort, employed only when the root causes of flight cannot be prevented or eliminated, and safe repatriation to the country of origin or to another site of temporary protection within a reasonable period of time cannot be effected. Resettlement in a third country is costly to the refugee, who must be uprooted once again and then reestablished in a society that is likely to be alien in culture, language, and other respects. It is also costly to the receiving country, which must either assist the refugee to assimilate successfully or run the social risks of her failure to do so. These costs are likely to be much higher than temporary protection, which can lead to repatriation in the not too distant future.

As we have just seen, however, repatriation in the short term is impossi-ble in a tragically large number of cases. This is especially true when the migration flow has been fueled by policies of uncompromising and per-haps permanent ethnic or religious persecution carried out by the regime in power in the country of origin. For persecuted minorities who have fled, the alternative to resettlement is to languish for many years in what amounts to a prison, isolated from normal social intercourse and eco-nomic activity and without the amenities of family life. In such cases, re-settlement—problematic as it is—may be the "least bad" remedy.

No one knows for sure how many of the world's refugees need resettle-ment. Uncertainty on this question, of course, largely reflects the ambigu-ity of "need" in this context, the contested factual and value judgments that give content to that term, and the political considerations that affect all estimates in this area.[98]

Only a few countries, however, now offer permanent resettlement to a significant number of refugees. The United States accepts by far the largest number of any country, at least in absolute terms.[99] In 1995 it ad-justed the status of 106,827 refugees to that of legal permanent resi-dent.[100] If asylee adjustments are included, the total rises to more than 114,664 in 1995.[101] Sweden, which accepts more refugees and asylees in proportion to its population than any other country, did so for about 36,400 people in 1993; Canada, with a population almost four times Sweden's, gave relief to only half as many (18,400), while Australia, with twice Sweden's population, accepted fewer than one-fourth as many

(8,800). The Netherlands and the United Kingdom each accepted about 10,000, while Germany accepted 16,000. In both the United States and Europe, there are signs that political changes may soon reduce the number of such offers.[102] Nor are other resettlement countries immune from many of the political pressures that may limit future refugee and asylum admissions in the United States.[103]

The vast majority of countries, however, make few or no resettlement offers even though some of them have ample resources for doing so. Japan, which enjoys the second largest economy in the world, provides a particularly striking example of resistance. Japan subscribed to the Refugee Convention in 1981 and enacted implementing legislation the next year. Nevertheless, in the thirteen years between 1982 and May 1995, Japan granted asylum to only 208 refugees—an average of sixteen per year. It also resettled 8,679 Indochinese refugees.[104] Finally, Japan extends "special permission to stay" to a small number (393 in 1991, for example) of deportable Chinese and other Asians, a group considered "de facto refugees."[105] Japan does score higher in terms of financial and material assistance to international refugee-aid agencies[106]—a point to which I shall return.

This extreme concentration of resettlement offers in a few countries means that when refugee emergencies occur (as they increasingly do), UNHCR and voluntary refugee organizations move reflexively (like Claude Rains' order in *Casablanca*) to "round up the usual suspects." Such a response is perfectly understandable and rational; after all (as Willie Sutton noted in explaining why he robbed banks), "that's where the money is." This approach, however, is becoming more inadequate and futile in a world of seemingly endless refugee emergencies in which prompt, safe repatriation is often impossible, and temporary protection is shunned by countries fearing, with some reason, that it could become permanent and thus attract even more migrants.

IV. THE PROPOSAL: PROPORTIONAL BURDEN-SHARING

What, then, is to be done? My proposal seeks a refugee protection system that can simultaneously achieve four major objectives: (1) maximization of protection resources; (2) observance of human rights principles; (3) respect for political constraints; and (4) administrative simplicity. Before explaining the proposal, I shall briefly discuss each of these goals.

Maximization of Resources Available for Protection. The system should maximize the total resources available for the genuine protection of refugees. I view this as the paramount objective; its primacy justifies compromising, where necessary, other important but less central goals. Protection resources can be maximized in two ways: by drawing new resources into the system and by better utilizing whatever resources exist. Thus, as many states as possible should participate in the protective system, not just those that possess a particular resource (such as cash, space, or ethnic diversity) or that happen to abut a refugee-producing area. In addition, the system should create incentives to use those resources most effectively. Specifically, it should encourage each state to allocate whatever resources it possesses or can mobilize to the refugee-protection strategy or strategies—root cause, temporary protection-cum-repatriation, and resettlement—that can be achieved to the greatest extent at the least cost.

Observance of Human Rights Principles. The system should ensure that refugees actually receive the protection to which international human rights law already entitles them. Failing that—and recognizing that the current system often falls far short on this score—their treatment should at least be no worse than it is now.

Respect for Political Constraints. The system should acknowledge the important political constraints that will inevitably continue to shape any meaningful international regime of refugee protection, and its institutions and practices should take due account of those constraints. These constraints are quite formidable, and I have no wish to minimize them. Some of them might seem inimical to more expansive refugee protection; they appear to be decidedly unpromising materials for policy reform. Yet, as I explain below, we can hope to turn three of these constraining conditions—the abiding forces of state sovereignty and self-interest, the growing vulnerability of *all* states to unwanted refugee influxes, and the diversity of states' traditions and resources for dealing with refugee flows—to some advantage. Indeed, any reform must come to terms with these conditions. A market-oriented approach is peculiarly capable of exploiting them.

Administrative Simplicity. Consistent with its other goals, the system should adopt a decentralized decisionmaking structure, leaving as much initiative as possible to individual states. It should seek to minimize the informational requirements and other transaction costs of the system's decisionmakers.

The proposal consists of five main structural elements: (1) agreement by states in a region on a strong norm that all ought to bear a share of temporary protection and permanent resettlement needs proportionate to their burden-bearing capacity; (2) a process for determining the number of those who need such protection; (3) a set of criteria for allocating this burden among states in the form of quotas; (4) a market in which states can purchase and sell quota compliance obligations; and (5) an international authority to administer the quota system and regulate this market. I shall discuss each of these elements and then identify some of the implementation and enforcement issues that would need to be resolved for the system to work.

In noting these implementation issues, I wish to emphasize what will be obvious to any well-informed reader: Many additional details must be addressed before the scheme can be fully realized. I recognize, of course, that the devil is often in the details. Nevertheless, I think that I am justified in assuming that should agreement be reached on the main outlines of these five structural elements, the rest can, through negotiation, be worked out. Accordingly, I do not dwell on the details here.

The Principle of Burden-Sharing

As noted in section I, international practice in the area of refugee protection reveals the existence of what might be called a weak norm of burden-sharing. A number of international instruments and scholarly analyses proclaim the importance of such a norm and exhort states to observe it. On the more mundane level of international practice, refugee-receiving states have entered into a number of arrangements in recent decades to share the burdens of major refugee crises, notably the CPA in Indochina[107] and the 1989 Conference on Central American Refugees.[108]

This burden-sharing norm, however, is manifestly weak. In the international instruments in which it can be discerned, the burden-sharing imperative is essentially precatory and hortatory; even its most energetic scholarly exponents like Goodwin-Gill seem to view it more as a moral aspiration than as a legally binding duty on all states. No effort has been mounted to enforce the norm against the numerous states that ignore it. Even in the war in the former Yugoslavia, which was waged with appalling ferocity in the very heart of Europe, the burden of protecting refugees was shared only to a very limited extent, with Croatia, Slovenia, and Germany bearing the brunt of it.[109]

Nevertheless, the moral and prudential foundations for imposing such a duty seem sturdy enough to establish a more robust burden-sharing regime. Joanne Thorburn advances three arguments for this norm, based on human rights, states' self-interest, and the *non-refoulement* principle:

> [F]orcibly moving the people, albeit for protection purposes, would be questionable from a human rights perspective. . . . The statist argument would find support in upholding the right to control admission, as people would not be arriving at the borders of one's own (distant) State because their level of protection would be sufficient in countries close to the State of origin (thanks to financial assistance and logistical support), and because the development and integrity of the first country of asylum would also be supported. However, the primary arguments for burden-sharing lie in support of the principle of *non-refoulement* . . . and in its necessity as an accompaniment to a firmly established norm of temporary protection. . . . *Refoulement,* even by proxy, is to be avoided at all costs.[110]

There is another justification for the burden-sharing norm based on the adventitious character of most refugee crises. Refugee flows usually occur with a suddenness, violence, and magnitude that can swiftly overwhelm the resources of a first-asylum state that is only linked to the flow by an accident of nature—its fortuitous proximity to the source country. In this respect, refugee emergencies resemble natural disasters like earthquakes and tornadoes, calamities as to which the norm of international solidarity and burden-sharing is relatively strong. The relationship of first-asylum states to refugee flows, of course, does not always possess this random, fortuitous character. In some cases, the first-asylum state, far from being an innocent bystander, bears some causal and hence moral responsibility for refugee flows; it may even have fanned or instigated the unrest that unleashed the crisis. The first-asylum state may hope to use the refugees' flight to discredit or destabilize the source country regime (for example, American policy toward Castro's Cuba and Zaire's policy toward Rwanda), or it may have revanchist designs on the source country (for example, Indian and Pakistani policies in Kashmir). Like some societies plagued by certain natural disasters,[111] first-asylum states sometimes bring refugee crises on themselves.

The possibility that some first-asylum states are complicit in refugee flows should surely be taken into account in designing and administering a reformed system of refugee protection. Indeed, imposing a binding obligation to bear some of the burdens that such a state causes might reduce its propensity to instigate refugee crises in the first place. Even so, the more compelling fact is that first-asylum states ordinarily are not in any morally meaningful sense responsible for their plight. Recognition of this is an important building block in the necessary structure of justification and political support for a norm of universal burden-sharing.

If the innocent helplessness of most first-asylum states is a morally constructive support for this norm, another fact—that different states face somewhat different risks of becoming a first-asylum country—tends to undermine political support for the norm. This risk differential makes it difficult to secure agreement on, much less compliance with, the norm because it reinforces the incentives of relatively insular[112] and hence low-risk states to avoid burden-sharing by free-riding on the self-interested efforts of the higher-risk states, leaving the latter to bear all of the burdens. This process of defection by low-risk states undermines the viability of any system, like the current one, that relies on voluntary burden-sharing and generates very weak incentives to cooperate. The analogy to the problem of adverse selection in the insurance context—in which those presenting relatively low risks will not participate in insurance pools that charge them average-risk premiums—is apt. No burden-sharing scheme, including the "refugee crisis insurance" approach proposed here, can be effective unless this problem of differential risks is squarely addressed.

Generally speaking, there are only two possible solutions to this problem. The first is to increase the estimates by traditionally insular states of their risk of becoming a first-asylum country. The second is to strengthen the other non-risk related incentives of all states, but especially of those at low risk of refugee flows, to participate in burden-sharing efforts. Both approaches are difficult to implement. Nevertheless, recent developments have rendered them, especially the first, somewhat more promising.

The risk that *any* state will become a first-asylum country is growing. The economic, spatial, and geopolitical barriers that until recently inhibited mass refugee flows are falling. Virtually all states realize that their territories are potential targets of sudden and possibly large refugee movements—with all of the attendant risks, political and otherwise, that such movements pose to the regime in power. Today, no state is immune; even island nations like Japan and Australia are vulnerable to spasmodic in-migration from the mainland. Ironically, this reality, which is certainly regrettable from the insular states' perspective, presents an opportunity to increase the acceptance of burden-sharing.

The change in risk has been most dramatic in Germany and Japan. The Basic Law of Germany expressly provides that it is not a country of immigration,[113] and the nation's history prior to 1989 was consistent with this tenet. Beginning in 1989, however, a huge influx of asylum seekers into Germany[114] dramatically challenged this tradition. Immigration and refugee policy has become a central issue in German politics. With restrictionist parties gaining ground, Germany amended its Basic Law in 1993 to limit severely asylum seekers' rights. Despite these efforts, however, the number of asylum seekers in Germany remains quite large.[115]

Like Germany, Japan has only recently begun to consider seriously the need to fashion an immigration and refugee policy.[116] Although it still receives few refugee claims, they are increasing—as is the number of foreigners, legal and illegal, living in Japan.[117] Perhaps more important, Japan is experiencing growing concerns about potential political convulsions in China, Hong Kong, and North Korea that could quickly send millions of refugees streaming across the short distance that separates Japan from mainland east Asia.[118]

For states like Germany, previously protected by the Iron Curtain but now a country of first asylum on a massive scale, and Japan, no longer protected by its geography from becoming a first-asylum state, the strategic implications of their new vulnerability are immense. No longer can they simply free ride on other states' policies of refugee control and management to protect them from major influxes into their own territories. Indeed, states' new interdependence goes beyond this; historically insular states are now more likely to face refugee flows resulting from the restrictive practices of other states.[119]

Thus, states previously at low risk of becoming first-asylum countries may now find a cooperative strategy far more attractive than they would have only a few years ago. Under this refugee-crisis insurance approach, all states arrange to bear some refugee protection burdens so that none will be saddled with a refugee crisis that it must bear alone. The German and Japanese experiences can serve as vivid lessons for other states that have resisted burden-sharing in the belief that they are still immune from large refugee flows.

The incentives for burden-sharing based on motives other than fear of becoming a first-asylum state remain weak in most regions. The traditional willingness of many sub-Saharan African states, with UNHCR assistance, to offer temporary protection to refugees from neighboring countries is the greatest exception. Pakistan's protection of millions of Afghani refugees during the 1980s is another, although pressure and aid from the United States were instrumental in eliciting this response. Once we move beyond temporary protection to permanent resettlement, as noted above, only Scandinavia, the United States, Canada, and a few other states offer it to a significant number of refugees.

Precisely because the altruistic motives for burden-sharing are so weak, these powerful states have strong reasons to induce others to cooperate by manipulating the formidable carrots and sticks that the powerful states control. In the past, these states, actuated by a combination of humanitarian and deeply self-interested motives, have managed to persuade recalcitrant first-asylum states like Thailand, Hong Kong, and Pakistan to protect temporarily (although the period often proved to be quite protracted) refugees on their territories.[120] As international economic developments improve industrialized states' leverage over first-asylum states with respect to trade concessions, technical assistance, and access to financial and other support, this approach, which entails the tactical use of political pressure, negotiation, and resource transfers, may bear additional fruit.

The success of a proportional burden-sharing system depends critically on the relatively powerful states' ability to use this leverage more skillfully and forcefully to induce broader participation in the system as refugee flows increase. This is likely to be most practicable in a regionally organized system.[121] In any event, one should recall that the current system of protection is equally dependent on the more powerful states exercising leverage and transferring resources to persuade the weaker first-asylum states to harbor refugees. A proportional burden-sharing system can only improve the chances that such influence would be effectively deployed.

This examination of the structure of incentives for refugee burden-sharing does not at all minimize the political obstacles that would impede its implementation, but it provides some hope that the prospects for gaining broader agreement on a more robust burden-sharing norm could improve in the future. The next question is: What should be the actual content of that norm?

The norm should express a principle of fairness in the distribution of refugee protection burdens. Specifically, it should satisfy three criteria of fairness: consent, broad participation, and proportionality.

Consent is essential. No state should be obliged to participate in the burden-sharing scheme unless it voluntarily undertakes to do so. This is a concession not only to practical politics but also to a concern that states both feel a genuine commitment to the enterprise and take responsibility for its success or failure. As the discussion immediately above suggests, a state may consent for a variety of reasons. Its consent is not ordinarily vitiated by the fact that it feels constrained to participate because of pressures exerted by other, more powerful states. States in the international system routinely deploy carrots and sticks in order to influence the decisions of other states and actors; only in the most extreme case would such inducements amount to duress negating consent.

Broad participation in a proportional burden-sharing scheme by consenting states is justified on the basis of each state's membership in an international community, which entails certain minimal rights and obligations defined by international law, including the duty to protect refugees. If the scheme is carried out on a regional basis, as I propose, participation is likely to be widespread, if not universal, within that region because of the more firmly entrenched patterns of intraregional influence and the relative homogeneity of wealth and values within regions.[122] A broadly participatory arrangement has several advantages: It minimizes each state's burden by distributing it among many states, and it overcomes the free rider and adverse selection problems by making it very difficult for states to opt out. Consequently, it eliminates the demoralization that participants experience when they perceive that they have been "suckered" by the defection of others.[123]

The proportionality principle is both a norm of fairness and a constraint dictated by political prudence. It demands that a state's share of the burden be limited to its burden-bearing capacity relative to that of all other states in the international community. Rough proportionality is probably essential to both consent and broad participation. Taken together, these three values imply a norm that all states in a region must shoulder some of the burden but that none must shoulder a burden that it cannot in fairness bear.

The Needs Assessment Process

In order to allocate the burden of refugee protection, we must first consider how the overall burden is to be defined, determined, and used as the basis for assigning quotas.

The overall burden is defined as the number of refugees who need to be offered protection—either temporary refuge or permanent resettlement—during a given time period. This number would be calculated by an interna-

tional agency to be described below,[124] and would be adjusted as unanticipated refugee emergencies occurred. Suffice it to say here that the agency
must be equipped to conduct the necessary investigations, make the requisite factual findings, administer and enforce the quotas, and regulate the
quotas market with due regard to changing circumstances.

Two difficult, inevitably controversial issues are embedded in this definition: the number of people seeking protection who are to be treated as
refugees, and the number of those refugees who need either temporary protection or permanent resettlement (rather than immediate repatriation).
Both issues, however, already arise under the current system and can be resolved, as they are now, through a combination of factual analysis, calculated conceptual ambiguity, and old-fashioned negotiation. As a formal
matter, the first issue—refugee status—is a legal one requiring application
of the refugee definition under the Convention or its domestic law equivalent.[125] To varying extents in different states, asylum adjudications exhibit
such formalism.[126] In contrast, decisions about which individuals are to be
temporarily or permanently protected are relatively ad hoc; they focus less
on the legal refugee definition than on the number of people that the protecting state can handle and, in the case of resettlement, on the putative
refugee's social and political acceptability to the receiving state. Accordingly, many of those selected for temporary or permanent protection would
probably fail to qualify as refugees in the more legalistic setting of asylum
adjudication. This practice suggests that the international agency can resolve the issue of refugee status *for purposes of this scheme* through the relatively informal, low-cost modalities that UNHCR, the first-asylum states,
and other states (often with the assistance of NGOs) now use to make protection decisions.[127]

The agency must then calculate a worldwide total of refugees who need
temporary protection and a total of those who need permanent resettlement, and then allocate those totals among participating states by assigning
a quota to each. The notion of "need" that must inform such a calculation
is bound to be controversial. To some extent, need is in the eye of the be-
holder, as evidenced by the frequent disagreements that now arise over this
issue between (and within) UNHCR, potential protecting states, and
NGOs.[128] Under the current system, UNHCR determines how many slots
are needed and proceeds to solicit offers from states that it thinks can be
persuaded to offer protection. In resisting these entreaties, states may dispute UNHCR's assessment of need, as well as assert their inability to accept
more refugees. If further negotiations ensue, the parties may articulate competing conceptions of need; hopefully, some agreement on numbers (if not
on the underlying conceptions) may be reached.

Under the proposal, the agency would proceed in a similar fashion. The
stakes in its needs assessments, however, would be much higher than they

are now because the assessments would generate the overall numbers to determine each state's binding quota. For this reason, it would be essential for the agency to render its needs assessments more transparent and to establish procedures enabling states to contest the findings on which their shares would be premised. Both needs assessments and procedures for challenging them are common in many areas of social policy and administrative law. Their design in the protection context should pose no special difficulties, other than the political ones owing to the weaker enforcement mechanisms in the international realm and the delays that such challenges might entail. The current system elides enforcement problems, of course, but only because it relies entirely on voluntary protection offers extended by a relatively small number of states.

The agency's determination as to how many people need only temporary protection and how many instead need resettlement is, of course, a very difficult one, requiring much information that is hard to obtain and even harder to verify, as well as predictions that may be little more than educated guesses. For the same reason, the line between temporary and permanent refuge is not easily maintained; as with the TPS Salvadorans,[129] many refugees cannot be repatriated by the protecting state despite its energetic efforts to do so.

Again, it is important to recognize that the current system must make the same kinds of difficult determinations so that UNHCR can plan the allocation of its limited resources and negotiate with potential protecting states. An additional advantage of a burden-sharing system, however, is that those states—fearing that erroneous predictions and determinations could leave them with more (or more permanent) refugees than they initially bargained for—would have strong incentives to ensure that the determinations are accurate, that other participating states bear their fair shares and minimize the necessity for permanent resettlement, and, most importantly, that temporary protection does not become permanent without the state's genuine consent.

The Criteria for Allocating the Protection Burden

In order to implement the proportionality principle discussed earlier, the quota should be based exclusively on what I shall call the protection criterion, which is designed to measure the capacity of the state in question to provide refugees with the most minimal safeguards and amenities to which they are entitled under the Refugee Convention. They primarily include food, clothing, shelter, and physical security.[130]

In the kind of regional, consensual burden-sharing scheme that I propose, the participating states would of course be free to adopt whatever protection criterion (or criteria) they preferred. Nevertheless, national wealth is a compelling index. Protective capacity is largely, though not exclusively, a function of national wealth. Human rights law aspires to assure refugees the most basic necessities of life and personal security, and a state's wealth is the single best surrogate for those factors that actually determine its ability to provide these necessities, directly or indirectly. National wealth is also readily quantifiable, albeit not without some controversy around the edges,[131] and it is a factor so closely related to national prestige that states are unlikely to succeed in minimizing it in a strategic effort to reduce their share of refugee burdens.

Other plausible criteria lack the administrative advantages of a wealth criterion. Consider the example of assimilative capacity.[132] One might want states' quotas to reflect their different propensities to assimilate refugees and other foreigners. The notion of assimilation, however, is notoriously hard to define or gauge objectively.[133] Indeed, the scholars who study it disagree strenuously about why, how, and when it occurs.[134] There are also normative objections to an assimilation criterion. Although it is highly desirable for states to facilitate affirmatively the integration of foreigners to whom they offer permanent resettlement, states are under no international legal duty to assure them full integration; states are only obligated to provide basic safeguards such as the right to work and to be free from discrimination.[135] Full assimilation moreover, is fundamentally incompatible with a regime of temporary protection—relief that states will only provide if they believe that it will terminate within a reasonably short period of time and thus before full integration occurs. As noted in section III, maintaining the credibility of *temporary* protection is essential to the viability of the protection system as a whole. Finally, a criterion that would enlarge states' quotas if they succeed in assimilating foreigners would perversely punish states for their openness and generosity.

The attractiveness of national wealth as the sole criterion for assigning refugee protection quotas is especially great in a system like the one I propose here, which would allow a state to pay other states to provide those protection services that it cannot or will not provide on its own territory. For this reason, a state's wealth should probably trump other objective factors such as population density and land mass.[136] Although these factors may well affect the ease with which a state can protect or resettle refugees on its own territory, these factors are probably best taken into account as they are reflected in the prices that states are willing to pay to transfer their burden to other states. For example, Malaysia and Singapore are countries of relatively great wealth but with high population densities, small land mass, and severe ethnic tensions that refugees might further inflame. These countries would be assigned large quotas but would probably offer a high price to shift the protection burden elsewhere.

Two exemptions from the quota system should be provided, and neither is likely to be controversial in practice. First, no quota should be assigned to a state that engages in systematic violations of human rights, nor should such states be permitted to purchase other states' quotas. Although the reason for this principle is obvious, some objections to it are also obvious. Applying the criterion in a world in which the number of repressive states remains tragically large would require some elusive and morally dubious distinctions. A few relatively easy cases exist (Iraq and North Korea, for example), but the gradations of brutality between these and many other regimes are subtle, and line-drawing will surely be both difficult and controversial. Furthermore, that states will view participation in the protection quota system as a burden rather than a benefit creates a perverse incentive: The exemption, by relieving states of a burden, could seem to reward human rights violations and hence encourage them. Although a state could only qualify for the exemption by being labeled as a human rights violator, this obloquy, which already attaches to such states, has manifestly failed to reform their odious conduct and is even less likely to do so when asserted as part of a refugee protection scheme.

In the context of the regional, consensual arrangement that I propose, this perverse incentive would be irrelevant. In such a scheme, the regional powers would have to agree on which states would participate and under what conditions. The regional leaders would surely be under great internal and external pressure to exclude the worst human rights violators.[137] Dissenting states need not join, and the rogue states themselves would hardly complain about being exempted from burden-sharing obligations.

The second exception should be for states whose wealth falls below some minimal level, as determined by international agencies.[138] Again, the justification is obvious: If such states cannot assure basic sustenance to their own people, they can hardly provide effective protection to strangers. This second exemption can overlap with the first, as demonstrated by the example of Haiti, which is both destitute and a persistent human rights violator.

Apart from these two exemptions, temporary adjustments to a country's wealth-driven quota may be the best that the system can manage by way of further refining the criterion. Certain exigent conditions substantially impairing a state's ability to accept or pay for refugee protection—for example, a state of war or natural disaster—might justify a temporary quota reduction or even a suspension. For similar reasons, the system should reduce a state's quota to reflect the number of refugees who are already on its territory and to whom it offers either asylum or temporary protection of a specified duration. Such a credit, and the incentives that it creates for the receiving state, would also minimize the emotional and economic costs of moving refugees, who have already suffered at least one dislocation, from an asylum state to another state.[139]

If such temporary quota adjustments were permitted, of course, states would press hard to obtain relief under them. Each adjustment, moreover, would entail vexing definitional and measurement problems.[140] Refinement of the quota system through adjustments of this kind, then, would inevitably increase the administrative complexity of the system.

A Market in Refugee Protection Quotas

Would states be interested in paying others to protect refugees? The short answer is that they already are doing so. In some refugee crises like Rwanda, some relatively wealthy states contribute funds to the first-asylum state to support its protection efforts *in situ*. Although these delegations of protection resources and responsibilities are certainly better than nothing, they suffer from a number of limitations. The delegation transactions are inevitably ad hoc, with each transaction having to be organized and coordinated by UNHCR, a dedicated but sluggish and highly politicized bureaucracy. They invite strategic behavior by states with conflicting interests hoping to free ride on the efforts of others.

A market system cannot eliminate these conditions, but it can hope to leverage certain constraints on refugee protection into an improved system. Just as increasing refugee flows, by exposing even traditionally insular states to the risk of sudden influxes, might encourage them to participate in the system of refugee protection, a market system might transform two other real-world constraints into important refugee policy virtues. First, state actors are motivated largely by their perceptions of national self-interest, broadly defined; they are unlikely to adopt humanitarian policies that are inconsistent with those perceptions. Second, states vary enormously in both the attitudes and the resources that they bring to refugee policy. A few states willingly devote substantial resources to refugee protection while other states do little but pass the buck.

Although reformers cannot count on changing either states' motivations or states' heterogeneity, they *can* devise mechanisms to guide states' self-interest into channels conducive to humanitarian goals. These mechanisms can encourage states to exploit their heterogeneity through exchanges that serve both their self-interest and the public interest in refugee protection. A properly regulated market in refugee protection quotas promises to accomplish both of these ends.

Once a state receives its quota, it must decide whether it will discharge it by offering protection to refugees (either temporary safe haven or permanent resettlement) on its own territory and, if so, which form of protection it will provide. It must then identify the particular refugees whom it will protect. In addition to domestic political considerations, this selection process now entails a number of interactions—interviews, investigations, consultations, and negotiations—with UNHCR, other potential receiving states, the first-asylum state, NGOs, and of course the particular refugees who are candidates for protection.

Under my proposal, the state would have an additional option. Rather than protect the quota refugees itself (presumably, but not necessarily, on its own territory), it could transfer part or all of its quota obligation to another state[141] in a voluntary, public transaction. In effect, the transferor state would pay the transferee state, which might not be a member of the regional burden-sharing system. The transferor state would be purchasing a discharge of its obligation from the transferee. The payment presumably would take the form of cash, but it could, in principle, be any resources that the transferee values enough to accept: credit, commodities, development assistance, technical advice, weapons,[142] political support, or some combination of these assets.

At first blush, it might seem preferable simply to create a centrally administered refugee protection fund into which each state would be obliged to pay a sum equal to its share under the protection criterion. The central authority would then contract with individual states for protection services. This approach, however, entails at least two important disadvantages. First, it would restrict the acceptable currency of trade to cash, thereby limiting the number and flexibility of possible transactions. The proposed system, in contrast, would permit a transferee state to accept not only cash but also any other resources, including political support and other hard-to-monetize assets, that it values more than cash. Second, a centralized system would be more complex and involve higher transaction costs than a more decentralized system in which state-to-state negotiations and transactions would predominate. For these reasons, states are more likely to accept the burden-sharing norm if it is effectuated through a market system.

Why might states enter into such transactions? As in any voluntary exchange, the parties will only do so if the exchange makes each of them better off, and it is entirely possible that no deals would in fact be struck. Even in this case, refugee protection would still be better off than under the existing system because of the quota state's commitment to its initial quota. Here, the transferor can only induce the transferee to accept the transferor's obligation by paying the transferee enough to compensate it for the additional burden of accepting the transferor's quota. This is precisely why interstate heterogeneity, with respect to both their attitudes toward refugees and their resources for dealing with refugee burden, can be a policy virtue.

Consider the example of Japan. Any regional system that included Japan would certainly assign it a large quota; after all, its people are the eighth wealthiest per capita in the world and the wealthiest in Asia.[143] With remarkably homogeneous population and no tradition of refugee protection immigration, or assimilation of foreigners, Japan would presumably be eager to purchase a discharge of its large protection obligation from another country—perhaps Australia, New Zealand, or another Pacific Rim state—and at a high price, reflecting both its high cost of living and its determination to maintain its ethnic homogeneity.[144]

Ethnically homogeneous, densely populated, and somewhat xenophobic states like Japan are not the only ones that might be willing to pay to be relieved of their burdens. The United States in effect did this in response to the 1994 exodus from Cuba when it persuaded Panama and several islands in the region to accept about 9,000 refugees, albeit only on a temporary basis.[145] Canada, Australia, New Zealand, Scandinavia, many European Union nations, Brazil, and other high-quota states with low population densities and a tradition of receiving and assimilating refugees and other immigrants would also be competing in regional or larger markets.

Like all other immigrant-receiving societies, these states are now facing strong public pressures to admit fewer refugees and immigrants. A quotas market would offer them a flexible solution to this political dilemma. It would enable them to respond to these restrictionist pressures not by reducing the level of refugee protection that their humanitarian traditions demand but by actually *increasing* it. This is because the high-quota states that would likely be purchasers of quota discharges also have high prices for most commodities, products, and services that refugees need. The costs per refugee are bound to be much higher in these states than almost anywhere else in the world. Refugees are entitled only to basic protection from persecution, not residence in the society of their choice. Human rights policy should seek neither more nor less than this.

By facilitating voluntary trades, moreover, the quota market could reduce the overall cost of the refugee protection system, giving it more "bang for the buck." First, it would tend to move protection programs from higher-cost states to lower-cost ones, enabling *more* refugees to be protected for any given resource level than under the existing system. Second, by increasing the number of states in a region that participate in the refugee protection system (as either buyers or sellers of discharge quotas), the system would reflect in the quota's market price the costs of shifting refugees from the state of first asylum to another place; hence, those costs would be minimized. In this way, high-quota states would seek to discharge their quotas by paying states of first asylum or neighbors of such states to protect those refugees where they are already located. Third, the quota price would reflect the risk that protection, initially meant to be temporary, will evolve into the more costly situations of long-term custody and permanent resettlement. Thus, transferor states, wishing to minimize the price they must pay to induce transferees to assume their burden, would have an interest in maintaining the integrity of temporary protection, which in turn is essential to the viability of any voluntary refugee protection system, including the current one.

The other side of the market—potential transferee states—should be reasonably crowded. All states want, and most desperately need, the hard currency that the high-quota states would presumably use to pay for their quota discharges, although transferee states might also value other forms of payment. Some potential transferee states have not been notably receptive to refugees but already have ethnically diverse populations and may have vast empty spaces (and residential controls) for temporary protection or re-settlement. Russia and Brazil are examples. Even a wealthy state with a siz-able quota of its own might nevertheless be willing to accept some addi-tional refugees, especially if its costs of doing so are fully, or perhaps even more than fully, covered by a transferor's payment. The state's motive might be humanitarian, ideological, ethnic, or geopolitical, rather than, or in addition to, the mercenary pursuit of hard currency.[146]

A potential source of uncertainty in a quotas market is the identity of the particular refugees who comprise a state's tradable quota.[147] Ordinarily, states do not accept refugees for temporary protection or resettlement until they have interviewed them and compiled a more or less particularized dossier. Under the proposed system, this information might be even more valuable; several states, not just one, would want it in order to decide whether and at what price to trade.

States considering whether to buy or sell quotas would seek to use such information to predict the economic, social, and political effects of such a trade Just as states under the current system usually give careful considera-tion to precisely which individuals or groups they are being asked to pro-tect, states under the proposal would pay particular attention to whether they have historical ties to certain refugees based on language, ethnicity, or other relationships to the receiving state. They will value whatever data on the refugees' social class, level of education, ethnicity, age, religion, family status, and any other demographic variables that may help them predict how quickly those refugees will assimilate, how productive they will be, which public services they will consume, and so forth. If states value such information but cannot obtain it, their costs and risks of trading will in-crease.

Amassing the information should not be too costly. First-asylum states already gather enough data to determine refugee status or otherwise decide what to do with the individual. Moreover, no state will seek information that is not worth the cost of gathering and assessing it. Refugees may want to limit uncontrolled access to personal information about themselves, fear-ing not only loss of privacy but also reprisals by their state of origin. These concerns can probably be met through confidentiality requirements.[148]

Another problem—that such information lends itself to discriminatory group judgments by receiving states—seems inescapable. Certainly it exists under the current system. A state's willingness to accept refugees depends in part on how it evaluates the refugees' prospects for early return or, if reset-tlement is necessary, for assimilation and productivity in the receiving state. These evaluations turn on the states' assessments of the demographic characteristics of different racial and ethnic groups and on the states' historical ties to those groups.

Although such assessments invite prejudicial and discriminatory judgments that would be odious in any other context, it is hard to see how they can be avoided here. Virtually every state that admits immigrants discriminates on the basis of national origin (source country), social class (skill or educational level), and ethnicity (family, linguistic, or cultural ties). The relatively few states that agree to protect refugees engage in a discriminatory selection process in which they choose how many refugees, and which ones, they will accept.[149] The haggling is particularly intense where permanent resettlement, with its higher stakes, is proposed.

The political reality is that states would be even more reluctant to accept refugees for protection if they could not pick and choose in this fashion. Perhaps they could be induced to agree on a "blind" allocation process behind a Rawlsian veil of ignorance. Would this be preferable? It seems doubtful. The fact is that certain affinities—religious, linguistic, ethnic, and occupational—between a receiving state and refugees tend to facilitate larger quotas, more generous treatment (in the case of temporary protection), and more rapid assimilation (in the case of resettlement). The proposed burden-sharing system seeks to make a virtue of this necessity by using a quotas market, in which such affinities would be reflected in quota prices, to attract more states and more resources into the vital work of refugee protection.

This issue probably cannot be resolved without further analysis and experience. The most important empirical question is how specific the information about the refugees in the quota must be in order to meet the demands of potential trading states. The answer depends largely on the relative costs and benefits of obtaining more specific information. Some states might be satisfied with broad demographic data on group composition; others might insist on the kind of refugee-specific identifying information that raises confidentiality and safety concerns. Such preferences probably vary from state to state.[150] A state's demand for refugee-specific information will also be affected by whether it offers only temporary protection, in which case particularized information is less important, or permanent resettlement, in which case the state will usually require it.

The problem of discriminatory refugee selection is not a new one, and the proposed burden-sharing scheme should not be faulted for failing to offer a neat solution that earlier efforts could not manage to devise. The CPA, the most comprehensive burden-sharing program yet established, allocated refugees through a process of intensive negotiation among the participating states in which certain demographic affinities were informally recognized as legitimate bases for assigning particular groups of refugees to one state rather than to another. Although all states would prefer that "their" refugees possess such affinities, some states were more insistent on them than others. In the end, the United States was perhaps the least insistent, accepting many refugees whom other states would not take.[151]

An International Authority

The proposal entails certain tasks that only an agency can perform. The agency must gather information about refugee protection needs, assign quotas to the states, develop policies to facilitate the market in quotas, disseminate information about market transactions, and deploy whatever authority the states grant it (or it can muster informally) to ensure that refugees' rights under international law are fully protected.

Although the states that would establish burden-sharing schemes might wish to assign these tasks to a new or existing regional agency, UNHCR is an obvious candidate to carry them out. UNHCR does not now assign quotas or supervise a market, but it already performs other functions that have allowed it to amass enormous expertise in refugee protection. There are good reasons, therefore, to entrust the quota and market responsibilities to UNHCR and to provide it with the resources and authority necessary to execute them.[152] There are also reasons to expect that UNHCR's effectiveness would improve under the proposed scheme, as the participating states would have strong incentives to strengthen UNHCR's capacity by providing it with adequate resources and political support.[153]

The agency should disseminate information about market transactions, but it need not otherwise devote much attention to policing them. Sovereign states should be presumed to be fully capable of protecting their own transactional interests in this market. What states cannot be relied upon to protect, however, are the interests of the refugees who enter their territory, which to some degree conflict with the states' interests in minimizing the burdens of refugee admissions. Although the states must retain the primary responsibility for the welfare of those refugees, the agency has crucial roles of advocacy and perhaps enforcement in pressing the states to observe international legal principles governing the treatment of refugees. Precisely how the agency plays these roles depends in part on the formal authority that the agency receives from the states and the informal leverage that it can generate.

In addition, the agency must help to resolve certain policy issues surrounding the structure and performance of the quotas market. Two such issues—applications for temporary quota adjustments and the specificity of the information about refugees—have already been discussed. Others are certain to arise. The transactions themselves, however, should be negotiated and effectuated state to state, not through the agency as intermediary.

V. A RESPONSE TO (ANTICIPATED) CRITICS

A number of objections to a market in refugee-protection quotas can be readily anticipated. In this part, I respond to the three most likely ones: (1) unworkability; (2) quality of protection; and (3) commodification. Each of these objections raises legitimate concerns. Most of them can be met in the design of the new system. For a few, doubts do remain. Again, however, these doubts apply at least as strongly to the existing system.

The Unworkability Objection

The first objection proceeds from the argument that the scheme is politically unacceptable and thus practically unworkable. Agreement among states is necessary to establish the system, yet states, so the argument goes, have no incentive to conclude such an agreement because a quota system would limit the freedom of action that they now enjoy and impose additional burdens on them. If states actually had the desire to create such a system, they would already have done so. Furthermore, a system of quotas would be complex and difficult to administer. Finally, it would be impossible to enforce such a system in the absence of a central entity possessing the requisite legal authority and coercive power. No such entity exists in the international sphere. This unworkability objection really consists of three somewhat distinct points concerning incentives, administrability, and enforceability. I have already discussed these to some extent. I shall consider them now in greater detail.

Incentives.   The logic of the claim about incentives is contingent on the circumstances specified by the observer. Any structure of incentives is inevitably contextual, a function of the conditions and choices that confront the decisionmaker at a particular point in time.

I have shown that the refugee context is indeed changing in ways that are altering the objective risks that states face, their perceptions about such risks, and their policy choices. The key change is the apparently permanent refugee crisis. No state is wholly immune from this crisis, which is already affecting how states perceive their risks of becoming a country of first asylum. These new perceptions, I suggest, should make states more receptive than they have previously been to a form of burden-sharing, a strategy that I have termed refugee crisis insurance. Today, even (or perhaps especially) a traditionally insular state might rationally prefer to agree in advance to accept a limited number of refugees in exchange for an assurance that other states will relieve it of any additional burden in the event of a refugee emergency that suddenly transforms it into a first-asylum country. Finally, as discussed below,[154] the states with the greatest stakes in a broader distribution of refugee protection burdens are precisely the ones that possess the largest stock of carrots and sticks.

Thus, the incentives to support such a burden-sharing strategy are now in place. Whether states will in fact act on them, of course, is an entirely different question; one must never underestimate the durability of old perceptions and policies. Nevertheless, the refugee pressures that have been building on some traditionally insular states like Germany, Japan, Australia, and New Zealand, and the growing sense of urgency—even crisis—among some of these states is evidence that the new incentives are affecting state behavior. The rise of at least embryonic regional refugee burden-sharing (and burden-avoiding) arrangements in Europe[155] and North America provides additional evidence of such a transformation.[156]

Administrability. It is certainly true that quota systems can be difficult to operate. They require an administrative agency to resolve a number of methodological, empirical, and normative questions, to implement the system in the face of many practical and political obstacles, and to make adjustments to accommodate constantly changing conditions. That the scheme would be consensual at its inception—that states would participate only if it served their interests—would reduce, but not eliminate, these obstacles.

The best evidence of such a system's administrability would be the operation of analogous schemes in other areas of public policy. During the last decade, many proposals have been made in which a regulatory authority would permit regulated entities to trade entitlements or obligations as a way to improve the regulated activity's allocative efficiency.[157] A few of these proposals would necessitate international agreements.[158] My proposal for tradable refugee-protection quotas draws on this approach.

Unfortunately, only a few such trading schemes have yet progressed much beyond the brainstorming stage, and none of them is either fully developed or entirely analogous to what I am proposing here. Nevertheless, two market-oriented schemes of this general kind, New Jersey's "fair share" affordable housing program and emissions trading under the Clear Air Act, are of some interest to refugee-policy reformers because they rely on assigned quotas, allow trading of those quotas, and have already been implemented to some extent.

The New Jersey program grew out of an earlier decision by the state supreme court in the seminal *Mount Laurel* litigation.[159] There, the court held that the state constitution required each municipality in the state to provide its fair share of affordable housing to people of low and moderate income. The state subsequently enacted a statute[160] to systematize these obligations and established a Council on Affordable Housing to implement the fair-share scheme. As part of this scheme, now municipalities may, under certain circumstances, enter into regional contribution agreements (RCAs) in which municipality A pays municipality B to discharge up to 50% of A's fair-share obligation. RCAs, it was hoped, would encourage rehabilitation of the existing and often substandard housing stock in the central cities.[161]

As implemented, the New Jersey scheme can hardly be said to be an unqualified success; commentators have given it mixed reviews, including some harsh criticism.[162] Although a number of RCAs have been concluded, they apparently provide for only a modest number of housing units,[163] and this seems to be true of the fair share program as a whole. Much of the difficulty stems from disputes over the fair shares and from the ease with which developers and municipalities can circumvent program requirements.[164]

Another market-oriented system that is already in place is emissions trading under the 1990 Clear Air Act amendments.[165] Under this program, utilities that reduce their emissions below a prescribed level may, under certain circumstances, either "bank" the excess reductions for their own future use or sell them as allowances to other utilities that face higher abatement costs. As with New Jersey's fair share program, the reviews of emissions trading are mixed. In contrast to the New Jersey program, however, virtually all commentators endorse the policy of emissions trading and agree that the savings in regulatory compliance costs have already been substantial. The main criticism seems to be that the program has failed to realize its full potential, largely because of market and regulatory uncertainty that discourages more extensive trading.[166] Efforts are afoot to broaden the use of emissions-trading mechanisms—extending into the international arena.[167]

It is hard to know precisely what lessons, if any, refugee-policy reformers should draw from the experiences of the domestic housing and emissions control programs and the emerging international environmental accords. These programs are similar to a refugee-quota scheme in a few respects but different in many others.

All of these market-based schemes impose obligations and then permit the obligors to trade those obligations to others. Each is designed to derive greater social benefit (affordable housing, pollution control, refugee protection) from a given level of resources. Each seeks to take account of the heterogeneity among the obligors (communities, polluters, and countries) and to turn it to social advantage. Both the New Jersey program and my refugee quota proposal are based on still-controversial norms of equitable burden-sharing, although they concern radically different goods (housing and protection from persecution) that are allocated in altogether different ways. In the housing program, both quota allocation and compliance measurement are plagued by definitional problems.

These problems, however, might not hobble a refugee-quota scheme in which strict legal definitions of "refugee" are of less practical importance.[168] Such a scheme, moreover, may not require the kind of complex technocratic knowledge that pollution-control agencies must possess in order to administer an emissions-trading system effectively.

Enforceability. Once states agree to participate in a refugee-quota scheme, monitoring compliance should not be particularly difficult, as UNHCR can readily count refugees, verify their destinations, and record transactions among states. Enforcement, however, would be far more problematic. Subscribing states would presumably have the same mixed motives to comply as they do in the case of other treaty obligations. These motives balance a desire to sustain a scheme of international cooperation to which they have agreed and that they believe furthers their national interest, and a desire to win or retain the approbation of actual or potential trading partners and politico-military allies, against a desire to free ride and retain their autonomy.

As with other international agreements, enforceability will depend largely on the degree to which powerful states wish to see the system implemented and are prepared to press other states to comply. I have argued that in this case, those with the greatest stakes in the scheme's success are the states that now feel obliged to accept refugees for permanent resettlement, as well as certain other nonresettlement states like Japan that might value refugee crisis insurance nonetheless. Happily, these are also the states that possess the most powerful levers for securing compliance with the quotas. Whether they would in fact use their influence for this purpose, of course, is a separate question. Once again, however, it is worth emphasizing that international cooperation is no less essential to the effectiveness of the *current* system.

I have proposed that the burden-sharing system initially be established on a regional basis. Participation by more states would of course be desirable and should be a goal for the future, but a scheme developed by a small number of powerful states in a region would, as noted earlier, have distinct advantages. These states could establish whatever conditions and criteria they deem necessary to protect their vital national interests. These interests would surely include their desire to discourage free rider behavior by other, nonparticipating states by penalizing their recalcitrance and rewarding their cooperation. If the scheme were successful—if it managed to diffuse refugee crises and to distribute protection burdens more broadly and fairly—other states might wish to join this market or to form markets of their own, thereby gradually enlarging the pool of burden-sharing states.[169]

I have also proposed that the new system of refugee protection be consensual, a feature of the current system and indeed of almost all collaborations in the international sphere. Today, states decide to protect refugees if and to the extent that they wish, for their own reasons, to do so. This is not to say, of course, that they enjoy complete freedom of action. Receiving states decide to protect refugees only after balancing a variety of considerations, including the seriousness with which they regard their obligations under the Refugee Convention. Some of their reasons are humanitarian;[170] others are not. Some states may conclude that they have little choice but to acquiesce in other states' requests to participate, backed up by positive or negative inducements. The proposed system would be no different. Indeed, I have just suggested that its viability depends on the willingness of powerful receiving states to deploy these inducements, if necessary, in order to enforce the quotas.

The Quality-of-Protection Objection

A more serious question relates not to the number of refugees who would be protected under the proposed system but to the *quality* of protection that would be provided in the receiving states. Under the current voluntary system, receiving states may fail to provide refugees with the full protections to which international law entitles them. Such failures, of course, are far more common with respect to the protection of those who claim asylum or other forms of temporary protection than with respect to resettled refugees, who usually become eligible for permanent legal status in short order.[171] Even so, it would not be surprising if states that have traditionally volunteered to protect refugees tend to treat them better than states that agree to do so for the first time and in exchange for compensation.

This is a genuine risk, but it is not peculiar to the quota-market proposal. Indeed, the risk attaches to any move toward more universal burden-sharing that brings previously nonparticipating states into the refugee-protection system. There are several techniques for minimizing this risk; they cannot wholly eliminate it.

First, states that pay others to fulfill their quotas cannot thereby divest themselves of the duty to ensure that the rights of their quota refugees are fully protected. They should be under an independent, continuing legal responsibility to see that the states with which they deal also protect those rights.[172] They could enforce this responsibility through contractual provisions, liens on receiving states' assets, and diplomatic remedies.

Second, the payments to the receiving state should not be made through an initial lump-sum transfer. Instead, the pressure for continuing compliance with human rights and other obligations can be maximized by making payments on a periodic basis. Again, the problem of ensuring that resources that the donor provides for refugee protection are in fact used for that purpose, rather than being drained off by corruption or inefficient administration, is a ubiquitous one, especially in the impoverished regions in which many refugee crises arise. It is not at all peculiar to the proposed burden-sharing scheme.

Third, the administering agency, whether it be UNHCR or another, should be given wide-ranging authority to monitor and to publicize the treatment of resettled refugees in light of humanitarian standards. Paying states must ensure that the agency receives the resources it needs to carry out its essential monitoring and reporting functions. By drawing more states into the protection system and by imposing on transferors as well as transferees a continuing responsibility for the proper expenditure of protection funds, the proposed system should increase support for the agency's activities.

The proposed expansion of the refugee-protection system beyond the traditional receiving states raises a related quality problem. The quota transfers permitted under a market system increase the probability that a refugee will end up being offered protection in a state in which she simply does not want to be. The states that the market newly draws into the system are likely to be poorer, more geographically isolated, ethnically different, and have different social policies than the traditional receiving states.

A refugee offered protection by a relatively unattractive state is placed in an unenviable position. She may have few options, all of them undesirable. She can reject the offer and remain where she is, in perhaps indefinite limbo, hoping that something better comes along. She can try to return home, which may be dangerous or even suicidal. Or she can accept the offer and receive protection in a country in which she thinks she will be unhappy.

Under the current system, a refugee confronts essentially the same options, with the difference being that there is a higher ex ante probability that the offering state will be an attractive one in which to live, temporarily or permanently. The refugee's options are limited because her rights under international law are limited. She is entitled only to *non-refoulement* and the other basic protections accorded by the Refugee Convention. She has no right to receive those protections in any particular state. Many refugees struggle, against great odds, to move from the state that initially offered them protection to one in which they prefer to live. Many succeed in doing so. Refugees, however, have no rights *qua* refugees to be protected in one state rather than in another. To create such a right would certainly reduce the willingness of states to grant protection, and it is almost inconceivable that the international community will ever do so.

A system of quotas (marketable or not) is designed to draw more states into the refugee-protection system and to increase the number of refugees receiving protection, but the quality of this protection may be reduced if the newly participating states are permitted to be less hospitable to refugees. This tension between the total amount of protection (in the sense of the number receiving it) and the quality of protection enjoyed by those who receive it transcends the marketable quota proposal; it applies, *mutatis mutandis,* to any reform that seeks to broaden refugee burden-sharing.

I believe that the paramount goal for refugee policy should be to maximize the number of individuals receiving basic protection against threats to their lives and freedoms.[173] Maximizing the quality of life enjoyed by those who receive that basic protection is highly desirable, of course, but it remains secondary to this primary purpose. Those who hold different normative priorities will view the proposal less favorably, but they will be hard pressed, I believe, to devise a better one.

The Commodification Objection

A final objection is directed not at the idea of quotas per se but at the moral implications of a system of marketable refugee quotas. This objection holds that such a market would allow and encourage states to traffic in human beings—and desperately vulnerable human beings at that—and that this offends common morality.[174]

For four reasons, my response to this objection is brief. First, the objection is a familiar one. It is made whenever the market is used to allocate scarce goods or activities—organ transplants, education, environmental controls, communications spectra, childbearing, and low-cost housing, to name a few examples—that have traditionally been allocated, at least ostensibly, through administrative or other "nonmarket" mechanisms.[175]

Second, the commodification objection implies that the relevant comparison is between a callous market-based system that would arbitrarily allocate refugees to diverse places and fates and a more rational system that allocates them according to some exalted principle of justice. In reality, of course, the existing refugee system does not even pretend to approach such an ideal. Rather, it is a system that—in common practice, if not in law—allows states of first asylum to decide whether and how to protect the individuals who manage to reach them and allows a handful of other states to select the small number of refugees whom they will accept for resettlement, usually based on their judgments about the refugees' prospects for assimilation. This system leaves the majority of refugees to languish indefinitely in dehumanizing, squalid camps or to be repatriated to conditions of possible persecution and almost certain suffering. Given the harsh reality of a dehumanizing status quo, a commodification objection to the proposed reform seems quite beside the point.

Third, the proposed system is perfectly compatible with whatever regulatory protections and market constraints are thought conducive to securing overriding public values. This is not to say, however, that any such constraint could be imposed without sacrificing other goals, including states' willingness to participate in the burden-sharing system.[176] Here, as elsewhere, the market exacts its price; there is no free lunch. But it is to say that we can and should seek an optimal mix of the conflicting values.

Finally, the commodification argument would fail even on its own terms if the market-based system actually succeeded in protecting more refugees, with a quality of protection no worse, and at a lower cost, than in the current system. Although new schemes seldom work exactly as planned, and prudence thus dictates caution on the part of reformers (including confining the proposal to a regional, consensual demonstration), I have adduced strong reasons to believe that the proposed scheme could indeed produce each of these advantages.

CONCLUSION

The need for improved refugee protection is both manifest and growing. The existing system, jerry-built to address conditions that have changed dramatically since its inception, exhibits a number of major flaws. At the most general level, the two most important flaws include a failure to furnish at least temporary protection to a large number of refugees who desperately need it and an unfair distribution of burdens among states able to provide protection. The maintenance of even this unsatisfactory system ultimately depends on the willingness of the relatively powerful industrial nations to use their leverage—their array of carrots and sticks—to induce the first-asylum states to offer temporary protection and, where permanent protection is necessary, to arrange for a limited number of resettlement slots in their own countries.

Equitable burden-sharing among states is a noble vision but not a new one. What is required to instantiate it is a system of norms, incentives, and institutions that can mobilize the necessary protection resources from states that will always be reluctant to commit them, especially if they believe that the protection will be permanent, not temporary. No system can eliminate this reluctance; it is endemic to states' narrow conceptions of their national self-interest. But the refugee burden-sharing scheme—by proposing a regionally-based, consensual arrangement combining a quota system that distributes refugee burdens among the wealthier states with a market option that can redistribute protection resources to other states that can more effectively use them to harbor more refugees—promises to increase the overall level and quality of protection. Like many promises, its hopes might not be fully realized, but even so it could hardly leave refugees worse off than they are now. In view of both the deplorable status quo and the potential for human rights gains, can we afford not to try?

14

Alien Rumination:
What Immigrants Have
Wrought in America

Alien Nation: Common Sense About America's Immigration Disaster. By Peter Brimelow. New York: Random House, 1995. Pp. xix, 327. $24.00.

It's a damn good thing for Peter Brimelow and his son, Alexander James Frank Brimelow, that Alexander was born in this country in 1991. Peter, a recently naturalized Briton, obviously loves the boy and wants him to live in the United States with Peter and his Canadian wife. But if Alexander had been born elsewhere, he would not be an American citizen, and if his dad had his way with our immigration policy, perhaps *none* of the Brimelows, dad included, could have entered as immigrants. The Brimelows are fortunate that the law did not and does not reflect Peter's radically anti-immigration prescriptions. And so, I shall argue, are the rest of us.

Part of the allure of this high-spirited,[1] chatty, often personal,[2] but otherwise uncharming book is that the author acknowledges such ironies. Indeed, he skillfully exploits them to construct a case for radical reform of immigration policy that verges on total elimination of immigration to the United States. Thus, he ruefully tells us that he feels "slightly, well, guilty that [Alexander's] fellow Americans had so little choice" in conferring a citizenship that Alexander, like many children of illegal aliens and temporary visitors, acquired through the fortuity of birth on American soil.[3] He shrugs off the prospect (now happily hypothetical in his own case) that when Congress adopts his proposal to cut off legal immigration entirely, even the nuclear family of an American citizen could not immigrate to the United States. Had that been the law when he came, he says in his amiable, no-big-deal style, "I would probably be writing a book on Canadian immigration policy right now."[4]

Although it is tempting to dismiss this book as another ideological tract, one to which only the already-converted will attend, that would be a mistake.[5] The book must be taken seriously, first, because it is already influencing the public debate on immigration.[6] *Alien Nation* has grand ambitions. It not only raises fundamental questions about immigration's effect on the past, present, and future of American society (which is common enough in this era of apocalyptic politics) but also proposes to *answer* them (which is more unusual). Brimelow wishes to jettison the basic structure of our immigration policy established by the Immigration and Nationality Act Amendments of 1965.[7] The 1965 law abolished the national origins quotas, which had been in effect since 1921,[8] replacing them with a system that allocated hemisphere-specific limits among seven preference categories (based on skills, family relationships, and refugee status) and in which all countries of origin in the eastern hemisphere were subject to the same 20,000-immigrant limit.[9] The immigration reform laws enacted in 1978, 1986, and 1990 preserved the essential structure (while altering the details) of this system.[10]

Brimelow proposes to end this system in favor of "a drastic cutback of legal immigration."[11] This proposal is perhaps the only instance of understatement in a book suffused with hyperbole. Calling his plan a drastic cutback is rather like calling Jack the Ripper unfriendly. Brimelow would stop all immigration immediately (but temporarily) and seems to propose a permanent termination of all family-based, refugee, and asylee immigration.[12] Presumably, he would permit only skills-based immigration, but he does not indicate how many of these immigrants he would admit. Of all the reform proposals advanced during this season of discontent, Brimelow's are surely among the most radical.[13]

Another reason to take *Alien Nation* seriously is its assertion that race[14] ought to matter in immigration policy. In the superheated environment in which racial issues are debated (and often evaded) today, they continue to be perhaps the most divisive and incendiary in American society. In the immigration policy context, they are explosive. Until the 1950s, racism pervaded and polluted American public law. Until only thirty years ago, it defined the very structure of our immigration law. Even today, the major receiving nations, all democracies, have embedded ethnocultural favoritism in their immigration and citizenship policies.[15] In Europe, even more virulent forms of racism and xenophobia increasingly taint immigration politics.[16]

Racism in the United States has declined dramatically in recent decades, despite frequent denials of this fact.[17] I believe—although the point is certainly arguable[18] and much turns on difficult definitions—that racism as such no longer plays a crucial role in immigration law; certainly it plays a less significant role than it did before 1965. Even so, immigration fundamentally shapes a number of racially charged policy questions, such as the future level and composition of the population, affirmative action, multi-cultural education, and legislative districting.[19]

Indeed, when commentators discuss how immigration affects labor markets, public budgets, urban development, political strategy, population growth, and the environment, they frequently refer to statistical data that break down the empirical effects of immigration, such as welfare utilization or fertility rates, by race. The public does not need experts to inform it that the proportion of nonwhites in the population is growing; the "browning" of America is obvious to anyone who walks down the street, rides a subway, or visits a classroom in almost any large city.

Nevertheless, the immigration debate has carefully elided discussion of the normative questions raised by these current and future demographic shifts: Are these changes good or bad for American society? Should they be slowed, accelerated, or left undisturbed? Which kinds of arguments support these evaluations? Our delicate discursive etiquette in matters of race consigns such questions largely to outspoken nativists such as Patrick Buchanan and to those who wish to pursue eugenic goals through immigration restriction.[20]

In more polite, punctilious company, these issues are left to evasive innuendo—or utter silence. Yet if the immigration debate is to have intellectual integrity and contribute to sound policy, this void must be filled. We must somehow learn to discuss racial questions candidly and fearlessly, but also with respect, sensitivity, and humility. This need is especially compelling in the immigration policy debate. After all, three decades after the national origins quotas were repealed, we still select most immigrants according to their national origins. We do so explicitly in our refugee, "diversity," and nation-specific (e.g., Cuban) programs, and implicitly in our family-based and legalization programs.[21] And individuals' national origins, of course, are highly correlated with race.[22]

Brimelow wishes to advance this debate but doubts that he will receive a fair hearing. He expects to be labeled a racist, which he archly defines as *"anyone who is winning an argument with a liberal."*[23] His prediction, if not his definition, is surely correct. Race is very much on his mind.[24] But is he a racist? Since Brimelow himself raises the question of his own racism and draws the reader's attention to it, a reviewer is tempted to seek an answer. The issue of his motivation, however, is an unwelcome diversion from the merits of Brimelow's claims, and I relegate it to a long endnote.[25]

In the end, the more interesting, significant, and policy-relevant issue is not the attitudes that underlie Brimelow's claims but the validity of those claims. If Brimelow's argument that the 1965 Immigration Act has been a national calamity were correct, we would be extraordinarily myopic and perverse to ignore or deny that fact—even if his argument were infected by racism. For reasons that I shall explain in the remainder of this review, I believe that his claim is false—or at least premature. But while *Alien Nation* is a bad book, it is also a valuable one—all the more so because it is so seductively easy to read. On the way to its erroneous conclusions, it makes many important points that are easily overlooked or have been driven underground in current immigration debates. It forces us to think more clearly about how and why his arguments are wrong. And it reminds us to resist the patriotic smugness and national self-delusion that come so easily to Americans and to be vigilant to assure that Brimelow's dire prophecies are not fulfilled.

The book's argument can be reduced to five distinct but related empirical claims whose significance can only be understood in the light of certain normative assumptions about the nature and purposes of American society. The first is a claim about *demography;* it asserts that immigration to the United States has reached unprecedented levels that are problematic in part because of the racial composition of the post-1965 flow. The second is a claim about *carrying capacity;* it holds that these high immigration levels are stretching American society's environmental resources (broadly defined) beyond the breaking point. The third is a claim about *economic impacts;* it contends that the post-1965 immigrants fail to pull their weight in the labor market and drain off scarce fiscal resources. The fourth is a claim about *cultural assimilation;* it states that the post-1965 immigrants are not embracing American values as completely or as swiftly as their predecessors did. The fifth is a claim about *politics;* it maintains that the post-1965 immigrants are altering the terms of political discourse in ways that weaken the American polity and call into question its viability as a nation-state. I shall discuss each of these claims in turn.

I. Demography

Brimelow emphasizes that total immigration to the United States, legal and illegal, is "at historic highs."[26] As Brimelow recognizes, the significance and truth of this assertion turn on several issues.[27] Should immigration be measured in absolute terms or relative to something else, such as the total or foreign-born population? Is it more meaningful to measure immigration on an annual basis or over longer periods of time? How many illegal aliens are being counted? Should immigration be measured net of permanent departures by aliens and U.S. citizens, and if so, how many departures are there? Except for legal admissions, which require the Immigration and Naturalization Service (INS) to issue visas, none of these indices is based on hard, reliable data; all can be, and often are, contested.

Admissions figures tend to fluctuate from one year to another, confounding efforts to discern significant trends on the basis of short-term changes.

For example, the admissions total in 1991 was approximately 1.8 million;[28] it then declined over the next four years to 720,000 in 1995[29] (when the INS had expected the total to increase again[30]). These fluctuations often reflect temporary special factors, including the evolution of particular short-term programs. The most important example is the legalization program under IRCA. This one-time spike in the admissions totals produced dramatic increases in the admissions totals beginning in 1989 but leveling off in 1992. IRCA legalizations, however, have had little effect on the figures since 1993,[31] and, for political reasons, such a legalization is unlikely to be repeated in the foreseeable future.[32]

Brimelow, then, is right to focus on longer-term trends. He is also correct to include illegal aliens in the total. Data on the number of illegal aliens are controversial and inexact, although expert estimates have narrowed considerably in recent years.[33] Estimates are based largely on extrapolations from the number of aliens apprehended at the Mexican border and from census surveys. Both methods are problematic.[34] Moreover, the gross category of illegal aliens must be broken down into subgroups for more precise, meaningful policy analysis. For example, different policies are needed to deal with the two, roughly equal, categories of illegal aliens: those who enter the United States illegally ("entrants without inspection" [EWIs]) and those who enter legally on temporary visas but then become illegal when they violate the terms of their visas ("overstays"). As another example, illegal aliens differ in how long they remain in the United States. Many illegals are temporary "sojourners," the duration of whose stays in the United States depends on seasonal, family, and economic factors, or are "commuters" who cross the border frequently. A growing share of the illegal flow from Mexico, however, now consists of "settlers"—mostly women and children planning to live with their families in the United States more or less permanently.[35] Because settlers' prolonged, illegal residence in the United States affects American society in more complex and significant ways than does the residence of sojourners, they pose the greatest challenges to politicians and policymakers.

In discussing illegal aliens, Brimelow is somewhat sloppy with the data, such as they are. Noting both the 1.3 million illegals apprehended by the Border Patrol in 1993[36] and estimates that it catches about one-third of those attempting to cross, he suggests that "a remarkable *2 to 3 million* illegal immigrants may have succeeded in entering the country in 1993."[37] But this suggestion ignores two well-known phenomena: multiple apprehensions of the same individuals who make repeated attempts until they cross successfully and sojourners who travel back and forth across the border repeatedly but are sometimes apprehended. Both of these common situations inflate the number of illegals. More important, he cites a "cautious" INS estimate that "300,000 to 500,000" net illegals remain each year.[38] His source for this estimate, however, is an unnamed INS spokesman, and the estimate is higher than the published estimates—300,000 is the figure most commonly used by researchers in the field, including INS researchers[39]— that he could have readily cited.

A similar slippage occurs when he discusses *emigration* by U.S. citizens and permanent residents, which of course bears on the total of *net* immigration. The best estimates are that 1.6 million emigrated during the decade of the 1980s, an outflow that has been steadily increasing since the 1940s and equaled the number emigrating during the 1920s.[40] Emigration seems to be accelerating during the 1990s.[41] He seeks to minimize this factor by stating that the post-1965 immigrants are less likely to emigrate than their pre-1920 predecessors, a trend that he attributes to the growth of the welfare state.[42] He may be correct, but the data do not establish his claim. First, the emigration data do not distinguish between noncitizen emigrants who were once immigrants and emigrants who were U.S. citizens (some of whom were never immigrants). Second, the decline in emigration began in the 1930s (if measured in absolute terms) and in the 1940s (if measured as a proportion of immigration).[43] It thus began long before the late 1960s, when Brimelow's two *bêtes noires*—the post-1965 immigration and the major growth in the welfare state—occurred. This chronology casts some doubt on his welfare-state explanation for declining emigration rates.

In a sense, however, these are mere details; they do not contradict Brimelow's position that the current level of net legal immigration is, by historical standards, quite high in absolute terms. The 1994 net legal immigration of just over 600,000 (804,000 immigrants minus 195,000 emigrants) is almost three times higher than the annual figures during the 1950s (for Brimelow, the last halcyon period before the Fall), when net legal immigration averaged just over 209,000.[44] It is also almost twice the level recommended by the politically astute, blue-ribbon Select Commission on Immigration and Refugee Policy only fifteen years ago.[45] Even the figure of 600,000 immigrants understates recent growth, of course, because it fails to include *illegal* immigrants, of whom there presumably were relatively few prior to the mid-1960s and almost none in the early decades of the century.[46] Adding 300,000 *resident* illegal aliens to the immigrant population each year[47] produces a grand total of at least 900,000 new resident immigrants each year, net of emigration. This number is high indeed, at least in absolute terms.

If we consider current immigration in *relative,* rather than absolute, terms—that is, new admissions or total foreign-born as a percentage of the total U.S. population—Brimelow's claim that immigration is at historically high levels must be qualified somewhat, as he acknowledges.[48] But even when viewed in these relative terms, the recent inflows have been substantial. Although the legal immigrants who entered in recent years constituted only 3.1% of the total U.S. population during the 1980s (the comparable shares for the first three decades of this century were 10.4%, 5.7%, and 3.5% respectively),[49] the steady accumulation of immigrants over time has produced a growing cohort of foreign-born in the United States. In 1994, over 22 million people, 8.7% of the total U.S. population, were foreign-born.[50] Although the percentage of the foreign-born remains far below the 13.2% share it composed in 1920, it is the highest percentage since then, and the foreign-born share has almost doubled since 1970, when it was 4.8%.[51] The fact that one out of every eleven persons in the United States is a first-generation immigrant gives immigration a much higher political and media profile today than it possessed only a quarter-century ago, when fewer than one in twenty were foreign-born.

Brimelow, however, does not simply ground his demand for drastic restriction on the size of the post-1965 cohort. He also claims that this newer immigration is fundamentally different from that which preceded it in two other respects: its continuity and its racial composition.

Continuity. One of the book's principal themes is that America has not always been a country that admitted immigrants. The traditional notion that there has been a steady stream of immigrants to the United States is one of those hoary, politically useful (to some) myths. The truth is that immigration to the United States has always come in waves—that is, until Congress unleashed the *tsunami* of 1965.[52] Beginning in the colonial period, immigration exhibited recurrent cycles of growth and decline. The many peaks and valleys were sensitive to conditions in Europe and job opportunities in the United States. When jobs were plentiful, immigrants came, many only as sojourners; when jobs were scarce, many of the earlier immigrants returned to the old country, and few new immigrants arrived. This punctuated pattern of immigration—occasional spurts followed by short-term "pauses" or longer "lulls"[53]—resulted mostly from the convulsions of war and the business cycle.[54] This pattern was also socially benign. Like the period between meals, the pauses and lulls facilitated digestion, a process that would have been far more dangerous and uncomfortable had the newcomers entered America's maw in large and constant gulps. Americans could more readily accept immigrants, who in turn had the time, space, and incentive to assimilate swiftly into American society.

Like almost every other good thing in Brimelow's account, however, this Edenic paradise of leisurely assimilation ended abruptly in (you guessed it!) 1965. Far from being wave-like, the post-1965 immigration has waxed but never waned; even now it shows no sign of receding.[55] The flow has been both continuous and continually rising (short-term fluctuations aside). In particular, the business cycle has had little effect on this immigration flow.[56] Brimelow has a ready explanation for this new development: In addition to jobs, the welfare magnet both attracts immigrants and keeps them here.[57] If

Brimelow is correct about this—if immigrants' motives have changed and the business cycle no longer disciplines immigration flows—the implications for both immigration and welfare policy would be far-reaching. But is it true?

Brimelow seeks to persuade us with strong assertions and vivid charts that draw our attention to the contrasting peaks and valleys before 1965 and the continuous ramping upward thereafter.[58] The unwary reader, however, should be forewarned: There is less to this evidence than meets the eye.[59] First, the major declines in immigration occurred during periods of either world war (1915–20, 1940–45) or deep economic depression (after 1873 and 1893, and during the 1930s).[60] Because we have managed since 1965 to avoid both of these evils—a point to which I shall return in the Conclusion—Brimelow cannot show that the historical responsiveness of immigration to the business cycle no longer operates. Only a new world war or depression can test his claim.

Second, the pre-1965 trough may not have been as deep as the numbers suggest. No numerical restrictions on immigration from the western hemisphere even existed before 1965, and thus any number of Mexicans could enter the United States legally by paying a fee, passing a Spanish literacy test, and obtaining a labor certification. Presumably, many did not bother to do so and instead entered illegally, which could not have been too difficult at a time when the Border Patrol was much smaller and less effective than it is today. Even if many did not enter the United States illegally, they were not counted in the totals contained in the official statistics. It is, therefore, a delicious irony, unremarked by Brimelow, that the same 1965 Act that he so thoroughly deplores also imposed a numerical restriction very much to his liking.

Third, the charts do not really tell us much about whether the causes of immigration fluctuations changed over time. We know that other things did not remain equal; for example, the legal rules governing immigration were in flux. Shortly after numerical limits on immigration were established in the mid-1920s,[61] the Great Depression drove immigration levels down, and World War II kept them low. Thus, the numerical caps could not really have begun to bite until the late 1940s, more than twenty years after their inception, at which point a different, more complex mix of factors (including massive refugee resettlements) were shaping immigration flows.

Finally, Brimelow's claim that the welfare state explains immigration's relentless rise during the post-1965 period is hard to square with the fact that this ramping up began in the 1950s, long before the Great Society expansion of the welfare state commenced.

Nevertheless, Brimelow might be correct that the business cycle no longer regulates immigration flows as it once did,[62] and that a legally mandated pause in immigration would enable the United States to better integrate the large post-1965 cohort. Such a new pause might facilitate the successful assimilation of this cohort, much as the pre-1920s cohort benefited from the earlier lull. A new pause might also ease immigration-related social anxieties resulting from the constant addition of newcomers.[63] Group mobility theory, the historical pattern of assimilation, and common sense lend some plausibility to this notion. It is intriguing that immigrants themselves—by a large majority—believe that immigration should either be kept at present levels or reduced, and support for this position increases with their time in the United States.[64] Whether immigrants possess some special insight into how large-scale, continuing immigration retards the assimilation of recent immigrants, or simply wish for selfish reasons to pull up the ladder now that they have climbed aboard, is unclear.

The attractiveness of a pause, however, depends in part on how the pause is defined and on its duration. Brimelow's approach is to permit either no immigration or only skills-based admissions (the reader can't be sure).[65] Others, however, will see no magic, and much mischief, in terminating *all* family-based and humanitarian admissions. For those categories, a more modest reduction in immigration, one that is temporary and whose overall effects can then be gauged, would almost certainly reconcile the competing considerations better than complete cessation.

Brimelow's effort to shift the burden of proof to defenders of immigration by appealing to social risk aversion also relies on a simplistic all-or-nothing approach. On the final page of his book, in a section entitled "What If?" Brimelow argues that immigration's uncertain effects argue for terminating or radically restricting it. If immigration advocates turn out to be wrong, he suggests, we will be left with many disastrous and perhaps irreversible consequences, whereas if the restrictionists are wrong, the worst that will happen is that the United States must deal with a labor shortage.[66] Risk aversion is a perfectly legitimate policy criterion, and if one shared Brimelow's views of immigration's effects, one might well accept this effort to shift the burden of proof. If instead one believes, as I do, that legal immigration is on the whole desirable, the more relevant policy criterion—one that should be particularly congenial to a conservative like Brimelow—becomes "if it ain't broke, don't fix it"—or, more precisely, "if it's just partly broke, just fix that part."

Racial Composition. To Brimelow, the most disturbing aspect of the Fall is the changing racial complexion of the United States. Before 1965, he notes, immigrants came overwhelmingly from the traditional source countries of northern and western Europe. In those glory days, "not all immigrants were alien to American eyes," and "native-born Americans were receiving continuous ethnic reinforcement."[67] But since the abandonment of the national origins quotas in 1965, the vast majority of newcomers have been Hispanic and Asian,[68] with a significant new black inflow from Africa and the non-Spanish Caribbean. In what he calls the Pincer Chart,[69] he shows (while acknowledging the uncertainties of long-term demographic projections) that whites, who were 81% of the population in 1790 and 75.7% in 1990, will decline to a bare majority (52.7%) in 2050.[70] Well before then, moreover, Hispanics will replace blacks as the largest single minority group. Brimelow then has the immigration liberal pose the key question: "*So what? Why do you care so much about race?*"[71] This is the essential question, and Brimelow provides several answers. In particular, he points to the reinforcement and distortion of affirmative action effected by immigration and to immigration's threat to social cohesion. Because these issues impinge most significantly on cultural assimilation and political power, however, I defer discussion of them to sections IV and V.

II. Carrying Capacity

Continued immigration, Brimelow despairs, will be a demographic and environmental disaster for the United States.[72] Nevertheless, although his warnings are certainly worth attending to, his predictions are highly arbitrary and unrealistic; he aims more to shock than to persuade. Interestingly, his predictions bear a striking resemblance to certain modes of argument— use of simplistic extrapolations from present to future, disregard for the complexity and subtlety of social adaptations, and presentation of stark doomsday scenarios—that conservatives properly mock when environmentalists and other social reformers advance them.

The centerpiece of Brimelow's analysis is a chart that he calls "The Wedge,"[73] which relies on projections developed by Leon Bouvier, a respected demographer and leading immigration restrictionist.[74] Had we terminated all immigration in 1970, Brimelow's "Wedge" purports to show, the U.S. population in 2050 would have been 244 million (i.e., less than the current total). But continuing immigration at present levels, he predicts, will produce a total in 2050 of 383 million, of which 36% will be post-1970 immigrants and their descendants. The "Wedge" consists of the additional 139 million Americans who will have descended from post-1970 immigrants,[75] unneeded and unwanted bodies that will place an unprecedented strain on the natural and human environments. He also predicts that more immigrants, especially those from the Third World whom the post-1965 rules have brought here, will bring new (and in some cases, old) diseases, high rates of fertility and crime, and low rates of education and skill. They will crowd out the rest of us, swamping our classrooms, extending our slums, polluting our air, and destroying our amenities and communities.[76] These dire consequences, he says, are already occurring.

Straight-line extrapolations from the present could indeed yield 383 million people in fifty-five more years. This is a lot of people, and the prospect of somehow squeezing all of them into our schools, beaches, parking spaces, and housing stock is not a pleasant one. Doing so would surely strain our natural and social environments. But straight-line extrapolations in such matters seldom prove to be correct. For all the scientific gloss of hard numbers, demography is as much art as science. Long-term demographic projections, like economic ones, are necessary and often valuable. Nevertheless, they necessarily assume that human choices are more fixed than they actually are and that the future will therefore be much like the recent past and present (except, of course, for such changes as the demographer can envision and accurately predict). Wise demographers know and say that this assumption is false, but they usually have little choice but to proceed as if it were true.

Demographic projections such as those cited by Brimelow emphasize the population-increasing effects of those immigrant groups whose fertility rates are higher than the fertility rates of natives. These higher rates reflect the greater proportion of immigrants, relative to the general population, who are in their childbearing years, cultural factors, and other causes. When high-fertility groups' share of the immigration stream and of the total U.S. population increases, the projected future population of the United States increases accordingly. This "shifting shares" phenomenon—the larger proportion in the population of high-fertility groups such as Filipinos, southeast Asians, and some Hispanics—drives much of the prediction of future U.S. population growth.[77]

This argument, however, resembles earlier "race suicide" theories that immigration historians and demographers have convincingly debunked by showing that immigrant fertility rates generally converge with those of the native population.[78] The important question, therefore, is how quickly this occurs. It appears that when women from high-fertility countries migrate to the United States, they both reduce and delay their childbearing to the point at which their fertility rates approach the overall U.S. norm. Indeed, compared to demographically similar native women, their rates sometimes are lower.[79] Admittedly, immigrants do accelerate U.S. population growth; since 1980, net immigration has accounted for about 37% of population growth.[80] But the extent and speed of their contribution to that growth in the future are difficult to predict and easy to exaggerate.

Much of Brimelow's concern about carrying capacity seems to relate to the dangers of overcrowding.[81] Even thirty years after the dreaded deluge began, however, the United States remains a country with a relatively low population density.[82] This concern does not simply reflect the vast uninhabited (and perhaps uninhabitable[83]) spaces in the American West. Even America's largest and densest cities are thinly populated relative to other cities in the world, including the most famously attractive ones.[84] Indeed, the population density of New York City is about half what it was in 1910;

other major cities are also less densely populated.[85] We have a long way to go before we reach density levels that other Western democracies find perfectly acceptable, even desirable. Our standards of acceptable density may be different from those in Europe, but our standards are not immutable, as the historical urbanization, suburbanization, and "edge city" cycles in the United States attest.

Demographic extrapolations from the present to the future are further confounded by the dynamics of markets, politics, and other powerful social processes that respond to developments that impose widespread social costs. These processes do not sit idly by while change unfolds but instead shape and constrain change, thereby altering its future trajectory. Demographic models cannot readily incorporate this fact, which is nicely captured in "Stein's Law" (stated by economist Herbert Stein): If a trend can't go on like this indefinitely, it won't.[86] Population growth, for example, bids up the prices of housing, education, and other goods; people therefore tend to have fewer children,[87] other things being equal.[88] If increased job competition pushes immigrants' unemployment high enough for long enough, they will tend not to migrate here. If competition for natural resources and other environmental goods becomes more intense, those goods will become more costly, which both rations their use and attracts additional supply; these behavioral responses in turn tend to reduce the price. If policymakers perceive that population growth harms the environment, the economy, and other areas of public concern, they will propose policy changes accordingly.

I am not suggesting that we can blithely count on these responses to eliminate any adverse effects of population growth—far from it. How well society reacts to these developments depends on the quality of information flows, the nature of politics, the efficiency of markets, and other factors. Even if optimal outcomes are unlikely under these conditions, however, Brimelow's dire predictions should be taken with more than a grain of salt. If our politics and markets are supple and responsive enough to react swiftly and intelligently to population pressures and other strains on carrying capacity, the future need not unduly arouse our fears. Indeed, since 1965, our social institutions have performed reasonably well in this regard, refuting the Chicken Littles of environmental pessimism.[89]

III. ECONOMIC IMPACTS

Brimelow acknowledges the rich contributions that the pre-1965 immigrants have made to the American economy.[90] He insists, however, that the post-1965 cohort is altogether different. Relying heavily and uncritically on the work of labor economist George Borjas, he argues that "the effect of the 1965 reform has been *to uncouple legal immigration from the needs of the U.S. economy.*"[91] This claim is actually a composite of four separate claims. The first is that labor market skills play a small and shrinking role in admissions policy. Second, the post-1965 cohort is less skilled than earlier cohorts. Third and related, the post-1965 cohort drains the economy more than earlier cohorts because its members, especially illegal aliens, are more likely to demand public assistance and displace native workers. Fourth, this displacement imposes particularly heavy burdens on current and potential African-American workers.

The first claim is correct. A major theme of the debate surrounding the Immigration Act of 1990 was the need to increase the level and relative share of skills-based admission.[92] In the end, however, the Act only slightly increased the share of these admissions. In 1994, only 15% of admissions were skills-based; moreover, roughly half of these consisted of skilled immigrants' accompanying family members, who may themselves lack skills needed in the United States. Family ties accounted for 62% of the admissions.[93] Because the 1990 Act substantially increased both the total number of immigrants and the numbers authorized for each immigrant category, the absolute number of skills-based immigrants did grow, thus obscuring how minimally the share of skills-based admissions had increased. Family unity, it appears, continues to trump all other immigration policy values.[94] Pending legislation would increase the relative weight of labor market skills, a reform whose advantages are widely appreciated.[95]

The second claim—that the "quality" of immigrants to the United States has declined since the 1965 reforms—is harder to assess. Good data on immigrant labor markets are hard to come by, and analyses are very sensitive to methodology. More to the point, labor economists disagree about the nature and validity of the data, methodology, and conclusions used by Borjas and other immigration analysis. There are several areas of dispute. One concerns the extent to which the "immigrant" category should be disaggregated. Different subcategories of immigrants—family-based admittees, skills-based admittees, refugees/asylees, age groups, source region or country groups, legals versus illegals—in a given cohort exhibit quite different characteristics. Lumping some or all of these subcategories together can significantly affect the outcome of the analysis. Reliance on census data, which employ rather crude, self-reported ethnic categories and almost certainly understate income, is also controversial.

Several generalizations growing out of labor market research do support some of Brimelow's concerns. Many post-1965 immigrants are highly educated, indeed, far more so than the native population. Many others are more skilled in *absolute* terms than the immigrants who preceded them, but because the native population's skills have increased even more in absolute terms and because lower skilled groups comprise a larger share of the total immigration flow, the "quality" gap has widened in *relative* terms.[96] Most of the immigrants who entered illegally—those who qualified for the amnesty under IRCA and those who have entered illegally since then—are low-skilled Mexicans. The education level of Mexican-origin immigrants, even among those who are naturalized U.S. citizens, is very low; overall, it averages about seven and a half years of schooling.[97] Other relatively low-skilled immigrant groups are Asian refugees and the elderly.[98] On the other hand, the recent arrivals also include better educated individuals—predominantly nonrefugees from Asia, Africa, and the Middle East—who should help to reduce the gap in the future.[99] This effect, however, will be gradual because their numbers remain relatively low. Again, pending legislation is likely to increase the skill levels of future immigrant cohorts.

Brimelow's third claim is that post-1965 immigrants inflict a net loss on the economy, taking into account the combined effects of their use of public services, their displacement of native workers, their tax payments, and their contribution to productivity. This claim is also difficult to assess precisely, as the existing studies seldom employ comparable definitions, measures, data sets, and methodologies.[100] For example, the outcomes of labor market impact analyses depend on whether the studies assume that particular labor markets (usually metropolitan areas) are closed systems, or whether they instead consider the significant possibility (given the high degree of internal labor mobility in the U.S. economy) that immigrant concentrations in one area induce some native workers to leave that area and discourage other natives who might otherwise migrate there from doing so.

Another controversial question of great political interest concerns immigrants' use of public services and benefits. Immigrant households are somewhat more likely to use welfare (AFDC and SSI) than native ones. Although this differential is small (7.5% of natives, 8.7% of immigrants), it increased during the 1980s as immigrant utilization rates grew and native rates declined. And in a very recent survey, immigrants *self-report* much higher utilization rates.[101] A number of earlier studies had found that if one controls for socioeconomic variables, immigrants were less likely than otherwise demographically similar natives to receive AFDC and SSI.[102] A very recent study using 1990 data indicates that this pattern of lower immigrant welfare utilization continues to be true for AFDC but not for SSI.[103] Immigrants now receive SSI at higher rates than demographically similar natives, a development that has generated strong public and congressional reaction.[104] Like the growing relative quality gap discussed earlier, the higher immigrant utilization of SSI is mostly due to the very large Mexican cohort and to the Asian *refugee* cohort, whose utilization rates more than doubled during the 1980s.[105]

A number of studies have attempted to determine whether immigrants on balance benefit or burden the U.S. economy. Brimelow, citing a highly disputed analysis by Donald Huddle[106] and a puzzling "back-of-the-envelope" estimate by Borjas, obviously thinks that the burdens predominate.[107] Urban Institute researchers Jeffrey Passel and Rebecca Clark recently reviewed the estimates made by Huddle and by state and local governments seeking reimbursement of immigration-related costs from the federal government.[108] Passel and Clark severely criticize these estimates for systematically understating tax collections from immigrants; overstating service costs for immigrants; failing to take account of the economic value generated by immigrant entrepreneurs and immigrant consumer spending; overstating job displacement impacts; overstating the size of the immigrant population, especially illegals; and ignoring the fact that natives also use more in services than they pay in taxes.[109] In particular, they find that Huddle underestimates the taxes paid by immigrants by $50 billion![110] Correcting this error alone, Passel and Clark argue, would defeat the claim that immigrants cost more than they contribute. Indeed, they estimate that the post-1970 immigrants—legal, amnestied, and undocumented—generate a surplus of $27.4 billion a year, not including nontax economic benefits.[111]

The large gap between these estimates reflects some quite technical methodological judgments by researchers. It would be foolish to allow immigration policy to turn on such judgments, especially since neither Huddle's cost estimate nor Passel and Clark's benefit estimate would count for much in a $7 trillion economy. Even so, there is no denying the *political* significance of these numbers: Public attitudes toward immigration are less favorable to the extent that immigrants are perceived to impose even small burdens on the economy and on taxpayers. Recent congressional actions confirm a strong consensus that immigrants (or their sponsors) should at least pay for themselves.[112]

The fourth claim—that post-1965 immigrants may displace many African-American workers[113]—might seem almost self-evidently true. After all, low-skilled immigrants and low-skilled blacks would appear to compete for a shrinking number of low-skill jobs. The terms of this competition, moreover, often favor even non-English speaking immigrants, especially illegals. Immigrants are accustomed to, and may accept, lower wages, and many employers perceive them to be more reliable, hard-working, and docile than native black workers.[114]

Much depends on the extent to which immigrant labor is a substitute for or a complement to native labor. If immigrant labor is a substitute, immigrants would increase unemployment among blacks (who unlike unsuccessful immigrants have no other home to which to return) and would, other things being equal, drive down wage levels for those blacks who are hired. Such effects would be consistent with studies indicating that real wages have declined for low-skill workers during much of the post-1965 period, and especially with studies concluding that recent immigration has contributed to the widening earnings gap between high-skill and low-skill workers.[115] But to the extent that immigrant labor instead complements native labor, immigrant labor would increase job opportunities for natives, including blacks. This increase might occur if immigrants fill labor niches that native workers are abandoning or if immigrants develop new entrepreneurial enclaves. There is evidence that both of these possibilities often occur.[116] Indeed, during the 1980s, immigrant groups seem to have competed more with each other than they did with native workers.[117]

Empirical studies have consistently failed to establish significant immigration-induced harm to native black workers.[118] Nevertheless, various methodological limitations of those studies, as well as subsequent changes in economic and immigration factors, mean that such effects cannot be ruled out.[119] The harmful effects, if any, appear to be much too small to justify a radical change in immigration policy on this ground alone.

IV. CULTURAL ASSIMILATION

Brimelow suggests that the post-1965 immigrants bear, and presumably transmit to their children, different and less attractive values than did the earlier waves of immigrants.[120] Although he is not clear precisely which values he has in mind, he presumably prefers those that most other people admire—honesty, industry, family stability, morality, education, optimism about the future, and respect for law and legitimate authority.[121] And although he is a bit vague about the indicia of the decline in immigrants' moral values, he does mention three areas of particular concern: crime, limited English proficiency (particularly among Hispanics), and high illegitimacy rates (particularly among Mexican-Americans).[122] Each of these three areas is certainly worth worrying about. Immigrant crime may be even worse than he suggests, and his concern about illegitimacy rates, at least among some immigrant groups, is warranted. On the other hand, his conclusions about limited English proficiency are exaggerated, and he fails to discuss the risk of second-generation attraction to underclass culture, which in the long run may be the most serious cultural problem of all. I discuss each of these areas in turn.

Crime

The incidence of immigrant crime is significant, if only because the number of immigrants is large. Most immigrant crime is drug-related.[123] Although the number of criminal aliens under law enforcement supervision in the United States is impossible to establish precisely, it has increased approximately ten-fold since 1980, imposing substantial costs of arrest, detention, and deportation. A 1993 congressional study estimated that 450,000 deportable criminal aliens were either incarcerated, on parole, or on probation in federal, state, and local jurisdictions.[124] A more conservative compilation of various federal and state estimates suggests that at least 270,000 deportable aliens are under criminal justice supervision.[125] Newly convicted aliens, of course, constantly replenish and enlarge this population. Illegals account for over half of the deportable aliens in state prisons.[126] Quite apart from other law enforcement costs, the costs of incarcerating alien criminals are high. The operating cost alone of a prisoner-year in federal prisons was estimated in early 1994 to be about $19,000.[127] If this cost were applied to the 100,000 deportable criminal aliens imprisoned in federal, state, and local facilities,[128] it would mean nearly $2 billion in annual incarceration costs.

Although the systematic data on point are somewhat dated, legal immigrants do not appear to commit any more crime than demographically similar Americans; they may even commit less, and that crime may be less serious.[129] Nor does today's immigrant crime appear to be worse than in earlier eras. The immigrants who flooded American cities around the turn of the century (the ancestors of many of today's Americans) were also excoriated as congenitally vicious and unusually crime-prone, not only by the public opinion of the day but also by the Dillingham Commission, which Congress established to report on the need for immigration restrictions.[130] The evidence suggests that those claims were false then, and similar claims appear to be false now.[131]

These historical and demographic points, however, are largely irrelevant to the contemporary political debate, which is concerned with the here and now. Media reports about criminal activity by Asian street gangs,[132] Latin American drug lords,[133] Islamic terrorists,[134] and Russian mafiosi[135] are profoundly disturbing to the American public and surely fuel restrictionist sentiment. In its concern about immigrant crime, as in other respects, the public often fails to differentiate between legal and illegal aliens.

Two abysmal policy lapses of the federal government have aggravated this political response. First, the government has failed to police the border and the interior effectively against illegal aliens, some of whom commit crimes after entry. Second, the government has failed to expel those legal and illegal immigrants who have been convicted of deportable offenses in the United States and who are already in governmental custody. The INS succeeded in deporting 31,000 criminal aliens in 1995,[136] approximately five times as many as it deported in 1989,[137] but this still amounts to just over 10% of the deportable aliens under criminal justice supervision. The federal government is now addressing both of these problems. The Border Patrol has been rapidly expanded[138] and is implementing some new enforcement techniques.[139] The INS, spurred by state and congressional pressures, is finally taking active steps to expedite the removal of criminal aliens; through a combination of new funds and special efforts, the agency hopes to deport 58,000 criminal aliens in 1996.[140] Increased efforts by the

Border Patrol, however, have been unsuccessful in the past.[141] The effectiveness of the new campaign, therefore, remains to be seen. Most recently, the Clinton administration proposed to bar companies that violate the immigration laws from receiving federal contracts.[142]

English Language

On the question of immigrants' acquisition of English-language proficiency, however, Brimelow stands on weaker ground. To be sure, he is correct that English proficiency is a precondition to full participation in the economic, political, and cultural aspects of American society. A recent four-country empirical study confirms the conventional wisdom: Dominant-language fluency is highly correlated with labor market returns, especially in the United States.[143] Dominant-language fluency is also important, even if not essential, to immigrants' full participation in the political process, which, despite some legal requirements for minority-language voting materials, is still conducted largely in English.

Brimelow refers to census data indicating that 47% of the U.S. foreign-born population does not speak English "very well" or "at all" and that 71% of foreign-born Mexicans report not speaking it "very well."[144] English fluency is probably the most important step to, and index of, full integration and participation in American society. It would indeed be a disturbing danger signal, and an augury of further linguistic fragmentation, if newcomers were not learning English at an acceptable rate. In any event, the American public is manifestly unwilling to accept this risk.[145]

Brimelow's figures, however, actually tell us little about the prospects for the linguistic assimilation of post-1965 immigrants, much less about how the new immigrants' progress compares to that of their predecessors. The reason is that those figures fail to distinguish between the first and second generations. Yet Americans hold the first generation to a much lower assimilation standard than that to which they hold succeeding ones.[146]

Brimelow overlooks the historical reality that first-generation immigrants have *always* been slow to acquire good English proficiency. This phenomenon is especially common if they arrived as adults, arrived recently, think that they are likely to return, are refugees rather than economic or family migrants, had little earlier exposure to English, had little schooling, or live in a minority-language enclave.[147] The post-1965 immigrants exhibit some of these variables more than earlier ones did, while exhibiting other variables less. Even as to first-generation immigrants, however, English use appears to be quite high.[148]

It is the English fluency of the *second* generation—those born in the United States or brought here as small children by foreign-born parents—that is critical to immigrants' integration and to society's cultural coherence. A recent analysis by Portes and Schauffler summarizes the historical pattern:

> In the past, almost every first generation's loyalty to their ancestral language has given way to an overwhelming preference for English among their children.

*   *   *

> [I]n no other country have foreign languages been extinguished with such speed. In the past, the typical pattern has been for the first generation to learn enough English to survive economically; the second generation continued to speak the parental tongue at home, but English in school, at work and in public life: by the third generation, the home language shifted to English, which effectively became the mother tongue for subsequent generations.
>
> This pattern has held true for all immigrant groups in the past with the exception of some isolated minorities.[149]

Powerful evidence of the second generation's continued progress in mastering English appears in Portes and Schauffler's recent empirical study of English-language proficiency among eighth- and ninth-grade second-generation students from many Caribbean, Latino, and Asian nationality groups in the Miami area, which has a larger proportion of foreign-born residents than any other American city. According to their data, gathered in 1992, fully 99% of the students reported that they spoke, understood, read, and wrote English "very well" or "well"; only 1% knew little or no English.[150] Time in the United States and ethnic-enclave residency were the most important independent variables; parental education and occupational and class status were unimportant. Moreover, the children's preference for daily communication in English over their parental language was overwhelming—even among recent arrivals, and especially among those living in communities in which the parental language was dominant.[151] The evidence on post-1965 immigrants' English fluency, then, belies Brimelow's animadversions, at least as far as the crucial second generation is concerned.[152]

Illegitimacy

In contrast, his concern about the high illegitimacy rates among some immigrant groups is amply warranted. He approvingly cites Michael Lind to the effect that "Hispanic 'family values' are another immigration enthusiast's myth—Mexican-American out-of-wedlock births, for example, are more than twice the white rate, at 28.9 percent."[153] Other evidence suggests that Mexican, Latin American, and Caribbean immigrant nonmarital fertility rates are much higher than those for immigrants from Asia and Europe.[154]

If such rates accurately indicate the incidence of children growing up in single-parent families, the rates would herald bleak life prospects for those children and hence for the quality of American life more generally. To those who would extenuate high alien illegitimacy on the ground that illegitimacy among black Americans is far higher and illegitimacy among white Americans is rising precipitously. Brimelow offers a compelling rejoinder: "[W]hat's the point of immigrants who are no better than we are?"[155]

Immigrants' cultural impact on American society, however, is a function both of the values that they bring with them to the United States and of those that they *acquire* here as they rub shoulders with Americans. Although Brimelow focuses entirely on the former, the latter are probably more important in the long run. Some evidence on what happens to immigrants' behavior and values as they rub shoulders with Americans is profoundly disturbing. Illegitimacy rates for some immigrant groups—for example, Caribbean immigrants, who tend to live closest to inner-city native minority populations with high illegitimacy rates—seem to *increase* the longer they are in the United States.[156] According to a recent study by demographer Frank Bean,[157] divorce rates, a subject that Brimelow fails to mention, reinforce this pattern. The study indicates that Hispanics, most of whom are Mexicans, exhibit lower divorce rates in their countries of origin than demographically similar U.S. natives do. Divorce rates rise, however, among the second generation here, and by the third generation, divorce rates are equal to those of U.S. natives.[158]

Recent research on second-generation immigrants suggests that these examples may simply illustrate a more general dynamic of cultural transfer. In this pattern, first- and second-generation immigrants, particularly second-generation children, are inducted into American subcultures that transmit some of that subculture's social pathologies to the newcomers. In this way, dysfunctional behavior that is relatively rare in the country of origin may, with exposure to that subculture, become more common among immigrant children to mimic the American norm.

Some sociologists of immigration, notably Alejandro Portes, describe this as a downward or "segmented" assimilation process.[159] Most new immigrants locate in areas that bring their children disproportionately into close contact with native minorities. Many of these natives, who may be the children and grandchildren of immigrants unable to escape from the inner city, suffer from prejudice, disadvantage, joblessness, and a variety of social pathologies that foster a cluster of self-defeating attitudes and behaviors, including negative views of education that contrast sharply with the optimism and socially adaptive strategies that immigrants usually bring with them and seek to transmit to their children. These natives, enraged and defeated by their blocked mobility, can powerfully influence—and contaminate—the values of the new immigrants' children, especially in the shared school environment. Portes starkly depicts the problem:

> The confrontation with the culture of the inner-city places second generation youth in a forced-choice dilemma: to remain loyal to their parents' outlook

and mobility aspirations means to face social ostracism and attacks in schools; to become "American" means often to adopt the cultural outlook of the underclass and thus abandon any upward mobility expectations based on individual achievement.[160]

In this context, Portes says, the best option for today's first generation may be to join dense immigrant communities where their children (the second generation) can "capitaliz[e] on the moral and material resources that only these communities can make available."[161] There the children may gain the breathing space and support they need to develop the skills that can move them securely into the American mainstream.[162] But if they fail to develop these skills, the children may succumb to the adversarial culture that surrounds, and insidiously penetrates, the immigrant enclave and may turn for solace to a negatively reconstituted ethnic culture that widens the differences between the second generation and their native counterparts.[163]

For our sake and the sake of the new immigrants, we must pray that they can enable their children to resist these seductions. If the new immigrants succeed in doing so, their children—like most (though not all) second generations have in the past—will in all likelihood enter the mainstream of American society, and Brimelow will have no cause for complaint. If the children fail, however, their future—and ours—may be even bleaker than Brimelow imagines. Although he does not discuss this possibility or the second-generation problem more generally, his argument clearly implies that the risk of failure is one that America can and should avoid either by eliminating immigration altogether or by limiting it to groups that are already so successful when they arrive that their children are relatively invulnerable to the blandishments of underclass culture.

V. POLITICS

Brimelow believes that the post-1965 immigration is already sapping the strength of the American political system. Some of his fears—for example, irredentist movements by Mexican immigrants to reunite the Southwest with Mexico and Mexican revanchism seeking to manipulate the continuing allegiance of Mexican-Americans[164]—are fatuous and even insulting in their depiction of the latter as pawns whose disloyalty Mexico City could successfully exploit. He warns that neither major party can count on being helped electorally by immigration and that continuing our current pro-immigration policies may spark a voter revolt that could strengthen an already budding third-party movement.[165] The Democrats and Republicans, of course, well understand this: Both the Clinton administration and the Republican majority in Congress are supporting reforms that, while different in some respects, would significantly restrict and restructure legal immigration.[166]

The political specter that haunts him most darkly, however, is balkanization.[167] The fragmentation of nation-states, both real or imagined,[168] into ethnic shards—a process observed in Lebanon, the former Soviet Union and Yugoslavia, many African states, and perhaps even Canada—has become a leitmotif of the post–Cold War world. This unraveling of political authority, often accompanied by massive human rights violations, brutal warfare, economic immiseration, and suppression of political and religious dissent, is an exceedingly dangerous development.

Could it happen here? Brimelow and many other Americans think so, and they believe that post-1965 immigration has increased the odds. Brimelow cites programs or cultural attitudes that create incentives for groups to exaggerate their differences, and he denounces the "New Class," which, he claims, wants to devolve the nation-state into ethnic tribes or to transcend the nation-state in the name of universal human rights.[169]

He mentions five specific policies that are effecting "the deconstruction of the American nation as it existed in 1965."[170] The first, of course, is the policy of immigration itself.[171] But how could the mere fact of immigration, even racially heterogeneous immigration, threaten national unity? After all, most of those who have *chosen* America presumably identify at least as strongly with its ideals and institutions as those who just happened to be born here. Especially in the first generation, many might continue to identify strongly with their country or culture of origin, but that was also true of the Germans, the Irish, the Jews, and even Brimelow's own group, the English.[172] Brimelow does not show that the new immigrants are somehow less patriotic than earlier ones or than native-born Americans are today. (Recall that he himself is a recent immigrant swiftly transformed into a flag-waving American). Indeed, new evidence suggests the contrary.[173]

He mentions four other balkanizing policies: bilingualism, multiculturalism, affirmative action, and a "systematic attack on the value of citizenship."[174] Unfortunately, he fails to provide any clear definitions, useful distinctions, or other analysis for the genuinely thoughtful, open-minded reader. Nevertheless, I believe that he is right to worry that these policies are weakening our coherence as a polity.[175] In seeking to use these policies to discredit immigration, however, Brimelow poses a seductive but perniciously false choice. Immigration may have encouraged the adoption of such policies, but it does not require them; we can reject them and still have immigration. If they are misguided policies, as in some respects they are, we can and should reform or repeal them without holding immigration hostage. We must instead evaluate immigration on its own merits. Brimelow might resist such a separation, of course, arguing that immigration by groups other than white "Anglo-Saxons" assures that the United States will maintain such policies, even if they prove to be perverse. I have more confidence, however, in the responsiveness and corrigibility of the

American policymaking process. Recent reactions against the more extreme versions of these misguided policies are already taking hold, and I believe that my confidence will ultimately prove justified.

Bilingualism

I noted earlier that the crucial second generation of new immigrants seems to be acquiring both competence in and a preference for English, much as their predecessors did.[176] Still, it would be most imprudent to ignore the danger signals raised by evidence suggesting that government-sponsored bilingual education programs have subordinated pedagogical goals, such as improving student performance in school by facilitating rapid English fluency, to the ideological purpose of strengthening the child's identification with her presumed ethnic culture.[177] In my view, ethnic cultural retention is a perfectly appropriate goal when pursued privately by parents and without public aid or interference, but it has no place in the governmental agenda of a society as pluralistic and liberal as ours. Most disturbing of all are recurring indications that this deformation of bilingual education may actually retard the English fluency, the educational progress, and hence the assimilation prospects of already disadvantaged immigrant children.[178] My present point, however, is that we can and should reform bilingual education without abandoning immigration.[179]

Multiculturalism

Multiculturalism can take many forms, with vastly different social consequences. A limited multicultural policy affirms the social value of diverse cultural traditions and practices, protects individuals' and groups' freedom to engage in them, and incorporates diversity values into public school curricula, holidays, and national symbols. A more ambitious multiculturalism goes beyond recognition and respect of such traditions to define, preserve, and reinforce group differences through law.

The limited forms of multiculturalism are essential in a pluralistic democracy in which ethnic pride can be personally enriching, group strengthening, and socially integrative.[180] These forms should not weaken newcomers' ability or desire to achieve minimal levels of social assimilation, or exacerbate inter-group conflict.[181] Limited multiculturalism need not degenerate into the intolerance, humorlessness, hypersensitivity, and bogus essentialism that insists that group membership, rather than individual character and personality, is our most defining and precious attribute.[182]

In criticizing more expansive policies of multiculturalism that deploy the law to entrench and even construct group differences, Brimelow parrots an already palpable and increasingly effective public impatience with their excesses.[183] This impatience is salutary so long as it does not in turn breed its own parochialism and intolerance.[184] In a vibrant democracy like ours, policies such as multiculturalism tend to engender their own repudiation and ultimate reversal precisely because enthusiasts push them beyond any sensible limits.

Quite apart from the growing political opposition to perverse versions of multiculturalism, some purely demographic considerations make rigid racial division of the kind that Brimelow predicts most unlikely. First, the racial data that Brimelow cites rely on self-ascriptions that are themselves remarkably changeable over time and on highly arbitrary racial categories that grow less and less meaningful over time.[185] This phenomenon is particularly true of nonblack groups. Most Hispanics, the largest ethnic minority grouping, identify themselves as white.[186] Furthermore, racial and ethnic boundaries blur as people of different groups marry. Exogamy, already high between some groups in the United States, has been increasing for all. Black-white marriage rates (the smallest exogamy category) more than quintupled between 1968 and 1988, rising from only 1.6% of all marriages involving an African-American to 8.9%. Exogamy between blacks and other groups and between whites and other groups has also been increasing.[187] Exogamy between American-born Asian women and non-Asian men is strikingly high, reaching 41.7% in 1990.[188]

The conventional demographic projections that Brimelow uses do not account for these remarkable (and in my view, highly desirable) trends, which seem likely to continue or even accelerate in the future.[189] Such analyses assume that "exogamy is nonexistent by assuming single ancestry offspring, usually taking the father's racial status as the marker."[190] A recent analysis that does seek to take exogamy (but not the other sources of shifting racial identities) into account shows that doing so can make an enormous difference in racial composition projections.[191] The study simulated future racial composition by factoring differential exogamy rates into the analysis and projecting the effect of those rates over multiple generations. If all mixed ancestry persons were classified as single ancestry and self-identified as white, the number of non-Hispanic whites could be 31 million people (nearly 15%) larger than under the conventional census projection by the year 2040.[192]

My point is not that whites therefore have less to fear from demographic change. Rather, the very *meaning* of the traditional racial categories that structure such fears is rapidly becoming obsolete. Social attitudes and choices are evidently catching up to this demographic reality. Static, rigid, self-perpetuating policies of affirmative action and multiculturalism, premised on these obsolete meanings and categories, are already proving to be reactionary, not liberating.

To return to the larger point: Militant, mindless multiculturalism can be a destructive ideology that one should oppose on a variety of empirical and normative grounds. Immigration, even the post-1965 immigration, does not require such folly. Policies calculated to foster, or at least not impede, immigrants' assimilation to the dominant American culture without suppressing their ethnic ties continue to be the best antidote to balkanizing pressures.[193]

Affirmative Action

Brimelow complains that, as the demographic pincers close, affirmative action will place Alexander, his white son, at even more of a disadvantage than the poor lad labors under today. But like multiculturalism, race-based affirmative action—at least in its strongest, nonprocessual forms—is a policy with a doubtful political future. The Clinton administration, for example, has not fought very hard for it.[194] But if affirmative action is plainly on the defensive in Congress, the courts, and public opinion, it also enjoys the political advantage of any long-standing, institutionalized program.[195]

Brimelow neither defines affirmative action nor engages in a detailed analysis of it, but he is clear that the post-1965 immigration renders it even more problematic than it would otherwise be. I emphatically agree.[196] Until the recent assault on affirmative action in Congress and the Supreme Court, the policy steadily expanded from the protection of blacks in the employment setting to the protection of new groups in new contexts. The new groups include immigrants who happen to possess the protected demographic characteristics, such as race, even though they did not personally suffer the historical discrimination that prompted affirmative action's solicitude for American blacks or descend from those who did. In my view, this policy is impossible to justify, even if one is not the father of a white child, and especially if one is the father of a black one.

This Review is not the place to analyze the merits and demerits of affirmative action in particular domains or in general.[197] Only affirmative action's connections to the post-1965 immigration concern me here. Affirmative action has benefited the post-1965 immigrants in at least two senses. First, affirmative action programs now confer protected status on the millions of immigrants who happen to be members of currently favored groups. Second, the rhetoric of affirmative action was used to legitimate and augment the power of ethnic interest group politics, spawning a program of so-called "diversity" admissions—wholly unwarranted, in my view[198]—that adds 55,000 visas each year for immigrants from countries whose nationals supposedly have been disadvantaged by the 1965 law.[199]

In contrast, the racially diverse post-1965 immigration has been decidedly *bad* for affirmative action. I predict that recent immigration, far from serving as a firm buttress for future affirmative action policies as Brimelow believes, will eventually contribute to their demise. Immigration has undermined race-based affirmative action programs by revealing and then magnifying the moral, political, and empirical weaknesses of some of their under-pinnings.[200] First, immigration enlarges the beneficiary pool to include immigrants who, unlike American blacks, cannot claim that they themselves have suffered historically rooted discrimination here, but who nevertheless are entitled by affirmative action programs to compete with Americans for program benefits. This phenomenon not only dilutes the programs' benefits (such as they are) but also undermines their moral integrity.

Second, the group-based nature of the claims that affirmative action programs endorse inevitably invites attention to the fact that some immigrant groups, including some that arrived after 1965, endured harsh discrimination based on religion, language, class, and race, yet have managed to achieve greater economic and social progress than have many American blacks.[201] This record of achievement is bound to weaken the claim of many traditional civil rights activists that policies such as affirmative action are essential to individual and group progress. Third, immigration renders transparent the illogic, even absurdity, of the racial classifications and methodologies on which the integrity of such programs ultimately rests.[202] Finally, as Brimelow points out, the growth of "new minorities, each with their own grievances and attitudes—quite possibly including a lack of guilt about, and even hostility toward, blacks"—casts an ominous shadow over the long-term political prospects of affirmative action and its capacity to promote interracial reconciliation.[203]

Brimelow unaccountably ignores another realm, voting rights, in which immigration erodes the coherence of affirmative action. Under the Voting Rights Act of 1965,[204] the U.S. Department of Justice, with the acquiescence of Congress and the federal courts, has frequently insisted that legislative district boundaries be drawn to maximize the number of seats safely controlled by representatives of racial minorities. Many legal scholars and political scientists question the wisdom, legality, and representational efficacy of this practice,[205] and some political commentators blame it for many of the devastating Democratic losses in the 1994 congressional elections.[206] The Supreme Court recently subjected the Justice Department's policy to heightened constitutional scrutiny.[207]

The post-1965 immigration renders affirmative action districting of this kind even more problematic. By multiplying the number of residentially concentrated ethnic groups that can assert claims to a limited number of safe legislative seats, immigration has intensified intergroup conflict and made negotiated solutions to these inevitably bitter disputes much more difficult. While Asian-origin voters are unlikely in the near future to achieve the numbers and concentrations needed to qualify for this form of relief, Hispanic-Americans, whose numbers are increasing more rapidly than the black population, have already crossed that threshold in a number of jurisdictions and will soon do so in others.[208]

The flaw in Brimelow's logic should now be clear. Whatever one's evaluation of the merits of race-based affirmative action programs and whatever the bearing of immigration on those programs, they can and should be considered separately from the issue of immigration policy. We can choose to have immigration without choosing the kind of affirmative action that discredits immigration by association.

Citizenship

Part of "the deconstruction of the American nation" that Brimelow laments results from a "[s]ystematic attack on the value of citizenship, by making it easier for aliens to vote, receive government subsidies, etc."[209] The content of "etc." appears in his call, *inter alia,* for fundamental changes in our approach to citizenship. They include a new Americanization campaign modeled on the programs of the first two decades of this century, an English-language requirement for new immigrants and stricter enforcement of the existing English requirement for naturalized citizens, constitutional amendments eliminating birthright citizenship for the native-born children of illegal aliens and prescribing English as our official language, and possibly the lengthening of the residency period for naturalization to as long as the fourteen years required under the Alien and Sedition Act of 1798 and repealed in 1801.[210]

Brimelow presents these ideas in a manner that treats them more as rallying points and political slogans than as serious, thoughtful proposals for change. He shows no interest in analyzing the evidence bearing on them, the substantial objections that might be made to them, or the features that might be necessary to make them politically palatable or practically implementable. He simply presents items on his laundry list.

Brimelow's *ipse dixits* will therefore be of little value to policymakers. Nevertheless, some of the items on his list do deserve serious consideration; indeed, some are already receiving it. An example is the issue of birthright citizenship for illegal alien children, which is now under active discussion in Congress.[211] Political scientist Rogers Smith and I coauthored a book analyzing this very question. We argued that the Citizenship Clause of the Fourteenth Amendment,[212] properly interpreted, permits Congress to regulate or even eliminate birthright citizenship for such children if it wishes.[213] We noted that whether Congress *should* prospectively eliminate birthright citizenship, and, if so, *how* to go about it, entail genuinely difficult normative, empirical, and policy questions.[214] We expressed a particular concern (shared by our critics[215]) that such a policy change risks creating a destitute, highly vulnerable, more or less permanent caste of pariah children who, due to ineffective INS border and interior enforcement, might remain in that condition for the rest of their lives in the United States.[216] We proposed strategies to avert this grim possibility, including an amnesty for many then-illegal aliens.[217] Nevertheless, this concern remains deeply troubling, especially today when the number of illegal alien residents in the United States may exceed four million and a new amnesty is politically inconceivable. The ever-insouciant Brimelow, however, appears not to have even considered the extremely difficult problems that this situation creates.

His proposal for an "official English" amendment is an even more telling example of his aversion to analysis. Because a similar policy has already been adopted in twenty-two states,[218] some evidence about how it actually works already exists. Brimelow fails to cite this evidence, which indicates that the policy has had no practical effect—except, perhaps, to convince many Hispanic-Americans, who already have overwhelming incentives to acquire English fluency, that they are unwelcome in their new country.[219]

A new "Americanization" program—if designed to foster immigrants' social and linguistic integration without the paternalism, cultural intolerance, and outright racism that tainted many of the early twentieth century campaigns[220]—might well be desirable. At a minimum, such an effort should significantly augment the woefully inadequate public resources now available for teaching English to adult immigrants.[221] The government should also abandon its traditional passivity with respect to naturalization and instead emphasize its benefits to immigrants.[222] Again, however, Brimelow does not trouble to explore seriously the programmatic content of an Americanization policy.[223]

In truth, his discussion of citizenship is really a diversionary tactic. His real agenda is something he portentously calls "the National Question."[224] He wishes to affirm his belief in a distinctive American nation-state in contrast to the one-worlders who, out of misguided guilt or bland cosmopolitanism, would dismantle our borders and throw open our doors to all comers—the more the merrier, the poorer the better.

This target, of course, is a straw man. There are indeed a smattering of academics, ethnic advocates, immigration lawyers, and militant multiculturalists who, if judged by their rhetoric, seem to fit this description.[225] But, as Brimelow surely knows, they are outliers—no more representative of immigration enthusiasts than Brimelow is of restrictionists. (I know of no restrictionist in Congress, for example, who proposes to go to zero immigration, as Brimelow seems to do.[226]) Americans vigorously disagree about precisely what Americanism consists of. They always have;[227] presumably they always will. Our core political identity is more elusive than that of, say, Japan, Germany, or Sweden—nation-states whose ethnic solidarities have powerfully shaped their self-understandings.[228] But while Americans struggle over the contemporary meaning of Americanism,[229] only a handful would deny that the United States is a distinctive polity that must protect its national sovereignty, nourish its culture, choose among its potential immigrants, and thus turn many away from its shores.

CONCLUSION

Brimelow claims that American society has fallen into crisis since the new immigrants arrived and that they are responsible for its decline. I have sought to demonstrate that most of his factual claims are either wrong or fail to justify his radical policy prescriptions. For those whom I have not yet convinced, I wish to use this concluding section to test his overarching claim—that the post-1965 immigration flow has been an unequivocal plague on American society. I propose to do so by offering a (necessarily incomplete) answer to the following question: How does the state of American society today compare to its state in 1965, when the new immigrants began coming and when the Fall (according to Brimelow) therefore began? Briefly stated, my answer is that we are in most important respects a far better society than we were before these immigrants arrived. Their contribution to this progress is striking in the growth of the economy, the expansion of civil rights and social tolerance, and the revitalization of many urban neighborhoods. Moreover, these immigrants bear little blame for the great exception to this progress: the increase in the social pathology afflicting some inner-city subcultures.[230] Just as Brimelow cannot prove that the post-1965 immigrants *caused* certain social conditions in America to be worse than they would otherwise have been, it would be impossible for me to show how much of our post-1965 progress they *caused*. The evidence strongly suggests, however, that the post-1965 immigrants contributed to it.

Brimelow's answer to the question, of course, is very different. To him, the America of 1965 was an Edenic paradise compared to today[231]—relatively crime-free, economically prosperous, normatively coherent, politically stable, linguistically unified, demographically stable, and ecologically sustainable. Most important, it was overwhelmingly white. By 1995, the newcomers had changed all that, bringing us a society marked by drugs, violent crime, economic decline, debased family life, a babel of languages, clashing value systems, racial conflict, political divisions, a population bomb, a crowded, degraded environment—and swarthy complexions. No wonder Brimelow anguishes about America's present and about his son Alexander's future![232]

Brimelow's depressing, hand-wringing account of today's America, although common enough among conservatives and liberals alike, is profoundly distorted. It is true that the new immigration coincided with some extremely negative developments in American life. The most important of these is the erosion of family structure, which has blighted the lives of an immense number of children born out of wedlock and raised in single- or no-parent households[233] by caretakers who depend on public assistance and who are often only children themselves. Most of what is most pernicious about American society today—its high levels of street crime, drug

use, racial fears, domestic violence, welfare dependency, public health men-
aces such as AIDS, educational failure, and high unemployment among
low-skill youth—derives from this fundamental pathology of family structure. There is no gainsaying its deeply corrosive effects on American life.

It is also true, however, that little of this pathology can be attributed to the
new immigrants. To be sure, many of them commit drug-related crimes;
some sub-groups, mainly Asian refugees, have relatively high welfare rates;
and some others, notably Mexican-Americans, have high illegitimacy rates.
These behaviors are indeed troubling, as is the fact that they seem to increase
the more that the new immigrants interact with Americans.[234] Still, these
grim patterns must be kept in perspective: Relatively few of the new immigrants commit crimes, and the vast majority of these are drug-related; we are
not *supposed* to select refugees for their skills; and the groups with high illegitimacy rates are comprised disproportionately of illegal aliens, many of
whom can be excluded in the future by better border control policies.

What about the other side of the ledger, which Brimelow assiduously ignores? If the post-1965 immigrants have contributed to some of America's
failures, have they not also contributed to some of our post-1965 successes? If so, do not these successes contradict Brimelow's alarums about
the state of the American polity?

The truth is that the last three decades have witnessed some remarkable
advances in American life. While causality in such matters is extremely
complex and elusive, the new immigrants can claim some credit for many
of these advances. Most plausibly, they have contributed to our continued
if slow economic growth,[235] the dramatic rise in the public's tolerance for
minorities (including dark-skinned aliens) and its support for racial integration and equality,[236] the renaissance in many previously declining urban
neighborhoods,[237] and the diversification and enrichment of many aspects
of American culture. Beyond these advances, however, are social improvements that bespeak a robust polity, one that contradicts Brimelow's vision
of political dissolution and decline attributable to the new immigrants.[238] I
shall mention only three areas of improvement: the environment, politics,
and the quality of life.

Environment

Brimelow blames the new immigrants for the deterioration of the American
environment.[239] In fact, however, the quality of the American environment
today is vastly superior to its state in 1965, before these immigrants arrived. Whether the concern is air pollution (indoor or outdoor), water quality, deforestation, pesticides, and other chemical risks, radiation hazards,
food quality, land preservation, historic preservation, wetlands, farmland,
energy efficiency, toxic waste, depletion of raw materials, lead paint, acid

rain, or many other conditions, the levels of risk and environmental degra-
dation today are lower, often much lower, than they were in 1965.[240] These
improvements rank as one of the greatest triumphs of private mobilization
and public policy in our history. Insofar as immigrants contributed to the
economic growth that made these policies fiscally and hence politically sustainable, they helped to improve the environment. At the very least, they
did not prevent such gains from being realized.

Politics

In 1965, blacks and other disadvantaged minorities played at best a marginal role in the American political system. For almost a century, they had
been routinely denied the vote guaranteed to them by the Fifteenth Amendment, and there were relatively few racial minority officeholders. There
were also few female officeholders, although women had received the franchise almost a half-century earlier. Three decades later, blacks, Asians, Hispanics, women, the disabled, elderly, gays and lesbians, and other minorities are full participants in the political system at all levels of government.
Their organizations have led largely successful struggles to enact a plethora
of laws—the Voting Rights Act of 1965,[241] the Age Discrimination in Employment Act of 1967,[242] the Age Discrimination Act of 1975,[243] the Education of the Handicapped Act of 1975,[244] the Americans with Disabilities
Act of 1990,[245] the Civil Rights Act of 1991,[246] and many others—designed
to prevent discrimination and otherwise advance their group interests.

As a result of these developments, the American political system today is
far more participatory and responsive to minority interests than it was in
1965.[247] If the level of party discipline in both major parties in Congress is
any measure of coherence, American politics today is also more coherent
and less fragmented than it has been for decades.[248] This partisanship reflects and reinforces a growing ideological polarization between the parties
that tends to sharpen policy issues, widen voters' choices, and increase accountability. The bellicosity of partisan politics today is part of the price
that we pay for these virtues, and it is well worth it.

Taken together, these changes have transformed the American state into
a more robust democracy than ever before. They have helped to shape a
polity that is far more just and responsive to far more people than it was
before the new immigrants came.

Quality of Life

I have already noted the enormous economic growth that has occurred
since 1965, growth that translates into higher disposable income and living
standards for virtually all Americans.[249] It is important to emphasize that

even the millions still mired in poverty—a group that, according to the best, consumption-based estimates, is less than half the percentage of the population that it was in 1961—enjoy an improved standard of living.[250] With the enactment and extraordinary expansion of the Food Stamp program, hunger as traditionally understood has been essentially eliminated from American life.[251] The proportion of housing units that are substandard declined from 16% in 1960 and 8.4% in 1970 to practically zero today.[252] Life expectancy for those born in 1992 was nearly five years longer than for those born in 1970.[253] Both the quantity and quality of medical care have improved enormously since 1965, and the rapid growth of the Medicare and Medicaid programs has enabled low-income people to share in those gains. Infant mortality rates dropped steadily during the post-1965 period; they fell by more than half between 1970 and 1991.[254] The percentage of Americans who completed four or more years of college nearly tripled between 1960 and 1993.[255] The rising quality of many public goods, such as recreational facilities, highways, low-cost entertainment, and (as noted above) the environment, also increased the value of Americans' consumption, albeit in ways not captured by the national income accounts.[256] Finally, the risk of a large-scale war claiming American lives and treasure—a tragic reality in 1965—has diminished almost to the vanishing point today.

These gains in the quality of life since 1965 are remarkable by any standard. All things considered, they may even exceed the gains during the pre-1973 period, when the American economy, as conventionally measured, was expanding at a faster rate. Even when set against the alarming increase in family dissolution and its dire consequences, these gains remain impressive. This dissolution, moreover, principally affects those Americans condemned to live in or in close proximity to the underclass, a group that still constitutes a relatively small share (approximately one to two percent) of the population. The small size of the share, while no consolation to those who comprise it or must reside near its members, nevertheless puts even this great failure into a somewhat broader, more hopeful perspective.

The quality-of-life gains since 1965 for the vast majority of Americans, then, have been enormous, perhaps unparalleled. It is impossible to know, of course, whether those gains would have been even larger or more widespread had we admitted fewer or different immigrants during this period.[257] What we do know is that the post-1965 immigrants, whom Brimelow condemns as afflictions and parasites, did join American society, and that we are now a more just, diverse, and prosperous society today than we were then. We can also be certain that many of the values that immigrants, the new as well as the old, brought with them will be essential to our continued vigor and progress. Today and tomorrow, even more than yesterday, America desperately needs what so many immigrants possess—optimism and energy, orientation to the future, faith in education as the ladder upward, hunger for their own and their children's success, and devotion to a dynamic, hopeful vision of America that has lost focus for many native-born citizens.

We must reform immigration policy to meet our changing needs. In particular, policy should assure that a larger share of the immigration flow consists of individuals who are most likely to succeed in the American economy of the twenty-first century. But it will take much, much more than this book to convince me that we should eliminate or radically reduce that flow. Immigration, including the post-1965 wave, has served America well. If properly regulated, there is every reason to expect that it will continue to do so.

Notes

Chapter 1

1. Most of the numbers that follow in this section are drawn from US Department of Justice (1997).

2. In principle, none of the illegals arriving after 1981 should have been eligible for the amnesty program, which established a cut-off arrival date of 1 January 1982.

3. FAIR's former executive director Roger Conner now heads a group (the American Alliance for Rights and Responsibilities) that advocates so-called communitarian norms, especially the promotion of public safety and public values in local public spaces. Here, too, the board members are decidedly mainstream in status and largely liberal in their politics.

4. Employing an unusual methodology, they elicited the respondents' answers to standard survey questions and then followed up with additional questions in a process designed to resemble, albeit crudely, the give-and-take of ordinary conversation about public issues. Sniderman and Piazza found that the respondents' views on race-oriented issues differed considerably from issue to issue. That is, attitudes about affirmative action were not the same as attitudes about fair-housing policies or about government spending on behalf of minorities. For my purposes, the more interesting finding is that respondents' initial views on issues (except for affirmative action) changed when those views were even weakly challenged or met with additional information. The authors summarized this finding as follows: "Finally, and perhaps most importantly, the positions that whites take on issues of race are pliable to a degree never suspected. Substantial numbers—on some issues as many as four in every ten—can be talked out of the positions they have taken by relatively weak counter-arguments, affirmative action not surprisingly being a major exception," (Sniderman Piazza: 13–14).
A somewhat analogous positional shift appears in a recent *New York Times*/CBS opinion poll on welfare reform. When the respondents were asked about their attitudes toward government "spending on welfare," 48 percent favored cuts, and only 13 percent favored increases. But when they were asked about "spending on programs for poor children," 47 percent favored increases, and only 9 percent favored cuts (DeParle).

5. Indeed, the word *ambivalent* appears in the title of a comprehensive survey of public attitudes toward immigration (Simon and Alexander) and in the subtitle of a recent study of Mexican immigrants' political identities in the United States (Skerry).

6. Some of these attitudinal distinctions are arguably inconsistent. Although respondents believe that immigrants take jobs away from Americans, for example, they also believe that immigrants take jobs that Americans do not want and that immigrants threaten neither their own jobs nor the jobs of people whom they know (Simon and Alexander).

7. Even more interesting, roughly similar patterns have been found from polling over time in Canada, Australia, Britain, and France. The survey data discussed in this and the preceding paragraph appear in Simon.

8. Similar questions can be raised about the enactment of the Immigration Reform and Control Act of 1986, which was expansionist on balance although it contained important con-

trol measures, notably employer sanctions. For a discussion of both the 1986 and 1990 acts and the role of ideas in immigration politics, see Schuck (1992).

9. This point is not necessarily contradicted by California's adoption of Proposition 187, for the measure was directed not at legal immigrants but at illegal ones, about whom political attitudes are considerable different (Schuck, 1995). The political significance of Proposition 187 is discussed in Chapter 6.

Chapter 2

1. The early immigration cases in the Supreme Court adopted this premise unequivocally. See, e.g., Fong Yue Ting v. United States, 149 U.S. 698, 711 (1893) ("The United States are a sovereign and independent nation, and are vested by the Constitution with the entire control of international relations, and with all the powers of government necessary to maintain that control and to make it effective."); Nishimura Ekiu v. United States, 142 U.S. 651, 659 (1892) ("It is an accepted maxim of international law, that every sovereign nation has the power, as inherent in sovereignty, and essential to self-preservation, to forbid the entrance of foreigners within its dominions, or to admit them only in such cases and upon such conditions as it may see fit to prescribe.") (citation omitted).

2. Cf. M. Walzer, Spheres of Justice 32 (1983) (pointing out that in Latin and some other ancient languages, strangers and enemies were designated by a single word).

3. See, e.g., Dames & Moore v. Regan, 453 U.S. 654 (1981).

4. Although undocumented aliens may sue in the courts and enjoy certain substantive rights, see Plyler v. Doe, 457 U.S. 202 (1982), many of their rights are unenforceable by them as a practical matter. See generally, e.g., Developments in the Law—Immigration Policy and the Rights of Aliens, 96 Harv. L. Rev. 1286, 1437 (1983) [hereinafter cited as Developments].

5. The classic study is J. Higham, Strangers in the Land: Patterns of American Nativism, 1860–1925 (1955).

6. L. Hartz, The Liberal Tradition in America 3–14 (1955).

7. See id. In practice, of course, a considerable portion even of American society—most notably slaves and, to some degree, females—were denied this liberty. See infra notes 27–31 and accompanying text.

8. See infra notes 25–32 and accompanying text.

9. See generally, J. Higham, supra note 5.

10. See infra notes 93–108, 130–48 and accompanying text.

11. Brown v. Board of Educ., 347 U.S. 483 (1954), may be viewed as initiating the changes that flowered during the 1960's.

12. See, e.g., L. Tribe, American Constitutional Law 277–84 (1978); Lopez, Undocumented Mexican Migration: In Search of a Just Immigration Law and Policy, 28 UCLA L. Rev. 615 (1981); Rosberg, The Protection of Aliens from Discriminatory Treatment by the National Government, 1977 Sup. Ct. Rev. 275; Developments, supra note 4. Evidence that these norms have taken root in other areas of the law is provided, for example, by the expanded scope of constitutional equal protection, the enactment of civil rights statutes protecting minorities and women, and the general broadening of tort liability. From another perspective, of course, these developments may be—and have been—viewed as moves away from universal norms toward a regime of group rights. See generally G. Garson, Group Theories of Politics ch. 2 (1978).

13. "Most of our public law—both substantive and procedural—grows quite directly out of private law and corresponding efforts to treat the government as a defendant in a private lawsuit." Sunstein, Judicial Relief and Public Tort Law (Book Review), 92 Yale L.J. 749, 758 (1983) (reviewing P. Schuck, Suing Government: Citizen Remedies for Official Wrongs (1983)). Sunstein goes on to assert that "that model is breaking down," id., a proposition with which I agree.

14. Thus, between the 1870s and the second decade of this century, Northern and Western Europe's share of the immigrant population declined from 73.6% to 17.4%. See M. Bennett, American Immigration Policies: A History 31 (1963).

15. Id. at 31–34, 36–39.

16. See W. Lafeber, The New Empire (1963); A. Schlesinger, The Age of Roosevelt: The Crisis of the Old Order 17–26 (1957).

17. F. Harper & F. James, The Law of Torts 1435–40 (1956).

18. See P. Schuck, Suing Government: Citizen Remedies for Official Wrongs 36–39 (1983).

19. For an explanation of the limited concept of duty in tort law during that period, see F. Harper & F. James, supra note 17, at 1430–32; see also Ames, Law and Morals, 22 Harv. L. Rev. 97, 103–05 (1908).

20. Nishimura Ekiu v. United States, 142 U.S. 651, 659 (1892) (citation omitted).

21. F. Harper & F. James, supra note 17, at 1447–59.

22. See 2 R. Phillimore, Commentaries Upon International Law 3–7 (3d ed. 1882); E. de Vattel, The Law of Nations 174–78 (1797).

23. See generally M. Gordon, Assimilation in American Life chs. 4, 5 (1964).

24. See generally J. Kettner, The Development of American Citizenship, 1608–1870 (1978) (discussing citizenship issues).

25. At least 48 million immigrants reached the United States between 1821 and 1978. See Select Comm'n on Immigration and Refugee Policy, U.S. Immigration Policy and the National Interest 96 (1981) [hereinafter cited as SCIRP Staff Report].

26. See J. Kettner, supra note 24, ch. 4. Although there was some local opposition to the naturalization of Jews, a 1740 English statute allowed Jews and other groups to obtain the rights of British subjects. Id. at 116–17.

27. Id. at 236. The preconditions for naturalization for white persons generally have remained easy to satisfy throughout our history, with only a few exceptions. See E. Hutchinson, Legislative History of American Immigration Policy, 1798–1965, at 12–16 (1981) (the Alien and Sedition Act interlude); J. Kettner, supra note 24, at 245–46 (requirement to renounce aristocratic titles); SCIRP Staff Report, supra note 25, at 88 (literacy test, first imposed during World War I). In 1790, the first federal naturalization act conferred citizenship only on a "free white person." J. Kettner, supra note 24, at 236. In 1870, Congress extended the naturalization laws to "aliens of African nativity and to persons of African descent." E. Hutchinson, supra, at 58.

28. This principle long antedated the fourteenth amendment of the Constitution, see J. Kettner, supra note 24, at 287–88, but was confirmed by both the amendment and the Civil Rights Act of 1866, ch. 31, 14 Stat. 27. See United States v. Wong Kim Ark, 169 U.S. 649 (1898). It does not embrace certain categories of individuals born here but not subject to United States jurisdiction: diplomats, alien enemies in hostile occupation, persons born on foreign ships in American waters, and Indians owing direct allegiance to tribes. Id. at 693; see also J. Kettner, supra note 24, at 287–333.

29. 8 U.S.C. § 1401(c) (1982). But see Rogers v. Bellei, 401 U.S. 815 (1971) (fourteenth amendment citizenship clause does not apply to individuals born abroad to American citizens). The statute at issue in Bellei imposed a requirement that a foreign-born person must reside in the United States for five years before reaching an age of twenty-eight years, in order to claim citizenship. This restriction has now been deleted by amendment. See Act of Oct. 10, 1978, Pub. L. No. 95–432, 92 Stat. 1046.

30. Osborn v. Bank of the United States, 22 U.S. (9 Wheat.) 738, 827 (1824) (dictum); J. Kettner, supra note 24, at 287 (sole exception being eligibility for Presidency).

31. But note the long history of deprivation of black voting rights and of continuing permissibility of property requirements, discussed in the legislative history of the Voting Rights Act of 1965, 42 U.S.C. §§ 1971, 1973–1973p (1976). See H. Rep. No. 439, 89th Cong., 1st Sess. 8–13 (1965), reprinted in 1965 U.S. Code Cong. & Ad. News 2437, 2439–44.

32. See, e.g., Plyler v. Doe, 457 U.S. 202, 210 (1982); Yick Wo v. Hopkins, 118 U.S. 356, 369 (1886). Even during the classical period, aliens did not necessarily relinquish those rights when, after leaving the jurisdiction of the United States, they attempted to reenter. See, e.g., Kwong Hai Chew v. Colding, 344 U.S. 590, 596 n.5 (1953) (quoting Bridges v. Wixon, 326 U.S. 135, 161 (1945)).

33. A. Bickel, The Morality of Consent 54 (1975). Rogers Smith has noted that the very universality of liberalism's moral principles, along with its couching of them in terms of personal human liberties, makes it difficult for liberal theory to give nationality and nationalism any central place in its notions of personal identity and political purpose. The craving for national self-determination may be seen by liberals as a natural part of human psychology, but one's particular nationality is viewed as a contingent characteristic, of secondary moral importance.

R. Smith, The Dilemmas of American Citizenship 1–2 (unpublished manuscript on file with author) (citing I. Berlin, Nationalism, *in* Against the Current 338–41 (1980)) (footnotes omitted).

34. A. Bickel, supra note 33, at 36. Bickel also failed to consider the possibility that under contemporary conditions, perpetuating a liberal policy of easy access to citizenship and legal rights may require a less liberal, more restrictive immigration policy. See infra notes 465–76 and accompanying text.

35. A. Bickel, supra note 33, at 35.

36. Sugarman v. Dougall, 413 U.S. 634, 651–52 (1973) (Rehnquist, J., dissenting).

37. U.S. Const. art. II, § 1, cl. 5.

38. U.S. Const. art. III, § 2, cl. 1.

39. U.S. Const. amends. XIV, § 2, XV, § 1.

40. See J. Kettner, supra note 24, ch. 7.

41. See Korematsu v. United States, 323 U.S. 214 (1944); see also Report of the Commission on Wartime Relocation and Internment of Civilians, Personal Justice Denied (1982).

42. R. Smith, "One United People": Discriminatory Citizenship Laws and the American Quest for Community, 1800–1937, at 22–23 (unpublished manuscript on file with author).

43. Scott v. Sandford, 60 U.S. (19 How.) 393 (1856).

44. U.S. Const. amend. XIV; Civil Rights Act of 1866, ch. 31, 14 Stat. 27; see also J. Kettner, supra note 24, at 300–33. Categorical racial exclusions from naturalized citizenship continued, however. In 1922, for example, a unanimous Supreme Court construed a 1906 statute limiting naturalization to "free white persons" and aliens of African nativity or descent, to exclude a Japanese alien. Ozawa v. United States, 260 U.S. 178 (1922).

45. 42 U.S.C. § 1973 (1976).

46. James Kettner observes: "The peculiar 'domestic dependent nation' status of the tribes thus ultimately served the purposes of those who wished to maintain control over Indians without fully incorporating them into the community of citizens. Because the tribes were 'domestic' and 'dependent,' white laws could be extended over them. Yet such extension did not constitute the kind of protection that elicited allegiance and sustained citizenship as long as political and judicial authorities considered the tribes, in some sense, 'nations' whose members were aliens. The logic of combining dependency and wardship with the idea of a separate allegiance and nationality was perhaps inconsistent; but it sufficed to exclude the Native Americans from the status and the privileges of American citizenship." J. Kettner, supra note 24, at 299–300.

47. 182 U.S. 244 (1901).

48. Id. at 279–80.

49. See Cabranes, Citizenship and the American Empire, 127 U. Pa. L. Rev. 391, 486 n.460 (1978) (giving statutory citations).

50. 258 U.S. 298 (1922).

51. Id. at 308. Absent such a move, of course, Puerto Ricans cannot vote. *Balzac* seems fully consistent with Congress's intention in enacting statutory citizenship for Puerto Ricans. See Cabranes, supra note 49, at 428–33.

52. Another category of American citizens is sometimes excluded not simply from enjoying the rights normally associated with that status but even from the right to reside in the United States. This category includes citizen children of deportable alien parents. See, e.g., INS v. Jong Ha Wang, 450 U.S. 139 (1981) (per curiam).

53. Yick Wo v. Hopkins, 118 U.S. 356, 368–69 (1886) (Chinese laborers entitled to protection against racial discrimination by municipal authorities in administration of ordinance.).

54. The Japanese Immigrant Case, 189 U.S. 86, 100–01 (1903) (construing a statute to require that such an alien at least be afforded a rudimentary administrative hearing before being deprived of liberty).

55. See, e.g., Exec. Order No. 11, 935, 5 C.F.R. § 7.4 (1983) (upheld in Mow Sun Wong v. Campbell, 626 F.2d 739 (9th Cir. 1980), cert. denied, 450 U.S. 959 (1981)).

56. See, e.g., Heim v. McCall, 239 U.S. 175 (1915).

57. Oyama v. California, 332 U.S. 633 (1948).

58. See, e.g., Developments, supra note 4, at 1400–33.

59. See Ng Fung Ho v. White, 259 U.S. 276, 281–85 (1922); The Japanese Immigrant Case, 189 U.S. 86, 101 (1903).

60. See generally J. Higham, supra note 5; Hofstadter, The Pseudo-Conservative Revolt, *in* The Radical Right 63–80 (D. Bell ed. 1963). The Founding Fathers were certainly not exempt. In 1753, for example, Benjamin Franklin warned against assimilating the Germans in Pennsylvania: "Those who came hither are generally the most stupid of their own nation, and as ignorance is often attended with great credulity, when knavery would mislead it, and with suspicion when honesty would set it right; and, few of the English understand the German language, and so cannot address them either from the press or pulpit, it is almost impossible to remove any prejudices they may entertain. Not being used to liberty, they know not how to make modest use of it." Vialet, A Brief History of U.S. Immigration Policy 6 (Library of Congress 1980).

61. Laws to prohibit the admission of poor and indigent immigrants were passed by Massachusetts colony as early as 1645 and 1655. E. Hutchinson, supra note 27, at 390. The Immigration Act of 1875, ch. 141, 18 Stat. 477, prohibited the importation of prostitutes.

62. Immigration Act of 1917, ch. 29, § 3, 39 Stat. 874, 877.

63. Immigration Act of 1924, ch. 190, § 11, 43 Stat. 153, 159–60; Immigration Act of 1921, ch. 8, § 2, 42 Stat. 5, 5–6.

64. Immigration and Nationality Act of 1952, ch. 477, § 212(a)(28), 66 Stat. 163, 184–86 (codified as amended at 8 U.S.C. § 1182(a)(28)(1982)); id. § 311, 66 Stat. 239 (codified as amended at 8 U.S.C. § 1422 (1982)).

65. For a summary of the statutory history, see E. Hutchinson, supra note 27, at 366–79. There were, of course, some blanket admissions, especially after World War II. These included the Displaced Persons Act of 1948, ch. 647, 62 Stat. 1009, and a number of special refugee programs. For discussions of the latter, see Congressional Research Service, U.S. Immigration Law and Policy: 1952–1979, at 15–24, 46–48, 58–59, 76–78 (1979).

66. Immigration and Nationality Act of 1978, Pub. L. No. 95–412, § 1, 92 Stat. 907 (amending Immigration and Nationality Act of 1952, § 201(a)) (codified as amended at 8 U.S.C. § 1151 (1982).

67. U.S. Const. amends. V, XIV.

68. E.g., Kwong Hai Chew v. Colding, 344 U.S. 590 (1953); Bridges v. Wixon, 326 U.S. 135 (1945).

69. U.S. Const. amend. XIV, § 2.

70. 130 U.S. 581 (1889).

71. Id. at 606.

72. Nishimura Ekiu v. United States, 142 U.S. 651, 660 (1892).

73. See Johnson v. Robison, 415 U.S. 361, 373–74 (1974) (an administrative decision is judicially reviewable despite a statutory no-review provision where the statutory language and

legislative history do not provide "the 'clear and convincing' evidence of congressional intent required by this Court before a statute will be construed to restrict access to judicial review") (citing Abbott Laboratories v. Gardner, 387 U.S. 136, 141 (1967)).

74. Consider this utterance in a 1977 decision by the Court: "At the outset, it is important to underscore the limited scope of judicial inquiry into immigration legislation. This Court has repeatedly emphasized that 'over no conceivable subject is the legislative power of Congress more complete than it is over' the admission of aliens. Our cases 'have long recognized the power to expel or exclude aliens as a fundamental sovereign attribute exercised by the Government's political departments largely immune from judicial control. Our recent decisions have not departed from this long-established rule.'" Fiallo v. Bell, 430 U.S. 787, 792 (1977) (citing *The Chinese Exclusion Case,* 130 U.S. 581 (1889)) (citations omitted). The opinion, after quoting Justice Frankfurter's observation in Galvan v. Press, 347 U.S. 522 (1954), that in support of Congress's plenary power over aliens, "there is not merely 'a page of history'... but a whole volume," went on to state that the Court would not "reconsider this line of cases." 430 U.S. at 793 n.4.

75. *Fiallo,* 430 U.S. at 793.

76. Consular decisions to deny visas, for example, are highly discretionary yet wholly immune from judicial review. See, e.g., Pena v. Kissinger, 409 F. Supp. 1182 (S.D.N.Y. 1976). The State Department, however, has created a system of administrative review. See 22 C.F.R. § 42.130 (1983); Note, Consular Discretion in the Immigrant Visa-Issuing Process, 16 San Diego L. Rev. 87, 101 (1978).

As recently as 1981, the Court upheld the refusal of the Attorney General to suspend the deportation of alien parents and their two children, both of whom happened to be American citizens. In doing so, it emphasized that the immigration authorities were entitled to construe the statutory standard for suspension narrowly if they wished, and criticized the court of appeals for encroaching on their discretion. INS v. Jong Ha Wang, 450 U.S. 139 (1981) (per curiam).

Even more recently, the Court refused to estop the INS from deporting an alien after having failed for 18 months to act upon an application for a visa, during which time his eligibility for the visa had evaporated. "Enforcing the immigration laws, and the conditions for residency in this country is becoming more difficult," the Court noted, and "[a]ppropriate deference must be accorded" to the INS as "the agency primarily charged by Congress to implement the public policy underlying these laws." INS v. Miranda, 103 S. Ct. 281, 284 (1982).

77. In The Japanese Immigrant Case, 189 U.S. 86 (1903), for example, the Court construed the immigration statute to require a hearing before deportation. See also Kwong Hai Chew v. Colding, 344 U.S. 590 (1953); Bridges v. Wixon, 326 U.S. 135 (1945).

78. At least one commentator speaks of "a striking discontinuity between discourse and doctrine" in the exclusion area. Developments, supra note 4, at 1314. For reasons discussed infra notes 86–92 and accompanying text, I find the discontinuity during the classical period to have been slight, but hardly striking. Another commentator has pointed out that this deference has not taken the form, common in "political questions" cases, of declining to reach the merits. "The deference shown legislative and executive action is based on a finding that such action was within their constitutional powers, not on a determination that the subject matter was beyond judicial competence." Note, Constitutional Limits on the Power to Exclude Aliens, 82 Colum L. Rev. 957, 969 n.86 (1982).

79. See, e.g., In re Gault, 387 U.S. 1 (1967) (juveniles); Miranda v. Arizona, 384 U.S. 436 (1966) (criminal suspects); Brown v. Board of Educ., 347 U.S. 483 (1954) (blacks).

80. See, e.g., Boutilier v. INS, 387 U.S. 118 (1967) (upholding Congress's power to exclude homosexual aliens); Abel v. United States, 362 U.S. 217 (1960) (use of INS warrant to facilitate FBI search of suspected spy's hotel room does not violate fourth amendment if agencies cooperated in "good faith"). In Flemming v. Nestor, 363 U.S. 603 (1960), the Court, though sharply divided, upheld a statute that denied social security retirement benefits to an alien who

had legally resided in the United States for 43 years, benefits to which he had contributed for two decades. The statute denied these benefits because he had been deported for being a Communist Party member during the 1930's—a time when mere membership was not illegal. Id. at 621 (Black, J., dissenting).

It seems highly doubtful that the Court would have upheld such a retroactive confiscation for Party membership had it been imposed upon a citizen rather than an alien. Although the Warren Court did not decide such a case itself, the lower federal courts and some state courts of that era repudiated somewhat analogous—and arguably less objectionable—efforts to deprive subversives of certain program benefits. See, e.g., Wellman v. Whittier, 259 F.2d 163 (D.C. Cir. 1958) (finding no express congressional intent to require Communist Party members to forfeit veterans benefits); Lawson v. Housing Auth., 270 Wis. 269, 70 N.W.2d 605, cert. denied, 350 U.S. 882 (1955) (public housing).

81. See, e.g., J. Crewdson, The Tarnished Door: The New Immigrants and the Transformation of America 113–41 (1983); Developments, supra note 4, at 1364–66.

82. Congress, for example, often passes private-bill legislation to provide immigration benefits for particular named aliens. See, e.g., P. Schuck, The Judiciary Committees 255–65 (1975).

83. See, e.g., Immigration and Nationality Act of 1952, § 212, 8 U.S.C. § 1182 (1982); El-Werfalli v. Smith, 547 F. Supp. 152 (S.D.N.Y. 1982) (exclusion of alien on reentry on basis of confidential information); cf. Immigration and Nationality Act of 1952, § 215, 8 U.S.C. § 1185 (1982).

84. See Fiallo v. Bell, 430 U.S. 787, 796 (1977).

85. See id.; Mathews v. Diaz, 426 U.S. 67 (1976); Kleindienst v. Mandel, 408 U.S. 753 (1972).

86. See Fiallo v. Bell, 430 U.S. 787 (1977) (plaintiffs included citizens making constitutional equal protection claim); Kleindienst v. Mandel, 408 U.S. 753 (1972) (constitutional claim based on citizen coplaintiffs' first amendment rights).

87. M. Edelman, The Symbolic Uses of Politics (1964).

88. See, e.g., Chy Lung v. Freeman, 92 U.S. 275 (1875) (state may not tax or regulate immigrants). But see, e.g., Cabell v. Chavez-Salido, 454 U.S. 432 (1982) (state may require citizenship as a condition of public employment as probation officer); De Canas v. Bica, 424 U.S. 351 (1976) (state may restrict private employment of illegal aliens).

89. See, e.g., United States v. Nixon, 418 U.S. 683 (1974) (executive and judicial branches; issue of presidential privilege); Youngstown Sheet & Tube Co. v. Sawyer, 343 U.S. 579 (1952) (legislative and executive branches; issue of lawmaking power); Myers v. United States, 272 U.S. 52 (1926) (legislative and executive branches; issue of presidential power to remove executive officer).

90. See, for example, the adjustment of status authority under the Immigration and Nationality Act of 1952, § 245, 8 U.S.C. § 1255 (1982). For a discussion of the way in which the INS has exercised this authority, see Diver, The Optimal Precision of Administrative Rules, 93 Yale L.J. 65, 92–97 (1983); Sofaer, The Change-of-Status Adjudication: A Case Study of the Informal Agency Process, I J. of Legal Stud. 349 (1972). The INS has further expanded INS discretion by its practice of publishing only certain of its decisions as "precedents." See Diver, supra, at 95.

91. See, e.g., 8 U.S.C. § 1225(c) (1982). The predecessor of § 1225(c) was the statute upheld in United States ex rel. Knauff v. Shaughnessy, 338 U.S. 537 (1950).

92. Youngstown Sheet & Tube Co. v. Sawyer, 343 U.S. 579, 635–36 (1952) (Jackson, J., concurring).

93. Nishimura Ekiu v. United States, 142 U.S. 651, 660 (1892). Or in the more pointed formulation: "Whatever the procedure authorized by Congress is, it is due process as far as an alien denied entry is concerned." United States ex rel. Knauff v. Shaughnessy, 338 U.S. 537, 544 (1950).

94. See L. Tribe, supra note 12, at 284. The Harvard Developments Note contends, however, that during the classical period the Court recognized some constitutional limitations on the exclusion power, its rhetoric to the contrary notwithstanding. Developments, supra note 4, at 1314–23. In fact, the cases that it cites do not refute the position taken here. Kwock Jan Fat v. White, 253 U.S. 454 (1920), Tang Tun v. Edsell, 223 U.S. 673 (1912), and Chin Yow v. United States, 208 U.S. 8 (1908), while exclusion cases, involved claims of United States citizenship, which have long been considered sui generis. See, e.g., Ng Fung Ho v. White, 259 U.S. 276, 284–85 (1922). Wong Wing v. United States, 163 U.S. 228 (1896), was a deportation case and involved not simply exclusion but expulsion plus *punishment*. Elting v. North German Lloyd, 287 U.S. 324 (1932), involved not an alien challenging her exclusion but a vessel challenging a fine that had been administratively imposed. Gegiow v. Uhl, 239 U.S. 3 (1915), holds only that judicial review of legal issues involving construction of the immigration statute is permissible. There is no suggestion in that opinion that such a holding is required by due process, although such a result is surely possible. See Crowell v. Benson, 285 U.S. 22, 49–50 (1932).

95. E.g., Landon v. Plasencia, 103 S. Ct. 321, 325–26 (1982).

96. In exclusion proceedings, for example, the burden of proof is on the alien, not the government, see 8 U.S.C. § 1361 (1982), and the availability of discretionary relief is far more limited. Compare id. § 1226 (appeal to the Attorney General from final exclusion decisions) and id. § 1183 (aliens excludable because likely to become public charges may be admitted at the discretion of the INS upon posting a bond) and id. § 1182(h) (aliens excludable for having committed crimes may secure waivers on account of hardship to a legal resident or citizen spouse or child in the United States) with, e.g., id. § 1254(a) (discretion of Attorney General to suspend deportation for hardship) and id. § 1253(h) (discretion of Attorney General to withhold deportation because of threat of persecution). The excludable alien, moreover, cannot designate the country to which she will be deported, as she can in deportation proceedings. Compare id. § 1253(a) (deportation) with id. § 1227(a) (exclusion). The appellate process exhibits yet another difference between deportation and exclusion: an alien in deportation proceedings can appeal to a federal court of appeals, while an alien in exclusion proceedings can seek review only through habeas corpus. Id. § 1105a(a), (b).

97. See Immigration and Naturalization Serv., U.S. Dep't of Justice, 1979 Statistical Yearbook 66–67; infra notes 212–27 and accompanying text.

98. Congress eventually enacted such a provision in 1996.

99. 338 U.S. 537 (1950).

100. 345 U.S. 206 (1953).

101. Mr. Justice Jackson in dissent noted that "if the Government has its way he seems likely to be detained indefinitely, perhaps for life, for a cause known only to the Attorney General." Id. at 220. Mezei was finally paroled after some three years of detention following an inquiry by a special panel of distinguished attorneys that recommended release. See W. Gellhorn, Individual Freedom and Governmental Restraints 36–38 (1956).

102. Indeed, the Attorney General refused to permit even the trial court to examine the "confidential information" in camera. 345 U.S. at 228 n.9 (Jackson, J., dissenting).

103. See, e.g., Hart, The Power of Congress to Limit the Jurisdiction of Federal Courts: An Exercise in Dialectic, 66 Harv. L. Rev. 1362, 1387–96 (1953), reprinted in P. Bator, P. Mishkin, D. Shapiro & H. Wechsler, Hart & Wechsler's The Federal Courts and the Federal System 330, 348–56 (2d ed. 1973); Martin, Due Process and Membership in the National Community: Political Asylum and Beyond, 44 U. Pitt. L. Rev. 165, 173–80 (1983).

104. Recent efforts to portray these decisions as anomalies include, for example, Rodriguez-Fernandez v. Wilkinson, 654 F.2d 1382, 1388 (10th Cir. 1981); Developments, supra note 4, at 1322–23. Compare supra note 74.

105. See, e.g., Landon v. Plasencia, 103 S. Ct. 321, 329–30 (1982); Fiallo v. Bell, 430 U.S. 787, 792 (1977).

106. 8 U.S.C. § 1182(a)(27) (1982).

107. See supra note 93.

108. 8 U.S.C. § 1225(c) (1982). The Court has never decided on the extent to which this decision is judicially reviewable. Recently, an excellent federal district court judge who possesses a detailed knowledge of immigration law, see Sofaer, supra note 90, ruled that a court may "inquire as to the Government's reasons" but may not "prob[e] into their wisdom or basis. If the Court finds that the Government acted on a facially legitimate and bona fide reason, its inquiry is complete." El-Werfalli v. Smith, 547 F. Supp. 152, 153 (S.D.N.Y. 1982).

109. Some classifications to which this discussion applies are not, strictly speaking, made on the basis of alienage; instead of distinguishing between citizens and aliens, classifications often distinguish between subcategories of aliens. See, e.g., Toll v. Moreno, 458 U.S. 1, 25 (1982) (Rehnquist, J., dissenting) (domiciled nonimmigrant aliens who hold G-4 visas); Mathews v. Diaz, 426 U.S. 67 (1976) (upholding classification of aliens on basis of residency status and length of residence); Narenji v. Civiletti, 617 F.2d 745 (D.C. Cir.) (upholding classification of aliens on basis of nationality), cert. denied, 446 U.S. 957 (1980).

110. See, e.g., Schweiker v. Wilson, 450 U.S. 221 (1981) (statutory classification of mentally ill patients by whether cared for in a public or private institution held a rational basis for denying certain welfare benefits); Parham v. Hughes, 441 U.S. 347 (1979) (statutory classification precluding father of an illegitimate child from suing for child's wrongful death held a rational means of proving paternity). How close the means-end relationship must be when the classification is on the basis of alienage is a question that need not be addressed here. For a discussion of the rational basis/strict scrutiny controversy surrounding this still unresolved question, see Note, A Dual Standard for State Discrimination Against Aliens, 92 Harv. L. Rev. 1516 (1979). The issue is further complicated by uncertainty concerning whether it is to be addressed under equal protection principles or under a preemption analysis. See, e.g., Note, State Burdens on Resident Aliens: A New Preemption Analysis, 89 Yale L.J. 940 (1980) [hereinafter cited as Note, State Burden]; Note, The Equal Treatment of Aliens: Preemption or Equal Protection, 31 Stan. L. Rev. 1069 (1979).

111. Mathews v. Diaz, 426 U.S. 67, 80 (1976); see also Fiallo v. Bell, 430 U.S. 787, 792 (1977).

112. See The Chinese Exclusion Case, 130 U.S. 581 (1889).

113. The Immigration Act of 1924, ch. 190, § 11, 43 Stat. 153, 159–160, established a quota system based on national origins, replacing the interim system set up by the 1921 statute. See Immigration Act of 1921, ch. 8, § 2, 42 Stat. 5, 5–6. The national origins quota scheme continued in force, with modification, see Immigration and Nationality Act of 1952, ch. 477 §§ 201–207, 66 Stat. 163, 175–81 until 1965. See Act of Oct. 3, 1965, Pub. L. No. 89–236, § 21(e), 79 Stat. 911, 920 (repealing national origin quotas and substituting separate quotas for Eastern and Western Hemispheres). The 1952 act provided that total annual immigration should not exceed one sixth of one percent of the number of inhabitants in the United States in 1920, Immigration and Nationality Act of 1952, § 201(a), 66 Stat. at 175, and it set a special limit on aliens from the "Asia-Pacific Triangle," id. § 202(b), 66 Stat. at 177.

114. See E. Hutchinson, supra note 27, at 294–95.

115. See, e.g., Examining Bd. of Eng'rs v. Flores de Otero, 426 U.S. 572 (1976) (citizenship requirement for practice in civil engineering held unconstitutional); Miranda v. Nelson, 413 U.S. 902 (1973) (mem.) (state's dismissal of employees on account of alienage held unconstitutional); Yick Wo v. Hopkins, 118 U.S. 356 (1886) (city ordinance discriminating on basis of race held unconstitutional).

116. See, e.g., Kleindienst v. Mandel, 408 U.S. 753 (1972) (upholding denial of a visa to Marxist scholar from Belgium).

117. Compare Sugarman v. Dougall, 413 U.S. 634 (1973) (citizenship requirement for state civil service held unconstitutional), and Graham v. Richardson, 403 U.S. 365 (1971) (state de-

nial, of welfare benefits to resident aliens held unconstitutional), with Mow Sun Wong v. Campbell, 626 F.2d 739 (9th Cir. 1980) (presidential order excluding noncitizens from the federal civil service held constitutional), and Matthews v. Diaz, 426 U.S. 67 (1976) (alien ineligibility provision of Medicare program held constitutional). Classifications relating to American Indians comprise a separate category.

118. See, e.g., Fiallo v. Bell, 430 U.S. 787, 792 (1977); Mathews v. Diaz, 426 U.S. 67, 81–82 (1976); Rosberg, supra note 12.

119. See Note, A Madisonian Interpretation of the Equal Protection Doctrine, 91 Yale L.J. 1403, 1419–25 (1982).

One suspects that this doctrinal discontinuity, as well as confusion over whether alienage classifications under state law are "suspect" or not, see supra note 110, are important factors inclining the Court increasingly to emphasize preemption rather than equal protection principles in such cases. Such an analysis finds state law unconstitutional under the supremacy clause, U.S. Const. art. VI, cl. 2, on the theory that the issue has been preempted by federal law. See, e.g., Toll v. Moreno, 458 U.S. 1, 17 (1982).

120. For an account of those subcommittees during the 92d and 93d Congresses, see P. Schuck, supra note 82.

121. As of 1979, the four states with the largest alien population were California (26%), New York (15%), Texas (8%), and Florida (7%). Immigration and Naturalization Serv., U.S. Dep't of Justice, 1979 Statistical Yearbook 84 (1979).

122. See, e.g., Reinhold, Hispanic Leaders Open Voter Drive, N.Y. Times, Aug. 9, 1983, at A15, col. 1.; Hispanic Power Arrives at the Ballot Box, Bus. Wk., July 4, 1983, at 32; Gurwitt, Widespread Political Efforts Open New Era for Hispanics, 40 Cong. Q., 2707 (1982); see also Miller, The Political Impact of Foreign Labor: A Re-evaluation of the Western European Experience, 16 Int'l Migr. Rev. 27 (1982) (describing political influence of aliens who lack voting rights).

123. See supra notes 36–39 and accompanying text.

124. U.S. Const. art. I, § 9, cl. 1. For an historical analysis of the dispute over whether this provision was intended to affect the power of Congress to regulate free immigration and/or the domestic slave trade, see Berns, The Constitution and the Migration of Slaves, 78 Yale L.J. 198 (1968).

125. U.S. Const. art. I, § 8, cl. 4. See L. Henkin, Foreign Affairs and the Constitution (1972).

126. See, e.g., Note, State Burden, supra note 110, at 944–46.

127. See, e.g., Chy Lung v. Freeman, 92 U.S. 275, 280 (1875).

128. For an enumeration of several additional governmental interests in differentiating on the basis of alienage, see, e.g., Hampton v. Mow Sun Wong, 426 U.S. 88, 104 (1976). None seems terribly persuasive, much less compelling. Even the most plausible, the incentive-to-naturalize interest, could be achieved by a narrower classification that would not disqualify aliens who had formally declared their intentions to naturalize pursuant to 8 U.S.C. § 1445(f) (1982).

129. This deference to governmental interests is perhaps especially evident with respect to admission criteria. Given a strictly limited visa policy in the face of essentially unlimited demand for visas, the government is obliged to choose among putative immigrants, sometimes on rather arbitrary grounds. What rational principle, for example, could justify Congress establishing a different numerical ceiling for the Eastern and Western Hemispheres? See Pub. L. No. 89–236, § 21(e), 79 Stat. 911, 920 (1965), amended by Act of Oct. 5, 1978, Pub. L. No. 95–412, 92 Stat. 907, 907 (replacing hemisphere quotas with a single, worldwide quota) (codified at 8 U.S.C. § 1151(a) (1982)).

130. Bugajewitz v. Adams, 228 U.S. 585, 591 (1913). Earlier, in Fong Yue Ting v. United States, 149 U.S. 698, 730 (1893), the Court had written: "The order of deportation is not a punishment for crime. It is not a banishment, in the sense in which that word is often applied to the expulsion of a citizen from his country by way of punishment. It is but a method of en-

forcing the return to his own country of an alien who has not complied with the conditions upon the performance of which the government of the nation, acting within its constitutional authority and through the proper departments, has determined that his continuing to reside here shall depend."

131. The Court has sometimes insisted that considerations of administrative cost and convenience cannot diminish constitutional rights, e.g., Bounds v. Smith, 430 U.S. 817, 825 (1977) ("[T]he cost of protecting a constitutional right cannot justify its total denial."), but it is perfectly clear that in fact and in law they do, e.g., Mathews v. Eldridge, 424 U.S. 319 (1976) (administrative burdens a factor in determining whether Social Security benefit termination proceeding comports with due process).

132. The Court has never questioned this doctrine, reaffirming it at least as recently as 1977. See Ingraham v. Wright, 430 U.S. 651, 668 (1977).

133. U.S. Const. amend. VI.

134. U.S. Const. art. I, § 9, cl. 3.

135. See, e.g., Galvan v. Press, 347 U.S. 522, 530–32 (1954) (ex post facto clause does not apply to deportation because it is not punishment); Harisiades v. Shaughnessy, 342 U.S. 580, 594–95 (1952) (same); see also Woodby v. INS, 385 U.S. 276, 284–86 (1966) (no requirement of proof beyond a reasonable doubt); Dymytryshyn v. Esperdy, 285 F. Supp. 507, 510 (S.D.N.Y.) (prohibition against bills of attainder inapplicable to noncriminal proceeding), aff'd, 393 U.S. 77 (1968). See generally United States v. Ward, 448 U.S. 242, 251–54 (1980).

136. See infra note 146 and accompanying text (exclusionary rule); Developments, supra note 4, at 1385, 1386–89 (burden of proof). In the Japanese Immigrant Case, 189 U.S. 86, 100–02 (1903), the Court held that due process did not require judicial review of summary deportation. Had the Court instead conceived of the proceeding as criminal in nature, judicial review would have been constitutionally required. See U.S. Const. amend. VI.

137. See, e.g., 8 U.S.C. § 1252(a) (1982). In Kennedy v. Mendoza-Martinez, 372 U.S. 144, 168 (1963), the Court identified incarceration as a factor supporting the conclusion that the sanction is punitive in nature. See also United States v. Janis, 428 U.S. 433, 447 n.17 (1976). But see United States v. Ward, 448 U.S. 242, 249–51 (1980) (a penalty is not criminal where Congress does not so intend).

138. See Note, Deportation and Exclusion: A Continuing Dialogue Between Congress and the Courts, 71 Yale L.J. 760, 789 n.143 (1962).

139. For example, an alien deported because of her affiliation with the Communist Party may be precluded from acquiring American citizenship. See 8 U.S.C. §§ 1251(a)(b), 1424(c) (1982).

140. See, e.g., Kennedy v. Mendoza-Martinez, 372 U.S. 144, 160–61 (1963).

141. Under 8 U.S.C. § 1253(h) (1982), a deportable alien may not, with some exceptions, be returned to her country if the Attorney General determines that her life or freedom would be threatened there on account of race, religion, nationality, membership in a particular social group, or political opinion.

142. 8 U.S.C. § 1253(a)(1)–(7) (1982) enumerates the categories of countries to which a deportable alien must or may be deported, and gives the Attorney General much flexibility concerning the countries to which she can be sent. 8 U.S.C. § 1227(a) (1982) gives the Attorney General similar flexibility regarding the deportation of excluded aliens.

143. Justice Douglas, no friend to euphemism, likened deportation to the ancient practice of banishment: "Banishment is punishment in the practical sense. It may deprive a man and his family of all that makes life worth while. Those who have their roots here have an important stake in this country. Their plans for themselves and their hopes for their children all depend on their right to stay. If they are uprooted and sent to lands no longer known to them, no longer hospitable, they become displaced, homeless people condemned to bitterness and despair." Harisiades v. Shaughnessy, 342 U.S. 580, 600 (1952) (Douglas, J., dissenting).

144. 8 U.S.C. § 1326 (1982). In practice, few of these cases are prosecuted unless the alien is thought to be a smuggler, has been deported several times before, or other aggravating factors are present, such as assault on a police officer. Letter from Edwin Harwood to Peter H. Schuck (July 28, 1983) (copy on file at the offices of the Columbia Law Review).

145. Even the Court has occasionally blushed while reaffirming the pretense that deportation is not punishment. See Galvan v. Press, 347 U.S. 522, 531 (1954) ("[S]ince the intrinsic consequences of deportation are so close to punishment for crime, it might fairly be said also that the *ex post facto* Clause, even though applicable only to punitive legislation, should be applied to deportation. But the slate is not clean.") (footnote omitted).

146. The statutes and regulations governing deportation proceedings afford many due process protections. The government bears the burden of proof. The alien has the right to counsel and the right to adduce evidence and to cross-examine witnesses. The alien also is entitled to notice, a hearing, a decision on the record, and judicial review. See 8 U.S.C. §§ 1105a, 1252 (1982); 8 C.F.R. §§ 242.1–.23 (1983). But the deportation laws fail to provide some protections that due process has been thought to require in other quasi-criminal contexts, such as trial before an independent judge and a jury of one's peers, see infra notes 167–89 and accompanying text, free legal assistance for indigents, see, e.g., Aguilera-Enriquez v. INS, 516 F.2d 565 (6th Cir. 1975), cert. denied, 423 U.S. 1050 (1976), the right to compel the production of relevant evidence, see supra notes 99–102, 108 and accompanying text, the exclusion of illegally obtained evidence, see, e.g., Abel v. United States, 362 U.S. 217 (1960), and the right to clear notice of the substantive standards to be applied, see, e.g., Boutilier v. INS, 387 U.S. 118 (1967).

147. The absence of such safeguards places the government in a position analogous to that of a traditional creditor or lessor who could enforce the voluntarily undertaken obligations of his debtor or lessee through self-help remedies, such as ex parte replevin, attachment and execution, or eviction. See, e.g., Brunswick Corp. v. J & P, Inc., 424 F.2d 100 (10th Cir. 1970) (replevin); Wheeler v. Adams Co., 322 F, Supp. 645 (D. Md. 1971) (same). In the classical tradition, the risk of error, unfairness, or indignity characteristic of such procedures, see Fuentes v. Shevin, 407 U.S. 67 (1972), is subordinated to the interest of the government in speedy enforcement of its claim. See generally Mashaw, Due Process and Its Discontents (unpublished manuscript on file with the author).

148. See infra notes 255–58 and accompanying text.

149. Although the INS and the courts routinely employ the term "detention" to describe the practice of holding aliens pending initiation and completion of exclusion and deportation proceedings, the length of many detentions and the conditions of confinement suggest that the term "imprisonment" more accurately depicts reality. See Jean v. Nelson, 711 F.2d 1455, 1500 n.51, reh'g en banc granted, 714 F.2d 96 (11th Cir. 1983). The following discussion will use the less inflammatory term. Cf. Korematsu v. United States, 323 U.S. 214, 223 (1944) ("[W]e deem it unjustifiable to call [assembly and relocation centers] concentration camps with all the ugly connotations that term implies. . . .").

150. E.g., 8 U.S.C. §§ 1222–1227, 1252 (1982).

151. 345 U.S. 206 (1953).

152. The trio of cases involving the curfew, evacuation, and detention imposed upon American citizens of Japanese descent during World War II are not discussed here because they were exercises of the war power, not the power to regulate immigration. See Ex parte Mitsuye Endo, 323 U.S. 283 (1944); Korematsu v. United States, 323 U.S. 214 (1944); Hirabayashi v. United States, 320 U.S. 81 (1943).

153. *Mezei*, 345 U.S. at 217. Justice Jackson, also dissenting, did Justice Black one better: "Government counsel ingeniously argued that Ellis Island is his 'refuge' whence he is free to leave in any direction except west. That might mean freedom, if only he were an amphibian! Realistically, this man is incarcerated by a combination of forces which keep him as effectually

as a prison, the dominant and proximate of these forces being the United States immigration authority. It overworks legal fiction to say that one is free in law when by the commonest of common sense he is bound." Id. at 220.

154. Id. at 209.

155. Id. at 215.

156. Id. at 216.

157. During 1952, a total of almost 39,000 aliens were detained; in the New York district, the average length of detention was 39 days. Maslow, Recasting Our Deportation Law: Proposals for Reform, 56 Colum. L. Rev. 309, 360 (1956).

158. Carlson v. Landon, 342 U.S. 524 (1952).

159. See, e.g., United States ex rel. Daniman v. Shaughnessy, 117 F. Supp. 388 (S.D.N.Y. 1953); United States ex. rel. Klig v. Shaughnessy, 94 F. Supp. 157 (S.D.N.Y. 1950) (reasoning in substance disapproved in United States ex rel. Yaris v. Esperdy, 202 F.2d 109 (2d Cir. 1953)).

160. See Jean v. Nelson, 711 F.2d 1455, 1469, reh'g en banc granted, 714 F.2d 96 (11th Cir. 1983).

161. Leng May Ma v. Barber, 357 U.S. 185, 190 (1958). Even if parole were arbitrarily denied, however, the courts, as deferential to the immigration authorities as ever, see supra notes 74–92 and accompanying text, would not intervene to grant it. See, e.g., In re Cahill, 447 F.2d 1343 (2d Cir. 1971).

162. See Jean v. Nelson, 711 F.2d 1455, 1464–65, reh'g en banc granted, 714 F.2d 96 (11th Cir. 1983). The 1981 detention policy, invalidated on several grounds in *Jean* and reimposed on a different legal footing in 1982, has survived initial legal challenge. Ishtyaq v. Nelson, No. 82–2288 (E.D.N.Y. Oct. 4, 1983).

163. Telephone interview with Howard Brown, Office of Planning and Analysis, INS (May 10, 1983).

164. See e.g., Jean v. Nelson, 711 F.2d 1455, 1500 n.51 (quoting from the Special Master's Report on the Haitians in detention), reh'g en banc granted, 714 F.2d 96 (11th Cir. 1983).

165. Indeed, in Leng May Ma v. Barber, 357 U.S. 185 (1958), in a remarkably niggardly construction of the statute, the Court refused even to protect the alien's right of *nonrefoulement,* one of the most basic rights conferred by international law. See Final Act and Convention of the United Nations Conference of Plenipotentiaries on the Status of Refugees and Stateless Persons, art. 33, U.N. Doc. A/CONF. 2/108, U.N. Sales No. 1951.IV.4 (1951), to which the United States acceded in 1968, see infra note 400.

Although *Mezei* and *Leng May Ma* were exclusion cases, there is no reason to believe that classical immigration law viewed protracted detention pending deportation any differently, so long as due process was observed prior to confinement. See United States ex rel. Hyndman v. Holton, 205 F.2d 228 (7th Cir. 1953); United States ex rel. Bryant v. Shaughnessy, 122 F. Supp. 326 (S.D.N.Y. 1954).

166. 345 U.S. at 216.

167. See, e.g., Withrow v. Larkin, 421 U.S. 35 (1975). Mixture of functions in particular cases, however, may be so unfair as to violate due process or equal protection principles. See, e.g., Gibson v. Berryhill, 411 U.S. 564 (1973); Cinderella Career and Finishing Schools, Inc. v. FTC, 425 F.2d 583 (D.C. Cir. 1970).

The administrative law judges who hear disability claims under the Social Security Act, 42 U.S.C. §§ 301–1397 (1976 & Supp. V 1981), arguably combine these functions to some degree in that they gather evidence and develop the facts as well as adjudicate the claims. Id. § 405(b), (g). This procedure was upheld, albeit without much reasoning, over due process and Administrative Procedure Act challenges. See Richardson v. Perales, 402 U.S. 389, 408–10 (1971).

168. The INS caseload is staggering. Each year, the INS adjudicates more than 1.5 million petitions for various benefits. Immigration and Naturalization Serv., U.S. Dep't of Justice, Asy-

lum Adjudications: An Evolving Concept and Responsibility for the Immigration and Naturalization Service 24 n.* (internal memo 1982) (copy on file at the offices of the Columbia Law Review) [hereinafter cited as INS Asylum Study].

169. Approval by an independent magistrate prior to arrest and detention, constitutionally required of the police, is ordinarily not required of the INS. 8 U.S.C. §§ 1252(a), 1357(a)–(c) (1982); Abel v. United States, 362 U.S. 217 (1960). But see Blackie's House of Beef, Inc. v. Castillo, 467 F. Supp. 170 (D.D.C. 1978), aff'd, 659 F.2d 1211 (D.C. Cir. 1981), cert. denied, 455 U.S. 940 (1982).

170. In the vernacular of the statute, they are called "special inquiry officer[s]." 8 U.S.C. § 1101(b)(4) (1982).

171. For a discussion of some of the informal patterns of prosecutorial influence over the immigration judge corps, see Roberts, Proposed: A Specialized Statutory Immigration Court, 18 San Diego L. Rev. 1, 7–11 (1980).

172. 339 U.S. 33, modified, 339 U.S. 908 (1950).

173. Id. at 46.

174. 5 U.S.C. §§ 551–576 (1982).

175. 339 U.S. at 46.

176. A deportation hearing involves issues basic to human liberty and happiness and, in the present upheavals in lands to which aliens may be returned, perhaps to life itself. It might be difficult to justify as measuring up to constitutional standards of impartiality a hearing tribunal for deportation proceedings the like of which has been condemned by Congress as unfair even where less vital matters of property rights are at stake. Id. at 50–51.

177. Marcello v. Bonds, 349 U.S. 302 (1955). The statute did allow a hearing officer a limited prosecutorial role. See infra note 183.

178. See H.R. 6652, 80th Cong., 2d Sess., 94 Cong. Rec. 6374 (1948). The bill, H.R. 6652, was returned to the House Judiciary Committee, 94 Cong. Rec. 6374 (1948), which reported the bill out without amendment within two weeks. H.R. Rep. No. 2140, 80th Cong., 2d Sess. (1948). No further action was taken.

179. 5 U.S.C. §§ 554, 556–557 (1982). With certain enumerated exceptions, the hearing officer must be independent in at least three senses. First, she cannot "consult a person or party on a fact in issue, unless on notice and opportunity for all parties to participate." Second, she cannot "be responsible to or subject to the supervision or direction of an [agency] employee or agent engaged in the performance of investigative or prosecuting functions." Third, no agency employee "engaged in the performance of investigative or prosecuting functions . . . in a case may . . . in that or a factually related case, participate or advise in the decision . . . except as witness or counsel in public proceedings." Id. § 554(d).

180. In addition to these policy considerations, there were legal arguments as well centering around the contention that Congress had never intended for the APA to apply to immigration hearings and that certain exceptions from the separation-of-functions provisions were applicable. H.R. Rep. No. 2140, 80th Cong., 2d Sess. 1–6 (1948).

181. Supplemental Appropriation Act of 1951, ch. 1052, 64 Stat. 1044, 1048 (1950) (exempting deportation and exclusion proceedings from the Administrative Procedure Act, ch. 324, §§ 5, 7–8, 60 Stat. 237, 239 (1946), repealed by Immigration and Nationality Act of 1952, ch. 477, § 403(a)(47), 66 Stat. 163, 280.

182. Immigration Act of 1917, ch. 29 §§ 16–17, 39 Stat. 874, 885–87, repealed by Immigration and Nationality Act of 1952, ch. 477, § 403(a)(13), 66 Stat. 163, 279.

183. 8 U.S.C. § 1252(b) (1982). The statute, however, expressly permits the hearing officer, inter alia, to "present and receive evidence, interrogate, examine, and cross-examine the alien or witnesses." Id.

184. Id. This was not the last time that Congress would reject the APA model for deportation proceedings. In 1961, it overruled court decisions applying the APA's judicial review provisions to immigration cases. See Woodby v. INS, 385 U.S. 276, 282–83 (1966) (Clark, J., dissenting).

185. 349 U.S. 302 (1955).

186. U.S. Const. amend. V.

187. 349 U.S. at 306–07.

188. "When the Constitution requires a hearing, it requires a fair one, one before a tribunal which meets *at least* currently prevailing standards of impartiality." *Wong Yang Sung,* 339 U.S. at 50 (emphasis added). Because the deportation tribunal did not meet even the recently enacted APA's standards of impartiality, id. at 36, the *Wong Yang Sung* Court could invalidate the INS procedure without reaching the question of whether the Constitution mandated some level of impartiality, as reflected in a particular tribunal structure, beyond that then required by the APA. This was the question the Court evaded in *Marcello.*

189. 349 U.S. at 311.

190. See supra notes 21–22 and accompanying text.

191. R. Merton, Social Theory and Social Structure 510–42 (1968).

192. See H. Kissinger, American Foreign Policy 55–58 (1969); C. Vance, Hard Choices: Critical Years in America's Foreign Policy (1983).

193. See, e.g., Asylum Adjudication: Hearings Before the Senate Subcomm. on Immigration and Refugee Policy, 97th Cong., 1st Sess. 46–61 (1981) (statement of I. Kurzban); Scanlan, Regulating Refugee Flow: Legal Alternatives and Obligations under the Refugee Act of 1980, 56 Notre Dame Law. 618, 627–29 (1981).

194. Great Britain admitted approximately 7,000 refugees in 1980, but only about 3,000 in 1981. Australia admitted about 22,000 in 1981–1982 and about 17,000 in 1982–1983. Telephone interview with U.N. High Comm'n on Refugees (Oct. 26, 1983).

195. See, e.g., R. Burt, Taking Care of Strangers (1979).

196. See L. Fransman, British Nationality Law and the 1981 Act 45–49 (1982); supra note 194.

197. Bureau of Census, U.S. Dep't of Commerce, Historical Statistics of the United States: Colonial Times to 1970, at 224 (1975). See generally E. Denison, Accounting for the United States Economic Growth: 1929–1969, at 11 (1974).

198. See, e.g., Reimers, Recent Immigration Policy: An Analysis, *in* The Gateway: U.S. Immigration Issues and Policies 13 (B. Chiswick ed. 1982) [hereinafter cited as The Gateway].

199. For discussion of occupational preferences and labor certification, see Goldfarb, Occupational Preferences in the U.S. Immigration Law: An Economic Analysis, *in* The Gateway, supra note 198, at 412.

200. For discussion of the Bracero program, see The H-2 Program and Non-Immigrants: Hearing Before the Subcomm. on Immigration and Refugee Policy of the Senate Comm. on the Judiciary, 97th Cong., 1st Sess. (1981); Morgan & Gardner, Potential for a U.S. Guest-Worker Program in Agriculture: Lessons from the Braceros, *in* The Gateway, supra note 198, at 361.

201. See Fogel, Illegal Aliens: Economic Aspects and Public Policy Alternatives, 15 San Diego L. Rev. 63, 68–69 (1977); Wachter, The Labor Market and Illegal Immigration: The Outlook for the 1980's, 33 Indus. & Lab. Rel. Rev. 342, 350–54 (1980).

202. See generally E. Denison, Accounting for Slower Economic Growth: The United States in the 1970's (1979).

203. Compare, e.g., Piore, Impact of Immigration on the Labor Force, 98 Monthly Lab. Rev. 41, 43 (May 1975) (arguing that undocumented aliens are hired to fill gaps in the secondary labor market), with, e.g., M. Wachter, supra note 203, at 343, 350–54 (arguing that undocumented workers depress the wages of the low-skilled American work force).

204. See Piore, supra note 203, at 43.

205. See Simon, The Overall Effect of Immigration on Natives' Incomes, *in* The Gateway, supra note 198, at 314.

206. The classic study is D. North & M. Houston, The Characteristics and Role of Illegal Aliens in the U.S. Labor Market: An Exploratory Study 142–49 (1976). Compare Reinhold, Taxes Aliens Pay to Texas Found to Top Benefit, N.Y. Times, Nov. 15, 1983, at A17, col. 1

("A new study in Texas has found that [illegal immigrants] contribute far more to the state's coffers in taxes than they take out in health, welfare and other publicly financed services."), with The Jobs Illegal Aliens Take From Americans, N. Y. Times, Dec. 3, 1983, at 22, col. 4 (letter to the editor disputing Texas study and arguing on the basis of recent INS research that, assuming only 21% of illegal aliens displace Americans from jobs, they cost over $13 billion more per year than they pay in taxes).

207. Immigration to the United States: Hearings Before the Select Comm. on Population, 95th Cong., 2d Sess. 183–90 (1978).

208. See Goldfarb, supra note 199, in The Gateway, supra note 198, at 412, 432–40 (discussion of the relationship between doctor shortage and immigration policy). But see Kaye, Danilov & McDonald, Alien Physicians and Their Admission into the United States, 16 San Diego L. Rev. 61, 62–64 (1978) (congressional discussion of the foreign medical graduate).

209. See U.S. Comptroller General, Report to the Senate Committee on the Budget: Impact of Illegal Aliens on Public Assistance Programs: Too Little Is Known, app. 2, at 17 (1977).

210. See, e.g., INS Efficiency Legislation: Hearing on H.R. 2043 Before the Subcomm. on Immigration, Refugees, and International Law of the House Comm. on the Judiciary, 97th Cong., 1st Sess. 174–183 (1981); Goldfarb, supra note 199, in The Gateway, supra note 198, at 412, 417–21; Kaye, Danilov & McDonald, supra note 208, at 66–69.

211. See supra notes 8–9 and accompanying text.

212. The legal definition of refugees, of course, is much narrower. See 8 U.S.C. § 1101(a)(42) (1982).

213. U.S. Comm. for Refugees, World Refugee Survey 1982, at 40–41 (1982). The number of refugees in Africa, for example, increased from 750,000 in 1967 to 6.5 million in 1981. Id.

214. The Presidential determination for fiscal 1983 was 90,000, see Presidential Determination No. 83–2 (Oct. 11, 1982), reprinted in 2 Fed. Imm. L. Rep. (CCH) ¶ 14,010 (Aug. 1983), but only about 60,000 are expected to be accepted, see N.Y. Times, Sept. 27, 1983, at A3, col. 2. For fiscal 1984, the administration has proposed a refugee limit of 72,000. Presidential Determination No. 83–11 (Oct. 7, 1983).

215. This figure includes only those who were under the guardianship of the allied armies: about seven million were eventually repatriated but approximately one million remained in the allied zones. See S. Rep. No. 950, 80th Cong. 2d Sess., reprinted in 1948 U.S. Code Cong. & Ad. News 2028, 2035.

216. INS Asylum Study, supra note 168, at 3–5.

217. 39 Fed. Reg. 41,832 (1974).

218. 8 U.S.C. §§ 1157–1159 (1982).

219. INS Asylum Study, supra note 168, at 6; Martin, The Refugee Act of 1980: Its Past and Future, 1982 Mich. Y.B. of Int'l Legal Stud. 91, 109.

220. INS Asylum Study, supra note 168, at 18.

221. See Aleinikoff, Aliens, Due Process and 'Community Ties': A Response to Martin, 44. U. Pitt. L. Rev. 237, 253–56 (1983). The current, much larger, backlog is discussed in Chapter 1. The status of the Mariel Cubans who did not have serious criminal records was subsequently regularized by Congress. Some of the criminal Mariels remain in federal custody.

222. See, e.g., In re Sibrun, 19 I. & N. Dec. No. 2932 (B1A Jan. 20, 1983) ("Generalized oppression by a government of virtually its entire populace does not come within those specified grounds."); see also Immigration Reform: Hearings Before the Subcomm. on Immigration, Refugees, and International Law of the House Comm. on the Judiciary, 97th Cong., 1st Sess. 622–701 (1981) (hearings on asylum) [hereinafter cited as 1981 House Hearings].

223. See infra notes 321–39 and accompanying text. 1981 House Hearings, supra note 224, at 622–701: INS Asylum Study, supra note 168, at 66.

224. See supra notes 156–61 and accompanying text.

225. See infra notes 376–401 and accompanying text for further discussion.

226. Chapter 1 discusses the current asylum claiming process.

227. Chapter 1 discusses the current illegal alien population.

228. See, e.g., King, Mexican Mohey Crisis Impels New Surge of Aliens to Texas, N.Y. Times, Mar. 19, 1983, at A1, col. 2. ("The Border Patrol is inundated, and the 2,000-mile border has turned into something more like a series of commuter stations than an international boundary.").

229. Winerip, Smuggling of Aliens by Canadian Route to U.S. Is Increasing. N.Y. Times, May 1, 1983, at A1, col. 3.

230. During the early part of 1983, Border Patrol apprehensions averaged 30% above the previous year. Departments of Commerce, Justice, and State. The Judiciary, and Related Agencies Appropriations for 1984: Hearings Before a Subcomm. of the House Comm. on Appropriations, Department of Justice, 98th Cong., 1st Sess. 690 (1983) (testimony of Alan C. Nelson, Comm'r, INS); see also N.Y. Times, Apr. 9, 1983, at A12, col. 4 (apprehensions during March 1983 at the southern border the highest for any single month).

231. On July 30, 1981, for example, the Attorney General addressed a joint congressional subcommittee, testifying that "[w]e have lost control of our borders. We have pursued unrealistic policies. We have failed to enforce our laws effectively." Administration's Proposals on Immigration and Refugee Policy: Joint Hearing Before the Subcomm. on Immigration, Refugees, and International Law of the House Comm. on the Judiciary, and the Subcomm. on Immigration and Refugee Policy of the Senate Comm. on the Judiciary, 97th Cong., 1st Sess. 6 (1981) (testimony of Att'y Gen. William French Smith).

232. It has been estimated that those who reside temporarily in the United States stay for six to 48 months. SCIRP Staff Report, supra note 25, at 544.

233. See United States v. Wong Kim Ark, 169 U.S. 649 (1898) (fourteenth amendment grounds). British law, in contrast, states that a person born in Britain will be a citizen if one parent at birth is a citizen or is settled in Britain, or can become a citizen if either parent does so while the child is a minor. British Nationality Act, 1981, ch. 61, §§ 1, 3. Previous British law conferred citizenship at birth unconditionally. See British Nationality Act, 1948, 11 & 12 Geo. 6, ch. 56, § 4; see also Sandifer, A Comparative Study of Laws Relating to Nationality at Birth and to Loss of Nationality, 29 Am. J. Int'l L. 248, 253–59 (1935) (discussing the widespread application of the *jus sanguinis* principle in civil law countries).

234. Piore, supra note 203; see also Immigration to the United States: Hearings before the Select Comm. on Population, 95th Cong., 2d Sess. 183–90 (1978) (statement of Burdette Wright). For an interesting example of an important public benefit newly extended to undocumented aliens, see Cummings, California Law Gives Aliens Lower College Costs, N.Y. Times, Dec. 6, 1983, at A22, col. 2 (resident illegal aliens may attend University of California system at reduced tuition rates, considerably lower than what out-of-state American citizens must pay).

235. For a discussion of the role of churches in harboring and supporting illegal aliens, see Austin, More Churches Join in Offering Sanctuary for Latin Refugees, N.Y. Times, Sept. 21, 1983, at A18, col. 1.

236. For an analysis of recent polling data bearing on this question, see Harwood, Alienation: American Attitudes toward Immigration, Pub. Op., June/July 1983, at 49.

237. But see Lopez, supra note 12, at 639–72 (historically, United States government and American employers actively encouraged Mexicans to immigrate here).

238. Obviously, Americans do not always vote along ethnic lines. Nevertheless, ethnic identification continues to be a powerful force in American politics. See Hispanic Power Arrives at the Ballot Box, Bus. Wk., July 4, 1983, at 32; Into the Mainstream: Widespread Political Efforts Open New Era for Hispanics, 40 Cong. Q. 2707 (1982). But the implication of the growing Hispanic political power for immigration policy is ambiguous. See Graham, Illegal Immigration and the New Restrictionism, 12 Center Mag., May–June 1979, at 54–64. Also, polls taken among blacks and Hispanics, both citizen and noncitizen, show they favor restriction of legal immigration and harsher policies toward illegal immigrants. 1 Fed. Imm. L. Rep. (CCH) Update No. 29, at 3–4 (Aug. 8, 1983).

239. Chapter 1 discusses current demographic projections.

240. See, e.g., Schmidt, Denver Election Widens Circle of Hispanic Leaders, N.Y. Times, June 23, 1983, at A16, col. 1. For an analysis of Hispanic voting power, see Kirschten, The Hispanic Vote—Parties Can't Gamble that the Sleeping Giant Won't Awaken, 15 Nat'l J. 2410 (1983).

241. See, e.g., Pear, Immigration and Politics: Hispanic Bloc's Fears Key to Failure of Bill, N.Y. Times, Oct. 6, 1983, at Al, col. 1; Hispanic Leaders Oppose Sanctions, 1 Fed. Imm. L. Rep. (CCH) Update No. 1, at 3 (Feb. 28, 1983); Coleman, Hispanics Hit Immigration Revision, Wash. Post, Feb. 26, 1983, at A9, col. 1.

242. See generally Schuck, Book Review, 90 Yale L.J. 702, 717–20 (1981) (reviewing The Politics of Regulation (J. Wilson ed. 1980)).

243. Smothers, Two Parties Woo Votes of Hispanic Americans, N.Y. Times, Sept. 17, 1983, at A7, col. 1.

244. American Enterprise Institute for Public Policy Research, Illegal Aliens: Problems and Policies 12 (1978).

245. An estimated 60% of refugees who have come from Southeast Asia since 1975 are concentrated in forty counties. Placement Policy Task Force, Office of Refugee Resettlement, Dep't of Health and Human Servs., Concept Paper on Refugee Placement Policy (1981). The concentration of Cuban, Haitian and Salvadoran refugees in south Florida and New York, of course, is especially striking.

246. See Harwood, supra note 236.

247. Chapter 1 discusses the statutory reforms enacted by Congress during the 1980's–1990's in response to this anxiety.

248. Kennedy, Form and Substance in Private Law Adjudication, 89 Harv. L. Rev. 1685 (1976).

249. Id. at 1733–35.

250. Id. at 1735–36.

251. Id. at 1736–37.

252. 182 U.S. 244 (1901), discussed supra text accompanying note 47.

253. See supra notes 29–34 and accompanying text.

254. See supra notes 9–11 and accompanying text.

255. McAuliffe v. Mayor of New Bedford, 155 Mass. 216, 220, 29 N.E. 517, 517–18 (1892).

256. That initial entry by an alien is quintessentially a privilege, explicitly characterized as such, has been a cardinal principle from the Court's earliest immigration decisions, see, e.g., *The Chinese Exclusion Case*, 130 U.S. 581 (1889), down to the Court's last Term, see Landon v. Plasencia, 103 S. Ct. 321 (1982).

257. See Van Alstyne, The Demise of the Right-Privilege Distinction in Constitutional Law, 81 Harv. L. Rev. 1439 (1968), and cases discussed therein.

258. To oversimplify a bit, the distinction continues to do service, albeit often sub rosa, in the Court's determinations concerning whether a protected property or liberty interest exists and if so, what process is due before it can be infringed. See, e.g., Smolla, The Reemergence of the Right-Privilege Distinction in Constitutional Law: The Price of Protesting Too Much, 35 Stan. L. Rev. 69 (1982), and cases discussed therein.

259. The historical character of this phenomenon is traced in Yeazell, Group Litigation and Social Context: Toward a History of the Class Action, 77 Colum. L. Rev. 866 (1977).

260. See Fishkin, The Boundaries of Justice, 27 J. Conflict Resolution 355, 358–61 (1983) ("To the extent one gives independent weight . . . to a special class of persons within the [nation's] boundary, one is departing from the liberal paradigm for theories of justice."); supra note 33 and accompanying text.

261. See supra text following note 12.

262. Kennedy's "altruist" ethos, which he opposes to individualism, includes values similar to those that I have termed "communitarian." Altruism, however, implies a particular kind of motivation that may or may not underlie communitarian values. Moreover, Kennedy applies his theoretical framework only to the private law of contracts. Kennedy, supra note 248, at 1685.

263. G. Gilmore, The Death of Contract 65, 87–90 (1974). Historically, one might regard this as the next stage of an earlier movement, that from status to contract. See H. Maine, Ancient Law 163–65 (1864).

264. See Rakoff, Contracts of Adhesion: An Essay in Reconstruction, 90 Harv. L. Rev. 1174, 1190–97 (1983); Lublin, Legal Challenges Force Firms to Revamp Ways They Dismiss Workers, Wall St. J., Sept. 13, 1983, at 1, col. 6.

265. Compare G. Gilmore, supra note 263, at 42–44 (discussing the traditional view), with Kronman, Mistake, Disclosure, Information and the Law of Contracts, in The Economics of Contract Law 114–121 (1979) (discussing the emerging view).

266. I. MacNeil, The New Social Contract: An Inquiry into Modern Contractual Relations (1980).

267. See Kennedy, supra note 248, at 1751.

268. See, e.g., Trentacost v. Brussel, 82 N.J. 214, 412 A.2d 436 (1980).

269. Restatement (Second) of Torts § 335 (1965); Harper & James, supra note 17, at 1443–44.

270. See, e.g., Tarasoff v. Board of Regents, 17 Cal. 3d 425, 551 P.2d 334 (1976).

271. See, e.g., Cobbs v. Grant, 8 Cal. 3d 229, 502 P.2d 1 (1972).

272. See, e.g., Employee Retirement Income Security Act of 1974, §§ 401–404, 29 U.S.C. §§ 1101–1104 (1976 & Supp. V 1981) (fiduciary duties of insurers).

273. Stewart, The Reformation of American Administrative Law, 88 Harv. L. Rev. 1669, 1671–76 (1975).

274. Id. at 1676–88.

275. Id. at 1711–802.

276. Chayes, The Role of the Judge in Public Law Litigation, 89 Harv. L. Rev. 1281, 1304–13 (1976); Stewart, supra note 273, at 1723–56.

277. See, e.g., Motor Vehicle Mfrs. Ass'n v. State Farm Mut. Auto. Ins. Co., 103 S. Ct. 2856 (1983).

278. P. Schuck, supra note 18, ch. 7; Chayes, supra note 276, at 1298–301.

279. See generally Reich, The New Property, 73 Yale L.J. 733 (1964).

280. See generally Chayes, supra note 276; Stewart, supra note 273.

281. See P. Schuck, supra note 18, at 1–29; Chayes, supra note 276, at 1284; Fiss, The Supreme Court, 1978 Term—Foreword: The Forms of Justice, 93 Harv. L. Rev. 1, 24–28 (1979).

282. See, e.g., infra notes 285–332, 385 and accompanying text. Group litigation on behalf of aliens was made possible by, and itself facilitated, the creation of "public interest" law centers specializing in aliens' rights, such as the Haitian Refugee Center in Florida.

283. See, e.g., J. Ely, Democracy and Distrust 14–22 (1980).

284. MacNeil calls these "supracontract norms," MacNeil, supra note 266, at 70, while Kennedy, with much the same phenomena in mind, refers to "altruistic" values, Kennedy, supra note 248, at 1717–22. For discussions of nonmarket values in administrative law, see Stewart, Regulation in a Liberal State: The Role of Non-Commodity Values, 92 Yale L.J. (July 1983 forthcoming); Schuck, Regulation, Non-Market Values and the Administrative State, 92 Yale L.J. (July 1983 forthcoming).

285. 457 U.S. 202 (1982).

286. 347 U.S. 483 (1954).

287. The implications of the *Plyler* decision for the constitutionality of Proposition 187 in California is analyzed in Chapter 6.

288. *Plyler,* however, appears to depart from conventional equal protection analysis. The Court acknowledged that, strictly speaking, the case involved neither a "suspect class" nor a "fundamental right." 457 U.S. at 223. Under the Court's precedents, therefore, it should have simply asked whether the state statute had a "rational basis." See, e.g., San Antonio Indep. School Dist. v. Rodriguez, 411 U.S. 1 (1973); Railway Express Agency v. New York, 336 U.S. 106 (1949). Instead, the Court insisted that Texas could sustain its statute only by showing that "it furthers some substantial goal of the State." *Plyler,* 457 U.S. at 223. The doctrinal anomaly thus presented lends some credence to a broader interpretation of *Plyler.*

289. U.S. Const. amend XIV.

290. Id. amend XIX.

291. See The Japanese Immigrant Case, 189 U.S. 86 (1903), discussed supra note 77.

292. The plaintiff children in these cases are special members of this class of undocumented aliens. Persuasive arguments support the view that a state may withhold its beneficence from those whose very presence within the United States results from their own unlawful conduct. These arguments do not apply with the same force to classifications imposing disabilities on the minor children of such illegal entrants. Those who elect to enter our territory by stealth and in violation of our law should be prepared to bear the consequences. But their children are not comparably situated. "[Parents] 'have the ability to conform their conduct to societal norms,' and presumably the ability to remove themselves from the State's jurisdiction; but [their] children . . . 'can affect neither their parents' conduct nor their own status.'" *Plyler,* 457 U.S. at 220 (quoting Trimble v. Gordon, 430 U.S. 762, 770 (1977)).

293. Id. at 221–23.

294. See De Canas v. Bica, 424 U.S. 351 (1976).

295. See supra note 52.

296. See, e.g., Lopez, supra note 12, at 645–46 (noting historical pattern of recruiting of Mexican aliens in Southwestern States; Developments, supra note 4, at 1453 (discerning an "unspoken policy of inviting undocumented aliens into the country to contribute to the economy").

297. *Plyler,* 457 U.S. at 225–26.

298. 8 U.S.C. § 1325 (1982).

299. In fiscal 1983, the Border Patrol apprehended one million aliens attempting to cross the border illegally. Wash. Post, Oct. 22, 1983, at A3, col. 1. On October 21, 1983, the INS Commissioner announced that next year he will seek supplemental appropriations for a 50% increase in Border Patrol personnel. Id.

300. See General Accounting Office, Report to the Congress by the Comptroller General of the United States: Illegal Aliens: Estimating their Impact on the United States 22 (1980); General Accounting Office, Report to the Senate Committee on the Budget by the Comptroller General of the United States: Impact of Illegal Aliens on Public Assistance Programs: Too Little is Known (1977).

301. 424 U.S. 351 (1976).

302. Id. at 356–63.

303. *Plyler,* 457 U.S. at 225–26. Indeed, in *De Canas,* unlike in *Plyler,* there was a plausible ground for arguing that the state law was in fact inconsistent with the immigration statute, yet the Court sustained the former as "consistent" with the latter. 424 U.S. at 363–65.

304. *Plyler,* 457 U.S. at 226.

305. The employer sanction provision that is the centerpiece of the pending immigration reform law probably cannot meet such a test either. General Accounting Office, Report to the Senate Subcommittee on Immigration and Refugee Policy, Committee on the Judiciary by the Comptroller General of the United States: Administrative Changes Needed to Reduce Employment of Illegal Aliens 22 (1981). For comparison with foreign countries, see General Accounting Office, Report to the Senate Subcommittee on Immigration and Refugee Policy, Committee on the Judiciary by the Comptroller General of the United States: Information on the Enforcement of Laws Regarding Employment of Aliens in Selected Countries (1982).

306. See also Ruiz v. Blum, 549 F. Supp. 871 (S.D.N.Y. 1982) (invalidating restrictions on participation by illegal aliens in publicly subsidized day care).

307. By denying parents employment, the statute in *De Canas* surely harmed their innocent children. It is possible, of course, to argue that the relationship between the statute and the harm to children was significantly less direct in *De Canas* than in *Plyler*. But both harms are eminently foreseeable, intended as disincentives to illegal immigration, and therefore direct. On the other hand, a distinction might be drawn between the immediate economic harm caused by the statute in *De Canas*, see supra note 294, and the real but more, attenuated economic harm that would result from a statute that denied, for example, educational benefits to undocumented alien parents, see supra note 292.

308. To be sure, the Court analyzes *Plyler* as a fourteenth amendment case, continues to cite approvingly Mathews v. Diaz, 426 U.S. 67 (1976), and emphasizes the plenary power of Congress in this field, see *Plyler*, 457 U.S. at 210–25. Nevertheless, much of the *Plyler* Court's equal protection analysis would seem to cast doubt upon a congressional enactment that barred undocumented children from public schools receiving federal assistance. This is particularly true of the arguments about innocent children, id. at 219–20, the uncertainty of deportation for any particular illegal alien—what the Court calls "an inchoate federal permission to remain," id. at 226—the policy's ineffectiveness, id. at 228, the de minimis effect on educational quality, id. at 229, and the long-term effects of deprivation, id. at 230.

309. Earlier decisions, beginning with The Japanese Immigrant Case, 189 U.S. 86 (1903), had conferred certain procedural rights upon excludable or deportable aliens, but not substantive rights.

310. The Texas statute in *Plyler* extended education benefits to lawfully admitted aliens and citizens, including children born here to illegal aliens, 457 U.S. at 245 n.4 (Burger, C.J., dissenting), and aliens who were in the process of obtaining documentation, id. at 205 n.2 (Opinion of the Court).

311. The Supreme Court's epochal decision in INS v. Chadha, 103 S. Ct. 2764 (1983), cannot be counted an exception. *Chadha* invalidated the legislative veto provision contained in 8 U.S.C. § 1254(c)(2) (1982), part of the immigration statute's suspension-of-deportation section, holding it severable from the rest of the act. But the decision was clearly preoccupied with broad constitutional principles rather than with anything peculiar to immigration law. The Court's criticisms of the legislative veto are unquestionably stronger with respect to the narrow, nonpolicy, adjudicative decision presented in the deportation setting than they are in most other statutory contexts, where broad national policy is at issue. See, e.g., Elliott, INS v. Chadha: The Administrative Constitution, the Constitution, and the Legislative Veto, 1983 Sup. Ct. Rev. (forthcoming). Indeed, were it not for the conventional characterization of deportation as a "civil" proceeding, see supra notes 130–36 and accompanying text, the legislative veto as applied in *Chadha* might well constitute a bill of attainder. Nevertheless, the Court resisted the suggestion, see 103 S. Ct. at 2788–89 (Powell, J., concurring); id. at 2792–93 (White, J., dissenting) (both objecting to the breadth of the holding), that it limit its holding to the particular statute before it. If all legislative veto provisions violate the Constitution, as the Court seems to believe, no plausible basis exists for excepting the immigration statute.

For what it is worth, the Court reaffirmed "the plenary authority of Congress over aliens." It may or may not be significant that the Court then immediately added that Congress has plenary authority *whenever* it has legislative jurisdiction. Id. at 2779.

312. See e.g., Fernandez-Roque v. Smith, 567 F. Supp. 1115 (N.D. Ga. 1983).

313. 563 F. Supp. 157 (D.D.C. 1983).

314. Since the Immigration Act of 1990, EVD-type relief has been regulated by statute under the label of "temporary protected status" (TPS).

315. 8 C.F.R. § 244.2 (1983). Plaintiff also challenged another alleged practice—the routine recommendation of denial of El Salvadoran asylum claims without regard to their individ-

ual merits. *Employees Union,* 563 F. Supp. at 161; Plaintiff's Memorandum of Points and Authorities in Opposition to Motion to Dismiss at 16–17. The court failed to discuss this claim.

316. Asylum may be unavailable for any of a number of reasons. The threatening conditions, for example, may not constitute a kind of "persecution" enumerated by the Refugee Act of 1980, § 201, 8 U.S.C. § 1101(a)(42) (1982). They may be too generalized or random to satisfy the Act's requirement that asylum be granted only for persecution directed at the particular individual who claims that status. 8 U.S.C. § 1158. The claimant may have been "firmly resettled" elsewhere and therefore ineligible for asylum hereunder. § 1101(a)(42). See, e.g., Rosenberg v. Yee Chien Woo, 402 U.S. 49 (1971); In re Portales, 18 1. & N. Dec. No. 2905 (BIA 1982).

317. INS Asylum Study, supra note 168, at 66.

318. Plaintiff's Memorandum of Points and Authorities in Opposition to Motion to Dismiss at 23, *Employees Union.*

319. 5 U.S.C. § 553 (1982) establishes certain procedures for agency rulemaking.

320. 563 F. Supp. at 161–63; Plaintiff's Memorandum of Points and Authorities in Opposition to Motion to Dismiss at 16–24.

321. 563 F. Supp. at 160; Defendants' Memorandum of Points and Authorities in Support of Motion to Dismiss at 7–9.

322. See Fiallo v. Bell, 430 U.S. 787 (1977); Kleindienst v. Mandel, 408 U.S. 753 (1972).

323. See, e.g., Schuck, Suing Our Servants: The Court, Congress, and the Liability of Public Officials for Damages, 1980 Sup. Ct. Rev. 281, 368.

324. *Employees Union,* 563 F. Supp. at 160. This phrase was actually extracted from a letter written by a State Department official in response to Senator Kennedy's letter to Secretary of State Haig criticizing the Administration's EVD policy: "While fighting in some areas has been severe, El Salvador has not suffered the same level of *widespread fighting, destruction and breakdown of public services and order* as did for example, Nicaragua, Lebanon or Uganda at the time when voluntary departure was recommended by the Department and granted by INS for nationals of those countries." Letter from A. Drischler, Acting Ass't Secretary for Congressional Relations, to Senator Edward Kennedy (Apr. 17, 1981) (emphasis added) (explaining why EVD was not granted to El Salvadorans), reprinted in 128 Cong. Rec. S831 (daily ed. Feb. 11, 1982).

325. Government's Motion to Dismiss at 7–9, *Employees Union.*

326. First, independent objective indices for the standard would be necessary, such as casualties, extent of destruction, change in the quality of public services and order, and political conditions. Then, available data from other countries would have to be gathered and compared to these indices.

327. Even if the necessary indices and data were made available to a court, neither the alien plaintiff nor the court would be likely to possess the resources to independently assess them. Moreover, in evaluating plaintiff's equal protection claim, the court must decide what other country or countries are "similarly situated" to the country to whose nationals the EVD, if granted, would apply. Yet it is not clear how the court would make such a judgment.

328. *Employees Union,* 563 F. Supp. at 161.

329. Id. Although the judge stated that the government had failed to allege that the case "specifically presents a situation in which it is essential that the United States speak with one voice," id., he earlier noted that the government had contended that prudential considerations "such as a need for the government to speak with a single voice," in combination with other factors, rendered the case nonjusticiable, id. at 160.

330. Id. at 161–62.

331. A nonbinding resolution calling upon the Reagan administration to grant Salvadorans extended voluntary departure was recently adopted by Congress as part of the State Department appropriations bill for 1984–1985. See H.R. 2915, § 1012, 129 Cong. Rec. H10,236,

H10,249 (daily ed. Nov. 17, 1983). Bills to bind the Administration in that regard have been introduced. S.2131, H.R. 4447, 98th Cong., 1st Sess. (1983).

332. See P. Schuck, supra note 18, ch. 7.

333. See infra notes 388–399 and accompanying text.

334. 103 S. Ct. 321 (1982).

335. Id. at 327–29; see also Rosenberg v. Fleuti, 374 U.S. 449 (1963); Kwong Hai Chew v. Colding, 344 U.S. 590 (1953). One commentary seems to regard *Landon* as a significant and welcome departure from earlier doctrine, particularly the Court's decisions in Shaughnessy v. United States ex rel. Mezei, 345 U.S. 206 (1953), discussed supra notes 100–02, 151–61 and accompanying text; and United States ex rel. Knauff v. Shaughnessy, 338 U.S. 537 (1950), discussed supra text accompanying note 99. See Developments, supra note 4, at 1319–20, 1323. This view, however, neglects the clear language of *Rosenberg,* 374 U.S. at 460, the fact that the absence in *Mezei* was lengthy and therefore distinguishable, and that *Knauff* did not involve a returning permanent resident at all. It is of interest that the Court in *Landon* cites both *Knauff* and *Mezei.* 103 S. Ct. at 329–30. Indeed, in one respect, *Landon* may limit the procedural protections available to the returning permanent resident, for the Court there holds for the first time that the question of her "entry"—that is, of excludability—can be decided in an exclusion rather than deportation proceeding. 103 S. Ct. at 325–29. The Court strongly suggests that the process which is due in that proceeding may be less than that which would apply in the deportation setting. Id. at 330. For a very recent lower court decision extending the *Fleuti* approach to a nonimmigrant seeking to remain in the United States after an INS-approved departure and return, see Joshi v. INS, No. 83–1614 (4th Cir. Oct. 27, 1983) (deportation rather than exclusion proceedings appropriate for addressing merits of claim).

336. *Plasencia,* 103 S. Ct. at 327–30. In so doing, the Court cited with apparent approval United States ex rel. Knauff v. Shaughnessy, 338 U.S. 537 (1950). 103 S. Ct. at 329–30. The Court also distinguished, on the basis of the length of absence, Shaughnessy v. United States ex rel. Mezei, 345 U.S. 206 (1953). 103 S. Ct. at 330. Finally, the Court once again embraced the rights-privilege distinction: "an alien seeking initial admission . . . requests a privilege and has no constitutional rights regarding his application, for the power to admit or exclude aliens is a sovereign prerogative." Id. at 329.

337. 551 F. Supp. 960 (E.D.N.Y. 1982), appeal dismissed sub nom. Phelisna v. Sava, No. 83–2034 (2d Cir. Apr. 29, 1983).

338. Id. at 963.

339. See id. at 962–63 (discussing Thack v. Zurbrick, 51 F.2d 634 (6th Cir. 1931), and citing United States ex rel. Giacone v. Corsi, 64 F.2d 18 (2d Cir. 1933)).

340. See supra notes 109–29 and accompanying text.

341. 541 F. Supp. 569 (N.D. Cal. 1982), aff'd sub nom. Hill v. INS, 714 F.2d 1470 (9th Cir. 1983). For a contrary holding see In re Longstaff, 716 F.2d 1439 (5th Cir. 1983) (since homosexual could have been admitted only through error, he had not been "legally" granted residency).

342. Boutilier v. INS, 387 U.S. 118 (1967). The district court in *Lesbian/Gay Freedom Day,* 541 F. Supp. at 584–85, distinguished *Boutilier* on the ground that Congress had not intended to freeze the exclusion of homosexuals into the statutory category—aliens afflicted with sexual deviation, or a mental defect—but wanted the exclusion to be subject to changing medical opinion.

343. 541 F. Supp. at 585–88.

344. Kleindienst v. Mandel, 408 U.S. 753, 768–70 (1972). The district court distinguished *Mandel* on the ground that here, unlike in *Mandel,* the government had advanced no "facially legitimate and bona fide reason" for the exclusion. *Lesbian/Gay Freedom Day,* 541 F. Supp. at 585–86 (quoting *Mandel,* 408 U.S. at 770).

345. As discussed in chapter 4, Congress in 1990 limited somewhat the ideological and status grounds for exclusion and deportation.

346. Kleindienst v. Mandel, 408 U.S. 753 (1972); Shaughnessy v. United States ex rel. Mezei, 345 U.S. 206 (1953); United States ex rel. Knauff v. Shaughnessy, 338 U.S. 537 (1950); Nishimura Ekiu v. United States, 142 U.S. 651 (1892).

347. Pub. L. No. 96–212, § 201(a), 94 Stat. 102 (1980).

348. Kleindienst v. Mandel, 408 U.S. 753, 769 (1972).

349. See, e.g., City of Akron v. Akron Center for Reproductive Health, Inc., 103 S. Ct. 2481, 2495–2516 (1983); Christensen v. Wisconsin Medical Bd., 551 F. Supp. 565, 568–70 (W.D. Wis. 1982).

350. See, e.g., Bolger v. Youngs Drug Prods. Corp., 103 S. Ct. 2875, 2881–85 (1983); United States v. Dickens, 695 F.2d 765, 772–74 (3d Cir. 1982), cert. denied, 103 S. Ct. 1792 (1983).

351. The Court in Kleindienst v. Mandel, 408 U.S. 753, 769–70 (1972), seemed to approve of this approach, however reluctantly. Thus, while upholding the government's position, the Court invited the kinds of challenges presented by *Lesbian/Gay Freedom Day* by recognizing the government's obligation to justify its exclusion and by analyzing those justifications, however superficially, for their facial legitimacy and bona fides.

352. 426 U.S. 67 (1976).

353. 430 U.S. 787 (1977).

354. 426 U.S. 88 (1976).

355. For criticism of the Court's approach in this case, see Schuck, Organization Theory and the Teaching of Administrative Law, 33 J. of Legal Educ. 13, 17 (1983). Even the result in *Hampton* was ephemeral; it was quickly reversed. See Exec. Order No. 11,935, 5 C.F.R. § 13 (1983), reprinted in 5 U.S.C. § 3301 app. at 384 (1976) (upheld in Mow Sun Wong v. Campbell, 626 F.2d 739 (9th Cir. 1980), cert. denied, 450 U.S. 959 (1981)). The Court's decision in *Diaz,* announced on the same day as *Hampton,* thus seems to be of hardier stock. Indeed, even state laws barring aliens from state employment seem to enjoy considerable constitutional legitimacy today, at least where the classification can be depicted, however implausibly, as manifesting the state's conception of its "political community." See Cabell v. Chavez-Salido, 454 U.S. 432, 447 (1982).

356. *Diaz,* 426 U.S. at 82.

357. *Fiallo,* 430 U.S. at 794–95 (quoting Kleindienst v. Mandel, 408 U.S. 753, 769–70 (1972), discussed supra notes 344–48, 351).

358. The classic example, of course, is the doctrine of heightened scrutiny of classifications affecting "discrete and insular minorities," rooted in a mere footnote. United States v. Carolene Prods. Co., 304 U.S. 144, 152 n.4 (1938). See generally J. Ely, supra note 283; Lusky, Footnote Redux: A *Carolene Products* Reminiscence, 82 Colum. L. Rev. 1093 (1982); Powell, *Carolene Products* Revisited, 82 Colum. L. Rev. 1087 (1982).

359. See, e.g., Rogers v. Bellei, 401 U.S. 815, 830 (1971); Afroyim v. Rusk, 387 U.S. 253, 257 (1967).

360. 457 U.S. 202 (1982), discussed supra notes 285–310 and accompanying text.

361. That criterion has been viewed by the Court as crucial to rationalize the series of cases, beginning with Graham v. Richardson, 403 U.S. 365 (1971), that involve *state* alienage classifications. The most recent of these cases is Cabell v. Chavez-Salido, 454 U.S. 432, 447 (1982).

362. 563 F. Supp. 157 (1983), discussed supra notes 313–32 and accompanying text.

363. See supra notes 145–48, 255–58 and accompanying text. Deportation under the individualistic ideology can also be analogized to a creditor's summary enforcement of contract rights. See supra note 147.

364. Lopez-Mendoza v. INS, 705 F.2d 1059 (9th Cir. 1983) (en banc), petition for cert. filed, 52 U.S.L.W. 3294 (U.S. Sept. 22, 1983) (No. 83–491).

This decision is especially significant in light of the Supreme Court's growing opposition to the exclusionary rule. See, e.g., Rawlings v. Kentucky, 448 U.S. 98 (1980); United States v.

Payner, 447 U.S. 727 (1980); see also Illinois Migrant Council v. Pilliod, 531 F. Supp. 1011 (N.D. Ill. 1982).

365. International Ladies' Garment Workers' Union v. Sureck, 681 F.2d 624 (9th Cir. 1982), cert. granted sub nom. INS v. Delgado, 103 S. Ct. 1872 (1983).

366. Aguilera-Enriquez v. INS, 516 F.2d 565, 569 n.3 (6th Cir. 1975), cert. denied, 423 U.S. 1050 (1976). One commentator has concluded that a right to appoint counsel has been created in effect for asylum claimants facing deportation. See infra note 397.

367. See infra notes 385–90 and accompanying text.

368. The 1996 amendments, discussed in Chapter 1, contained many examples of such resistance.

369. See Developments, supra note 4, at 1384–95.

370. United States v. Ward, 448 U.S. 242, 251 (1980), created such a quasi-criminal category in a nonimmigration context. See Wheeler, The Constitutional Case for Reforming Punitive Damages Procedures, 69 Va. L. Rev. 269, 322–51 (1983); see also Woodby v. INS, 385 U.S. 276, 285 (1966) (a deportation proceeding requires a higher degree of evidence despite its noncriminal nature).

371. See, e.g., Francis v. INS, 532 F.2d 268 (2d Cir. 1976); Noel v. Chapman, 508 F.2d 1023 (2d Cir.), cert. denied, 423 U.S. 824 (1975).

372. See, e.g., Developments, supra note 4, at 1395–98.

373. Total apprehensions in 1996 exceeded 1.6 million.

374. See infra notes 431–33 and accompanying text.

375. See Petition for Writ of Certiorari at 17 n.10, INS v. Lopez-Mendoza, filed, 52 U.S.L.W. 3268 (U.S. Sept. 22, 1983) (No. 83–491). For a discussion of the effect of procedures on decision quality in the context of the social security disability program, see J. Mashaw, Bureaucratic Justice 106–23 (1983). Professor Mashaw has also analyzed this question in the context of the Aid to Families with Dependent Children program during the early 1970's. See Mashaw, The Management Side of Due Process, 59 Cornell L. Rev. 772, 776–91, 811–15 (1974) (due process hearings of little value to AFDC claimants); see also infra notes 451–52 and accompanying text.

376. See, e.g., Louis v. Nelson, 544 F. Supp. 973, 975–76 (S.D. Fla. 1982), aff'd sub nom. Jean v. Nelson, 711 F.2d 1455, reh'g en banc granted, 714 F.2d 96 (11th Cir. 1983).

377. See supra note 164.

378. Although the Eighth Amendment's prohibition of "cruel and unusual punishment," U.S. Const. amend. VIII, does not apply prior to conviction, Fifth Amendment due process requirements do. U.S. Const. amend. V. See City of Revere v. Massachusetts Gen. Hosp., 103 S. Ct. 2979 (1983).

379. 8 U.S.C. § 1158 (1982). Indeed, the provisions of the Refugee Act have recently been held to require INS to provide an asylum hearing even to stowaways, who are denied an exclusion hearing under 8 U.S.C. § 1182(a)(18) (1982) of the immigration statute. See Yin Sing Chun v. Sava, 708 F.2d 869 (2d Cir. 1983).

380. 8 U.S.C. § 1253(h) (1982).

381. See supra notes 315–17 and accompanying text.

382. See Nicholas v. INS, 590 F.2d 802 (9th Cir. 1979) (INS district director has affirmative duty to recommend deferred action status where she feels it is appropriate; court will review her decision for abuse of discretion). But cf. Pasquini v. Morris, 700 F.2d 658 (11th Cir. 1983) (deferred action guidelines confer no substantive right and court will only review for abuse of discretion).

383. See P. Schuck, supra note 82, at 255–65.

384. See INS Asylum Study, supra note 168, at 20–26; Aleinikoff, supra note 221, at 254–56.

385. These transgressions include violations of due process and equal protection under the fifth amendment, U.S. Const. amend. V, and of 8 U.S.C. §§ 1252(b), 1253(h) (1982). See Hai

ian Refugee Center v. Smith, 676 F.2d 1023 (5th Cir. 1982) (rights of alien seeking political asylum held sufficient to invoke due process guarantees); Fernandez-Roque v. Smith, 567 F. Supp. 1115 (N.D. Ga. 1983) (INS violated due process clause by not providing detained excludable aliens with procedurally adequate hearings); Louis v. Nelson, 544 F. Supp. 973 (S.D. Fla. 1982) (INS detention program violated equal protection clause), aff'd sub. nom. Jean v. Nelson, 711 F.2d 1455, reh'g en banc granted, 714 F.2d 96 (11th Cir. 1983); Orantes-Hernandez v. Smith, 541 F. Supp. 351 (C.D. Cal. 1982) (INS violated due process clause by not advising aliens of their right to apply for political asylum); Nunez v. Boldin, 537 F. Supp. 578 (S.D. Tex.) (same), appeal dismissed, 692 F.2d 755 (5th Cir. 1982).

386. The 1996 amendments to the immigration statute severely restricted the availability of judicial relief from detention through habeas corpus or other forms of judicial review.

387. See Developments, supra note 4, at 1366–68.

388. See Jean v. Nelson, 711 F.2d 1455, 1472, reh'g en banc granted, 714 F.2d 96 (11th Cir. 1983).

389. See Haitian Refugee Center v. Smith, 676 F.2d 1023 (5th Cir. 1982).

390. See Orantes-Hernandez v. Smith, 541 F. Supp. 351 (C.D. Cal. 1982); Nunez v. Boldin, 537 F. Supp 578 (S.D. Tex.), appeal dismissed, 692 F.2d 755 (5th Cir. 1982).

391. See Rodriguez-Fernandez v. Wilkinson, 654 F.2d 1382 (10th Cir. 1981); Fernandez-Roque v. Smith, 567 F. Supp. 1115 (N.D. Ga. 1983). But see Palma v. Verdeyen, 676 F.2d 100 (4th Cir. 1982) (upholding an indefinite detention of an alien after an unsuccessful attempt to deport him).

392. 567 F. Supp. 1115 (N.D. Ga. 1983).

393. Id. at 1120, 1140.

394. Id. at 1139.

395. It is arguable that Congress intended to create these new rights when it acceded to the 1967 Protocol Relating to the Status of Refugees, Nov. 1, 1968, 19 U.S.T. 6224, T.I.A.S. No. 6577, 606 U.N.T.S. 267. But neither the Protocol nor the Handbook on Procedures and Criteria for Determining Refugee Status (1979), which is recognized as an authoritative explication of the Protocol, mentions these rights. Even article 26 of the 1951 Convention relating to the Status of Refugees, 189 U.N.T.S. 137, which the United States in the 1967 Protocol has undertaken to apply, provides for freedom of movement only for "refugees," who are "lawfully within the country," not for those whose status has not yet been determined. See Bertrand v. Sava, 684 F.2d 204, 219 (2d Cir. 1982) ("the Protocol affords the petitioners no rights beyond those they have under our domestic law").

396. Orantes-Hernandez v. Smith, 541 F. Supp. 351 (C.D. Cal. 1982).

397. Martin, supra note 103, at 171. Martin also suggests that the lower courts have in effect, if not in law, created a right to free appointed counsel by requiring expeditious hearings while also enjoining deportation hearings in which the alien lacks counsel. Id. at 219–20.

398. 8 C.F.R. § 208.3(b) (1983) ("asylum requests shall also be considered as requests for withholding exclusion or deportation").

399. Fernandez-Roque v. Smith, 567 F. Supp. 1115 (N.D. Ga. 1983).

400. 8 U.S.C. § 1158 (1982).

401. Id. § 1253(h)(1) (precluding deportation "if the Attorney General determines that such alien's life or freedom would be threatened in such country on account of race, religion, nationality, membership in a particular social group, or political opinion"). The showing that an alien must make to qualify for withholding of deportation under this provision is somewhat different, and less demanding, than that for asylum. Cf. 8 U.S.C. § 1101(a)(42)(A) (asylum requires showing of "persecution" or a "well-founded fear of persecution").

402. Under Leng May Ma v. Barber, 357 U.S. 185 (1958), aliens paroled into the country are not deemed to have "entered." See supra notes 160–61 and accompanying text.

403. See Marcello v. Bonds, 349 U.S. 302 (1955), discussed supra notes 185–89 and accompanying text.

404. The distinctions between the rights of asylum claimants and other aliens becomes understandable in these terms as well. One with a valid claim to asylum, almost by definition, has no other place to go.

405. 676 F.2d 1023 (5th Cir. 1982).

406. Haitian Refugee Center v. Civilett, 503 F. Supp. 442, 519–23 (S.D. Fla. 1980), aff'd sub nom Haitian Refugee Center v. Smith, 676 F.2d 1023 (5th Cir. 1982).

407. See Roberts, supra note 171, at 7–11; Wasserman, Some Defects in the Administration of Our Immigration Laws, 21 Law & Contemp. Probs. 376, 380–81 (1956); Developments, supra note 4, at 1364–66.

408. 48 Fed. Reg. 8038–40 (1983).

409. In 1990, an independent corps of asylum adjudicators was established by regulation.

410. See supra notes 285–402 and accompanying text. For examples and a discussion of the causes and consequences of this development, see P. Schuck, supra note 18, at 35–53.

411. See, e.g., Kleindienst v. Mandel, 408 U.S. 753, 770 (1972). For a discussion of the "law of leeways," see K. Llewellyn, The Bramble Bush 156–57 (1930).

412. Government Accounting Office, Prospects Dim for Effectively Enforcing Immigration Laws i–v (1981): see also supra notes 385–91 and accompanying text.

413. Immigration and Nationality Act of 1952, ch. 477, 66 Stat. 163 (codified as amended in 8 U.S.C. §§ 1101–1503 (1982)).

Chapters 1 and 4 discuss a series of important statutory changes enacted between 1986 and 1996.

414. See supra notes 6–8, 26–31 and accompanying text.

415. Immigration Act of 1924, ch. 139, § 11, 43 Stat. 153, 159 (repeal 1952); Immigration Act of 1917, ch. 301, § 3. 39 Stat. 874, 877. See supra notes 62–63 and accompanying text.

416. Morgan & Gardner, Potential for a U.S. Guest-Worker Program in Agriculture: Lessons from the Braceros, in The Gateway, supra note 198, at 361.

417. Chapters 1, 4, and 5 discuss these schemes.

418. See British Nationality Act, 1981, ch. 61. The 1981 Act, for example, restricts the extension of citizenship to persons born in the United Kingdom to those born to a British citizen or resident. Id. § 1. Prior law extended citizenship based on birth without restriction. See British Nationality Act, 1948, ¶908.

419. "[I]n a world of hierarchy, bureaucracy, and constituency," MacNeil notes, "[t]he law . . . is constitutional and administrative law and the law of political relations, more than the law of contract to which generations of American lawyers have been accustomed." I. Mac-Neil, supra note 266, at 84.

420. Even the expansion of fault-based tort liability, as powerful a trend as one finds in our law, has not been a steady one. See, e.g., M. Horwitz, The Transformation of American Law, 1780–1860, at 67–108 (1977) (describing nineteenth century tort law as limiting liability in order to provide a subsidy to economic interests). But see Schwartz, Tort Law and the Economy in Nineteenth-Century America: A Reinterpretation, 90 Yale L.J. 1717, 1722–34 (1981) (nineteenth century tort law was solicitous toward victims).

421. See generally, e.g., W. Ascher, Forecasting: An Appraisal for Policy-Makers and Planners (1979).

422. See generally P. Schuck, supra note 18, at 257.

423. In this respect, it resembles contract law and differs from most of tort law.

424. See INS v. Chadha, 103 S. Ct. 2764, 2774–75 (1983) (Congress established legislative veto over deportation suspensions to alleviate "intolerable" burden of private bills); id. at 2805–06 (White, J., dissenting) (same).

425. See, e.g., Jay v. Boyd, 351 U.S. 345 (1956) (suspension of deportation is not a matter of right, but a matter of grace); Comment, Congressional Review of Suspension of Deportation and the Doctrine of Separation of Powers, 19 San Diego L. Rev. 177 (1981); Comment, A

Suspension of Deportation: A Revitalized Relief for the Alien, 18 San Diego L. Rev. 65 (1980); Comment, Suspension of Deportation: Illusory Relief, 14 San Diego L. Rev. 229 (1976).

426. Perhaps the most celebrated practitioner of this strategic art is Carlos Marcello, who at this writing remains in the United States despite an order of deportation entered affirmed by the Supreme Court in 1955, and based upon a 1938 narcotics conviction. For the latest chapter in this never-ending epic, see Marcello v. INS, 694 F.2d 1033 (5th Cir.), cert. denied, 103 S. Ct. 3112 (1983), and for a synopsis of events up to 1981, see United States ex rel. Marcello v. District Director, 634 F.2d 964, 973–79 (5th Cir. 1981).

427. See Harwood, Can Immigration Laws Be Enforced?, 72 Pub. Interest 107, 109 (1983).

428. See, e.g., King, Flood of Bogus I.D. Papers Imperils Plan to Curb Aliens, N.Y. Times, Sept. 9, 1983, at A1, col. 1. The prevalence and importance of document fraud surely would be increased by enactment of the Simpson-Mazzoli immigration bill, which would create programs of employer sanctions and amnesty for illegal aliens based upon personal identification documents. See infra note 446.

429. As Chapter 1 discusses, the INS budget grew steadily during the 1980s and dramatically during the mid-1990s.

430. See N.Y. Times, Sept. 14, 1983, at A26, col. 1 (2800 Border Patrol officers); Telephone interview with the Office of the Sergeant at Arms of the Congress (Dec. 22, 1983 (1222 Capitol building security guards). The INS is seeking a significant increase in Border Patrol resources. See supra note 299.

431. See Harwood, supra note 427, at 109–10.

432. Id. at 111, 116.

433. Id. at 116.

434. See Lopez-Mendoza v. INS, 705 F.2d 1059, 1089–92 (9th Cir. 1983) (en banc) (Alarcon, J., dissenting), petition for cert. filed, 52 U.S.L.W. 3294 (U.S. Sept. 22, 1983) (No. 83–491). To be sure, the exclusionary rule has often been applied in immigration cases. Id. at 1064–65. But its use under current conditions could raise novel administrative problems. With respect to appointed counsel, see supra note 397.

435. 567 F. Supp. 1115 (N.D. Ga. 1983). See discussion supra notes 392–94 and accompanying text.

436. See Martin, supra note 397, at 180–81 (data from West Germany).

437. See, e.g., Harwood, Immigrant Bill Alien to Reality, N.Y. Times, Sept. 5, 1983, at 19, col. 4; King, supra note 428.

438. See supra note 222 and accompanying text.

439. See, e.g., Jean v. Nelson, 711 F.2d 1455, 1462–63, reh'g en banc granted, 714 F.2d 96 (11th Cir. 1983); Fernandez-Roque, 567 F. Supp. 1115 (N.D. Ga. 1983).

440. Letter from T. Alexander Aleinikoff to Peter H. Schuck (Aug. 25, 1983) (copy on file at the offices of the Columbia Law Review). Aleinikoff adds: "When we add to this the perceived political necessity of labelling refugees from friendly countries as 'illegal aliens' (Salvadorans) and illegal aliens from enemies as 'refugees' (Cubans), no wonder things are as confused as they are." Id.

441. See, e.g., supra notes 426–40 and accompanying text.

442. Their effectiveness, however, remains in serious doubt. For example, both programs could be subverted by massive document fraud. See Comment, Illegal Immigration: Employer Sanctions and Related Proposals, 19 San Diego L. Rev. 149, 164 (1981); King, supra note 428.

443. 457 U.S. 202 (1982).

444. N. Y. Times, Sept. 11, 1983, at A29, col. 1.

445. See Austin, More Churches Join in Offering Sanctuary for Latin Refugees, N.Y. Times, Sept. 21, 1983, at A18, col. 1.

446. Subsequent legislation, particularly the 1996 reform discussed in Chapters 1 and 5, has increased these sanctions.

447. For a rare example of such a challenge, see INS v. Chadha, 103 S. Ct. 2764 (1983).

448. As David Martin puts it, the private interests at stake are "off the charts," in terms of the balancing test of Mathews v. Eldridge, 424 U.S. 319, 334–35 (1976). Martin, supra note 103, at 190. This is also true in § 243(h) cases, which involve withholding of deportation because of the threat of persecution, 8 U.S.C. § 1253(h) (1982). See, e.g., Stevic v. Sava, 678 F.2d 401 (2d Cir. 1982) (deportation); Fernandez-Roque v. Smith, 567 F. Supp. 1115 (N.D. Ga. 1983) (detention); Hotel & Restaurant Employees Union, Local 25 v. Smith, 563 F. Supp. 157 (D.D.C. 1983) (extended voluntary departure).

449. 457 U.S. 202 (1982).

450. 563 F. Supp. 157, 160–61 (D.D.C. 1983).

451. See, e.g., P. Schuck, supra note 18, chs. 6 & 7; Altman, Implementing a Civil Rights Injunction: A Case Study of *NAACP v. Brennan,* 78 Colum. L. Rev. 739 (1978); Diver, The Judge as Political Powerbroker: Superintending Structural Change in Public Institutions, 65 Va. L. Rev. 43 (1979); Frug, The Judicial Power of the Purse, 126 U. Pa. L. Rev. 715 (1978). Moreover, unlike the typical structural injunction case, in which a state agency confronts the combined power of the federal government, a federal court ordering immigration reforms would oppose the United States Department of Justice, and perhaps the Congress as well. In that posture, successful implementation of the decree would be especially problematic.

452. See supra notes 423, 426–50 and accompanying text.

453. See supra notes 70–92, 371–73 and accompanying text.

454. See generally Chassman & Rolston, Social Security Disability Hearings: A Case Study in Quality Assurance and Due Process, 65 Cornell L. Rev. 801 (1980).

455. See supra notes 373–75, 434–40 and accompanying text.

456. See, e.g., Fiallo v. Bell, 430 U.S. 787 (1977) (upholding the definition of "child" under 8 U.S.C. § 1101(b)(1) (1982) as excluding illegitimate children who seek preference by virtue of the child's relationship with the father); Kleindienst v. Mandel, 408 U.S. 753 (1972) (upholding the refusal of the Attorney General to waive ineligibility for entry into the United States of a foreign journalist who was barred under 8 U.S.C. §§ 1182(a)(28)(D), (G)(v) & (d)(3)(A) (1982) as an advocate or publisher of the "doctrines of communism").

457. For a general exploration of remedial flexibility, see P. Schuck, supra note 18, ch. 8. For an application of the clear statement approach in a quasi-immigration case, see Kent v. Dulles, 357 U.S. 116 (1958) (holding that the Secretary of State may not refuse to issue a passport because of the applicant's political views, absent an explicit congressional provision).

458. See generally P. Schuck, supra note 18, at 143–46. According to Professor Diver's analysis, many categories of INS decisions are susceptible to this form of control. Diver, supra note 90, at 92–97, 106–09.

459. Friedrich, The Concept of Community in the History of Political and Legal Philosophy, in Community (Nomos II) 20 (1959).

460. See B. Ackerman, Social Justice in the Liberal State 89–95 (1980).

461. See C. Beitz, Political Theory and International Relations 161–76 (1979); Fishkin, supra note 260, at 358–61.

462. Yick Wo v. Hopkins, 118 U.S. 356, 369 (1886).

463. Aristotle, Politics, Bk. I, ii 8–12, at 111–13 (W. Bollard trans. 1877).

464. See discussion in Friedrich, supra note 459, at 7–12.

465. T. Hobbes, Leviathan 56–58 (Oakeshott ed. 1962); J. Locke, The Second Treatise of Government 62–64 (J. Gouch ed. 1946).

466. J. Rousseau, The Government of Poland 5–9 (W. Kendall trans. 1972).

467. M. Walzer, supra note 2, at 62.

468. Mutatis mutandis, it begins to approach Roberto Unger's "countervision" of contract law, in which "the initial, tentative definition of any entitlement must now be completed by a second stage. Here the boundaries are drawn and redrawn in context according to judgments

of both the expectations generated by the specific situation of interdependence and the impact that a particular exercise of a right might have upon other parties to the relationship or upon the relationship itself." Unger, The Critical Legal Studies Movement, 96 Harv. L. Rev. 561, 639–40 (1983). Indeed, to some commentators, even clear positive law is no limitation upon the vast transformational power of communitarian values. See, e.g., Lopez, supra note 12, at 696 ("No matter how strongly our formal laws deny it, our conduct creates the obligation [to undocumented Mexican workers]."). For several thoughtful efforts to refine the concept of community as applied to contemporary immigration law, see id.; Aleinikoff, supra note 221; Martin, supra note 103.

469. See SCIRP Staff report, supra note 25, at 296.

470. U.S. Bureau of the Census, Statistical Abstract of the United States: 1982–1983 (1982).

471. As discussed in Chapter 1, the percentage of foreign-born in the U.S. is now approaching 10%.

Chapter 3

1. For our purposes, the period of "the 1980s" began with the Mariel boatlift from Cuba in the early spring of 1980 and ended with the enactment of the Immigration Act of 1990, Pub. L. No. 101–649, 104 Stat. 4978 (codified as amended in scattered sections of 8, 18, 26, 29, and 42 U.S.C.) (1990 Act). See Peter H. Schuck, *The Politics of Rapid Legal Change: Immigration Policy in the 1980s,* in 6 STUDIES IN AMERICAN POLITICAL DEVELOPMENT 37, 44–49 (Stephen Skowronek & Karen Orren eds., Spring 1992; reprinted as Chapter 4 of this volume).

2. Pub. L. No. 96–212, 94 Stat. 102 (codified as amended in sections of 8, 20, 22, 42, and 50 U.S.C.) (Refugee Act).

3. 100 Stat. at 3359.

4. 104 Stat. at 4978.

5. Congress enacted other immigration legislation which, though more limited in scope, also could be considered significant reform. See Immigration Marriage Fraud Amendments of 1986, Pub. L. No. 99–639, 100 Stat. 3537 (codified as amended in scattered sections of 8 U.S.C.) (IMFA) (increasing sanctions for persons who obtain legal immigrant status through fraudulent marriages), *amended by* 1990 Act § 702, 104 Stat. at 5086; Anti-Drug Abuse Act of 1988, Pub. L. No. 100–690, § 7343(a)(4), 102 Stat. 4181, 4470 (codified as amended in scattered sections of 8 U.S.C.) (Anti-Drug Abuse Act) (requiring the detention of all aliens in deportation proceedings who have been convicted of an "aggravated felony").

6. See David A. Martin, *Reforming Asylum Adjudication: On Navigating the Cast of Bohemia,* 138 U. PA. L. REV. 1247, 1249–53 (1990).

7. See THOMAS ALEXANDER ALEINKOFF & DAVID A. MARTIN, IMMIGRATION: PROCESS AND POLICY 109–10 (Interim 2d ed. 1991). To reinforce these changes, the Justice Department in 1990 adopted new regulations providing for nonadversarial adjudication of asylum claims by a group of specially-trained asylum officers who are outside the district director's office. See Asylum and Withholding of Deportation Procedures, 55 Fed. Reg. 30,674 (1990) (to be codified at 8 C.F.R. pts. 3, 103, 208, 236, 242, and 253). However, the immigration court retains exclusive jurisdiction over asylum claims raised in exclusion or deportation proceedings.

8. See note 68 infra and accompanying test in original source.

9. See test accompanying notes 140–196 infra in original source.

10. See. e.g., GEORGE J. BORJAS, FRIENDS OR STRANGERS?: THE IMPACT OF IMMI-GRANTS ON THE U.S. ECONOMY (1990); LAWRENCE H. FUCHS, THE AMERICAN KALEIDO-

SCOPE: RACE, ETHNICITY, AND THE CIVIC CULTURE. (1990); JULIAN L. SIMON, THE ECONOMIC CONSEQUENCES OF IMMIGRATION (1989); Edmonston et al., *supra* note 3, at 11–28 in original source.

11. See e.g., Linda S. Bosniak, *Exclusion and Membership: The Dual Identity of the Undocumented Worker Under United States Law,* 1988 WIS L. REV. 955; Neil A. Friedman, *A Human Rights Approach to the Labor Rights of Undocumented Workers,* 74 CAL. L. REV. 1715 (1986).

12. See e.g., Arthur C. Helton, *Political Asylum Under the 1980 Refugee Act: An Unfulfilled Promise,* 17 U. MICH. J.L. REF. 243 (1984); Stephen H. Legomsky, *Political Asylum and Theory of Judicial Review,* 73 MINN. L. REV. 1205 (1989).

13. See. e.g., John A. Scanlan, *Aliens in the Marketplace of Ideas: The Government, the Academy, and the McCarran-Walter Act,* 66 TEX. L. REV. 1481 (1988); Steven R. Shapiro, *Ideological Exclusions: Closing the Border to Political Dissents,* 100 HARV. L. REV. 930 (1987).

14. See generally Peter H. Schuck, *The Transformation of Immigration Law,* 84 COLUM. L. REV. 1 (1984).

15. See id.; Schuck, *supra* note at 84–86.

16. See Schuck, *supra* note 1, at 41, 47–49.

17. While we recognize that the term "alien" may have a pejorative connotation to some readers, we feel its use is appropriate in a survey of immigration litigation. The term is defined by statute, see 8 U.S.C. § 1101(a)(3) (1988) (defining an "alien" as "any person not a citizen or national of the United States"), and has a specific and narrow meaning in immigration law. We use it only in that sense.

18. See note 74 infra (access to counsel) and text accompanying note 21 *infra* (discussion of the winnowing process) in original source.

19. This type of litigation selection bias conceivably could affect our data in several ways. First, it could occur when more pro-alien law results in a caseload composed both of fewer strong claims by aliens (because the INS no longer bothers to oppose them) and more weak ones (because the favorable legal climate invites aliens to assert more marginal claims). Under such a scenario, at some point the aliens' overall litigation success rate would begin to decline as the stronger claims dropped out of the system and aliens lost more of the marginal ones. Indeed, such a decline could occur even if more aliens (in absolute numbers) were winning their cases than under the earlier, less favorable, law.

Second, to the extent that aliens can select the jurisdiction in which they litigate, a similar selection effect might occur in a court perceived to be more pro-alien than others. For instance, the Ninth Circuit has been perceived, correctly, as being more protective of alien rights than courts in other circuits. Interview with Sara Campos, Staff Attorney, San Francisco Lawyers' Committee for Urban Affairs, in San Francisco, Cal. (May 11, 1992) (noting that aliens in deportation or exclusion proceedings often seek, and are granted, changes of venue to California); see note 23 infra and accompanying text in original source. If the perceived litigation advantage were large enough, aliens might even more to that jurisdiction in anticipation of future litigation. The opposite effect would occur if the INS viewed particular jurisdictions as pro-government, as 8 U.S.C. § 1252(c) (1988) grants the Attorney General the authority to transport detained aliens out of the circuit in which they are apprehended. This discretion is limited, however, and courts have generally tried to prevent the INS from using this authority to forum shop. See, e.g., Maldonado-Cruz v. United States Dept, of Immigration & Naturalization, 883 F. 2d 788, 791 (9th Cir. 1989) (applying law of the circuit with which alien had most contact prior to being transferred by INS).

Because we lack independent data on the strength of aliens' underlying claims that are necessary to control for these selection factors, they could affect our analysis. On the other hand, the possibility of such bias is diminished for several reasons. First, any effect that litigation selection has on the areas that we seek to analyze would largely be limited to our assessment of litigation outcomes, and many of the other topics we discuss, such as caseload, criminal cases, and remands would not be affected. It is unclear even whether and to what extent our discussion of outcomes would change, especially in exclusion and deportation cases, where pre-litigation settlement patterns are quite different from those in general civil cases. See infra.

Second, the selection effect would affect the analysis of some categories of litigation more than others. For example, it might not significantly affect our data on undocumented immigrants, who have always had powerful incentives to challenge exclusion and deportation orders, regardless of pro-alien or pro-government trends in immigration law. For example, aliens in deportation proceedings are entitled to an automatic stay pending judicial review of any deportation orders, and can be employed during that period. See note 51 infra in original source. Under most circumstances, they would be no worse off than if they had not sought judicial review. At the other extreme, the propensity of aliens and others to initiate "affirmative challenges," see text accompanying notes 140–196 infra in original source, is likely to be far more sensitive to substantive changes in immigration law, and hence more susceptible to selection effects. Falling in between these two extremes are asylum claims. Aliens who make asylum claims while remaining in INS detention pending the outcome of litigation bear a greater cost in seeking judicial review; the aliens' prospects for success would probably influence their propensity to litigate somewhat more than if they were free to work during that period.

A third implication of this type of selection effect is that some of our findings become even more noteworthy. If a selection effect systematically reduces the proportion of strong claims litigated relative to weak ones, then our conclusions that aliens' litigation success rates have increased over time is correspondingly more striking, since the higher success rates have arisen from cases presumably weaker on average than those in earlier years.

Another potential source of litigation selection bias is the possibility that the cases that proceed to final judgment are systematically different than the settled cases, which are presumably far more numerous and important in the aggregate. See George L. Priest & Benjamin Klein, *The Selection of Disputes for Litigation,* 13 J. LEGAL STUD. 1 (1984). Under the Priest & Klein model, which was developed to explain litigation patterns in civil damage actions, the lawyers on both sides are assumed to be fully informed about the strength of the claims and equally capable of predicting outcomes. *Id.* at 9. Each side compares its expected returns from litigation with the coats of litigation and makes a settlement offer. *Id.* at 12–17. The cases with relatively predictable outcomes are settled, leaving to be litigated only those cases in which the outcome is relatively uncertain. *Id.* If this model were applicable to our data on court litigation, any general inferences drawn about immigration cases would almost certainly be misleading, since most of these cases never reach court. We believe, however, that the Priest & Klein model is inapplicable to immigration litigation. First, it assumes the parties have equal interests in the outcome; It does not apply to litigation in which the stakes are very different, such as when one of the parties is a repeat player. In immigration litigation, the INS is the epitome of the repeat player, while the alien plays only once. (Private immigration lawyers, to be sure, also are repeat players of a sort, another complication for which the model does not account.). Second, the pattern of case settlement in the immigration area, especially in exclusion and deportation cases, is skewed by two factors: (a) the strong incentives that an alien, particularly one not in detention, has to remain in the United States as long as possible and therefore not to settle even the weakest of cases; and (b) the many types of discretionary relief, such as voluntary departure and parole, that the INS may grant aliens in order to avoid litigating particular claims.

20. For some purposes we combine the 1989 and 1990 cases into a single dataset, 1989–1990, which represents a large body of recent decisions. In some instances, however, we wish to make year-to-year comparisons; in those situations, we either use the data for only one of the years, or we derive the "1989–1990 average" by aggregating the data for both years and dividing by two.

21. Many commentators and practitioners believe that the Ninth Circuit is significantly more sympathetic than any other circuit to the claims of aliens, particularly those seeking asylum. See. e.g., Sana Loue, *Alien Rights and Government Authority: An Examination of the Conflicting Views of the Ninth Circuit Court of Appeals and the United States Supreme Court,* 22 SAN DIEGO L. REV. 1021 (1985); Carolyn P. Blum, *The Ninth Circuit and the Protection of Asylum Seekers Since the Passage of the Refugee Act of 1980.* 23 SAN DIEGO L. REV. 327 (1986).

22. 467 U.S. 837 (1984).

23. Our sample size here is too small for our findings about remands to be statistically significant. Indeed, of the 23 cases remanded during 1989, we were able to complete the coding sheet on only 13. Even with this limited sample, however, we hope to convey a general sense of how the INS, BIA, and immigration judges handle immigration cases on remand. *See* notes 278–292 infra and accompanying text in original source.

24. See notes 234–239 *supra* and accompanying text in original source.

25. For several suggested solutions to a roughly analogous problem, see JERRY L. MASHAW, BUREAUCRATIC JUSTICE: MANAGING SOCIAL SECURITY DISABILITY CLAIMS 194–209 (1983).

26. Even a list confined to book-length critiques during the last decade is a long one. *See. e.g.,* JOHN CREWDSON, THE TARNISHED DOOR: THE NEW IMMIGRANTS AND THE TRANSFORMATION OF AMERICA (1983); HARWOOD, *Supra* note 51 in original source; MILTON D. MORRIS, IMMIGRATION: THE BELEAGUERED BUREAUCRACY (1985); THE PAPER CURTAIN: EMPLOYER SANCTIONS' IMPLEMENTATION, IMPACT, AND REFORM (Michael Fix ed, 1991); SELECT COMM'N ON IMMIGRATION AND REFUGEE POLICY, U.S. IMMIGRATION POLICY AND THE NATIONAL INTEREST: THE FINAL REPORT AND RECOMMENDATIONS OF THE SELECT COMMISSION ON IMMIGRATION AND REFUGEE POLICY WITH SUPPLEMENTAL VIEWS BY COMMISSIONERS 70–75 (1981) [hereinafter SELECT COMM'N REF.] The U.S. General Accounting Office has issued a number of critical evaluations of the INS in recent years. *See, e.g.,* UNITED STATES GENERAL ACCOUNTING OFFICE, IMMIGRATION MANAGEMENT: STRONG LEADERSHIP AND MANAGEMENT REFORMS NEEDED TO ADDRESS SERIOUS PROBLEMS (1991); UNITED STATES GENERAL ACCOUNTING OFFICE, IMMIGRATION MANAGEMENT: IMMIGRATION AND NATURALIZATION SERVICE LACKS READY ACCESS TO ESSENTIAL DATA (1990).

27. Again, this particular observation is not a novel one. See ALEINIKOFF & MARTIN, *supra* note 9, at 110–11 in original source; see also SELECT COMM'N REF., *supra* note 26, at app. G (analysis of the INS' administrative problems, including its combination of enforcement and service functions). Our findings, however, confirm the widespread impression that the problem has not yet been solved.

28. Commendably, the Justice Department took a number of important steps during the decade to separate INS functions. In 1983, for example, it established the immigration court in the EOIR outside the INS. See note 9 *supra* and accompanying text in original source. In implementing IRCA's legalization program, the INS attempted to create buffers between its law enforcement operation and its adjudication of amnesty claims. In 1990, it established a specialized corps of asylum adjudicators, who report to a central office in INS headquarters, rather than to the district directors. See Asylum and Withholding of Deportation Procedures, 55 Fed. Reg. 30,674, 30,680 (1990) (to be codified at 8 C.F.R. pts. 3, 103, 208, 236, 242, and 253).

Unfortunately, these efforts have not been wholly effective. Post-IRCA buffers between enforcement and legalization activities did not prevent the INS from violating the amnesty provisions of the law. See notes 228 & 233 *supra* in original source. As to the recent changes in the asylum adjudication system, at least one insider fears that the tendency of the INS' law enforcement function to affect its asylum adjudications has not been eliminated; that person has expressed concern that the INS General Counsel, who continues to render legal advice to the new unit, will project an "enforcement mentality" into asylum adjudicators' interpretations of the

Refugee Act. Confidential Telephone Interview with an asylum officer in the INS' Central Office for Refugees, Asylum, and Parole (Nov. 11. 1991).

One might argue, of course, that the INS violations resulted from conditions that have little to do with the failure to separate enforcement and service, such as inadequate resources, poor legal advice, uncertain legislative guidance, or excessive delegation to the district directions. We are still agnostic on this question but suspect that the argument has some force.

29. *See* Asylum and Withholding of Deportation Procedures, 55 Fed. Reg. 30.674 (1990) (to be codified at 8 C.F.R. pta. 3, 103, 208, 236, 242, and 253); *see also* note 297 *Supra* in original source.

30. *See* Frank J. Prial, *200 Aliens Seeking Asylum Could Be Paroled in a Test,* N.Y. TIMES, Apr. 29, 1990, at 28.

31. *See* UNITED STATES IMMIGRATION AND NATURALIZATION SERVICE, BASIC LAW MANUAL ASYLUM (1991).

Chapter 4

1. On the Progressive Era, see Stephen Skowronek, *Building a New American State: The Expansion of National Administrative Capacities, 1877–1920* (Cambridge: Cambridge University Press, 1982). On the New Deal, see Arthur M. Schlesinger, Jr., *The Age of Roosevelt: The Crisis of the Old Order* (Boston: Houghton Mifflin, 1957), *The Age of Roosevelt: The Coming of the New Deal* (Boston: Houghton Mifflin, 1958), and *The Age of Roosevelt: The Politics of Upheaval* (Boston: Houghton Mifflin, 1960). On the Great Society, see Milton Viorst, *Fire in the Streets: America in the 1960s* (New York: Simon and Schuster, 1979). On the 1970s, see Haynes B. Johnson, *In the Absence of Power: Governing America* (New York: Viking Press, 1980); and Joseph A. Califano, Jr., *Governing America: An Insider's Report from the White House and the Cabinet* (New York: Simon and Schuster, 1981).

2. Most of Reagan's major legislative successes—tax reform and deregulation, for example—largely effectuated a return to earlier laissez-faire policies. It does not gainsay his considerable political achievement in winning these changes to point out that, unlike the many unprecedented Progressive and New Deal reforms, Reagan's were modeled on earlier policies.

3. Congress began limiting immigration in 1875, when it barred convicts and prostitutes. Idiots, lunatics, and paupers were added to the list in 1882, which was the same year that the first Chinese Exclusion Act was passed. The Gentlemen's Agreement of 1907 barred Japanese workers. Additional restrictions were added in the Immigration Act of 1917, enacted over President Wilson's veto. For a summary of this history, see Vernon M. Briggs, Jr., *Immigration Policy and the American Labor Force* (Baltimore: Johns Hopkins University Press, 1984), ch. 2.

4. The 1965 law enlarged the overall quota for Eastern Hemisphere countries slightly (from 154,000 to 170,000), but it also imposed a quota on Western Hemisphere countries (120,000) for the first time. This new quota followed hard on the heels of the termination of the Bracero program in 1964. Briggs, *Immigration Policy,* pp. 63–64.

5. On interest group liberalism, see Theodore J. Lowi, *The End of Liberalism, The Second Republic of the United States.* 2d ed. (New York: Norton, 1979). On incrementalism, see Charles E. Lindblom, "The Science of Muddling Through," *Public Administration Review* 19 (1959): 79. On rational choice, see William H. Riker, *The Theory of Political Coalitions* (New Haven: Yale University Press, 1962). On the new institutionalism, see, e.g., James G. March and Johan P. Olsen, *Rediscovering Institutions: The Organizational Basis of Politics* (New York: Free Press, 1989), emphasizing the rational choice account of institutions; and Rogers M. Smith, "Science, Non-Science, and Politics: On Turns to History in Political Science," in *The Historic Turn in the Human Sciences,* ed. T. McDonald (Ann Arbor: University of Michigan Press, forthcoming), emphasizing the historical account of institutions.

6. For an illuminating discussion on this point, see Rogers M. Smith, "If Politics Matters: Implications for a 'New Institutionalism'" (Unpublished paper presented at the 1991 Annual Meeting of the American Political Science Association).

7. For an elegant, somewhat analogous effort to "test" competing explanatory paradigms—there, of the administrative process rather than of legislative politics—see Jerry Mashaw, "Explaining Administrative Process: Normative, Positive, and Critical Stories of Legal Development," *Journal of Law, Economics & Organization* 6 (1990): 267.

8. For another, provocative example of rapid policy change in the last decade, see R. Shep Melnick, "Separation of Powers and the Strategy of Rights: The Expansion of Special Education." unpub. ms., 1990. Melnick asks, "How did advocates for the handicapped manage to pass legislation transforming special education without the advantages of presidential leadership, party support, lobbying by established interest groups, or a significant shift in public opinion?" (p. 5) Part of his answer, like part of mine, is court litigation. But he also points to a more unusual explanation not relevant to the immigration case: the expansive effects of both federalism and separation of powers.

9. On the concept of normal politics, see Bruce A. Ackerman, "The Storrs Lectures: Discovering the Constitution," *Yale Law Journal* 93 (1984): 1013.

10. The relative insignificance of the White House's political role in influencing immigration legislation during the 1980s is discussed *infra,* text accompanying note 59.

11. The Democrats have controlled the House and the Senate since the 1950s, except for 1981–87, when the Republicans controlled the Senate.

12. In this respect, political conditions here resembled those in Western Europe, where restrictionist attitudes of an even more resolute, virulent stripe prevailed—and continue to prevail—and where the countervailing forces favoring expansion are much weaker. See infra note 38.

13. See Senator Simpson's supplemental statement in U.S. *Immigration Policy and the National Interest: The Final Report and Recommendations of the Select Commission on Immigration and Refugee Policy with Supplemental Views by Commissioners* (U.S. Government Printing Office, 1981) (hereinafter SCIRP Final Report), Appendix B, at p. 411.

14. Alan Simpson (an interested observer, to be sure) insisted that IRCA was "not nativist, not racist and not mean" (Robert Pear, "Drive to Revamp Immigration Law is Gaining," *New York Times,* December 2, 1982, p. A28). Buchanan's campaign did revive nativist and vaguely racist themes, but they seemed to attract only a limited, politically marginal audience.

15. See, e.g., Craig R. Whitney, "Big British Fight Shapes Up On Hong Kong Emigre Plan," *New York Times,* January 10, 1990, p. A1; Stephen Kinzer, "A Wave of Attacks on Foreigners Stirs Shock in Germany," *New York Times,* October 1, 1991, p. A1; Alan Riding, "France Imposes a Tighter Political Refugee Policy," *New York Times,* February 14, 1991, p. A11; and "Australia Cuts Immigration," *FAIR Immigration Report,* August 1991 (citing *Financial Times,* May 1, 1991). See also Alan Riding, "French Right Hits a Nerve With Immigration Plan," *New York Times,* November 24, 1991, p. 12. (although polls indicate only 15 to 17 percent of voters support the openly nativist National Front, over 30 percent share its views on immigration; President Mitterand said France has reached "the threshold of tolerance" on immigration) "German Social Democrats Signal Openness to Limits on Refugees," *New York Times,* March 13, 1992, p. A10. (main opposition party to support constitutional change to restrict refugees).

16. See, e.g., William H. Riker, *The Art of Political Manipulation* (New Haven: Yale University Press, 1986).

17. A forthcoming article describes this as "a somewhat neglected topic in contemporary political science" (Peter A. Hall, "Policy Paradigms, Social Learning, and the State: The Case of Economic Policymaking in Britain," in *Comparative Politics,* 1992). For a review essay, see Charles M. Levine, "Where Policy Comes From: Ideas, Innovations, and Agenda Choices," *Public Administration Review* 45 (1985): 255. The Reagan agenda, however, encouraged the study of ideas in politics, and some fine studies have resulted. See, e.g., Martha

Derthick and Paul J. Quirk, *The Politics of Deregulation* (Washington, D.C.: Brookings Institution, 1985) (deregulation); David A. Stockman, *The Triumph of Politics: How the Reagan Revolution Failed* (New York: Harper & Row 1986) (supply-side economics); Robert A. Katzmann, *Institutional Disability: The Saga of Transportation Policy for the Disabled* (Washington, D.C.: Brookings Institution, 1986) (right to integrative equality); and Mark J. Roe, "Political Elements in the Creation of a Mutual Fund Industry," *University of Pennsylvania Law Review* 139 (1991): 1469 (idea of fragmenting economic power drove legislation barring Wall Street control of industry). Robert Katzmann maintains that the Chicago School's ideas about competition drove the Federal Trade Commission's programmatic changes in antitrust policy during the 1980s (personal communication to author). For a pre-Reagan era example, see Peter Steinfels, *The Neoconservatives: The Men Who Are Changing America's Politics* (New York: Simon and Schuster 1979) (neoconservatism). For an example from British politics, see Hall, "Policy Paradigms."

18. Peter A. Hall, ed., *The Political Power of Economic Ideas: Keynesianism Across Nations* (Princeton, N.J.: Princeton University Press, 1989), pp. 4, 361–62.

19. See Gil Loescher and John A. Scanlan, *Calculated Kindness: Refugees and America's Half-Open Door, 1945 to the Present* (New York: Free Press, 1986), p. 153; Ruth Wasem, *Asylum and Temporary Protected Status Under U.S. Immigration Law,* (Cong. Research Service, June 14, 1991) p. 8, fig. 2. Although the data cited by Wasem cover only 1946–89, the level of refugee admissions prior to 1946 was lower than in the postwar period.

20. *1990 Statistical Yearbook of the Immigration and Naturalization Service,* p. 97, chart G. (hereinafter cited as 1990 INS Yearbook). The 1977 figure dropped to fewer than 25,000.

21. See Lawrence H. Fuchs, "The Reactions of Black Americans to Immigration," in *Immigration Reconsidered: History, Sociology, and Politics,* ed. Virginia Yans-McLaughlin (New York: Oxford University Press, 1990).

22. The original chairman, former Governor Reuben Askew, resigned shortly after the commission began to accept the position of U.S. Trade Representative.

23. For example, Judi Hanson, *UPI,* July 31, 1981.

24. This phrase, which would become popular to the point of triteness, appears to have been coined by Senator Alan Simpson in a SCIRP press conference, reported by Richard L. Strout, "U.S. Immigration Dilemma: Is There Too Much 'Compassion,'" *Christian Science Monitor,* December 9, 1980, p. 4. Simpson also used it in his separate statement appended to the SCIRP final report. See SCIRP Final Report, p. 413.

25. SCIRP Final Report, p. 411. For example, Simpson proposed an annual cap on legal admissions of 400,000 to 550,000, with the number to be lower until the flow of illegal aliens was substantially reduced. Even Simpson's higher figure (550,000) would have been lower than the legal immigration level (if refugee adjustments of status are included) in 1981, the year in which Simpson was writing.

26. The White House, however, remained uneasy about employer sanctions, which threatened to turn businesspeople into law enforcers. For the evolution of employer sanctions legislation, see *1982 Congressional Quarterly Almanac,* Washington, D.C.: Congressional Quarterly Inc., p. 405; and *1983 Congressional Quarterly Almanac,* p. 287.

27. In 1981, Huddleston had introduced S. 776, the Immigration and National Security Act of 1981, which would have established a cap of 350,000 on all legal immigration, including refugees and immediate relatives. His August 1982, proposal was an amendment to S. 2222, the first Simpson-Mazzoli bill. Simpson opposed Huddleston's amendment and it was defeated by a vote of 35–63. The 1982 admissions figures can be found in *1989 INS Yearbook,* p. 1, table 1.

28. In this essay, I use the conventional "diversity" label to describe a set of provisions—enacted in IRCA, extended in 1988, and further extended and refined in the 1990 act—that give favored treatment to nationals from countries that were "underrepresented" or "disadvantaged" in the post-1965 immigrant flows. As discussed *infra,* text accompanying notes 91–98, these labels can be somewhat misleading.

29. Calls for the repeal of the employer sanctions, which began soon after IRCA was implemented, have grown more insistent as they have been bolstered by studies that purport to show that the sanctions have caused additional employment discrimination against Hispanic and Asian workers. See, e.g., Adam Clymer, "Bill Would Alter Immigration Law," *New York Times,* September 21, 1991, p. 7 (a bipartisan coalition of senators, led by Hatch and Kennedy, introduce legislation to repeal sanctions). The proponents of repeal tend to be those who opposed sanctions initially. Even before the repeal legislation (S. 1734 and H.R. 3366) was introduced, the Black Leadership Forum denounced it. See *FAIR Immigration Report,* September 1991, p. 1.

30. Between IRCA and the 1990 act, Congress did pass the Anti-Drug Abuse Act of 1988, Pub. L. 100-690 (2nd sess.), which made it easier to deport aliens convicted of drug-related and other "aggravated felonies." Although this statute was certainly restrictive in this sense, its narrow focus on criminal offenders makes it somewhat irrelevant to the more general pro-immigrant trend discussed in this essay.

31. Not counting the almost 900,000 amnestied aliens who adjusted to legal status in 1990 and swelled the number of legal admissions for that year, the United States admitted a total of 529,120 aliens: 231,680 nonquota immigrants (i.e., immediate relatives, special immigrants, etc.); 214,550 under the family preferences; 53,729 under the occupational preferences; 20,371 under the program for aliens from countries "adversely affected" by the 1965 act; and 8,790 under the so-called diversity program. As discussed in Chapter 1, by 1996, long after the 1986 amnesty had ceased to effect the total significantly, the number of admissions had increased to 915,000: 445,253 non-quota immigrants; 294,174 under the family preferences; 117,499 under the occupational preferences; and 58,790 under the diversity program. This does not include refugees and asylees who were admitted but not yet adjusted to the status of permanent resident, but it does not include the 128,565 refugees and asylees who were admitted in prior years and adjusted their status in 1996.

32. See, *Interpreter Releases* 68 (August 30, 1991): 1116 (family unity provisions of the act); and Katherine Bishop, "U.S. Policy on Salvadoran Immigrants is Attacked," *New York Times,* May 20, 1991, p. A10 (temporary protected status provisions of the act). In late December, after the statutory deadline had expired, INS officials reported to Senator Simpson's staff that more than 180,000 Salvadorans had been granted this status. *Interpreter Releases* 69 (January 17, 1992): 88.

33. American Baptist Churches v. Thornburgh, 760 F. Supp. 796 (N.D. Cal. 1990).

34. The administration also extended this status to Somalis in September, 1991.

35. The most recent published analyses are in the collection of papers entitled *The Paper Curtain: Employer Sanctions' Implementation, Impact, and Reform,* ed. Michael Fix (Santa Monica, Calif.: Rand Corp., 1991). The editor summarizes these impact analyses as follows: "[T]hree years after enactment, the law had yet to bring about broad compliance or to stem significantly the tide of undocumented migration to the U.S." (p. 21). See also David Johnston, "Border Crossings Near Old Record; U.S. to Crack Down," *New York Times,* February 9, 1992, p. 1.

36. *1990 INS Yearbook,* table 1.

37. The vote was 89–8 in the Senate and 264–118 in the House. Some of the votes on recent immigration reform legislation were close. For example, IRCA passed the House by only 238–173, and the Refugee Act of 1980 passed the House by 207–192. The votes to override President Truman's veto of the McCarran-Walter Act of 1952 were 57–26 in the Senate and 278–113 in the House.

38. Another factor exacerbating the crisis was the growing hostility to refugees (and immigrants more generally) by other potential countries of second asylum, especially in Europe. Their hostility increased during the 1980s, contrary to the situation in the United States. See, e.g., Center for Immigration Studies, "Immigration to the U.K.: A Closing Door," *Scope* (Fall-Winter 1990–1991): 7; Craig R. Whitney, "Big British Fight Shapes Up on Hong Kong

Emigre Plan," *New York Times,* January 10, 1990, p. Al; Alan Riding, "France Imposes a Tighter Political Refugee Policy," *New York Times,* February 14, 1991, p. All; Alan Riding, "France Sees Integration as Answer to View of Immigrants as Taking Over,'" *New York Times,* March 24, 1991, p. 3; David Binder, "Flood of Foreigners Seeking Asylum Angers West Germans," *New York Times,* August 11, 1990, p. 3; Serge Schmemann, "Germans Fear Becoming Eastern Europe's Keeper," *New York Times,* December 9, 1990, sec. 4 p. 1; Stephen Kinzer, "Swiss Voting Results Reflect Anti-Immigrant Mood," *New York Times,* October 27, 1991, p. 11; and Center for Immigration Studies, "Immigration in Sweden: Refugees on the Rise," *Scope* (Summer 1991): 14 (describing 1989 law tightening asylum procedures); Alan Cowell, "Attacks on Immigrants Raise Concern in Italy," *New York Times,* February 9, 1992, p. 21.

39. Loescher and Scanlan, *Calculated Kindness.*

40. Doris Meissner, "Reflections on the U.S. Refugee Act of 1980," in *The New Asylum Seekers: Refugee Law in the 1980s,* ed. David A. Martin (Dordrecht: Martinus Nijhoff Publishers, 1988), p. 61.

41. According to Lawrence Fuchs, "no major immigration legislation has ever passed the Congress . . . which was initiated primarily by the Executive branch . . ." Fuchs, "The Corpse That Would Not Die: The Immigration Reform and Control Act of 1986," *Revue Europeenee des Migrations Internationales* 6 (1990): 111, 114.

42. Bureau of the Census demographers who consulted with the Select Commission placed the figure at somewhere between 3.5 and 6 million, a more defensible figure that the major media began to use. (Fuchs, "Corpse," p. 66 and source there cited).

43. Harris N. Miller, "'The Right Thing to Do': A History of Simpson-Mazzoli," in *Clamor at the Gates: The New American Immigration,* ed. Nathan Glazer, (San Francisco: ICS, 1985) pp. 53–54.

44. In addition to public officials, certain special interests in the immigration area—labor, Asian-Americans, and Mexican-Americans—were represented directly Fuchs, "Corpse," p. 115.

45. Lawrence Fuchs, "Immigration Reform in 1911 and 1981: The Role of Select Commissions," *Journal of American History* 70 (1983): 58, 61–65.

46. Letter to author, November 4, 1991.

47. This is evident in the numerous invocations of the commission's recommendations and authority during the final debate on the 1990 act. *Congressional Record,* S17105–S17118 (October 26, 1990) 101st Cong., 2d Sess., Vol. 136, No. 149—Part 2; and H12358 (October 27, 1990) 101st Cong. 2d Sess., Vol. 136, No. 150.

48. The "odd couple" description comes from Lawrence Fuchs, who worked closely with both senators during this period both as executive director of the Hesburgh Commission and later as consultant (telephone conversation, June 12, 1991). Their collaboration was executed and extended through the friendship between their staff aides, Jerry Tinker and Richard Day (telephone conversation with Muzaffar Chishti, Director of Immigration Project, International Ladies' Garment Workers' Union, December 4, 1990).

49. Miller. "Right Thing," p. 49.

50. Fuchs interview.

51. Fuchs, telephone interview, June 12, 1991. Simpson adverted to this problem in his supplemental statement to the SCIRP Final Report. There, in introducing the issue of ethnic patterns, he noted that "I am about to enter into a very sensitive area and there is some risk that what I will say may be misunderstood" (p. 414).

52. During Senator Kennedy's tenure as chairman of the full committee, he had abolished the subcommittee, preferring to handle immigration matters in the full committee.

53. Unlike Simpson, he had not served on the Hesburgh Commission and his views had not been shaped, as Simpson's had, by its deliberations.

54. Miller, "Right Thing," p. 56. After 1986, control in the House would pass from Rodino and Mazzoli to newer members—Howard Berman, Bruce Morrison, Barney Frank, and

Charles Schumer—all urban liberals with strong personal and constituent commitments to immigration expansion. All but Morrison were also instrumental in the final stages leading to the enactment of IRCA.

55. The discussion of Congress's treatment of immigration legislation between 1981 and 1984 is largely based upon Miller's account, ibid.; Aristide R. Zolberg, "Reforming the Back Door: The Immigration Reform and Control Act of 1986 in Historical Perspective," in *Immigration Reconsidered,* ed. Yans-McLaughlin p. 315, and various issues of *Congressional Quarterly.*

56. SCIRP Final Report, at II.B.1 (pp. 61–69), II.C (pp. 72–81), and VI.E (pp. 226–29).

57. Fuchs, "Corpse," p. 116.

58. Among these issues were the need for an overall numerical cap on legal admissions, the number to be admitted each year, the timing of legalization, and the fifth preference (for siblings of U.S. citizens) (SCIRP Final Report, pp. 411–23).

59. Telephone interview with Richard Day, Counsel to Senator Simpson, November 15, 1991. According to Day, Simpson complained publicly about the White House's indifference, complaints that the White House may have wanted those in the business community who opposed Simpson's proposals to hear. In addition to Attorney General Smith, George Bush, then vice president, offered to help Simpson gain access to the president if needed. The White House's passivity on immigration issues persisted, however, when Bush became president.

60. Personal interview, March 12, 1991.

61. SCIRP Final Report p. 3: "We recommend closing the back door to undocumented/illegal migration [and] opening the front door a little to accommodate legal immigration in the interests of this country." See also p. 82; and "Notre Dame's President Offers Solution on Aliens," *New York Times,* August 24, 1981, p. A12: quoting SCIRP Chairman Hesburgh: "In a word, we think the front door to America, the legal door, should be opened a bit wider and the back door, the illegal one, closed."

62. "Congress Jump-starts a Corpse," *New York Times,* October 12, 1986, p. A22 (editorial).

63. Robert Pear, "President Signs Landmark Bill on Immigration," *New York Times,* November 7, 1986, p. A12.

64. The phrase is taken from Fuchs, "Corpse."

65. The requirement that amnesty applicants have resided in the United States since 1982, however, was much more stringent than the residence requirements of most European amnesty programs, such as Italy's 1990 program, which reached back only to December 31, 1989. See David A. Martin, "Of Immigration Laws, Families, and Apple Prices," *Virginia Law School Report,* p. 23, 24 (Winter 1992); Doris Meissner, Dimitri Papademetriou and David North, *Legalization of Undocumented Aliens: Lessons from Other Countries* (Carnegie Endowment for International Peace, 1986).

66. Fuchs, "Corpse," p. 124.

67. The Immigration Marriage Fraud Amendments, Pub. L. 99-639, were passed only four days later. While these provisions were undeniably severe and excessively rigid (the harshest of them would be amended in the Immigration Act of 1990), they were directed at a particular abuse—sham marriages designed to circumvent the immigration preference system—and do not denote a general animus against aliens.

68. See John Kingdon, "Ideas, Politics, and Public Policies (Paper presented at 1988 Annual Meeting of American Political Science Association, Washington, D.C.).

69. See discussion *infra,* text accompanying notes 114–116.

70. Despite use of the term "business," business interests in immigration policy were by no means monolithic. This point is discussed *infra,* text following note 77.

71. See Zolberg, "Reforming," pp. 317–18. On the historical treatment of the Mexican border, see also Gerald P. Lopez, "Undocumented Mexican Migration: In Search of a Just Immigration Law and Policy," *U.C.L.A. Law Review* 28 (1981): 615.

72. Fuchs, "Corpse," p. 115.

73. On fraud in the agricultural worker legalization program, see Roberto Suro, "False Migrant Claims: Fraud on a Huge Scale," *New York Times,* November 12, 1989, p. 1. Unions such as the ILGWU, which had many members who were undocumented, favored a more generous amnesty.

74. See, generally, Kirk Victor, "Labor Pains," *National Journal* 23 (1991): 1336.

75. Morrison interview.

76. Letter to author from Lawrence Fuchs, November 4, 1991.

77. In the areas of public education and health care, for example, business interests were in the vanguard of reform efforts. See, e.g., John E. Chubb and Terry M. Moe, *Politics, Markets and America's Schools* (Washington, D.C.: Brookings Institution, 1990), p. 13; Linda E. Demkovich, "Public and Private Pressures to Control Health Care Costs May be Paying Off," *National Journal* 16 (1984): 2390.

78. In Simpson's view, the preference gave siblings an unwarranted advantage in the immigration competition, one that actually cut against family unification values by reducing family members in the old country (Day interview). The Hesburgh Commission had been divided on this politically delicate issue, with all of the elected officials except Simpson favoring retention of the fifth preference (Fuchs letter).

79. *Congressional Quarterly Weekly Report,* February 27, 1988, p. 518. The Hesburgh Commission did not favor any point system (Fuchs letter).

80. The Hesburgh Commission, over the strong objection of its chairman, had recommended such a provision (Fuchs letter).

81. Simpson's bill, however, would not have counted immediate relatives against skills-based or "independent" admissions.

82. Pub. L. 100-658.

83. As discussed supra note 30, the 1988 act was directed at a particular evil and does not really contradict the general pro-immigration thrust during the last half of the decade.

84. Morrison interview.

85. Telephone interview, August 27, 1991.

86. Ibid.

87. Indeed, as Simpson's Senate aide points out, he had sponsored employer sanctions, and the Chamber of Commerce opposed the final version of all three Simpson-Mazzoli bills (Letter to author from Richard Day and Carl Hampe, October 29, 1991 [hereinafter Day/Hampe letter]).

88. The current controversy over whether the Cubans, who have received relatively favored treatment since the early days of the Castro regime, should continue to enjoy it is an example. See, e.g., "The Stick Congress Gave Castro," *New York Times,* August 15, 1991, p. A22 (editorial urging repeal of the Cuban Adjustment Act). Concerning the strikingly different treatment of Cubans and Haitians, see Anthony DePalma, "For Haitians, Voyage to a Land of Inequality," *New York Times,* July 16, 1991, p. A1.

89. See, e.g., Carole J. Uhlaner, "Perceived Discrimination and Prejudice and the Coalition Prospects of Blacks, Latinos, and Asian Americans," in *Racial and Ethnic Politics in California,* ed. Bryan O. Jackson and Michael B. Preston (Berkeley, Calif.: IGS Press, 1991), p. 339; and Charles Henry and Carlos Muñoz, Jr., "Ideological and Interest Linkages in California Rainbow Politics," in Jackson and Preston, *Racial and Ethnic Politics,* p. 323.

90. Today's newcomers include both high-naturalizing groups (Asians) and low-naturalizing groups (Hispanics). See Peter H. Schuck, "Membership in the Liberal Polity: The Devaluation of American Citizenship," *Georgetown Immigration Law Journal* (1989) pp. 9–10.

91. See Robert Pear, "Major Immigration Bill Is Sent to Bush," *New York Times,* October 29, 1990, p. B10, col. 4.

92. State Department Message no. A-178 (September 28, 1990), pp. 10–11. The fifth ranking country was Indonesia (8 percent). All other countries had less than half as many visas as Indonesia (Thomas Saenz, "The Development of Diversity Immigration Laws" [Unpublished manuscript, May 28, 1991], p. 8 n. 27 [on file with author]).

93. Ibid., p. 2. The next five countries were Pakistan (9 percent), Egypt (5 percent), Peru (5 percent), Trinidad and Tobago (4 percent), and Poland (3 percent).

94. See David Reimers, "An Unintended Reform: The 1965 Immigration Act and Third World Immigration to the United States," *Journal of American Ethnic History* 3 (1983): 9, 16. Recent research on the 1965 Act, however, suggests that those new flows were neither unexpected nor unintended. See Gabriel J. Chin, "The Civil Rights Revolution Comes to Immigration Law: A New Look at the Immigration and Nationality Act of 1965," 75 N.C. L. Rev. 273(1996).

95. An estimated 44 percent of the diversity visas will go to Europeans, a larger share than under the OP-1 program. Immigrants from Northern Ireland are also advantaged by a provision that treats that country as separate from Great Britain for purposes of the diversity program. (See Saenz, "Immigration Laws," pp. 10–11).

96. The diversity provisions will benefit not only new immigrants from these groups but also a large number who came on nonimmigrant visas during the 1980s and remained illegally. See Pear, "Major Immigration Bill."

97. To be sure, the diversity provisions will also benefit some immigrants from African and Asian nations, just as the earlier OP-1 ("Berman") program had done.

98. Although President Bush vetoed the legislation and his veto was sustained in the Senate, he later implemented the protections through administrative action.

99. The idea of legislating separate immigration streams had been proposed earlier by the Select Commission in its Final Report (at II.B.1., p. 111) and by Senator Simpson in his legislative proposals.

100. Letter.

101. Insiders sometimes called this the "Italian preference" because of the ardor with which Italian-Americans, so intensely committed to extended family, had used it to bring over their siblings in the past.

102. For a chronology of this reform *see Interpreter Releases* 68 (March 18, 1991): 305–07.

103. Morrison interview.

104. Day/Hampe letter.

105. "Democrats for Vitality" *Wall Street Journal,* October 1, 1990, p. A14; "Stonewall Simpson," October 12, 1990, p. A14; Michael J. Boskin letter to the Editor, October 16, 1990, p. A27; and Simpson letter to the Editor, October 18, 1990, p. A17.

106. Simpson apparently played little or no role in bringing the White House around. Day interview, January 7, 1992.

107. Simpson, following the much-discussed Workforce 2000 report, assumed that unskilled domestic labor would be in surplus. He also believed that unskilled aliens would quickly abandon the jobs that had justified their green cards and move on to something better (Day/Hampe letter).

108. As Morrison recalls, "Simpson wanted to make me pay six times over for the Irish and the other diversity provisions, which provided quasi-amnesty for Irish, Poles, and others" (Morrison interview).

109. Day/Hampe letter. Senator Kennedy did not state his "bottom line," presumably because the bill was obviously going to include higher overall admissions and more generous benefits for the Irish than he had ever believed possible.

110. Telephone interview with Jerry Tinker, Staff Director, Immigration and Refugee Affairs Subcommittee, Senate Judiciary Committee, January 28, 1992; telephone interview with Bonnie Maguire, legislative assistant, Subcommittee on Immigration, Refugees, and International Law, March 11, 1992.

111. "The Administration didn't need softening at this point—they wanted the bill" (Day/Hampe letter). According to the ILGWU lobbyist, the administration's desire for the bill reflected the fact that it had some other foreign policy fish to fry, including its fear (exploited by President Duarte) that El Salvador might fall to the rebels if it was deprived of the remittances from its nationals in the United States, and its desire to provide safe haven to Liberians, Kuwaitis, and Lebanese (Chishti interview).

112. Chishti interview. In May 1991, when fewer Salvadorans than expected applied for TPS, Moakley helped pressure the INS into lowering the application fees and introduced new legislation that would extend the application period. The fees were lowered and a four-month extension (until October 31, 1991) was signed by the president in July 1991, by which time over 100,000 applications had been received by the INS. (*Interpreter Releases* 68 [July 1991]: 790). This was still far below the 500,000 who had earlier been thought to be eligible (*Interpreter Releases* 68 [January 1991]: 97).

113. *Congressional Record* S17109 (October 26, 1990). 101st. Cong., 2d Sess., Vol. 136, No. 149—Part 2.

114. Chishti interview.

115. See, generally, Fuchs. For a very recent example, see Sam Roberts, "Reshaping of New York City Hits Black-Hispanic Alliance," *New York Times,* July 28, 1991, p. 1 (on the City Council redistricting conflict).

116. Telephone interview with Richard Day, Counsel to Senator Simpson, October 25, 1991.

117. Simpson was also exasperated with some of the liberals in the House delegation, whom he felt were continually raising the stakes and altering their demands after he had struck a deal with them.

118. *Id.* For the IRCA precedent, see supra section IV ("Political Entrepreneurship").

119. Here, as in most earlier key votes on this legislation, the Democrats favored the bill much more consistently than the Republicans, and Northern Democrats did so more than Southern Democrats. Nevertheless, support for it cut broadly across partisan lines. See *Congressional Quarterly,* November 3, 1990, p. 3764.

120. See Kingdon, "Ideas, Politics."

121. Ibid., pp. 5–6.

122. The theory about the political functions of ideas advanced in the following discussion borrows from Peter Hall (*Political Power,* chs. 1 and 14), who distinguishes the "economics-centered," "state-centered," and "coalition-centered" influences of ideas. I identify some additional functions that Hall fails to mention, and because I am interested in how ideas influenced immigration policy rather than fiscal policy (Hall's principal focus), my classification is somewhat different.

123. See Steven Kelman, *Making Public Policy: A Hopeful View of American Government* (New York: Basic Books, 1987), chs. 10, 11.

124. For a comparison between the way in which Cubans and Haitians are treated under U.S. immigration laws, see *supra* note 88.

125. See, for example, Tamar Lewin, "Study Points to Increase in Tolerance of Ethnicity," *New York Times,* January 8, 1992, p. A12 (between 1964 and 1989 "social standing" of almost all groups increased, especially Asians and blacks).

126. Hall, *Political Power,* pp. 10–12.

127. See, e.g., Suzanne Garment, *Scandal: The Crisis of Mistrust in American Politics* (New York: Times Books, 1991). (new ideas about relation between public and private morality). On measuring the rate and direction of legal change, see George L. Priest, "Measuring Legal Change," *Journal of Law, Economics & Organization* 3 (1987): 193 (using ratio of parties' settlement demands and offers to measure legal change).

128. Olmstead v. United States, 277 U.S. 438, 485 (1928) (dissenting opinion).

129. In summarizing the role of ideas on immigration politics, I have used the word "elites" advisedly. Most ordinary Americans revere the nation's immigrant past and admire individual immigrants whom they know, but they do not favor an expansionist immigration policy. This was true prior to the 1980s and it almost certainly remains true today. Individuals with high educational and professional status who participate actively in policy debates and are deeply influenced by intellectual currents are different. Elite public opinion in the 1980s, as articulated by liberal and conservative editorialists alike, strongly endorsed pro-immigration reforms, and their views exerted considerable influence in Congress and the upper reaches of the

executive branch. See Miller, "Right Thing," pp. 57, 66; and Fuchs interview. For a review of editorial opinion on immigration before 1980, see Rita J. Simon, *Public Opinion and the Immigrant: Print Media Coverage, 1880–1980* (Lexington, Mass.: Lexington Books 1985).

130. This section draws heavily on the analysis in Peter H. Schuck, "The Transformation of Immigration Law," *Columbia Law Review* 84 (1984): 1; and Peter H. Schuck, "The Emerging Political Consensus on Immigration Law," *Georgetown Immigration Law Journal* 5 (1991): 1, 9. See also Hiroshi Motomura, "Immigration Law after a Century of Plenary Power: Phantom Constitutional Norms and Statutory Interpretation," 100 *Yale Law Journal* 545 (1990).

131. For a statistical analysis of changing patterns of immigration adjudication in the appellate courts between 1979 and 1990, see Peter H. Schuck and Ted H. Wang, "Immigration in the Courts During the 1980s," a study conducted for the Administrative Conference of the United States (1992). But c.f., Francis v. INS, 532 F.2d. 268 (2d Cir. 1976) (holding INA 212 (c) unconstitutional as applied); Tapia-Acuna v. INS, 640 F.2d. 223 (9th Cir. 1981) (same); INS v. Chadha, 462 U.S. 919 (1983) (holding unconstitutional legislative veto in INA, 244).

132. For example, Haitian Refugee Center v. Smith, 676 F.2d 1023 (5th Cir. 1982).

133. Plyler v. Doe, 457 U.S. 202 (1982).

134. For example, Abourezk v. Reagan, 785 F.2d 1043 (D.C. Cir. 1986), *aff d without opinion,* 484 U.S. 1 (1987).

135. For example, Landon v. Plasencia, 459 U.S. 21 (1982). As discussed in Chapter 1, the 1996 Immigration reform law limited these rights and narrowed judicial review.

136. See Schuck, "Membership in the Liberal Polity." As discussed in Chapters 1, 5, and 8, the 1996 welfare reform and immigration reform laws sharply reversed this trend.

137. American-Arab Anti-Discrimination Committee v. Meese, 714 F. Supp. 1060 (C.D. Cal. 1989). This decision was later reversed by the appellate court, but only after the Immigration Act of 1990 had repealed the provision in question. 1940 F.2d 445 (9th Cir. 1991).

138. See sources cited by Hall, "Policy Paradigms" p. 22 n. 23.

139. For example, Julian L. Simon, *The Economic Consequences of Immigration* (Oxford, U.K.: B. Blackwell 1989); and Idem, "More Immigration Can Cut the Deficit," *New York Times,* May 10, 1990, p. A33, col. 1. Although Simon favors essentially unlimited immigration, he (following some other economists) has also proposed implementing a more limited system by auctioning off visas. See discussion of this proposal in Schuck, "Emerging Political Consensus," pp. 17–18.

140. See Morrison and Chisti interviews. See also, Fuchs letter, "I think that even pro-immigration policy makers such as Kennedy and Paul Simon don't believe that, whether or not Julian Simon does."

141. See, Robert Bach and Doris Meissner, *America's Labor Market in the 1990's: What Role Should Immigration Play?* (Carnegie Endowment for International Peace, June 1990), p. 15.

142. George J. Borjas, *Friends or Strangers: The Impact of Immigrants on the U.S. Economy* (New York: Basic Books, 1990), p. 222. See the discussion of these points in Schuck, "Emerging Political Consensus," pp. 27–30.

143. In two respects, the share of labor-related visas is actually smaller. First, another 880,000 admissions that are not labor related (attributable to aliens adjusting status under the IRCA amnesty provisions) should be added to the denominator for 1990, which would reduce the share of labor-related visas to under 4 percent. *1990 INS Yearbook,* p. 41. (On the other hand, the amnesty admissions will decline to zero within a few years.) Second, as with the pre-1990 law, *most* of the labor-related visas are not really based on the possession of labor skills but are allocated to the family members of visa-holding workers. See *1990 INS Yearbook* table 4.

144. The SCIRP staff's revision of the entire immigration statute, not included in the commission report, included changes in the exclusion provisions that did not carry the commission's imprimatur but were nonetheless useful in the later deliberations leading to the 1990 act. When the commission approved its final report, Simpson convinced the other commissioners that although he agreed that the traditional exclusions should be changed, the media

would run headlines suggesting that the commission wanted to admit gays and communists, which would undermine the commission's recommendations. Fuchs letter.

145. See Loescher and Scanlan, *Calculated Kindness.*

146. *1989 INS Yearbook* p. 98, table f.

147. See discussion *supra,* text accompanying notes 91–102.

148. Saenz, "Development of Diversity."

149. In sharp contrast to previous immigration legislation, which was not thought to require frequent or intensive review by Congress, the new law mandated a commission to report on immigration policy changes that might be needed in the future. Until the late 1970s, oversight of immigration administration (or much of anything else) by the judiciary committees, especially the Senate committee, was almost nonexistent. See Peter H. Schuck, ed. *The Judiciary Committees:* A Study of the House and Senate Judiciary Committees (New York: Grossman, 1975).

150. For a very recent example, see Leon F. Bouvier, *Peaceful Invasions: Immigration and Changing America* (Lanham, Md.: University Press of America, 1992), which its publisher describes as a "liberal limitationist" making the case for "humane restrictionism" *Scope,* Spring 1991, p. 1.

151. Musing about whether the outcome might have been different if an eloquent restrictionist like Sam Ervin had been in the Senate to argue the case, or if FAIR had possessed the intellectual leadership of the Immigration Restriction League in the early part of the century, former SCIRP director Lawrence Fuchs recently observed: "One is struck by the fact that there was no strong intellectual movement for restriction" (Letter).

152. For an effort to solve this puzzle in a different context, see Hall, "Policy Paradigms," pp. 7–8.

153. As Chou En-lai said when asked about the effects of the French Revolution, "It is too early to tell." The possibility of a sharp political backlash against expansionist immigration policies certainly cannot be ruled out, as other liberal democracies are learning today. See Rosemarie Rogers, *Responses to Immigration: The Western European Host Countries and Their Immigrants,* (unpub. ms., 1991); Craig R. Whitney, "Europeans Look for Ways to Bar Door to Immigrants," *New York Times,* December 29, 1991, p. 1; see also sources cited supra note 38.

Chapter 6

1. As discussed in Chapters 1 and 5, the 1996 immigration reform statute made this relief more difficult to obtain and rendered aggravated felons ineligible for it altogether.

2. As discussed in Chapter 5, the 1996 welfare reform law substantially reduced such benefits; some were restored in 1997.

3. The 1996 immigration reform statute strengthened the enforceability of these pledges.

4. As discussed in Chapters 1 and 8, naturalizations have risen dramatically.

Chapter 7

1. A. BICKEL, THE MORALITY OF CONSENT 54 (1975).

2. It is therefore surprising how little commentary it has received. This situation may be changing. *See, e.g.,* P. SCHUCK & R. SMITH, CITIZENSHIP WITHOUT CONSENT: ILLEGAL. ALIENS IN THE AMERICAN POLITY (1985); Aleinikoff, *Theories of Loss of Citizenship,* 84 MICH. L REV. 1471 (1986): T. Aleinikoff, Aliens, Citizens and Constitutional Membership (1987) (unpublished manuscript).

3. That policy is exclusionary (like the citizenship policies of all other states) but also relatively inclusive. For cross-national comparisons, *see* W. Brubaker, *Citizenship and Naturalization: Policies and Politics* in IMMIGRATION AND THE POLITICS OF CITIZENSHIP IN EUROPE AND NORTH AMERICA (W.R. Brubaker ed. 1989).

4. One may plausibly argue, for example, that the political dominion of the United States over its territory, and indeed the boundaries of the territory, were established arbitrarily and through immoral means; that cross-national inequalities of wealth are unjust and are sustained and exacerbated by exclusionary citizenship policies; that the primacy that liberalism accords to personal freedom implies that the parochial interests of the United States should yield to individuals' wishes (in some versions of liberalism, their "rights") to migrate and to join the American polity; and that accidents of birth, such as geography, cannot morally be used to allocate precious resources such as political membership. For arguments along one or more of these lines, see, e.g., B. ACKERMAN, SOCIAL JUSTICE IN THE LIBERAL STATE 89–95 (1980): M. WALZER, SPHERES OF JUSTICE: A DEFENSE OF PLURALISM AND EQUALITY (1983): C. BEITZ, POLITICAL THEORY AND INTERNATIONAL RELATIONS (1979); M. GIBNEY, STRANGERS OR FRIENDS: PRINCIPLES FOR A NEW ADMISSION POLICY (1986): Schuck, *Review of Gibney, Strangers or Friends: Principles for A New Admission Policy.* 81 AM. J. INT'T. LAW 782 (1987).

5. For an historical account, see J. KETTNER, THE DEVELOPMENT OF AMERICAN CITIZENSHIP, 1608–1870 (1970). As Kettner demonstrates, citizenship was also easily acquired during the colonial period and under the Articles of Confederation.

6. Dred Scott v. Sanford, 60 U.S. (19 How.) 393 (1857).

7. U.S. CONST., amend. XIV. § 1, cf. 1.

8. Birthright citizenship is the subject of Chapter 9.

9. The principal exceptions were most American Indians (i.e., those not living in white society), the children of foreign diplomats and belligerents, and children born on foreign vessels. For a discussion of these exceptions, see SCHUCK & SMITH, *supra* note 2, at 85, note 46.

Many thousands of pregnant Mexican women cross the border illegally each year to have their babies, presumably motivated in part by the desire to confer American citizenship upon the newborn children by the simple expedient of bearing them on American soil. The issue of whether these children should automatically acquire birthright citizenship is discussed in SCHUCK & SMITH, *supra* note 2, at 113–22, 128–40.

10. The statutory requirements are five years' residency, continuous residency since the filing of the naturalization petition, good moral character, attachment to constitutional principles, and being "well-disposed to the good order and happiness of the United States." 8 U.S.C. §§ 1423, 1427 (1970). The generous judicial interpretation of these requirements is exemplified by Girouard v. United States, 328 U.S. 61 (1946). However, although the formal judicial denial rate is only 3 percent, the INS administratively denied 27 percent of the naturalization applicants during the 1985–87 period. *See New Citizens in Limbo? One in Three Applicants for U.S. Citizenship Neither Pass Nor Fail,* NALEO Background Paper #8, 3–4 (1988).

11. Politicians of all stripes, responding to ethnic voters and advocacy organizations, as well as to the symbolic value of naturalization, press the INS to process more applicants for citizenship.

There is a genuine dispute about the reasons for the low naturalization rates of certain immigrant groups. But these rates cannot fairly be attributed either to politicians' opposition or to bureaucratic resistance by the INS. I certainly do not mean to deny that the INS could do more effective outreach to stimulate more naturalization petitions by eligible aliens. Its ability to do so, however, is largely a question of budgetary resources, not agency stonewalling. *See, e.g.,* North, The Long Gray Welcome: A Study of the American Naturalization Program (1985) (Report Prepared for the NALEO Educ, Fund, 1985).

12. U.S. Const., amend. XIV, § 1, cl. 2. In Mathews v. Diaz, 426 U.S. 67 (1976), the Supreme Court held that the equal protection principle embedded in the Fifth Amendment's Due Process Clause restricts the Federal Government less, at least with respect to alienage classifications, than it restricts state law alienage classifications through the Fourteenth Amendment.

13. *See* Westen, *The Empty Idea of Equality,* 95 HARV. L. REV. 537 (1982).

14. For a discussion of the relationship between membership and citizenship, *see* Aleinikoff, *supra* note 2, at 1488–89.

15. Again, the question of which rights are "basic" in this sense and thus ought to be protected for aliens as well as citizens is beyond the scope of this essay, except insofar as those rights have *already* been established for aliens under American law.

16. Resident aliens, however, are a special kind of minority. Unlike racial or religious groups, the attribute that defines resident aliens as a minority and disadvantages them is not only readily mutable but can be shed within a relatively short period of time (five years). And as future voters with ethnic allies in the existing citizen population, the risks to them of legally-imposed discrimination are somewhat reduced.

17. For the leading recent exposition, see I. BERLIN, TWO CONCEPTS OF LIBERTY (1958).

18. According to some studies, current *legal* immigration policy, by emphasizing family re-unification at the expense of needed labor market skills, has actually increased differentials with regard to education levels. *See* V. BRIGGS, JR., IMMIGRATION POLICY AND THE AMERICAN LABOR FORCE 85–86 (1984); Chiswick, *A Troubling Drop in Immigrant 'Quality'*, N.Y. Times, Dec. 21, 1986, § 3, at 3, col. 1. On the other hand, legal immigrants' economic progress appears to eliminate the income gap within a little more than a decade in this country. BRIGGS, *supra*, at 83–85 (reviewing empirical studies).

19. This formulation of the constitutional test for alienage classifications is an over-simplification for at least two reasons. First, it applies only to *state law* alienage classifications. Alienage classifications created by federal law are subject to less exacting judicial scrutiny. *See* Mathews v. Diaz, 426 U.S. 67 (1976). Second, even as to state law classifications, the Supreme Court may have abandoned this formulation in favor of federal preemption analysis of such classifications to determine whether the state law conflicts with a federal policy. Both of these refinements remain matters of considerable controversy among legal scholars.

Where the equal protection standard is not met, the government retains the choice concerning *how* to equalize—that is, whether to extend eligibility to include the previously excluded group or whether to equalize treatment by further restricting or eliminating eligibility altogether—so long as it can then satisfy the constitutional standard for justifying alienage classifications.

20. Schneider v. Rusk, 377 U.S. 163 (1964); Huynh v. Carlucci, 679 F.Supp. 61 (D.D.C. 1988) (invalidating federal regulations limiting access of certain groups of naturalized citizens to classified national security information). Naturalized citizens, unlike birthright citizens, remain subject to involuntary loss of nationality for misrepresentation in connection with the procurement of their naturalization. 8 U.S.C. § 1451 (1970); Kungys v. United States, 108 S.Ct. 1537 (1988); Chaunt v. United States, 364 U.S. 350 (1959). Naturalized citizens are also ineligible to be President. U.S. CONST., Art. 11, § 1, cl. 5.

21. *See, e.g.,* Graham v. Richardson, 403 U.S. 365 (1971). However, *temporary* resident aliens—a status created by the Immigration Reform and Control Act of 1986 for aliens who qualify under the Act's legalization provisions—are ineligible for a number of means-tested benefits for five years. This ineligibility continues during that period even though the alien may have adjusted to the status of permanent resident alien. 8 U.S.C. § 1255a(h) (1970).

22. *Compare, e.g.,* Cabell v. Chavez-Salido, 454 U.S. 432 (1982) (statutory citizenship requirement for California probation officers is valid) *and* Bernal v. Fainter, 467 U.S. 216 (1984) (citizenship requirement for notary public held invalid under 14th Amendment).

23. Some disadvantages, such as ineligibility to own federally regulated TV stations or obtain a pilot's license, constrain only a small number of people, although such restrictions are doubtless offensive to those subject to them.

24. Another exclusive right of citizens—to travel on a U.S. passport—chiefly concerns mobile aliens whose own nations may revoke or refuse to reissue their passports. Legal resident aliens, however, can usually obtain travel documents from the U.S. government. *See, e.g.,* 8 U.S.C. § 1203 (1970) (re-entry permits).

25. It is significant, however, that restrictions on aliens' right to vote are almost universal among the Western European democracies as well.

26. See Rosberg. *Aliens and Equal Protection: Why Not the Right to Vote?*, 75 MICH. L. REV. 1092 (1977).

27. Only a bare majority of Americans, after all, bother to exercise their right to vote even in presidential elections, and the percentage of eligible voters who cast ballots in other elections ordinarily is even lower. Indeed, it is irrational, strictly speaking, for *any* individual to vote, especially in our system of winner-take-all (i.e., no proportional representation) elections; the costs of doing so far exceed the likelihood that an individual vote will be decisive. *See* A. DOWNS, AN ECONOMIC THEORY OF DEMOCRACY ch. 13 (1957).

28. *See, e.g.,* Perkins v. Smith, 370 F.Supp. 134 (D.Md. 1974). *summarily off'd,* 426 U.S. 913 (1975).

29. Executive Order No. 11935 (1976). This restriction was upheld in Mow Sun Wong v. Campbell, 626 F.2d 789 (9th Cir.). *cert. denied,* 450 U.S. 959 (1981). Broad alienage restrictions on state civil service employment were invalidated in Sugarman v. Dougall, 413 U.S. 634 (1973).

30. *See supra* note 21 and cases cited there.

31. This term is defined to include the spouse, parents (if the citizen child is over 21), and unmarried children under 21. 8 U.S.C. § 1151(b) (1970).

32. 8 U.S.C. § 1153(a)(2) (1970). However, a spouse or unmarried child of an immigrating alien who accompanies or follows the immigrating alien shares his or her status and place on line. *Id.* § 1153(a)(8).

33. Again, the latter are subject to denaturalization. *See supra* note 18.

34. *See. e.g.,* INS v. Lopez-Mendoza, 468 U.S. 1032 (1984).

35. Harisiades v. Shaughnessy, 342 U.S. 580, 600 (1952) (Douglas, J., dissenting).

36. 8 U.S.C. § 1251(a) (1970). One commentator estimated that the statute creates 700 different grounds for deportation. Maslow, *Recasting Our Deportation Law: Proposals for Reform.* 56 COLUM. L. REV. 309, 314 (1956).

37. It is difficult to know which of these rights are protected by the Constitution, as most of them were created by statute well before the "due process revolution" of the late 1960's and 1970's expanded the *constitutional* basis for such rights. In this connection, it may be significant that the Supreme Court recently expanded the constitutionally secured procedural rights of returning resident aliens. Landon v. Plasencia, 459 U.S. 21 (1982).

It seems doubtful that Congress could eliminate many of these rights even if it wished to do so. *See. e.g.,* Verkuil, *A Study of Immigration Procedures,* 31 UCLA L REV 1141 (1984). Perhaps more important, the direction of congressional efforts is suggested by Congress's refusal during the most recent round of immigration law reform to adopt the "summary exclusion" provision, which would have limited the right of judicial review for excludable aliens.

This is not to say, however, that Congress never jeopardizes existing due process rights. Serious constitutional questions are raised by the provision of the 1986 marriage fraud legislation, Pub. L. 99–639, which denies an alien the right to obtain immediate relative or preference status by reason of a marriage entered into during exclusion or deportation hearings until the alien has resided outside the United States for two years. *See. e.g.,* Azizi v. Meese, Civil No. 11-87-957 AHN (D.Conn.).

38. In 1986, for example, only 23,000 individuals were formally deported out of a permanent resident alien population totaling many millions of people, and virtually all of those deportees were either illegal entrants, out-of-status nonimmigrants (i.e., temporary visitors), or convicted criminals. A far larger number (1.58 million) were expelled without formal proceedings, but almost all of these fell into the same three categories. *See* 1986 Statistical Yearbook of the Immigration and Naturalization Service 105. Relatively few expellees are in the United States for a significant length of time. *See* 1984 Statistical Yearbook 194.

Aliens who are fortunate enough to have competent legal representation may hope to escape deportation entirely even when they are clearly deportable. In the celebrated (but surely atypical) *Marcello* case, the INS spent more than 30 years attempting to deport an alien: as recently as 1986, he was here exhausting his appeals and the patience of the INS. *See* Marcello v. INS, 644 F.2d 1033 (5th Cir.), *cert. denied*, 464 U.S. 935 (1983).

39. *See e.g.,* Vance v. Terrazas, 444 U.S. 252 (1980) (in establishing loss of citizenship, government must prove intent to surrender U.S. citizenship); Kahane v. Shultz, 653 F. Supp. 1486 (E.D.N.Y. 1987) (government must show voluntary expatriating act by citizen showing intent to relinquish citizenship).

40. *See* INS, 1984 Statistical Yearbook 177.

41. Kungys v. United States, 108 S.Ct. 1537 (1988) (to denaturalize a naturalized citizen, government must show willful misrepresentation or concealment of material fact which resulted in procurement of citizenship).

42. 8 U.S.C. § 148(a)(1).

43. Dual citizenship is analyzed in Chapter 10.

44. *See* SCHUCK & SMITH, *supra* note 2, at chs. 1–3.

45. These figures are derived from data published in Proceedings of the First National Conference on Citizenship and the Hispanic Community, May 5, 1984, at 1–2, table 1.

46. *See* North, The Long Gray Welcome, *supra* note 10, at 42, exhibit 15.

47. Aliens may experience more delays and paperwork than citizens do in establishing their eligibility for benefits. This difference presumably does not loom large as a motive to naturalize, although I have been told by a friend, a Canadian national, that she naturalized in the United States out of a desire to utilize the faster-moving citizens line when passing through customs control at Kennedy Airport after an international flight.

48. INS 1986 Statistical Yearbook, *supra* note 37, at 76.

49. Although the INS does not publish data on naturalization rates, David North has calculated them for the 1976–85 period by comparing three-year rolling averages of immigrant flows to those naturalized eight years after the middle year of the three. *See* North, *supra* note 10. I have taken the analysis through the analysis through 1986, updating North's calculations using INS's corrected data. It indicates naturalization rates of 44 percent in 1982, 45.5 percent in 1983, 47 percent in 1984, 50 percent in 1985, and 55 percent in 1986. The recently concluded amnesty program, however, is unlikely to increase the naturalization rate and many well reduce it. *See infra* note 63.

50. *See* North, *supra* note 10, at 50, 54.

51. The out-of-pocket expenses, including the INS fee of $185 per application, lawyer's fees, and the cost of acquiring the necessary documentation, were also substantial.

52. These observations are based upon a preliminary evaluation of the amnesty program by D. Meissner and D. Papademetriou, *The Legalization Countdown: A Third Quarter Assessment, 1988* (Carnegie Endowment for International Peace).

53. *See* Plyler v. Doe, 457 U.S. 202 (1982). The applicability of these principles depends largely upon whether the alien is deemed to have "entered" the United States, in which case he or she can invoke due process protection, or has been apprehended at the border, in which case he or she cannot.

54. *See* SCHUCK & SMITH, *supra* note 2, at 73.

55. 8 U.S.C. §§ 1449 (certificate of naturalization), 1401(c), (d), (e), and (g) (citizenship at birth) (1970).

56. *See* SCHUCK & SMITH, *supra* note 2, at 94.

57. See Lopez, *Undocumented Mexican Migration: In Search of a Just Immigration Law and Policy.* 28 UCLA L. REV. 615 (1981).

58. The two most important measures were the employer sanction provisions of the 1986 Immigration Reform and Control Act, Pub. L. 99-603, and the Immigration Marriage Fraud Amendments of 1986. Pub. L. 99-639.

59. Smith and I have argued (*see supra* note 2) that the framers of the Citizenship Clause intended its "subject to the jurisdiction thereof" qualification to exclude those to whose presence or membership the nation has not consented. We contend that had illegal aliens constituted a recog-

nized category in 1868 when the Clause was adopted, the framers would also have excluded their native-born children from automatic birthright citizenship under the Clause, as they did most members of the Indian tribes. Quite apart from the Clause's legal meaning, however, the question remains whether the United States, contrary to the practice of most other liberal democratic nations, ought to grant citizenship to such children as a matter of policy. This policy question is complicated by the enactment of employer sanctions and legalization programs in 1986. Its resolution turns upon empirical and normative issues relating to the incentives for illegal migration and the dynamics and value of assimilation. These questions are beyond the scope of this essay.

60. Indeed, if the alien is prominent enough, the United States may be prepared to lower the price even more. In this, it follows the practice of the United Kingdom, which granted South African runner Zola Budd citizenship so that she could represent them in international competition.

61. A parallel development—the large (relative to other democracies) and growing proportion of citizens who are eligible to vote but fail to do so—creates the same kind of risk, although its actual effect on policy outcomes is a matter of some dispute.

62. Schauer, *Community, Citizenship, and the Search for National Identity.* 84 MICH. L. REV 1504 (1986).

63. WALZER, *supra* note 4, at 38.

64. See Schuck, *Immigration Law and the Problem of Community,* in CLAMOR AT THE GATES: THE NEW AMERICAN IMMIGRATION 305 (N. Glazer ed. 1985).

65. See Schuck, *The Transformation of Immigration Law,* 84 COLUM. L. REV. I (1984). And quite apart from the question of legal doctrine, the underlying naturalization rate, which affects as well as reflects the value attributed to citizenship, is unlikely to rise significantly in the foreseeable future. Although Asian-Americans (and their family members who later come here through "chain migration") can be expected to naturalize at relatively high rates, this effect may be overwhelmed by more than one million Mexicans who compromise at least 70 percent of those who will be legalized under the amnesty programs. These individuals (and those family members whom they bring in) will presumably continue to naturalize at low rates.

66. This is not to deny that efforts will sometimes be made to resuscitate citizenship as a distinctive, meaningful, and advantageous status. Indeed, the INS plans to propose legislation that would increase the incentives to naturalize by making it more difficult for permanent resident aliens, but not for citizens, to bring their families here and by reducing the required residence period for naturalization to three years. 65 INTERP. REL. 405 (1988).

The provision of the 1986 legislation that makes even permanent resident aliens temporarily ineligible for certain governmental benefits if they acquired their legal status through the amnesty program, 8 U.S.C. § 1255a(h), also increases the value of citizenship relative to permanent resident status. But since the period of statutory ineligibility continues for five years after legalization, a period during which the legalized alien is not yet eligible for naturalization, there is nothing that he or she can do to remove this particular disability and thus no greater incentive to naturalize.

67. In that context, the "entry doctrine" of traditional immigration law—the notion that an alien who has not yet "entered" the United States is to be regarded as standing at the border and is excludable without any procedural rights not conferred by Congress—remains an important, if quite objectionable, fiction. See Schuck, *supra* note 63, at 20–21.

Chapter 8

1. As I note infra, I mean to include in "sovereignties" both public and private governance regimes to which individuals may be subjected.

2. The number of legal immigrants actually admitted was 915,000 in 1996, 720,000 in 1995, 804,000 in 1994, and 904,000 in 1993.

3. The Immigration and Naturalization Service (INS) rejected 200,000 petitions in 1996; 965,000 petitions were pending in March 1997.

4. The globalization phenomenon, while important, is easily exaggerated. According to a very recent study, U.S.-based firms' share of world output outside the United States actually declined from 3 percent to 2 percent between 1977 and 1993, even as the domestic U.S. economy expanded. Robert Lipsey et. al, Internationalized Production in World Output, NBER Working Paper No. 5385 (1996).

5. *See* Peter H. Schuck, *The Message of 187*, Am. Prospect 85–92 (1995).

6. Some commentators maintain that the justifications for citizenship lie primarily in the international law realm; this status, they believe, has—or ought to have—little significance inside a nation's borders. *See, e.g.*, Stephen H. Legomsky, *Why Citizenship?*, 35 Va J. Int'l L. 279, 300 (1994). Chapter 6 discusses Proposition 187.

7. David Jacobson, Rights Across Borders: Immigration and the Decline of Citizenship 131 (1996). I discuss, and criticize, Jacobson's conception of "post-national citizenship." *See infra* page 202–205.

8. For each status, these rights are more expansive and valuable than the rights of those who occupy the status beneath it. The obligations attaching to these statuses, however, are not calibrated or distributed in quite the same way as rights. The obligations owed by citizens are not necessarily greater than those owed by lesser statuses; in some respects—such as the resident alien's paperwork obligations to the INS—citizen's duties may actually be *less* onerous.

9. *See* David A. Martin, *Due Process and Membership in the National Community: Political Asylum and Beyond*, 44 U. Pitt. L. Rev. 165–235 (1983).

10. Alexander M. Bickel, The Morality of Consent 54 (1975).

11. Peter H. Schuck, *Membership in the Liberal Polity*, 3 Geo. Immigr. L. J. 1 (1989). Much depends, of course, on what one means by "membership" and how full it must be in order to satisfy Bickel's terms. Women, for example, were citizens but lacked the franchise, at least in federal elections, until the ratification of the Nineteenth Amendment in 1920. Young adults only obtained the franchise in 1971 with the adoption of the Twenty-Sixth Amendment. A full, robust citizenship, moreover, demands more than the right to vote. *See* Rogers M. Smith, Civic Ideals: Conflicting Visions of Citizenship in U.S. Public Law (1997); Judith N. Shklar, American Citizenship: The Quest for Inclusion (1991).

12. Although the United Kingdom no longer strongly adheres to *jus soli*, France does. *See* Patrick Weil, La France et ses Etrangers (1995).

13. Customary exceptions to the *jus soli* rule exist: They include, for example, children born on foreign-flag vessels and children of diplomatic personnel.

14. Peter H. Schuck and Rogers M. Smith, Citizenship without Consent: Illegal Aliens in the American Polity (1985). Legislation to eliminate birthright citizenship in these circumstances was considered (but not adopted) in 1996 and the 1996 Republican Party platform called for a constitutional amendment for this purpose. I have opposed such measures under current conditions. *See Hearings Before the Subcomm. on Immigration and Claims and on the Constitution of the House Judiciary Comm., 103d Cong.* (1995) (statement and letter of Peter H. Schuck); Peter H. Schuck and Rogers M. Smith, Letter to the Editor, N.Y. Times, Aug. 11, 1996, at A14.

15. An INS study of the group of aliens who immigrated to the United States in 1977 found that 54 percent still had not naturalized by the end of 1995, 18 years later, when they had already been eligible for well over a decade. Moreover, most aliens who do naturalize do not apply until well after they become eligible; their median period of U.S. residency is now nine years. There are, however, important regional and country variations in speed of naturalization.

16. *See generally* Gerald L. Neuman, *Justifying U.S. Naturalization Policies* 35 VA J. Int'l L. 237 (1994); Peter H. Schuck, *Whose Membership Is It Anyway? Comments on Gerald Neuman*, 35 VA J. Int'l L. 321, 326 (1994). Chapter 10 discusses plural citizenships.

17. Peter J. Spiro, *Dual Nationality and the Meaning of Citizenship*, 46 Emory L.J. 1411 (1997).

18. 485 U.S. 759 (1988).

19. *See* Jamin Raskin, *Legal Aliens, Local Citizens: The Historical, Constitutional and Theoretical Meanings of Alien Suffrage*, 141 U. Pa. L. Rev. 1391 (1993); Gerald L. Neuman, *We Are the People: Alien Suffrage in German and American Perspective*, 13 Mich J. Int'l L. 259, 291–335 (1992); Gerald Rosberg, *Aliens and Equal Protection: Why not the Right to Vote?*, 75 Mich. L. Rev. 1092 (1977).

20. United States citizens, it should be noted, often do not vote; only forty-nine percent of those eligible to vote in the 1996 presidential election and thirty-eight percent of those eligible to vote in the 1994 congressional elections cast their ballots—a higher rate than in recent off-year elections.

21. For a case dealing with a similar issue in Canada, see *Lavoie v. The Queen* (1995) (upholding Canada's citizenship preference against a constitutional challenge).

22. Harisiades v. Shaughnessy, 342 U.S. 580, 600 (1951).

23. In 1996 only 54,000 aliens were formally deported or removed "under docket control" and virtually all of these were illegal entrants, out-of-status non-immigrants, violators of narcotics laws, or convicted criminals. The proportion of aliens removed who were charged with crimes or narcotics activity was 66 percent. A far larger number (1.5 million) were expelled without formal proceedings, but almost all of these fell into the same four categories. U.S. Dep't of Justice, Immigration and Naturalization Service, Statistical Yearbook for 1996 (1997). Moreover, relatively few of those who were deported or expelled had been in the United States for a long period of time. U.S. Dep't of Justice, Immigration and Naturalization Service, Statistical Yearbook for 1993 at 156 (1993).

24. *See* Peter H. Schuck & John Williams, *Deporting Criminal Aliens: The Pitfalls and Opportunities of Federalism*, 21 Harv. J. L. & Pub. Pol'y (forthcoming 1998). The agency, however, has improved its performance recently. *Id.*

25. First, so-called 'deeming' provisions apply to many federal and state benefit programs. Even an alien with a visa to enter as an LPR can be excluded if he is "likely at any time to become a public charge," that is, receive means-tested public assistance. An LPR or other alien already in the United States can be removed if he has become a public charge within five years of entry, unless he can show that his poverty was caused by conditions that arose after entry. Very few removals have been enforced under this provision. Entering aliens (except for refugees) must show that they will have a steady source of support through employment, family resources, or otherwise. If they cannot do so, a portion of the income of the entering aliens' U.S. resident sponsors (in the case of family-based immigrants) is deemed to be available to the alien for a number of years after arrival, which will ordinarily render him ineligible for public benefits. An alien who receives welfare would also encounter difficulty in sponsoring other family members as immigrants.

The 1996 welfare reform law extends the reach and enforceability of these deeming provisions, making fewer LPRs eligible for benefits even if they can survive the other new, more categorical restrictions on eligibility for new immigrants and for those already admitted but not yet naturalized citizens.

26. LPRs do enjoy the benefits of a special program, adopted as part of the compromise that led to the 1986 employer sanctions provisions, which bars job discrimination against aliens who are legally authorized to work. The 1996 amendments make proof of discrimination more difficult by requiring the alien to show the employer's discriminatory intent.

27. Indeed, this growth continued (except in the case of Aid to Families with Dependent Children) during the Reagan and Bush years. *See* Peter H. Schuck, *Against (and for) Madison: An Essay in Praise of Factions*, 15 Yale L. & Pol'y Rev. 553 (1997).

28. Among academics, Lawrence Mead and Mary Ann Glendon were two of the most outspoken advocates for this position. *See* Mary Ann Glendon, Rights Talk: The Impoverishment of Political Discourse (1991); Lawrence M. Mead, Beyond Entitlement: The Social Obligations of Citizenship (1986).

29. See Peter H. Schuck, *Membership in the Liberal Polity: The Devaluation of American Citizenship*, 3 Geo. Immig. L. J. 1 (1989).

30. See, e.g., Canada House of Commons, Canadian Citizenship: A Sense of Belonging: Report of the Standing Committee on Citizenship and Immigration (1994).

31. See, e.g., *id.* at 17.

32. For a discussion of these social forces, see Peter H. Schuck, *Introduction: Reflections on the Federalism Debate*, 14 Yale L. & Pol'y Rev. 1 (1996).

33. For leading and contrasting discussions of this development, see Evan McKenzie, Privatopia: Homeowner Associations and the Rise of Residential Private Government (1994); Richard T. Ford, *The Boundaries of Race: Political Geography in Legal Analysis*, 107 Harv. L. Rev. 1841 (1994); Robert C. Ellickson, *Cities and Homeowners' Associations*, 130 U. PA. L. Rev. 1519 (1982).

34. See, e.g., Peter Skerry, *Many Borders to Cross: Is Immigration the Exclusive Responsibility of the Federal Government*, 25 Publius 71 (1995); Gerald Neuman, *The Lost Century of American Immigration Law*, 93 Colum. L. Rev. 1833 (1993).

35. If anything, the courts, led by the Supreme Court, have reaffirmed this primacy in the last decade. For a review of some of the recent cases, see Stephen H. Legomsky, *Ten More Years of Plenary Power: Immigration, Congress, and the Courts*, 22 Hastings Const. L.Q. 925 (1995).

36. See, e.g., Peter J. Spiro, *The States and Immigration in an Era of Demi-Sovereignties*, 35 Va J. Int'l L. 121 (1994); Peter H. Schuck, *The Transformation of Immigration Law*, 84 Colum. L. Rev. 1, 14–30 (1984); Stephen H. Legomsky, *Immigration Law and the Principle of Plenary Congressional Power*, 1984 Sup. Ct. Rev. 255;.

37. 117 S.Ct. 38 (1996).

38. See League of United Latin American Citizens v. Wilson, 908 F. Supp. 755 (C.D. Cal. 1995). In November 1997, the 1996 federal district court reaffirmed its decision despite the intervening enactment of the welfare reform statute requiring states to discriminate against illegal aliens in the administration of certain social programs. This decision has been appealed.

39. See Peter Skerry, *Many Borders to Cross: Is Immigration the Exclusive Responsibility of the Federal Government*, 25 Publius 84 (1995).

40. See *id.* at 78–79.

41. See Peter J. Spiro, *The States and Immigration in an Era of Demi-Sovereignties*, 35 Va J. Int'l L. 121 (1994).

42. *Id.* at 162.

43. This development is not confined to the United States but is occurring in other developed nations as well.

44. 403 U.S. 365 (1971).

45. The favored groups are: refugees and asylum-seekers in their first five years in the United States, veterans and soldiers, and those who have worked in the United States for ten years and stayed off public assistance during that time.

46. As part of the budget compromise negotiated by President Clinton and Congress in July 1997, some of the SSI benefits, accounting for nearly half of the other cuts, were restored to legal immigrants who were receiving benefits on or before August 22, 1996.

47. 426 U.S. 67 (1976).

48. See, e.g., Abreu v. Callahan, 971 F. Supp. 799 (S.D.N.Y. 1997).

49. See Keys to Successful Immigration: Implications of the New Jersey Experience (Thomas J. Espenshade, ed., 1997); Scott McCartney and Karen Blumenthal, *Texas Strives to Avoid California's Mistakes, and It Is Prospering*, Wall St. J., Sept. 13, 1995, at A1.

50. See, e.g., Eric Schmitt, *Giuliani Criticizes G.O.P. and Dole on Immigration,* N.Y. Times, June 7, 1996, at B3. Some of the states mentioned (as well as others) have sued the federal government to recover billions of dollars that states have expended to educate, incarcerate, and hospitalize illegal aliens. All such suits have been dismissed and appeals are pending.

51. A similar analysis has been applied, *mutatis mutandis,* to many other areas of public policy in the United States. *See, e.g.,* Roberta Romano, The Genius of American Corporate Law (1993); *Symposium Issue on Federation,* Yale L. & Pol'y Rev. (1996); Daniel Esty, *Revitalizing Environmental Federalism,* 95 Mich. L. Rev. 570 (1995).

52. Yasemin Soysal, Limits of Citizenship: Migrants and Postnational Membership in Europe 136 (1994). Soysal notes that the idea of post-national citizenship has developed since the Second World War and especially during the last two decades. *Id.*

53. David Jacobson, Rights Across Borders: Immigration and the Decline of Citizenship 126–27 (1996).

54. *Id.*

55. I have borrowed this phrase and its connotation from Bruce Ackerman. *See* Bruce A. Ackerman, *The Storrs Lectures: Discovering the Constitution,* 93 Yale L. J. 1013–72 (1983).

56. See Yasemin Soysal, Changing Parameters of Citizenship and Claims Making: Organized Islam in European Public Spheres, Working Paper No. EUF 1996/4 (1996) [hereinafter *Soysal, Changing*].

57. I developed this theme almost fifteen years ago in an article that called attention to these judicial stirrings. Peter H. Schuck, *The Transformation of Immigration Law,* 84 Colum. L. Rev. 1, 14–30 (1984). Jacobson has also discussed some of these themes. David Jacobson, Rights Across Borders: Immigration and the Decline of Citizenship 131 (1996). In hindsight, I believe my conclusion that a "transformation" was occurring may have been somewhat premature, although important changes in judicial doctrine and attitude clearly did occur during the 1980s.

58. *See* Peter H. Schuck, *Public Law Litigation and Social Reform,* 102 Yale L. J. 1763 (1993). The swift overruling and narrowing of most of the "post-national" U.S. court decisions on behalf of long-detained criminal aliens that Jacobson cites confirms this point. *Id.* And while Plyler v. Doe, 457 U.S. 202 (1982), probably the most important "post-national" decision cited by him, remains intact, both its narrow majority and its reasoning leave it vulnerable to being either reversed or distinguished away, perhaps in the pending litigation challenging the constitutionality of Proposition 187. *See* Peter H. Schuck, *The Message of 187,* Am. Prospect 85–92 (1995).

59. See Peter Finley Dunne, Mr. Dooley's Opinions 26 (1901).

60. See Soysal, Changing, *supra* note 56, at 16. Although Soysal does not expressly refer here to the idea of post-national citizenship developed in her other work, she is clearly invoking it, as when she concludes: "[t]his shift in focus from national collectivity to particularistic identities . . . points to the emergence of a new basis for participation and the proliferation of forms of mobilization at various levels of polity, which are not imperatively defined by national parameters and delimited by national borders." *Id.*

61. For a magisterial account of these contests, see Rogers M. Smith, Civic Ideals: Conflicting Visions of Citizenship in U.S. Public Law (1997).

62. Peter H. Schuck, *Against (and for) Madison: An Essay in Praise of Factions,* 15 Yale L. & Pol'y Rev. 553 (1997).

63. Even in this mature form, most European (and American) analysts consider it a limited, laggard example of the species.

64. The most recent evidence bearing on this question is the decision to create a large new federal program to provide health care coverage to children who are uninsured. Adam Clymer, *Whitehouse and the G.O.P. Announce Deal to Balance Budget and Trim Taxes,* N.Y. Times, July 29, 1997, at A1.

Chapter 10

1. See Robert M. Cover, "The Supreme Court, 1982 Term: Foreword: Nomos and Narrative," *Harvard Law Review* 97 (1983): 4; Michael Walzer, *Spheres of Justice: A Defense of Pluralism and Equality* (New York: Basic Books, 1983); Sanford Levinson, "Constituting Communities Through Words That Bind: Reflections on Loyalty Oaths," *Michigan Law Review* 84 (1986): 1440.

2. Following convention, I use the terms *citizenship* and *nationality* interchangeably for most purposes in this discussion, although the legal distinction between the two concepts does become important below when I discuss how the law should treat the franchise; paradigmatically, citizens possess it but nationals do not. A recent essay urging that the two statuses be decoupled in order that their functional and normative aspects can be separated also observes that citizenship "attempts to encompass in one word a legal status, a state of mind, a civic obligation, an immigration benefit, an international legal marking, and a personal virtue." (Harvard Law Review)

3. I shall continue to refer to "dual" citizenship although, as noted below, triple and even more plural citizenships are becoming increasingly available to individuals as a result of the conjunction of modes for acquiring citizenship—and liberalizing ones at that—deriving from parentage, marriage, naturalization, and reacquisition of former nationalities.

4. Peter J. Spiro, "Dual Nationality and the Meaning of Citizenship," *Emory Law Journal* 46 (1997): 1435 (citing President James Buchanan's secretary of state, Lewis Cass).

5. In addition to the widespread adoption of no-fault laws for dissolving marriages, at least one state, Louisiana, has created a consensual, dual-track regime for regulating the conditions for divorce. See Kevin Sack, "Louisiana Approves Measure to Tighten Marriage Bonds," *New York Times*, June 24, 1997, 1.

6. Liberalization can occur in the country of first nationality (when that country does not denationalize its citizens for naturalizing elsewhere), in the country of second nationality (when it does not require naturalizing citizens to renounce their earlier nationality), or in both.

7. See T. Alexander Aleinikoff, *Citizen and Membership: A Policy Perspective* (Washington, D.C.: Carnegie Endowment for International Peace, 1997); Gerald L. Neuman, "Justifying U.S. Naturalization Policies," *Virginia Journal of International Law* 35 (1995): 237–278; Spiro, "Dual Nationality."

8. See, for example, Rogers M. Smith, *Civic Ideals: Conflicting Visions of Citizenship in U.S. History* (New Haven: Yale University Press, 1997); Peter H. Schuck and Rogers M. Smith, *Citizenship Without Consent: Illegal Aliens in the American Polity* (New Haven: Yale University Press, 1985); Stephen H. Legomsky, "Why Citizenship?" *Virginia Journal of International Law* 35 (1995): 279; T. Alexander Aleinikoff, "Citizens, Aliens, Membership and the Constitution," *Constitutional Commentary* 7 (1990): 9; Neuman, "Justifying U.S. Naturalization Policies."

9. In my view, citizenship can be justified, among other reasons, as creating an additional incentive to assimilate by acquiring a minimal competence in the dominant language, gaining a minimal understanding of (and hopefully a love for) the nation's institutions, and affirming a minimal allegiance to the polity. Such assimilation is of inestimable value both to American society and to aliens in the United States. See Peter H. Schuck, Expert Testimony in *Lavoie v. The Queen*, Federal Court of Canada, Trial Division, October 1994.

10. Peter H. Schuck, "The Re-Evaluation of American Citizenship," *Georgetown Immigration Law Journal* 12 (1997): 1. Also in *Challenge to the Nation-State: Immigration in Western Europe and the United States*, ed. C. Joppke (New York: Oxford University Press, 1998).

11. I mean this in the etymological sense of the word; the debate is addressing questions at the very root of the notion of citizenship.

12. Neuman, "Justifying U.S. Naturalization Policies," 237–278.

13. Schuck and Smith, *Citizenship Without Consent*; Spiro, "Dual Nationality."

14. U.S. General Accounting Office, "Naturalization of Aliens: INS Internal Controls," Testimony before Subcommittee on Immigration, Senate Judiciary Committee, May 1, 1997, GAO/T-GGD-97–98.

15. Katharine Q. Seelye, "20 Charged with Helping 13,000 Cheat on Test for Citizenship," *New York Times*, 28 January 1998, A12.

16. U.S. Congress, "Societal and Legal Issues Surrounding Children Born in the United States to Illegal Alien Parents," Joint Hearing before Subcommittee on Immigration and Claims and the Subcommittee on the Constitution, House Judiciary Committee, 104th Congress, 1st Session, December 13, 1995, Serial No. 50 (Washington, DC: Government Printing Office, 1996); U.S. Congress, Hearing before Subcommittee on Immigration and Claims, House Judiciary Committee, 105th Congress, 1st Session, June 25, 1997 (unpublished).

17. Neuman, "Justifying U.S. Naturalization Policies," 237–78; Spiro, "Dual Nationality"; Aleinikoff, *Citizen and Membership*; Noah Pickus, ed., *Immigration and Citizenship in the 21st Century* (Lanham, MD: Rowman and Littlefield, 1998).

18. Gerald L. Neuman, "Nationality Law in the United States and Germany: Structure and Current Problems," in *Paths to Inclusion: The Integration of Immigrants in the United States and Germany*, ed. Peter H. Schuck and Rainer Munz (Providence, RI: Berghahn Books, 1998). Neuman points out that "[b]efore the 1860s the U.S. was full of dual nationals who thought of themselves as Americans."

19. William Safire, "Citizen of the World," *New York Times*, May 16, 1983, A31. The flip side of this selfishness—Americans who acquire foreign nationalities and renounce their U.S. citizenship in order to avoid paying U.S. taxes—aroused such public resentment that Congress enacted a statute in 1996 to address the practice. See Ted J. Chiappari, "Expatriation Tax: Income Tax Liability of Expatriates and Departing Lawful Permanent Residents," in *1997–98 Immigration and Nationality Law Handbook, Vol. II* (Washington, DC: American Immigration Lawyers Association, 1997).

20. Alex Aleinikoff estimates that half a million children acquire dual citizenship in the U.S. *at birth* each year. See Aleinikoff, *Citizen and Membership*.

21. Aleinikoff identifies six discrete combinations of rules that can lead to dual citizenship. See Aleinikoff, *Citizen and Membership*. Peter Spiro notes that dual citizenship was expanded by the historical circumstances that states in the 19th century increasingly rejected other states' claims of perpetual allegiance, and that Europe's adoption of *jus sanguinis* in the 19th century coincided with the application by the U.S. of an almost absolute rule of *jus soli*. See Spiro, "Dual Nationality."

22. Spiro views this development as the third major challenge to the historic paradigms of nationality, following the spread of the principle of perpetual allegiance and the growth of liberal democratic states. See Spiro, "Dual Nationality."

23. Aleinikoff, *Citizen and Membership*.

24. Spiro, "Dual Nationality."

25. See Schuck and Munz, *Paths to Inclusion*, "Introduction." Germany is sharply divided on this question. The Free Democrats, Socialists, and Greens support dual nationality for children born of foreigners in Germany, with the children required to choose between German and foreign citizenship at age 18. The Christian Democrats and Christian Social Union strongly oppose dual nationality.

26. Eugene Goldstein and Victoria Piazza, "Naturalization, Dual Citizenship and Retention of Foreign Citizenship: A Survey," *Interpreter Releases* 73 (April 22, 1996): 517.

27. Aleinikoff, *Citizen and Membership*; Jorge A. Vargas, "Dual Nationality for Mexicans? A Comparative Legal Analysis of the Dual Nationality Proposal and Its Eventual Political and Socio-Economic Implications," *Chicano-Latino Law Review* 18 (1996): 1–58. Aleinikoff believes that the net effect of these two changes, which trade off more dual nationals in the first

generation against fewer in the second and subsequent ones, will be to produce fewer dual nationals eventually than under the old rules. Whether or not he is correct about this, the changes will surely encourage more Mexicans to naturalize in the U.S.

28. Spiro, "Dual Nationality"; Sam Dillon, "Mexico Woos U.S. Mexicans, Proposing Dual Nationality," *New York Times*, December 10, 1995, 16.

29. Some observers doubt that the new Mexican law will significantly affect naturalization rates in the U.S., arguing that discrimination against non-citizens in America is a more important factor driving naturalizations. See "Dual Citizenship, Domestic Politics and the Naturalization Rates of Latino Immigrants in the U.S.," Policy Brief, Tomas Rivera Center, June 1996.

30. Somini Sengupta, "Immigrants in New York Pressing Drive for Dual Nationality," *New York Times*, December 30, 1996, B1.

31. Until recently, as Spiro shows, states actively opposed, and contrived to limit their nationals' affiliations with other states through military, legal, and diplomatic means. He also points to the inconsistencies of some states' positions on dual citizenship, "attempt[ing] a rule of nationality from other states that they would not have for themselves." See Spiro, "Dual Nationality." I speculate that this practice is more difficult to effectuate today than it was when states were more willing to discriminate overtly in their legal regimes.

32. Rey Koslowski, comments at roundtable discussion on plural citizenship, Carnegie Endowment for International Peace, April 25, 1997.

33. Neil Lewis, "Reno Acts to Suspend Deportations," *New York Times*, July 11, 1997, A13.

34. Alejandro Portes, "Divergent Destinies: Immigration, the Second Generation, and the Rise of Transnational Communities," in *Paths to Inclusion*, ed. Schuck and Munz.

35. Indeed, Spiro notes that many states are now so eager for their nationals both to naturalize in economically advanced countries and to retain their ties to the state of origin that their nationality laws make it difficult or even impossible for their nationals to make an effective renunciation in the second state. In an arresting phrase, he calls this a "new perpetual allegiance," different from the old in that the states now *encourage* their nationals to acquire additional citizenships. He suggests that this development poses a dilemma for the second state if it wishes to minimize dual citizenship among its new members by requiring (as the U.S. now does *not* require) an effective renunciation. If the second state refuses to naturalize migrants from states that will not effectuate such a renunciation, then in effect no migrants from those states will be able to naturalize. This refusal would create political and diplomatic difficulties between the states and, by preventing naturalization, would impede the assimilation of these migrants. See Spiro, "Dual Nationality"; and also Dillon, "Mexico Woos U.S. Mexicans," 16.

36. T. Alexander Aleinikoff, "Theories of Loss of Citizenship," *Michigan Law Review* 84 (1986): 1471. See also *Kungys v. United States*, 485 U.S. 759 (1988).

37. Nancy F. Cott, "Marriage and Women's Citizenship: A Historical Excursion," unpublished manuscript, Yale University Department of History, 1996; Spiro, "Dual Nationality." The Supreme Court is now considering a further challenge to this gender bias in connection with the transmission of citizenship to illegitimate children. See *Miller v. Albright*, 96 F.3d 1467 (DC Cir.), cert. granted 117 S. Ct. 1551 (1997). The case was argued on November 11, 1997.

38. "Advice about Possible Loss of U.S. Citizenship and Dual Nationality," U.S. Department of State, reprinted in *Interpreter Releases* 67 (1990): 1093. Indeed, as David Martin has argued, the State Department not only tolerates dual citizenship through naturalization elsewhere by U.S. citizens but actually makes it more difficult for citizens to renounce their American citizenship by not effectuating renunciatory language in the other state's naturalization oath. David A. Martin, "The Civil Republican Ideal for Citizenship, and for Our Common Life," *Virginia Journal of International Law* 35 (1995): 301.

39. Aleinikoff, *Citizen and Membership*.

40. Spiro, "Dual Nationality." Aleinikoff notes that some of the problems associated with dual citizenship today could be ameliorated through bilateral agreements between states. See Aleinikoff, *Citizen and Membership*.

41. For another example of an *ex ante* interest that even an insular state may have in an international safety net regime (for refugees), see Peter H. Schuck, "Refugee Burden-Sharing: A Modest Proposal," *Yale Journal of International Law* 22 (1997): 243.

42. Schuck and Smith, *Citizenship Without Consent*; but see also Gerald L. Neuman, *Strangers to the Constitution: Immigrants, Borders, and Fundamental Law* (Princeton, NJ: Princeton University Press, 1996).

43. Schuck and Smith, *Citizenship Without Consent*; Peter H. Schuck, "Rethinking Informed Consent," *Yale Law Journal* 103 (1994): 899.

44. A commission reviewing Canada's dual citizenship law recommended in 1994 that both new "involuntary" dual citizens and naturalizing citizens "accord primacy" to their Canadian nationality. Canada House of Commons, "Canadian Citizenship: A Sense of Belonging," Report of the Standing Committee on Citizenship and Immigration (June 1994), 15.

45. *Rogers v. Bellei*, 401 U.S. 815 (1971). Some have expressed concern that a liberal dual citizenship policy might encourage the proliferation of second- and third-generation dual citizenship in the U.S. by permitting those who naturalize in America to transmit their U.S. citizenship through *jus sanguinis* to children and grandchildren who live elsewhere and have no other ties to the U.S. Congress could respond to this risk, if it exists, by enacting the kinds of residency requirements for *jus sanguinis* citizens that *Bellei* upheld.

46. *Afroyim v. Rusk*, 387 U.S. 253 (1967).

47. Usually, but not always. Well into the 20th century, aliens were permitted to vote in some states, and some municipalities permit them to vote in local elections—a practice that is common in Europe. Indeed, even undocumented aliens are entitled to vote in local school board elections in New York City. See Jamin Raskin, "Legal Aliens, Local Citizens: The Historical, Constitutional and Theoretical Meanings of Alien Suffrage," *University of Pennsylvania Law Review* 141 (1993): 1391.

48. *Schneider v. Rusk*, 377 U.S. 163 (1964).

49. Levinson, "Constituting Communities," 1465.

50. One possible explanation—that immigrants wishing to naturalize in the U.S. are aliens whose petitions give the government leverage over them that it lacks over Americans who are already citizens and wish to naturalize elsewhere—simply begs the central policy and perhaps constitutional questions of which conditions the polity can and, as a moral matter, should impose on the acquisition of citizenship through birth or consent, and why the status difference between the two groups should matter insofar as the supposed dangers of dual citizenship are concerned.

51. The U.S. has become increasingly aggressive in pursuing those who expatriate—thus ending their dual citizenship status (if they had it)—in order to minimize their U.S. tax obligation. Tax law changes enacted in 1996 are designed to defeat this stratagem. See Chiappari, "Expatriation Tax."

52. Neuman, "Nationality Law in the United States and Germany."

53. The confusion about standards results from the Supreme Court's severely fractured decision in *Kungys v. United States,* which attempted to define them. These standards may become clearer as a result of denaturalization cases that are being initiated in the wake of revelations that the INS has erroneously naturalized many ineligible aliens. See Seelye, "20 Charged with Helping 13,000 Cheat."

54. Neuman, "Justifying U.S. Naturalization Policies."

55. Peter H. Schuck, "Whose Membership Is It, Anyway? Comments on Gerald Neuman," *Virginia Journal of International Law* 35 (1995): 321.

56. For some parents of dual citizens, it also permits them to protect their children from the dangers of growing up in American ghettoes. Apparently, the children do not always want that option. See, for example, Larry Rohter, "Island Life Not Idyllic for Youths From U.S.," *New York Times*, February 20, 1998, A4 (describing "Dominican Yorks").

57. See Linda Basch, *Nations Unbound: Transnational Projects, Postcolonial Predicaments, and Deterritorialized Nation States* (Langhorne, PA: Gordon and Breach, 1985); Portes, "Divergent Destinies."

58. Recent empirical research suggests that naturalization affects English proficiency more strongly than any other indicator of durable attachment to the U.S. This effect, moreover, goes beyond the fact that one who naturalizes must already have acquired some English proficiency: "[a]lthough there is a modest English prerequisite for U.S. citizenship, it is hard to image that this effect outweighs the substantial propensity for naturalized citizens to want to make long-term investments in many forms of U.S.-specific capital, including learning English." Thomas J. Espenshade and Haishan Fu, "An Analysis of English-Language Proficiency Among U.S. Immigrants," *American Sociological Review* 62 (1997): 300.

59. See, for example, Spiro, "Dual Nationality," 101–2. That the ease of acquiring dual nationality increases immigrants' propensity to naturalize in the second state seems self-evident and has been reported by some observers in some countries. See Sengupta, "Immigrants in New York." Participants in the Carnegie Endowment workshop reported that the average period taken by Italians resident in Canada to naturalize there declined from 17 to 6 years after Italy permitted dual citizenship, and that the naturalization rate of Irish immigrants in Australia increased when Canberra eliminated from its naturalization oath an affirmation of loyalty to the British Crown. Mary Woods, Comments at roundtable discussion on plural citizenship, Carnegie Endowment for International Peace, April 25, 1997. But see Tomas Rivera Center, "Dual Citizenship."

60. Schuck, "Whose Membership Is It Anyway?" 329.

61. Levinson, "Constituting Communities."

62. Schuck and Munz, *Paths to Inclusion*.

63. Spiro, "Dual Nationality," 102–3.

64. The 1997 budget agreement will restore approximately half of these 1996 benefit cuts. See Robert Pear, "Legal Immigrants to Benefit Under New Budget Accord," *New York Times*, July 30, 1997, A17. President Clinton proposed in his January 1998 State of the Union message to fill much of the remaining gap. See Michael Fix and Wendy Zimmerman, "The Legacy of Welfare Reform" (working draft, The Urban Institute, February 1998).

65. Fix and Zimmerman, "Legacy."

66. Strictly speaking, of course, it is not dual citizenship per se that imposes these fiscal burdens, but rather the naturalization incentive created by a policy to deny benefits to aliens. Still, the effect is the same: a liberal dual citizenship policy will cost the government—*some* government—more in benefits. These costs, of course, should be offset by any corresponding social benefits, such as food stamps and SSI, that are generated by making these individuals eligible for these transfer programs.

67. The Canadian parliamentary committee cited this concern, among others. Canada House of Commons, "Canadian Citizenship," 15.

68. Recent examples are Sweden's effort to prosecute Argentine military officers for the death of a teenager who was a Swedish-Argentine dual citizen, and Spain's effort to prosecute Argentine military officers for the murder of Spanish-Argentine dual citizens.

69. Spiro, "Dual Nationality."

70. Depending on how one views these complex imbroglios, China's increasingly bellicose protests against Taiwan, which governs millions of people whom China views as Chinese citizens, and Russia's threats against the Baltic republics for their alleged discrimination against resident Russians, might be considered examples. As Neuman points out, these are often cases not of dual nationality but of single nationality individuals who reside outside their country but have ethnic ties to it. Neuman, "Nationality Law in the United States and Germany."

71. Under U.S. law, a dual citizen can certainly vote in American elections. Whether this citizen can also vote in the other state's elections depends on the law of that state. As noted earlier, the pending Mexican law will not permit Mexicans naturalizing in the U.S. to vote in

Mexican elections, although Mexico could amend its election law to allow them to do so, in effect rendering them citizens, not merely nationals, of Mexico. Mexico has already changed its election law to permit Mexican citizens who reside abroad to vote by absentee ballot.

72. The existence of Arrovian voting paradoxes does not substantially affect this argument.

73. Spiro, "Dual Nationality." Foreign politicians from major sending countries now frequently visit American communities in which their émigrés live, seeking to woo remittances, investments, and political support. See, for example, Patrick J. McDonnell, "San Salvador Mayor Visits Expatriates in L.A.," *Los Angeles Times*, November 19, 1997, 1.

74. Although the possibility that the church might harm U.S. interests seems far-fetched, the risks of other nongovernmental organizations doing so may be worth considering at a time when NGOs can wield enormous influence, even qualifying them for the Nobel peace prize. As Spiro points out, NGOs enjoy the freedom of action to undertake certain conduct that states are unlikely to engage in because of the legal, political, or diplomatic constraints under which they operate.

75. Peter Skerry, *Mexican-Americans: The Ambivalent Minority* (New York: Free Press, 1993).

76. Peter H. Schuck and Bruce Brown, "Lessons from Lippo," *Wall Street Journal*, February 27, 1997, A16.

77. It is always possible to finesse the question by simply assuming that those who have already lived as U.S. citizens have accepted that political identity through a kind of tacit consent. This argument from tacit consent is plausible, but problematic. See Schuck and Smith, *Citizenship Without Consent*; Levinson, "Constituting Communities."

78. I do not favor this approach, which is discussed in the final paragraph of this essay.

79. Albert O. Hirschman, *Exit, Voice, and Loyalty: Responses to Decline in Firms, Organizations, and States* (Cambridge, MA: Harvard University Press, 1970).

80. Obviously, there is room for interpretation here; if the criterion of an independent judiciary were used, for example, it is not clear that any of these countries (except perhaps India) would qualify. The others, in order of the number of immigrants sent, are Vietnam, China, Dominican Republic, Cuba, Ukraine, and Russia.

81. Canada House of Commons, "Canadian Citizenship."

82. The suspicion that many who naturalize do so for opportunistic reasons seems to animate a recent proposal to decouple functional citizenship (concerned with rights and duties) and nationality (concerned with affirming one's affective ties to the polity). (*Harvard Law Review*).

83. Some other reasons for increased naturalizations include an intensified INS efforts to encourage them, aliens' need to pay a fee for renewing their green cards that is only slightly lower than the naturalization fee, and the large cohort of those legalized under the amnesty provisions of the Immigration Reform and Control Act of 1986 who have only recently satisfied the time limits required for naturalization.

84. Aleinikoff, *Citizen and Membership*.

85. Aleinikoff, *Citizen and Membership*.

86. I shall not attempt here to define assimilation or to defend its importance as a preeminent value against which to assess immigration policy generally and dual citizenship policy in particular. I have discussed these matters elsewhere (Schuck, "Alien Rumination," *Yale Law Journal* 105 [1996]: 1987–95), and there is a voluminous literature on the subject.

87. Alex Aleinikoff finds it "interesting that this concern has never been stated for the 6,000–8,000 Canadians who naturalize in the United States each year, and have since 1977 been permitted to retain Canadian citizenship." Aleinikoff, *Citizen and Membership*. His innuendo—that racial animus distinguishes the two cases—may be correct, but the much larger number and perhaps residential concentration of naturalizing Mexicans, and their lesser command of English, might also contribute to and justify the different reactions.

88. Sengupta, "Immigrants in New York."

89. Schuck, "Whose Membership Is It, Anyway?"

90. Spiro, "Dual Nationality."

91. Spiro, "Dual Nationality."

92. "Traitor" is used here in its colloquial sense—as someone who betrays the nation—rather than its technical sense, which requires among other things that the traitor be a citizen of that nation. See *Kawakita v. United States*, 343 U.S. 717 (1952). For a nuanced discussion of treason and loyalty, including some cases in which citizenship was an issue, see George P. Fletcher, *Loyalty: An Essay on the Morality of Relationships* (New York: Oxford University Press, 1993), especially chap. 3.

93. Spiro, "Dual Nationality."

94. In such campaigns, of course, dual citizens are as entitled to serve in the armed forces as other citizens. Indeed, resident aliens may serve.

95. Indeed, Americans may also engage in such conduct on behalf of *democratic* regimes, even close allies of the U.S., as is demonstrated by the fascinating case of Jonathan Pollard, who illegally transferred U.S. military secrets to Israel—apparently in the belief that there was no conflict of interest.

96. For the classic exploration of the different ways of thinking about and institutionalizing relationships in which loyalty plays some role, see Hirschman, *Exit, Voice, and Loyalty.*

97. My colleague Akhil Amar points out that a U.S. citizen may not simultaneously be a citizen of more than one American state because this would give her two votes for Congress and the presidency rather than the one that her fellow citizens enjoy.

98. However, open primary states permit members of one political party to vote in the primary of another.

99. Many people, of course, use names that are different from their legal ones.

100. Neuman, "Justifying U.S. Naturalization Policies."

101. Other asymmetries may not be far off. The Commission on Immigration Reform, for example, considered whether to limit future immigrant admissions by restricting the right of newly naturalized citizens to petition for the admission of their relatives beyond the limits that apply to other citizens.

102. In fact, evidence from cognitive psychology strongly suggests that people who already possess a thing value it more than they would value the same thing if they did not yet possess it but hoped to acquire it. Hence they are more likely to defend it effectively.

103. As Levinson puts it, native-born citizens "are free to regard the Constitution as an abomination and even support its violent replacement by a more agreeable substitute; naturalized citizens, however, are formally bound to swear that their new self-definition of being 'American' will include at least the propositions laid out in their oath. . . ." Levinson, "Constituting Communities," 1463. Neuman does seem to view this asymmetry as problematic. "Justifying U.S. Naturalization Policies," 253–63.

104. This assumes, of course, that good moral character is defined in a minimalist fashion. This has not always been the case.

105. As a glance at the naturalization statute reveals, the United States has long done so with respect to eligibility standards. Rights have not been exempt from discrimination. The most important example is voting rights, which were withheld from citizen women until the 19th Amendment, and are still withheld from citizen felons and citizen children under the age of eighteen.

106. Neuman suggests that their concerns may be pretextual and "often a tactic for preventing naturalization of Mexicans." Gerald L. Neuman, letter to author dated August 18, 1997. As noted earlier, Aleinikoff harbors the same suspicion. In any event, nothing in my analysis turns on whether or not they are correct.

107. Aleinikoff, *Citizen and Membership.*

108. Schuck and Smith, *Citizenship Without Consent.*

109. After circulating several drafts of this essay containing my proposal, I learned that Lawrence Fuchs in recent congressional testimony had made a similar one and that the Commission on Immigration Reform had recommended an oath like the one favored by Fuchs. We all

emphasize the requirement of a primary loyalty to the U.S. I go beyond them, however, in seeking to specify (not necessarily in the oath itself) the duties that should define that primary loyalty.

110. Some evidence of oathtakers' seriousness, were it needed, appears in the report that Irish naturalization rates in Australia rose when applicants were no longer required to swear allegiance to the British Crown.

111. Levinson, "Constituting Communities," 1459.

112. For what it is worth, Congress seems to agree; only recently and reluctantly did it permit the INS, and not just judges, to conduct the ceremony and oathtaking.

113. This clause seems superfluous unless it means to affirm a state of emotion or veneration that might strengthen the inclination, already required, to support and defend the Constitution and laws.

114. Whether this duty should be characterized as "exclusive" loyalty to the U.S. or merely "primary" loyalty is not clear. It is exclusive in the sense that it overrides any other duties in the unlikely event of conflict, but it is primary in the sense that, precisely because conflict is unlikely, it can easily coexist with duties to others. In any event, nothing turns on the distinction.

115. The notion of a hierarchy of claims appears in the very same provision of the Immigration and Nationality Act that prescribes the naturalization oath. Section 337 of the statute, in defining "religious training and belief" for purposes of an exception to the duty to bear arms, provides that the phrase means a "belief in a relation to a Supreme Being involving duties that are superior to those arising from any human relation . . ." The Canadian parliamentary committee, which as noted earlier would require that certain new dual citizens accord "primacy" to their Canadian nationality, does not define what such primacy means or would entail.

116. Stephen H. Legomsky, letters to the author dated August 21, 1997, and September 2, 1997.

117. There are at least two recent examples: an American who was briefly the president of Yugoslavia, and another who is now president of Latvia (but has relinquished his U.S. citizenship). While this duty is important, however, it is likely to be implicated so rarely that it need not be mentioned explicitly in the renunciation oath, which should retain its solemn dignity and lofty generality insofar as possible.

118. Legomsky, letters to the author dated August 21, 1997, and September 2, 1997.

119. To be sure, one can imagine a scenario in which a government-private entity conflict would be more troubling than a government-government conflict—for example, if the other state were an insignificant one that could not harm U.S. interests but the private entity were a multinational corporation with global interests that could harm the U.S.—but such a possibility does not invalidate the prophylactic rule that I am proposing to govern the vast majority of situations.

120. Lawrence Fuchs writes, "I do not worry about the asymmetries required between naturalized citizens and native born Americans. Not every inconsistency can be fixed." Letter to the author dated September 12, 1997.

121. I wish to be clear that I am generally opposed to loyalty oaths, and I am not advocating them here. Indeed, my point is that one's revulsion against loyalty oaths should lead one to resist requiring them of others. Moreover, if Congress does require an oath of existing citizens, it must choose its words very carefully in order to avoid violating Justice Robert H. Jackson's canonical precept: "If there is any fixed star in our constitutional constellation, it is that no official, high or petty, can prescribe what shall be orthodox in politics, nationalism, religion, or other matter of opinion or force citizens to confess by word or act their faith therein" (*West Virginia State Board of Education v. Barnette*).

Chapter 11

1. The 1997 amnesty, as discussed in Chapter 1, will facilitate the legalization of these individuals.

2. I analyze these issues at greater length in Peter H. Schuck, "Reflections on the Effects of Immigrants on African-Americans—and Vice Versa," in *Help or Hinderance: The Economic Implications of Immigration for African Americans* (D. Hamermesh and F. Bean, eds.) New York: Russell Sage Foundation (1998): Chap. 13.

3. As discussed in Chapters 1, 5, and 8, the 1996 welfare reform law significantly restricted legal aliens' eligibility for public benefits.

Chapter 12

1. *See* p. 43 n.181 (citing DIANA DEARE, U.S. BUREAU OF THE CENSUS, GEOGRAPHICAL MOBILITY: MARCH 1990 TO MARCH 1991 (Current Population Reports P20–463, 1992)). Sowell adds that internal migrations by Americans exceed all migrations by all foreigners to the U.S. P. 43.

2. His books include ETHNIC AMERICA: A HISTORY (1981), PREFERENTIAL POLICIES: AN INTERNATIONAL PERSPECTIVE (1990), RACE AND CULTURE: A WORLD VIEW (1994), and RACE AND ECONOMICS (1975).

3. This was notably true of the Indians in Africa, p. 316, the Italians in Argentina, pp. 152–53, and the Jewish, Chinese, and Parsee Indian middleman minorities everywhere, pp. 29–32.

4. Sowell notes that Chinese workers on rubber plantations were more than twice as productive as their Malay counterparts at the same unskilled jobs. P. 191.

5. For example, Sowell refers to the willingness of immigrant groups to extend credit, on the basis of refined knowledge and judgment of individuals' ability to repay, to those rejected by conventional lenders. *See, e.g.,* pp. 33, 318.

6. He assumes throughout that economic success is praiseworthy in itself and also is conducive to success in other realms, such as politics and high culture. As noted below, he insists that the causality runs in this direction and not the other way around. *See infra* note 47 and accompanying text.

7. Sowell is not too clear on this point, but his descriptions of occupational patterns seem to indicate that the Chinese, pp. 228–29, Indians, p. 368, and Jews, pp. 306–07, were the classic middleman minorities in almost all of their destination countries, while the Germans, p. 103, and Japanese, p. 137, were more likely to concentrate initially in agriculture. The Italians, at least in the United States, primarily entered the construction trades. Pp. 163–64.

8. In the German case, for example, he focuses on the German migrations to Russia, the United States, Brazil, Paraguay, and Australia; the chapter on Indians develops their experience in Uganda, Kenya, South Africa, Guyana, Trinidad, the United States, Malaysia, Sri Lanka, and Fiji.

9. A comparison of economic patterns and achievements *among* the six groups would have been an interesting and perhaps illuminating extension of his analysis, even if such a comparison had to be confined, for methodological reasons, to an individual country like the United States in which all groups reside in large numbers. Such a comparison might have also provided an important comparative benchmark—(relative) economic *failure*—which is missing from Sowell's account except insofar as he compares the economic performance of each of the six groups to the sometimes inferior performance of the natives of the group's destination countries. Unfortunately, however, he does not pursue this line of inquiry.

10. Sowell cites studies showing that over a period of 10 to 15 years, Black, White, and Chinese migrants to the United States and to Canada and Britain have risen beyond parity with the native populations. P. 38. A recent study comparing immigrant and native earnings in the United States finds a mixed picture in which Japanese, Korean, and Chinese immigrants begin with wages much lower than native-born workers and reach parity with them within 10 to 15 years, Europeans begin with comparable wages and remain at parity, and Mexicans en-

ter with very low wages and never catch up. *See* ROBERT F. SCHOENI ET AL, THE MIXED ECONOMIC PROGRESS OF IMMIGRANTS at xiv (1996).

11. This was notably true of the Italians, who constituted perhaps the largest emigration from a single country in history. Pp. 173–74.

12. He does not explicitly compare the six groups' levels of performance, but considers each notably successful. See *supra* note 9.

13. See discussion of sex ratios *infra* notes 31–33 and accompanying text.

14. For example, Sowell observes that the Japanese migrants to Hawaii originated in different and poorer regions of Japan than those who migrated to the mainland United States. P. 119. These local intracountry-of-origin differences in migration patterns were especially important in Italy. For example, northern Italian migrants in the 1901–13 period, Sowell reports, overwhelmingly went to European destinations while 91% of the southern Italians, virtually all unskilled workers, crossed the Atlantic. Pp. 141, 143.

Within each country of origin, the geographical sources of migration were diverse but also sometimes highly concentrated. For example, most Italian immigrants to Australia before World War II came from relatively unpopulated areas of Italy; more than half of the Indian migrants to the Middle East in 1979 came from Kerala state, which contained less than 3% of India's population. P. 5. Of the pre–World War I Chinese immigrants to the United States, a majority came from Toishan, just one of 98 districts in Kwangtung province. P. 177.

But the migration patterns were sometimes even more localized than this. Thus Sowell reports that "rates of emigration varied enormously between very similar provinces and villages in Italy, even when they were located near each other, for one community might have overseas contacts and the next community not." P. 145 (endnote omitted).

15. Sowell notes that more than 90% of all Japanese in the Western Hemisphere lived in just two countries, Brazil and the United States, p. 113, and 90% of Jews in the world live in just five countries, with nearly three-quarters of the total living in the United States and Israel, p. 234.

16. The temporal dimension of migrant flows also affects their destinations, and these shifts can be sharply discontinuous. Sowell observes that half of the Germans who left from 1816 to 1830 emigrated to South America, but after 1830 about 90% went to the United States. P. 52.

17. For example, the Volga Germans were actively recruited and subsidized by Catherine the Great, who hoped to use their settlements as models of efficient agriculture that the Russian peasants might emulate. P. 59. They encountered great hostility, however, at the local level. Pp. 59–60.

18. "Virtually no wealthy people emigrated from India to Africa," Sowell reports, "even though there have been Indians who acquired great wealth in various African countries." P. 313. Few of the Italians who emigrated to the western hemisphere possessed skills when they arrived. P. 174.

19. I have already noted that the absence of analysis regarding group failures, in a study focusing on group successes, constitutes an analytical failing of the book. *See supra* note 9.

20. Pp. 371–72. He adds that "[R]acial, ethnic, or national minorities who have owned or directed more than half of particular industries in particular nations have included not only the six groups considered here but also the Lebanese in West Africa, Greeks in the Ottoman Empire, Britons in Argentina, Belgians in Russia, and Spaniards in Chile. Minority predominance in particular industries and occupations has been common at local levels as well. In the early nineteenth century, over half the newspapers in Alexandria were owned by Syrians. In the Russian Empire in the eighteenth century, Armenians owned 209 of the 250 cotton cloth factories in the province of Astrakhan. Beginning in the 1960s, most of the installers of underground cable in Sydney, Australia were Irish. In the 1990s, more than four-fifths of all the doughnut shops in California were owned by people of Cambodian ancestry. P. 372 (endnotes omitted).

21. In support of this cultural capital hypothesis, Sowell cites evidence indicating that Black-White differences in the United States in income and infant mortality rates decline or disappear when one controls for important cultural variables. Pp. 382–83.

22. The firestorm of controversy that erupted over RICHARD J. HERRNSTEIN & CHARLES MURRAY, THE BELL CURVE (1994) is merely the most recent skirmish in a long war over the meaning and use of I.Q. scores.

23. *See generally* DANIEL J. KEVLES, IN THE NAME OF EUGENICS (1985). For a recent review of these arguments in the immigration context, see Dorothy Nelkin & Mark Michaels, *Biological Categories and Border Controls: The Revival of Eugenics in Anti-Immigration Rhetoric,* 17 INTL. J. OF SOCIOL. & SOC. POLY. (Spring 1997).

24. His list of cultural commitments is long and often quite specific. "Cultures differ," he notes, "in the relative significance they attach to time, noise, safety, cleanliness, violence, thrift, intellect, sex, and art. These differences in turn imply differences in social choices, economic efficiency, and political stability." P. 379. He adds that "language and physical appearance . . . fertility patterns, technology, philosophy, social customs, and institutions of government" will also vary by culture. P. 380.

25. Interestingly (and perhaps inconsistently), Sowell maintains that the Italians in Argentina were far more entrepreneurial than their native-born counterparts, especially in retailing. Pp. 152, 154. He also cites the remarkable fact that the foreign-born owned 60% of all the real estate in Buenos Aires earlier in this century. P. 154.

26. *See* Paul A. Samuelson, *The Pure Theory of Public Expenditure,* 36 REV. ECON. & STAT. 387 (1954) (defining public goods as goods that can be enjoyed in common such that one individual's consumption does not affect the amount of the good available to another individual).

27. Pp. 36–37. One might add that those at the very bottom are likely to lack the sense of optimism required to undertake the arduous project of migration.

28. Pp. 42–43. This theory bears an interesting relationship to George Borjas's claim that high-skill immigrants tend to move from areas of higher income equality to areas of lower income equality (where their skills will yield a greater return) and that low-skill immigrants move in the opposite direction (so that they will be less disadvantaged). *See* GEORGE J. BORJAS, FRIENDS OR STRANGERS: THE IMPACT OF IMMIGRANTS ON THE U.S. ECONOMY 16–18 (1990).

29. Sowell cites estimates that nearly 24 million of the 30 million people who left the Indian subcontinent in the century after the mid-1830s returned and that 60% of the southern Italian, Croatian, and Slovenian immigrants to the United States during the early 20th century returned home. P. 25.

30. These remittances are immense and constitute major elements of the economies of the countries of origin. Sowell reports some striking data on this. *See, e.g.,* pp. 21–22, 114, 145.

31. Even today, barriers to intermarriage also exist *within* some of the immigrant groups, such as Indians, along the lines of language or religion. *See* p. 332. Sowell notes, however, that caste lines among migrating Indians became less important in some destination countries like Guyana, Trinidad, and Malaysia. Pp. 333, 349. Interestingly, he relates the differential survival of caste distinctions in various destination countries to the length of the voyage there, which compromised the physical separation on which such distinctions rely. P. 351.

32. Pp. 95–96. The most extreme male imbalance may have been among the Chinese in the United States during the late 19th century when the sex ratio reached 27:1. As a result, the Chinese population steadily declined. Pp. 220–21.

33. Sowell reports that 97% of Italian men in 1920 were married to Italian wives and that even as late as 1950 this was still true of more than three-quarters of them. P. 162.

34. Upper estimates of mortality rates during the middle passage approach 30 percent. *See* HERBERT S. KLEIN, THE MIDDLE PASSAGE: COMPARATIVE STUDIES IN THE ATLANTIC SLAVE TRADE 137, 265–68 (1978); *see also* DAVID ELTIS, ECONOMIC GROWTH AND THE ENDING OF THE TRANSATLANTIC SLAVE TRADE (1987).

35. Sowell mentions as examples the expulsions of Jews from medieval Europe, Indian Chettyars from Burma, Moriscoes from Spain, and Indians and Pakistanis from Uganda. P. 46. I have already mentioned the Japanese internments in the United States, some of which were initiated by Latin American countries (although not Brazil) that sent their Japanese residents to the United States for internment. *See* p. 134.

36. For a crude taxonomy of restrictionist attitudes, including xenophobia, see Peter H. Schuck, *The Treatment of Aliens in the United States, in* PATHS TO INCLUSION: THE INTEGRATION OF MIGRANTS IN THE UNITED STATES AND GERMANY (Peter H. Schuck & Rainer Munz eds., 1998). For another account of xenophobia, see Gerald L. Neuman, *Aliens as Outlaws: Government Services, Proposition 187, and the Structure of Equal Protection Doctrine,* 42 UCLA L. REV. 1425 (1995).

37. That discrimination often also redounds, with a just perversity, to the perpetrators' disadvantage by depriving them of the benefits of the immigrants' skills provides but cold comfort to the victims.

38. See *supra* note 29.

39. The same mixed picture was provided by the most widely read earlier work comparing the progress of different immigrant groups in the United States. *See* NATHAN GLAZER & DANIEL PATRICK MOYNIHAN, BEYOND THE MELTING POT: THE NEGROES, PUERTO RICANS, JEWS, ITALIANS, AND IRISH OF NEW YORK CITY (1970).

40. Myron Weiner, *Nations Without Borders: The Gifts of Folk Gone Abroad,* 75 FOREIGN AFF. 128, 131–32 (1996) (reviewing MIGRATIONS AND CULTURES: A WORLD VIEW).

41. Originality, of course, is a matter of degree. Sowell's emphasis on the distinctive characters and cultures of groups, on the geophysical origins of these differences, and on their behavioral effects has many illustrious antecedents. *See* 1 & 2 BARON DE MONTESOUIEU, THE SPIRIT OF LAWS (Special Edition 1984); BERNARD BAILYN, THE PEOPLING OF BRITISH NORTH AMERICA: AN INTRODUCTION (1986); THOMAS JEFFERSON, NOTES ON THE STATE OF VIRGINIA (1995).

42. See *supra* note 17.

43. This has been the experience of the Chinese in Malaysia, for example. *See* p. 197. On the other hand, many Chinese entrepreneurs have evaded these preference restrictions by employing Malay fronts in so-called "Ali-Baba" enterprises. P. 196.

44. See discussion of middleman functions, *supra* note 7 and accompanying text.

45. *See, e.g.,* Amy L. Chua, *The Privatization-Nationalization Cycle: The Link Between Markets and Ethnicity in Developing Countries,* 95 COLUM. L. REV 223, *passim* (1995).

46. Sowell reports that "[t]he Chinese in Indonesia have long been considered the most assimilated Chinese community in Southeast Asia but this has not prevented them from being also the most repeatedly and violently attacked." P. 205. He also notes that despite the economic success of the Chinese in Indochina, an estimated 70% of the one million refugees who left Vietnam in the late 1970s were Chinese, and half of Kampuchea's Chinese population of 400,000 were killed during this period. Pp. 212–13.

47. Sowell ascribes this pattern to the immigrant Germans in the United States and in Australia, pp. 79, 97, the Japanese in Canada and Peru, pp. 124–25, 128, 137, the Italians in Argentina and elsewhere, p. 155, and the Jews and the Chinese almost everywhere, p. 218. On the other hand, some of his data seem inconsistent with this pattern. He notes, for example, that the overseas Chinese were disproportionately active in union and Communist movements in Southeast Asia and that the same was famously true of Jewish immigrants. P. 190. He also traces Indian political activism in Kenya. Pp. 325–26.

48. Even in New York City at the height of their migration there, the Italians constituted only 7.4 percent of the population. P. 161.

49. Chinese immigrants have experienced such recrimination throughout southeast Asia. Pp. 181–213. Indians suffered at the hands of independence movements both in Africa, where they had supported such movements, p. 326, and in Ceylon, where they had remained aloof from politics, pp. 356–58.

50. Sowell points out, for example, that Fiorello LaGuardia, the popular mayor of New York City for more than a decade, failed to carry the Italian vote in his 1941 re-election campaign against an Irish opponent. P. 166. This single example, of course, hardly establishes Sowell's claim; indeed, many contrary cases in which ethnic solidarity at the polls was decisive could readily be cited. *See, e.g.,* DONALD L. HOROWITZ, ETHNIC GROUPS IN CONFLICT *passim* (1985).

51. Pp. 232–33. To support this claim, Sowell points to the Chinese experience: in countries (like Indonesia) where this generally apolitical group was more politically active, it did not seem to do better. Pp. 205–06. Without more, however, this assertion is hardly persuasive, as it does not consider the possibility that the Chinese, absent their political action, would have done even worse. Still, there is much to be said for Sowell's general claim, and other commentators have concurred in it. *See* BORJAS, *supra* note 28; GLAZER & MOYNIHAN, *supra* note 39.

52. I say "traditionally" because the immigration policies adopted by those relatively few destination countries that now accept immigrants on a normal flow basis have increasingly tended to require immigrants to possess levels of education, occupational skill, language, or wealth that may already rival or exceed those of the native-born population. At the very least, these requirements will enable new immigrants to achieve parity within a relatively short time. *See* SCHOENI ET AL., *supra* note 10.

53. A vast literature exists on the subject. The classic study in the U.S. context is MILTON M. GORDON, ASSIMILATION IN AMERICAN LIFE (1964). For recent analyses of the subject in the U.S. and German contexts, see PATHS TO INCLUSION, *supra* note 36.

54. These creative and destructive tensions are, of course, the sources of great literary and artistic creations in every immigrant society.

55. See BORJAS, *supra* note 28, at 169–76.

56. See Alejandro Portes, *Children of Immigrants: Segmented Assimilation and Its Determinants, in* THE ECONOMIC SOCIOLOGY OF IMMIGRATION: ESSAYS ON NETWORKS, ETHNICITY, AND ENTREPRENEURSHIP 248, 250–51 (Alejandro Portes ed., 1995).

57. See, e.g., YEN LE ESPIRITU, ASIAN AMERICAN PANETHNICITY: BRIDGING INSTITUTIONS AND IDENTITIES (1992); BILL ONG HING, MAKING AND REMAKING ASIAN AMERICA THROUGH IMMIGRATION POLICY 1850–1990 (1993).

58. See, e.g., PETER SKERRY, MEXICAN-AMERICANS: THE AMBIVALENT MINORITY (1993); JAMES Q. WILSON, NEGRO POLITICS (1960).

59. See the immigration provisions of the Illegal Immigration and Immigrant Responsibility Act of 1996, Pub. L. No. 104–208, 110 Stat. 3009; the Anti-Terrorist and Effective Death Penalty Act of 1996, Pub. L. No. 104–132, 110 Stat. 1215; and the Personal Responsibility and Work Opportunity Reconciliation Act of 1996, Pub. L. No. 104–103, 110 Stat. 55.

60. See *supra* note 59 and accompanying text.

61. The reasons for both optimism and concern are discussed in Chapter 14.

Chapter 13

1. The word "refugees," of course, carries several different meanings. In this Article, I shall generally use the word in its broadest connotation to characterize individuals who have fled their country for one reason or another and believe that they cannot or should not return to it in the near future, although they may hope to do so if conditions permit. In this usage, the category is narrower than both "migrants" (whom I think of simply as people on the move) and "immigrants" (who have left their country intending to reside permanently in some other country). It is much broader, however, than the technical legal category of refugee defined in the Convention Relating to the Status of Refugees, July 28, 1951, art. 1, para. A, 189 U.N.T.S. 137, 152 [hereinafter 1951 Refugee Convention], and in U.S. immigration law, *see* 8 U.S.C. § 1101(a)(42) (1994). When I write of refugees in what follows, I mean to use the term in its broader, nonlegal connotation except when the context indicates the contrary.

2. *World Refugee Statistics,* WORLD REFUGEE SURVEY: 1995 IN REVIEW (1996), at 3, 4 tbl.1. Many millions more are internally displaced. *See id.* at 6 tbl.3. Other estimates vary. *The New York Times* reports a February 1995 count by the United Nations High Commissioner for Refugees (UNHCR) estimating that 23 million refugees had crossed borders and another 26 million were displaced in their own countries. According to this report, "I in every 115 people on earth is now on the run or in some kind of exile." Barbara Crossette, *This Is No Place Like Home,* N.Y. TIMES, Mar. 5, 1995, at D3. On the other hand, *Immigration Review* reports that UNHCR recognizes 14.4 million refugees, down 25% from the 18.2 million classified as refugees in 1993. 24 IMMIGR. REV., Winter 1996, at 7, 7. I shall not attempt to reconcile these figures; even the lowest estimates present an immense human tragedy and awesome policy challenge.

3. A recent empirical study of the sources and causes of refugee flows to the United States indicates that these factors have changed significantly in the last quarter century. Wars and political persecution (other than from ethnic conflicts) are less important causes of refugee flows than they were in 1969. Although the number of countries and conflicts generating refugee flows has changed little since then, what has principally changed is the number of refugees per conflict, which in turn reflects increasing levels of violence per conflict due to the growth in antipersonnel mines and small arms weapons. The rise in the number of refugees per conflict remains even after one controls for population growth and easier transportation. For purposes of the present discussion, the most important implications of the increased violence and the kinds of weapons employed are that they have multiplied the total refugee flow and made repatriation of refugees much more difficult. See Myron Weiner, *Bad Neighbors, Bad Neighborhoods: An Inquiry into the Causes of Refugee Flows, 1969–1992, in* MIGRANTS, REFUGEES, AND FOREIGN POLICY: U.S. AND GERMAN POLICIES TOWARD COUNTRIES OF ORIGIN (Rainer Münz & Myron Weiner eds., forthcoming 1997).

4. The notion of "compassion fatigue" was coined during the 1970s to reflect this psychological reality. Only this can account for the current passivity of the Clinton administration with respect to the appalling refugee crisis in eastern Zaire. *See* Iain Guest, *How and When To Intervene for Humanity,* CHRISTIAN SCI. MONITOR, Dec. 2, 1996, at 19 (noting that American failure to define policy in Zaire leaves desperate refugees trapped).

5. On the growing predominance of the internally displaced, see Weiner, *supra* note 3.

6. See Raymond Bonner, *New Road to West for Illegal Migrants,* N.Y. TIMES, June 14, 1995, at A12.

7. The Refugee Convention defines a refugee as a person with a "well-founded fear of being persecuted for reasons of race, religion, nationality, membership in a particular social group, or political opinion, is outside the country of his nationality and is unable or, owing to such fear, is unwilling to avail himself of the protection of that country." 1951 Refugee Convention, *supra* note 1, art. 1, para. A(2). This does not cover the bulk of migrants fleeing the conditions listed in the first paragraph of this Article.

8. The methods for processing refugees in Europe were harmonized in the Dublin Convention and the Second Schengen Agreement. Convention Applying the Schengen Agreement of 14 June 1985 Between the Governments of the Benelux Economic Union, the Federal Republic of Germany, and the French Republic on the Gradual Abolition of Checks at Their Common Borders, June 19, 1990, 30 I.L.M. 84 [hereinafter 1985 Schengen Agreement]; Convention Determining the State Responsible for Examining Applications for Asylum Lodged in One of the Member States of the European Communities, June 15, 1990, 30 I.L.M. 427 [hereinafter 1990 Dublin Convention]. The 1990 Dublin Convention establishes uniform procedures for processing asylum applicants, and the 1985 Schengen Agreement contains rules for determining one "responsible state" to process each application. *See* James C. Hathaway, *Harmonizing for Whom? The Devaluation of Refugee Protection in the Era of European Economic Integration,* 26 CORNELL INT'L L.J. 719, 722–28 (1993); Gerald L. Neuman, *Buffer Zones Against Refugees: Dublin, Schengen, and the German Asylum Amendment,* 33 VA. J. INT'L L. 503, 506–09 (1993). By rel-

egating asylum seekers to one asylum application and adjudication in Europe, these agreements are likely to decrease the level of refugee protection. The United States and Canada are planning to enter into a similar "country of first arrival" agreement. *See Canada, U.S. Release Joint Draft Agreement on Refugee Claims,* 72 INTERPRETER RELEASES 1614 (1995).

9. Several recent developments in the United States might increase the pressures here, quite apart from the more secular growth in refugee movements throughout the world that inevitably affect the United States. These developments include the amendment of the statutory "refugee" definition to include persecution for resistance to coercive population control methods, *see* Illegal Immigration Reform and Immigrant Responsibility Act of 1996 (IIRIRA), Pub. L. No. 104–132, § 601, 110 Stat. 1214 (amending 8 U.S.C. § 1101(a)(42)), the granting of some of the rapidly growing number of asylum applications from Mexicans, *see* Sam Verhovek, *In a Shift, U.S. Grants Asylum for 55 Mexicans,* N.Y TIMES, Dec. 1, 1995, at A1 (citing increase in applications from 122 in 1990 to 6397 in 1993 to 9304 in 1995, while grants increased from zero in 1993 to 54 in 1995), and the much-publicized grant of asylum to a woman from Togo based on her fear of clitoridectomy, *see* In re Kasinga, Interim Dec. No. 3278 (B.I.A. 1996); Celia W. Dugger, *Board Hears Asylum Appeal in Genital-Mutilation Case,* N.Y. TIMES, May 3, 1996, at B5 (estimating that more than 85 million women in world are subject to clitoridectomy). On the other hand, other provisions of IIRIRA adopted new procedures that are intended to restrict the availability of asylum. *See* IIRIRA § 601 (amending 8 U.S.C. § 1158).

10. For recent examples of sovereignty skeptics, see JEAN-MARIE GUEHENNO, THE END OF THE NATION-STATE (Victoria Elliot trans., 1995); DAVID JACOBSON, RIGHTS ACROSS BORDERS: IMMIGRATION AND THE DECLINE OF CITIZENSHIP (1996); YASEMIN N. SOYSAL, LIMITS OF CITIZENSHIP: MIGRANTS AND POSTNATIONAL MEMBERSHIP IN EUROPE (1994); Claudio Grossman & Daniel D. Bradlow, *Are We Being Propelled Towards a People-Centered Transnational Legal Order?* 9 AM. U. J. INT'L L. & POL'Y L (1993); Aristide R. Zolberg, *Changing Sovereignty Games and International Migration,* 2 IND. J. GLOBAL LEGAL STUD. 153 (1994); see also David A. Martin, *Effects of International Law on Migration Policy and Practice: The Uses of Hypocrisy,* 23 INT'L MIGRATION REV. 547, 548 (1989) (citing sources suggesting that doctrine of sovereign discretion over immigration is fundamentally erroneous). A related genre of commentary on sovereignty emphasizes its transcendence by economics-driven regionalism. *See, e.g.,* KENICHI OHMAE, THE END OF THE NATION STATE: THE RISE OF REGIONAL ECONOMIES (1995).

11. As noted below, "temporary" protection often turns out to be permanent. On the other hand, refugees receiving "permanent" resettlement might—should conditions in their country of origin change—later wish or (if they are not yet citizens) be required to repatriate. *See infra* notes 77–78 and accompanying text.

12. For example, it would deal with the growing problem of the internally displaced. *See* Weiner, *supra* note 3.

13. One possible objection to organizing this proposal on a regional basis—that it would further balkanize international relationships that are already divided along economic, racial, and ethnic lines for which regions are proxies—seems weak. Regional bloc formation reflects large geopolitical and global economic forces. Moreover, it is gradually giving way to a more integrated system, as suggested by the recent expansions of NAFTA, MERCOSUR, NATO, the EU, and other groupings that were initially more geographically limited than they are now, as well as by proposals to extend them further in the future. To the extent that regional arrangements entail problems, my scheme is not intended to solve them. By emphasizing the interdependence and mutual interests of different regions, however, it might even improve their relationships, as mutually beneficial market transactions tend to do. The issue of discrimination by states in the trading of protection quotas is discussed in *infra* text accompanying notes 148–49.

14. James C. Hathaway, *Reconceiving Refugee Law as Human Rights Protection,* 4 J. REFUGEE STUD. 113, 126–28 (1991) (proposing international protection system that removes

national interdiction schemes and directly involves international supervisory agency in protective measures taken pending viability of safe return to state of origin).

15. *See, e.g.,* Guy S. Goodwin-Gill, *Refugees: The Functions and Limits of the Existing Protection System, in* HUMAN RIGHTS AND THE PROTECTION OF REFUGEES UNDER INTERNATIONAL LAW 149, 165–73 (Alan E. Nash ed., 1987); Gil Loescher, *The International Refugee Regime: Stretched to the Limit?,* 47 J. INT'L AFF. 351, 376–77 (1994).

16. *See, e.g.,* MYRON WEINER, THE GLOBAL MIGRATION CRISIS: CHALLENGE TO STATES AND TO HUMAN RIGHTS (1995) (presenting recent and comprehensive analysis of these developments).

17. *See* 1951 Refugee Convention, *supra* note 1.

18. On international refugee law, see generally GUY S. GOODWIN-GILL, THE REFUGEE IN INTERNATIONAL LAW (1983); ATLE GRAHL-MADSEN, THE STATUS OF REFUGEES IN INTERNATIONAL LAW (1972). On domestic asylum law, see generally 6 CHARLES GORDON ET AL., IMMIGRATION LAW AND PROCEDURE § 137 (1996).

19. Some conventions have adopted broader refugee definitions. Conclusion 3 of the Cartegena Declaration classifies as refugees persons "[who] have fled from their country because their life, safety, or liberty have been threatened by widespread violence, foreign aggression, domestic conflict, massive violation of human rights or other situations that have seriously disturbed public order." Cartegena Declaration, *quoted in Annual Report of the Inter-American Commission on Human Rights, 1984–85,* Organization of American States, OEA/Ser. L/V/II.66/Doc. 10, rev.1, at 179–82 (1985). The Organization of African Unity added the following language to the definition of refugee: "every person who, owing to external aggression, occupation, foreign domination or events seriously disturbing public order in either part or the whole of his country of origin or nationality, is compelled to leave his place of habitual residence in order to seek refuge in another place outside his country of origin or nationality." OAU Convention Governing the Specific Aspects of Refugee Problems in Africa, Sept. 10, 1969, art. I, para. 2, 1001 U.N.T.S. 45, 47; *see also supra* note 9 (discussing amendment of U.S. refugee definition to include those fleeing coercive population control).

20. The armed attacks by exiled Rwandan Hutu militias against Tutsis in Zaire is a recent example, *see, e.g.,* Nicholas D. Kristof, *Rwandans, Once Death's Agents, Now Its Victims,* N.Y. TIMES, Apr. 13, 1997, at A1 (noting continued refugee crises and persistent ethnic battles among exiles), as is the suspected killings of refugees by Zairian rebels, *see* Raymond Bonner, *New Refugee Crisis Builds in Zaire,* N.Y. TIMES, May 14, 1997, at A8 (reporting that Kabila's rebels may have participated in killings). Unfortunately, there are many others. *See, e.g., Cuban Refugees Riot in Cayman Islands Camp,* N.Y. TIMES, Apr. 18, 1995, at A7; Edward A. Gargan, *200 Vietnamese Refugees Flee Detention Camps in Hong Kong,* N.Y. TIMES, May 11, 1996, at A4 (reporting on riots, arson, hostage-taking, escapes); Douglas Jehl, *Israeli Barrage Hits U.N. Camp in Lebanon, Killing at Least 75,* N.Y. TIMES, Apr. 19, 1996, at A1; Eric Schmidt, *Cuban Refugees Riot in Panama,* N.Y. TIMES, Dec. 9, 1994, at A1; Philip Shenon, *Khmer Rouge Said To Harass Refugees,* N.Y. TIMES, Mar. 26, 1992, at A3 (discussing Khmer Rouge attacks on refugee camps in Thailand and Cambodia).

21. For instance, refugee seamen are accorded the right to "sympathetic consideration to their establishment on [a contracting state's] territory." 1951 Refugee Convention. *supra* note 1, art. 11. With respect to movable and immovable property, *see id.* art. 13, and with respect to rights of self-employment, *see id.* art. 18, refugees are to receive "treatment as favourable as possible," *id.* arts. 13, 18. Refugees are accorded the right to freedom of movement "subject to any regulations applicable to alien generally in the same circumstances." *Id.* art. 26. Refugees "lawfully in [a state's] territory" may not be expelled "save on grounds of national security or public order." *Id.* art. 32.

22. *See, e.g.,* G.J.L. COLES, PROBLEMS ARISING FROM LARGE NUMBERS OF ASYLUM-SEEKERS: A STUDY OF PROTECTION ASPECTS 36–40 (1986); GERASSIMOS FOURLANOS, SOVEREIGNTY AND THE INGRESS OF ALIENS 155, 159–61 (1986); Howard Adelman, *Obli-*

Notes

gation and Refugees, in HUMAN RIGHTS AND THE PROTECTION OF REFUGEES UNDER IN-
TERNATIONAL LAW, supra note 15, at 73, 73–87; James C. Hathaway & R. Alexander
Neve, Making International Refugee Law Relevant Again: A Proposal for Collectivized and
Solution-Oriented Protection, 10 HARV. HUM. RTS. J. (forthcoming 1997).

23. There are a number of such instruments. See, e.g., U.N. CHARTER art. 49 (declaring
that members "shall join in affording mutual assistance in carrying out the measures decided
upon by the Security Council"); 1951 Refugee Convention, supra note 1, art. 150 (considering "that the grant of asylum may place unduly heavy burdens on certain countries, and that
a satisfactory solution of a problem of which the United Nations has recognized the international scope and nature cannot therefore be achieved without international cooperation"); 3
THE COLLECTED TRAVAUX PREPARATOIRES OF THE 1951 GENEVA CONVENTION RELAT-
ING TO THE STATUS OF REFUGEES 114 (Alex Takkenberg & Christopher C. Tahbaz eds.,
1990) (recommending "that Governments continue to receive refugees in their territories and
that they act in concert in a true spirit of international co-operation in order that these
refugees may find asylum and the possibility of resettlement"); infra Section V.

24. See, e.g., GOODWIN-GILL, supra note 18, at 101–26, 215–34.

25. Howard Adelman, for example, argues for burden-sharing in the following terms:
"[U]nless states that claim to hold to this principle of justice collectively share the burden of
extending that principle to individuals outside the orbit of any state and lacking protection,
the situation will tend to destabilize, particularly in those states most vulnerable in their commitment to protecting their own citizens. In sum, self-interest, when combined with its uni-
versalization into an abstract principle, dictates an obligation to refugees." Adelman, supra
note 22, at 84.

26. The Dublin, Schengen, and U.S.-Canada agreements, see supra note 8, are burden-
sharing mechanisms, but they seek to restrict protection, not expand it. The three primary examples of large-scale burden-sharing—the CPA in southeast Asia, the International Conference on Assistance to Refugees in Africa, and the International Conference on Central
American Refugees—are discussed in Hathaway & Neve, supra note 22.

27. See generally INDEPENDENT COMM'N ON INT'L HUMANITARIAN ISSUES,
REFUGEES: THE DYNAMICS OF DISPLACEMENT (1986). Some smaller, regional resettlement
programs based on burden-sharing principles have also been somewhat successful.

28. For a criticism of the CPA's human rights deficiencies, see James C. Hathaway, Labelling the "Boat People": The Failure of the Human Rights Mandate of the Comprehensive
Plan of Action for Indochinese Refugees, 15 HUM. RTS. Q. 686 (1993).

29. See, e.g., Draft Declaration and Comprehensive Plan of Action, June 14, 1989,
reprinted in Indochinese Refugees Conference Held in Geneva, DEP'T ST. BULL., Oct. 1989,
at 69, 71 [hereinafter CPA]; Fact Sheet: Association of Southeast Asian Nations (ASEAN), 3
DEP'T ST. DISPATCH 601, 602 (1992).

30. See Astri Suhrke, Indochinese Refugees: The Law and Politics of First Asylum, in
REFUGEES AND WORLD POLITICS 136, 145 (Elizabeth G. Ferris ed., 1985). From 1975 until
the 1979 conference, only 200,000 Indochinese refugees were processed for international resettlement. See UNHCR: Report of the Secretary General, U.N. GAOR, 34th Sess., Agenda
Item 83, at 5, U.N. Doc. A/34/627 (1979). By May 1979, countries had committed to resettling only 125,000 worldwide. See Court Robinson, Sins of Omission: The New Vietnamese
Refugee Crisis, WORLD REFUGEE SURVEY: 1988 IN REVIEW (1989), at 5, 6. At the time of
the 1979 conference, 350,000 Indochinese remained in refugee camps in the region. See
UNHCR: Report of the Secretary General, supra, at 5.

31. UNHCR: Report of the Secretary General, supra note 30, at 5.

32. See Robinson, supra note 30, at 6.

33. See, e.g., Foreign Relations Authorization Act, Pub. L. No. 100–204, § 904, 101 Stat.
1331, 1402–03 (1987). First-asylum countries consisted primarily of members of the

Association of Southeast Asian Nations (ASEAN)—including Indonesia, Malaysia, the Republic of the Philippines, Singapore, and Thailand—as well as Hong Kong.

34. The principal resettlement countries included the United States, Canada, Australia, and France.

35. Mutual self-interest among Central American countries moving toward peace also accounted for the success of the 1989 Conference on Central American Refugees. *See* Hathaway & Neve, *supra* note 22.

36. See, e.g., Bill McCollum, *Land Vietnamese in Thailand—An Inadequate Response,* WORLD REFUGEE SURVEY: 1985 IN REVIEW (1986), at 19, 20; *see also The Refugee Act of 1980 and Its Implementation, Statement Before the House Judiciary Comm.* (Apr. 30, 1980), *in* 19 I.L.M. 700 (statement of Ambassador Victor H. Palmieri) [hereinafter Palmieri].

37. Suhrke, *supra* note 30, at 145; *cf.* Hathaway & Neve, *supra* note 22 (noting U.S. desire to punish and isolate Vietnam).

38. See, e.g., Suhrke, *supra* note 30, at 136–37; *see also* Court Robinson, *Buying Time: Refugee Repatriation from Thailand,* WORLD REFUGEE SURVEY: 1992 IN REVIEW (1993), at 18.

39. The ODP, for instance, served those with family members in the United States and other Western countries. *See* Kenneth J. Conboy, *An American Agenda for the Geneva Conference on Indochinese Refugees,* Heritage Foundation Reports, No. 104, June 2, 1989, *available in* LEXIS, News Library, Arcnws File.

40. Atle Grahl-Madsen, *Protection of Indochinese Refugees, in* ROUND TABLE ON HUMANITARIAN ASSISTANCE TO INDO-CHINA REFUGEES AND DISPLACED PERSONS 69, 70 (International Inst. of Humanitarian Law ed., 1980).

41. See Suhrke, *supra* note 30, at 139.

42. See id. at 145. UNHCR's expenses were covered mainly by donations from Japan and the United States. *See id.* The costs of running the camps were significant. For instance, in 1979 Hong Kong spent $14 million to establish and run camps. *See* Roda Mushkat, *Hong Kong: Refugees and Displaced Persons—The Hong Kong Experience, in* ROUND TABLE OF ASIAN EXPERTS ON CURRENT PROBLEMS IN THE INTERNATIONAL PROTECTION OF REFUGEES AND DISPLACED PERSONS 96, 97 (International Inst. of Humanitarian Law ed., 1980).

43. See Ingrid Waller, *Social Assistance and Integration Programs in the USA, in* ROUND TABLE ON HUMANITARIAN ASSISTANCE TO INDO-CHINA REFUGEES AND DISPLACED PERSONS, *supra* note 40, at 20, 20. By March 1979, France had accepted over 62,000 refugees, Canada over 47,000, and Australia over 37,000. *See id.* By the end of that year, 290,000 refugees had been resettled in the United States alone. *See id.*

44. See Robinson, *supra* note 30, at 6; *see also* Suhrke, *supra* note 30, at 139.

45. See Robinson, *supra* note 30, at 7.

46. See id. at 6. More than half of the refugees were resettled in the United States. By 1991, the United States had resettled 1,127,401 Indochinese refugees—745,576 of whom were Vietnamese. *See U.S. Has More Than 1.1 Million Refugees from Indochina,* AGENCE FRANCE PRESSE, Dec. 19, 1991, at 2. The rest of the refugees were divided among other resettlement countries. In addition, 280,000 Vietnamese who fled to China were permanently resettled there. *See East Asia and the Pacific,* WORLD REFUGEE SURVEY: 1989 IN REVIEW (1990), at 51, 53.

47. See *East Asia and the Pacific,* WORLD REFUGEE SURVEY: 1988 IN REVIEW (1989), at 49, 55; Robinson, *supra* note 30, at 8.

48. From 1979 to 1989, the United States contributed over half a billion dollars to the care and support of Indochinese refugees. *See* Lawrence S. Eagleburger, Statement at the International Conference on Indochinese Refugees (June 18, 1989), *reprinted in* DEP'T ST. BULL., Oct. 1989, at 69, 70. In addition, the United States spent several billion dollars in resettlement costs. According to a 1989 State Department estimate, the United States spends $7000 for each refugee resettled—$2000 for transportation and resettlement and $5000 for social ser-

vices. See Robert Pear, *U.S. Raises Quota of Soviet Refugees by Cutting Asians'*, N.Y. TIMES, Jan. 12, 1989, at A1. Considering that the United States resettled over 1.1 million refugees, its financial contribution to the resettlement effort was significant. Japan also contributed significant financial resources to the resettlement effort. *See 11 Billion Yen Aid To Be Offered to Indochina Refugees*, JAPAN ECON. NEWSWIRE, July 6, 1985, *available in* LEXIS, News Library, Arcnws File (reporting Japan's pledge to cover half of cost of UNHCR general relief programs for Indochinese refugees and to donate additional 11 billion yen to these refugees). Japan, however, did not accept many refugees for resettlement. From 1979 until 1991, less than 8000 refugees were resettled in Japan. See *East Asia and the Pacific*, WORLD REFUGEE SURVEY: 1991 IN REVIEW (1992), at 56, 61.

49. In a 1980 speech, the U.S. Coordinator for Refugee Affairs stated: "President Carter's pledge to double our rate of resettlement of Indochinese refugees to 14,000 a month was a critical factor in generating new resettlement pledges by over 20 countries at the Geneva conference last July. Support from the international community encouraged Southeast Asian countries to begin once again to grant asylum to all new arrivals." Palmieri, *supra* note 36, at 700.

50. See *East Asia and the Pacific*, WORLD REFUGEE SURVEY: 1990 IN REVIEW (1991), at 60, 64.

51. See id. at 62.

52. See Robinson, *supra* note 30, at 6. Vietnam did so to protest a backlog of 22,000 cases. *See id.*

53. See id.; see also Phan Quang Tue, *Going Back Against the Tide*, RECORDER, Dec. 19, 1991, at 6.

54. This holds true in other refugee contexts as well. As one commentator has aptly noted, "[u]nilateral deterrence pushes the problem onto a neighbour." Barry N. Stein, *The Nature of the Refugee Problem, in* HUMAN RIGHTS AND THE PROTECTION OF REFUGEES UNDER INTERNATIONAL LAW, *supra* note 15, at 47, 65. As an example, Stein cites a one-year jump in Norway's asylum caseload from 300 to 8000 applicants after neighboring countries closed their borders. *Id.* (citing Jeff Crisp, *Norway: Asylum Policy: The Humanitarian Dilemma*, REFUGEES, Aug. 1987, at 13, 14); see also Dennis Gallagher et al., *Temporary Safe-Haven: The Need for North American-European Responses, in* REFUGEES AND INTERNATIONAL RELATIONS 333, 335–36 (Gil Loescher & Laila Monahan eds., 1989) (discussing interconnectedness of asylum policies and examples). This point also applies to the actions of resettlement countries. For instance, when the United States was sluggish in fulfilling its ODP resettlement commitments, Vietnam retaliated by halting the program. See *supra* note 52 and accompanying text. Similarly, when the United States reduced its ODP ceiling in 1989 to accommodate refugees from the former Soviet Union, Vietnam responded by suspending discussions on allowing 50,000 former political prisoners and their families to emigrate. See Robinson, *supra* note 30, at 10.

55. See, e.g., Robinson, *supra* note 30, at 7–8; Suhrke, *supra* note 30, at 148. According to Robinson, the "reasons for flight [were] compelling and varied, but it is fair to say that virtually all have left, not in search of asylum, but in search of resettlement." Robinson, *supra* note 30, at 8 (citing study by Ford Foundation).

56. The CPA dealt only with Vietnamese and Lao refugees. Negotiations regarding Cambodian refugees (who were included in earlier resettlement programs) were conducted separately.

57. See CPA, supra note 29, para. E(9)(b). See generally Robinson, supra note 38; Hiram A. Ruiz, *The CPA: Tempestuous Year Left Boat People Adrift*, WORLD REFUGEE SURVEY: 1995 IN REVIEW (1996), at 82.

58. CPA, *supra* note 29, para. D(6).

59. See id. para. E(9) (containing multi-year commitment to resettle all Vietnamese who arrived in temporary asylum camps prior to agreed date). The United States, for instance, agreed to resettle 22,000 of the 52,000 long-stayers. *See* Eagleburger, *supra* note 48, at 70. Australia committed to resettling 11,000 long-stayers. *See East Asia and the Pacific, supra* note 46, at 51.

60. CPA, *supra* note 29, para. E(9)(a). Specifically, the CPA named the following countries as resettlement candidates: Australia, Austria, Belgium, Canada, Denmark, Federal Republic of Germany, Finland, France, Ireland, Italy, Japan, Luxembourg, the Netherlands, New Zealand, Norway, Spain, Sweden, Switzerland, United Kingdom, and the United States. *Id.*

61. See Ruiz, *supra* note 57, at 82. From the beginning of the CPA in 1989 until the 1995 meeting, approximately 80,000 Vietnamese were resettled in the West, and over 72,000 others were repatriated to Vietnam. *See id.*

62. See id.

63. *Id.* at 82–83.

64. *Id.* at 83.

65. I exclude the strategy of altering the legal definition of "refugee." Because narrowing the definition would deny protection to some individuals who deserve and desperately need it, virtually all proposals for change urge that the definition be broadened. *See, e.g.,* Frederick B. Baer, *International Refugees as Political Weapons,* 37 HARV. INT'L L.J. 243 (1996); Isabelle R. Gunning, *Expanding the International Definition of Refugee: A Multicultural View,* 13 FORDHAM INT'L L.J. 35, 72–85 (1990). Whatever the merits of broadening the refugee definition, however, such a reform would simply multiply the problems discussed in the text. *See supra* note 19 (discussing broader refugee definitions).

66. For example, Professor Peter J. Spiro, writes: "Of course there are still some pretty nasty regimes scattered here and there, but without the backbone that communism provided, they are likely, at least in most cases, not to last forever, so that temporary protection should suffice for those fleeing such conditions. I think it's unlikely that we will witness anything like the Vietnamese refugee crisis anytime soon." Letter from Peter J. Spiro, Professor, Hofstra University, to the author 1 (July 1, 1996) (on file with author).

67. See Weiner, *supra* note 3.

68. Participants in a research consortium based at York University's Centre for Refugee Studies are elaborating a strategy for refugee law reform based on a commitment to rights-regarding temporary protection and dignified repatriation. *See generally* James C. Hathaway, *Can International Refugee Law Be Made Relevant Again?,* WORLD REFUGEE SURVEY: 1995 IN REVIEW (1996), at 14.

69. See James C. Hathaway, *Root Causes as Refugee Protection: A Chimerical Promise?, in* IMMIGRATION AND EUROPEAN UNION: BUILDING ON A COMPREHENSIVE APPROACH 117, 117–21 (S. Perrakis ed., 1995).

70. Examples include famines, which are sometimes caused or at least exacerbated by inefficient agricultural policies and distribution systems, and floods, which sometimes reflect perverse patterns of tidal land development.

71. Even in relatively democratic societies, such traditions appear to play an important role in differentiating political and economic outcomes. *See* ROBERT D. PUTNAM, MAKING DEMOCRACY WORK: CIVIC TRADITIONS IN MODERN ITALY 183–85 (1993) (noting that social capital is dominant factor).

72. It is not simply physical invasions of a state's territory that the norm of state sovereignty constrains. The norm also prevents a state that has borne the costs of another state's refugee-generating policies or practices from suing the source state to recover those costs. Establishing such a cause of action could—assuming that the source state's causal responsibility could be proved and the resulting judgment could be enforced—render a root cause strategy far more effective. The freezing of Iraq's assets abroad and the embargo on its crude-oil sales after the Persian Gulf War were modest steps in that direction. By way of analogy, consider other intergovernmental transfer obligations: the U.S. government's obligation under the 1995 unfunded mandate legislation to reimburse state and local governments for their costs of complying with certain federally-imposed requirements, *see* Unfunded Mandates Reform Act of 1995, Pub. L. No. 1044, 109 Stat. 48, and the Elizabethan poor laws' provision for communi-

ties receiving destitute residents of other communities to charge the latter for certain maintenance costs, even to the point of litigatio, *see, e.g.,* MICHAEL KATZ, THE UNDESERVING
POOR 11–12 (1989). *But see* International Law Ass'n, *Draft Declaration of Principles of International Law on Compensation to Refugees and Countries of Asylum* (Report of the 64th
Conf., 1991), *reprinted in* 64 INT'L L. PROC. 333 (1991).

73. These instances include the creation after the Persian Gulf War of a "safe zone" in
northern Iraq to protect the Kurdish minority there, and the U.S. invasion of Haiti to restore
President Aristide. Another example is the ill-fated ECOMOG involvement in Liberia. See,
e.g., Hugh Dellios, *No More Rwandas? U.S. Proposal for All-African Peacekeeping Force
Draws Fire,* CHI. TRIB., Oct. 8, 1996, at 3 (noting corruption and partisanship of ECOMOG
troops).

74. See, e.g., James F. Smith, *NAFTA and Human Rights: A Necessary Linkage,* 27 U.C.
DAVIS L. REV. 793, 800–01 n.22, 841 n.202 (1994).

75. See Christopher Mitchell, *The Impact of U.S. Policy on Migration from Mexico and the
Caribbean, in* MIGRANTS, REFUGEES, AND FOREIGN POLICY: U.S. AND GERMAN POLICIES
TOWARD COUNTRIES OF ORIGIN, *supra* note 3.

76. See *NAFTA, Non-Trade Related Issues: Immigration,* MEX. TRADE & L. REP., Nov.
1993, at 9, 11 (noting that economic development may, in short term, increase migration).

77. For some statistics on voluntary and involuntary repatriations, see *World Refuges Statistics, supra* note 2, at 7 tbls. 5, 6.

78. See, e.g., John Kifner, *Conflict in the Balkans: A Holocaust Rescuer Is Herself Rescued
from Siege of Sarajevo,* N.Y. TIMES, Feb. 8, 1994, at A15 ("Many [members of Sarajevo's
Jewish community] arrived here carrying the keys to their homes in Spain in the belief that
they would soon return there, and many of the keys have been handed down through many
generations."); Sebastiao Salgado, *War Without End,* N.Y. TIMES MAG., July 30, 1995, at 24
(reporting that 40,000 Vietnamese boat people remain in detention camps after 20 years). For
the Palestinian refugees who lived in and wish to return to what is now Israel, repatriation is
not in sight after almost half a century. This is admittedly an unusual case.

79. See, e.g., Gargan, *supra* note 20 (reporting that refugees in Hong Kong rioted when
faced with repatriation to Vietnam); James C. McKinley, Jr., *Some Rwandan Exiles Can't Go
Home Again,* N.Y. TIMES, Feb. 7, 1996, at A8 (reporting that because of fear of reprisals,
Hutu refugees refuse to return despite harsh conditions in camps and campaign by UNHCR to
convince them of safe conditions at home); Seth Mydans, *In Thai Camps, Fear of Burmese
Troops Grows,* N.Y. TIMES, Mar. 3, 1997, at A3 (describing new policy of Thai government
that only women, children, and elderly among Burmese refugees will be allowed to stay in
Thailand).

80. See Steven Erlanger, *U.S. and Hanoi Agree To Give Boat People One Last Chance,* N.Y.
TIMES, May 15, 1996, at A13; *see also* Gargan, *supra* note 20.

81. See 8 U.S.C. § 1158(b) (1994). This cessation provision follows article 1(C)(5) of the
1951 Refugee Convention, *surpa* note 1.

82. See, e.g., GRUNDGESETZ [Constitution] [GG] art. 16(a)(4) (F.R.G.) ("The implementation of measures terminating a person's sojourn shall . . . be suspended by the court only
where serious doubt exists as to the legality of the measure. . . .").

83. See Joan Fitzpatrick, *Flight from Asylum: Trends Toward Temporary "Refuge" and Local Responses to Forced Migrations,* 35 VA. J. INT'L L. 13, 16 (1994).

84. It is sometimes called temporary refuge, temporary asylum, or temporary safe haven.
Those who receive it are sometimes called de facto refugees. This is to be distinguished from
the creation of "safe areas" for refugees in the state of origin, as the United States and its allies
did in Iraq after the Persian Gulf War. For a discussion of other variants of safe haven, see
Weiner, *supra* note 3 (distinguishing among models in which powerful third country controls
safe territory elsewhere [Guantanamo], self-administered safe zones within country of origin

(Kurds in Iraq), and internationally protected safe zones within country of origin [Bosnia]). As Fitzpatrick notes, temporary refuge "has become more regularized and formalized, assuming an unaccustomed prominence in the refugee policies of European states." Fitzpatrick, *supra* note 83, at 16; see also Joanne Thorburn, *Transcending Boundaries: Temporary Protection and Burden-Sharing in Europe,* 7 INT'L J. REFUGEE L. 459 (1995).

85. Joan Fitzpatrick and others criticize temporary protection as simply one more transparent device (like detention, denial of work permits, and other such policies) to constrict migrants' access to the rights and remedies established for Convention refugees. *See, e.g.,* Fitzpatrick, *supra* note 83, at 16–18; Harold Hongju Koh, *America's Offshore Refugee Camps,* 29 U. RICH. L. REV. 139 (1994) (chronicling, describing, and criticizing U.S. temporary protection policies toward Haitians and Cubans); see also Gerald L. Neuman, *Recent Trends in United States Migration Control,* 38 GERMAN Y.B. INT'L L. 284, 288–98 (1995) (discussing Koh article).

86. Just as the United States procured such space in the Caribbean, so European and Asian states could do so in their regions. Section 604 of IIRIRA excepts from the statutory right to apply for asylum those aliens who can be removed, pursuant to a bilateral or multilateral agreement, to a third country that is "safe" (as defined by the provision). See Illegal Immigration Reform and Immigrant Responsibility Act of 1996 (IIRIRA), Pub. L. No. 104–132, § 604, 110 Stat. 1214 (amending 8 U.S.C § 1158).

87. The United States, for example, spent $1 million per day to maintain its refugee camps on the Guantanamo Bay Naval Base. *See U.S. Policy Toward Cuba: Hearings Before the W. Hemisphere Subcomm. of the Senate Foreign Relations Comm.* (1995) (statement of Peter Tarnoff, Under Secretary for Political Affairs), *reprinted in* 6 U.S. DEP'T ST. DISPATCH 446, 451 (1995); Gillian Gunn, *Over Troubled Waters: U.S. Policy Toward Cuba Has Changed, but Does the President Know It?,* WASH. POST, May 21, 1995, at C2. In 1979, Hong Kong spent $14 million to establish and run camps. See Mushkat, *supra* note 42, at 97. In the view of some knowledgeable observers, even these expenditures have not produced adequate conditions. Professor Koh, who represented the migrants on Guantanamo against the U.S. government, calls for "shelters capable of withstanding the elements; refugees housed in family groups and allowed freedom of movement within the camps; private voluntary agencies, nongovernmental organizations, and the United Nations High Commissioner on Refugees, not the United States military, running the camp's religious, education [sic], and recreational services; the United States Public Health Service and not the military providing health care; with mail and phone access made available to the refugees, along with ready access of press, human rights monitors, volunteer religious organizations, and doctors. Social activities at the camps—education, religion, books, recreation, intracamp communication and the like—must be greatly expanded to maintain morale and reduce tensions and frustration. . . . The access of lawyers and legal counseling is as important to the success of these camps as medical counseling." Koh, *supra* note 85, at 171–72.

88. Virtually all proponents of temporary protection say far more about protection than about its temporary aspect. *See, e.g.,* Thorburn, *supra* note 84. Yet it is clear that states will not provide this remedy unless they believe that the burden will indeed be short-lived. Professor James C. Hathaway is a rare academic voice who acknowledges and seeks to deal with this reality. *See* Manuel A. Castillo & James C. Hathaway, *Temporary Protection, in* RECONCEIVING INTERNATIONAL REFUGEE LAW (James C. Hathaway ed., forthcoming 1997).

89. See 8 U.S.C.A. § 1254a note (West Supp. 1997) (Special Temporary Protected Status for Salvadorans, originally enacted as Immigration Act of 1990, Pub. L. No. 101–649, § 303, *amended by* Pub. L. No. 102–65, 105 Stat. 322 (1991); Pub. L. No. 104–208, div. C, tit. III, § 308(g)(I), (g)(6)(A), 110 Stat 3009 (1996)).

90. For a summary history of Salvadoran TPS, see THOMAS ALEXANDER ALEINIKOFF ET AL., IMMIGRATION PROCESS AND POLICY 889–96 (3d ed. 1995); *id.* at 100 (Supp. 1997).

91. Under the amnesty legislation enacted in November 1997, these individuals are eligible to apply for cancellation of removal under the relatively liberal standards that applied before the 1996 immigration reform law went into effect. See Chapter 1.

92. Some 149,500 new applications were filed in fiscal year 1995, up slightly from 146,400 in fiscal year 1994. *See Congress: Immigration, Welfare, Minimum Wages,* MIGRA-TION NEWS, Aug. 1996, at 8, <http://migration.ucdavis.edu/By-Month/MN-Vol–3–96/MN_Aug_96.hmtl//RTFT.C3>.

93. KATHLEEN NEWLAND, U.S. REFUGEE POLICY: DILEMMAS AND DIRECTIONS 27 (1995).

94. The same was not true of the Haitian refugees at Guantanamo. *See generally* Terry Coonan, *America Adrift: Refoulement on the High Seas,* 93 U. CIN. L. REV. 1241 (1995).

95. See Neuman, *supra* note 85, at 293–97.

96. See Olaf F. Reerman, *Readmission Agreements, in* IMMIGRATION ADMISSIONS: THE SEARCH FOR WORKABLE POLICIES IN GERMANY AND THE UNITED STATES (K. Hailbronner et al. eds., forthcoming 1997).

97. See Alan Cowell, *German Court Upholds Laws To Limit Foreigners Seeking Refuge,* N.Y. TIMES, May 15, 1996, at A5 (noting that Constitutional Court upheld third-country transit rules).

98. See *World Refugee Statistics,* WORLD REFUGEE SURVEY: 1994 IN REVIEW (1995), at 42, 43 tbls. 1, 2.

99. As a percentage of refugee and asylum admissions to total population, however, the United States ranked fifth behind Sweden, Canada, Australia, and Denmark in 1994. *See id.* at 46 tbl.9.

100. See U.S. DEP'T OF JUSTICE, IMMIGRATION AND NATURALIZATION SERV., 1995 STATISTICAL YEARBOOK OF THE IMMIGRATION AND NATURALIZATION SERVICE 83 tbl.26 (1997).

101. See id. at 91 tbl.32.

102. In what could be an augury of restrictions to come, Congress's blue-ribbon Commission on Immigration Reform recommended in June 1995 that the annual refugee quota, which was 112,000 in 1995, be reduced to 50,000. *See* U.S. COMM'N ON IMMIGRATION REFORM, LEGAL IMMIGRATION: SETTING PRIORITIES 131 (1995). The Commission believed that this change would still accommodate at least twice as many Convention refugees as under the current quota, which resettles many who are now accepted under a lower standard but who would not qualify as Convention refugees. *See id.*

103. See *infra* text accompanying notes 112–18.

104. By way of comparison, Canada, with one-fourth of Japan's population, resettled more than 136,000 Indochinese. The United States, with twice Japan's population, resettled about 820,000, but this partly reflected, of course, the special role of the United States in the Vietnam War. *See* ISAMI TAKEDA, JAPAN'S RESPONSES TO REFUGEES AND POLITICAL ASYLUM-SEEKERS 3, 6 (International Migration Working Paper Series, 1995).

105. See id. at 9, 11 tbl.2.

106. See *World Refugee Statistics, supra* note 97, at 45–46 tbls. 8, 10.

107. See *supra* section III.

108. For a discussion of this burden-sharing arrangement, see Hathaway & Neve, supra note 22; see also Dennis Gallagher, *The Evolution of the International Refuges System,* 23 IN-T'L MIGRATION REV. 579, 590–91 (1989); Rosemarie Rogers, *The Future of Refugee Flows and Policies,* 26 INT'L MIGRATIONS REV. 1112, 1133–34 (1992).

109. See Thorburn, *supra* note 84 (discussing Croatian and Slovenian efforts but unaccountably failing to mention Germany's granting of temporary refuge to hundreds of thousands of Croatians displaced by war there).

110. *Id.* at 476–77.

111. See *supra* text accompanying note 3.

112. The word "insular" here simply refers to a condition of relative immunity from large migration flows, whether the barriers to such flows are geographical or geopolitical.

113. See Rainer Münz & Ralf Ulrich, *Changing Patterns of German Immigration, 1945–1994, in* MIGRANTS PAST, MIGRANTS FUTURE: GERMANY AND THE UNITED STATES (Klaus Bade & Myron Weiner eds., forthcoming 1997). The *Aussiedler,* people of German ancestry whose families have lived in eastern Europe, often for centuries, are not really exceptions, as they are considered German by blood and culture and are permitted to acquire German citizenship more or less automatically upon their return to Germany. *See id.*

114. Munz and Ulrich provide the statistics. See id.

115. The total in 1994 was 127,000, well below the 438,000 who applied in 1992. See id.

116. Like Germany's willingness to accept *Aussiedlers,* Japan now accepts *nikkeijin,* people of Japanese ancestry living abroad, many of them in South America. *See* Myron Weiner, *Opposing Visions: Migration and Citizenship Policies in Japan and the United States, in* TEMPORARY WORKERS OR FUTURE CITIZENS? JAPAN AND U.S. MIGRATION POLICIES (M. Weiner & T. Hanami eds., New York University Press 1998).

117. See id. at 10 tbl.1. The Japanese Justice Ministry estimated that there were 285,000 foreigners living illegally in Japan in 1995. *See Japan's Foreign Residents and the Quest for Expanded Political Rights* JEI REP., July 19, 1996, *available in* LEXIS, World Library, Allwid File (noting continuing hostility to foreigners and immigration); *see also* Mayumi Itoh, *Japan's Abiding Sakoku Mentality,* Orbis, Mar. 22, 1996, *available in* 1996 WL 13459521 (noting that, as of January 1995, approximately 1.6 million foreigners resided in Japan). Notwithstanding Japanese resistance to increasing numbers of foreign residents, a looming labor shortage may necessitate more immigration. *See Japan's Foreign Residents and the Quest for Expanded Political Rights, supra; Migration Issues in APEC,* ASIAN MANAGER, Jan. 1, 1997, *available in* 1997 WL 10097043.

118. See Weiner, *supra* note 115; see also Andrew Pollack, *Beckoning Foreign Investors, North Korea Opens the Door a Crack, to Capitalism,* N.Y. TIMES, Sept. 19, 1996, at D1 ("Some experts fear that North Korea could collapse, sending millions of refugees streaming to South Korea, China and Japan.").

119. This occurred most dramatically whenever Thailand, Hong Kong, and other first-asylum states for Indochinese refugees engaged in pushbacks or announced new restrictions, thereby channeling the refugee flow to Malaysia, Singapore, Japan, Australia, and other potential havens in the region.

120. During the conflict in the former Yugoslavia, the states of the European Union pressed Croatia and Slovenia, first-asylum states for refugees from Bosnia and Herzegovina, to maintain the refugees there rather than diverting them westward. Croatia and Slovenia did so, incurring large fiscal and domestic political costs. See Thorburn, *supra* note 84, at 473–76.

121. In Africa, the Organization of African Unity might constitute such an organization. Alternatively, South Africa, which is the continent's wealthiest state and has become a major destination for refugees, might lead such an effort.

122. The qualifier "relative" is important, as the examples of impoverished Haiti and communist Cuba in the North American-Caribbean region demonstrate.

123. As discussed *infra* in text accompanying notes 136–37, the principle of broad participation in this context should be subject to two exceptions.

124. See *infra* section V.

125. The Refugee Act of 1980, 8 U.S.C. § 1101(a)(42) (1994), defines "refugee" as a person with a "well-founded fear of persecution on account of race, religion, nationality, membership in a particular social group, or political opinion." This definition does not include "any person who ordered, incited, assisted, or otherwise participated in the persecution of any person" on account of the same factors. *Id.* This mirrors the definition in the 1951 Refugee

Convention. See 1951 Refugee Convention, *supra* note 1, art. 1, para. A(2). Section 604 of IIRIRA in effect narrows the refugee definition by barring several additional categories of aliens from applying for asylum. *See* IIRIRA, Pub. L. No. 104–132, § 604, 110 Stat. 1214 (amending 8 U.S.C. § 1158).

126. The formalism of asylum procedures differs considerably among countries. The U.S. system is by far the most formal. *See* David Martin. *The Obstacles to Effective Internal Enforcement of the Immigration Laws in the United States, in* IMMIGRATION ADMISSIONS: THE SEARCH FOR WORKABLE POLICIES IN GERMANY AND THE UNITED STATES, *supra* note 95.

127. The contrast between the resources expended on formal asylum adjudication and those expended on actual refugee protection is striking. See Hathaway & Neve, *supra* note 22.

128. See *Refugees in Eastern Zaire and Rwanda: Hearings Before the House Comm. on Int'l Relations, Subcomm. On Int'l Operations and Human Rights,* 105th Cong. (1996), *available in* LEXIS, Legis Library, Cngtst File (statement of Roger P. Winter, Dir. U.S. Comm. for Refugees) (noting wide disparities in refugee numbers); Thomas W. Lippman, *Governments, Aid Groups Divided over Refugee Crisis in Zaire,* WASH. POST, Nov. 22, 1996, at A41 ("Some relief organizations accused the Clinton administration of playing down the crisis to wiggle out of its commitment to send troops for an international military rescue mission. But American officials said that numbers compiled by the U.N. High Commissioner for Refugees (UNHCR) were exaggerated.").

129. See *supra* text accompanying notes 90–92.

130. I emphasize the importance of the minimality of these safeguards and amenities to any realistic scheme of burden-sharing and protection. Although the ultimate goal is to integrate fully resettled refugees into the host society once it is concluded that safe repatriation cannot be effected, the initial conditions of maintenance should maximize the number of people who can be minimally protected for a given expenditure, rather than protecting fewer refugees at higher levels of amenity. Protection implies safety before comfort.

131. National wealth can be measured in different ways. Some of the many indices include gross national product, per capita national product, GNP adjusted for quality-of-life or social indicators, potential wealth, etc.

132. Another example—consideration of a state's own responsibility for refugee flows—would also be very difficult to apply. Such a criterion would be confounded by all of the notorious complexities and indeterminacies of social process, historical causation, international morality, and international polities.

133. One might try to devise measures of assimilation based on indices of ethnic conflict with particular societies, patterns of in- and out-migration, levels of political and social participation by minority groups, naturalization rates, and the like. Even if such measures could be compiled, they would be so crude as to be unacceptable to the states involved.

134. See, e.g., Richard D. Alba, *Assimilation, Exclusion, or Neither? Models of Incorporation Immigrants in the United States, in* PATHS TO INCLUSION: THE INTEGRATION OF MIGRANTS IN THE UNITED STATES AND GERMANY (Peter Schuck & Rainer Münz eds., 1998) (discussing different models).

135. See 1951 Refugee Convention, *supra* note 1, art. 3 ("The Contracting States shall apply the provisions of this Convention to refugees without discrimination as to race, religion or country of origin.") Most rights conferred by the Convention are not mandatory upon contracting states, see *supra* note 21 and accompanying text, and contracting states are only required "as far as possible" to "facilitate the assimilation and naturalization of refugees," 1951 Refugee Convention, *supra* note 1, art. 34. This fact reduces the force of the displacement of voluntarism objection. See *infra* section VI.

136. Multi-factor criteria could certainly be devised. In connection with the conflict in the former Yugoslavia, for example. Germany proposed a formula for allocating protection burdens among the European Union states. According to Joanne Thorburn, the proposal was

"based on the size of the population of Member States, the size of their territory and the amount of their Gross Domestic Product, all as a percentage of the Union total, leading to figures guiding the percentage number of people from a mass influx of displaced persons which each State should take. This indicative figure would be modified according to the Member State's contribution to peace-keeping forces and its particular use of foreign and security policy measures in the country of origin. The reaction from other Member States was sceptical, not surprisingly since the proposing State is the one whose burden would be relieved by the institution of such a mechanism, whereas others would find themselves faced with more persons in need of protection." Thorburn, *supra* note 84, at 476 (footnote omitted).

137. It is true, as Joan Fitzpatrick observes, that even human rights violators "may in fact be safe harbors for certain groups of refugees." Letter from Joan Fitzpatrick, Professor, University of Washington to author 1 (June 27, 1996) (on file with author). She mentions Zaire and the Rwandan Hutu, and Iran and the Iraqi Kurds as examples. *Id.* Whether such states could participate would be a matter for the regional groups to resolve.

138. The United Nations Development Programme compiles cross-national indices on wealth in its Human Development Index. U.N. DEV. PROGRAMME, HUMAN DEVELOPMENT REPORT 15–22 (1995) [hereinafter HUMAN DEVELOPMENT REPORT] (measuring factors such as life expectancy at birth, educational attainment, including adult literacy and school enrollment, and income); *see also* Barbara Crosette, *U.N. Documents Inequities for Women as World Forum Nears,* N.Y. TIMES, Aug. 18, 1995, at A3.

139. The regional character of the proposed burden-sharing scheme encourages consideration of such factors. For example, if refugees are to be temporarily protected or permanently resettled, it is clearly preferable to do so in the region from which they came, other things being equal. The operation of the quotas market is likely to reinforce the salience of this neighborhood factor by providing a premium to states for taking refugees who can more easily be returned once the need for protection ceases. Robert Ellickson has suggested a higher quota for neighboring states on the theory that they are likely to have the greatest influence over most of the conditions that spawn refugee crises nearby; increasing their quotas to reflect this factor, he argues, will strengthen their incentives to prevent those conditions from producing refugee flows. Interview with Robert C. Ellickson, Professor of Law, Yale Law School, in New Haven, Conn. (Feb. 19, 1996).

140. For example, crediting a state's quota to reflect its protection of those refugees who are already on its territory might require distinguishing between refugees and ordinary immigrants. In countries like the United States, drawing this distinction often requires a complex, costly adjudication. Even then it is somewhat arbitrary.

141. Or states, since the quota might be fractionated for purposes of trading.

142. The transfer of weapons would be subject, of course, to nonproliferation requirements.

143. See HUMAN DEVELOPMENT REPORT, *supra* note 137, at 19 tbl. 1.1. Some small oil countries also have extremely high per capita wealth. Qatar and the United Arab Emirates ranked third and fourth respectively, in real GDP per capita in 1992. See id. at 20 tbl.1.2.

144. See, e.g., Sheryl DuWunn, *Japan Worries About a Trend: Crime by Chinese,* N.Y. TIMES, Mar. 12, 1997, at A4 (noting that large relative increase in illegal immigrants from China and immigrant-related crime "'shakes the very foundation of the Japanese government'").

145. See Koh, *supra* note 85, at 155. According to Bronson McKinley, a senior State Department official involved in negotiating the agreement with Panama, the cost to the United States was quite high.

146. Germany's willingness to accept hundreds of thousands of Croatian refugees, for example, is explicable in these terms. If the transaction were "identity-blind," however, certain motivations such as ethnic commonality would be weakened. This issue is discussed below.

147. The problem arises, of course, with respect to two groups of refugees—those who would compose the quota initially assigned to a state and those who would compose the quotas for a potential transferee state might be willing to bargain. An analogy to poorly specified property rights is apt.

148. U.S. law protects the confidentiality of asylum applicants by limiting disclosure of the asylum application and identifying details. *See* 8 C.F.R. § 208.6 (1995). Presumably, regional burden-sharing arrangements could provide similar safeguards.

149. At the time of this writing, the U.S. government is considering the resettlement of Kurdish refugees from northern Iraq on the basis of whether they previously worked for the United States. See Steven Lee Myers, *U.S. To Help Free Refugees in Iraq,* N.Y. TIMES, Sept. 13, 1996, at A1.

150. States may differ in the extent to which they view refugee resettlement as a type of immigration program in which they make judgments on a highly individualized basis about refugees' assimilability, as distinguished from more generalized, categorical judgments.

151. See *supra* text accompanying notes 62–64.

152. The coordinating role of intergovernmental agencies, notably UNHCR and UNDP, has been very important to the success of burden-sharing arrangements. See Hathaway & Neve, *supra* note 22.

153. This was the case during the CPA, when the United States and other participating states extended UNHCR's responsibilities to include establishing and administering holding camps. See Eagleburger, *supra* note 48, at 69–70.

154. See *infra* text accompanying notes 168–69.

155. See 1985 Schengen Agreement, *supra* note 8; see also Reerman, *supra* note 95.

156. See Hathaway & Neve, *supra* note 22.

157. For some examples of this approach, see Michael Klausner, *Market Failure and Community Investment: A Market-Oriented Alternative to the Community Reinvestment Act,* 143 U. Pa. L. Rev. 1561, 1580–92 (1995) (proposing tradable community investment obligations); Edmund L. Andrews, *F.C.C. Plan, with a Twist, To Require Educational TV,* N.Y. TIMES, Apr. 1, 1995, at 38 (proposing tradable children's educational programming requirements); Peter Passell, *A Venerable Peanut Subsidy May Be Target of Republicans,* N.Y. TIMES, Dec. 1, 1994, at D2 (noting plan to make peanut marketing quotas tradable within counties); Peter Passell, *Big Government and the Big 3 Pass the Air Pollution Buck,* N.Y. TIMES, Oct. 20, 1994, at D2 (proposing tradable auto emission reduction obligations); Peter Passell, *One Answer to Overfishing: Privatize the Fisheries,* N.Y. TIMES, May 11, 1995, at D2 (planning to create fishing rights quotas).

158. See, e.g., Richard B. Stewart & Jonathan B. Wiener, *The Comprehensive Approach to Global Climate Policy: Issues of Design and Practicality,* 9 ARIZ. J. INT'L & COMP. L. 83 (1992) (proposing to reduce greenhouse gases).

159. Southern Burlington County NAACP v. Township of Mount Laurel, 456 A.2d 390 (N.J. 1983); Southern Burlington County NAACP v. Township of Mount Laurel, 336 A.2d 713 (N.J. 1975).

160. Fair Housing Act of 1985, N.J. STAT. ANN. §§ 52:27D–301 to –329 (West 1986 & Supp. 1992).

161. See JESSE DUKEMINIER & JAMES I. KRIER, PROPERTY 1126 (3d ed. 1993).

162. *Id.* at 1127–28 (discussing studies in summary fashion).

163. See NEW JERSEY COUNCIL ON AFFORDABLE HOUS., STATUS OF MUNICIPALITIES, 1989–1999 (1997).

164. For a discussion of the outcome of the *Mount Laurel* case, see Ronald Smothers, *After Landmark Ruling, Slow and Painful Progress,* N.Y. TIMES, Mar. 3, 1997, at B1; Ronald Smothers, *Decades Later, Town Considers Housing Plan for the Poor,* N.Y. TIMES, Mar. 3, 1997, at B5; Ronald Smothers, *Mt. Laurel Votes To Build Homes for the Poor,* N.Y. TIMES, Apr. 12, 1997, at B1.

165. 1990 Amendments to Clean Air Act, Pub. L. No. 101–549, §§ 401–413, 104 Stat. 2399, 2584–635 (codified at 42 U.S.C. § 7651 (1994)).

166. See, e.g., U.S. GEN. ACCOUNTING OFFICE, GAO/RCED–95–30, AIR POLLUTION: ALLOWANCE TRADING OFFERS AN OPPORTUNITY TO REDUCE EMISSIONS AT LESS COST,

ch. 3 (1994), *available at* http://frwebgate.access.gpo.gov/cg . . . txt&directory =/diskb/wais/ data/gao; Robert W. Hahn & Gordon L. Hester, *Marketable Permits: Lessons for Theory and Practice,* 16 Ecology L.Q. 361, 401–06 (1989); Peter Passell, *Illinois Is Looking to Market Forces To Help Reduce Its Smog,* N. Y. TIMES, Mar. 30, 1995, at D2 (noting that environmentalists believe program has succeeded beyond expectations).

167. See, e.g., DANIEL DUDEK & JONATHAN WIENER, OECD, JOINT IMPLEMENTATION, TRANSACTION COSTS, AND CLIMATE CHANGE (1996); Daniel Dudek et al., *Technology-Based Approaches Versus Market-Based Approaches, in* GREENING INTERNATIONAL LAW 182 (Phillippe Sands ed., 1993) (discussing voluntary Climate Control accord); Stephen Kinzer, *U.S. Utilities Helping Czechs To Curb Greenhouse Gases and Air Pollutants,* N.Y. TIMES, Sept. 18, 1995, at A8 (noting that utilities anticipate "joint implementation" law allowing domestic pollution credits for achieving pollution reductions abroad); Peter Passell, *For Utilities, New Clear-Air Plan,* N.Y. TIMES, Nov. 18, 1994, at D1 (suggesting that transaction between Arizona and New York utilities may lead to global market system); Peter Passell, *Yawn. A Global-Warning Alert. But This One Has Solutions,* N.Y. TIMES, Feb. 13, 1997, at D2 (describing international emissions trading system to reduce greenhouse gases).

168. For discussion of refugee definitions, see *supra* notes 1, 19.

169. For a similarly incremental approach to an incomplete market in climate change risks, see THOMAS C. HELLER, JOINT IMPLEMENTATION AND THE PATH TO A CLIMATE CHANGE REGIME 11–14 (Robert Schuman Centre at the European Univ. Inst., Jean Monnet Chair Paper No. 23, 1995).

170. The Scandinavian countries, for example, do not take in refugees because of U.S. pressure; they do so out of a long, autonomous tradition of refugee protection.

171. The efforts by Zaire and Burundi to force Hutu refugees to return to Rwanda are tragic examples of the failure to protect those seeking temporary protection. *See* McKinley, *supra* note 79.

172. This responsibility could be analogized to a company's continuing liability—imposed by contract, statute, or common law—for certain risks associated with particular assets it sells to another.

173. This goal is recognized in section 243(h) of the Immigration and Nationality Act, 8 U.S.C. § 1253(h) (1994), which implements article 33 of the 1951 Refugee Convention. Section 243(h) provides that "the Attorney General shall not deport or return any alien . . . to a country if the Attorney General determines that such alien's life or freedom would be threatened in such country on account of race, religion, nationality, membership in a particular social group, or political opinion." *Id.*

174. For an elaboration of such an argument in the context of rent control, see Margaret Jane Radin, *Market-Inalienability,* 100 HARV. L. REV. 1849, 1878, 1918 (1987); Margaret Jane Radin, *Residential Rent Control,* 15 PHIL. & PUB. AFF. 350 (1986). For a response to Radin, see Richard A. Epstein, *Rent Control and the Theory of Efficient Regulation,* 54 BROOK. L. REV. 741, 770–74 (1988).

175. For classic discussions of alternative decision processes for allocating such goods, see GUIDO CALABRESI & PHILIP BOBBITT, TRAGIC CHOICES (1978); ROBERT A. DAHL & CHARLES LINDBLOM, POLITICS, ECONOMICS, AND WELFARE (1976). The phrase "at least ostensibly" and the scare quotes around "nonmarket" are intended to convey a recognition that these other processes, including politics and legal structures, usually conceal rather than eliminate the market's operation. This fact is in accord with public choice theory and with empirical studies in areas as diverse as campaign finance, interest group behavior, the regulatory process, judicial elections, and litigation.

176. For example, a requirement that interstate transactions be "identity-blind," *see supra* notes 145–48 and accompanying text, might discourage some ethnically homogeneous states from participating.

Chapter 14

1. Jack Miles aptly refers to it as "bottled brio." Jack Miles, *The Coming Immigration Debate,* Atlantic Monthly, Apr. 1995, at 130, 131 (reviewing Peter Brimelow. Alien Nation: Common Sense About America's Immigration Disaster (1995) [hereinafter Alien Nation).

2. Too personal, In some respects—a point noted by Jack Miles in his largely admiring review. *See Id.* at 140.

3. Alien Nation. *supra* note 1, at 4. On birthright citizenship, see *Hearing Before the Sub-Comm. on Immigration and Claims and the Subcomm. on the Constitution of the House Comm. on the Judiciary,* 104th Cong., 1st Sess. (Dec. 13, 1995) (statement of Peter H. Schuck, Professor, Yale Law School) [hereinafter Schuck Testimony]; Letter from Peter H. Schuck, Professor, Yale Law School, & Rogers Smith, Professor, Yale University, to House Subcomm. on Immigration and Claims and House Subcomm. on the Constitution of the House Comm. on the Judiciary (Feb. 14, 1996) (supplementing Dec. 1995 testimony) (on file with author) [hereinafter Supplemental Letter].

4. Alien Nation, *supra* note 1, at 263.

5. For example, in his review of the book, Aristide Zolberg expresses surprise and dismay as to "[w]hy this journalistic broadside has received such respectful treatment." Aristide Zolberg. Book Review, 21 Population & Dev. Rev. 659, 659 (1995). A number of other readers have been similarly dismissive.

6. The media and Congress have already given it much prominence, and it is bound to receive more attention as we approach two seismic political events: congressional action on immigration reform legislation and the 1996 election campaign. For a sampling of Brimelow's appearances on national television programs, see *Booknotes* (C-SPAN television broadcast, June 11, 1995), *cited in Reuters Daybook,* June 11, 1995, *available in* LEXIS. News Library, Curnws File; *Charlie Rose* (PRS television broadcast, Apr. 20, 1995). *transcript reprinted in* LEXIS, News Library, Curnws File (transcript no. 1360); *Crossfire* (CNN television broadcast, July 4, 1995). *available in* LEXIS, News Library, Curnws File (transcript no. 1398); *Firing Line: Resolved: All Immigration Should Be Drastically Reduced* (PBS television broadcast, June 16, 1995), *discussed in* Walter Goodman, *Television Review: An Immigration Debate's Real Issue.* N.Y. Times, June 15, 1995, at C20; *MacNeil/Lehrer NewsHour: Alien Nation* (PBS television broadcast, Aug. 16, 1995), *available in* LEXIS, News Library, Curnws File; *The McLaughlin Group* (television broadcast, Aug. 1995), *discussed in* Susan Douglas, *Snide Celebrations: Network TV Political Talk Shows and Women's Rights,* Progressive, Oct. 1995, at 17, 17. Brimelow has also testified before Congress. *See Immigration Issues: Hearing Before the Subcomm. on Immigration and Claims of the House Judiciary Comm.,* 104th Cong., 1st Sess. (May 17, 1995).

7. *See* Alien Nation, *supra* note 1, at 258. The 1965 amendments, Act of Oct. 3, 1965, Pub. L. No. 89–236, 79 Stat. 911 (codified as amended in scattered sections of 8 U.S.C.), modified the landmark Immigration and Nationality Act of 1952, ch. 477, 66 Stat. 163 (codified as amended at 8 U.S.C. §§ 1101–1523 [1988 & Supp. 1994]).

8. *See* Immigration Act of 1921, ch. 8, 42 Stat. 5. Congress adopted the national origins quotas in provisional form in 1921, *id.* § 2, 42 Stat. at 5–6, and codified them as a permanent system in 1924, Immigration Act of 1924, ch. 190, § 11, 43 Stat. 153, 159–60.

9. Act of Oct. 3, 1965, §§ 1–3, 8, Pub. L. No. 89–236, 79 Stat. at 911–14, 916–17.

10. *See* Immigration Act of 1978, Pub. L. No. 95–412, 92 Stat. 907; Immigration Reform and Control Act of 1986, Pub. L. No. 99–603. 100 Stat. 3359; Immigration Act of 1990, Pub. L. No. 101–649, 1990 U.S.C.C.A.N. (104 Stat.) 4978.

11. Alien Nation, *supra* note 1, at 262.

12. *Id.* at 262–63. I say "seems" because he is not altogether clear about how far he is prepared to go in restricting immigration. Brimelow proposes severe cutbacks in each category that would still preserve the category in some form, but he also says that, in the end, complete elimination is the preferred policy. *Id.* Either Brimelow has not considered the possibility that some of these changes—especially a refusal to allow genuine asylees to enter the United States—would

violate human rights conventions to which the United States is a signatory, or he does not care if they do.

13. Brimelow, however, is not as radical as Michael Lind, who, to protect the earnings of native-born Americans, advocates zero net immigration. See Michael Lind, The Next American Nation: The New Nationalism and the Fourth American Revolution 321–22 (1995). I should add that Lind's book is both provocative and excellent, although its brief discussion of immigration policy is among its weakest sections.

14. Brimelow's discussion does not distinguish clearly between race, which connotes a close phenotypic affinity among people, and ethnicity, which connotes a cultural affinity, albeit one in which skin color might play an important cohesive role. He uses the terms more or less interchangeably. He assumes that there are well-defined races in the United States today, that they are accurately represented by Census data, and that they bear race-specific cultural values and behavioral propensities of a kind that would or should be relevant to immigration policy. These beliefs are as dangerous as they are false. For a critique of these assumptions, see id. at 118–27.

15. Both the ethnocultural conception of nationhood and the contrasting political conception are traced in Rogers Brubaker, Citizenship and Nationhood in France and Germany (1992).

16. See generally Controlling Immigration: A Global Perspective (Wayne A. Cornelius et al. eds., 1994) [hereinafter Controlling Immigration] (comparing immigration policy and politics of immigration of Western democracies).

17. For recent reviews and analyses of the evidence, see William G. Mayer. The Changing American Mind: How and Why American Public Opinion Changed Between 1960 and 1988. at 22–28 (1992); Benjamin I. Page & Robert Y. Shapiro, The Rational Public: Fifty Years of Trends in America's Policy Preferences 68–81 (1992); Byron M. Roth, Prescription for Failure: Race Relations in the Age of Social Science 45–72 (1994). See generally Abigail Thernstrom & Stephan Thernstrom. *The Promise of Racial Equality* in The New Promise of American Life 88, 88–101 (Lamar Alexander & Chester E. Finn, Jr. eds., 1995) (discussing indicia of racism and measures of political and economic progress of African-Americans). Particularly interesting is the increase during the 1980s in the proportion of whites and blacks who said that they had a "fairly close friend" of the other race. In 1989, two-thirds of whites reported having a fairly close black friend, up from 50% in 1981. Similarly, 69% of blacks said that they had a fairly close white friend in 1981; by 1989, this number had increased to 80%. *Id.* at 95; see also D'Vera Cohn & Ellen Nakashima. *Crossing Racial Lines,* Wash. Post. Dec. 13, 1995, at A1 (discussing newspaper poll that indicates that more than three-quarters of Washington area 12- to 17-year-olds say they have close friend of another race). On the other hand, a recent study finds that at least one aspect of traditional prejudice—the stereotype of blacks as lazy—is still widespread and contributes to whites' opposition to welfare. Martin Gilens, *Racial Attributes and Opposition to Welfare,* 57 J. Pol. 994 (1995).

18. The most arguable exceptions, such as the contrast between the immigrant-friendly Cuban Adjustment Act. Pub. L. No. 89–732, 80 Stat. 1161 (1966) (codified as amended at 8 U.S.C. §§ 1101(b)(5), 1255 (1988)), and the often harsh treatment of Haitians, are over-determined; they can also be explained on geopolitical and ideological grounds. For opposition to the Cuban emigrées' advantages under the Cuban Adjustment Act, see The Stick Congress Gave Castro, N.Y. Times, Aug. 15, 1991, at A22 (editorial). Haitians have experienced a more hostile reception. See Anthony DePalma, For Haitians, Voyage to a Land of Inequality. N.Y. Times, July 16, 1991, at A1. This differential was much noted—and decried—during the Haitian refugee crisis that followed the Haitian military's overthrow of the government of President Jean-Bertrande Aristide in 1991. See, e.g., Bob Herbert, In America: Fasting for Haiti, N.Y. Times, May 4, 1994, at A23.

Some observers also attribute much of the support for Proposition 187 in California to racism. See, e.g., Kevin R. Johnson, An Essay on Immigration Politics, Popular Democracy, and California's Proposition 187: The Political Relevance and Legal Irrelevance of Race, 70 Wash. L. Rev. 629, 650–61 (1995); Gerald L. Neuman, Aliens as Outlaws: Government Ser-

vices, Proposition 187, and the Structure of Equal Protection Doctrine, 42 UCLA L. Rev. 1425, 1451–52 & n. 125 (1995). There is room, however, for genuine disagreement about the significance of the Latino support for the measure. *Compare* Peter H. Schuck, *The Message of 187.* Am. Prospect, Spring 1995, at 85, 89–90 (viewing support of significant minority of Latinos for Proposition 187 as evidence of nonracist nature of support for measure) *with* Johnson. *supra,* at 650–61 (viewing fact that majority of Latinos opposed it as evidence of racism). A federal district court in California has partially enjoined the enforcement of Proposition 187 on constitutional grounds. See League of United Latin Am. Citizens v. Wilson, 908 F. Supp. 755 (C.D. Cal. 1995).

19. See Infra text accompanying notes 76–93 (racial composition): 180–97 (bilingualism and multiculturalism): 198–207 (affirmative action); 208–12 (legislative districting).

20. For a recent review of these eugenic arguments, see Dorothy Nelkin & Mark Michaels. Biological Categories and Border Controls: The Revival of Eugenics in Anti-Immigration Rhetoric (Sept. 12, 1995) (unpublished manuscript, on file with author).

21. The national origins of family-based admissions follow these of the petitioning U.S. *citizens* or legal resident aliens. For example, the beneficiaries of the massive legalization program, many of whom may now petition on behalf of their family members, were disproportionately from Mexico and other Central American nations. *See* Frank D. Bean et al., Opening and Closing the Doors: Evaluating Immigration Reform and Control fig. 5.1 at 69, fig. 5.2 at 71 (1989).

22. Usually, but not always. Almost half of the immigrants from Africa are white. Telephone Interview with Professor Frank D. Bean, Population Research Center, University of Texas at Austin (Nov. 22, 1995).

23. Alien Nation, *supra* note 1, at 10–11. He immediately adds, "Or, too often, a libertarian. And, on the Immigration issue, even some confused conservatives." *Id.* at 11.

24. Thus, he is both impressed and obviously dismayed by the fact that "when you enter the INS waiting rooms you find yourself in an underworld that is not just teeming but is also almost entirely colored." *Id.* at 28. He never says why this disturbs him. Similarly, he insists that "[i]t is simply common sense that Americans have a legitimate interest in their country's racial balance." *Id.* at 264. Frankly, I do not understand why that is so, why race per se should matter.

Unfortunately, his racial awareness does not distinguish him from most Americans today; we seem obsessed with the subject. The difference may be that Brimelow does not simply believe that race *does* matter. See, e.g., Cornel West, Race Matters (1993); *see also* Peter H. Schuck, *Cornell West's Race Matters: A Dissent,* Reconstruction, 1994 No. 3, at 84 (book review) (praising West's open discussion of controversial race issues but criticizing specifics of West's analysis). He also believes that it *should* matter—a lot.

25. After making his quip about liberals, Brimelow offers a serious definition. Racism, he writes, is "committing and stubbornly persisting in error about people, regardless of evidence." Alien Nation, *supra* note 1, at 11. He calls this "the only rational definition" of racism. *Id.* Having noted the question of his own racism and then defined the term, he immediately dismisses the charge on the ground that he is open to evidence. This auto-acquittal, however, is not entirely satisfying. For one thing, his definition of racism as nothing more than an obdurately erroneous methodology of inference is peculiar and evasive. It fails to distinguish racism from many other more morally acceptable, but still regrettable, forms of cognitive error. It also ignores the substantive content of racist views, which of course is their chief point of interest. In common understanding and parlance, racism is a belief in the inherent superiority of one's race, almost invariably accompanied by feelings of animus or contempt toward members of other races. This definition would distinguish racism from what Dinesh D'souza calls "rational discrimination"—discrimination based not on hostility but on the need to act without full information, which would be costly to acquire, and thus on the basis of generalizations (or stereotypes) that are certain to be wrong in many, perhaps even most, individual cases. See Dinesh D'souza, The End of Racism: Principles for a Multiracial, Society (1995).

In this common-sense understanding of racism, it is hard to say whether *Alien Nation* is a racist book. Brimelow's genial discussion reveals an acute sense of racial pride and difference but little outright animus or contempt; his breezy, loose-jointed writing style, which makes no pretense of analytical rigor, leaves it maddeningly unclear precisely what he is claiming. Key concepts such as race and cultural assimilation remain ill- or undefined. His conclusions about group superiority refer to a group's culture, national origin, ethnicity, or class rather than to its race or genetic endowment as such. For example, he notes that street crime is related to "present-orientation." which he says varies among different ethnic groups, and that "[i]nevitably, therefore, certain ethnic cultures are more crime prone than others." Alien Nation, *supra* note 1, at 184. He then refers to the disproportionate arrest rates among blacks. *Id.* Nowhere, however, does he claim that blacks or other disfavored groups are genetically inferior. *See id.* Specifically, he disavows any intention to rely on the claims about racial differences in IQ emphasized in Richard J. Herrnstein & Charles Murray, The Bell Curve: Intelligence and Class Structure in American Life (1994), although he is careful not to disavow the claims themselves. See Alien Nation, *supra* note 1, at 56 n.*.

On the other hand, the book's central, frequently reiterated claims—that the post–1965 immigrants are diluting the predominantly white "Anglo-Saxon" Protestant stock that made America great and that this gravely threatens American society—certainly resemble claims of racial (or at least national origin) superiority, despite Brimelow's disclaimers. And he seems rather eager to define blacks out of the original American nation (much as Chief Justice Taney infamously and tragically did in the *Dred Scott* decision, see Scott v. Sandford, 60 U.S. (19 How.) 393 [1857]) to support his point that America was essentially white and European until the despised 1965 law was implemented. See Alien Nation, *supra* note 1, at 66–67. For that matter, Brimelow also ignores the presence of substantial numbers of persons of Mexican descent in the Southwest following the U.S. annexation of the region. Nor does Brimelow's lily-white vision of pre-1965 America square with the influx of Chinese and Japanese into California and the West after the Civil War. An interesting contrast is presented by the scrupulously and emphatically *nonracist* discussion of many of these same points by Michael Lind. *See* Lind, *supra* note 13, at 259–98.

26. Alien Nation, *supra* note 1, at 29.

27. See id. at 29–49.

28. 1994 INS Statistical Yearbook, *supra* note 29, tbl. 1.

29. The figures for these years include IRCA legalizations, of which there were only 6,000 in 1994. *Id.* tbl. 4.

30. Telephone Interview with Michael Hoefer, Chief of Demographic Analysis, Immigration and Naturalization Service (Sept. 20, 1995) [hereinafter Telephone Interview with Hoefer]. The 1994 decline also reflected the termination of certain special programs and other factors. *Id.* For what it's worth, the INS expects legal immigration to increase in 1996. Telephone Interview with Michael Hoefer, Chief of Demographic Analysis, Immigration and Naturalization Service (Apr. 2, 1996).

31. 1994 INS Statistical Yearbook, *supra* note 29, at 19. The legalization program is also contributing to the enormous growth in naturalization petitions that began in 1995, as the program's beneficiaries are now completing the five-year residency period required for naturalization. *See* Seth Mydans. *The Latest Big Boom: Citizenship,* N.Y. Times, Aug. 11, 1995, at A12. In contrast, the program for dependent family members of legalized aliens added about 34,000 in 1994, down from 55,000 in 1993. 1994 Immigration Report, *supra* note 31, tbl. 2. The program will continue to contribute significantly to the totals for years to come due to the enormous "overhang" of such dependents waiting for visas.

32. A much smaller amnesty, however, was enacted in 1997 and applies to more than 400,000 undocumented aliens from Central America.

33. *See* Jeffrey S. Passel, *Commentary: Illegal Migration to the United States—The Demographic Context, in* Controlling Immigration, *supra* note 16, at 113, 114–15. Unless otherwise

indicated, the discussion of illegal aliens is based on Frank D. Bean et al., *Introduction* to Undocumented Migration to the United States: IRCA and the Experience of the 1980s. 1, 1–10 (Frank D. Bean et al. eds., 1990): Thomas J. Espenshade, *Unauthorized Immigration to the United States.* 21 Ann. Rev. Soc. 195 (1995); and Telephone Interview with Hoefer, *supra* note 35. The other essays in the Bean volume are quite useful empirical studies of illegal immigration.

34. See Passel, *supra* note 37, at 114–15.

35. See Wayne A. Cornelius, *From Sojourners to Settlers: The Changing Profile of Mexican Immigration to the United States, in* U.S. Mexico Relations: Labor Market Interdependence 155, 155–95 (Jorge A. Bustamante et al. eds., 1992).

36. The number declined to 1.09 million in 1994. Immigration & Naturalization Serv., U.S. Dep't of Justice, INS Fact Book: Summary of Recent Immigration Data tbl. 14 (1995).

37. Alien Nation, *supra* note 1, at 33.

38. *Id.* at 27, 33–34.

39. Robert Warren, Estimates of the Undocumented Immigrant Population Residing in the United States, by Country of Origin and State of Residence: October 1992, at 13 (Apt. 1995) (unpublished paper presented at Population Association of America conference, San Francisco, on file with author); Telephone Interview with Hoefer, *supra* note 35. A restrictionist group argues for a figure of 400,000 on the basis of a recent Census Bureau report. *See* John L. Martin, How Many Illegal Immigrants? 1 (Center for Immigration Studies Backgrounder No. 4–95, 1995).

40. Telephone Interview with Hoefer, *supra* note 35.

41. Ashley Dunn, *Skilled Asians Leaving U.S. for High-Tech Jobs at Home,* N.Y. Times, Feb. 21, 1995, at A1, B5 (reporting that Census Bureau estimates 195,000 foreign-born Americans emigrate each year, highest since World War I).

42. See Alien Nation, *supra* note 1, at 39.

43. See Statistics Div., Immigration & Naturalization Serv., U.S. Dep't of Justice, Immigration Fact Sheet 4 (1994) [hereinafter Immigration Fact Sheet ("Emigration"); Telephone Interview with Hoefer, *supra* note 35.

44. This figure is obtained by subtracting the INS emigration data from the 1950s, see Immigration Fact Sheet, *supra* note 47, from INS immigration data from that decade, see 1994 INS Statistical Yearbook, *supra* note 29, tbl. 1.

45. See Subcommittee on Immigration and Refugee Policy of the Senate Comm. on Judiciary & Subcomms, on Immigration, Refugees and International Law of House Comm. on the Judiciary, Final Report of the Select Commission on Immigration and Refugee Policy, 97th Cong., 1st Sess. 30 (1981) (statement of Rev. Theodore Hesburgh) (recommending cap on legal immigration of 350,000).

46. The impetus for the large increase in illegal migration to the United States is usually attributed to the termination of the Bracero program in 1964. On the Bracero program, see generally Kitty Calaviia, Inside the State: The Bracero Program, Immigration, and the I.N.S. (1992). There presumably were some illegal aliens early in the century—those who evaded the nonnumerical restrictions imposed by federal law since 1875 and by state law since much earlier. See generally Gerald L. Neuman, *The Last Century of American Immigration Law (1776–1875),* 93 Colum. L. Rev. 1833 (1993) (explaining pre–1875 immigration laws). As to the latter category, however, see Schuck Testimony, *supra* note 3, at 2 n.2.

47. This illegal immigration accounts for at least one-third of all population growth due to Immigration. Espeashade, *supra* note 37, at 200–01.

48. Alien Nation, *supra* note 1, at 35–38, 43–45.

49. For this figure, see the graph entitled "Rate of immigration by decade, 1820–1990" in John J. Miller & Stephen Moore. *The Index of Leading Immigration Indicators, in* Strangers at Our Gate: Immigration in the 1990s, at 100, 103 (John J. Miller ed., 1994) (citing Bureau of the Census, U.S. Dep't of Commerce, Statistical Abstract of the United States 1992 tbl. 5 [1992]). These figures are clearly based only on legal immigration.

50. Bureau of the Census, U.S. Dep't of Commerce, March 1994 Current Population Survey, *cited in* Martin, *supra* note 43, at 1.

51. Bureau of the Census, U.S. Dep't of Commerce, Statistical Abstract of the United States 1994 tbl. 54 (1994) [hereinafter 1994 U.S. Statistical Abstract. This percentage approximates the foreign-born share of 8.6% in Germany in 1994. Rainer Münz & Rolf Ulrich, *Changing Patterns of Migration: The Case of Germany, 1945–1994, in* Opening the Door: U.S. and German Policies on the Absorption and Integration of Immigrants (Peter H. Schuck et al. eds., forthcoming 1996) [hereinafter Opening the Door] (Münz & Ulrich manuscript at 34, on file with author). The foreign-born share in Canada is much higher. See Controlling Immigration, *supra* note 16, tbl. A.9 at 420 (15.4% share in 1986).

52. Brimelow's account of immigration waves appears primarily in Alien Nation, *supra* note 1, at 29–33.

53. 1994 INS Statistical Yearbook, *supra* note 29, tbl. 1 at 25.

54. See infra text accompanying notes 62–64.

55. Alien Nation, *supra* note 1, at 38. Unless, of course, Congress enacts pending legislation to restrict legal immigration. See infra note 170 and accompanying text.

56. *Id.* at 33. Nathan Glazer makes the same claim. See Nathan Glazer, *Immigration and the American Future*, Pub. Interest. Winter 1995, at 45, 53 ("The rise and fall of the business cycle and employment still plays some role in immigration, but it is a surprisingly small one").

57. Alien Nation, *supra* note 1, at 33, 39, 42.

58. See. e.g., id. chart 1 at 30–31, chart 2 at 32. Brimelow calls chart 2 "a ramp . . . or a springboard." *Id.* at 33 (ellipsis in original).

59. I mean this literally, as well as figuratively. The charts are sealed in a way that can easily mislead the reader. The scale makes the troughs seem deeper than they were in absolute terms, and the scale exaggerates the significance of the inevitable short-term fluctuations. Brimelow's *trompe l'oeil* is particularly egregious in chart 1, see id. at 30–31, chart 3, see id. at 34, and chart 5, see id. nt 42, although this problem plagues many of his diagrams.

60. See 1994 INS Statistical Yearbook, *supra* note 29, tbl. 1.

61. As noted above, nonnumerical restrictions had constrained immigration even before Congress began to regulate immigration in 1875. See *supra* note 50.

62. For some supporting evidence, which the authors view as "preliminary," see James F. Hollifield & Gary Zuk, The Political Economy of Immigration: Electoral, Labor, and Business Cycle Effects on Legal Immigration in the United States, 11–16 (Sept. 1995) (unpublished paper presented at migration workshop sponsored by Institute for Migration and Ethnic Studies, University of Amsterdam, on file with author).

63. See Alien Nation, *supra* note 1, at 211–16. For example, he points to historical patterns of increased intermarriage of Chinese immigrants and whites in the South after immigration had been interrupted for a long period of time. *Id.* at 270.

64. *The Immigrant Experience,* Am. Enterprise, Nov.-Dec. 1995. at 102, 103 (relating May–June 1995 survey in which 66% of immigrants here for decade or less expressed this view). The comparable figure for non-immigrant Americans, according to a different survey in June 1995, was 89%. Id.

65. See *supra* notes 12–13 and accompanying text. *Compare* Alien Nation, *supra* note 1, at 261 (proposing that only immigrants with skills be admitted) *with id.* at 261–62 (proposing moratorium on immigration, or a lull at minimum).

66. *Id.* at 275.

67. *Id.* at 59. This historical vision of a white brotherhood into which earlier waves of white immigrants from southern and eastern Europe were readily inducted is, of course, a wholly misleading and pernicious account of the undisguised hostility that greeted so many of those who happened to he swarthier, poorer, and religiously different than the Americans of that time and who Brimelow, without recognizing the irony, now includes in the desirable "white" category. See generally Nathan Glazer & Daniel Patrick Moynihan, Beyond the Melt-

ing Pot: The Negroes, Puerto Ricans, Jews, Italians, and Irish of New York City 137–216 (2d ed. 1970); John Higham, Strangers in the Land: Patterns of American Nativism, 1860–1925 (Rutgers Univ. Press, 2d ed. 1988) (1955). In contrast to Brimelow, some strident conservatives forthrightly acknowledge this history of discrimination. See, e.g., Thomas Sowell, Ethnic America: A History (1981).

68. Immigration analysts commonly speak of "Hispanics" and "Asians." It is exceedingly important, however, to recognize the enormous ethnic, linguistic, religious, national origin, and other diversities within these broad groupings, and even within narrower classifications such as South Asians. Indeed, these diversities are so great as to render such labels virtually meaningless for most purposes, and often misleading. The Census Bureau and other researchers have adopted these rubrics and use them to organize important immigration data. Political actors have also found them quite serviceable. See Yen Le Espiritu, Asian American Panethnicity: Bridging Institutions and Identities 112–33 (1992): Peter Skerry, Mexican-Americans: The Ambivalent Minority 25–26 (1993); Kevin R. Johnson, *Civil Rights and Immigration: Challenges for the Latino Community in the Twenty-First Century*, 8 La Raza L. J. 42. 67–72 (1995). Not surprisingly, the law has fallen into line. In this essay, I reluctantly accede to these most arbitrary and distorting, but largely inescapable, conventional rubrics.

69. The pincer image refers to two arms—one consisting of Hispanics, the other consisting of blacks and Asians—bearing down upon the white population and gradually squeezing it into a minority position.

70. Alien Nation, *supra* note 1, chart 12 at 63. Oddly, he counts Hispanics (21.1% in 2050) as nonwhites in the Pincer Chart, yet only four pages later he notes that almost half of all Hispanics in the 1990 census counted themselves as whites, *id*. at 67, and he subsequently points out, quite rightly, the larger absurdity of a "Hispanic" category, *id*. at 218. Although he does not say so, the "Asian" rubric is even more absurd, as it aggregates into one meaningless category groups that do not even share a common language, as do Hispanics.

71. *Id*. at 66.

72. The demographic parade of horribles that results from immigration is a recurrent theme of Brimelow's book. For his discussion of the environmental consequences in particular, see *id*. at 187–90.

73. See id. chart 8 at 47.

74. For an example of Bouvier's empirical work, see Leon F. Bouvier & Lindsey Grant. How Many Americans? Population, Immigration and the Environment (1994). Other restrictionist writings draw heavily on this work. See. e.g., Roy Beck, Re-Charting America's Future: Responses to Arguments Against Stabilizing U.S. Population and Limiting Immigration (1994) (citing six Bouvier sources throughout book).

75. See Alien Nation, *supra* note 1, at 47.

76. *Id*. at 151–55, 186–90.

77. See, e.g., Bouvier & Grant, *supra* note 78, at 73; Leon Bouvier, Immigration and Rising U.S. Fertility: A Prospect of Unending Population Growth 2–11 (Center for Immigration Studies Backgrounder No. 1–91, 1991).

78. See Tamara K. Hareven & John Modell, *Family Patterns, in* Harvard Encyclopedia of American Ethnic Groups 345, 348–49 (Stephan Thernstrom et al. eds., 1980) [hereinafter Harvard Encyclopedia].

79. See, e.g., Francine D. Blau. *The Fertility of Immigrant Women: Evidence from High-Fertility Source Countries, in* Immigration and the Work Force 93, 126 (George J. Borjas & Richard B. Freeman eds., 1992) [hereinafter Immigration and the Work Force]. A recent study claims that the experience of immigrant women in struggling against discrimination significantly reduced their fertility in the United States. *See* Thomas J. Espenshade & Wenzhen Ye, *Differential Fertility Within an Ethnic Minority: The Effect of "Trying Harder" Among Chinese-American Women*, 41 Soc. Probs. 97 (1994).

80. Espenshade, *supra* note 37, at 201: Passel, *supra* note 37, at 116. An additional 20% of U.S. population growth resulted from births to immigrants.

81. Alien Nation, *supra* note 1, at 188–89.

82. In 1994, the United States had 74 people per square mile, compared to 623 in the United Kingdom and 275 in France, which are hardly countries that one thinks of as crowded. 1994 U.S. Statistical Abstract, *supra* note 55, tbl. 1351.

83. I say "perhaps" because throughout American history, land previously thought to be uninhabitable was successfully developed for residential and other uses. Sections of Washington, D.C., and many other American cities were reclaimed from swampland, and cities such as Los Angeles, Salt Lake City, and Las Vegas were built in the most forbidding desert conditions.

84. In 1992, the population per square mile in New York City, the most densely populated in the United States, was 11,482; the corresponding densities for London and Paris were 10,490 and 19,883, respectively. The figure for Hong Kong, the most densely populated—and one of the richest—in the world, was 250,524. 1994 U.S. Statistical Abstract, *supra* note 55, tbl. 1355.

85. Chicago was slightly more densely populated in 1990 than in 1920, but less so than in 1930. I am grateful to Professor Thomas Muller for supplying me with these data, which are based on his research comparing figures from the first few decades of this century as reported in the 1930 U.S. census with population data for 1992.

86. See, e.g., Herbert Stein, *Health Care Basics,* San Diego Union-Trib., May 29, 1994, at G1.

87. This has been the pattern in other countries such as Japan, where housing is scarce.

88. This *ceteris paribus* condition, of course, applies to all such predictive statements.

89. See infra notes 243–44 and accompanying text.

90. See Alien Nation, *supra* note 1, at 216 ("[T] he American experience with immigration has been a triumphant success.").

91. *Id.* at 141.

92. See Peter H. Schuck, *The Politics of Rapid Legal Change: Immigration Policy in the 1980s,* 6 Stud. Am. Pol. Dev. 37, 86–89 (1992).

93. Telephone Interview with Hoefer, *supra* note 35.

94. Schuck, *supra* note 96, at 88.

95. *E.g.,* S. 1394, 104th Cong., 1st Sess. (1995), which passed the Senate Subcommittee on Immigration on Nov. 29, 1995. See 72 Interpreter Releases 1605 (Dec. 4, 1995). Senator Simpson's effort to reduce employment-based admissions has failed. See Eric Schmitt, *Author of Immigration Measure in Senate Drops Most Provisions on Foreign Workers,* N.Y. Times, Mar. 8. 1996, at A20.

96. See George J. Borjas, *National Origin and the Skills of Immigrants in the Postwar Period, in* Immigration and the Work Force, *supra* note 83, at 17.

97. Frank D. Bean et al., *Educational and Sociodemographic Incorporation Among Hispanic Immigrants to the United States, in* Immigration and Ethnicity: The Integration of America's Newest Arrivals 73, this. 3.1, 3.2 at 81–82 (Barry Edmonston & Jeffrey S. Passel eds., 1994) [hereinafter Immigration and Ethnicity]. Although this figure is based on census data from 1986 and 1988, the same data indicate that the education level of the Mexican-origin groups declined substantially from that of earlier cohorts of Mexican-origin immigrants, thereby "lend[ing] support to the contention that at least some immigrant groups are less skilled than either other immigrant groups or earlier entrants for the same group." *Id* at 86. These data suggest that "immigration no longer selects for relatively better educated Mexicans." *Id.* at 93. Another disturbing finding is that the educational attainment of third-generation Hispanics, a group dominated by Mexican-Americans, was actually lower than that of their parents, suggesting that the hard-won progress of the second generation does not necessarily continue in the third. *Id.* at 94; *cf. infra* notes 150–56 and accompanying text (noting

need to distinguish among first, second, and third generations of immigrants in evaluating linguistic assimilation).

98. For a comparative study of the skill levels of Asian immigrant national groups that uses years of education as a proxy for skill, see Sharon M. Lee & Barry Edmonston. *The Socioeconomic Status and Integration of Asian Immigrants, in* Immigration and Ethnicity, *supra* note 101, at 101, 112–14 & tbl. 4.3 at 113.

99. Alejandro Portes, Divergent Destinies: Immigration, Poverty, and the Second Generation 7 (Sept. 1995) (unpublished paper prepared for German-American Project on Immigration and Refugees, on file with author).

100. For a discussion of this problem as it appears in the leading studies, see Georges Vernez & Kevin F. McCarthy. The Costs of Immigration to Taxpayers: Analytical and Policy Issues (RAND Center for Research on Immigration Policy, MR–705-Ff/1F, 1996).

101. Eighteen percent of those in the United States for a decade or less have received food stamps. Medicaid, AFDC, and similar aid; 22% of those in United States for 11–20 years have received such aid; and 17% of those in United States for 21 years or more have benefited from such programs. See *The Immigrant Experience, supra* note 64 at 103.

102. Of course, even if this pattern of lower incidence of welfare utilization by immigrants were true, it would simply raise anew the question of immigrant "quality." See discussion *supra* notes 100–03 and accompanying text.

103. See Michael Fix & Jeffrey S. Passel. *Who's on the Dole? It's Not Illegal Immigrants.* L.A. Times, Aug. 3, 1994, at B7 (summarizing results of study based on 1990 census data).

104. See. e.g., *Welfare Revision: Hearing Before Human Resources Subcomm. of House Ways and Means Comm.,* 104th Cong., 1st Sess. (Jan. 27, 1995) (statement of Jane L. Ross, Director, Income Security Issues, General Accounting Office) (detailing dramatic growth in immigrants' claims), available in LEXIS, News Library. Curnws File: Ashley Dunn, *For Elderly Immigrants, a Retirement Plan in U.S.,* N.Y. Times, Apr. 16, 1995 at I (same). Pending legislation in both houses of Congress would restrict immigrants' SSI eligibility. See S. 269, 104th Cong., 1st Sess. § 203 (1995); II.R. 4, 104th Cong., 1st Sess. § 202 (1995).

105. Frank D. Bean et al., Country-of-Origin, Type of Public Assistance and Patterns of Welfare Recipiency Among U.S. Immigrants and Natives, 17–18 & tbl. 4 at 30 (unpublished paper of Population Research Center, University of Texas-Austin, on file with author). The authors note that the absolute increase in Mexican SSI use reflected the great increase in the number of Mexican immigrants during the decade rather than any increased propensity of the average Mexican immigrant to use it. *Id.* at 13–14. Indeed, the rate of SSI use among Mexican immigrants actually declined over the decade. Nevertheless, the sheer growth in the Mexican cohort, coupled with its higher-than-immigrant-average utilization rate, drove the overall immigrant rate higher. *Id.* On the other hand, the number of Asian refugees has already declined and may be even lower in the future. See 1994 INS Statistical Yearbook, *supra* note 29, at 75 (supplying statistics for Vietnamese and Laotian refugees, two of largest Asian refugee groups).

106. Donald Huddle, The Costs of Immigration (July 1993) (unpublished paper prepared for the Carrying Capacity Network, on file with authors). For a sampling of the controversy surrounding Huddle's analysis, see Jane L. Ross, Illegal Aliens—National Net Cost Estimates Vary Widely. GAO/HEHS–95–133 (July 25, 1995), available in LEXIS, News Library, Curnws File.

107. See Alien Nation, *supra* note 1, at 151–53.

108. Jeffrey S. Passel & Rebecca L. Clark, How Much Do Immigrants Really Cost? A Reappraisal of Huddle's "The Cost of Immigrants" (Feb. 1994) (unpublished research report, on file with author).

109. See id.

110. *Id.* at 3.

111. *Id.* at 2. In turn, the Center for Immigration Studies, which has worked closely with Huddle, has responded to Passel and Clark with new estimates, focusing on immigrants' future claims against Social Security, that find a net burden of $29.1 billion. Center for Immigration Studies, The Costs of Immigration: Assessing a Conflicted Issue 1, 19 (Center for Immigration Studies Backgrounder No. 2–94, 1994). The Center and other restrictionists have often pointed in recent years to the faltering economy in California, where a large percentage of the post–1965 immigrants have settled, as evidence of their negative economic effects. It remains to be seen how the strong resurgence of California's economy, see James Sterngold, *Recovery in California Wears a New Costume,* N.Y. Times, Jan. 2, 1996, at C10, will affect these restrictionist arguments.

112. Congress is insisting that sponsors of family-based immigrants be legally responsible in the event that the immigrants become destitute. *See* S. 269. 104th Cong., 1st Sess. § 204 (1995); H.R. 4, 104th Cong., 1st Sess. [session] 503 (1995).

113. Alien Nation, *supra* note 1, at 174–75.

114. See, e.g., Joleen Kirschenman & Kathryn M. Neckerman, *'We'd Love to Hire Them, But . . .': The Meaning of Race for Employers, in* The Urban Underclass 203, 204 (Christopher Jencks & Paul E. Peterson eds., 1991). For a vivid illustration of this point, see Mary C. Waters, Black Like Who? (forthcoming 1996) (finding West Indians preferred to African-Americans as employees).

115. See George J. Borjas, *The Economic Benefits from Immigration,* 9 J. Econ. Persp. 3, 10 (1995) (citing other studies).

116. See Thomas Muller, Immigrants and the American City 166–85 (1993).

117. See Elaine Sorensen & Frank D. Bean, *The Immigration Reform and Control Act and the Wages of Mexican Origin Workers: Evidence from Current Population Surveys,* 75 Soc. Sci. Q. 1, 16 (1994).

118. After claiming that the post–1965 immigration has contributed to the economic woes of black workers, Alien Nation, *supra* note 1. at 173–75. Brimelow exhibits some caution, saying that it is "at least a possibility," *id.* at 175. His discussion is entirely one-sided on this point. Reviewing the studies in 1989, Robert Reischauer concluded that "careful and sophisticated analyses by a number of social scientists provide little evidence that immigrants have had any significant negative impacts on the employment situation of black Americans." Robert D. Reischauer, *Immigration and the Underclass,* 501 Annals Am. Acad. Pol. & Soc. Sci. 120, 120 (1989) (abstract). A recent study by the U.S. Bureau of Labor Statistics, however, finds that recent high levels of immigration are depressing the wages of low-skilled workers. See *Immigrants Contribute to Rising Gap Between Rich and Poor,* FAIR Immigration Report, Feb. 1996, at 6 (citing David Jaeger, Skill Differentials and the Effect of Immigrants on the Wages of Natives [Bureau of Labor Statistics, U.S. Department of Labor Working Paper No. 273, 1995]). The study does not appear to have examined the effects of immigration specifically on low- and unskilled African-American workers.

119. These possibilities are discussed in Frank D. Bean et al., *Labor Market Dynamics and the Effects of Immigration on African Americans, in* Blacks, Immigration and Race Relations (Gerald Jaynes ed., forthcoming) (manuscript at 5–18, on file with author), which concludes that immigration into tight labor markets might reduce black unemployment, while immigration into loose ones might increase it.

120. See Alien Nation, *supra* note 1, at 178–90, 211–18.

121. See. e.g., Waters, *supra* note 118 (finding these values to be preferred by immigrants' employers and co-workers).

122. *Id.* at 88–89, 145 (English proficiency): *id.* at 181 (illegitimacy); *id.* at 182–86 (crime).

123. An estimated 75% of the aliens in federal prisons, compared to 56% of the U.S. citizens there, are incarcerated for drug-related charges. *Criminal Aliens: Hearing Before the Subcomm. on International Law, Immigration and Refugees of the House Comm. on the Judi-*

ciary, 103d Cong., 2d Sess. 165 (1994) [hereinafter *1994 Criminal Aliens Hearing*] (testimony of Kathleen Hawk, Director, U.S. Bureau of Prisons).

124. *Criminal Aliens in the United States: Hearings Before the Permanent Subcomm. on Investigations of the Senate Comm. on Government Affairs,* 103d Cong., 1st Sess. 12 (1993) [hereinafter *1993 Criminal Aliens Hearing*].

125. See John Williams, The Criminal Alien Problem 1 n.2 (Oct. 20, 1995) (memorandum on file with author).

126. A recent statistical study of foreign-born state inmates found that approximately 45% were illegal aliens. See Rebecca L. Clark et al., Fiscal Impacts of Undocumented Aliens: Selected Estimates for Seven States tbls. 3.2, 3.4 (1994). The INS estimates that 20% of foreign-born state inmates are not deportable at all. *Removal of Criminal and Illegal Aliens: Hearings before the Subcomm. on Immigration and Claims of the House Judiciary Comm.,* 104th Cong., 1st Sess. (Mar. 23, 1995) (testimony of T. Alexander Aleinikoff, General Counsel, Immigration and Naturalization Service), *available in* LEXIS, News Library, Curnws File [hereinafter Aleinikoff Testimony]. This figure suggests that the remaining 35% of foreign-born inmates are deportable aliens who are not in illegal status.

127. See *1994 Criminal Aliens Hearing, supra* note 127, at 133 (statement of Rep. Richard H. Lehman).

128. Aleinikoff Testimony, *supra* note 130.

129. The data, such as they are, appear in Julian L. Simon, The Economic Consequences of Immigration 102–03 (1989).

130. On the Dillingham Commission, see Maldwyn Allen Jones, American Immigration 152–57 (2d ed. 1992).

131. See Simon, *supra* note 133, at 102–03.

132. See, e.g., John Kifner, *Immigrant Waves From Asia Brings an Underworld Ashore,* N.Y. Times, Jan. 6, 1991, at 1 (reporting on Asian gangs in New York).

133. See, e.g., Clifford Krauss, *Drug Arrests in Colombia Lead to Killings in Queens,* N.Y. Times, Nov. 25, 1995, at 1.

134. See, e.g., Joseph P. Fried, *Sheik and 9 Followers Guilty of a Conspiracy of Terrorism,* N.Y. Times, Oct. 2, 1995, at A1.

135. See, e.g., Selwyn Raab, *Influx of Russian Gangsters Troubles F.B.I. in Brooklyn,* N.Y. Times, Aug. 23, 1994, at A1.

136. See Steven A. Holmes, *Large Increase in Deportations Occurred in '95,* N.Y. Times. Dec. 28, 1995, at A1.

137. See *1993 Criminal Aliens Hearing, supra* note 128, at 77.

138. The Border Patrol now includes 5000 officers, and Congress has instructed the INS to add 1000 more on the Mexican border. Migration News (Jan. 1996) (migrant news PLM <migrant@primal.ucdavis.edu>).

139. For example, in the El Paso, Texas, sector of the U.S.-Mexico border, the INS in September 1993 Implemented "Operation Hold-the-Line," in which Border Patrol Officers were stationed every hundred yards or so along the border. See Joel Brinkley, *A Rare Success at the Border Brought Scant Official Praise,* N.Y. Times, Sept. 14, 1994. at A1. The deployment reduced apprehensions of illegals from 700 to around 200 per day. Wayne A. Cornelius et al., *Introduction: The Ambivalent Quest for Immigrant Controls, in* Controlling Immigration, *supra* note 16, at 3, 35. A 1994 study of "Operation Hold-the-Line," however, determined that the program had not deterred long-distance immigration, diverting such immigration instead to other crossing points along the border. James Bornemeier, *El Paso Plan Deters Illegal Immigrants,* L.A. Times, July 27, 1994, at A3, A15 (discussing report prepared by Frank Bean and others for U.S. Commission on Immigration Reform).

The INS has also staged simulations at the southern border of an immigration deluge provoked by an internal crisis in Mexico. Sam Dillon, *U.S. Tests Border Plan in Event of Mexico Crisis,* N.Y. Times, Dec. 8, 1995, at B16.

140. Aleinikoff Testimony, *supra* note 130; see also Holmes, *supra* note 140, at D18 (detailing INS's increased efforts).

141. See Espenshade, *supra* note 37, at 211–12 (citing data and reasons for failure of enforcement efforts). Espenshade points out that once an illegal immigrant has taken up residence in the interior, "the annual probability of being apprehended is roughly 1–2%." *Id.* at 212. Immigration control efforts in Europe have also been generally ineffective. *See generally* Controlling Immigration, *supra* note 16, at 143–97.

142. See Robert Pear, *Clinton to Ban Contracts to Companies that Hire Illegal Aliens,* N.Y. Times, Jan. 23, 1996, at A12.

143. Barry R. Chiswick & Paul W. Miller, *The Endogeneity Between Language and Earnings: International Analyses,* 12, J. Labor Econ. 246, 278–79 (1995).

144. Alien Nation, *supra* note 1, at 88–89.

145. Twenty-two states have already adopted "official English" laws. Joyce Price, *English-Only Advocates Sense Momentum; See Passing Chance for Proposed Bills,* Wash. Times, Sept. 7, 1995, at A2 (listing 22 states). Senator Robert Dole has proposed such a rule at the federal level, *id.,* and other presidential contenders will not be far behind. Indeed, President Clinton signed such a law for Arkansas when he was governor of that state. *Campaign English from Senator Dole,* N.Y. Times. Sept. 10, 1995, § 4, at 16. While Dole originally pledged, if elected, to seek to eliminate federal support for bilingual education, see id., he subsequently toned down his rhetoric to permitting bilingual education programs "'that ensure that people learn English in a timely fashion,'" Margot Hornblower, *Putting Tongues in Cheek: Should Bilingual Education Be Silenced?* Time, Oct. 9, 1995, at 40, 42. Congress recently held hearings on English as the common language of the United States. *House Holds Hearing on English as the Common Language,* 72 Interpreter Releases 1542 (1995).

146. Alejandro Portes puts the point this way: "[F]irst-generation immigrants are not regarded generally as poor, no matter what their objective situation is, because they are seen as somehow different from domestic minorities. The same is not true of their children who as U.S. citizens and full participants in American society, are unlikely to use a foreign country as a point of reference or as a place to return to. Instead, they will be evaluated and will evaluate themselves by the standards of their new country." Portes, *supra* note 103, at 15.

147. Chiswick & Miller, *supra* note 147, at 278–79. In another paper based on Australian data. Chiswick and Miller show that "ethnic network" variables—particularly the existence of an ethnic press, proximity of relatives, and spouse's origin language—are more important than the mere fact of living in a minority-language enclave in explaining dominant-language fluency. Barry R. Chiswick & Paul W. Miller, Ethnic Networks and Language Proficiency Among Immigrants (1995) (unpublished manuscript, on file with author).

148. In a 1995 survey, 81% of immigrants living in the United States for more than 20 years report using "English at home most often"; for those in their first decade, the figure is 49%. *See The Immigrant Experience, supra* note 68, at 103.

149. Alejandro Portes & Richard Schauffler, *Language and the Second Generation: Bilingualism Yesterday and Today,* 28 Int'l Migration Rev. 640, 641, 643 (1994) (citing sources).

150. *Id.* at 647. The authors state that "self-reports of language ability, unlike other individual characteristics, are both reliable and valid." *Id.* at 646 (citing sources).

151. *Id.* at 647, 652. Indeed, the authors note that because fluent bilingualism is increasingly an economic asset, the loss of parental-language fluency may pose a greater risk for today's second generation than the nonproblem of inadequate English. *Id.* at 659. This preference for English was even stronger among Cuban children, who were educated in bilingual schools at the core of an ethnic enclave. *Id.* at 652.

Brimelow does cite (incorrectly, *see* Alien Nation, *supra* note 1. at 306 n.4) a study of second-generation schoolchildren in the San Diego and Miami areas that found that Mexican-American children, including those who claimed to be proficient in English, nevertheless retained and preferred to speak the parental language (Spanish) to a much greater degree than children from other nationality groups did. See Rubén G. Rumbaut, *The Crucible Within: Ethnic Identity. Self-Esteem, and Segmented Assimilation Among Children of Immigrants,* 28 Int'l Migration Rev. 748, tbl. 3 at 768 (1994).

152. Despite the much higher Spanish preference rate of the Mexican-American children in the Rumbaut study, they are not really an exception. Their English fluency was only slightly lower than some foreign-language groups and was higher than several others, especially some Asian groups. Rumbaut, *supra* note 155, tb1. 3 at 768. Spanish-language speakers, especially Mexicans, tend to have higher parental-language retention rates, especially if they live near the border, interact with frequent border crossers, live in a community constantly being replenished by first-generation Spanish-speaking immigrants, or adopt an adversarial stance toward Anglo society. By the third generation, however, virtually everyone is monolingual. See Alejandro Portes & Rubén G. Rumbaut, Immigrant America: A Portrait 183 (1990).

153. Alien Nation, *supra* note 1, at 181.

154. Charles Hirschman, *Problems and Prospects of Studying Immigrant Adaptation from the 1990 Population Census: From Generational Comparisons to the Process of "Becoming American,"* 28 Int'l Migration Rev. 690, 708–10 (1994). The rates among Asian refugees, however, are much higher than for other Asians. *Id.* at 710.

155. Alien Nation, *supra* note 1, at 184.

156. Hirschman, *supra* note 158, at 711.

157. See Frank D. Bean et al., Socioeconomic and Cultural Incorporation and Marital Disruption Among Mexican Americans (Sept. 1995) (unpublished paper, on file with author).

158. *Id.* at 26–27. Frank Bean and his colleagues attribute the rise in divorce rates in the second and third generations to the special uncertainties and vulnerabilities surrounding the immigration experience in the United States that keep families together in the first generation. *Id.* at 25–26. Even in the third generation, the Hispanic divorce rate does not exceed that of U.S. natives, whereas the black divorce rate is higher than the U.S. average. Nevertheless, this dynamic could have worrisome implications for Mexican-American progress in the United States. As the authors put it, "The greater marital stability of lower socioeconomic status immigrants, when included in average rates of marital disruption, leads to what some might term a falsely rosy picture." *Id.* at 26.

159. See Alejandro Portes & Min Zhou, *The New Second Generation: Segmented Assimilation and Its Variants,* 530 Annals Am. Acad. Pol. & Soc. Sci. 74, 74 (1993).

160. Portes, *supra* note 103, at 17 (citations omitted).

161. *Id.* at 23.

162. Portes and Zhou have found empirical evidence for this form of self-consciously delayed assimilation among the Cuban and Punjabi Sikh enclaves in South Florida and California, respectively, contrasting the experiences of these groups to the less protected, downwardly assimilating Haitians in Miami, and Mexicans and Mexican-Americans in central California. See Portes & Zhou, *supra* note 163, at 87–91.

163. See Bean et al., *supra* note 101, at 76–77. The Mexican-American experience in educational attainment, furthermore, suggests that continued progress beyond the second generation is by no means assured. *See supra* note 101 and accompanying text.

164. See Alien Nation, *supra* note 1, at 193–95. For another discussion of this possibility, see Leon Bouvier, What If . . . ? Immigration Decisions: What Could Have Been. What Could Be 15 (1994).

165. See Alien Nation, *supra* note 1, at 195–201. As precedent, Brimelow points to the brief rise of the Know-Nothings' American party in the 1850s. He emphasizes that the Know-Nothings, while rabidly anti-Catholic, did not in fact seek to restrict immigration and placed a higher priority on abolition. *Id.* at 12–13, 200.

166. See Steven A. Holmes, *House Panel Keeps Intact Bill to Restrict Immigration,* N.Y. Times, Oct. 12, 1995, at A20 (discussing Republican bill to restrict legal immigration); Robert

Pear, *Clinton Embraces a Proposal to Cut Immigration by a Third,* N.Y. Times, June 8, 1995, at B10 (reporting President Clinton's endorsement of proposal by Commission on Immigration Reform to reduce legal immigration by one-third).

167. See Alien Nation, *supra* note 1, at 123–33.

168. The term "imagined" is taken, of course, from Benedict Anderson's coinage. See Benedict Anderson, Imagined Communities: Reflections on the Origin and Spread of Nationalism (2d ed. 1991).

169. See Alien Nation, *supra* note 1, at 230–32. Brimelow defines the "New Class" (a term he explicitly borrows from Irving Kristol, see Irving Kristol., Two Cheers for Capitalism 26–31 (1978)) as "the professionals who run and benefit from the state . . . and its power to tax." *Id.* at 230. For an avowedly liberal critique of the balkanizing tendencies of contemporary society that rejects this distinction between the "new class" and other powerful class interests, see Lind, *supra* note 13, at 327.

170. Alien Nation, *supra* note 1, at 219.

171. Id.

172. Indeed, the fact that many of the new immigrants are refugees fleeing cruel regimes in harsh societies, which Brimelow insists was not true in the good old days, *id.* at 246, suggests that the newcomers' loyalties are, if anything, less conflicted than those of their predecessors.

173. See *The Immigrant Experience, supra* note 68, at 101 (relating 1995 survey data fmm June 1995 that indicate that immigrants' belief in American values is as great or greater than that of natives).

174. Alien Nation, *supra* note 1, at 219.

175. Brimelow fails to mention another policy—racially defined and gerrymandered legislative districting—that I believe is perhaps even more dangerous because it reinforces racialist thinking and creates perverse incentives for political behavior, and because it is especially difficult to dislodge once it is in place. See infra notes 208–12 and accompanying text.

176. See *supra* notes 153–56 and accompanying text.

177. For instances of this ideological subordination, see, for example, Stephanie Gutmann. *The Bilingual Ghetto: Why New York's Schools Won't Teach Immigrants English.* City J., Winter 1992, at 29; Abigail M. Thernstrom, *E Pluribus Plura—Congress and Bilingual Education,* Pub. Interest. Summer 1980, at 3. I say "presumed" because of claims that assignment to bilingual classes sometimes reflects nothing more than the school's ascription of ethnicity to the child based on her surname. For an example of this practice, see Gutmann, *supra,* at 29.

178. See Toby L. Bovitz, *Bilingual Education in New York No Longer Serves Students.* N.Y. Times, Mar. 23, 1995, at A24 (letter to editor from bilingual psychologist in school system): Sam Dillon, *Report Faults Bilingual Education in New York.* N.Y. Times, Oct. 20, 1994. at Al; Gutmann, *supra* note 181, at 29; Jacques Steinberg, *Lawsuit Is Filed Accusing State of Overuse of Bilingual Classes,* N.Y. Times, Sept. 19, 1995, at B6 (reporting suit by parents' group). But see Maria Newman, *Schools are Likely to Stop Automatic English Testing.* N.Y. Times, Feb. 27, 1996, at B3 (describing plan to terminate automatic testing of children with Spanish surnames for possible placement in bilingual programs).

179. Legislation pending in Congress would greatly restrict or even eliminate bilingual education. See, e.g., H.R. 1005, 104th Cong., 1st Sess. § 3(a) (1995) (repealing former Bilingual Education Act, 20 U.S.C. §§ 3281–3341 [1994]); see also Hornblower, *supra* note 149, at 42 (detailing congressional and administration positions on bilingual education). To the extent that these changes would eliminate even genuinely transitional, short-term bilingual education entirely, they may go too far.

180. Canada, for example, has made multiculturalism a constitutionally-protected value. Can. Const. (Constitution Act. 1982). Pt. 1 (Canadian Charter of Rights and Freedoms), 1 27 ("This Charter shall be interpreted in a manner consistent with the preservation and enhancement of the multicultural heritage of Canada."). The U.S. Supreme Court has also protected

the right of religious and ethnic minorities to preserve their cultural practices. *E.g.,* Pierce v. Society of Sisters of the Holy Names of Jesus and Mary, 268 U.S. 510 (1925) (invalidating Oregon law requiring children between ages of eight and 16 to attend public school): Meyer v. Nebraska, 262 U.S. 390 (1923) (striking down Nebraska statute prohibiting teaching of languages other than English and instruction in languages other than English).

181. Glazer, *supra* note 60, at 46–47.

182. For a spirited attack on this "ideal of authenticity" and on the contrived character of many multiculturalists' symbols, see Lind, *supra* note 13, at 122–27.

183. For alarming and sometimes tragi-comical examples by insightful observers, see Richard Bernstein, Dictatorship of Virtue: Multiculturalism and the Battle for America's Future (1994); Lynne V. Cheney, Telling the Truth: Why Our Culture and Our Country Have Stopped Making Sense—and What We Can Do About It (1995).

184. See, e.g., Mary Lefkowitz, Not out of Africa: How Afrocentrism Became an Excuse to Teach Myth as History (1996).

185. See, e.g., Lind, *supra* note 13, at 118–37; Mary C. Waters, Ethnic Options: Choosing Identities in America 16–51 (1990); Christopher A. Ford, *Administering Identity: The Determination of "Race" in Race-Conscious Law,* 82 Cal L. Rev. 1231, 1239–40 (1994).

186. The percentage of white-identifying Hispanics depends in part on the structure of the survey instrument and the methodology of the questioner. Bureau of the Census, U.S. Dep't of Commerce, Current Population Reports, Series P23–182, Exploring Alternative Race-Ethnic Comparison Groups in Current Population Surveys 2–3 (1992). For an historical survey of the changing racial and ethnic questions in the census, including the mutability of Hispanic self-identification, see Stephan Themstrom, *American Ethnic Statistics, in* Immigrants in Two Democracies: French and American Experience 80, 100 n.5 (Donald L. Horowitz & Gérard Noiriel eds., 1992) (reporting that 21.1% of people who identified with Spanish-origin group in 1971 gave different origin just one year later: 12% of all those who self-identified as Hispanic had abandoned it).

187. For these exogamy data, see Frank D. Bean et al., The Changing Demography of U.S. Immigration Flows: Patterns, Projections, and Contexts 13 (July 1995) (unpublished paper presented at Conference on German-American Migration and Refuges Policies, on file with author).

188. See id. tbl. 4.

189. In a curious, brief discussion of interracial marriage, he acknowledges that it would lend to dissipate the Pincers' pressure and then adds the following "*BUT*" (italics and capitalization in original): "while more Hispanics are intermarrying, the proportion of all Hispanic marriages has fallen, swamped by the sheer growth of the Hispanic population." Alien Nation, *supra* note 1, at 274. The meaning and relevance of this observation escape me.

190. Bean et al., *supra* note 192, at 14.

191. *See* Barry Edmonston et al., Ethnicity, Ancestry, and Exogamy in U.S. Population Projections, (Apr. 1994) (unpublished paper presented before Population Association of America, on file with author).

192. *See* Bean et al., *supra* note 192, at 14–15 (summarizing findings in Edmonston et al., *supra* note 195, at 28). The actual number would depend on how such individuals self-identify in reporting to the census. This in turn may depend on how the Census Bureau resolves the issue of whether a mixed ancestry category should be established. On the Census Bureau's approach to this question, see Lawrence Wright, *One Drop of Blood,* New Yorker, July 25, 1994, at 46.

193. For two discussions of this question, see Ford Found., Changing Relations: Newcomers and Established Residents in U.S. Communities (1993); Opening the Door, *supra* note 55. The first of these would change the focus from immigrants' *assimilation* to their *accommodation,* defined as "a process by which all sides in a multifaceted situation. Including established residents and groups at different stages of settlement, find ways of adjusting to and supporting

one another." Ford Found., *supra,* at 4. To the extent that this change is an exhortation to receiving communities to welcome immigrants, it is benign, but to the extent that it is meant to shift the initiative for, and the principal burdens of, assimilation from immigrants to the established community, it is probably misguided and will engender resistance.

194. See, e.g., Paul M. Barrett, *Pentagon Move to Hurt Minority Builders,* Wall St. J., Oct. 25, 1995, at B2 (reporting that Defense Department. Small Business Administration, and other agencies are curtailing affirmative action programs); Steven A. Holmes, *White House to Suspend a Program for Minorities,* N.Y. Times, Mar. 8, 1996, at A1 (ordering three-year suspension of minority and female set-aside programs for contracts).

195. The struggle to limit affirmative action will be extended and will proceed differently in different policy domains. *See, e.g.,* B. Drummond Ayres Jr., *Efforts to End Job Preferences Are Faltering.* N.Y. Times, Nov. 20, 1995, at A1. My criticisms of affirmative action do not refer to policies that require employers, universities, and other entities to engage in more broadranging recruitment processes, which I strongly support. These policies are not seriously in question. Rather, I am concerned with policies that either require, or as a practical matter demand, quotas or preferences based on race.

196. See Peter H. Schuck, *The New Immigration and the Old Civil Rights,* Am. Prospect, Fall 1993, at 102, 108–11.

197. No one can gauge precisely the overall social effects of race-based affirmative action on its supposed beneficiaries. There are, however, reasons to believe that the net effects are either inconsequential or negative. For example, Thomas Sowell, who has written extensively on affirmative action both in the United States and abroad, has compared the pre- and postaffirmative action periods and found that black employment gains were actually greater during the earlier period. Thomas Sowell, Preferential Policies: An International Perspective 113, 115 (1990). In a recent study comparing protected minorities' employment patterns in private firms that adopted either "identity-conscious" (making race relevant) or "identity-blind" (merit-based) personnel decisions, the authors (both strong affirmative action proponents) found that by most measures, improvement in the groups' employment status was not affected by identity-conscious interventions. Alison M. Konrad & Frank Linnehan, *Formalized HRM Structures: Coordinating Equal Employment Opportunity Or Concealing Organizational Practices?* 38 Acad. Mgmt. 1. 787 (1995).

On the negative side, members of protected groups whose genuine, hard-won achievements on the job and in universities are unfairly depreciated because of the supposed favoritism ascribed to affirmative action have suffered much personal indignity, reputational harm, and psychic injury as a result. The social damage to relations between the races has been incalculably great, in my view. According to a recent study, white opposition to affirmative action now encompasses the liberal core of the Democratic party; it is just as strong among those most committed to racial equality as among those least committed to such values. See Martin Gilens et al., Affirmative Action and the Politics of Realignment 3–4 (Apr. 1995) (unpublished conference paper prepared for annual meeting of Midwest Political Science Association, on file with author). One fervently hopes that this damage is not irreversible.

198. The beneficiaries of this program, after all, come from countries that were unfairly *favored* by the pre–1965 immigration policy. For a general critique of diversity programs, including this one, see Stephen II. Legomsky, *Immigration, Equality and Diversity,* 31 Colum. J. Transnat'l. L. 319, 330–35 (1993).

199. Many of these countries, of course, were *advantaged* by the pre–1965 law. In fact, the chief beneficiaries of this program, as was intended at the time of enactment, are the Irish, for whom 41% of the diversity vises were reserved during 1992–94. See Schuck, *supra* note 96, at 71–72.

200. See Schuck, *supra* note 200, at 108–11 (noting invidious group comparisons invited by race-based affirmative action, and favoring class-based remedies instead); see also Richard

D. Kahlenberg, *Equal Opportunity Critics,* New Republic, July 17 & 24, 1995, at 20 (noting that some opponents of race-based affirmative action are beginning to embrace class-based preferences). Class-based affirmative action also has its critics, *see, e.g.,* Michael Kinsley. *The Spoils of Victimhood,* New Yorker, Mar. 27, 1995, at 62, 65–66, and would be difficult to implement, see, e.g., Sarah Kershaw, *California's Universities Confront New Diversity Rules,* N.Y. Times, Jan. 22, 1996, at A10 (discussing problems in applying class-based criteria).

201. See Nathan Glazer, Affirmative Discrimination: Ethnic Inequality and Public Policy 168–205 (1975); Nathan Glazer, *Immigrants and Education, in* Clamor at the Gates: The New American Immigration 213 (Nathan Glazer ed., 1985) [hereinafter Clamor at the Gates]; Ivan Light, *Immigrant Entrepreneurs in America: Koreans in Los Angeles, in* Clamor at the Gates, *supra,* at 161; Peter I. Rose, *Asian Americans: From Pariahs to Paragons, in* Clamor at the Gates, *supra,* at 181; Schuck, *supra* note 200, at 107. For a microscopic view of these invidious comparisons as they operate in the workplace, see generally Waters, *supra* note 118.

202. See, e.g., Ford, *supra* note 189, at 1234 ("However analytically 'soft' a particular classification may be, making it a centerpiece of government resource-allocation will require that it be 'hardened' dramatically."); Wright, *supra* note 196, at 46.

203. Alien Nation, *supra* note 1, at 65 (emphasis omitted). This possibility seems especially great among Asian-Americans, who tend to be more conservative politically than African-Americans.

204. 42 U.S.C. §§ 1971–1973p (1988 & Supp. 1993).

205. See, e.g., Lani Guinier, The Tyranny of the Majority: Fundamental Fairness in Representative Democracy 41–70 (1994); Carol. M. Swain, Black Faces, Black Interests: The Representation of African Americans in Congress, at vii–ix. 193–225 (1993); Abigail Thernstrom, Whose Votes Count?: Affirmative Action and Minority Voting Rights (1987); James F. Blumstein, *Racial Gerrymandering and Vote Dilution: Shaw v. Reno in Doctrinal Context,* 26 Rutgers L.J. 517 (1995); Schuck, *supra* note 200, at 105–11; Peter H. Schuck, *What Went Wrong with the Voting Rights Act,* Wash. Monthly, Nov. 1987, at 51. Other scholars have enthusiastically endorsed it. See, e.g., Bernard Grofman et al., Minority Representation and the Quest for Voting Equality 131–37 (1992); Luis R. Fraga, *Latino Political Incorporation and the Voting Rights Act, in* Controversies in Minority Voting: The Voting Rights Act in Perspective 278 [Bernard Grofman & Chandler Davidson eds., 1992) (hereinafter Controversies in Minority Voting] Pamela S. Karlan, *The Rights to Vote: Some Pessimism About Formalism,* 71 Tex. L. Rev. 1705, 1737–40 (1993); Allan J. Lichtman, *Redistricting, in Black and White,* N.Y. Times, Dec. 7, 1994, at A23.

206. See. e.g., Juan Williams, *Blocked Out in the Newt Congress: The Black Caucus Regroups as Jesse Mulls a Third Party Bid,* Wash. Post, Nov. 20, 1994, at C1.

207. The leading cases are Shaw v. Reno, 113 S. Ct. 2816 (1993), and Miller v. Johnson, 115 S. Ct. 2475 (1995).

208. See Hugh Davis Graham, *Voting Rights and the American Regulatory State, in* Controversies in Minority Voting, *supra* note 209, at 177, 195–96. On growing Asian-American political activism, see Steven A. Holmes, *Anti-Immigrant Mood Moves Asians to Organize,* N.Y. Times, Jan. 3, 1996, at A1.

209. Alien Nation, *supra* note 1, at 219 (emphasis omitted). The key, he writes, is "[a]voiding the Romans' mistake of diluting their citizenship into insignificance." *Id.* at 267.

210. *Id.* at 264–67.

211. See Schuck Testimony, *supra* note 3; Supplemental Letter, *supra* note 3; see also Neil A. Lewis, *Bill Seeks to End Automatic Citizenship for All Born in the U.S.,* N.Y. Times, Dec. 14, 1995, at A26.

212. U.S. Const. amend. XIV, § 1.

213. Peter H. Schuck & Rogers M. Smith, Citizenship Without Consent: Illegal Aliens in the American Polity 5, 72–89 (1985); see also Peter H. Schuck, *Membership in the Liberal Polity: The Devaluation of American Citizenship,* 3 Geo. Immigr. L.J. 1 (arguing that

birthright citizenship and minimal incentives for aliens to naturalize have lowered value of U.S. citizenship).

214. Schuck & Smith, *supra* note 217, at 90–115.

215. The most probing criticisms—although not persuasive in our view—are found in Gerald L. Neuman, Strangers to the Constitution: Immigrants, Borders and Fundamental Law (forthcoming 1996) (manuscript at 473–535, on file with author); David A. Martin, *Membership and Consent: Abstract or Organic?* II Yale J. Int'l L. 278 (1985). But see Peter H. Schuck & Rogers M. Smith, *Membership and Consent: Actual or Mythic? A Reply to David A. Martin,* II Yale J. Int'l L. 545 (1986).

216. See Schuck & Smith, *supra* note 217, at 97–100. 136–37.

217. *Id.* at 99, 135. Our book was published well before Congress enacted such an amnesty in the 1986 IRCA legislation. We recommended such a measure in the book.

218. See discussion *supra* note 149 and accompanying text; *see also Montana Law on English.* N.Y. Times. Apt. 3, 1995, at B8 (describing law that makes English official language of state government). *But see Court Strikes Language Law.* N.Y. Times, Dec. 9, 1994, at A18 (relating decision of Ninth Circuit that invalidated on First Amendment grounds amendment to Arizona Constitution requiring state employees to speak only English on job).

219. See Jack Citrin, *Language Politics and American Identity.* Pub. Interest, Spring 1990, at 96, 108 ("The instrumental consequences of state and local 'official English' legislation are virtually nil, and in the absence of a genuine threat to the status of English, the formal subordination of other languages is mainly divisive.").

220. For a description of the Americanization movements of the first two decades of the twentieth century, see Philip Gleason, *American Identity and Americanization, in* Harvard Encyclopedia, *supra* note 82, at 31, 39–41, 57–58 (entry and bibliographic sources).

221. Such classes are chronically over-subscribed, and the waiting lists are long. David Leanhardt, *Immigrants' Hopes Converge on English Class: Eager to Break Language Barrier. Would-Be Students Overwhelm Programs for Adults,* Wash. Post, July 25, 1994, at B1; Deborah Sontag, *English as a Precious Language: Immigrants Hungry for Literacy Find That Classes Are Few,* N.Y. Times, Aug. 29, 1993, at 29.

222. The current INS administration is already instituting such a change, with some success. Its timing could hardly be better. For reasons having little to do with the INS's new effort and much to do with the threat to legal immigrants' public benefits posed by pending legislation and an imminent change in Mexico's own citizenship law, *see* Sam Dillon, *Mexico Woos U.S. Mexicans. Proposing Dual Nationality,* N.Y. Times, Dec. 10, 1995, § 1, at 16 (discussing proposed Mexican constitutional amendment that would permit Mexicans living in United States to retain Mexican nationally upon becoming U.S. citizens), a stunning increase in the number of naturalization petitions is now occurring. See, e.g., Louis Freedberg, *Citizenship Wave Surprises INS: Applications Pour in as Immigrants Act to Protect Benefits,* S.F. Chron., Apr. 13, 1995, at A1, A23 (detailing increase in naturalization petitions in INS's San Francisco district and in United States). The total for 1995 will probably exceed one million.

One presumes that Brimelow opposes this development, since he thinks that naturalization should be a far more protracted process and therefore applauds the Know-Nothings' battle cry: "Nationalize, then naturalize." Alien Nation, *supra* note 1, al 12–13, 265. I believe that the current five-year minimum period, which is already longer than those in a number of immigrant nations, has served us well. In any event, most naturalizing immigrants take longer than five years. See 1994 INS Statistical Yearbook, *supra* note 29, tbl. K at 128.

223. For a recent, thoughtful exploration of some normative issues concerning citizenship, see the papers on that subject in Symposium, *Immigration Law and the New Century: The Developing Regime,* 35 Va. J. Int'l. L. 1 (1994).

224. See Alien Nation, *supra* note 1. at 232. 264–67.

225. For scholars advocating open borders, or at least a strong presumption in favor of them, see, for example, Bruce A. Ackerman, Social Justice in the Liberal State 89–95 (1980);

Joseph H. Carens, *Aliens and Citizens: The Case for Open Borders,* 49 Rev. Pol. 251 (1987); R. George Wright, *Federal Immigration Law and the Case for Open Entry,* 27 Loy. L.A. L. Rev. 1265 (1994).

226. Even the group Negative Population Growth, which is radical enough to want to reduce the U.S. population to 125–150 million (about half its present size), proposes legal immigration of up to 100,000 per year. *See* advertisement in New Republic, Oct. 23, 1995, after 37. But see Lind, *supra* note 13, at 206–07 (discussing proposals for increased immigration).

227. See Gleason, *supra* note 224, at 39–41.

228. For an interesting effort by one immigrant to define Americanism, see Ted Morgan, On Becoming American (1978).

229. For one such effort that strongly eschews "Anglo-centric" conceptions of the American nation (such as Brimelow's), see Lind, *supra* note 13, at 352–88.

230. I say "little," not none. Aliens' drug-related crime, *see supra* notes 127–46 and accompanying text, is the principal exception.

231. He tells us that he and his brother "gave it an A+." Alien Nation, *supra* note 1, at 221.

232. He says that "we still give it an A+" but then adds "what's left of it." *Id.* By this qualification he presumably means the part that the new immigrants have not yet destroyed.

233. A March 1995 Census Bureau report indicates that 30.8% of families with children were headed by a single parent in 1994; the corresponding rate was 13% in 1970. Of the 11.5 million such families, the vast majority—9.9 million—were headed by women. *2-Parent Families Increasing in U.S.,* N.Y. Times, Oct. 17, 1995, at A17.

234. See *supra* notes 160–67 and accompanying text. Other American (mis)behaviors also seem to rub off on immigrants. For example, the prostate cancer rate among Japanese men increases markedly when they immigrate to the United States, apparently because of their change to a high-fat diet here. The prostate cancer rate per 100,000 increased from eight for men in Japan to 30 for first-generation Japanese immigrants in Los Angeles and to 34 for second-generation immigrants; among white men in Los Angeles it is 66. Jane Brody, *Low-Fat Diet in Mice Slows Prostate Cancer,* N.Y. Times. Oct. 18, 1995, at C13.

235. The per capita gross national product increased almost 60% in constant dollars between 1965 and 1993: per capita disposable income increased almost 75% during the same period. 1994 U.S. Statistical Abstract, *supra* note 55, tbl. 691.

236. See sources cited *supra* note 17.

237. See, e.g., Muller, *supra* note 120, at 151–60; Louis Winnick, New People in Old Neighborhoods: The Role of New Immigrants in Rejuvenation New York's Communities (1990).

238. Brimelow's narrative of decline is commonplace today. It is also told by some who would probably agree with him on little else. See, e.g., Charles A. Reich, Opposing the System (1995).

239. Alien Nation, *supra* note 1, at 187–90.

240. For a detailed discussion of these changes, see generally Gregg Easterbrook, A Moment on the Earth: The Coming Age of Environmental Optimism (1995); Aaron Wildavsky, But is it True? A Citizen's Guide to Environmental. Health and Safety Issues (1995): The True State of the Planet: Ten of the World's Premier Environmental Researchers in a Major Challenge to the Environmental Movement (Ronald Bailey ed., 1995).

241. 42 U.S.C. §§ 1971–1973p (1988 & Supp. 1993).

242. 29 U.S.C. §§ 621–634 (1988 & Supp. 1993).

243. 42 U.S.C. §§ 6101–6107 (1988).

244. 20 U.S.C. §§ 1400–1485 (1994).

245. 42 U.S.C. §§ 12101–12213 (Supp. 1993).

246. Civil Rights Act of 1991, Pub. L. 102–166, 105 Stat. 107 (codified at scattered sections of 42 U.S.C.).

247. Indeed, one can argue that it is *too* responsive to special interests of all kinds and insufficiently deliberative.

248. See Adam Clymer, *With Political Discipline. It Works Like Parliament.* N.Y. Times, Aug. 6, 1995, § 4, at 6 (analyzing high level of party discipline among congressional Republicans and resulting improvement in discipline among congressional Democrats).

249. See *supra* note 239.

250. See Daniel T. Slesnick, *Gaining Ground: Poverty in the Postwar United States,* 101 J. Pol. Econ. 1. tbl. 3 at 16 (1993). As the share of the poor has diminished, moreover, the ranks of the wealthy have swelled. According to one estimate, the number of families with earnings of over $100,000 in constant dollars has increased from slightly more than 1 million in 1967 to 5.6 million in 1993. David Frum, *Welcome, Nouveaux Riches,* N.Y. Times, Aug. 14, 1995, at A15. For a recent account of the improved living conditions of the rural South Carolina poor between the 1960s and today, see Dana Milbank, *Up from Hunger: War on Poverty Won Some Battles as Return to Poor Region Shows,* Wall St. J., Oct. 30, 1995, at A1.

251. For an account of this development, see R. Shep Melnick, Between the Lines: Interpreting Welfare Rights 183–232 (1994). The quality of life for the most destitute Americans, including the homeless and panhandlers, has improved dramatically as well. *See* Robert C. Ellickson. *Controlling Chronic Misconduct in City Spaces: Of Panhandlers, Skid Rows, and Public-Space Zoning,* 105 Yale L.J. 1165, 1190–91, 1203–04 (1996).

252. John C. Weicher, *Private Production: Has the Rising Tide Lifted All Boats?, in* Housing America's Poor 45, 46 (Peter D. Salins ed., 1987). The data also indicate that blacks have shared in these improvements: "The percentage of black households lacking complete plumbing plunged and the percentage living with more than one person per room dropped from 28.3% in 1960 to 9.1% in 1980. The available data indicate that these auspicious trends have continued since 1980. The residential situation of the institutionalized poor has also improved as prisons, mental hospitals, and similar accommodations have become much more livable." Robert C. Ellickson, *The Untenable Case for an Unconditional Right to Shelter,* 15 Harv. J.L. & Pun. Pol. 17, 27 (1992) (footnotes omitted).

253. 1994 U.S. Statistical Abstract, *supra* note 55, tbl. 114.

254. *Id.* tbl. 120. The decline was almost as rapid for blacks and other nonwhites. Id.

255. Steven A. Holmes, *A Generally Healthy America Emerges in a Census Report,* N.Y. Times. Oct. 13, 1994, at B13.

256. The Inadequacy of many of the dominant measures of public and private wealth, income, and consumption is an old complaint. *See, e.g.,* Peter Passell, *Economic Scene,* N.Y. Times, Oct. 12, 1995. D2 (reviewing previous and current criticisms of national income accounting).

257. The difficulty of this question is not eased much by *A Tale of Ten Cities: Immigration's Effect on the Family Environment in American Cities,* a report coauthored by demographer Leon Bouvler and Scipio Garling and published by the Federation for American Immigration Reform in November 1995. Federation for American Immigration Reform, A Tale of Ten Cities: Immigration's Effect on the Family Environment in American Cities (1995). This report compares the quality of life in five pairs of matched cities, each pair of which includes a high- and a low-immigration city. The report finds in the low-immigration cities a much better quality of life, as measured by nine categories of variables: education, income, occupation, home life, housing, cultural adaptation, crime, community, and health, Comparisons of this kind, however, usually suffer from methodological weaknesses that make causal inferences highly problematic, especially the inability to control for the many variables that make the paired cities different for nonimmigration reasons. For a critique of the methodology of this report, see John E. Berthoud, FAIR's "A Tale of Ten Cities": A Fair Analysis? (Nov. 1995) (unpublished report by vice president of Alexis de Tocqueville Institution, on file with author). In addition to this serious problem, *A Tale of Ten Cities* selected high-immigration cities with large concentrations of *illegal* aliens, which inevitably distort the data. It also ignored the fact that, while most immigration-related costs are borne locally, most immigration-generated benefits (e.g., increased tax revenues and economic efficiency) are realized at higher levels.

Bibliography

Chapter 1

DeParle, Jason (1994), "Despising Welfare, Pitying its Young," *New York Times,* 18 December, E5.

Dunn, Ashley (1994), "Skilled Asians Leaving US for High-tech Jobs at Home," *New York Times,* 21 Feb., p. A1.

Espenshade, Thomas J. (1994), "Can Immigration Slow US Population Aging?," *Journal of Policy Analyses and Management,* 13, p. 759.

Espenshade, Thomas J. and Hempstead, Katherine (1997), "Contemporary American Attitudes Toward US Immigration", *International Migration Review,* 30 (Summer): 535–70.

Higham, John (1970), *Strangers in the Land: Patterns of American Nativism, 1860–1925,* 2nd edn (New York: Atheneum).

Lewontin, Richard C. (1995), "Sex, Lies, and Social Science," *New York Review of Books,* 20 Apr. p. 24

New York Times. (1994), "Americans in 2020: Less White, More Southern," 22 April, p. A1.

Schuck, Peter H. (1992), "The Politics of Rapid Legal Change: Immigration Policy in the 1980s," *Studies in American Political Development,* 6: pp. 37–92.

_____ (1995), "The Message of 187", *American Prospect,* no. 21, pp. 85–92

_____ (1996), "Alien Rumination", *Yale Law Journal,* 105, no. 7: pp. 1963–2012.

Simon, Rita J. (1995), "Immigration and Public Opinion," Paper presented at National Legal Conference on Immigration and Refugee Policy, Washington, DC, 30 Mar.

Simon, Rita J., and Susan H. Alexander (1993), *The ambivalent Welcome: Print Media, Public Opinion, and Immigration* (Westport, CT: Praeger).

Skerry, Peter (1993) *Mexican Americans: The Ambivalent Minority* (New York: Free Press).

Sniderman, Paul, and Thomas Piazza (1993), *The Scar of Race* (Cambridge: Harvard University (Press).

US Department of Justice (1996), *US Immigration and Naturalization Service, 1995; Statistical Yearbook* (Washington, DC: US Government Printing Office).

_____ (1997), *Immigration and Naturalization Service, 1996 Statistical Yearbook* (Washington, DC: US Government Printing Office).

Warren, Robert, and Kraly, Ellen Percy (1985), *The Elusive Exodus: Emigration from the United States* (Washington, DC: Population Reference Bureau).

Chapter 10

Afroyim v. Rusk, 387 U.S. 253 (1967).

Aleinikoff, T. Alexander. 1997. *Citizen and Membership: A Policy Perspective.* Washington, D.C.: Carnegie Endowment for International Peace.

_____. 1990. "Citizens, Aliens, Membership and the Constitution." *Constitutional Commentary* 7: 9.

_____. 1986. "Theories of Loss of Citizenship." *Michigan Law Review* 84: 1471.

Basch, Linda. 1985. *Nations Unbound: Transnational Projects, Postcolonial Predicaments, and Deterritorialized Nation States.* Langhorne, Pa.: Gordon and Breach.

Canada House of Commons. 1994. "Canadian Citizenship: A Sense of Belonging." Report of the Standing Committee on Citizenship and Immigration, June.

Chiappari, Ted J. 1997. "Expatriation Tax: Income Tax Liability of Expatriates and Departing Lawful Permanent Residents." In *1997–98 Immigration and Nationality Law Handbook.* Vol. 2. Washington, D.C.: American Immigration Lawyers Association.

Cott, Nancy F. 1996. "Marriage and Women's Citizenship: A Historical Excursion." Department of History, Yale University. Unpublished manuscript.

Cover, Robert M. 1983 "The Supreme Court, 1982 Term. Foreword: Nomos and Narrative." *Harvard Law Review* 97: 4.

Dillon, Sam. 1995. "Mexico Woos U.S. Mexicans, Proposing Dual Nationality." *New York Times,* December 10, p. 16.

Espenshade, Thomas J., and Haishan Fu. 1997. "An Analysis of English-Language Proficiency Among U.S. Immigrants." *American Sociological Review* 62: 288.

Fletcher, George P. 1993. *Loyalty: An Essay on the Morality of Relationships.* New York: Oxford University Press.

Fuchs, Lawrence. 1997. Letter to author, September 12.

Goldstein, Eugene, and Victoria Piazza. 1996. "Naturalization, Dual Citizenship and Retention of Foreign Citizenship: A Survey." *Interpreter Releases* 73 (April 22): 517.

Harvard Law Review. 1997. "Note: The Functionality of Citizenship." 110: 1814.

Hirschman, Albert O. 1970. *Exit, Voice, and Loyalty: Responses to Decline in Firms, Organizations, and States.* Cambridge: Harvard University Press.

Koslowski, Rey. 1997. Comments at roundtable discussion on plural citizenship, Carnegie Endowment for International Peace, April 25.

Kungys v. United States, 485 U.S. 759 (1988)

Legomsky, Stephen H. 1997. Letters to author, August 21 and September 2.

———. 1995. "Why Citizenship?" *Virginia Journal of International Law* 35: 279.

Levinson, Sanford. 1986. "Constituting Communities Through Words That Bind: Reflections on Loyalty Oaths." *Michigan Law Review* 84: 1440.

Lewis, Neil. 1997. "Reno Acts to Suspend Deportations." *New York Times,* July 11, p. A13.

Martin, David A. 1995. "The Civil Republican Ideal for Citizenship, and for Our Common Life." *Virginia Journal of International Law* 35: 301.

Neuman, Gerald L. 1997a. Letter to author, August 18.

———. 1997b. "Nationality Law in the United States and Germany: Structure and Current Problems." In *Paths to Inclusion: The Integration of Migrants in the United States and Germany,* edited by Peter Schuck and Rainer Münz (Providence, R.I.: Berghahn Books).

———. 1996. *Strangers to the Constitution: Immigrants, Borders, and Fundamental Law.* Princeton: Princeton University Press.

———. 1995. "Justifying U.S. Naturalization Policies." *Virginia Journal of International Law* 35: 237–278.

Pear, Robert. 1997. "Legal Immigrants to Benefit Under New Budget Accord." *New York Times,* July 30, p. A17.

Pickus, Noah. 1998. *Immigration and Citizenship in the Twenty-First Century.* Lanham, Md.: Rowman and Littlefield.

Portes, Alejandro. 1997. "Divergent Destinies: Immigration, the Second Generation, and the Rise of Transnational Communities." In *Paths to Inclusion: The Integration of Migrants in the United States and Germany,* edited by Peter Schuck and Rainer Münz (Providence, R.I.: Berghahn Books).

Rogers v. Bellei, 401 U.S. 815 (1971).

Sack, Kevin. 1997. "Louisiana Approves Measure to Tighten Marriage Bonds." *New York Times,* June 24, p. 1.

Safire, William. 1985. "Citizen of the World." *New York Times,* May 16, p. A31.

Schneider v. Rusk, 377 U.S. 163 (1964).

Schuck, Peter H. 1997a. "The Re-Evaluation of American Citizenship." *Georgetown Immigration Law Journal* 12: 1. Also in *Challenge to the Nation-State: Immigration in Western Europe and the United States,* edited by Christian Joppke (Oxford and New York: Oxford University Press, 1998).

_____. 1997b. "Refugee Burden-Sharing: A Modest Proposal." *Yale Journal of International Law* 22: 243.

_____. 1995. "Whose Membership Is It, Anyway? Comments on Gerald Neuman." *Virginia Journal of International Law* 35: 321.

_____. 1994a. Expert testimony in *Lavoie v. The Queen,* Federal Court of Canada, Trial Division, October.

_____. 1994b. "Rethinking Informed Consent." *Yale Law Journal* 103: 899.

Schuck, Peter H., and Bruce Brown. 1997. "Lessons from Lippo." *Wall Street Journal,* February 27, p. A16.

Schuck, Peter, and Rainer Münz, eds. 1997. *Paths to Inclusion: The Integration of Migrants in the United States and Germany.* Providence, R.I.: Berghahn Books.

Schuck, Peter H., and Rogers M. Smith. 1985. *Citizenship Without Consent: Illegal Aliens in the American Polity.* New Haven: Yale University Press.

Sengupta, Somini. 1996. "Immigrants in New York Pressing Drive for Dual Nationality." *New York Times,* December 30, p. B1.

Skerry, Peter. 1993. *Mexican-Americans: The Ambivalent Minority.* New York: The Free Press.

Spiro, Peter J. 1997. "Dual Nationality and the Meaning of Citizenship." *Emory Law Journal* 46: 1411.

Tomas Rivera Center. 1996. "Dual Citizenship, Domestic Politics and Naturalization Rates of Latino Immigrants in the U.S." Policy Brief, June.

U.S. Congress. 1997. Hearing before the Subcommittee on Immigration and Claims, House Judiciary Committee. 105th Congress, 1st Session, June 25, 1997. Unpublished.

_____. 1996. "Societal and Legal Issues Surrounding Children Born in the United States to Illegal Alien Parents." Joint Hearing before the Subcommittee on Immigration and Claims and the Subcommittee on the Constitution, House Judiciary Committee. 104th Congress, 1st Session, December 13, 1995. Serial No. 50. Washington, D.C.: Government Printing Office.

U.S. Department of State. 1990. "Advice about Possible Loss of U.S. Citizenship and Dual Nationality." Reprinted in *Interpreter Releases* 67: 1093.

U.S. General Accounting Office. 1997. "Naturalization of Aliens: INS Internal Controls." Testimony before the Subcommittee on Immigration, Senate Judiciary Committee, May 1, GAO/T-GGD-97-98.

Vargas, Jorge A. 1996. "Dual Nationality for Mexicans? A Comparative Legal Analysis of the Dual Nationality Proposal and Its Eventual Political and Socio-Economic Implications." *Chicano-Latino Law Review* 18: 1–58.

Walzer, Michael. 1983. *Spheres of Justice: A Defense of Pluralism and Equality.* New York: Basic Books.

West Virginia State Board of Education v. Barnette, 319 U.S. 624, 642 (1943).

Index

Abraham, Spencer, 147
Administrative Procedure Act of 1982
  (APA). *See* Legislation
Administrative review, 69
"Adversely affected" countries, 116
Afroyim v. Rusk, 227, 228, 235
Aid to Families with Dependent
  Children (AFDC), 192, 194, 256
Alien and Sedition Acts, 220, 352
Alienkoff, Alexander, 72, 237
Alien Nation, 326–358. *See also*
  Brimelow, Peter
Aliens. *See* Immigration
American Civil Liberties Union
  (ACLU), 122, 126
American Federation of
  Labor–Congress of Industrial
  Organizations (AFL-CIO), 113,
  114, 118, 120
American Immigration Lawyers'
  Association, 115
Americans with Disabilities Act of
  1990. *See* Legislation
Amnesty. *See* Immigration, amnesty
Amnesty International, 139
Anderson, Benedict, 183
Anti-Terrorism and Effective Death
  Penalty Act of 1996 (AEDPA). *See*
  Legislation
Armey, Richard, 6, 142
Ascription. *See* Citizenship, ascriptive
  view of
Asylees. *See* Immigration
Attorney General, 57–58, 67, 75

Balzac v. People of Porto Rico, 27
Bean, Frank, 345
Bennett, William, 6, 142, 158
Bickel, Alexander, 26, 27, 163, 184

Bilingualism. *See* English language
Black, (Justice) Hugo, 36
Board of Immigration Appeals (BIA),
  62, 66–67, 75
Booz, Allen, & Hamilton, 133
Border control, 45–46, 83, 98, 102,
  106, 112, 125, 142, 145, 157,
  180, 181, 183–184, 202, 213,
  295, 342, 352
  public attitudes toward, 71–72, 130
  and sovereignty, 46, 56, 183–184
Border Patrol, 70, 72, 140, 146, 156,
  330, 343
Borjas, George, 278, 339
Boskin, Michael, 124
Bouvier, Leon, 335
Bracero program, 12, 28, 67–68, 104,
  113
Brandeis, (Justice) Louis D., 131
Brennan, (Justice) William J., 149–151
Brimelow, Peter, xv, 326–358
Brooks, Jack, 116, 118, 123, 125, 126
Brown v. Board of Education, 54
Brumer, Senator, 125
Bryant, John, 124
Buchanan, Patrick, 6, 141
Burden of proof, 60, 132
Bush, Governor George, 142

California, xiii, 33, 47, 72, 89, 104,
  112, 141, 142, 143, 147, 153,
  155, 190, 253. *See also*
  Proposition 187
Calvin's Case, 208–209
Campbell, Tom, 133
Carter administration, 64, 97, 103
Carter, Jimmy (President), 101
Carter, Stephen, 262
Cato Institute, 133

Chain migration. *See* Family
    unification
Chinese Exclusion Act of 1882. *See*
    Legislation
The Chinese Exclusion Case, 29
Citizens, xii, 1
    differences among, 26–27
    differences between non-citizens
        and, 26
    equality of birthright and
        naturalized, 26, 241
    equality with non-citizens, 26
    rights of, 26–27, 29, 173, 184, 227,
        242
Citizenship, 147, 352–353
    advantages of, 163, 186–190, 225
    ascriptive view of, 207–209, 211,
        215, 218
    birthright, xiii, 142, 161, 164, 170,
        177, 179, 182, 185, 193, 207,
        212, 220, 226, 236, 241, 247
    for children of illegal aliens born in
        the U.S., 142, 170–171, 182, 193,
        212–213, 214–215, 221, 352
    concept of, 26, 217
    and consent, 168–171, 209–211,
        213, 244
    and definition of national
        community, 25–26, 161, 177–178
    descent, 26, 179, 185, 207, 226,
        236, 241, 247
    devaluation of, xiii, 161, 171–175,
        177, 186, 192–193, 220
    difficulty of obtaining, 25–26, 67,
        163, 171, 184
    in the domestic domain, 178,
        184–193
    dual. *See* Plural citizenship
    in English law, 208
    in the federal system, 177,
        193–202
    in the international domain,
        177–178, 179–184
    and liberal society, 26
    loss of, 168, 186, 208, 211, 226
    marriage analogy, 217–218,
        240–241, 243
    plural. *See* Plural citizenship
    "post-national," 178, 202–205
    public attitudes toward, 163,
        172–174, 176, 184, 192, 240
    reevaluation of, xiii, 161, 176–206,
        220
    right of expatriation, 212
*Citizenship Without Consent: Illegal
    Aliens in the American Polity*,
    161, 215
City of Richmond v. J.A. Croson, 254
Civil liberties and rights, 95–96, 103,
    120
Civil Rights Amendments of 1991. *See*
    Legislation
Civil rights movement, 191, 249
    conflict with immigrants, 255–257
    political influence of, 255, 257–261,
        261–262
    problems in, 252, 256–257
Clark, Rebecca, 340
Classical conception of immigration,
    xii, xiv, 17, 20–21, 22–39, 48, 53,
    73
    and the "civil" nature of
        deportation, 34–35, 62–63,
        167
    and consent-based obligation, 45,
        48, 60, 68
    and the equal protection principle,
        32–34
    and the extraconstitutional status of
        exclusion, 31–32, 59–61, 136
    and judicial deference, 29–31, 34
    and non-independent adjudication,
        37–39
    and the power to classify aliens,
        32–34
    and the power to detain, 35–37
    and property law 23–24
    and the restrictive ideal of the
        national community, 25–29, 34,
        37, 45, 48, 49, 77
    and sovereignty, 37, 45, 48, 56, 134
    tensions in, 69
Clean Air Act Amendments of 1990.
    See Legislation

Clinton administration, 90, 182, 343, 346

Clinton, Bill (President), 140, 142, 143, 252

Coke, Sir Edward, 207–209

Cold War, 183, 191

Communitarian
conception of immigration, xiv, 17, 21–22, 24–25, 54–67
legal order, 50–51, 69
tensions in, 69
values, 51, 53, 66, 73, 78

Community (also national community), 25, 37, 41, 54–57, 61–62, 72, 76–80, 161, 171–173, 174, 184, 208, 238
immigrants relationship to, 35, 46, 171–172
and legal status, 25
restrictive ideal of, 25–29, 34, 45, 48, 77

Conference on Central American Refugees (1989), 303

Congress, xii, xiii, 1, 29, 34, 39, 55, 59, 72, 76, 89–90, 93, 133, 136, 139, 144, 153, 159, 198–199, 261, 298
committee structure, 117
delegation of immigration authority, 31
legislation. *See* Legislation
in the 1980s, 91–138
and paradigms of causal explanation advanced by political scientists, 92–96
policy-making by, 91–93
power to regulate immigration, 39, 56, 61–62, 103, 132, 186, 188, 227
restrictionists' failure in 1996, 10, 14
restrictionists' influence in, 114
shaping definition of national community, 28

Comprehensive Plan of Action and Orderly Departure Program in Southeast Asia (CPA), 284–285, 287, 290–293, 296, 303

Consent, 20–21, 23–24, 37, 45, 48, 49, 50, 51, 60, 61, 65, 66, 78, 163, 165, 168–171, 178, 225–227

Constitution
and citizenship, 164
and exclusion, 31–32, 59–61, 78, 136, 167
and federal power over immigration, 33–34, 39, 186
rights guaranteed under, 34
See also Citizenship; Equal protection; Procedural rights

"Contract with America," 141

Cornelius, Wayne, 153

Council on Affordable Housing, 319

Countries of first asylum, 100, 101, 289, 291, 304

Courts, xii, xiv, 17, 19, 28, 29, 41, 53, 64–65, 81, ch. 3, 93, 102, 203, 254–255
and judicial deference, 29–31, 34, 50, 57–59, 61–62, 67, 74, 75, 83, 174
lower, 57, 62, 65, 67
role of, 73–76, 132

Cousins, Norman, 7

Cover, Robert, 217

Cronkite, Walter, 7

De Canas v. Bica, 56, 57

DeConcini, Senator Dennis, 126

Democrats, 105, 106, 107, 109, 110, 111, 115, 116, 126, 142, 262, 346, 351

Denationalization. *See* Citizenship, loss of

Deportation. *See* Enforcement, removal; Immigration, deportation

Deterrence of illegal immigration, 45, 70–73

Devolution, 193–195

Dillingham Commission, 11, 103, 342

Douglas, (Justice) William O., 167, 189

Downes v. Bidwell. See The Insular Cases

Dred Scott case, 27, 149, 213

Dual citizenship. *See* Plural citizenship

Due process. *See* Procedural rights

Duties. *See* Legal duties

Education, 146
  bilingual, 147, 190, 191, 261
  public. *See* Immigration, public
    services and benefits and
Eliade, Mircea, 183
Enforcement, 45, 55–56, 109, 136,
    143
  and adjudication, 66–67, 82
  anti-discrimination program, 13,
    107, 109, 110, 130, 137, 251
  cancellation of removal, xiv, 15, 69,
    144, 145, 154
  criminal aliens, removal of, 13, 15,
    139, 144, 153
  deportation. *See* Enforcement,
    removal; Immigration,
    deportation
  detention, xiv, 15, 35–37, 59–60,
    63–66, 74
  discretionary relief. *See*
    Enforcement, cancellation of
    removal
  effectiveness of, 70–71, 99, 129,
    130, 139, 142, 152, 159, 181,
    342, 352
  employee verification system, 105,
    106, 125, 126. *See also*
    Identification cards
  employer sanctions, 13, 72, 84, 98,
    99, 103, 105, 106, 107, 110, 113,
    114, 126, 129, 130, 152, 343
  exclusion, 31–32, 50, 59–61, 77.
    See also Enforcement, removal
  formal deportation vs. "voluntary
    departure," 70
  judicial review of, xiv, 1, 15, 17,
    144, 174
  of labor certification, 43
  legalization, 105, 107, 109, 113,
    129, 140, 328
  marriage fraud aliens, removal of,
    13, 122, 140
  parole, 36, 100, 101
  and public opinion, 47–48
  risk of removal, 167
  removal, xiv, 15, 29, 44, 57–59,
    62–66, 74, 75, 84, 116, 131, 145,
    167

  stay of deportation, 44, 57–59
  summary removal. *See* Enforcement,
    removal
English language, xiii, 8, 94, 142, 147,
    155, 190–191, 220, 238, 250,
    343–344, 348, 352, 353
Equal protection, 27–28, 32–33, 53,
    54, 57, 77, 130, 132, 151, 157,
    163, 164–167, 170, 173, 174,
    187, 196, 251, 254
  exceptions to, 166–167
  and relevant differences, 164
  and tension between equality and
    liberty, 165
  and tension between
    majoritarianism and minority
    rights, 165
European Free Trade Area, 180
European Union, 180
Executive Office for Immigration
    Review (EOIR), 67, 82, 83
Expansionism. *See* Immigration, public
    attitudes toward
Expatriation. *See* Citizenship, loss of
Extended Voluntary Departure (EVD),
    57–59, 74, 75, 99

Family unification, 95, 98, 103, 114,
    115, 117, 119, 121, 122, 124,
    125, 131, 133, 134–135, 136,
    138, 158, 166, 182, 188, 254,
    327, 328, 334, 338
Federal Communications Commission,
    221
Federal preemption, 57, 186–188, 197
Federal subsidies to states, 107, 111,
    117, 157
Federation for American Immigration
    Reform (FAIR), 7, 94, 97, 98,
    110, 111, 142
Fernandez-Roque v. Smith, 65, 71, 74
Fiallo v. Bell, 61
Field, (Justice) Stephen, 29
Florida, 47, 97, 101, 104, 112, 156,
    200, 255
Food stamps, 143, 194, 205, 256,
    357

Foreign policy considerations, 29, 74, 75, 119, 196
  constraining of, 40–41
  and judicial deference, 31, 58–59
  See also Immigration, and foreign policy; Globalization
Fourteenth Amendment. *See* Citizenship; Equal protection; Procedural rights
Frank, Barney, 109, 122–123, 127
Fuchs, Lawrence, 103, 122

General Accounting Office (GAO), 109, 146
Gere, Richard, 123
Gill, 303
Gingrich, Newt (Speaker of the House of Representatives), 6, 142, 158
Globalization, 95, 114, 132, 134, 174, 180–181, 220
Goodwin-Gill, 303
Gramm, Phil (Senator), 109
Great Society, 91, 194
Group litigation. *See* Impact litigation
Guestworkers. *See* Labor, agricultural; Temporary workers
Guinier, Lani, 255

Habeas corpus, 29, 64, 144
Haitian Refugee Center v. Smith, 66
Hall, Peter, 96, 130
Hampton v. Mow Sun Wong, 61
Hardwood, Edwin, 70
Hartman, David, 240
Hathaway, James C., 287
Hayakawa, S.I., 7
Hegel, Fredrich, 240
Helms, Jesse, 124, 296
Heritage Foundation, 133, 159
Hesburgh Commission (also SCRIP), 97, 98, 103, 104, 105, 113, 129, 331
Hesburgh, Father Theodore, 97
Higham, John, 6
Hirschman, Albert, 236
Holmes, (Justice) Oliver Wendell, Jr., 49

Hotel & Restaurant Employees Union, Local 25 v. Smith, 57–59, 62, 74
House of Representatives, 105, 119
  Agriculture Committee, 107
  Education and Labor Committee, 107, 118
  Energy and Commerce Committee, 107
  Foreign Affairs Committee, 121
  Immigration subcommittee, 116, 142
  Judiciary Committee, 105, 107, 108, 116
  Rules Committee, 106, 107, 108, 123, 126
  Ways and Means Committee, 119
H–2 program, 68, 110, 113
Huddle, Donald, 339
Huddleston, Walter (Dee) (Senator), 98, 111
Hudson Institute, 133
Human rights, 66, 77, 78, 95, 101, 128, 133, 135, 165, 204, 210, 233, 284, 302, 303, 334
Human rights advocates. *See* Interest groups

Ideas, role in policy, 95, 111, 128–137
  and belief changing, 129
  and coalition building, 128–129
  and dissonance reducing, 130–131
  and policy design, 135–137
  and policy purpose, 133–135
  and regime reinforcing, 130
  and rule of law, 131–133, 135, 162
  and symbol mobilizing, 129–130
Identification cards, 126–127, 156, 261
Ideological exclusion, 83, 99, 122, 130, 136, 141
Illegal aliens. *See* Immigration, illegal.
Illegal Immigration Reform and Immigrant Responsibility Act of 1996 (IIRIRA). *See* Legislation
Illinois, 47
Immigrants. *See* Immigration
Immigration, and immigrants

affirmative action and, xiii, 147, 191, 250, 251, 258–260, 267–268, 350–352

"alien protection jurisprudence" hypothesis, 17, 83–87

amnesty, xiv, 12, 13, 15, 72, 98, 99, 106, 108, 110, 113, 140, 141, 145, 170, 179, 182, 188–189, 212, 352–353

assimilation of, xiii, 25, 171, 190, 220, 228, 237–238, 244, 249, 278–279, 334, 341–346, 353

asylum and asylees, xii, xiv, 1, 43–45, 65, 74, 82, 83, 85, 86–87, 92, 97, 99, 100, 131, 132, 141, 144, 145, 156, 254, 327

bars to aliens' return to U.S., 15

and business cycle, 332–334

caps, 116, 117, 118, 122, 125, 135

carrying capacity, 335–337

caseload, 63

children of, 55, 132, 151

civil rights and, xiii, 103, 104, 120, 130, 191, 249, 251–263

"classical" conception of. *See* Classical conception of immigration

classifications, xii, 32–34, 61–62, 166

"communitarian" conception of. *See* Communitarian conception of immigration

and the community, 46, 184

controls on, history of, 11–15

courts and. *See* Courts

criminal, 13, 116, 126, 139, 140, 142, 143, 144, 146, 147, 157, 341–343

culture and, 268–271, 275

demographics, xii, 3–4, 23, 42, 47–48, 54, 63–64, 82, 89, 92, 146, 156, 162, 181–182, 252, 253, 267–268, 271–273, 329–335

deterrence of illegal. *See* Deterrence of illegal immigration

deportation, 34–35, 62–63, 75. *See also* Enforcement, removal

and discrimination, xiii, 13, 61–62, 89, 159, 188, 199, 200, 273–275

diversity program, 13, 14, 99, 117, 118, 119, 135, 140, 254, 327, 328

effects on economy, 155, 337–341, 339, 356–358

effects on low-income Americans, 7

enforcement. *See* Enforcement

and the environment, 335, 337, 355–356

external effects on, 102

and foreign policy, 19, 31, 100, 119

geographic concentration of, 11, 12, 33, 47, 102, 119, 197, 213, 253

illegal, xi, xvii, 12, 45–46, 55, 69, 95, 98, 103, 107, 113, 114, 125, 129, 131, 133, 139, 141, 142, 145–146, 149, 151, 153, 154, 160, 167, 170, 179, 181, 200, 330–331

and illegitimacy, 344–346

immigrants attitudes toward, 9

incarceration of, 35–37, 64

integration. *See* Immigration, assimilation of

judges, 37–39, 82

law. *See* Immigration Law

lawyers for immigrants, xiv, 83, 114

legal admissions system, 13–14

legal residents, xii, 65, 158, 167, 177, 179, 184, 188–189

legislation. *See* Legislation

legitimacy of, 67, 69–73, 87, 216

litigation. *See* Immigration litigation

moral claims of, 19, 35, 46, 157, 184, 213, 215

multiculturalism and, xiii, 7, 70, 172, 181, 190–191, 203, 250, 279, 347–348, 348–350

new (post–1965), xii, 89, 140, 329, 331, 332–334, 337, 346, 350

in other countries, 68, 92, 141, 149, 156, 169, 175, 179, 185, 190, 191, 193, 205, 214, 280

political influence of, 30, 33, 47–48, 73, 253, 276–278, 346–354 politics of, xiii, 1, 10–11, 19, 31, 32, 103, 117, 139, 141, 356

public attitudes toward, xii, xiii, 4–11, 20, 23, 33, 47–48, 73, 92, 94–95, 98, 99, 102, 103, 107, 111, 112, 114, 130, 132, 137, 139–140, 141, 143, 147, 149, 155, 172–174, 181–182, 183, 190, 220, 257–261, 342

and public safety, 94, 183

public services and benefits and, xiii, 55, 90, 110, 113, 117, 132, 136, 139, 141, 142, 143, 150, 151, 153, 182, 186, 189–190, 192, 199–200, 225, 256, 338, 339–340, 357

quotas, 28, 33, 78, 89, 97, 110, 128, 129, 135, 136, 140, 145, 252

refugees. *See* Refugees

relationship to government, 67, 195

rights of, 1, 19, 30, 64, 65, 130, 132, 173, 179, 227. *See also* Equal protection; Procedural rights

role of ideas. *See* Ideas, role in policy

role of President, 31, 58–59

role of states in, 30–31, 150, 186–187, 197, 225

and sovereignty, 19, 23–24, 48, 59, 134

success of, 264–281

and technological change, 191, 220, 221

undocumented. *See* Immigration, illegal

volume and characteristics of, 3–4, 23, 36–37, 54, 63–64, 67, 69, 80, 82, 92, 99, 136, 140, 150, 156, 171, 179, 181–182, 224, 252, 329–332

as workers, 83, 106, 136, 141, 182, 191, 255–256, 276–278, 327

Immigration Act of 1917. *See* Legislation

Immigration Act of 1921. *See* Legislation

Immigration Act of 1924. *See* Legislation

Immigration Act of 1990. *See* Legislation

Immigration and Nationality Act of 1952. *See* Legislation

Immigration and Nationality Act of 1978. *See* Legislation

Immigration and Nationality Amendments of 1965. *See* Legislation

Immigration and Naturalization Service (INS), 30, 37–39, 45, 64–65, 66–67, 70, 82, 83, 123, 124

abuses, 73, 75, 139, 154, 298

collaborative relationships, 87

efficiency, 72, 130, 140, 142, 146, 342–343, 352

errors, 74

policies, 75–76, 82, 99

resources, 72

Immigration law

distinctiveness of, 19–20, 21, 39, 50, 68, 81

pressures for change in, 39–54

transformation of, ch. 2

Immigration litigation, 82–87, 99

Immigration Marriage Fraud Amendments of 1986. *See* Legislation

Immigration Reform and Control Act of 1986. *See* Legislation

Impact litigation, 52–53, 64, 84–87

Incrementalism, 92

"Independent" workers, 115

Individualism, 24, 48–50, 78. *See also* Liberalism

The Insular Cases, 27, 49

"Interest group liberalism," 92

Interest groups, 91, 93, 94–95, 136

balance of, 110–127

blacks, 127, 261

business, 73, 92, 103, 111, 113–119, 129, 133, 231

environmental, 94, 107, 142, 147

ethnic, 103, 107, 115, 118, 119–122, 141

growers, 103, 105, 107, 108, 109,
 112–113
Hispanic, 103, 104, 106, 107, 108,
 109, 112, 121–122, 126, 127,
 252, 261, 262
human rights advocates, 115,
 122–127
Irish, 115, 116, 120
organized labor, 94, 104, 107, 111,
 113–119, 126, 147
population control, 94, 142
strength of, 111
See also Civil rights movement
"Interest representation" model of
 administrative law, 52
International community, 231, 289
International human rights, xiii, 128,
 233

Jackson, (Justice) Robert H., 31
Jacobson, David, 183, 202–204
Jencks, Christopher, 260, 263
Jordan, Barbara, 144
Judicial deference. *See* Courts, and
 judicial deference
Judicial review, 69
Jus Sanguinis. See Citizenship, descent
Jus Soli. See Citizenship, birthright
Justice Department, 67, 87, 123, 254,
 351

Kelly, Alex, 221
Kemp, Jack, 6, 142, 158
Kennedy, Duncan, 48
Kennedy, Edward (Senator), 97, 104,
 106. 107, 109, 114, 115, 116, 117,
 118, 124, 125, 126, 129
Kennedy, Randall, 262
Kettner, James, 209
Kirkland, Lane, 114
Kline, Garner, 105
Kristol, William, 142

Labor
 agricultural, 98, 107, 110, 113, 159
 certification, 43, 135
 displacement, 338, 340–341

high-skilled, 114, 115, 145
 illegal workers, 98, 254
 low-skilled, 114, 124, 338
 market, 42–43, 118, 133, 135, 155,
  191, 276–278, 338
 rights of workers, 83, 107, 108, 130
 skill of workers, 95, 129, 133, 135,
  136, 327
 standards, 43, 107, 130
 supply, 42, 82, 105, 113, 125, 129,
  155, 191
 unions, 43
Lamm, Richard, 7
Landon v. Plasencia, 60
Lautenberg, Senator Frank, 121
Law
 administrative, 52, 53, 64, 68, 75, 83
 confidence in, 45
 contract, 51
 immigration. *See* Immigration Law
 incentive structures created by, 69–71,
  117, 152, 212, 225
 private, 50, 51–52, 68
 public, 50
 theories of obligation in, 51–54, 61,
  66, 68
 tort, 51–52, 53
Lawyers Committee for Human Rights,
 87
Lazarus, Emma, 25
Legal duties, 50, 66, 68
Legal resident aliens. *See* Immigration
Legislation (listed chronologically)
 Chinese Exclusion Act of 1882, 6, 27,
  112, 261, 273
 Immigration Act of 1917, 27, 37, 38,
  67
 Immigration Act of 1921, 27
 Immigration Act of 1924, 27, 67
 National Origins Act of 1924, 11–12
 Immigration and Nationality Act of
  1952, 28, 38–39
 McCarran-Walters Act of 1952, 67
 Immigration and Nationality Act
  Amendments of 1965, 12, 92, 97,
  104, 105, 120, 136, 138, 190, 252,
  328
 Immigration and Nationality Act of
  1978, 28

Refugee Act of 1980, 1, 13, 14, 17, 44, 62, 64, 65, 72, 82, 99, 101, 104, 136, 138, 140

Administrative Procedure Act of 1982 (APA), 37–39

Simpson-Mazzoli immigration reform legislation, 31–32, 71, 76

Immigration Marriage Fraud Amendments of 1986, 13, 122

Immigration Reform and Control Act of 1986 (IRCA), xiv, 13, 82, 98, 99, 103, 104, 105, 106, 109, 110, 113, 114, 116, 118, 122, 123, 127, 130, 138, 159, 181, 254, 261

Moakley-DeConcini bill, 123, 125, 126

Americans with Disabilities Act of 1990, 252

Clean Air Act Amendments of 1990, 319, 320

Immigration Act of 1990, xiii, xiv, 10, 13, 14, 82, 89, 97, 98, 103, 120, 128, 133, 135, 137, 140, 145, 252, 254, 261, 338

Civil Rights Amendments of 1991, 252

Anti-Terrorism and Effective Death Penalty Act of 1996 (AEDPA), 142–143, 145

Illegal Immigration Reform and Immigrant Responsibility Act of 1996 (IIRIRA), xiv, 13, 14–15, 17, 143, 144, 145, 146

Personal Responsibility and Work Opportunity Reconciliation Act of 1996, xiv, 8, 187, 192, 197, 203, 232, 237

Nicaraguan Adjustment and Central American Relief Act of 1997, 158

Legitimacy, 69–73

Legomsky, Stephen, 245, 246

Lesbian/Gay Freedom Day Committee, Inc. v. INS, 60

Levinson, Sanford, 228, 232, 240, 243

Lewis, Tony, 139

Liberalism, 20, 68, 72, 76–78, 134, 163, 173
and consent, 24
and universal rights, 24, 27, 50, 72, 77, 165, 202, 210

Lincoln, Abraham, 6

Locke, John, 209–210

Los Angeles, 102, 147, 155, 187, 253, 255, 256, 260, 262

Loury, Glenn, 263

McCarran-Walters Act of 1952. *See* Legislation

McCarthy era, 177

MacNeil, Ian, 51

Marcello v. Bonds, 38

Mariel boatlift, 44, 94, 97, 101, 102, 131

Martin, David, 65, 184

Mathews v. Diaz, 61–62, 158, 200

Mazzoli, Romano, 105, 106, 115, 116, 117

Media, 93

Medicare and Medicaid, 186, 194, 204, 357

Meese, Edwin, 109

Mexican American Legal Defense and Education Fund, 139

Miami, 102, 117, 255, 256

Migrations and Cultures: A World View, 264–281

Moakley-DeConcini bill. *See* Legislation

Moakley, Joseph (Representative), 123, 126

Morrison, Bruce, 106, 114, 116, 117, 118, 119, 120, 121, 123, 124, 125, 129, 133, 135, 137

Mount Laurel litigation, 319

Murdoch, Rupert, 221

National Association for the Advancement of Colored People (NAACP), 252

National community. *See* Community

National Community Service Corps, 192

National identity. *See* Community

Nationalism, 23

National Origins Act of 1924. *See*
Legislation
Nationhood, 25. *See also* Community
Nativism. *See* Immigration, public
attitudes toward
Naturalization, 159, 177, 179, 185,
225, 237, 242
demographics, 168
disadvantages of, 169, 187
incentives to, 163, 166–167, 169,
187, 188–189, 192–193, 227
oath, 243
volume, 168–170
Natural rights, 50, 79
Neuman, Gerald, 229, 241
New Deal, 91, 194, 205
"The New Institutionalism," 92
New Jersey, 47, 143, 319
New York City, 255, 256, 260, 336
New York (state), 33, 47, 104, 143, 147
New York Times, 139
Nicaraguan Adjustment and Central
American Relief Act of 1997. *See*
Legislation
Ninth Circuit, 62, 84, 85, 86
Non-governmental organizations
(NGOs), 289, 308, 312
Non-refoulement, duty of, 289, 297,
303
North American Free Trade Agreement
(NAFTA), 141, 180, 295

O'Connor, (Justice) Sandra Day, 154
O'Croidan, Daire, 115
O'Neill, Tip (Speaker of the House of
Representatives), 106, 107, 120
Orderly Departure Program (ODP), 290,
291, 292. *See also* Comprehensive
Plan of Action
Organization of Chinese Americans, 121

Passel, Jeffrey, 340
The Passenger Cases, 195
Personal Responsibility and Work
Opportunity Reconciliation Act of
1996. *See* Legislation
Piazza, Thomas, 8

Plenary power doctrine, 194–195. *See
also* Congress; Federal preemption
Plural citizenship, xiii, 162, 177, 185,
217–247
benefits, 230–232, 243
contemporary debate, 220–224
costs, 232–242
demographics of, 221, 236–237
effects of, 224–225
laws of other countries, 222–223,
235, 236–237
and loyalty, 238–240, 243, 244–247
motives for retaining, 222, 228, 237
and national community, 236, 238
reforms of, 242–247
renunciation, 222, 223, 226, 229,
244
Plyler v. Doe, 54–57, 62, 68, 72, 74,
150–154
Policy making, 91–93
Porter, Roger, 124
Portes, Alejandro, 279, 345–346
President. *See* Immigration, role of
President
Price, Hugh, 263
Private law. *See* Law, private
Privilege, 62. *See also* Right-privilege
distinction
Procedural rights, 27–28, 31–32, 35,
37–39, 45, 52, 53, 57, 60, 62–66,
69, 70, 74–75, 91, 96, 131, 132,
144, 153, 157, 163, 167–168,
170, 173, 174, 179, 225, 254
Property rights, 23–24, 53
Proposition 187, xiii, 6, 89, 141, 147,
149–162, 182, 197, 234
constitutionality of, 150–154
focus on illegal aliens, 155
and *Plyler v. Doe*, 150–154
and public attitudes toward
immigration, 149
Public law. *See* Law, public

Racism, 327. *See* Immigration, public
attitudes toward
Raspberry, William, 263
Rational choice theory, 92, 93, 96

Reagan administration, 64, 97, 124, 126
"Reagan Revolution," 91
Reagan, Ronald (President), 105–106
Reform of Refugee Protection, 293–301
  economic development, 295–296
  eliminating root causes, 285, 294–296
  prompt repatriation, 285, 296–297
  temporary protection, 285, 297–300
  permanent resettlement, 285, 300–301. *See also* Refugee Burden Sharing
Refugee Act of 1980. *See* Legislation
Refugee Burden Sharing, 285–287, 301–317
  administration, 287, 302–303, 307–309, 309–312, 318–322
  anticipated objections, 287, 318–325
  capacity, 310–312
  creation of a market, 286, 312–317
  incentives to participate, 285–286, 303, 312–317, 318–319
  proportionality, 285, 303–307, 309–312
  regional character, 285–286, 309, 311, 321
  safeguards, 309, 311, 316, 322–324
Refugee Convention, 309, 322
Refugees, xii, xiv, 97, 100, 103, 104, 114, 130, 134, 159, 327
  ability to qualify for asylum status, 44, 287–288, 297
  costs, 289, 291, 302
  current regime for protecting, 282, 283, 287–290
  demographics, 43–45, 97, 119, 130, 142, 282, 283, 289–290, 304
  public opinion on, 130, 288
  receiving regions, 283, 288, 289, 304, 312
  risk of receiving, 304–306
  safeguards for, 297
  source countries, 43, 44, 146, 190, 205, 295
  volume, 43–45, 97, 130, 153, 205, 282, 304

  See also Comprehensive Plan of Action; Immigration; Reform of Refugee Protection; Refugee Burden Sharing
Rehnquist, (Justice) William, 154
Reno v. Shaw, 255
Replenishment workers, 108, 113
Republicans, 106, 107, 109, 116, 133, 141, 142, 147, 158, 194, 254, 262, 346
Restrictionism. *See* Immigration, public attitudes toward
"Restrictive nationalism." *See* Classical conception of immigration; Immigration, public attitudes toward
Right-privilege distinction, 48–50
Rights
  of groups, 50, 174, 204, 258–260
  See also Immigration and immigrants, rights of; Liberalism, and universal rights
Rodino, Peter, 105, 108, 115, 116, 126
Rogers v. Bellei, 227
Roybal, Ed, 126

SALT II accord, 100
Sanctuary, 738
Scalia, (Justice) Antonin, 154
Schauer, Fred, 172
Schlesinger, Arthur, 147
Schneider v. Rusk, 241
Schumer, Charles, 108, 109, 125
Select Commission on Immigration and Refugee Policy (SCRIP). *See* Hesburgh Commission
Senate, 110, 115, 123
  Immigration subcommittee, 147
  Judiciary Committee, 117
Separation of powers, 91
Shaughnessy v. United States ex rel. Mezei, 32, 36
Sierra Club, 7, 147
Simon, Julian, 133
Simon, Rita, 9
Simpson, Alan (Senator), 104–105, 106, 107, 108, 109, 110, 115, 116,

117, 118, 123, 124, 125, 126, 127, 129, 158
Simpson-Mazzoli immigration reform legislation. *See* Legislation
Skocpol, Theda, 263
Smith, Christopher (Representative), 296
Smith, Lamar, 142, 147
Smith, Rogers, 170, 215, 352
Smith, William French, 98, 105
Sniderman, Paul, 8
Solarz, Steven, 121
Sovereignty, 19, 23–24, 37, 39, 41, 45, 46, 48, 50, 52, 59, 60, 66, 68, 152, 177, 196, 284
and judicial deference, 30–31
Sowell, Thomas, 264–281
Soysal, Yasemin, 202–204
Spanish-American War, xi
Spiro, Peter, 198, 232, 233, 234–235, 238
Starr, Paul, 263
States. *See* Immigration, role of states in
Steele, Shelby, 263
Steering Committee of the International Conference on Indochine Refugees, 293
Stewart, Richard, 52
Structural relief, 75. *See also* Impact litigation
Substantive justice, 66
Supplemental Security Income (SSI), 90, 142, 158, 194, 205
Suspension Clause, 144
Swain, Carol, 255

Taxpayers, 42
Technological innovation, 43, 221
Temporary protected status (TPS), 126, 254, 299
Temporary workers, 108, 112, 114, 115, 117, 118, 119, 125, 159, 181
Territorial control. *See* Border control
Terrorism, 183
Texas, 33, 47, 104, 112, 117, 142, 153, 156, 256, 262
Thomas, (Justice) Clarence, 154

Thornburn, Joanne, 303
Thurmond, Strom (Senator), 104, 105
Tianamen Square, 121
Transnational communities, 230
Treaty of Paris, xi
Treaty of Rome, 180
Two Treatises of Government, 209

Unz, Ron, 155
Unanticipated consequences, law of, xi
Undocumented aliens. *See* Immigration, illegal
United Nations High Commissioner for Refugees (UNHCR), 289, 290, 291, 292, 301, 308, 309, 312, 317, 321, 323
United States
citizens. *See* Citizens
citizenship. *See* Citizenship
competitiveness, 114, 133, 134
Congress. *See* Congress
Constitution, xi, 1. *See also* Constitution
demographics of, 41, 82, 95, 142, 162, 249, 252, 253, 262, 335, 349
emergence as a world power, 23
erosion of foreign policy power, 40–41
as a first-asylum country, 101
Japanese and Japanese-Americans, treatment of, 6, 104
Louisiana Purchase, xi
racial attitudes in, 8
source countries, xi, 12
territories, xi, 27
United States Commission on Immigration Reform, 144, 145, 188
Urban and industrial development, 20
Urban Institute, 340–341
U.S. English, 7
United States ex rel. Knauff v. Shaughnessy, 32
United States v. Lopez, 196

Vietnam War, 183
Virginia, 154

Voting Rights Act of 1965, 27, 254, 351

Wall Street Journal, 124, 133
Walzer, Michael, 79, 172, 210
Wang, Theodore, 17
Warren Court, 30
Washington, 187
Watergate, 91, 117
Wattenburg, Ben, 133
Welfare state, 98, 102, 136, 142, 143, 178, 182, 184, 191–192, 194, 199–200, 205, 220, 331. *See also* Legislation, Personal Responsibility and Work

Opportunity Reconciliation Act of 1996
West, Cornel, 260, 263
Wilson, Pete (Governor of California, Senator), 108, 141, 149, 155, 159, 181, 234
Wilson, William Julius, 260, 263
"Wilson workers," 108
Wong Yang Sung v. McGrath, 37–39
Work authorization, 98

Xenophobia. *See* Immigration, public attitudes toward